Mormonism Under the Microscope

Mormonism Under the Microscope

"The Devil Is in the Details"

Volume III

by

Joel M. Allred

Mountain Press
P.O. Box 58544
Salt Lake City UT 84158-0544

PUBLISHED 2020. PRINTED AND BOUND IN CHINA.

FIRST EDITION

ISBN: 978-0-9773955-9-0

Library of Congress Control Number: 2016915076

Consult with uncertainty.

Find peace in probabilities.

Present courage to commotion.

A mind is a terrible thing to close.

Transcend the forms that lifted you.

When institutionalized, the religion embodies an assertion of; the exclusive possession of truth, an elitist identity, a separation from others who are not members of the group, the growth of intolerance toward others, and actual hostility toward those who do not conform to their beliefs and behaviors. This is accompanied by efforts to convert those outside of their ranks. Under the guise of caring for others, the religion is then dedicated to the perpetuation of itself.

Walter Kania

The field of Mormon history is a hall of mirrors, full of distorted and incomplete reflections of nearly any event.

John G. Turner

[H]is honesty, courage and intelligence got the better of his ideology; he understood his former beliefs with the hard-won wisdom of the disillusioned.

Tribute to Fouad Ajami, (1945-2014), Bret Stephens

CONTENTS

Foreword

Foreword

Mormon polygamy, a doctrine first described in or about 1831, then more fully described in writing in 1843, credits Jesus, Christianity's unmarried pastor, as the author of the controversial principle. On August 12, 1843, the written revelation on celestial (plural) marriage was secretly read to the Nauvoo High Council – thought to be a carefully selected group of confidential men – by Joseph Smith's brother, Hyrum Smith.[1] The description of that meeting failed to report that the astonishing new principle had been discussed. Nor did Minutes report that some Nauvoo High Councilmen (William Marks, Leonard Sobey, Austin Cowles[2]) rejected Hyrum and the revelation, thus turning their backs on the prophet Joseph Smith's unpredictable Lord. The consequences of this 1843 communication were instantly and inevitably divisive.

With the private dissemination of the oral contents of what only very much later became Section 132 of the Doctrine and Covenants, Joseph Smith redefined the commonly accepted nature of sin and became the lord and master of Mormon marriage. The message conveyed to Joseph by the God of Abraham, Isaac and Jacob provided as follows: "For behold, I reveal unto you a new and an everlasting covenant; and if ye abide not that covenant, then are ye damned; for no one can reject this covenant and be permitted to enter into my glory."[3]

The revelation assigned God's glory to the practice of polygamy. The rudiments of plurality, in the beginning, became known only to such highly favored men and women as could be trusted not to tell the truth. This new and everlasting covenant (Mormon polygamy) wasn't published in the Doctrine and Covenants with the other

---

[1]"Hyrum Smith reasoned upon said Revelation for about an hour . . . and then enjoined it upon said Council, to receive and acknowledge the same, or they would be damned." (Affidavit, Thomas Grover to notary James Jack, 6 July 1869, reproduced at *The Nauvoo City and High Council Minutes*, John S. Dinger ed. [Salt Lake City: Signature Books, 2011], 467-68 n 61).

[2]On that day, August 12, 1843, Austin Cowles, one of the dissenters, didn't know that his already married daughter, *Mrs.* Elvira Anna Cowles (Holmes) had also secretly married a second husband (Joseph Smith), becoming one of Smith's polyandrous wives on June 1, 1843.

[3]Doctrine and Covenants (1957), 132:4.

revelations until 1876. Although the practice of polygamy was
involuntarily and publicly suspended in and after 1890, the great,
sublime, beautiful, and glorious revelation described by Joseph's
God remains in its appointed place in the modern Doctrine and
Covenants, prepared to guide the domestic relationships of faithful
Saints, husbands, "wives and concubines" in a Mormon afterlife.[4]

A previous revelation explained:

> In the celestial glory there are three heavens or
> degrees; And in order to obtain the highest, a man
> must enter into this order of the priesthood [meaning
> the new and everlasting covenant of marriage]; And
> if he does not, he cannot obtain it. He may enter into
> the other, but that is the end of his kingdom; he
> cannot have an increase.[5]

Polygamy is a commandment directed to those who want "to enter
into" the celestial glory of God in the highest division of heaven. To
those who aspire to become gods.

Mormon polygamy is assigned in its entirety to Joseph's Lord
(meaning Jesus). Joseph's revelator, the God of Abraham, Isaac and
Jacob, commanded the practice of polygamy. And when Joseph was
slow to react, that same God is supposed to have sent an angel with a
drawn sword to enforce the reluctant prophet's compliance. Early
Mormons, who called Jesus a polygamist and roundly condemned
monogamy, understood that Joseph's Lord stood behind this new
and powerful everlasting celestial/plural marriage covenant.
Mormon polygamy was going to be the governing principle in Latter-
day Saint heaven. It is the order of the afterlife. Although suspended
for now in various inhospitable climes, Mormons believe it will be
fully reembraced to the glory of God in the life to come. Joseph will
have his hundreds of wives, some of them historic (including married
non-Mormon women to whom he is nonconsensually sealed), and the
biological children of his polyandrous wives with their other
husbands, and so will his monstrously married successor, Brigham

---

[4]Ibid., 132.
[5]Ibid., 131:1-4.

Young. Smith and Young are the authors of and the exemplars for the Mormon iteration of the common Christian principle that "families are forever." Polygamy is the unwelcome element in that tender equation.

Emma Smith Calls Foul

Emma Smith told William E. McLellin in 1847 in Nauvoo, Illinois, after the death of Joseph Smith, "that she knew her husband practiced both adultery and Spiritual Wifery! And that she also knew that he had the Polygamic revelation."[6] The revelation, as Emma correctly surmised, was about polygamy. Emma knew, and told McLellin, that her husband's creditors "proved [obligations]" against Joseph Smith's bankrupt estate, in Carthage, Hancock County, Illinois, that exceeded the sum of $200,000, against which there was "not a dollar to pay the debt!" An average family at that time earned about $400 a year. She knew and reported that the "$40,000 for goods in New York" and Joseph Smith and Sidney Rigdon's "fines for banking without a charter" in Ohio were not ever paid.[7] On April 18, 1842, Joseph and Hyrum Smith, residents of Nauvoo, Illinois, filed petitions for bankruptcy.[8]

While Emma knew about Fanny Alger (Joseph's housemaid) and the identity of a handful of Joseph's plural wives some time after the earliest encounters, she didn't begin to know the down and dirty details of her husband's extraordinary private life. For her, apparently, the rule of Sarah, requiring the consent of the first wife to take other wives, polygamous wives, didn't apply. "The Female Relief Society which Joseph had organized in mid-March 1842 with Emma as president, was quickly diverted from charitable offices to the purging of iniquity."[9] It is almost farcical to learn later in life

---

[6]William E. McLellin, Letter to John L. Traughber, 14 December 1878, in *The William E. McLellin Papers: 1854-1880*, eds. Stan Larson and Samuel J. Passey, foreword by George D. Smith (Salt Lake City: Signature Books, 2008), 515.

[7]Ibid.

[8]D. Michael Quinn, *The Mormon Hierarchy: Origins of Power* (Salt Lake City: Signature Books in association with Smith Research Associates, 1994), 634.

[9]Fawn McKay Brodie, *No Man Knows My History: The Life of Joseph Smith the Mormon Prophet*, 2d ed., rev. and enl. (New York, NY: Alfred A. Knopf, 1972), 305.

that Emma's leadership colleagues in that "select society of the virtuous" were unanimously implicated in the greatly secret less-than-sacred practice of polygamy while Emma was in the dark. "Assisting her in the leadership of the society were some of the ablest women in the church: Mrs. Elizabeth Ann Whitney, Mrs. Sarah M. Cleveland, Elvira Cowles, and the poetess Eliza R. Snow."[10] Joseph Smith had secretly married *Mrs.* Sarah M. Kingsley (Howe Cleveland) some time before "March 1842." He married Eliza R. Snow on June 29, 1842. He married Sarah Ann Whitney, the daughter of Elizabeth Ann Whitney, on July 27, 1842, and *Mrs.* Elvira Anna Cowles (Holmes) on June 1, 1843.[11]

Sarah Ann Whitney, seventeen years old, was married to the thirty-six year old Joseph Smith by her father, Newel K. Whitney, in the presence of her mother, Elizabeth Ann Whitney, Emma's Second Counselor in the Relief Society Presidency. Sarah Ann, Smith's sixteenth wife, was sealed to the prophet on the day of their marriage, July 27, 1842. She became one of no less than twenty-three (and more probably twenty-five) women who were sealed (pledged for eternity) to Joseph Smith before he was ever sealed to Emma Smith, his legal wife, on May 28, 1843.[12]

Emma Smith refused to follow the branch of the divided Church, the schism led by Brigham Young, after the death of Joseph Smith. She was humiliated by the conduct of her husband and hated polygamy. From July 17, 1831, the date first unmistakably associated with the secret practice of polygamy, until June 27, 1844, the date of his death, Joseph Smith never publicly admitted he ever practiced polygamy. Emma Smith told her children in an important interview in the presence of her second husband near the end of her life that their father never practiced polygamy. The blame for the origin of that nasty principle, she said, rested with a wicked Brigham Young.

---

[10]Ibid., 306.

[11]George D. Smith, *Nauvoo Polygamy: " . . . but we called it celestial marriage"* (Salt Lake City: Signature Books, 2008), 621-23.

[12]Ibid. Maria Lawrence and Helen Mar Kimball were sealed to Smith on dates not entirely certain but *circa* May 1843.

Introduction

The Nineteenth-Century Roots of Mormon Polygamy

Church members' secrets set them apart from the world, sealed them up to one another through things arcane, and fortified them in their confidence that they were the special friends of God.[1]

B. Carmon Hardy

DECADES OF DECEPTION

Nineteenth-century Saints believed that plural marriage (polygamy) was just what Joseph Smith privately said that it was, "the most holy and important *doctrine* ever revealed to man on [the] earth."[2] It was the "chief cornerstone" of the "restored" church. In that early era, the controversial "doctrine" survived the death of the prophet to become nineteenth-century Mormonism's "most distinctive signature."[3] The Latter-day Saints considered plural marriage "a prescription for health, an antidote for immorality, and a key to history and government."[4] The Mormon Pentecost, a lively movement rooted in "the conviction that old things were passing away," found an "outlet for some of its fires in sexual behavior."[5]

---

[1]B. Carmon Hardy, *Solemn Covenant: The Mormon Polygamous Passage* (Urbana, Chicago: University of Illinois Press, 1992), 364.

[2]Richard S. Van Wagoner, *Mormon Polygamy: A History* (Salt Lake City: Signature Books, 1986), iii.

[3]B. Carmon Hardy, *Doing the Works of Abraham: Mormon Polygamy – Its Origin, Practice, and Demise*, vol. 9 of *Kingdom in the West: The Mormons and the American Frontier* (Norman, OK: The Arthur H. Clark Company, 2007), 109.

[4]Hardy, *Solemn Covenant: The Mormon Polygamous Passage*, xviii.

[5]Ibid., 3. "Wherever inspirationist religion thrives, spiritual license is easily converted to other entitlements." "[T]he times were ablaze with sexual consideration."

Brigham Young informed his followers that Joseph Smith and
Oliver Cowdery learned about "The Principle" (polygamy) in 1829
while they were translating the Book of Mormon. Brigham H.
Roberts, "The Defender of the Faith," the husband of three wives
and the father of fifteen children, said that there "was indisputable
evidence that within a year of the books publication Joseph Smith
became convinced plural marriage was a correct principle."[6]   In
about 1831, Smith secretly "approved intermarriage with Indian
women" (Lamanites). Already married Mormon men were told to
take Indian women as plural wives. "There is evidence that during
the 1830's Smith inaugurated the practice of taking plural wives in
his own private life." If that happened in the 1830s, as some
scholars surmise, it happened without Emma Smith's knowledge or
consent. By nineteenth-century reckoning, this interracial Mormon
Indian mixing was calculated "to whiten the skin of Indian
offspring and make them more 'delightsome.'"[7] "Beyond the early
date of the proposal [a directive to intermarry with Indian women],
it is significant that Joseph looked upon plural marriage as a
eugenic instrument."[8] That point is further elucidated in this book
at Appendix A.

"Great Basin Saints" (Brigham's particular followers) were taught
that Jesus was a polygamist, and Brigham reported that Mother
Eve was but "one of Adam's wives." Those Utah Territory Saints,
like the prophet Joseph in his time, formalized "marriage and
divorce without civil authority"; informal alliances (sexual consent
relationships) were not uncommon when relationships were
solemnized "without deputization from the state."[9]   Brigham
Young's version of Joseph Smith's theocracy roundly disparaged
monogamy. As Professor Hardy explains, it offered Joseph Smith-
approved   polygamy-based   panaceas   for   "the   disheveled
[monogamous] condition of the family, the want of affection
between many husbands and their spouses, and the loss of
patriarchal authority in the home."[10] Hardy further explains that
Mormon polygamists during the reign of Brigham Young "viewed

---

[6]Ibid., 5.
[7]Ibid.
[8]Ibid.
[9]Ibid., 6.
[10]Ibid., 7-8.

non-Mormon monogamists as hypocritically conducting 'their sexual intercourse by lustful feelings' instead of 'the pure and holy feelings of procreation.' Their vision combined a plurality of wives with male dominance and a disciplined, reproductively purposed sexuality . . . ."[11]

God was always at the center of Joseph's polygamy. Smith told his private polygamous elite, a quiet bunch, that an angel with a drawn sword commanded him to practice plurality at the risk of the loss of his life. He made similar but secret representations to some individual women in order to make them feel secure. On this particular issue, Joseph's God denied to Joseph's followers the right to freely decide. In Mormon lore the heavenly messenger made it clear that God himself was the author of Mormon polygamy. Smith didn't reduce the full-blown revelation on polygamy to writing until July 1843. The document was not made public until 1852, and it was not formally included in the *Doctrine and Covenants* until 1876.[12] The cynical provisions that preceded the inclusion of the 1843 "Polygamic revelation" in all editions and printings of the Doctrine and Covenants until 1876 were canonized by the voice of the Church. Those provisions said that the members of the Church practiced nothing but traditional monogamous marriage. The doctrine of polygamy, presently in a state of suspense, is carefully preserved in the Doctrine and Covenants (Section 132). Mormonism's polygamous founders are vicariously sealed (married or assigned for eternity) to hundreds of women, whether those women were previously married or single. Then further, Mormon or not is not really an issue. Mormons intend to practice "this great, sublime, beautiful and glorious doctrine"[13] unrestrained by the laws of the Gentiles in a Mormon afterlife. The vaunted concept of the Mormon family both then and now presumes the restoration of the polygamous principle.

Twenty-first century Saints have no choice but to defend the character of Joseph Smith, the untrustworthy Prophet of the Restoration (the man at the center of everything). That must also

---

[11]Hardy, *Doing the Works of Abraham: Mormon Polygamy*, editor's note, 109.

[12]Hardy, *Solemn Covenant: The Mormon Polygamous Passage*, 9.

[13]Orson Pratt, quoted in Hardy, *Doing the Works of Abraham: Mormon Polygamy*, 79.

include a duty to support the character of another equally tarnished figure, Brigham Young, who is only just now admitted by one very important Mormon scholar to have been "more violent and coarse than the man Mormons have known."[14] The historical Brigham was very different than the glorified figure presented to them by their prophets and apostles for close to one hundred seventy-five years. For those who can't forget the injudicious conduct of those two rough men, for troubled Saints who now see darkness and deceit where others see only light and truth, modern scholarship has brought to light issues and facts concealed and suppressed for the better part of two hundred years. This all serves to describe a shameful betrayal of trust.

John G. Turner's seminal study of Brigham Young (published by a division of the Harvard University Press in 2012) offers stunning new insight into the life and times of Brigham Young. After reporting that "Sermons published in the *Journal of Discourses* eliminated much of Young's color, coarseness, and profanity while presenting his ideas in more polished form," Turner offers a new and different kind of biography one hundred and thirty-five years after the death of Brigham Young. His Preface states: "[G]reater access to church-controlled primary sources differentiates this study from all previous biographies save [Leonard] Arrington's [a worshipful apologetic tome]."[15]

Multigenerational Latter-day Saints are now obliged to defend unconscionable conduct objectionable in any current context in order to protect doctrines imposed on them without consent as children to guide them as adults. They cannot countenance evidence of moral transgression in the lives and teachings of Joseph Smith and Brigham Young without catching themselves in a disastrous error. No person writing on Mormon themes can fail to explore the impact of polygamy. This book will attempt to describe issues and events of interest associated with that controversial doctrine while noting that those issues are treated to more

---

[14]Richard L. Bushman, Endorsement, Dust Jacket, John G. Turner, *Brigham Young: Pioneer Prophet* (Belknap Press of Harvard University Press, 2012). "The story Turner tells in this elegantly written biography will startle and shock many readers. . . . [T]he book will require a reassessment of Brigham Young the man."
[15]Ibid., viii.

comprehensive analysis in the works of what is an impressive group of polygamy scholars.[16]

In an introduction to his remarkable book *Solemn Covenant: The Mormon Polygamous Passage*, B. Carmon Hardy described some of his objectives. After the secret period, up to 1852 and prior to the Manifesto (1890), early Mormon rhetoric portrayed monogamy as the discredited province of "[w]horemasters" and prostitutes, a consequence of "prostitution and moral rot," the predictable result of "Apostate, Hypocritical Christianity."[17] Then Hardy reports a demeaning cynical consequence of the Manifesto. While publicly pretending to discontinue such performances (polygamy), church leaders authorized new plural marriages within and outside the United States both before and after 1890. Hardy goes on to say he will explore the Mormons' vision of the polygamous ideal, the consequences of their public dishonesty, and their attempt to preserve the polygamous ideal for the eternities. His work describes Mormonism's astonishing transformation into a determined advocate of the previously harshly disparaged monogamous ethic.[18]

Such astonishing transformations are far from unusual; they are forced by circumstances. Hard times demand hard choices. Many victims of cognitive dissonance may sympathize with the sentiments

---

[16]Fawn McKay Brodie, *No Man Knows My History: The Life of Joseph Smith the Mormon Prophet*, 2d ed., rev. and enl. (New York, NY: Alfred A. Knopf, 1972). Linda King Newell and Valeen Tippets Avery, *Mormon Enigma: Emma Hale Smith, Prophet's Wife, "Elect Lady," Polygamy's Foe – 1804-1879* (Garden City, N.Y.: Doubleday & Company, Inc., 1984). Van Wagoner, *Mormon Polygamy: A History*. Hardy, *Solemn Covenant: The Mormon Polygamous Passage*. Todd Compton, *In Sacred Loneliness: The Plural Wives of Joseph Smith* (Salt Lake City: Signature Books, 2001). Hardy, *Doing the Works of Abraham*. George D. Smith, *Nauvoo Polygamy: " . . . but we called it celestial marriage"* (Salt Lake City: Signature Books, 2008). Newell G. Bringhurst and Craig L. Foster, *The Persistence of Polygamy: From Joseph Smith's Martyrdom to the First Manifesto, 1844-1890* (USA: John Whitmer Books, 2013). Brian C. Hales and Laura H. Hales, *Joseph Smith's Polygamy: Toward a Better Understanding* (Draper, UT: Greg Kofford Books, 2015). *See also* D. Michael Quinn, "LDS Church Authority and New Plural Marriages, 1890-1904," *Dialogue: A Journal of Mormon Thought*, vol. 18 no. 1, (Spring 1985): 9-105.
[17]Hardy, *Doing the Works of Abraham*, 86.
[18]Hardy, *Solemn Covenant*, xviii.

of Zina Diantha Huntington (Jacobs) (Smith) (Young), the polygamous domestic possession in consecutive stints of Henry Jacobs, Joseph Smith and Brigham Young. "The thoughts of my heart or the emotions of my minde," Zina opined, "causes my very head to acke."[19]

As scholars continued to dismantle the whitewashed versions of the modern Church's history, and in 2016 in a protected setting, one Mormon scholar and Smith biographer Richard L. Bushman became philosophical: "I think that for the Church to remain strong it has to reconstruct its narrative," Bushman said to a group of faithful friends. "The dominant narrative is not true; it can't be sustained." Prideful in his candor and while testing the boundaries of permissible dialogue, he then proceeded to say, "The Church has to absorb all this new information or it will be on very shaky grounds and that's what it is trying to do and it will be a strain for a lot of people, older people especially. But I think it has to change."[20] Older people are those most particularly affected because they haven't forgotten what they were taught.

Thoughtful Latter-day Saints, including prophets and apostles, expect to practice polygamy in a Mormon afterlife. Section 132 of the Doctrine and Covenants, Emma Smith's polygamic revelation and canonized Mormon scripture, is undeniable proof of that. To criticize the polygamic revelation for its polygamous content, even today, may subject troubled modern Saints to excommunication.[21] Up to the present day, various modern prophets (Joseph Fielding Smith, Harold B. Lee, Howard W. Hunter, Ezra Taft Benson, Russell M. Nelson) continue to be sealed to more than one wife in temple sealing ceremonies after the first wives are dead. Russell M. Nelson, installed as the new prophet in 2018, is one of no less than

---

[19]Zina Huntington quoted in Turner, *Brigham Young: Pioneer Prophet*, 136. Spoken in 1845, the year "Brigham Young was sealed to Zina."

[20]Jonathan Ellis, "Transcript of Claudia and Richard Bushman's Remarks at Faith Again" (12 June 2016, accessed 6 February 2018), available from https://medium.com/ @ jellistx / transcript-of-claudia-and-richard-bushmans-remarks-at faith-again-e9d03bdea0e3; Internet, p. 16.

[21]John Dehlin, "Kirk and Lindsay Van Allen – Facing Church Discipline for Rejecting Polygamy D&C 132," Episode 530 (8 April 2015, accessed 6 February 2018), available from http://www.mormonstories.org/kirk-and-lindsay-van-allen-facing-church-discipline-for-rejecting-polygamy-dc-132/; Internet, 22 pages.

twelve celestial polygamist prophets. There are also routine sealings of other less distinguished modern Mormon men, including apostles. Many regular male members have been sealed by the power of the priesthood for eternity to more than one woman in rites that Latter-day Saints recognize to be eternal. They intend to have their plural wives in a Mormon eternity, and they have so declared.

While the temporal practice of polygamy for more than one living wife at a time has been involuntarily suspended, it is believed that it will ultimately be required for everyone who hopes to achieve a presence in the highest division of the Celestial Kingdom, where the faithful priesthood holders, all of them men, expect to practice the plurality principle in the physical presence of polygamous gods.[22] Section 132, the polygamous commandment, remains in effect as an eternal principle.

No one can expect to understand Mormonism, where it has been and what it has become, without first understanding the plurality principle, known to include both "wives and concubines."[23] Section 132 embraces the concept of concubines. Did Joseph Smith expect any woman he met, including already married women with legal husbands, to marry him for time and eternity? For *time* (when the married women were to be shared by Joseph and their legal husbands) and for *eternity* (when the married women and their biological children belonged to Smith and not to their husbands and biological fathers)? Here we see the architect of Mormonism's concept of the eternal family protecting marriage in his own peculiar and unsustainable way. Joseph Smith was sealed, bonded for eternity, to hundreds of women, including historical celebrities such as Madam Victor Hugo, Charlotte Corday, Queen Maud of Scotland, St. Helene, the mother of Constantine, Matilda, an Empress of Germany, St. Therese and various others. No, Joseph didn't expect every woman he was interested in to marry him. He expected some of them, like Mrs. Orson (Sarah) Pratt and Sidney Rigdon's unmarried daughter Nancy, at least at first, to be

---

[22]Bruce R. McConkie, *Mormon Doctrine*, 2d ed. (Salt Lake City: Bookcraft, 1966), 578. "Obviously the holy practice will commence again after the Second Coming of the Son of Man and the ushering in of the millennium." (Ibid.).

[23]Doctrine and Covenants, 132:1.

something other and less than "wives," probably concubines.

Until the year 2019, Mormon women wore veils in Mormon temples and swore to obey their husbands; God favored Adam and neglected "Eve." From at least 1831 (Brigham Young said from 1829) until at least 1852, for the period of Joseph Smith's lifetime and then until long after his death, Latter-day Saints deceived each other and almost everyone else about the teaching and practice of "The Principle."

Eternal Polygamy Lives

Twelve Mormon prophets are now known to have been sealed for eternity to more than one woman. Four of them, call them *"celestial polygamists,"* more modern men – Harold B. Lee, Howard W. Hunter, Joseph Fielding Smith and Russell M. Nelson – took second or third wives after their first or second wives died. Seven other earlier and consecutive polygamous prophets, mostly bearded men who guided the fortunes of the Church from 1830 to 1945, were married and sealed to about one hundred forty women in ceremonies that governed those strange relationships for both time and eternity. Those 1830-1945 prophets' plural marriages and sealings occurred on earth, where polygamy was actively practiced during all or part of their lifetimes. All of the first seven Mormon prophets, like Old Testament figures, had multiples of wives simultaneously. Those first seven prophets fathered about two hundred thirty-three children.

Ezra Taft Benson was a special case. He served as the Secretary of Agriculture in the Cabinet of President Dwight D. Eisenhower, and then as the thirteenth President (and Prophet) of the Church of Jesus Christ of Latter-day Saints. His particular situation sheds light on issues already discussed, including that prominent prophet's conception of the afterlife. Benson, who had a living legal wife, was privately sealed to a second wife, Eva Amanda Benson, in the temple in the presence of his living wife in the 1950s.[24] Sixty

---

[24]Ezra Taft Benson, *Diary*, 25 April 1950. For context and a full citation, *see* Gary James Bergera, "'Weak-Kneed Republicans and Socialist Democrats': Ezra Taft Benson as a U.S. Secretary of Agriculture, 1953-61, Part 2," *Dialogue: A*

years after the Manifesto, Benson was sealed for eternity to his cousin, a woman who had never been married and died without a husband. Benson's living wife, Flora, met him at the altar and stood proxy for Benson's plural wife in a vicarious ceremony that bound the three of them together as husband and wives for eternity. The ceremony, which recognized the principle of plurality (celestial polygamy), was performed by Elder Joseph Fielding Smith, who later became the tenth President (and Prophet) of the Church of Jesus Christ of Latter-day Saints.

All of these marriages, including the plural marriages of five modern Mormon prophets – Harold B. Lee, Howard W. Hunter, Joseph Fielding Smith, Ezra Taft Benson and Russell M. Nelson – involved celestial sealings, couplings for eternity. Can anyone doubt that those modern prophets, like those earlier prophets, expected to have their plural wives in a life to come?[25]

While Mormon men can still be married and sealed to a second wife after the first wife dies, Mormon women can not be sealed to a second husband after the first husband dies. Mormon men married for a second or third time in the temple after the death or deaths of eternal companions can be sealed to a second or third wife, only if the new wife is not already sealed (bound by some prior ceremony to someone else for eternity). Some second marriages in the temple are only for time (when the woman is already sealed to someone else); other second marriages in the temple are for time and eternity (when the woman is not already sealed to someone else). Joseph Smith was posthumously sealed to Fanny Alger, the wife of Solomon Custer, in a Utah temple in 1899 after Custer's death. By Mormon reckoning, Smith will have Custer's wife (and Custer's biological children with Fanny Alger Custer) for eternity in a Mormon afterlife.[26] Brigham Young was ultimately sealed to

---

Journal of Mormon Thought, vol. 41 no. 4 (Winter 2008), 55-95. *See, e.g.*, Lindsay Hansen Park, "Who Are the Real Mormons?" (22 August 2016, accessed 18 September 2018), available from http://www.patheos.com/blogs/yearofpolygamy /2016/08/many-mormonisms/; Internet, p. 7 of 8.

[25]"My lovely Joan was sent to me: So Joan joins Fern,/That three might be, more fitted for eternity./'O Heavenly Father, my thanks to thee.'" (Harold B. Lee, a poem which appeared in the *Deseret News* [Church Almanac, 1974], 17).

[26]There was no record of Joseph Smith ever having been sealed to Fanny Alger during their lifetimes. In fact, the young hired domestic left the Smith

Martha Brotherton (who had refused his proposal in life), with Martha's sister Mrs. Parley P. (Elizabeth Brotherton) Pratt acting as proxy in a vicarious ceremony for an unconsenting Martha, in the endowment house after Martha's death.[27] In life, eighteen-year-old Martha had fled Nauvoo and Mormonism in horror, then sometime later exposed Brigham Young and Joseph Smith for their efforts to force her to surrender herself to Brigham Young and polygamy.

While Section 132 doesn't specifically preclude the marriages and sealings of monogamous couples for time and eternity, it is not *the monogamic revelation*. It was specifically designed to provide for the marriages, sealings and couplings ("wives and concubines") of polygamous Saints. In Mormonism's private polygamous period, and for a long time after the 1852 public disclosure of the practice of polygamy, monogamy was viewed with contemptuous disdain. *Celestial marriage was plural marriage*. Section 132 of the Doctrine and Covenants, commanding the practice of polygamy as part of every edition of the Doctrine and Covenants since 1876, provides undeniable evidence of Mormonism's polygamous future. Mormonism's families are forever, but they are also polygamous. Mormon leaders today do not openly advertise the society's polygamous future but know it is true. It is clear from its content that "the 1843 revelation was a selective accumulation of the prophet's thought on the subject" of the plurality of wives and concubines.[28] The revelation doesn't fit the monogamous mold. Only the welcome imposition of the United States anti-polygamy laws forced the Mormons to have one wife for one husband.

---

household and married a non-Mormon after what Oliver Cowdery called a "dirty, nasty, filthy affair." On April 4, 1899, under the supervision of President Lorenzo Snow, Fanny Alger was sealed to Joseph Smith in order – it was said – to create a record of their sealing. (*See* 4 April 1899, Book D, 243, Salt Lake Temple Sealing Records, GS Film, 184, 590). Mormons accept Oliver Cowdery's testimony as a witness to the Book of Mormon. Why shouldn't they accept Oliver Cowdery's testimony that Joseph Smith's relationship with Fanny Alger was a "dirty, nasty, filthy affair"?

[27]On 27 August 1842, the *Wasp*, a Nauvoo newspaper, described Martha Brotherton and several other "mean harlots." On 1 August 1870, while he was still the prophet and following her death, she was nonconsensually sealed to Brigham Young. (Salt Lake Endowment House Records, Van Wagoner, *Mormon Polygamy*, 230-31).

[28]Hardy, *Solemn Covenant*, 10.

Knowledgeable Latter-day Saints recognize this interference of the Gentiles as an only temporary imposition, however, something to be followed until they can reinstate "the law of heaven."

Old Testament Polygamy

Nineteenth-century Saints were taught that the "ancient men of God [Abraham, Isaac (Isaac had but one wife, Rebecca, and no concubines) and Jacob, Moses, David and Solomon] were justified in taking plural wives and concubines."[29]   They were not only justified but commanded to comply.   Joseph's revelation states: "[A]nd it was accounted unto . . . [them] for righteousness . . . and they have entered into their exaltation . . . and sit upon thrones, and are not angels but are gods."   Joseph's polygamous Lord (the unequivocal sponsor of "The Principle") unambiguously stated that "those who have this law revealed to them must obey the same."[30] Failure to comply created a consequence.   Professor Hardy explains, "Clearly, polygamy represented more to the Saints than only an opportunity to broaden their sexual experience.   It was integral with their cosmology."[31]   It was a requisite element of the eternal family, a mandatory way station on the road to godhood.   It was for those destined to become not angels but rather Gods. Today's investigators and converts hear nothing of that.

A Sacred Order for Noble Spirits

Mormon polygamy was a commandment directed to the elect by the voice of God in 1843. It was first directed to a small group of the highly favored, and then to the Nauvoo High Council.   When the early Church decided to admit duplicity (utter dishonesty associated with the previously secret practice of polygamy) after decades of deceit (denial and obfuscation), its leaders were not contrite.   In 1852, speaking for Brigham Young and to the Church, Orson Pratt, when honor charged to address decades of dishonesty, changed the subject.   Instead of begging forgiveness from those the

---

[29]Ibid.
[30]Ibid., 10. *See, e.g.,* Doctrine and Covenants 132:3 ff. (1843).
[31]Hardy, *Solemn Covenant,* 10-11.

Mormon Under the Microscope

leaders of the Church had deceived from 1829 or 1831 to 1852, he paid homage to "the millions" of premortal spirits who "needed to be clothed with flesh before continuing their progress through eternity."[32] Polygamy, he said, was important to them.

> *. . . I have already told you that the spirits of men and women, all had a previous existence, thousands of years ago, in the heavens, in the presence of God; and I have already told you that among them are many spirits that are more noble, more intelligent than others, that were called the great and mighty ones, reserved until the dispensation of the fulness times, to come forth upon the face of the earth through a noble parentage . . . ."[33]*

Those who had been held in reserve, saved to emerge in the last days because of their extraordinary worthiness, required "a noble parentage." The elect, those so called and chosen, were not mongrels to be parceled out thoughtlessly to the families of the great unwashed. According to Pratt,

> *The Lord has not kept them in store for five or six thousand years past, and kept them waiting for their bodies all this time to send them among the Hottentots, the African negroes, the idolatrous Hindoos, or any other of the fallen nations that dwell upon the face of the earth.[34]*

These noblest of all spirits "were reserved for birth into polygamous households."[35]

---

[32]Ibid., 15.

[33]Deseret News Extra, Containing A Revelation on Celestial Marriage (18 September 1852), 2:23 [3/1], cited at Hardy, *Doing the Works of Abraham: Mormon Polygamy*, 76, 79.

[34]Pratt, Ibid., emphasis added.

[35]Hardy, *Solemn Covenant*, 15, citing Florence Ivins Hyde, a plural wife of Apostle Moses Thatcher.

The "chief corner stone" of the Work

Hardy writes that the Latter-day Saints viewed with suspicion "the moral character of anyone outside the Mormon fold. Millenarianism [last days syndrome], with its portrayal of increasing wickedness in the last days, belief that polygamy alone could check lustful behavior, and the effects of geographic isolation contributed to the attitude."[36] After visiting Brigham Young, Horace Greeley reflected on this: "He [Young] assumed as undeniable that outside of the Mormon Church, married men usually kept mistresses – that incontinence is the general rule, and continence the rare exception."[37] The notion that "most non-Mormons" are ethically challenged persists even today.

The evils of monogamy – prostitution, disease, debilitation and lowered life expectancy[38] – were to be eliminated in society by the exertions of the followers of "The Principle." B. Carmon Hardy, stressing polygamy's sometimes forgotten preeminence, summed up "the most holy and important principle":

> *George Q. Cannon once said [in 1891] [that] it [polygamy] was a doctrine purposely revealed by God to bring His followers into conflict with the rest of the world and its established beliefs. Church spokesmen were earnest in saying the revelation on polygamy constituted the most significant truth given by God to man; that it was the family order of heaven; that sealing authority and plural marriage were indissolubly bound together; that it would regenerate*

---

[36]Hardy, *Doing the Works of Abraham*, 86, editor's note.

[37]Horace Greeley, *An Overland Journey, New York to San Francisco, The Summer of 1859* (New York: C.M. Saxton, Barker & Co.; San Francisco: H.H. Bancroft & Co., 1860), cited in Hardy, *Doing the Works of Abraham*, 86-87.

[38]When Rome imposed monogamy, when "the early Christians apostatized from the older, divinely approved practice of polygamy, among the Jews," by adopting Roman monogamy, "The result was prostitution and moral rot. Abortion, adultery, and divorce . . . ." ("Deceivers and Being Deceived," *Deseret Evening News*, 28 February 1881, 14:81 [2/1], quoted in Hardy, *Doing the Works of Abraham*, 86). According to Brigham Young, the "monogamic order of marriage, so esteemed by modern Christians . . ." was "a system established by a set of [Roman] robbers." (Remarks by President Brigham Young, *Deseret News* [Weekly], 6 August 1862, quoted in Hardy, *Doing the Works of Abraham*, 86).

*mankind, nurture a superior civilization, and
eliminate sexual wickedness.   Some believed that
failure to implement the doctrine would delay the
Second Coming of Christ. Thousands looked upon its
practice as "the chief corner stone" of the work.*[39]

And why would they have not? Joseph said that he asked the Lord
"to know and understand" how he justified his servants Abraham,
Isaac and Jacob, Moses, David and Solomon, "as touching the
principle and doctrine of their having many wives and concubines."
By way of response, Joseph's God commanded polygamy. "Go ye,
therefore," he said, "and do the works of Abraham; enter ye into
my law and ye shall be saved."[40] God commanded the practice with
"a penalty of damnation affixed to its rejection." So there it was –
no one could rightfully "call himself a Latter-day Saint without
accepting and practicing polygamy."[41]   Those Latter-day Saints
today who don't understand that this is so, that it also extends to
their own future in heaven, are either ignorant of their history or
just fooling themselves. Families may be forever, but in the case of
the Mormons they are also polygamous. See Appendix A.

---

[39]Hardy, *Solemn Covenant*, 18.
[40]Doctrine and Covenants 132:1, 32.
[41]*Journal of Discourses* 17:224-25 (Orson Pratt, 1874), quoted in Hardy,
Solemn Covenant, 19.

POLYGAMY

"Wherever inspirationist religion thrives, spiritual license is easily converted to other entitlements. Early Mormonism displayed little of the closely bricked theological edifice it presents today. Many areas of ritual and belief were, if not inchoate, yet under construction." (B. Carmon Hardy, Solemn Covenant, 3).

Joseph Smith, Jr., circa 1843, by Bathsheba W. Smith (1822 – 1910). Image source: Public domain, via Wikimedia Commons.

The prophet privately said that plural marriage was "the most holy and important doctrine ever revealed to man on the earth." Without obedience to that principle, he said, no one could attain to the fullness of exaltation in the life to come. Joseph's unmarried pastor was even more explicit: "For behold, I reveal unto you a new and an everlasting covenant [plural marriage]; and if ye abide not that covenant, then are ye damned; for no one can reject this covenant and be permitted to enter into my glory." (Doctrine and Covenants 132:4).

All civil (secular non-Mormon) marriages "are of no efficacy, virtue or force in and after the resurrection from the dead . . . [Doctrine and Covenants, 132:3]." "Marriage by secular authority is of effect during mortality only –Though the form of marriage should make it appear to be for time and eternity, the ordinance is not valid beyond the grave unless solemnized by the authority of the Holy Priesthood as the Lord directs . . . . [Preface, Section 132, Doctrine and Covenants (1957)]."

"How infinite are the possibilities of our nature when we reflect that these grave, unrebellious people, the waifs and findings of all lands, many of them dignified in apparel and culture, and steadily ascending in the scale of comfort and possessions, hold still with the tenacity of a moral purpose to the loose and spreading life of polygamy, preferring this fantastic reproduction like the Banyan's branches to the straight and peaceful unity of the European family." (George Alfred Townsend, Preface, Hardy, Solemn Covenant).

William E. McLellin. Image source: Public
domain via Wikimedia Commons.

Emma Hale Smith. Image source: Public domain,
via Wikimedia Commons.

William E. McLellin: *"I visited Mrs. Emma Smith in Nauvoo, in 1847. She told me plainly and frankly that her husband did receive and deliver the Polygamic revelation himself, and she knew he practiced its provisions. And she said she knew he had committed adultery with girls previous to that." (McLellin Papers, Letter to Traughber)*

JOSEPH SMITH

Joseph Smith married about thirty-eight women, not including Fanny Alger, during his lifetime. About nine of them were teenagers, and two of them were fourteen years old. Thirteen or fourteen of those women were already legally married, civilly covenanted to, supported by, living and cohabiting with other men when they also married him. No less than twenty-three of Joseph's women, and perhaps as many as twenty-five, were sealed to him before he was sealed to his legal wife, Emma Smith, and to his own biological children. He was married to about thirty-four women in about twenty-one months in 1842 and 1843. (George D. Smith, Nauvoo Polygamy)

Smith had married seventeen women before thirty-one witnesses testified in the Times and Seasons, at his request and while he was that publication's editor, that "Inasmuch as this church . . . has been reproached with the crime of fornication and polygamy: we declare that we believe that one man should have one wife; and one woman but one husband, except in case of death, when either is at liberty to marry again."

Joseph's witnesses testified that "we know of no other rule or system of marriage than the one published from the Book of Doctrine and Covenants" (unconditional monogamy), and "we know of no secret wife system" in this place. "We," twelve prominent Mormon men and nineteen prominent Mormon women, "do hereby certify and declare . . . that J.C. Bennett's 'secret wife system' is a disclosure of his own make." (Times and Seasons, October 1, 1842).

ORSON PRATT
"THE APOSTLE OF POLYGAMY"

"The Lord has not kept them [the preexistent spirits of "the great and mighty ones," "spirits that are more noble, more intelligent than others"] in store for five or six thousand years past [measured against the age of the earth] . . . waiting for their bodies all this time to send them among the Hottentots, the African negroes, the idolatrous Hindoos, or any other of the fallen nations that dwell upon the face of this earth. They are not kept in reserve in order to come forth to receive such a degraded parentage . . . ." (Deseret News, Extra)

"[W]hat will become of those individuals who have this law [polygamy] taught unto them in plainness if they reject it? . . . I will tell you, they will be damned saith the Lord God almighty . . . ." (Ibid.)

IN SUPPORT OF A POLYGAMOUS AFTERLIFE

Bruce R. McConkie: *"In the early days of this dispensation, as part of the promised restitution of all things, the Lord revealed the principle of plural marriage to the Prophet. Later the Prophet and leading brethren were commanded to enter into the practice, which they did in all virtue and purity of heart despite the consequent animosity and prejudices of worldly people. After Brigham Young led the saints to the Salt Lake Valley, plural marriage was openly taught and practiced until the year 1890. At that time conditions were such that the Lord by revelation withdrew the command to continue the practice, and President Wilford Woodruff issued the Manifesto directing that it cease. ("Discourses of Wilford Woodruff," pp. 213-218.)* **Obviously the holy practice will commence again after the Second Coming of the Son of Man and the ushering in of the millennium.** *" (Mormon Doctrine, 2 ed., 578).*

GEORGE Q. CANNON

"License to marry should not come from the priest but from the physician ["true and effectual reform must begin in the marriage bed"]. It [the improvement of the moral condition of the world] will be when the law forbids the unhealthy to beget children – when it compels every healthy man to marry – when a refusal to this will debar him from holding office – from voting – from sueing at courts at law – from making contracts – from following any learned profession – when it suffers no healthy girl to remain single after she becomes of proper age – when no whore shall be permitted to live – when illicit intercourse shall be punished with death . . . ." *(Appendix A)*

"[A]s long as monogamy is the law, bastardy, whoredom, and degeneracy will exist; and also their concomitants, irreligion, intemperance, licentiousness and vice of every kind and degree." *(Cannon, Editor, Western Standard)*

In 1871, Cannon, "a savvy political operative," was described in the New York Tribune as "stout of flesh, low of stature, rubicund [ruddy] of countenance, and ready of tongue." (John G. Turner)

HEBER C. KIMBALL

"For a man of God to be confined to one woman is small business; for it is as much as we can do now to keep up under the burdens we have to carry; and I do not know what we should do if we only had only one wife apiece." *(Deseret News)*

Some of Brigham Young's Wives. Image source: https://utahstories.com/
2010/08/in-defense-of-polygamy/

BRIGHAM YOUNG

Brigham Young had about fifty-five wives and fifty-five children. He was divorced or separated about fifteen or sixteen times from about fourteen or fifteen different women. About thirty-nine of his wives were married to other men before or after they married him. He was a second husband to about fifteen polyandrous women and his polyandry was sexual. He fathered one of his daughters with Zina Diantha Huntington (Jacobs) (Smith) (Young) after the death of Joseph Smith and during the lifetime of Henry Jacobs, who was Zina's legal husband and the biological father of her two sons. Young granted more than sixteen hundred divorces during his tenure as the leader of the Church.

MISOGYNY

Brigham Young: *"Great God! . . . . [female] council & wisdom . . . don't weigh as much with me as the weight of a Fly Tird."* *(Cleland and Brooks)*

Brigham Young's Estate: *When Brigham Young died, his will "apportioned the estate among nineteen classes of wives and children . . . ." What wasn't known was that Brigham Young had about thirty additional wives who were "not mentioned . . . in the will." No official provision appears to have been made for their support.*

POLYGAMY RULES

George Armstrong Hicks: *"There was one part of our faith that [was] more particularly put in practice than any of the rest, and that was polygamy. That, with some of our teachers, was the most prominent point of their faith [and Mormonism's "most distinctive" nineteenth-century signature]. The young girls of Spanish Fork were fairley besieged by men old enough to be ther fathers. The young women from 13 to 16 years of age were many of them sealed to men three times their own age. The girls were told that if any faithful man made them an offer of marriage, it was their imperative duty to except [accept] the offer. An old and tried man in the gospel [was] more capable of giving them a high degree of glory than a young and untried man."*

AARON JOHNSON

The Bishop at Springville was a man whose name was known to God. (Doctrine and Covenants 124:132). Married twelve times, his wives included eight teenagers. Johnson was plurally married to five of his nieces. He had eleven of his fifty-one children with Mary Ann Johnson, one of his brother's daughters. When they married he was thirty-nine and she was fourteen. He had five children with another niece, Harriett Fidelia Johnson. When they married he was forty-six and she was fifteen. He married three teenagers (ages fourteen, fifteen and nineteen) on his fiftieth birthday.

GEORGE D. WATT

On 5 January 1852, George D. Watt, Mormonism's first English convert and Brigham Young's stenographer and private clerk, married his half-sister, Jane Brown. George D. Watt and Jane Brown, who was but one of his six wives, shared the same mother, Mary Ann Wood. Together, these two half-siblings became the parents of three children. Watt was born in 1812; Jane Brown was born in 1828.

MORMON DOGGEREL VERSE

I have got but one lone wife
And I can get no more
The doctrine is, I can't be saved
Unless I've half a score.

JOHN TAYLOR

Brigham Young's successor, Mormon prophet John Taylor, was seventy-eight years old when he married twenty-six year old Josephine Elizabeth Roueche on December 19, 1886, six months before he died on July 25, 1887. She died in 1943.

Image source: Public domain,
via Wikimedia Commons.

LORENZO SNOW

President Lorenzo Snow was fifty-seven years old when he married fifteen-year old Sarah E. Minnie Jensen in 1871. They had five children together. He had his last child (Rhea Lucile Snow, born November 5, 1896) at the age of eighty-two.

Image source: Public domain,
via Wikimedia Commons.

ZINA DIANTHA HUNTINGTON (JACOBS) (SMITH) (YOUNG)

"The thoughts of my heart or the emotions of my minde causes my very head to acke."

Image source: Public domain,
via Wikimedia Commons.

NANCY RIGDON

Her marrying Joseph Smith "would not prevent her from marrying any other person."

ANOMALIES

George Armstrong Hicks: *"I once heard my mother say that she saw the Prophet and William Law's wife out carriage riding to gather [together] when Law was absent from home." "It was said that even the prophet Joseph . . . had the wives of leading men 'sealed' to him, and it was said that among the number was the wife of William Law, at least it was whispered around among the people and I believe the report to be true."*

George Armstrong Hicks: *"It was said that a girl thus 'sealed' ['spirituals'] might, if she choose and opertunity offerred, marry any yo[u]ng man she choose. Marriage was supposed to be for time only and the obligation would terminate at death, but 'sealing' was for eternity, and parties thus joined would hold the relationship of husband and wife in the next world. I am well acquainted with one woman by the name of Julia Parks who became the 'spiritual wife' of Dimic[k] B. Huntington in Nauvoo. A young man by the name of Wm. Lindsey courted and married her, never in the least expecting that she was the 'spiritual' of anyone. After several children were born, Julia confessed that she was the spiritual wife of Huntington."* Zina Huntington (Jacobs) (Smith) (Young) said that Lindsay married Parks at the home of Dimick B. Huntington, her brother, and it is known that Lindsay and Parks had eight children. Julia and her biological children with Lindsay will belong to Dimick Huntington in a Mormon afterlife. *"Hicks traveled to Utah with the Lindsays and so knew them well."* What Julia Parks did, Joseph told Nancy Rigdon (who refused his proposal) she could do. Marrying him, he said, would not preclude her marriage to any other person.

Joseph F. Smith Family. Image source: Public domain via Wikimedia Commons.

DON CARLOS SMITH

Ebenezer Robinson: *"He [Don Carlos] was a bitter opposer of the 'spiritual wife' doctrine which was being talked quite freely, in private circles, in his lifetime." "Any man who will teach and practice the doctrine of spiritual wifery will go to hell: I don't care if it is my brother Joseph."*

Ina Coolbrith, Daughter: *"He quietly made plans to go back to Kirtland in 1842, and was only prevented by his death."*

Image Source: http://josephsmithsr.com/doncarlos/

HYRUM SMITH

May 14, 1843: *"[O]nly the Devil would give a revelation approving 'wifes and concubines.'" (D. Michael Quinn)*

August 12, 1843: *In a meeting without written minutes, Hyrum read the revelation on plural marriage dated July 12, 1843. The revelation described the principle and doctrine of "many wives and concubines." "After reading the documents to the High Council, he admonished those who believed the words of the Revelation to 'go forth and obey the same, and be saved.' Those who rejected it would be 'damned.'" (Thomas Grover)*

Image Source: George Edward Anderson, 1860-1928, Public domain, via Wikimedia Commons.

Image source: Public domain, via Wikimedia Commons.

AGNES COOLBRITH (SMITH: DON CARLOS) (SMITH: JOSEPH) (SMITH: GEORGE A.) (PICKETT: WILLIAM)

"O! what a dupe I have been; what a dupe I have been."

PROPHETS PREY

"Go ye, therefore, and do the work of Abraham; enter ye into my law and ye shall be saved . . . . Abraham received concubines, and they bore him children . . . . David also received many wives and concubines, and also Solomon and Moses my servants, as also many others of my servants, from the beginning of creation until this time; and in nothing did they sin save in those things which they received not of me." (Doctrine and Covenants [1876], 132:32, 37-38).

RULON JEFFS HAD MORE THAN FIFTY WIVES

Rulon Jeffs, who became the prophet of the Fundamentalist Latter Day Saint Church (disciples who refused to suspend the practice of polygamy), attended the same high school as Gordon B. Hinckley, one of the Mormon prophets, and served a mission for the Church of Jesus Christ of Latter-day Saints in England, where he was a Secretary, Treasurer and Assistant to the President of the Mormon Mission. His first wife, Zola, was the daughter of Hugh B. Brown, who later became a member of the First Presidency of the Church of Jesus Christ of Latter-day Saints. Rulon was the father of two children with Zola, and the father of Warren Jeffs with one of his later wives. (Lindsay Hansen Park). Zola and Rulon were divorced in 1941.

Image Source: https://www.youtube.com/watch?v=lXP9t4rqZ4c

CANONIZED PLURALITY
ENDLESS INCREASE, ETERNAL GLORY

"This manifestation of divine light unfolding the purposes of God in the exaltation of His obedient children, making plain the celestial or eternal order of marriage, with endless increase and the extension of the glory of the sons of God, is the most momentous and magnificent unfoldment of the plans, purposes, and behests of the Almighty ever brought forth by the great seer of the nineteenth century [Joseph Smith]." (Deseret News)

Winston Blakemore, a modern polygamist, with some of his more than 149 children. Image source:
http://www.yan.vn/nguoi-dan-ong-co-145-nguoi-con-ruot-o-tuoi-60-103917.html

THOSE FAITHFUL FEW
MEN, WOMEN AND CHILDREN OF POLYGAMY

One scholar has referred to them in a sensitive way as useful, "as a reliquary of nineteenth-century Latter-day Saint life." Of them, he says, we see "Mormons who find in fundamentalist organizations a greater faithfulness to the doctrines and practices of the early church . . . ." (B. Carmon Hardy). Of them it might be said that they are the true followers of the prophet Joseph Smith, those who most appreciate the eternal and everlasting nature of celestial marriage, the order supposed by nineteenth century Saints to be at the heart and core of the Abrahamic covenant. They are "the ideological descendants of adherents who, a century ago, feared those changes that have become a part of twentieth-century Mormon belief." (Ibid.). They are those who heard their prophet's voice.

WARREN JEFFS

They strive to "defend polygamy's domestic configuration." They drink "from ancient springs." (Ibid., xviii-xix)

Warren Jeffs with a child bride.
Image source: Pinterest.com.

TWELVE POLYGAMOUS PROPHETS

HAROLD B. LEE

Image Source: https://www.mormonwiki.com/
File:Harold_B_Lee.jpg#filelinks

Harold B. Lee, who was just then an apostle, performed the marriage ceremony for this author and his wife. Seven of the prophets of the LDS Church (Joseph Smith, Brigham Young, John Taylor, Wilford Woodruff, Lorenzo Snow, Joseph F. Smith, and Heber J. Grant), those who led the Church from 1830 to 1945, actually practiced polygamy with about one hundred forty different women during their lifetimes. Five other LDS prophets (Joseph Fielding Smith, Harold B. Lee, Ezra Taft Benson, Howard W. Hunter, Russell M. Nelson), and some Mormon apostles including Dallin Oaks and L. Tom Perry, have been sealed to more than one woman in the temples, almost always after the death of an earlier wife. Those leaders expect to have more than one wife in the afterlife. The LDS Church did not abandon the "doctrine" of polygamy; it suspended the "practice" of polygamy in 1890, and then again (when that first effort failed) in 1904.

EZRA TAFT BENSON

"In 1950, Ezra Taft Benson [the thirteenth prophet] had himself sealed in marriage to his recently deceased [unmarried] cousin, Eva Amanda Benson – his living wife, Flora, standing in as proxy." Benson: "The Lord will richly bless her [Flora] for this act of unselfish love for Eva and me and the Kingdom." (Ezra Taft Benson, Diary, April 25, 1950, Dialogue, Winter 2008). Benson's sealing ordinance was performed by Elder Joseph Fielding Smith in the Salt Lake Temple. Smith later became the tenth President of the Church of Jesus Christ of Latter-day Saints. Benson was the great-grandson of a polygamist who married Desdemona Wadsworth Fullmer (Smith), one of Joseph Smith's plural wives, on January 26, 1846, shortly after the death of Smith. His father grew up in a polygamous household. (Lindsay Hansen Park)

Image Source: Public domain, via
Wikimedia Commons.

DESERET NEWS 1885

"However much the people might desire to do this [abandon polygamy], they could not without yielding every other principle, for it is the very key stone of our faith, and is so closely interwoven into everything that pertains to our religion that to tear it asunder and cast it away would involve the entire structure." ["Deseret News" quoted in Hardy, "Solemn Covenant," xix].

In and after 1890, "the church altered the phrase celestial marriage to mean simply a union for eternity." (Solemn Covenant, xxii). In its previous and scripturally correct manifestation, celestial marriage meant polygamous marriage. "[T]he times were ablaze with sexual consideration. ... We should naturally expect that such a pentecost would find an outlet for some of its fires in sexual behavior." (Ibid., 3). Polygamy "contributed to the social upheaval in Nauvoo, Illinois, and became the signature by which Mormons were known to the world after their removal to the Great Basin." (Ibid., xviii).

Front Page of the first issue of the *Deseret News*, published June 15, 1850. Image source: Public domain, via Wikimedia Commons.

"UTAH'S FIRST TEMPLE"
ST. GEORGE, UTAH

Joseph Smith and Brigham Young formulated divinely unchangeable deity-driven ceremonies, including Brigham Young's Last Testament (the "Lecture at the Veil") that until they were edited and revised contained highly incendiary rituals that prominently featured acrimonious attacks on evangelical Christianity, treasonous oaths against the government, potentially gruesome penalties, under the shield nudity and unanticipated covenants entered without the informed consent of the parishioner. The temple ceremony required the awkward misogynistic subservience of women wearing veils to their husbands. The "Lecture at the Veil" promoted the doctrine that Adam was God.

Image Source: Public domain, via Wikimedia Commons.

NAUVOO EXPOSITOR, JUNE 7, 1844

"We give this week to the following Preamble, Resolutions and Affidavits, of the Seceders from the Church at Nauvoo.-- The request is complied with on account of their deeming it very important that the public should know the true cause of their dissenting, as all manner of falsehood is spread abroad in relation to the schism in the Church. In our subsequent numbers several affidavits will be published, to substantiate the facts alleged."

ORDER OF DESTRUCTION

*"**City Council Resolution:** Resolved, by the City Council of the City of Nauvoo, that the printing office from whence issues the 'Nauvoo Expositor' is a public nuisance, and also all of said Nauvoo Expositors, which may be, or exist in said establishment, and the Mayor is instructed to cause said printing establishment and papers to be removed without delay, in such manner as he shall direct. Passed June 10th, 1844. George W. Harris, Prest. pro tem."*

__Order of Joseph Smith, Mayor (June 10, 1844):__ "To the Marshal of said City, greeting. You are hereby commanded to destroy the printing press from whence issues the Nauvoo Expositor, and pi the type of said printing establishment in the street, and burn all the Expositors and libelous handbills found in said establishment; and if resistance be offered to your execution of this order by the owner or others, demolish the house; and if anyone threatens you or the Mayor or the officers of the city, arrest those who threaten you, and fail not to execute this order without delay, and make due return thereon. By order of the City Council, JOSEPH SMITH, MAYOR."

Nauvoo Expositor Building, circa 1844. Image source: Public domain via Wikimedia Commons.

MARSHAL'S RETURN

"The within named press and type is destroyed and pied according to order, on this 10th of June, 1844, at about 8 o'clock p.m. J.P. Greene, C.M. [Danite, Brigham Young's brother-in-law], Headquarters, Nauvoo Legion, June 10th, 1844."

CHAPTER ONE

Visions and Revivals

[H]is word was received with the least confidence by those who knew him best. He could utter the most palpable exaggeration or marvelous absurdity with the utmost apparent gravity.

Pomeroy Tucker[1]

If God had not appeared to Joseph in 1820, or the Angel Moroni in 1823, this was, Joseph could come to appreciate, an oversight . . . which, after due consideration, he did not hesitate to amend.

Dale Morgan

. . . I was left [after the Vision] to all kinds of temptations, and mingling <with> all kinds of society I frequently <fell> into many foolish errors and displayed the weakness of youth and the corruption of human nature which I am sorry to say led me into divers temptations to the gratification of many appetites offensive in the sight of God.[2]

Joseph Smith

---

[1]Pomeroy Tucker Account (1867), Dan Vogel, ed., *Early Mormon Documents* (Salt Lake City: Signature Books, 2000), 3:93. "It is an interesting illustrative fact to be noticed in the history of Mormonism . . . that the origin of that extraordinary politico-religious institution is traceable to the insignificant little stone found in the digging of Mr. [Clark] Chase's well in 1819 [according to Willard Chase the stone was found in 1822]. *Such was the acorn of the Mormon oak.*" (Ibid., 3:99, emphasis added). A modern pundit disrespectfully attributed this fictitious quote to the prophet Joseph Smith: "I wouldn't say I've ever been a magician," he said, while looking at a stone in a hat pulled tight against his face, "but once I pulled an entire religion out of my hat."

[2]H. Michael Marquardt and Wesley P. Walters, *Inventing Mormonism: Tradition and the Historical Record* (n.p.: Smith Research Associates, 1998), Prologue, xiv-xv. From an extract from the Manuscript History penned in 1839 by James Mulholland before it was edited for publication.

CHARACTER AND CONFUSION

The 1838 "initial draft" of the *1838-39 History*, containing what metamorphosed to become the canonized account of the First Vision, "was written during a four-day period by George W. Robinson."[3]   Robinson was Sidney Rigdon's son-in-law, Nancy Rigdon's brother-in-law, Athalia Rigdon's husband, John C. Bennett's friend, a Danite Colonel,[4] a Nauvoo Legion General, a Church Recorder, Joseph Smith's Secretary, and a Scribe and Clerk to the First Presidency. In 1842, the same year the account of the vision he had partially penned was published, he left the Church.   General Robinson was thoroughly disenchanted and fearful for his safety. He would later become an apostle in another church. Joseph Smith's "early chroniclers," other men who carried the prophet's water and studied him, those who knew him best, also left.[5]   Smith's evacuees included Jesse Gause, Frederick G. Williams, Ezra Booth, William E. McLellin, John Whitmer, David Whitmer, Christian Whitmer, Jacob Whitmer, Peter Whitmer Jr., Hiram Page, Luke S. Johnson, Lyman E. Johnson, Martin Harris, John F. Boynton, Oliver Cowdery, Warren Cowdery, Warren Parrish, Thomas B. Marsh, Orson Hyde, John Corrill, Reed Peck, Benjamin Winchester and many less distinguished others, serious religious men, hall of fame founders. Many of Mormonism's most important and influential early disciples voted their changing convictions with scampering feet. A few of them (Luke S. Johnson, Oliver Cowdery, Thomas B. Marsh, Orson Hyde, Martin Harris) then later returned, but Johnson, Cowdery, Marsh and Martin Harris remained out of the Church until sometime after the death of the prophet.

"In 1839 [Robinson's initial draft of the *1838 History*] was copied by James Mulholland, another of Smith's scribes,[6] into what is known

---

[3]Marquardt and P. Walters, *Inventing Mormonism*, ix-x.

[4]D. Michael Quinn, *The Mormon Hierarchy: Origins of Power* (Salt Lake City: Signature Books in association with Smith Research Associates, 1994), 483.

[5]Sidney Rigdon left the Church, but not until after the death of Joseph Smith. Orson Hyde was out of favor and the Quorum for a short time.

[6]Former First Presidency Counselor William Law found the early death of Mulholland (in 1839, the same year Mulholland copied Robinson's initial draft of the history) suspicious. Dr. W. Wyl asked this question to Dr. William Law: "Have you had any knowledge of cases of poisoning in Nauvoo ordered by the

today as the Manuscript History of the Church: Book A-1. The A-1 book [the initial draft that became the Manuscript History] was revised before and after its first publication and is now considered to be Smith's official narrative."[7]   The provisions from the Manuscript History quoted in this chapter reflect the narrative as it was at first written by Mulholland in the last year of his life and "before it was edited for publication"[8] in the *Times and Seasons* in 1842. The Manuscript History, Mulholland's Manuscript History, which revised the unpublished initial draft, Robinson's initial draft, cleaned up in 1839 what was started in 1838 before the piece was published in 1842. The final product then became the founding story of the Church of Jesus Christ of Latter-day Saints. In 1842 Smith described, in what became the 1838-39 Canonized Pearl of Great Price Account, what happened after a vision supposed to have occurred "on the morning of a beautiful clear day early in the spring of Eighteen hundred and twenty." And what he further said preceded the vision of the angel in charge of the golden plates three-and-a-half years later in September 1823.[9]

Manuscript History: Book A-1 read as follows:

> *During the space of time which intervened between the time I had the vision and the year Eighteen hundred and twenty-three (having been forbidden to*

---

authorities?" Law: "I know that several men, six or seven, died under very suspicious circumstances. Among them were two secretaries of the prophet, Mulholland and Blaskel Thompson [1839, 1841]. I saw Mulholland die and the symptoms looked very suspicious to me, Dr. Foster, who was a very good physician, believed firmly that those six or seven men had been poisoned, and told me so repeatedly." (W. Wyl, Interview with William Law, 30 March 1887, *Salt Lake Tribune* [31 July 1887]). Joseph Smith later plurally married Mulholland's widow, Sarah Scott (Mulholland). After the death of James Mulholland (1839), and after the death of Joseph Smith (1844), Sarah was married for time to Heber C. Kimball, who was also proxy for Sarah's sealing to James Mulholland (but not to Joseph Smith). (George D. Smith, *Nauvoo Polygamy: " . . . but we called it celestial marriage"* [Salt Lake City: Signature Books, 2008], 623, 645 n 193).

[7]Marquardt and Walters, *Inventing Mormonism*, ix-x.

[8]Ibid.

[9]In the high-value Manuscript History Book A-1, the angel was identified as "Nephi," and not "Moroni," an error that was not inconsequential. The two religious leaders were separated in the Book of Mormon narrative by about a thousand years.

> *join any of the religious sects of the day, and being of*
> *very tender years and persecuted by those who ought*
> *to have been my friends, and to have treated me kindly*
> *and if they supposed me to be deluded to have*
> *endeavoured in a proper and affectionate manner to*
> *have reclaimed me) I was left to all kinds of*
> *temptations, and mingling <with> all kinds of society I*
> *frequently <fell> into many foolish errors and*
> *displayed the weakness of youth and the corruption of*
> *human nature which I am sorry to say led me into*
> *divers temptations to the gratification of many*
> *appetites offensive in the sight of God.*[10]

Those initial candid omissions intended to protect him from the follies of youth did not survive revision by Joseph or his redactors. The amended passage currently found in the canonized account now reads as follows:

> *I was left to all kinds of temptations; and, mingling*
> *with all kinds of society, I frequently fell into many*
> *foolish errors, and displayed the weakness of youth,*
> *and the foibles of human nature; which, I am sorry to*
> *say, led me into divers temptations, offensive in the*
> *sight of God. In making this confession, no one need*
> *suppose me guilty of any great or malignant sins. A*
> *disposition to commit such was never in my nature.*

---

[10]*Manuscript History, 1838-39,* (before the manuscript was edited for publication), reproduced at Marquardt and Walters, *Inventing Mormonism*, xiv-xv. *See, e.g., Times and Seasons* 3 (1842):749, quoted in Dale Morgan, *Dale Morgan on Early Mormonism: Correspondence & A New History*, ed. John Phillip Walker, with a Biographical Introduction by John Phillip Walker and a Preface by William Mulder (Salt Lake City: Signature Books, 1986), 250 (for a later correction see 375 n 10), emphasis added. The sound of this "corruption" is decidedly sexual. Note C – in the Manuscript History and added to the Pearl of Great Price Account of the First Vision of the Father and the Son after the account had been published without it in the *Times and Seasons* in 1842 – contained a third amendment (clarification), which was added to Joseph's "official" account. "'History,' A-1, pp. 132-33. 'Note C,' which appears in the later text, contains Joseph's qualification of his statement that he had been led into 'divers temptations,' wherein he asserts that 'in making this confession no one need suppose me guilty of any great or malignant sins . . . .'" (Dean C. Jessee, "The Early Accounts of Joseph Smith's First Vision," *BYU Studies* 9, no. 3 [Spring 1969]: 13, n 27, emphasis added).

But I was guilty of levity, and sometimes associated with jovial company, etc., not consistent with that character which ought to be maintained by one who was called of God as I had been. But this will not seem very strange to any one who recollects my youth, and is acquainted with my native cheery temperament.[11]

Joseph told Joshua the Jewish minister in 1835 that he had been told by an unnamed personage in about 1820 that his sins had been forgiven and that he was "filled . . . with Joy unspeakable."[12] When Joseph explained a second vision of the angel with the plates (that followed a first vision of the personages) to Joshua, it was described as another vision of angels in the night season after he had retired to bed. This Joseph, then about 17 years old, "was verry conscious that [he] had not kept the commandments" and "repented hartily" for all his "sins and transgression," humbling himself before "Him <whose eyes are over all things> . . . ."[13]

Documentational Timing

On April 27, 1838, in the state of Missouri, a recent emigrant by the name of Joseph Smith, just then an angry refugee from Kirtland, Ohio, commenced to dictate to a committee what would in time, after supplementation, become the official *History (the Manuscript History) of the Church of Jesus Christ of Latter-day Saints.* The original draft of this autobiographical narrative should have contained an account of the vision of the Father and the Son. Shortly after he arrived at Far West, Caldwell County, Missouri, Smith, Sidney Rigdon, Hyrum Smith and George W. Robinson drafted the initial opening section. By May 2 they had reached the account of Smith's obtaining the gold plates in September 1827.

---

[11]The Pearl of Great Price, Joseph Smith – History 1:28.

[12]Vogel, ed., *Early Mormon Documents*, 1:44, Joseph Smith Recital to Robert Matthews, 9 November 1835, Joseph Smith Diary, 9 November 1835, 23-26 (LDS Church History Library).

[13]Ibid.

"This first part is said to have not survived."[14] It may not have ever existed, but then again it may have found a place in some confidential section of those nineteenth-century archives.

Joseph Smith's handwritten 1832 Holographic Account of a Vision of the Son, a document concealed and suppressed by the highest leaders of the Church, survived to be reluctantly published one hundred thirty-three years later in 1965. That the first part of the high value April-May 1838 initial draft should somehow not have survived is highly improbable. Vogel reports that,

> The earliest history draft presented here begins abruptly with the baptisms of Smith and Cowdery in May 1829 and is evidently a continuation of the History begun in 1838 in Missouri. In the handwriting of James Mulholland, one of Smith's scribes, the twenty-five pages of text were probably written in Illinois soon after Smith's arrival in April 1839. Mulholland's earliest reference to writing for Smith was 10 June 1839 . . . .[15]

"The Manuscript History became the source for the various versions of Smith's published or official history."[16] Joseph Smith was thirty-two years old when he, counselors Sidney Rigdon and Hyrum Smith, and a scribe, George W. Robinson, prepared the preliminary draft of what would become the official *History of the*

---

[14]Joseph Smith, Diary, 27 April – 4 May 1838; cf. Faulring 1987, 176-80, cited by Dan Vogel, Editorial Note, Vogel, ed., *Early Mormon Documents*, 1:54, emphasis added.

[15]Vogel, ed., *Early Mormon Documents*, 1:54. James Mulholland, Diary, 10 June 1839, cited in Jessee, "The Early Accounts of Joseph Smith's First Vision," (1989), 231, 267. The information included in *Early Mormon Documents*, vol. 1, is from Dean C. Jessee's 1989 transcription (1989, 231-64). Mulholland died under suspicious circumstances on November 3, 1839, and Smith later married his widow.

[16]Vogel, ed., *Early Mormon Documents*, 1:55. Before Mulholland died on November 3, 1839, he started to prepare "a final draft of the opening portion of Smith's Manuscript History . . . . Mulholland apparently adapted this version from his and Robinson's earlier drafts of 1838 and 1839 . . . ." Other scribes, including Robert B. Thompson (who died on August 27, 1841), William W. Phelps and Willard Richards, followed Mulholland and finished the History. Smith lost two scribes to death in less than two years.

Church, a history that would grow to include the 1838-39 Pearl of Great Price Account of the 1820 vision of the Father and the Son. He was at least thirty-three years old when it was further continued, composed, adapted, recopied and revised in and/or after 1839, thirty-four years old when the earliest version was published by Orson Pratt in Scotland in 1840, thirty-six years old when the modern account was published in the *Times and Seasons* in Nauvoo in 1842, and even older when the account was still yet further amended after publication in and/or after 1843 or 1844.[17] All of this later revision suggests a lot of invention many years after the original event was supposed to have occurred in 1820. Smith was dead before the 1838-39 Pearl of Great Price Account finally achieved its now revered (and canonized) prominence as the founding story of the Mormon Church (the acceptance of which is necessary for baptism). The 1838-39 Pearl of Great Price Account was composed under volatile circumstances at stressful times. The 1842 *Times and Seasons* publication of the account followed the disastrous Zion Camp misadventure in 1834, the doctrinal, economic and social difficulties that surfaced at Kirtland, Ohio, in 1837, and the short nasty Missouri Mormon War in 1838.

Regarding the separate earlier reported vision of the Angel Moroni, there are three presently known primary accounts – (1) Joseph Smith History (1832), (2) Oliver Cowdery and Joseph Smith History (1834-35); and (3) Joseph Smith/Pearl of Great Price History of the Church (1838-39) – plus various other secondary accounts. Two of the secondary accounts are attributed to Lucy Mack Smith, Joseph Smith's mother, and to William Smith, his brother.[18] Joseph also described the gold plates events to Robert Matthews (Joshua the

---

[17]A precursor account mostly faithful to the substance of the 1838-39 Pearl of Great Price Account was published in Scotland in 1840 by Orson Pratt. The modern account was then published in the *Times and Seasons* (a Mormon publication edited by Joseph Smith) in Nauvoo, Illinois, in 1842. The Wentworth Account: 1842, a foreshortened version of the vision, was prepared after the 1838-39 Pearl of Great Price Account but was published in the *Times and Seasons* in Nauvoo in 1842, shortly before the Pearl of Great Price Account. Orson Pratt appears to have played some part in the creation of the Wentworth Account, language in which seems to have tracked in some particulars the language contained in the Pratt version of the vision reported in Scotland in 1840.

[18]William Smith was a founding Apostle of the Church of Latter Day Saints in 1835. He briefly became the Patriarch, succeeding his father (Joseph Sr.), and his brother (Hyrum), after Joseph's death.

Jewish Minister) in 1835.   Still another separate account was prepared by Joseph's dependable friend, Joseph Knight.

Atmospherics

On April 6, 1830, Joseph Smith was ordained "Prophet, Seer and Revelator" of what was at first called the Church of Christ.   On April 6, 1830, he was appointed "to be a translator [seer, a translator, etc. (Doctrine and Covenants 21:1)] ...."[19]   On April 6, 1830, the day the Church was organized, the Lord instructed the members to "give heed unto all his [Joseph's] words and commandments which he shall give unto you as he receiveth them, walking in all holiness before me.   For his word ye shall receive, as if from mine own mouth, in all patience and faith."[20]   David Whitmer was of the opinion that, "Brother Joseph being ordained as 'Prophet, Seer and Revelator' to the church" "was the first error that crept into the church."[21]   "Desiring . . . prominence . . . ," Whitmer said, "is not humility, but . . . pride; it is seeking praise of mortals instead of the praise of God."   "Satan surely rejoiced on that day."[22]   Whitmer, one of the Three Witnesses to the Book of Mormon, was sorely disappointed by that early turn of events.[23]

Joseph Smith didn't mention a vision of the Father and the Son when the Church was legally organized on April 6, 1830.   He didn't mention Levi, Aaron, Melchizedek, John the Baptist, Peter, James and John, Elias, Elijah or Priesthood.   "No one, friend or foe, in New York or Pennsylvania remembers either that there was 'great

---

[19]Doctrine and Covenants 21:1.

[20]Ibid., 21:4-5.

[21]David Whitmer, *An Address to All Believers in Christ: by A Witness to the Divine Authenticity of The Book of Mormon* (Richmond, MO: n.p., 1887; photographic reprint, Concord, CA: Pacific Publishing Company, 1993), 33-34.

[22]Ibid.

[23]"They [the members of the Church] were like the children of Israel wanting a king, and God gave them a king ["God allowed them to be answered according to their erring desires"] ["Remember also that *some revelations are of God; some revelations are of man; and some revelations are of the devil.*"], but it was to their final destruction.   He gave the church a leader, but it proved their destruction . . . and [produced the] final landing of the majority of them in the Salt Lake Valley in polygamy, believing that their leader had received a revelation from God to practice this abomination." (Ibid., 34, emphasis retained).

persecution' or even that Joseph claimed to have had a vision."[24]
The decades-long delayed 1842 report of the 1820 vision followed by
many years the young glass looker's checkered early career, his
persistent use of the chocolate-colored stone ("the acorn of the
Mormon oak"), the persistent practice of ritual magic and various
things occult, money digging, glass looking, fortune telling and the
petulant antics of the treasure-guardian "Nephi" or "Moroni," the
messenger assigned different names in different accounts.   The
1838-39 Pearl of Great Price Account followed Joseph's much
earlier tearful admission to his father-in-law (Isaac Hale) in the
presence of a friendly witness (Peter Ingersoll) in the 1820s that "he
could not see in a stone now, nor never could; and that his former
pretensions in that respect, were all false," after which Joseph
"promised to give up his old habits of digging for money and
looking into stones."[25] It was a promise he didn't begin to keep. He
subsequently translated the Book of Mormon and received some of
the early revelations by looking at the chocolate-colored stone in the
bottom of an old white stovepipe hat.

Before the 1838-39 Pearl of Great Price Account of the vision of the
Father and the Son was published in 1842, Joseph – who was
supposed to have obtained magic spectacles and golden plates – had
translated, published and revised the Book of Mormon and
corrected the King James Bible. By 1838-39 and before 1842,
Joseph had reported visitations from Nephi or Moroni, John the
Baptist, Peter, James and John, and many other heavenly
messengers, including but not limited to Jesus, Moses, Elias and
Elijah.[26] In the face of that extensive accumulation of supernatural

[24]Grant H. Palmer, *An Insider's View of Mormon Origins* (Salt Lake City:
Signature Books, 2002), 245.

[25]Peter Ingersoll, being first duly sworn, 9 December 1833, statement
reproduced in Eber D. Howe, *Mormonism Unvailed: Or, A Faithful Account of That
Singular Imposition and Delusion* (Painesville, OH: E.D. Howe, 1834; reprint, New
York: AMS Press Inc., 1977), 234-35.

[26]Paul R. Cheesman, "An Analysis of the Accounts Relating Joseph Smith's
Early Visions" (Master of Religious Education Thesis, Brigham Young University,
1965), 68. *See, e.g.,* Doctrine and Covenants 110:11-13 and headnote. "In addition
to the Father, Son, and Moroni, there were more than ten personage[s] involved in
the manifestations, according to Joseph Smith . . . ." Cheesman, the man who was
first allowed to reveal the long-suppressed first 1832 Account of the vision of the
Son more than one hundred and thirty years after the fact and in 1965, did not
specifically mention two of them, Elias *and* Elijah. (Ibid.).

recitals, he had inexplicably still not yet ever publicly described the 1820 vision of the Father and the Son. Before the 1838-39 Pearl of Great Price Account was locally published in 1842, Joseph claimed to have effectuated through the efforts of angels the restorations of the Aaronic, Patriarchal and Melchizedek Priesthoods. John the Baptist had supposedly conferred the lower (Aaronic) priesthood on Joseph Smith and Oliver Cowdery, and they had baptized each other and others. Peter, James and John had supposedly conferred the higher (Melchizedek) priesthood on Joseph Smith and Oliver Cowdery, and they had ordained each other and others. These accounts didn't exist until in and after 1834. It is important to recount that the Priesthood restoration events were retroactively described at the end of a revelation originally written years before (and also published years before) without them. The amendments, true to form, were unannounced. Furthermore, Elias had supposedly conferred the Patriarchal (Abrahamic) Priesthood on Joseph Smith and Oliver Cowdery, and Joseph Smith Sr. and Hyrum Smith had been ordained to the office of Presiding Patriarch. Hyrum had been ordained to succeed Joseph Sr. by Joseph Sr. just before Joseph Sr. died. Joseph had established priesthood quorums and restored and staffed the new Church, first as the "Church of Christ," then as the "Church of Latter Day Saints," and finally as the "Church of Jesus Christ of Latter-day Saints." The last two titles had millennial implications (failed millennial implications); and one of the titles faced criticism at the time because it omitted the name of Christ.

By 1838-39 Smith had placed the historic location of the Garden of Eden in Jackson County, Missouri, coincidentally the place of the final gathering, the place called Mormon Zion. He showed his followers where Adam went after he and Eve were expelled from the Garden and where Cain killed Abel, and he identified (but not until after others had first discovered) ancient Adam's altar. Adam wasn't symbolic; his story wasn't a myth. These events, their stated locations and the altar (an artifact of critical importance), like some of Smith's revelations, proved to Smith's satisfaction and to that of his followers that Adam and Eve, Cain, Abel, and others began and lived in North America. Thus the Western Hemisphere (not the Great Rift Valley) had really been the cradle of civilization. Adam, according to Joseph, was known as Michael in the preexistence.

Joseph Smith identified Elias and Elijah as two separate figures. Esaias *and* Isaiah were also identified as two separate figures. By 1838-39 and before 1842, Smith had supervised the publication of the 1833 Book of Commandments (containing selections from the more than seventy revelations he had already received), and he had collaborated with Cowdery in the preparation and publication of an extensive 1834-35 History, the first "authorized" history of the Church of Latter Day Saints. That history, "the first account published in a church periodical" (a series in the form of letters that appeared in the *Latter Day Saints' Messenger and Advocate*), was "later copied into Joseph Smith's journal and considered part of his own history."[27] Neither of those resources contained an account of the vision of the Father and the Son. Nor did they discuss the restoration of the Melchizedek Priesthood.

Kirtland Turmoil

After the Saints moved to Ohio, Joseph Smith ordered and supervised the construction of a temple in Kirtland. By this time he had received and published the revelations described in the Book of Doctrine and Covenants in 1835, and he had prepared ("*Prepared by the Prophet Joseph Smith*") or helped to prepare and passed upon the *Lectures on Faith* delivered to the School of the Prophets in Kirtland, Ohio, in 1834-35. The Three Witnesses to the Book of Mormon selected twelve founding members of the Quorum of the Twelve Apostles in 1835. Joseph, however, replaced one of the witnesses' choices (Brigham Young's brother, Phineas Young) before he was ordained with his own brother William Smith.

"A leadership crisis began in Kirtland on 7 November 1837,"[28] resulting in a number of "prominent apostasies," in large part because of various Book of Mormon issues. Martin Harris was excommunicated during the last week of December in 1837. It was a period of economic and doctrinal distress, a time of pain and disappointment. Frederick G. Williams, a Counselor in the First Presidency, the dependable soldier who penned the historical recitals associated with Joseph's Handwritten 1832 Account of the

---

[27]Marquardt and Walters, *Inventing Mormonism*, ix.
[28]Palmer, *An Insider's View of Mormon Origins*, 245.

first vision, left the Church. John Whitmer, one of the witnesses to the Book of Mormon, an early and important historian, was excommunicated in 1838. On March 25, 1838, Harris, one of the Three Witnesses, "told a public meeting [after Smith and Rigdon left Kirtland] that none of the witnesses had physically seen or handled the plates, that they had not seen the plates with their 'natural eyes.'"[29] Harris saw the plates, he said, like one sees a city through a mountain. The eight witnesses had been reluctant to sign their statement, according to Harris, because they hadn't seen or handled the plates. George A. Smith, who became an apostle in 1839, attended the meeting ("this last meeting" on March 25, 1838) where Martin Harris addressed certain issues concerning the plates. Harris's comments "triggered a discussion led by Warren Parrish. As a result of the spread of those unwelcome recitals, Apostles John F. Boynton, Luke Johnson, and other church members 'renounced the Book of Mormon.'"[30] Five days after that meeting, and on March 30, George A. Smith recounted those recent events in these terms: "'Last Sabbath, a division arose among the Parrish party about the Book of Mormon. John Boynton, W. Parrish, Luke Johnson and others said it was nonsense.'[31] Smith further recalled that about 'thirty . . . prominent Elders' belonging to the Parrish group, including Apostles Lyman Johnson, William McLellin, and others, 'renounce[d] the Book of Mormon and Joseph Smith.'"[32]

Warren Parrish, Joseph Smith's former highly favored scribe, was a prominent figure in the Kirtland revolt. Boynton called Mormonism a humbug from first to last.[33] By April 7, 1838, five of the apostles were said to be out of harmony or doubtful, including Joseph's younger brother, William Smith. A second Smith brother, Samuel H. Smith, in league with William, was troubled. On April 13, 1838, Apostles Luke S. Johnson, Lyman E. Johnson and John F.

---

[29]Ibid., 245-46.

[30]Ibid., 246.

[31]George A. Smith to Josiah Fleming, 30 March 1838, *Journal History of the Church* (Kirtland, OH: LDS Archives), quoted in Palmer, *An Insider's View of Mormon Origins*, 246.

[32]George A. Smith, 10 January 1858, *Journal of Discourses*, 26 vol. (London and Liverpool: 1854-86), 7:115, quoted in Palmer, *An Insider's View of Mormon Origins*, 246.

[33]Palmer, *An Insider's View of Mormon Origins*, 246-47.

Boynton were excommunicated or left the church.[34]   Oliver
Cowdery and David Whitmer were excommunicated on April 12
and 13, 1838. Hiram Page and Jacob Whitmer, two other Book of
Mormon witnesses, left the Church, and by the fall of 1838, Thomas
B. Marsh (the President of the Quorum of the Twelve Apostles)
and Orson Hyde (who would return to become a future President of
the Quorum of the Twelve Apostles) had also defected.[35]   Hyde,
Luke S. Johnson and Marsh later returned, in the case of Marsh not
until long after the death of Smith. Grant Palmer points out:

> *Within a month of Harris' comments, three of the*
> *apostles no longer believed in the Book of Mormon*
> *and two more were out of favor with the church . . . .*
> *All three witnesses to the Book of Mormon and three*
> *of the eight had defected. The entire Whitmer clan*
> *had left the church.*[36]

Before this debate raged, before the spirit soured and near to the
time of the Book of Mormon woes, the Kirtland Anti-Safety Society
failed. "Economic disillusionment over the failure of the Kirtland
Anti-Safety Society [Joseph's God-directed anti-Bank] may have
fueled the dissent, but doctrinal disillusionment stemming from
Harris's statement and the subsequent debate over the Book of
Mormon continued to smolder long afterwards."[37]   Joseph's
controversial domestic encounters with an amiable young domestic
by the name of Fanny Alger, who boarded with the Smiths, added
fuel to the fire.[38] Over time Joseph had several personal encounters
with household helpers who lived with him, Emma and the children
at home.

---

[34]Ibid., 247.

[35]Ibid., 248.

[36]Ibid., emphasis added.

[37]Ibid.

[38]Benjamin Johnson: She was "A varry nice & Comly young woman about
my own age[,] towards whoom not only mySelf but everyone Seemed partial for the
ameability of her character and it was whispered eaven then that Joseph Loved
her." (See Dean R. Zimmerman, *I Knew the Prophets: An Analysis of the Letter of
Benjamin F. Johnson to George F. Gibbs, Reporting Doctrinal Views of Joseph
Smith and Brigham Young* [n.l.: Horizon Publishers, 1976], 37-38, quoted in George
D. Smith, *Nauvoo Polygamy*, 46).

"During this time of apostasy, approximately three hundred left the Church, representing about 15 percent of the Kirtland membership."[39] It was exactly during this time of upheaval, when some church leaders begin doubting his mission as a prophet, that Smith chose "to connect his prophetic call"[40] to a vision independent of the recollections of undependable witnesses. After leaving Kirtland (and his creditors) in a cloud, and "On April 26 [1838] he renamed the church. The next day he started dictating a new first vision narrative"[41] that "appears to have shifted his [prophetic] call from 1823 [back] to 1820 . . . ."[42] Now the 1823 vision of the Angel Moroni, the original First Vision (even though it was not mentioned anywhere in the first edition of the Book of Mormon[43]), surrendered its early advantaged place to a new and previously unknown account of an 1820 vision of the Father and the Son. Early Mormons believed that the 1823 vision of the Angel Moroni was the First Vision.[44] This new and first public account of a First Vision narrative describing the Father and the Son was more impressive than the first unpublished account of Joseph's first encounter with deity, the 1832 Holographic epiphany. That 1832 Account was concealed and suppressed in the society's archives for one hundred thirty-three years, until 1965.[45] The new formerly unfamiliar First Vision narrative awkwardly supplanted the primacy of the 1823 vision of the Angel Moroni, but not before it borrowed lock, stock and barrel that first reported vision's classic account of a great Palmyra revival.

He announced that his initial calling had not come
from an angel in 1823, as he had said for over a

---

[39]Joseph Smith Jr., *The Papers of Joseph Smith: Journal, 1832-1842*, ed. Dean C. Jessee (Salt Lake City: Deseret Book Company, 1989-1992), 217-18 n 2, quoted in Palmer, *An Insider's View of Mormon Origins*, 248.

[40]Ibid., 245.

[41]Doctrine and Covenants 115:3-4; Jessee, ed., *The Papers of Joseph Smith: Journal, 1832-1842*, 232-33, quoted in Palmer, *An Insider's View of Mormon Origins*, 248.

[42]Palmer, *An Insider's View of Mormon Origins*, 245.

[43]Richard L. Bushman, with the assistance of Jed Woodworth, *Joseph Smith: Rough Stone Rolling* (New York: Alfred A. Knopf, 2005), 39.

[44]*See, e.g.*, Oliver Cowdery and Joseph Smith's 1834-35 History of the "rise" of the church, Oliver Cowdery (and Joseph Smith), "Letter to W.W. Phelps, Esq.," *Messenger and Advocate*, vol. 1 no. 1 (October 1834).

[45]Palmer, *An Insider's View of Mormon Origins*, 251-52.

decade, but from God the Father and Jesus Christ in 1820 (JS-History 1:28). This earlier date established his mission independent of the troubling questions and former witnesses associated with the Book of Mormon. Like the 1834-35 priesthood restoration recitals, the first vision version of April 1838 added significant material that bolstered his authority during a time of crisis.[46]

Drafting in Missouri

Kirtland was in chaos. The disgraced prophet left with Rigdon during the night in January 1838. He arrived in Missouri on March 14, 1838. Far West was flourishing when Smith arrived, and the Saints were at peace with their neighbors. The conflict at that moment in time was within (not outside of) the Church. On March 10, 1838, just before the fugitive prophet arrived, John Whitmer was excommunicated. On April 12 and 13, 1838, very shortly after the prophet arrived, Oliver Cowdery, David Whitmer, Lyman E. Johnson, Luke S. Johnson and John F. Boynton were excommunicated. Starting on April 27 and until May 4, 1838, Smith (assisted by others) dictated the "History of the Church," part of which then later and after revision became the 1838-39 Pearl of Great Price Account of Joseph's previously unknown 1820 vision of the Father and the Son, an account that was published in the *Times and Seasons* in 1842. Prepared in 1838-39, this account wasn't published until 1842.

In June the Danites, a secret society under the direction of Joseph Smith and Sidney Rigdon, was organized at Far West and Adam-ondi-Ahman. On June 17, 1838, not long after the prophets arrived, Rigdon delivered the notorious Salt Sermon. It was a harsh public condemnation of those perceived as disloyal to Smith and Rigdon. Rigdon compared the dissenters to salt that had lost its savor that was, he said, thenceforth good for nothing but to be cast out and trodden under foot of men. On June 19, after terrible threats against their lives and those of their families, Oliver

---

[46]Ibid., 251, emphasis added.

Cowdery, the Whitmers and Lyman E. Johnson fled from Caldwell County. In July, under the direction of Joseph Smith, Mormons violated an earlier agreement made by lesser figures not to expand their settlements in northwestern Missouri. On July 4, 1838, Sidney Rigdon delivered his "war of extermination" speech, a provocative message the Church would like to have forgotten composed in the office of the Presidency. In August, September and October, after Smith and Rigdon literally kicked a sleeping dog, theocratic Mormons and Missouri slave holders and republicans fought a short, nasty, brutal war in which the Mormons initially gave nearly as good as they got. They were equally ugly antagonists. On November 1, Joseph advised his Mormon troops to surrender.

Far West, that previous place of peace, was now in ruins, the people were scattered, and Joseph, Sidney and the Church were finished, not only in Far West, Adam-ondi-Ahman and DeWitt, but in the divinely promised place of the all-important Gathering, Independence and Missouri. Joseph Smith and all those who followed him were not welcome anywhere in the land of their earthly and eternal inheritance. Zion was lost and the prophets went to jail! Smith and Rigdon had quickly created the volatile circumstances that unsettled Far West and led to the Missouri debacle.

The later actual publication of modern Mormonism's founding story followed the beginning of missionary work, gatherings at Kirtland, Ohio; Independence, Far West, Adam-ondi-Ahman and DeWitt, Missouri, and the Mormon passage to Iowa and Illinois. Much history preceded the notice of this new and previously unannounced account. The 1842 publication of the 1838-39 Pearl of Great Price Account of a supposed 1820 vision of the Father and the Son followed dreadful oaths taken by fanatical Danites (Mormon thugs), a war between the Mormons and the state of Missouri, recriminations and hard time at the Liberty Jail. It followed Smith's escape, fugitive status for the Mormon prophet, reunification, the construction of the city-state called Nauvoo (at the place first called Commerce, Illinois) and the rise of Joseph's then next most intimate associate, Dr. John C. Bennett.

The publication of the founding story of the Mormon Church – an account market-tested in Scotland in 1840 – is actually an 1842 event in LDS American chronology. Joseph Smith had migrated from the occult to the sacred when the now canonized Pearl of Great Price Account of the 1820 vision was first presented to the faithful in the *Times and Seasons* at Nauvoo, Illinois, in April 1842. Historian Bushman writes: In the minds of Mormons today, the First Vision is an event of seismic importance. "[T]he events of that morning marked the beginning of the restoration of the Gospel and the commencement of a new dispensation."[47] The vision provided a new source of authority for a discredited prophet whose prophecies concerning Mormon money, the Anti-Bank in Ohio, the Gathering, Zion in Missouri and the redemption of Zion in Missouri had miserably failed. And it supplanted the vision of the Angel Moroni, that was until then the founding story of the Mormon Church.

Publishing in Scotland

Although the 1838-39 Pearl of Great Price Account was at least the fourth account of an 1820 vision of the deities, it was the only account besides the 1842 Wentworth Account (a shortened less detailed account of the same event) known to the members of the Church in the nineteenth century. Ordinary Mormons knew nothing of four other earlier versions of three other 1832 and 1835 accounts (none of which have ever been included in the Pearl of Great Price or canonized).

Members were taught for more than one hundred years that the Pearl of Great Price Account (including the 1840 Scottish account) was the only account of Smith's first encounter with deity and that the prophet told his story only once. The 1840 and 1842 accounts, and Wentworth, it is supposed, may be counted as one. When Joseph revisited the previous uncirculated private accounts of the vision in 1838 and 1839, he could not have appreciated how carefully future historians would look at every element of his various claims, including the specious claims of persecution, or how devastating their researches would be to the authenticity of the various accounts. When he did finally publish (market test) a

---

[47]Bushman, *Joseph Smith: Rough Stone Rolling*, 39.

version of the new account in 1840, it was not in Nauvoo, Illinois, then busy becoming the center of the Mormon universe, but rather in distant Scotland at the fringes of Mormon civilization and for the benefit of a tiny dispensable segment of the Mormon flock.

Why did Joseph Smith allow Orson Pratt to publish an account of the First Vision in a tiny congregation in Scotland years before the story was published for the benefit of a larger congregation in Nauvoo? For the same reason that Brigham Young directed Orson Pratt (in 1852) to reveal to the world the fact that the Mormons had taught, had practiced and were practicing polygamy, contrary to everything they had previously solemnly said with but one voice for more than twenty years. Orson Pratt, an honored member of the Mormon hall of fame, was bright but dishonest. He could put controversial facts, unbelievable deceptions, in the best possible light. Orson's older brother Parley told the leaders of the Church it was their duty to lie for the prophet.[48] The two Pratts were reliable disciples perfect for polygamy (or anything else). They were men who could be trusted not to tell the truth.

If Joseph's 1838-39 Account was preached anywhere or at any time prior to its 1840 publication in Scotland, it was probably done by the younger Pratt. It seems plausible to surmise that the vision was previewed at distance in a smaller less significant market, where failure was meaningless, in order to see how it would play in a larger more significant market, where failure wasn't an option. If that founding story could make it there – among the proud, the few, the prickly poorly informed Scots – it could probably make it anywhere. And if it couldn't make it there what had anyone lost?

---

[48]Sidney Rigdon in the June 18, 1845, *Messenger and Advocate*, an after-the-death-of-Joseph resource, described how Apostle Parley P. Pratt, in speaking of the means by which Church leaders should sustain Smith, advised that "we must lie to support brother Joseph, it is our duty to do so.'" (Richard S. Van Wagoner, *Mormon Polygamy: A History* [Salt Lake City: Signature Books, 1986], 235 n 12). "Not only were church leaders willing to violate the law to promote polygamy, they also did not hesitate to blacken the character of individuals who threatened to expose the secret practice of plural marriage." (Ibid.). Rigdon, out of the Church, angry with Joseph and opposed to polygamy, said, "How often these men and their accomplices stood up before the congregation, and called God and all the holy Angels to witness, that there was no such doctrine taught in the church; and it has now come to light." (Ibid., 72).

In 1842, twenty-two years after the alleged vision, Joseph Smith first publicly described the previously unknown event to the members of the American Church. His account was published in the *Times and Seasons* in Nauvoo two years before the prophet's death after it had been market tested in distant Scotland.

"A Great Awakening"

Since 1842 the Mormon Church has taught that Joseph Smith was initially prompted to retire to the woods in consequence of the circumstances associated with a religious revival that occurred in Palmyra, New York, in the year 1820. In actuality, there was no religious revival in Palmyra, New York, in the year 1820. Time and study have revealed stunning contradictions in Joseph Smith's 1838-39 Pearl of Great Price Account of an 1820 vision. Those findings challenge the traditionally accepted chronology of Mormonism's founding events. In 1820 – in what was said to have been the second year after the Smith family's move to Manchester, New York, and the year in which Joseph claimed he saw the Father and the Son – "there was in the place where we lived an unusual excitement on the subject of religion. It commenced with the Methodists, but soon became general among all the sects in that region of country."[49] Ministering "to the hunger of his followers for a stirring legend of his youth,"[50] Joseph dated the First Vision against that "unusual excitement." Methodists, Presbyterians and Baptists competed for converts and "great multitudes united themselves to the different religious parties . . . ."[51]

The founding story of the Church of Jesus Christ of Latter-day Saints (the 1838-39 Pearl of Great Price Account of an 1820 vision first brought to light in 1842) reported that the conversions of four members of Joseph's immediate family occurred during a great Palmyra revival.

> *I was at this time in my fifteenth year. My father's family was proselyted to the Presbyterian faith, and*

---

[49]The Pearl of Great Price, Joseph Smith – History 1:5.
[50]Morgan, *Dale Morgan on Early Mormonism*, 245.
[51]The Pearl of Great Price, Joseph Smith – History 1:5.

> *four of them joined that church, namely, my mother,*
> *Lucy; my brothers Hyrum and Samuel Harrison; and*
> *my sister Sophronia.*[52]

The revival also caused Joseph to retire to the woods and prompted him to make his first attempt to pray out loud. The revival framed the inquiry ("which of all the sects was right"), the vision and the response. It was (and is) the historical centerpiece of the founding story of the Church of Jesus Christ of Latter-day Saints. It was a temporal event against which the verisimilitude of Joseph's visionary claims has come to be measured. Dale Morgan argued that it provided objective content against which the vision's subjective content might be absolutely evaluated.[53]

The Boy Who Didn't Pray

Donna Hill, one of Smith's biographers, described his early religious life in faith-promoting terms: "The strict church requirements of Puritan communities did not prevail [in Manchester and Palmyra]. Nevertheless, like many others, the Smiths had remained intensely religious within the family circle."[54] What that meant, when unencoded, was that the Smiths (until some of them converted to the Presbyterian Church after and because of the death of Alvin) were not even church goers. "In every account of the Smith family life which we have from their own hands, faith and prayer were predominant," Hill reports.[55] Yet Pomeroy Tucker, a young printer apprentice employed by the *Palmyra Register* newspaper office who knew the Smiths and assisted with the printing of the Book of Mormon, called the Smith family "an illiterate, whisky drinking, shiftless, irreligious race of people . . . ."[56]

"Joseph Jr. said that his parents 'spared no pains' in the religious

---

[52]Ibid., 1:7, emphasis added.

[53]Morgan, *Dale Morgan on Early Mormonism*, 255.

[54]Donna Hill, *Joseph Smith: The First Mormon* (USA: Doubleday & Company, Inc., 1977; reprint, Salt Lake City: Signature Books, 1977, 1982, 1999), 44.

[55]Ibid.

[56]Pomeroy Tucker Account (1867), Vogel, ed., *Early Mormon Documents*, 3:93.

education of their children."[57] Yet in 1820, in his fifteenth year and "amidst" all of his "anxieties," this same Joseph Smith also said, "I had never as yet made the attempt to pray vocally."[58] Furthermore, his older brother Alvin didn't belong to a church and had never been baptized. None of the Smith children had been baptized. The family was dysfunctional. The mother was a Puritan, the father was a Universalist or a Unitarian, and possibly both. Their principles clashed. Alvin, also a treasure-seeking son, assumed the precarious role of family patriarch. Joseph Sr., a hard-drinking money-digging man and a Masonic seceder, was a weak patriarch. Father Joseph was in fact a family project. There were those who wanted him to be more than he was. "[F]aith and prayer were predominant"? Is that claim not highly improbable given what else Joseph has said? These incongruities materially affect everything he later claimed. While Joseph's later apologetic talk may heighten his narrative, with regard to the evidence it is quite preposterous.

"Lucy said years afterward that she had raised her children 'in the fear and love of God, and never was there a more obedient family.'"[59] Yet Joseph, confessing frailty, said that he had never before uttered a vocal prayer. And he admitted, at the height of his great spiritual experience, shortly after the vision in 1820, that he had succumbed to "the corruption of human nature" and "to the gratification of many appetites offensive in the sight of God."[60] Someone else later softened that admission to say, "I frequently fell into many foolish errors, and displayed the weakness of youth, and the foibles of human nature; which I am sorry to say, led me into divers temptations, offensive in the sight of God."[61]

Joseph's Awakening

In his one-hundred thirty year concealed and suppressed 1832 Holographic (handwritten) Account of a vision that didn't surface

---

[57]Hill, *Joseph Smith: The First Mormon*, 44.
[58]The Pearl of Great Price, Joseph Smith – History 1:14.
[59]Hill, *Joseph Smith: The First Mormon*, 45.
[60]Manuscript History, 1839, Mulholland, prior to editing for publication, quoted in Prologue, Marquardt and Walters, *Inventing Mormonism*, xiv-xv.
[61]The Pearl of Great Price, Joseph Smith – History 1:28.

until 1965, Joseph Smith said that he became interested in religion when he was about twelve years old. That was when his mind "become seriously imprest [p. 1] with regard to the all importent concerns for the well=fare of my immortal Soul."[62] Smith turned twelve on December 23, 1817. From "the age of twelve years to fifteen," he said he "pondered many things" in his heart.[63] But Josiah Stowell Jr., a friendly voice, rocked that boat to say that Joseph did not profess religion when they attended school together in Bainbridge, New York, during the winter of 1825-26. This was supposedly after the First Vision, after the Second Vision, and just before the Bainbridge money-digging trial in 1826.[64] Joseph was nineteen or twenty years old during the winter of 1825-26.

In Oliver and Joseph's 1834-35 first authorized and first published account of a first First Vision, the vision of the angel in charge of the plates, the then first account of Joseph's first encounter with a heavenly messenger, the collaborators initially declared that Joseph's "mind became awakened" because of the preaching of the Reverend George Lane during a great Palmyra revival that occurred in the "15th year" of Joseph's life. That would have been 1820.[65] That clearly meant – before anyone knew about some 1820 vision of the Father and the Son – that the *vision of the angel with the plates* and *the Palmyra revival* both occurred in 1820. But that was a mistake. The 1834-35 History was awkwardly corrected in a subsequent installment to change that equation and say that *the vision of the angel,* the *Palmyra revival* and *Joseph's religious awakening*, three separate important concerns, had actually occurred in "1823" in the "17th" year of Joseph's life.[66] Josiah Stowell Jr.'s later account also rocked that boat.

When Oliver Cowdery and Joseph Smith confidently moved the

---

[62]Joseph Smith Jr., *The Personal Writings of Joseph Smith*, ed. Dean C. Jessee (Salt Lake City: Deseret Book, 1984), 4.

[63]Ibid., 5.

[64]Josiah Stowell Jr. to J.S. Fullmer, 17 Feb. 1843, LDS Archives, published in *LDS Church News* (12 May 1985), 10.

[65]"Letter III" (Cowdery and Smith's 1834-35 History), *Messenger and Advocate*, vol. 1 no. 3 (December 1834), 42.

[66]Oliver Cowdery (and Joseph Smith), "Letter IV To W.W. Phelps, Esq." (Oliver Cowdery and Joseph Smith's 1834-35 History), *Messenger and Advocate*, vol. 1 no. 5 (February 1835), 78.

revival from 1820 to "the year 1823" in 1834, describing Joseph as sixteen and in his "seventeenth year" (when he was actually seventeen and in his eighteenth year), no ordinary Mormon had ever heard about a vision of the "crucifyed" Lord in 1821 or a vision of the Father and the Son in 1820. The colossal mistake made in the 1834-35 History, prepared with the full participation of the prophet Joseph Smith, had been caused, the correcting entry said, by "an error in the type." The mistake had been to place the revival that preceded the vision of the angel with the plates in 1820 in Joseph's "fifteenth year" rather than in 1823 in Joseph's seventeenth year. However, the 1834-35 History was wrong on both counts. The Reverend George Lane did not visit Palmyra to participate in a revival there until July 1824. Joseph's mind could not have been "awakened" to religion by the preaching of Reverend Lane until 1824 and 1825, when Joseph, then eighteen or nineteen, was in the nineteenth and twentieth years of his life. Reverend Lane was in Palmyra in 1824, and remained there until early 1825.

The 1838-39 Pearl of Great Price Account recorrected Joseph and Oliver's earlier correction. Now the revival was moved from 1823, where it had earlier landed because of an "error in the type," back to 1820, where it had briefly been before the "error in the type." So the 1820 revival became an 1823 revival before it became an 1820 revival for the second time. In this blatant revision of the facts, Joseph's religious awakening is now seen to have occurred not because of the preaching of the Reverend George Lane in 1823, when Joseph was seventeen, as the first authorized history of the Church said that it was, but rather because of that unannounced vision of the Father and the Son in 1820, when Joseph was fourteen years old. Now Joseph was prompted (this time by that double recorrected 1820 revival) to retire to the woods, having "never as yet made the attempt to pray vocally."[67] In Oliver and Joseph's 1834-35 History, preceded by their reckoning by an 1823 revival, there is no account of a vision of the Father and the Son. That is to say that in the first authorized history of the Church of Jesus Christ of Latter-day Saints prepared in 1834 and 1835 by Joseph Smith and Oliver Cowdery, there is no account of an 1820 vision of the Father and the Son.

---

[67]The Pearl of Great Price, Joseph Smith – History 1:14.

That carefully published history (practically the work of Joseph Smith) reported that Joseph's "mind became awakened" to religion because of, and "in common with others," by the powerful preaching of the Reverend George Lane, and not because of a visit of the Father and the Son, an event the founders' 1834-35 full account of the history of the rise of the Church didn't mention. Later in 1838-39 – when Joseph, without the help of the excommunicated Cowdery, turned history on its ear – everything suddenly changed. *"During this time of great excitement"* – speaking publicly in 1842 of that previously totally unknown account of that totally unfamiliar 1820 event – Joseph now changed the date of the great revival for the second time. "[M]y mind," he said, "was called up to serious reflection and great uneasiness; but though my feelings were deep and often poignant, still I kept myself aloof from all these parties, though I attended their several meetings as often as occasion would permit."[68]

Earlier in 1834-35, before the 1838-39 Pearl of Great Price Account began to be composed, Oliver and Joseph reported that Joseph's "mind became awakened" to the wonders of religion by the preaching of the Reverend George Lane during a great Palmyra revival that occurred in 1823 when Joseph was seventeen years old. This was just before a vision of the angel in charge of the golden plates. No one but Joseph Smith knew those things; Oliver Cowdery could do nothing more than to report them. In 1838-39 Joseph's mind was resupposed to have been awakened by a vision of the Father and the Son during a great Palmyra revival that occurred in 1820 when Joseph was fourteen years of age. Thus two separate visions that were years apart were now both preceded by the same great Palmyra revival.

Richard L. Bushman points to the one hundred and thirty-three year suppressed 1832 Holographic History (the account first published in 1965, the account which he is on record as having said that he favors) to support the proposition that "Joseph Smith Jr. began to be concerned about religion 'at about the age of twelve years,' in late 1817 or early 1818, when the aftereffects of the revival of 1816 and 1817 were still being felt."[69]   Does Joseph's

---

[68]The Pearl of Great Price, Joseph Smith – History 1:8, emphasis added.
[69]Bushman, *Joseph Smith: Rough Stone Rolling*, 37.

language in the 1838-39 Pearl of Great Price Account appear to describe the remote *"aftereffects"* of a revival that occurred three or four years before the 1820 vision in 1816 or 1817? Did Joseph's mother, brothers and sister join the Presbyterian church in 1816 or 1817? Did the Reverend George Lane lead a great revival then? Was Joseph's brother Alvin still alive? Does *"[d]uring this time of great excitement,"* does *"[i]n the midst of this war of words and tumult of opinions,"* does this *"great and incessant"* outcry appear to describe a fourteen year old 1820 boy "laboring under . . . extreme difficulties" caused by the *"aftereffects"* of a revival that occurred in Palmyra, New York, in 1816 or 1817 when he was ten or eleven? What is at issue here? Why is that early revival even mentioned here? Because Joseph's twenty-first century biographer recognizes that there was no Palmyra revival in 1820. Looking for any relevant revival before 1823, "1816 and 1817" is simply as good as it gets. Did Joseph mean to say that he consciously kept himself aloof from all these parties and acted upon these adult perceptions at the ages of ten or eleven? A boy who had never before uttered a vocal prayer?

Oliver and Joseph's 1834-35 History (requested by Joseph, prepared "under" his "close supervision," copied into his journal, considered part of his history and concerned with the angel in charge of the plates) confidently placed the Palmyra revival in 1823, when Joseph was seventeen and in the eighteenth year of his age. Joseph's 1838-39 Pearl of Great Price Account (concerned with a vision of the Father and the Son) confidently re-placed the Palmyra revival in 1820, when Joseph was fourteen in the fifteenth year of his age. History places the Palmyra revival, described at different times to have caused both of two separate events (the 1823 vision of the angel in charge of the plates and the 1820 vision of the Father and the Son), in 1824-25, during the ministry of the Reverend George Lane. This was during the ministry of the Reverend Benjamin Stockton, and after the death of Alvin Smith, when Joseph Smith was eighteen and nineteen in the nineteenth and twentieth years of his age.

Methodists

The 1824-25 revival "commenced with the Methodists."[70]   The
Reverend George Lane was the Presiding Methodist Elder in the
Ontario District from July 1824 to January 1825.   Joseph's 1832
Holographic Account of the First Vision of the Son does not forbid
him from joining a church, nor does it mention a revival or claim
persecution.[71] The Palmyra revival reported in the 1838-39 Pearl of
Great Price Account, on the other hand, said that Joseph "became
somewhat partial to the Methodist sect, and . . . felt some desire to
be united with them . . . ."[72] Thus the 1820 version of the vision of
the Father and the Son as reported in 1838-39, which described an
1820 revival, and the 1832 version of an 1821 vision of the Son but
not the Father as reported in 1965, that didn't describe any revival,
are seen to reflect contradictory facts. These two reports may not
seem to describe the same event. The conduct of the Smiths, at that
time, was more consistent with the 1832 vision, which didn't
preclude them from joining a church, than with the 1838-39 vision
which ultimately "forbade" the boy from joining a church. The
conclusion of that later report was that, "I had now got my mind
satisfied . . . that it was not my duty to join with any of them . . . ."

Grant Palmer recognized that,

> The Smith's religiosity [the pattern of their lives]
> after 1820 is consistent with the 1832 version [of the
> first vision].   First, Joseph was involved with a
> Methodist class in Palmyra as an exhorter. Second
> he reported that he "often" participated in the
> extended revival near his home in 1824-25. He said,
> "I attended their several meetings as often as
> occasion would permit, . . . [becoming] partial to the
> Methodist sect, and I felt some desire to be united
> with them;" (JS - History 1:8). During this revival
> Lucy, Hyrum and other family members joined the
> Presbyterian church where they remained active
> until September 1828. That same year, Joseph

---

[70]The Pearl of Great Price, Joseph Smith – History 1:5.
[71]Palmer, *An Insider's View of Mormon Origins*, 253.
[72]The Pearl of Great Price, Joseph Smith – History 1:8.

sought membership with the Methodists in Harmony, Pennsylvania. He and his parents, while believing prior to 1820 that none of the churches was true, did not consider any unworthy to join. Had Lucy heard her son say that Jesus Christ personally instructed him "to go not after them" [the message of the 1838-39 Account] and to not "join any" church because "all" of the ministers, creeds and churches "were an abomination in his sight," [the message of the 1838-39 Account of the 1820 vision] she and her several children certainly would not have joined the Presbyterians and worshiped with them from 1825 until 1828. Nor is it probable that Joseph would have participated with the Methodists between 1820-1828.[73]

Joseph caught "a spark of Methodism in the camp meeting, away down in the woods, on the Vienna road." Orsamus Turner recalled that Joseph Smith became "a very passable exhorter in evening meetings."[74] Pomeroy Tucker further recalled that "At one time he joined the probationary class of the Methodist church in Palmyra, and made some active demonstrations of engagedness, though his assumed convictions were insufficiently grounded or abiding to carry him along to the saving point of conversion . . . ." Tucker then further reports that Joseph soon withdrew "from the class."[75]

Twists and Turns – Competing Gravities

After this early flirtation with the Methodists at the camp meeting, long before there was an 1838-39 Account, Joseph's announced conclusion, according to Pomeroy Tucker, was that "all sectarianism was fallacious, all the churches on a false foundation, and the Bible a fable."[76] A boy who thought that every church was wrong and that the Bible was a fable might grow to become a

[73]Palmer, *An Insider's View of Mormon Origins*, 252-53.
[74]H. Michael Marquardt, *The Rise of Mormonism: 1816-1844* (Longwood, FL: Xulon Press, 2005), 48.
[75]Pomeroy Tucker Account (1867), Vogel, ed., *Early Mormon Documents*, 3:94.
[76]Ibid.

fourteen year old who had never uttered a prayer (the 1838 First Vision Account), a seventeen year old who didn't know "if a Supreme being did exist" (the 1834-35 Account) and a twenty year old who "didn't Profess religion" (Joseph Stowell Jr., 1825-26). Such a person might come to wonder, when and if ever awakened, if he was "accepted" of God. Such an one might very well yearn for "a full manifestation of divine approbation."[77]

The period between 1820 and 1823, like Smith's life to the age of fourteen, is a barren period for historians. In 1825 Hyrum Smith borrowed the chocolate-colored peepstone ("the acorn of the Mormon oak") back from Willard Chase. Joseph later used the mysterious stone to translate the Book of Mormon. Though requested back, the stone was never returned.

How can anyone hope to explain Joseph's encounter with Methodism in Harmony, Pennsylvania, in 1828 when he signed a class book and tried to join the Methodists after he met and married Emma Smith? This unexplained episode came after a Methodist minister was supposed to have treated his report of an 1820 vision "not only lightly but with great contempt."[78] And it occurred after he was supposed to have been explicitly forbidden from joining any of the sects ("for they were all wrong").[79] Because "their creeds were an abomination . . . . [because] those professors were all corrupt; . . . [because] they teach for doctrines the commandments of men . . . ."[80] In this demonstrable fondness for the Methodist sect, Joseph's mind is seen as far from "satisfied so far as the sectarian world was concerned."[81] Again, the evidence doesn't support an 1838-39 First Vision Account that wasn't publicly reported until 1842.

---

[77]"Letter IV" (Cowdery and Smith's 1834-35 History), *Messenger and Advocate*, vol. 1 no. 5 (February 1835), 78. "Within a few years after 1825 Joseph was apologizing for his 'former uncircumspect walk, and unchaste conversation, ...'" (Ibid., quoted in Morgan, *Dale Morgan on Early Mormonism*, 259).

[78]The Pearl of Great Price, Joseph Smith – History 1:21.

[79]"I asked the Personages . . . which of all the sects was right – and which I should join. I was answered that I must join none of them, for they were all wrong." And then, "He again forbade me to join with any of them; . . . ." (Ibid., 1:18-20). Thus, Smith was twice forbidden.

[80]Ibid., 1:19.

[81]Ibid., 1:26.

By the end of 1825 the 1824-25 Palmyra revival is over. Now a crystal-gazing money-digging Joseph "re-embraced" a forbidden lifestyle that "had given him a sense of power and control: treasure-seeing . . . with a vengeance."[82] In March of 1826, following yet another turn with Willard Chase's borrowed stone, after that supposed glorious morning and that non-existent tumultuous revival in 1820, and after the vision of the angel with the plates and that non-existent revival in 1823, Joseph found himself described as a "prisoner" in the courtroom of Justice Albert Neely in South Bainbridge, New York. He was charged to respond to the contentions that he was a "disorderly person" and an "Impostor." Before the prisoner Joseph Smith stood trial in Judge Neely's court in 1826, he had supposedly seen (as he would only much later say) the "crucifyed" Lord in 1821 (Joseph's 1832 Holographic Account), *or* two personages and many angels in 1820 (Joshua 1 and 2:1835), *or* a first visitation of angels in 1820 (Erastus Holmes:1835), *or* two personages, one of them a Father and the other a Son, in a vision "uncluttered by angels" in 1820 (1838-39 Pearl of Great Price Account). Furthermore, he will later say that he had seen and received instructions from the angel in charge of the golden plates at least four times in 1823, then again in 1824, then again in 1825. By 1826 and before those court proceedings, no man on earth could hope to match those supernatural credentials, if what he claimed to have experienced in the 1838-39 Account (reported in 1842) was true.

This had been his experience before he awkwardly described his money-digging improprieties without mentioning the tiniest element of this history to Justice Neely and a large audience in court in March of 1826. This extraordinary spiritual history, we may repeat, was innocently contradicted by Josiah Stowell Jr. in 1843: *"I also went to schoal with him one winter [1825-26] he was a fine likely young man & at that time [1826] did not Profess religion . . . ."*[83] Michael Morse (Joseph and Emma's brother-in-law), whose conclusion tracked that of the younger Stowell, told an interviewer in 1879 that *"Joseph at that time (about 1825) was a green, awkward,*

---

[82]Dan Vogel, *Joseph Smith: The Making of a Prophet* (Salt Lake City: Signature Books, 2004), 65.

[83]Josiah Stowell Jr. to J.S. Fullmer, 17 Feb. 1843, LDS Archives, published in *LDS Church News* (12 May 1985), 10, emphasis added.

and ignorant boy of about 19 yrs of age Says he <then> made no profession of religion."[84] There he was drawing circles with a magic dagger in search of "filthy lucre" and lost things with a peepstone in Harmony (Pennsylvania) in November of 1825; excavating for treasure with Josiah Stowell Sr. and Joseph Knight Sr. in Bainbridge and Colesville (New York) in 1826 and 1827; and entering his name on the class book at the Methodist Church in Harmony, Pennsylvania, in 1828, after his marriage to Emma Hale.

The vision "on which this whole cause turns"

The 1838-39 Pearl of Great Price Account of the First Vision of the Father and the Son, though no one knew about it until 1840 (Scotland) and 1842 (Nauvoo, Illinois), became the founding story of the Mormon Church. Every faithful Latter-day Saint is expected to defend this canonized story of the vision, no matter the cost. In the words of one distinguished Mormon First Vision scholar,

> *Belief in the vision is one of the fundamentals to which faithful members give assent. Its importance is second only to belief in the divinity of Jesus of Nazareth. The story is an essential part of the first lesson given by Mormon missionaries to prospective converts, and its acceptance is necessary before baptism.*[85]

A recent Mormon prophet, the now deceased Gordon B. Hinckley, described the First Vision's supreme importance on various important occasions to the members of the faith. The First Vision is

> *the hinge pin on which this whole cause turns. If the First Vision was true, if it actually happened, then the Book of Mormon is true.   Then we have the*

---

[84]William W. Blair Journal, RLDS Archives (8 May 1879) (Blair interviewed Michael Morse in Amboy, Illinois), quoted in Marquardt and Walters, *Inventing Mormonism*, 70 n 31, emphasis added.

[85]James B. Allen, "The Significance of Joseph Smith's 'First Vision' in Mormon Thought," *Dialogue: A Journal of Mormon Thought*, vol. 1 no. 3, (Autumn 1966): 1, emphasis added.

*priesthood.   Then we have the Church organization
and all of the other keys and blessings of authority
which we say we have.   If the First Vision did not
occur, then we are involved in a great sham.   Now, it
is just that simple.   Everything . . . turns on the reality
of that first vision . . . .*[86]

President Hinckley, who was the supreme leader of the Mormon
Church, then further reported at General Conference in October
2002 that: "Our whole strength rests on the validity of that vision.
It either occurred or it did not occur. If it did not, then this work is
a fraud . . . . [U]pon that unique and wonderful experience stands
the validity of this church."[87]

Falling from Grace – Spiraling Down

In the *1838-39 Pearl of Great Price Account,* when Joseph knelt to
pray in the spring of 1820, he said he was seized upon by some dark
power and entirely overcome by "an astonishing influence" that
bound his tongue so he could not speak. "Thick darkness gathered
around me, and it seemed to me for a time as if I were doomed to
sudden destruction."[88] After calling upon God

*to deliver me out of the power of this enemy, [and] at
the very moment when I was ready to sink into despair
and abandon myself to destruction – not to an
imaginary ruin, but to the power of some actual being
from the unseen world, who had such marvelous
power as I had never before felt in any being – just at
this moment of great alarm, I saw a pillar of light
exactly over my head, above the brightness of the sun,
which descended gradually until it fell upon me.*[89]

---

[86]Gordon B. Hinckley, "Messages of Inspiration from President Hinckley,"
Church News (1 Feb. 1997), 2, emphasis added.

[87]Gordon B. Hinckley, "The Marvelous Foundation of our Faith," *Ensign*
(October 2002), 80.

[88]The Pearl of Great Price, Joseph Smith – History 1:15.

[89]Ibid., 1:16, emphasis added.

"During the years following his audience with the Deities, Joseph, candid in his admissions of frailty, succumbed to the 'corruption' of his human nature, and to the 'gratification of many appetites' offensive in the sight of God."[90] In all of that Joseph didn't act like a boy who had seen the Son *or* the Father and the Son, Moroni *or* Nephi, and many angels. Does it seem likely that a boy who had seen what he said he saw and felt what he said he felt would so quickly succumb to the kind of temptation he chose to describe? Would an innocent fourteen-year-old boy who had seen and spoken to the Deities after he felt the "marvelous power" of the underworld so quickly fall from grace? Did this weak vessel grow to become the prophet of the dispensation of the fullness of times? Is this boy who early on had never spoken a prayer the most important boy on earth? Is this the fragile beginning of the man who would do more "save Jesus only, for the salvation of men in this world, than any other man" who ever lived?[91] Shall he decide who shall be permitted to enter the Kingdom of Heaven? Shall he become god to the spirits in the spirit world?

THE EPISTLE OF JAMES

William Smith (Joseph's younger brother and a founding member of the Quorum of the Twelve Apostles) remembered a powerful sermon delivered by the Reverend George Lane, the leader of the Methodists' Ontario Conference, during the Palmyra revival. It would be well to remember that Oliver and Joseph paid glowing tribute to Reverend Lane in their 1834-35 History. He had, they said (Joseph said because Cowdery never saw the Methodist Elder) a "manner of communication . . . peculiarly calculated to awaken the intellect of the hearer, and arouse the sinner to look about him for safety . . . ." His "discourses" during the revival in "1823" were what "awakened" Joseph's "mind" to the wonders of religion.

---

[90]Joseph Smith Jr., *History of The Church of Jesus Christ of Latter-day Saints*, B.H. Roberts, ed., 2d ed., rev., (Salt Lake City: The Deseret Book Company, 1978), 1:9-10, quoted in LaMar Petersen, *The Creation of the Book of Mormon: A Historical Inquiry* (Salt Lake City: Freethinker Press, 2000), 10. "Such candor was thought unnecessary by redactors. The offensive words were deleted from the official history of 1902 . . . ." (Ibid., n 20).

[91]Doctrine and Covenants 135:3.

Their history said: "[M]uch good instruction was always drawn from his discourses on the scriptures, and in common with others, our brother's mind became awakened."[92]

William Smith, who was equally impressed, described Reverend Lane and the revival: "In 1822 and 1823," William said, "the people in our neighborhood were very much stirred up with regard to religious matters by the preaching of a Mr. Lane, an Elder of the Methodist Church, and celebrated throughout the country as a 'great revival preacher.'"[93] A joint meeting of the congregations in the Smiths' neighborhood (a meeting sponsored by the Baptists, Methodists and Presbyterians) had "succeeded in stirring up quite a feeling, ..." One Reverend Stockton, the president of the meeting and a Presbyterian, wanted the converts to join the Presbyterian faith, "but as father [Joseph Smith Sr.] did not like Rev. Stockton very well, our folks hesitated and the next evening a Rev. Mr. Lane of the Methodists preached a sermon . . . ."[94] The unsurprising topic of the circuit-riding revivalist's powerful sermon (George Lane's sermon), according to William Smith, was: "'What church shall I join?' And the burden of his discourse was to ask God, using as a text, 'If any man lack wisdom let him ask of God who giveth to all men liberally [James 1:5].'"[95]

When he dictated the Pearl of Great Price Account of the First Vision in 1838-39, Joseph Smith described an 1820 quandary. He found himself, he said, caught up in the midst of a great revival. It was "[i]n the midst of this war of words and tumult of opinions" that he often said to himself, "What is to be done? Who of all these parties are right; or are they all wrong together? If any of them be right, which is it, and how shall I know it?"[96] Now, according to Joseph Smith in the canonized account of the vision offered to the

---

[92]Editor, "Letter III" (Cowdery and Smith's 1834-35 History), *Messenger and Advocate*, vol. 1 no. 3 (December 1834), 42.

[93]William Smith, *On Mormonism* (1883), Vogel, ed., *Early Mormon Documents*, 1:494.

[94]William Smith, interview with E.C. Briggs (1893), Vogel, ed., *Early Mormon Documents*, 1:513. This all occurred after the death of Alvin Smith on November 19, 1823. Joseph Sr. didn't like Reverend Stockton because of the sermon Stockton preached at the funeral of the unbaptized Alvin Smith in November 1823.

[95]Ibid., emphasis added.

[96]The Pearl of Great Price, Joseph Smith – History 1:10.

public for the first time more than twenty years later, something suddenly became crystal clear. "While I was laboring under the extreme difficulties caused by the contests of these parties of religionists, I was one day reading the Epistle of James, first chapter and fifth verse, which reads: *'If any of you lack wisdom let him ask of God, that giveth to all men liberally, and upbraideth not; and it shall be given him.'*"[97] With this remarkable discovery, a fortified Joseph was plain and simply overwhelmed. *"Never did any passage of scripture come with more power to the heart of man than this did at this time to mine. It seemed to enter with great force into every feeling of my heart."*[98] Wrought up by this splendid promise and in the midst of that great revival, Joseph retired to the woods in 1820 to ask the Lord "which of all the sects was right – and which I should join."[99]

But wait. Isn't that the question William Smith said that Reverend Lane encouraged his investigators to ask in a powerful sermon delivered at that memorable conference? Wasn't that the same scripture Reverend Lane described in a remarkable sermon attended by the Smiths? Did Joseph really just stumble upon that remarkable scripture in the Epistle of James one day while he "was laboring under the extreme difficulties caused by the contests of these parties of religionists," or did the Reverend George Lane point the way to that passage in his sermon in 1824? Wasn't that direction part and parcel of the Reverend Lane's contribution to the religious awakening of Joseph Smith? Was Joseph guided there by the Reverend Lane – guided to the question, guided to the process and guided to the answer – in a sermon the prophet's younger brother never forgot?

When Joseph Smith *dictated* his autobiography to a committee in 1838 and 1839, he said that he asked God the Father and Jesus Christ the same question William Smith said Reverend George Lane asked his congregation to ask in Palmyra, New York, in the midst of the great revival there. This previously unknown retroactive account of an alleged vision of the Father and the Son came eighteen or nineteen years after it was supposed to have

---

[97]Ibid., 1:11, emphasis retained.
[98]Ibid., 1:12., emphasis added.
[99]Ibid., 1:18.

occurred. It was then only published in the *Times and Seasons* in
1842, fully twenty-two years after the supposed occurrence.
Although it was then thought to have been the only known account,
we now know that there were at least four different versions of
three earlier unannounced accounts. If Joseph Smith simply
chanced upon the Epistle of James, it was only after he heard (or
heard from others who heard) the stirring discourse delivered by
Reverend Lane. Lane didn't come to Palmyra to participate in a
revival there until July 1824. William Smith's dates ("1822 and
1823"), while close to correct, were not correct. Everything that
William Smith described relating to George Lane, Benjamin
Stockton, the Epistle of James and the real Palmyra revival
followed the death of Alvin Smith in November 1823. Reverend
Lane's revival sermon, which followed by one day Reverend
Stockton's appeal to converts to join the Presbyterian Church, was
delivered in 1824 or 1825 when Lane was the Presiding Elder for
the Methodists at the Ontario Conference in Palmyra, New York.

DATING THE REVIVAL

During the Reverend Lane's revival in 1824, then still yet again in
Harmony (Pennsylvania) in 1828, Joseph Smith seriously
considered becoming a member of the Methodist Church. That
Joseph Smith entertained the idea of becoming a Methodist[100] at
Palmyra, New York, in and/or before 1824 and again at Harmony,
Pennsylvania, in 1828, contradicted Joseph's 1842 assertion that
Jesus commanded him in 1820 not to join any of the sects.[101] He
had got his mind "satisfied" in 1820, he said, "so far as the sectarian
world was concerned – that it was not my duty to join with any of
them, but to continue as I was until further directed."[102] But then it
must also be said that Joseph didn't really say any of those things
about "Jesus," "duty" or "the sectarian world," or document any of
those purported 1820 instructions, or prepare, publish or amend his
accounts of them, until 1838, 1839, 1840, 1842, 1843 and/or 1844.

---

[100]Oliver Cowdery joined the Methodist church after he left the Mormon
Church, and Emma Smith and her children attended the Methodist church after
the death of Joseph Smith.
    [101]Ibid., 1:19-20.
    [102]Ibid., 1:26.

It was perfectly logical that Joseph Smith should be inclined toward the Methodists. For as he and Oliver Cowdery specifically said in their first *authorized* history of the Church of Latter Day Saints, and as William Smith said after Joseph's death, the leader of the true revival, the hero of the true revival and the man who awakened Joseph's interest in religion was "the great revival preacher," the Reverend George Lane. Lane was a towering Methodist figure at a Palmyra revival now positively known to have occurred in 1824 and 1825, when Joseph was in the nineteenth and twentieth years of his age. Reverend Lane first traveled to his posting in Palmyra, New York, in 1824. He left his Palmyra ministry in January 1825 because of an illness in his family. This was *two years after* Joseph said in *1832* that an angel of the Lord "came and stood before me" on "the 22nd day of Sept. AD 1822,"[103] and one year after Joseph claimed in 1838-39 that the angel came on September 21, 1823.[104] It was only after this that Joseph Smith could possibly have heard the preaching of the Reverend George Lane.

It was the confusion caused by the great Palmyra revival described in the 1838-39 Pearl of Great Price Account that prompted Joseph Smith to ask God the Father and Jesus Christ, "two Personages, whose brightness and glory defy all description," "which of all the sects was right – and which I should join."[105] When he had asked the question and received the Deities' answer, Joseph described how he then proceeded to relate the details of that experience to one of the Methodist preachers.

> *Some few days after I had this vision, I happened to be in company with one of the Methodist preachers, who was very active in the before mentioned religious excitement; and, conversing with him on the subject of religion, I took occasion to give him an account of the vision which I had had. I was greatly surprised at his behavior; he treated my communication not only lightly, but with great contempt, saying it was all of the devil, that there were no such things as visions or*

---

[103]1832 Account, Jessee ed., *The Personal Writings of Joseph Smith*, 6-7, emphasis added.

[104]The Pearl of Great Price, Joseph Smith – History 1:28-29, emphasis added.

[105]Ibid., 1:17-18.

*revelations in these days; that all such things had
ceased with the apostles, and that there would never
be any more of them.*[106]

Yet eight years later Joseph put his name on a class book and tried
to join the Methodist Church. That was in Harmony, Pennsylvania,
after his marriage to Emma and after he said that he had acquired
the golden plates. His later story would have inexplicably placed
the plates and the Urim and Thummim (which he said that he
received in 1827) in his possession when he was trying to join the
Methodists in Pennsylvania in 1828. It seems safe to suppose that
this account of the Methodist preacher had reference to Reverend
Lane, the Presiding Methodist Elder, one of the architects of the
Palmyra revival, a great revival preacher and the person whose
sermons awakened our brother's mind[107] to the wonders of religion.
But it contained recitals Joseph didn't describe in his first
handwritten account of his first encounter with deity in 1832, or in
the 1834-35 History, or in four different versions of three other
unannounced accounts of the First Vision. What suggests that this
later ungracious 1838-39 Pearl of Great Price comment concerning
the Methodist preacher is a literary construct (like the story of the
random discovery of the Epistle of James), and not some verifiable
historical fact, is the fawning description assigned to the wonderful
Reverend Lane by Oliver Cowdery and Joseph Smith in their 1834-
35 History. In that carefully composed earlier account, prepared
about ten years after Reverend Lane's revival, nothing would
suggest that there was ever any kind of unsympathetic encounter
with Reverend Lane or any other Methodist preacher.

In 1834 Joseph and Oliver unequivocally praised the impressive
preaching of the charismatic Reverend Lane. Reverend Lane's
"great awakening" contributed to cause Joseph to begin "to reflect
and inquire, which of all these sects was right."[108] According to
William, "Joseph [—] [who was] then about seventeen years of age,
had become seriously inclined, though not 'brought out,' as the

---

[106]Ibid., 1:21., emphasis added.
[107]"Letter III" (Cowdery and Smith's 1834-35 History), *Messenger and
Advocate*, vol. 1 no. 3 (December 1834), 42.
[108]William Smith, *On Mormonism* (1883), Vogel, ed., *Early Mormon
Documents*, 1:495.

phrase was . . . ."[109] Oliver and Joseph amplified the performance
of Methodist Elder Lane (it is important to remember that only
Joseph knew these facts). A Mormon publication reported in 1834:

> *It is necessary to premise this account [Oliver and*
> *Joseph's 1834-35 First Authorized History of the*
> *Church] by relating the situation of the public mind*
> *relative to religion, at this time: One Mr. Lane, a*
> *presiding Elder of the Methodist church, visited*
> *Palmyra, and vicinity. . . . There was a great*
> *awakening, or excitement raised on the subject of*
> *religion, and much enquiry for the word of life. Large*
> *additions were made to the Methodist, Presbyterian,*
> *and Baptist churches. – Mr. Lane's manner of*
> *communication was peculiarly calculated to awaken*
> *the intellect of the hearer, and arouse the sinner to*
> *look about him for safety – much good instruction was*
> *always drawn from his discourses on the scriptures,*
> *and in common with others, our brother's mind*
> *became awakened.*[110]

This all described a pivotal event in Joseph's religious life. His
encounter with the Reverend Lane had been a turning point, not a
rebuke. In *1823* (Joseph and Oliver's date, but really Joseph's
date), when he "was about seventeen years of age," Joseph's mind,
by his own reckoning, *"became awakened"* to religion. According to
William, it was then – because of the revival (and not in 1820,
because of a vision that he had as of yet never described) – that his
brother *"began to reflect and inquire, which of all these sects was*
right."[111] What prompted this intensified concern? It was the
remarkable preaching of Reverend Lane, a "tallented man
possessing a good share of literary endowments, and apparent
humility."[112] Oliver and Joseph's 1834-35 History, which didn't

---

[109]Ibid., emphasis added.

[110]"Letter III" (Cowdery and Smith's 1834-35 History), *Messenger and
Advocate*, vol. 1 no. 3 (December 1834), 42, emphasis added.

[111]William Smith, *On Mormonism* (1883), Vogel, ed., *Early Mormon
Documents*, 1:495.

[112]"Letter III" (Cowdery and Smith's 1834-35 History), *Messenger and
Advocate*, vol. 1 no. 3 (December 1834), 42.

mention an 1820 vision of the Father and the Son [or an 1829 visit from Peter, James and John], did roundly praise Elder Lane . . . ."[113] Joseph's mind wasn't awakened by an 1821 visit of the "crucifyed" Lord, or by an 1820 vision of the Father and the Son. It rather seems that Joseph's mind was "awakened" in 1824 and 1825, the true years of the great Palmyra revival, by the impassioned preaching of one "great revival preacher."

That Reverend Lane's discourse stirred the people in Joseph's neighborhood is a fact fully supported by contemporaneous records. That he did so in 1822 and 1823 (according to William Smith[114]) or in 1823 (according to Oliver and Joseph[115]) is close, but history confirms it as 1824-25. The Palmyra revival described in the 1838-39 Pearl of Great Price Account of the First Vision of the Father and the Son as having occurred in 1820 when Joseph Smith was fourteen and the Palmyra revival described in the 1834-35 History of the vision of the Angel Moroni as having occurred in 1823 when Joseph Smith was seventeen actually occurred in 1824-25 when Joseph Smith was eighteen or nineteen. (Smith turned eighteen on December 23, 1823). The great Palmyra revival involving the Reverend Lane actually occurred in 1824-25 in the nineteenth and twentieth years of brother Joseph's life. Latter-day Saints may take that to the bank. As an astute historian noted:

> *Not in 1820 as the First Vision would have it, not in*
> *1823 as the Vision of the Angel Moroni would have it,*

---

[113]Ibid., 42. Lucy's 1845 "Preliminary Manuscript" described what she was supposed to have believed one year after Joseph's death. And William Smith's 1883 account described what William is supposed to have believed forty years after Joseph's death. William's bottom line was this: *The Reverend George Lane's preaching led to Joseph's prayer and first vision of an angel.* (William Smith, "On Mormonism," 1883, Vogel, ed., *Early Mormon Documents*, 1:494-495; and William Smith's interview with E.C. Briggs [1893], Ibid., 1:513). "According to William Smith, a visit from an angel was Joseph's first heavenly ministration and this occurred in 1823." (Petersen, *The Creation of the Book of Mormon*, 15). LaMar Petersen cites Hill, *Quest for Refuge*, 193 n 49, citing William Smith's account as printed in the July 1841 *New York Observer*. This Hill reference, Petersen notes, may refer, by reason of a transcriptional error, to the *Congregational Observer*.

[114]William Smith, *On Mormonism* (1883), Vogel, ed., *Early Mormon Documents*, 1:494-495.

[115]"Letter IV" (Cowdery and Smith's 1834-35 History), *Messenger and Advocate*, vol. 1 no. 5 (February 1835), 78.

but in 1824 began the revival which has left its indelible impress upon Mormon history. Decisive in fixing the accounts by Joseph Smith and his family within the framework of contemporary event is the memory that has come down to us of the Reverend George Lane, chief architect of the revival. Lane, prior to the fall of 1824, had never ridden the circuits of the Ontario District, and he was never to ride them again.[116]

From Lane's career only, and without reference to the abundant supporting evidence, it can be established that the revival which awakened Joseph to the importance of religion took place from four to five years after the Father and Son appeared to him, and from a year to a year and a half after the Angel Moroni came to his bedside to reveal his momentous calling.[117]

In 1823 Lane was living in the area of Wilkes-Barre, Pennsylvania, and was not appointed presiding elder of the Ontario District in which Palmyra was located until July, 1824. He presided only until January 1825 when illness in his family forced him temporarily to leave the ministry.[118]

---

[116]Morgan, *Dale Morgan on Early Mormonism*, 257, emphasis added. "George Peck, *Early Methodism Within the Bounds of the Old Genesee Conference From 1788 to 1828* (New York, 1860), 167, 234-238, 313, 447-449, 492-495, provides full details of Lane's life in the ministry . . . . *After laboring five years in the Susquehanna District, Lane was transferred to the Ontario [New York] District at the fifteenth meeting of the Genesee Conference in July 1824.*" (Ibid., 376-77 n 26, emphasis added).

[117]Morgan, *Dale Morgan on Early Mormonism*, 257, emphasis added.

[118]"For official confirmation of Lane's assigned field of labor, see *Minutes of the Annual Conferences* (1773-1828), 1:337, 352, 373, 392, 418, 446. In 1823 Lane was serving in the Susequehanna District in central Pennsylvania." (Quoted in Marquardt and Walters, *Inventing Mormonism*, 21 n 27 at 38-39). In 1819, Lane attended a business meeting (the Genesee Annual Conference) held at Vienna, fifteen miles from the Smith home. "The 'Journal' of the conference does not indicate that any preaching services were held, and there is no indication of any revival touched off at Vienna or Palmyra." (Ibid.).

. . . Lane was the Methodist presiding elder of the Ontario District [including Palmyra] from July 1824 until January 1825."[119]

Reverend Lane did not preach at an 1816-1817 Palmyra revival, and there was no Palmyra revival in 1820. *Joseph Smith could not have seen the Reverend George Lane or heard him preach before July 1824.*[120]

Moving the Revival

The 1838-39 Pearl of Great Price Account described a vision that occurred in the spring of 1820 as the result of a religious revival. Joseph was "an obscure boy, only between fourteen and fifteen years of age."[121] When did Joseph decide to retire to the woods and ask the Lord who "giveth to all men liberally, and upbraideth not"? "In the midst of this war of words [the revival] and tumult of opinions, I often said to myself: What is to be done?" What was his concern? "Who of all these parties are right; or, are they all wrong together? If any one of them be right, which is it, and how shall I know it?" Just exactly when did he decide to do something about it? "While I was laboring under the extreme difficulties caused by the contests of these parties of religionists [and during the revival], I was one day reading the Epistle of James . . . ."[122] These are hard religious times. This great revival – this "war of words," this "tumult of opinions," this "great and incessant" cry,[123] this

---

[119]Marquardt and Walters, *Inventing Mormonism*, 55, emphasis added.

[120]Mormon historian Larry C. Porter claimed to have gathered evidence to support the proposition that Reverend Lane "made trips to within fifteen miles of Palmyra several times between 1819 and 1824." (Fawn M. Brodie, *No Man Knows My History: The Life of Joseph Smith the Mormon Prophet*, 2d ed., rev. and enl. [New York, NY: Alfred A. Knopf, 1972], 410). That does nothing to change the facts surrounding the Palmyra revival. The Smiths joined the Presbyterian Church because of the revival, which occurred after the death of Alvin Smith on November 19, 1823. The "large additions" made to the Palmyra congregations and described by Joseph Smith were all made in 1824-25. There were no "large additions" made to the Palmyra congregations in 1820, a year when some of the Palmyra congregations actually lost members.

[121]The Pearl of Great Price, Joseph Smith – History 1:22.

[122]Ibid., 1:10-11.

[123]Ibid., 1:9-10.

"unusual excitement on the subject of religion" "in the place where [we] lived"[124] – caused the future Mormon prophet to retire to the woods there to receive, while the revival was raging, a vision of the Father and the Son. It all happened *"on the morning of a beautiful, clear day, early in the spring of eighteen hundred and twenty."*[125] Unless it did not. Does Joseph seem in the least uncertain about the 1820 date? The 1820 date is described in a history first composed in 1838, further composed in 1839, but not published until the early 1840s. Between the composition and publication of the grandiloquent account, there was ample opportunity for correction.

Internal Discrepancies

There are several different markers of time described in the official 1838-39 Pearl of Great Price Account of the First Vision. The year 1820 is the first and most obvious. Joseph Smith turned fourteen on December 23, 1819. He was fourteen in the spring of 1820 and turned fifteen, after the reported vision, on December 23, 1820. His description of his age at the time of the vision is unequivocal. A second marker, however, is this: Joseph dated the revival that prompted him to retire to the woods and pray in conflicting terms reflected in the same account. "Some time in the second year after our removal to Manchester, there was in the place where we lived an unusual excitement on the subject of religion."[126] "[T]he Smith family did not move onto their Manchester farm until 1822. The second year after this move would have been 1824, not 1820."[127] There was *no* revival in 1820, but there was a powerful revival like the one Joseph described in Palmyra "during the fall and winter of 1824-25,"[128] and Reverend Lane was there. Eighteen twenty-four (1824) was "the second year" after the Smith's "removal to Manchester," and the revival continued in 1825. The 1838-39 Pearl of Great Price Account of the First Vision is accordingly internally inconsistent on a number of counts. It first reports, with great certainty, that the vision occurred in the spring of 1820 during the

---

[124]Ibid., 1:5.
[125]Ibid., 1:14, emphasis added.
[126]Ibid., 1:5.
[127]Marquardt and Walters, *Inventing Mormonism*, 15.
[128]Ibid.

revival when Joseph Smith was fourteen years old and in his fifteenth year. It then said with equal certainty that the revival commenced in "the second year after our removal to Manchester," which was in 1824, when Joseph Smith was eighteen years old and in his nineteenth year.

History overwhelmingly supports the proposition that the actual Palmyra revival Joseph Smith erroneously described as one prologue to each of two separate visions (the 1820 First Vision of the Father and the Son and the 1823 vision of the Angel Moroni) occurred as an historical fact only once, in 1824 and 1825. Of that, given historical hindsight and recent research, there can be but very little room for doubt.

> *An examination of newspaper accounts, religious periodicals, church records, and personal narratives shows that there were no significant gains in church memberships or any other signs of revival in Palmyra in 1820. There was a stirring and momentous revival there with all the features that Joseph Smith's history mentions during the fall and winter of 1824-25.*[129]

The Presbyterian Palmyra revival history shows "revivals in 1817 and in 1824 but nothing in the intervening years."[130] "The revival over the winter of 1816-1817, which affected mainly the Presbyterian church of Palmyra, received coverage in at least a dozen periodicals, ... The 1824-25 revival likewise received enthusiastic write-ups in an equal number of publications."[131] In these same periodicals, there is "total silence" about any Palmyra revival having occurred between 1819 and 1821.[132] But Joseph later described religious excitement there at a time when there was none: "My mind," he said, "at times was greatly excited, *the cry and*

---

[129]Ibid., emphasis added.

[130]James H. Hotchkin, *A History of the Purchase and Settlement of Western New York, and the Rise, Progress and Present State of the Presbyterian Church in that Section* (N.Y.: M.W. Dodd, 1848), 378, quoted in Marquardt and Walters, *Inventing Mormonism*, 18.

[131]Ibid., 18-19. An imposing list of prominent publications containing accounts of the 1824-25 revival is found at 36 n 12.

[132]Ibid., 19. *See* n 13 on page 36 for a long list of periodicals examined "without finding a single reference to a Palmyra revival" between 1819 and 1821.

tumult were so great and incessant. "[133] Joseph Smith was feeling the "great and incessant" "cry and tumult" of the same impressive revival that caused his mother, two of his brothers and one of his sisters to join, in each of two separate accounts of different visions, the Western Presbyterian Church in Palmyra, New York. One account had it *before* Joseph had his First Vision of the Father and the Son in 1820, and another account had it *after* the death of Alvin Smith on November 19, 1823. Each account reports that the Smiths joined the Presbyterians, one in 1823 and another in 1820, because of the same great revival. Joseph's later story of an 1820 vision wasn't a small mistake.

> *Oliver Cowdery's [Oliver Cowdery and Joseph Smith's] 1835 account mentions that the extended revival began "in Palmyra and vicinity." Lucy elaborated: "About this time their was a great revival in religion and the whole neighborhood was very much aroused to the subject and we among the rest flocked to the meeting house." Palmyra's newspaper, the Wayne Sentinel reported the religious fervor in 1824-25. It was also commonplace for religious periodicals to report on revivals. Accordingly fifteen accounts of this 1824-25 revival have been found. There is not a single reference to a Palmyra revival between 1818 and 1821 in any of the major religious periodicals.*[134]

The 1824 date for the commencement of the Palmyra revival coincides perfectly with the Palmyra ministry of the Reverend George Lane. George Lane became the Presiding Elder of a Methodist circuit (that included Palmyra) in July of 1824,[135] and he left Palmyra in January 1825. That meant that "our brother's mind was awakened" some time after July of 1824 and some time before January 1825, in both cases after the death of Alvin, when Joseph Smith was eighteen or nineteen years old (and in the nineteenth and twentieth years of his age).

---

[133]The Pearl of Great Price, Joseph Smith – History 1:9, emphasis added.

[134]Palmer, *An Insider's View of Mormon Origins*, 243-44 and included cites, n 20-23, emphasis added.

[135]Marquardt and Walters, *Inventing Mormonism*, 21.

"Great Multitudes" Unite

In the 1838-39 Pearl of Great Price Account of the First Vision, Joseph Smith recalled that "great multitudes united themselves to the different religious parties, which created no small stir and division amongst the people . . . ."[136]   That controversial circumstance didn't occur in Palmyra, New York, after 1818 or before 1824. "Church membership rolls are carefully kept, and in most cases can still be traced."[137]   "[G]reat multitudes," including four members of Joseph's immediate family, did join the various churches as a result of the 1824-25 revival.[138]   Grant H. Palmer

---

[136]The Pearl of Great Price, Joseph Smith – History 1:5.

[137]Marquardt and Walters, *Inventing Mormonism*, 17.

[138]The Pearl of Great Price, Joseph Smith – History 1:5-9. Besides Joseph's explicit references, ancillary facts strongly suggest that the Smiths had joined the Presbyterian Church years before Joseph ever thought to describe an 1820 vision of the Father and the Son. Three unusual notes, notes denominated A, B and C, were added to Joseph's 1838-39 Manuscript History: Book A-1. Dean C. Jessee, Mormonism's Joseph scholar, speaking for the Church in a Mormon publication, met the criticisms of Mormonism's detractors with the following explanation.

> Since none of these insertions [notes A, B or C] appear in the first published account of this "History" [the 1838-39 Manuscript History: Book A-1] in the *Times and Seasons* in 1842, but the last two are included in the present printed text, critics have regarded this as an example of text tampering. It is doubtful from the content of the notes that they could have originated from anyone other than Joseph Smith.   More important, however, is the fact that all three of them appear in Book A-1 in Willard Richards' handwriting. Since his tenure as scribe on the "History" did not begin until December 1841 and was concluded in March 1844, it is plain that these three insertions were included during Joseph's supervision of the "History." [Jessee, "The Early Accounts of Joseph Smith's First Vision," *BYU Studies* 9, no. 3 (Spring 1969): 13 n 27].

Some time after the publication of the 1838-39 Pearl of Great Price Account of the First Vision in the *Times and Seasons* in 1842, Note B was added to the previously published account in subsequent printings, where it now remains. Note B "reads as follows . . . in our present printed text":

> When the light had departed I had no strength, but soon recovering in some degree. I went home, & as I leaned up to the fire piece Mother enquired what the matter was. I replied never mind all is well. – I am well enough off. *I then told my Mother I have learned for myself that Presbyterianism is not True.* – . . . . [Ibid., 12-13, emphasis added].

Why was that several years delayed addendum important to Joseph? Because his mother and three of his siblings had already joined the Presbyterian Church, by

concluded that "These facts best fit the 1824-25 local history rather than an 1820 setting. Lucy Smith mentioned that her participation in the revival came after Alvin's death in November 1823. She joined the Presbyterians, hoping for solace."[139]

> *The records report that 103 persons joined the Palmyra [Presbyterian] church in 1824-25, while only fourteen converted in 1820-21.*[140]

> *Palmyra Baptist Church records for 1818-25 reveal that the only conference year to show significant growth was September 1824 to September 1825, during which membership increased from 132 to 219. No other conference year between 1818-25 had an increase of more than a dozen convert baptisms.*[141]

> *According to Methodist records, 208 persons joined in the Ontario District, including Palmyra, in 1824-25, while there was a loss of membership in 1820-21 totaling 81 members.*[142]

"[D]uring the entire year of 1820," "the first Baptist Church in Palmyra" baptized only eight new members. "For the one year

---

that history's reckoning in 1820, but by all other reckonings after the death of Alvin. And why is it important here? Because those four Smiths didn't join the Presbyterian Church until some time after Alvin Smith's death in November of 1823. Note B, the latest possible addition to the canonized account, sheds further light on the unmistakable discrepancies that clearly attend Joseph Smith's anachronistic 1838-39 reconstituted telling of modern Mormonism's now most sacred 1820 event.

[139]Palmer, *An Insider's View of Mormon Origins*, 240.

[140]"Presbyterial Reports to the Synod of Geneva, 1812-1828," 89 (22 March 1821), 116 (23 Sept. 1825), Presbyterian Historical Society, Philadelphia, quoted in Ibid., 241 n 12, emphasis added.

[141]"The First Baptized [sic] Church in Palmyra," 1818-1825; and membership figures, *Minutes of the Ontario Baptist Association* (Rochester, N.Y.: Everard Peck, 1825), 5 (28 Sept. 1825), both at the American Baptist Historical Society, Rochester, N.Y.), quoted in Palmer, *An Insider's View of Mormon Origins*, 241 n 13, emphasis added.

[142]*Minutes of the Annual Conferences*, 1824 report: 466; 1825 report: 471; 1819 report: 330; 1820 report: 345; 1821 report: 366, quoted in Palmer, *An Insider's View of Mormon Origins*, 243 n 18, emphasis added.

period from October 1824[143] to the end of September 1825 there
were a total of 94 persons baptized, an increase of 87 members.
Membership increased from 132 to 219 (65 percent)."[144] In 1824-25
the *Methodists* for the Ontario circuit identified 208 new members
(for "the dozen or so preaching points serviced by a circuit-riding
preacher") in the summer of 1825 for the previous year. "In
contrast, the circuit had constantly lost members during the period
between 1819 and 1821 – twenty-six in 1819, six in 1820, and forty-
nine in 1821."[145]

In 1824-25 the *Presbyterians* (facts derived from reports from the
Geneva Presbytery) "show that by 21 September 1825, when figures
were in for a revival over the winter of 1824-25, '99 have been
admitted on examination.'" "In the congregation of Palmyra, the
Lord has appeared in his glory to build up Zion. More than a
hundred have been hopefully brought into the kingdom of the
Redeemer." Coincidentally "for the period between February 1820
and March 1821" there were "only fourteen additions to the
Western Presbyterian Church of Palmyra" (the church the Smiths
joined). "If four Smiths [had] joined that year, this left only ten
others to join all year."[146]

If the "unusual excitement on the subject of religion" commenced
some time "in the second year" after the Smiths "removal to
Manchester," as Joseph Smith reported,[147] it commenced in 1824.
A revival that commenced in 1824 creates a terrible problem for a
vision supposed to have occurred in the spring of 1820. Because the
revival commenced in 1824 and continued through 1825, Joseph
wasn't fourteen and in his fifteenth year, but rather eighteen or
nineteen and in his nineteenth or twentieth years. The revival
Joseph described in the 1838-39 Pearl of Great Price Account of an
1820 vision of the Father and the Son, the same revival Oliver and
Joseph described in their 1834-35 History of an 1823 vision of the

---

[143]The "awakening" for Baptists actually "began on 20 October 1824."
(Marquardt and Walters, *Inventing Mormonism*, 17 [citations at n 6 on 34]).

[144]Ibid., 17, citations at n 6 on 34.

[145]Ibid., 17, citations at n 7 on 34.

[146]Geneva Presbytery "Records," 2 Feb. 1820, Book C:37, and "Presbyterial
Reports to the Synod of Geneva," quoted in Marquardt and Walters, *Inventing
Mormonism*, 17-18.

[147]The Pearl of Great Price, Joseph Smith – History 1:5.

Angel Moroni, occurred as an historical fact in Palmyra, New York, in 1824 and 1825 – *after* the death of Joseph's brother Alvin in November of 1823, *after* Joseph said that he had a vision of the angel in charge of the plates on September 21, 1823, *after* the ministries of the Reverends George Lane and Benjamin Stockton commenced in 1824, and *after* Joseph claimed to have had a vision of the Father and the Son in the spring of 1820. The 1838-39 Pearl of Great Price Account of the First Vision of the Father and the Son is a theological construct. Started in 1838, further composed and amplified in 1839, published in Scotland in 1840, published in America in 1842, and amended (by means of those unusual notes) after publication in 1843 or 1844, it badly misdescribed the 1824-25 Palmyra revival.

The vision of the Father and the Son described by Joseph Smith in the 1838-39 Pearl of Great Price Account did not follow a Palmyra revival that started with the Methodists in 1824. Nor did it hearken *back* to an earlier Palmyra revival in 1816 or 1817 when Joseph was ten or eleven. Methodists didn't start two separate revivals; the first revival was a Presbyterian event. The Smiths didn't join twice, and the warring sectarian parties didn't get together twice. The 1838-39 Account placed the 1820 vision of the Father and the Son after four members of Joseph Smith's family became Presbyterians, an event that didn't occur as an historical fact until after the death of Alvin Smith on November 19, 1823. That anachronistic claim, central to this discussion, standing alone, should doom the vision. The secular history of those contentious events, supported by contemporaneous church membership records preserved by Baptists, Methodists and Presbyterians, confidently places the great Palmyra revival in 1824-25.

It cannot be said, as the 1838-39 Pearl of Great Price Account turned history on its head to say, that Lucy, Hyrum, Samuel and Sophronia Smith joined the Western Presbyterian Church in Palmyra in 1820.[148]

---

[148]As the modern church continues to teach. *See*, e.g., *Teachings of Presidents of The Church – Joseph Smith* (Salt Lake City, UT: The Church of Jesus Christ of Latter-day Saints, 2007), 29.

Historian Grant H. Palmer:

> *[I]t is unlikely that Lucy would have joined the Presbyterians in 1820 and then again in 1824-25. Nor is it likely that the Reverends Stockton and Lane would have worked together in the same area twice or that the Methodists, Presbyterians, and Baptists would have twice sponsored a joint revival that began in harmony and ended in turmoil and bitter sectarian strife.*[149]

Historian Dan Vogel:

> *No matter how anachronistic Smith's later story of the revival and his quest for the true church, the sequencing of events remained constant. There was a revival, followed by his family's conversion to Presbyterianism, followed by confusion over which church was right, then a determination to join none of them. This was Joseph's emotional chronology which, when placed in the historical setting of the 1824-25 revival, enables one to look not to 1820 or 1823 but to 1825 and beyond for the decisive moments when his claims became prohibitive of other sects and he assumed the task of founding the only true church.*[150]

Placed in historical perspective, the problem is this: The revival Joseph described actually occurred in 1824 and 1825, but the two different visions Joseph described as having been caused by the revival Joseph described occurred in 1820 and 1823. When Joseph Smith composed a new and unfamiliar account of an 1820 vision of the Father and the Son in 1838 and 1839 in the thirty-third and thirty-fourth years of his life, he created an impossible chronology.

---

[149]Palmer, *An Insider's View of Mormon Origins*, 244, emphasis added.
[150]Vogel, *Joseph Smith: The Making of a Prophet*, 63.

CHAPTER TWO

Presbyterian Smiths

*[W]e all with one accord wept over our irretrievable
loss [the death of Alvin], and we could "not be
comforted because he was not."*[1]

*About this time [Alvin died on November 19, 1823]
there was a great revival in religion, and the whole
neighborhood was very much aroused to the subject,
and we, among the rest, flocked to the meetinghouse
to see if there was a word of comfort for us that might
relieve our overcharged feelings.*[2]

Lucy Mack Smith

ALVIN'S DEATH

The Golden Plates Revival

Oliver and Joseph (Cowdery as scribe) reported in the *Messenger
and Advocate* (an official Mormon publication) in 1834-35 that a
Palmyra revival that occurred in 1823 caused Joseph's mother and
siblings to join the Presbyterian Church. "In this general strife for
followers, his mother, one sister, and two of his natural brothers,
were persuaded to unite with the Presbyterians."[3]   This was the
preamble to Joseph Smith and Oliver Cowdery's 1834-35 First
Authorized Account of the 1823 vision of the angel in charge of the
golden plates (it is the 1834-35 History). Lucy Mack Smith made it

---

[1]Lucy Mack Smith, *History of Joseph Smith by His Mother, Lucy Mack Smith:
The Unabridged Original Version – An Up-To-Date Reprint of the Original 1853
Edition in Its Entirety, With Additional Information from the Rough-Draft
Manuscript and Corrections Resulting from Subsequent Research*, comp. R. Vernon
Ingleton, with a foreword by Richard Lloyd Dewey (Arlington, VA; Provo, UT:
Stratford Books, 2005), 144.

[2]Ibid., 145.

[3]Oliver Cowdery (and Joseph Smith), "Letter III To W.W. Phelps, Esq."
(Oliver Cowdery and Joseph Smith's 1834-35 History), *Messenger and Advocate*,
vol. 1 no. 3 (December 1834): 42.

perfectly clear in her autobiography that her conversion and the conversions of three of her children – Hyrum, Samuel and Sophronia – occurred after the death of Alvin Smith, Lucy's favorite son, on November 19, 1823. That is a revelation to be remembered here. On that point, and at first, Joseph Smith, Oliver Cowdery and Joseph's mother, Lucy Mack Smith, were in total accord.

The Smiths joined the Presbyterians "hoping for solace."[4] Lucy, Hyrum, Samuel and Sophronia joined the Western Presbyterian Church in Palmyra during a well-documented revival that actually occurred as an historical fact in 1824 and 1825. That at least three of them remained active until 1828 and on the Presbyterian rolls until 1830 is confirmed by contemporaneous records still carefully kept.

Lucy Mack Smith in her history determined the chronology of early events in the following order: (1) Nephi (not Moroni) appeared and described the golden plates; (2) Alvin got suddenly sick and died; (3) "there was a great revival" in Palmyra; (4) Lucy, Hyrum, Samuel and Sophronia joined the Presbyterian Church. It is just that simple.

Lucy Mack Smith:

> . . . Alvin was cut open in order to discover, if it were possible, the cause of his death. On doing so they found the calomel lodged in the upper bowels, untouched by anything which he had taken to remove it and as near as possible in its natural state, surrounded as it was with gangrene . . . .

> *"Here," said he* [a doctor by the name of Robinson] *"is one of the loveliest youths that ever trod the streets of Palmyra, destroyed – murdered, as it were – by him at whose hand relief was expected; cut off from the face of the earth by a careless quack who even dared*

---

[4]Grant H. Palmer, *An Insider's View of Mormon Origins* (Salt Lake City: Signature Books, 2002), 240.

to trifle with the life of a fellow mortal."[5]

Thus did Alvin ("a youth of singular goodness of disposition – kind and amiable"[6]) succumb to an early event, an overdose of calomel administered by an inexperienced physician in a futile attempt to arrest the effects of "bilious colic."[7]   With Alvin's passing, "lamentation and mourning filled the whole neighborhood."[8]   "A vast concourse of people attended his obsequies, who seemed very anxious to show their sympathy for us in our bereavement."   In a passage crossed out in her rough-draft manuscript, Lucy said, "*The circumstance of this death aroused the neighborhood to the subject of religion.*"[9]   In the rough draft manuscript prepared in 1845, after the death of Joseph Smith, in a note that was not published in the 1853 first edition of her heavily censored autobiography, Lucy Mack Smith offered this description of the passing of Alvin.

> *Thus was our happiness blasted in a moment when we least expected the blow. . . . the poisoned shaft entered our very hearts' core and diffused its deadly effect throughout our veins.   We were for a time almost swallowed up in grief, so much so that it seemed impossible for us to interest ourselves at all about the concerns of life.   The feeling of every heart was to make speedy preparation to follow him who had been too much the idol of our hearts, and then, if it pleased God to take us also, we would receive the call as a favor at his hands from whom it came.*[10]

Alvin died two months after Joseph was supposed to have told his family about the golden plates (which he had seen but not then yet acquired).   Alvin didn't know before his death that there had been a

---

[5]Lucy Mack Smith, *History of Joseph Smith by His Mother, Lucy Mack Smith: The Unabridged Original Version*, comp. R. Vernon Ingleton, 142-43, emphasis added.   This is the version cited throughout this chapter.   "All but the first few words of this paragraph are crossed out in the rough draft manuscript."   The omitted words are italicized.

[6]Ibid., 142.

[7]Ibid., 139.

[8]Ibid., 142.

[9]Ibid., 143, emphasis added.

[10]Ibid., emphasis added.

vision of the Father and the Son, and neither did his mother, father or siblings. On September 22, 1823 (a date assigned to the vision of the visit of the Angel), Joseph Jr., Alvin and William Smith had been working in their father's field together. On November 19, 1823, Alvin Smith was dead. "Alvin manifested, if such could be the case," Lucy reports, "greater zeal and anxiety in regard to the record [by that to say the golden plates] that had been shown to Joseph than any of the rest of the family; in consequence of which we could not bear to hear anything said upon the subject."[11]

When Joseph spoke about the record after Alvin's death, it brought Alvin to their minds, he who had gone "to return no more in this life." "[W]e all with one accord wept over our irretrievable loss, and we could 'not be comforted, because he was not.'"[12] Mother Smith does not purport to describe Alvin's feelings about what was then an unknown and unreported 1820 vision of the Father and the Son. Now, with Alvin gone and in their sorrow, the Smiths look for solace in unfamiliar places at the revival in the meetinghouses. In what is yet another critically important entry found crossed out in Lucy's rough-draft manuscript prepared in 1845 and omitted by Lucy and/or her tenders from the 1853 edition of Lucy's biography for perfectly obvious reasons, the prophet's mother reported that,

> *About this time [when the Smiths could "not be comforted because he [meaning the departed Alvin] was not"] there was a great revival in religion, and the whole neighborhood was very much aroused to the subject, and we, among the rest, flocked to the meetinghouse to see if there was a word of comfort for us that might relieve our overcharged feelings.*[13]

This is after the angel "Nephi"[14] (then only later changed to become "Moroni") is supposed to have appeared to Joseph.[15] This is after

---

[11]Ibid., 143-44.

[12]Ibid., 144.

[13]Ibid., 145, emphasis added.

[14]Ibid., 123.

[15]Lucy recalled that the angel first spoke to Joseph on "the evening of the twenty-first of September 1823" (quoting Joseph) in these terms: "He called me by name and said unto me that he was a messenger sent from the presence of God to

the angel commanded Joseph to go to his father and tell him of the vision and commandments he had received.[16] This is after Joseph made known to his family "all that he had communicated to his father in the field"; after he had told them "of his finding the record" and of "what passed between him and the angel while he was at the place where the plates were deposited."[17] This is after the angel "Nephi" told Joseph, according to Lucy, that "There is not a true church on earth – no not one"; after Joseph told Alvin about the golden plates; *and after Alvin died on November 19, 1823, knowing nothing about a vision of the Father and the Son.*

Lucy Mack Smith:

> *Shortly after the death of Alvin, a man commenced laboring in the neighborhood to effect a union of the different churches, in order that all might be agreed and thus worship God with one heart and with one mind.*
>
> *This seemed about right to me, and I felt much inclined to join in with them; in fact, the most of the family appeared quite disposed to unite with their numbers; but Joseph, from the first, utterly refused even to attend their meetings, saying, "Mother, I do not wish to prevent your going to meeting, or any of the rest of the family's; or your joining any church you please; but do not ask me to join them. I can take my Bible and go into the woods and learn more in two hours than you can learn at meeting in two years, if you should go all the time."[18]*

Joseph Sr., unlike Joseph Jr., attended two or three meetings.

---

me and that his name was Nephi . . . ." (Ibid., 123). "Nephi is the name that appears in the manuscript [Joseph's Manuscript History]." Orson Pratt later changed that name in the manuscript with a footnote and an asterisk. Pratt initialed the change. It was supposed that there had been several references to "Moroni" in other early resources. This inexplicable mistake (Nephi in the manuscript) has been forgotten or ignored.

[16]The Pearl of Great Price, Joseph Smith – History 1:49.

[17]Lucy Mack Smith, *History of Joseph Smith*, 132.

[18]Ibid., 145-46, emphasis added.

"During this excitement Joseph [Jr.] would say it would do us no injury to join them, that if we did we should not continue with them long, for we were mistaken in them and did not know the wickedness of their hearts."[19] These comments were composed by Lucy and her tenders in 1845 shortly after Joseph's death. And it was during the great 1824-25 revival that Lucy and Joseph's siblings joined the Presbyterian Church. The "great revival" *followed* the death of Alvin Smith, *followed* the vision of the Father and the Son, *followed* the instructions of Jesus to Joseph in the Sacred Grove, and *followed* the repeated instructions of the angel to Joseph on the evening and in the morning of September 21 and 22, 1823.

The revival resupposed to have caused the vision of the Father and the Son, the same revival first supposed to have caused the vision of the angel in charge of the golden plates, actually *followed* both of those alleged events. And the report of the visit of the angel in charge of the golden plates *preceded* the report of the visit of the Father and the Son by many years. The actual sequence of the reported events occurred in the following order: (1) the September 21, 1823, vision of the Angel in charge of the golden plates (sometimes "Nephi," sometimes "Moroni"); (2) the death of Alvin Smith on November 19, 1823; (3) the 1824-25 Palmyra revival; (4) the 1824-25 conversions of Lucy, Hyrum, Samuel and Sophronia Smith; and (5) the *1838-39 Pearl of Great Price Account of the Vision of the Father and the Son*, a retroactively reported 1820 event supposed to have preceded by four or five years its duly reported cause (the 1824-25 Palmyra revival).

Alvin's Obsequies

Lucy Mack Smith lost Alvin on November 19, 1823 (two months after Joseph is supposed to have described September 21 and 22 visions of the angel in charge of the plates to his family, including Alvin). Alvin's death drove a grieving Lucy "to seek consolation in community religion."[20] Alvin's November 1823 services were held

---

[19]Ibid., 146.
[20]Dan Vogel, *Joseph Smith: The Making of a Prophet* (Salt Lake City: Signature Books, 2004), 56.

at the Western Presbyterian Church in Palmyra, New York, after which several members of the Smith family joined that particular church. The Reverend Benjamin Stockton (the future pastor of Lucy, Hyrum, Samuel and Sophronia Smith), the man who preached the funeral sermon, offended Alvin's father. "In delivering the funeral sermon, he could not resist preaching to the unconverted who were visiting his church for the first time."[21] Reverend Stockton "intimated very strongly" that Alvin, who didn't belong to a church and hadn't been baptized, had gone to hell. "Stockton's indiscretion incensed Joseph, Sr.,"[22] a man who held Universalist views.

In 1842, when Joseph first publicly reported that he had had *an 1820 vision* of the Father and the Son, he had to move the Palmyra revival he previously announced in the 1834-35 History to have occurred in 1823 back three years to the year 1820. He now reported, contrary to everything he had previously said, that Lucy, Hyrum, Samuel and Sophronia joined the Presbyterian Church during an 1820 revival, *before* Joseph retired to the woods and *before* that new and surprising previously unknown and unreported vision was supposed to have occurred.[23] That late-to-the-table claim was impossible because there was no revival in Palmyra, New York, in the year 1820. Alvin was alive for three-and-a-half years after Joseph said (but not until 1838-39 in writing, or 1842 in public) that he had seen the Father and the Son in 1820. But Alvin didn't know about the Father and the Son in 1820 or before his death in 1823, and Alvin didn't live to see Lucy, Hyrum, Samuel and Sophronia join the Presbyterian Church.[24] On his death bed, as recounted by his adoring mother, the vision of the Father and the

---

[21]Ibid., 55.

[22]Ibid., quoting William Smith.

[23]"When the light had departed [after the 1820 vision], I had no strength; but soon recovering in some degree, I went home . . . . I then said to my mother "I have learned for myself that Presbyterianism is not true." (Joseph Smith Jr., *History of The Church of Jesus Christ of Latter-day Saints*, B.H. Roberts, ed., 2d ed., rev., [Salt Lake City: The Deseret Book Company, 1978], 1:6). That wouldn't have made sense because Joseph's mother wasn't a Presbyterian until 1824 or 1825.

[24]While Lucy Mack Smith prominently mentioned Joseph Jr. and Joseph Sr.'s responses to her plan to join the Presbyterians, she said nothing about Alvin or his response, precisely because Alvin was dead before she, Hyrum, Samuel and Sophronia attended that revival in 1824-25 and joined the Presbyterian Church.

Son was never discussed. The conversions of his mother, Hyrum, Samuel and Sophronia found no place in his contemplation of death concerns.

The Smiths' Conversion

Joseph Smith was a month away from his eighteenth birthday when the Reverend Benjamin Stockton preached the funeral sermon for Alvin Smith.[25] The 1823 funeral took place three-and-a half years *after* Joseph later claimed that he had seen the Father and the Son in 1820, two months *after* Joseph later said that he had seen the Angel "Nephi" (or "Moroni") in 1823, and *before* Joseph's mother, Hyrum, Samuel and Sophronia joined the Presbyterian Church. Angered by the Reverend Stockton's insensitive sermon, Joseph Smith Sr. (who had attended two or three meetings to gratify Lucy) declined accepting any further invitations. He "peremptorily

---

[25]When the Reverend Benjamin Stockton preached the funeral service for Alvin Smith in November 1823, he was not yet the pastor of Palmyra's Western Presbyterian Church. "Stockton was pastor of the Skaneateles church in central New York from 4 March 1818 until 30 June 1822. He visited Palmyra for a speech to the Youth Missionary Society in October 1822, and the newspaper described him then as 'Rev. Stockton of Skaneateles.' He appeared again in the Palmyra paper when he performed a wedding on 26 November 1823, just a week after Alvin's death. According to William Smith, Stockton was present the previous week and preached Alvin's funeral sermon." (H. Michael Marquardt and Wesley P. Walters, *Inventing Mormonism: Tradition and the Historical Record* [n.p.: Smith Research Associates, 1998], 20). He did not become the pastor at the Palmyra Presbyterian Church until February 18, 1824, but appears to have been the pastor when Lucy and Joseph's siblings joined. And he appears to have been the "Presiding Pastor" at one of the revival meetings attended by the Smiths. Grant Palmer clarified this issue in these terms: "William Smith noted that his mother and family 'belong[ed] to the Presbyterian Church, of whome the Rev. Mr. Stoc[k]ton was the Presiding Pastor or Shepard.'" (Marvin S. Hill, "The First Vision Controversy: A Critique and Reconciliation," *Dialogue: A Journal of Mormon Thought*, vol. 15 no. 2 [Summer 1982]: 45 n 48). "*Presbyterian records confirm that Benjamin B. Stockton was the pastor of the Palmyra Presbyterian Church from mid-February 1824 to September 1827 and that he participated in the very successful revivals of 1824-25. The records report that 103 persons joined the Palmyra church in 1824-25, while only fourteen converted in 1820-21.*'" (Palmer, *An Insider's View of Mormon Origins*, 241 n 11, emphasis added). "For Rev. Stockton's installation, see the *Wayne Sentinel* (Palmyra, NY, 18, 25 Feb. 1824); for his release, see Geneva Presbytery 'Records,' 18 Sept. 1827 (C: 252-254; D:83-5), Presbyterian Historical Society, Philadelphia." (Ibid.).

refused, going any more, either for my gratification, or any other persons."[26] The two Josephs would not be counted among an impressive number of new converts joining Reverend Stockton's church in 1824-25.[27] At least three of the Smith siblings, more susceptible to Lucy's orthodox importunements and shocked to the core by the passing of Alvin, were also engaged in a search for solace. Lucy linked Alvin's death and the revival that followed to the conversion of herself and three of her children. She presented her case for joining a church during the "great revival" in ecumenical terms. Lucy wrote that Joseph Sr. "declined attending the meetings after the first but [he also] did not object to myself and such of the children as chose . . . <going or becoming> church members . . . < . . . if we wished>."[28]

Joseph Describes a Backdated 1820 Revival

The "great love" of the new converts for the different faiths "expressed at the time of their conversion, and the great zeal manifested by the respective clergy" who were "promoting this extraordinary scene of religious feeling," "let them join what sect they pleased," soon gave way to scenes of religious partisanship. As Joseph Smith wrote in his history:

> *[I]t was seen that the seemingly good feelings of both the priests and the converts were more pretended than real; for a scene of great confusion and bad feeling ensued – priest contending against priest, and convert against convert; so that all their good feelings one for another, if they ever had any, were entirely lost in a*

---

[26]Lucy Mack Smith, *Biographical Sketches of Joseph Smith the Prophet, and His Progenitors for Many Generations* (Liverpool, UK: S.W. Richards, 1853), 90, quoted in Dale Morgan, *Dale Morgan on Early Mormonism: Correspondence & A New History*, ed. John Phillip Walker, with a Biographical Introduction by John Phillip Walker and a Preface by William Mulder (Salt Lake City: Signature Books, 1986), 258.

[27]"The reference to Stockton is another among the innumerable evidences that it is the revival of 1824-25 that figures in Mormon history." (Morgan, *Dale Morgan on Early Mormonism*, 377 n 37).

[28]Lucy Mack Smith, Preliminary Manuscript (M.S.), quoted in Dan Vogel, ed., *Early Mormon Documents* (Salt Lake City: Signature Books, 1996-2003), 1:306-7.

strife of words and a contest about opinions.[29]

Professor Marvin S. Hill, an important Latter-day Saint scholar and a brother of one of Smith's biographers, provided this insightful overview:

> I am inclined to agree with him [Reverend Walters, a non-Mormon revival scholar] that the turmoil that Joseph describes that led to some family members joining the Presbyterians and that led to much sectarian bitterness, does not fit well into the 1820 context detailed by Bachman [Joseph's amended "context" detailed by Bachman]. For one thing, it does not seem likely that there would have been so much sectarian strife in 1820 and then have a joint revival where all was harmony in 1824. In addition, as Walters notes, Lucy Mack Smith says the revival where she became interested in a particular sect, came after Alvin's death, thus almost certainly in 1824 . . . . She would not be likely to make up such a personal reaction of her own or the family's, nor mistake the time when it happened. *I am persuaded that it was 1824 when Lucy [and Joseph's siblings] joined the Presbyterians, and that, of course, is a critical point for dating the revival . . . .*[30]

What Lucy Knew and When

Lucy Mack Smith and William Smith both described at different times the 1823 vision of the angel in charge of the plates as Joseph's First Vision, and so did the members of the early Church. Oliver and Joseph unequivocally described the vision of an angel in 1823 as Joseph's First Vision in that 1834-35 First Authorized History found in Joseph's journal, published in the *Messenger and Advocate* and then later republished "in the *Times and Seasons* without any

---

[29]The Pearl of Great Price, Joseph Smith – History 1:6, emphasis added.
[30]Marvin S. Hill speech, Sunstone Theological Symposium (1981), quoted in Jerald Tanner and Sandra Tanner, *Mormonism – Shadow or Reality?* (Salt Lake City: Utah Lighthouse Ministry, 1987), 162C, emphasis added.

thought of correction."[31] The 1834-35 History penned by Oliver Cowdery was "written at the Prophet's request and under his personal supervision." It was then published and republished "under" Joseph Smith's "direction."

In a post publication amendment to the 1842 publication of the 1838-39 Pearl of Great Price Account, Joseph (or someone) described twenty-two years after an 1820 vision how the fourteen-year-old Joseph was supposed to have told his mother that the Presbyterian Church wasn't true. The conversation was said to have occurred when Joseph returned to his home after the vision of the Father and the Son *in 1820*. That was three-and-a-half years before Alvin's death on November 19, 1823, at least four years before his mother, Hyrum, Samuel and Sophronia joined the Western Presbyterian Church, four or five years before the 1824-25 Palmyra revival, and at least ten years before the Smiths formally renounced their Presbyterian faith.

If Joseph had actually told his mother, an early faithful disciple, *in 1820* that he had learned for himself that "Presbyterianism is not true,"[32] his words had been ignored. Lucy joined the Presbyterian Church in 1824 or 1825 and remained an active member there from 1824-25 until 1828, and on the Presbyterian rolls until 1830. The earlier 1834-35 History, prepared by Joseph Smith and Oliver Cowdery, specifically (and with emphasis) dated the great revival as having occurred in 1823 when Joseph was seventeen years old and in the eighteenth year of his age. Joseph Smith, the person who knew, was the source of the date.

The Presbyterian Smiths, with the possible exception of Sophronia, remained active members of the Presbyterian Church until about September 1828,[33] which was approximately eight-and-a-half years

---

[31]Joseph Fielding Smith, *Doctrines of Salvation*, ed. Bruce R. McConkie, vol. 3 (Salt Lake City: Bookcraft, 1956), 236.

[32]The Pearl of Great Price, Joseph Smith – History, 1:20.

[33]Lucy Mack Smith and Joseph Smith Sr. traveled to Pennsylvania to meet Emma's family in about September of 1828. (Vogel, *Joseph Smith: The Making of a Prophet*, 147). They seemed to better understand what Joseph was about following this visit. "*. . . Lucy, Hyrum and Samuel stopped attending meetings at the Presbyterian church about this time.*" (Ibid., 148, emphasis added). Sophronia, who

after 1820. But their son and brother said in 1838 that 1820 was the year that he was twice forbidden by the deities in the strongest terms from joining any of the sects. Both the Presbyterian Smiths and the 1828 Methodist-friendly Joseph appear to have ignored this strongly stated twice repeated injunction (a command not publicly even described until the early 1840s). It was more than twenty years after 1820, and even then some time after the publication of the vision in the *Times and Seasons* in 1842, before Joseph said in a note attached to the manuscript that he told his mother in 1820, "*I have learned for myself that Presbyterianism is not true.*"[34] Lucy Mack Smith was not a member of the Presbyterian Church in 1820 or until after the death of Alvin, and Alvin was alive and well in 1820. Lucy Mack Smith's religious affiliation over the years that followed, from about 1824 to about 1828 and on the record until 1830, contradicts that dubious claim.

Both Lucy Mack Smith and William Smith, unlike Joseph, associated the indictment of the Christian churches with the vision of the angel in charge of the plates and not, as Joseph only very much later announced, with the vision of the Father and the Son. The admonition, according to Lucy, wasn't originally from God or Jesus; it was from "Nephi" or "Moroni." Joseph, twenty years later, moved the revival, changed the principals and reworked the facts in order to support the story of an earlier and unannounced 1820 vision. The other Smiths remembered what Joseph said to their family in September 1823. Neither Lucy nor William ever really made peace with the Mormon prophet's amended late-in-life creation, the committee-driven 1838-39 Pearl of Great Price Fourth Account of an 1820 vision of the Father and the Son. Neither did other early Mormon leaders, including Brigham Young.

Reversing the Irreversible

To successfully compose a new and previously unknown 1820 history in 1838 and 1839, based on new and previously unknown and unsupported claims, contradicting the memories of family and

---

had married Calvin Stoddard, seemed to have already stopped attending. (Ibid., 484).

[34]The Pearl of Great Price, Joseph Smith – History 1:20, emphasis added.

neighbors, friends and foes alike, was a formidable task. This now new "truth" was inconvenient in a number of ways. For one, how would Joseph explain his tardy recitals of allegedly distant events to his mother, Lucy Mack Smith, a woman of intellect who knew nothing about what was now seen to become a new and terribly late account of an 1820 vision of the Father and the Son?

After the delayed publication of the 1838-39 Pearl of Great Price Account in the *Times and Seasons* in 1842, several issues remained to be resolved. What Joseph Smith told his mother about this (new and unfamiliar) vision had to have been one of them. The Account, as it was first published in Nauvoo in 1842, did not include this clarification ("*I have learned for myself that Presbyterianism is not true*"[35]), an after-the-fact statement intended to describe an 1820 conversation between Joseph and his mother.[36] The report of that 1820 conversation came four years after the drafting of the history of the canonized vision of the Father and the Son commenced in 1838, three years after the earliest draft was revised and amplified in 1839, and more than twenty-two years after the 1820 vision was supposed to have occurred. The manuscript of the "History" containing the Pearl of Great Price Account included three notes designated A, B and C, two of which, notes B and C, were added to the text of the 1838-39 Pearl of Great Price Account *after* that account had been published for the first time in the *Times and Seasons* in 1842 without them. Note B, one of those undated notes, contained the particular Presbyterian passage supposed to have been addressed to Joseph's mother in 1820.

The insertions (post-publication amendments) to the *Times and Seasons* First Vision Account were created as notes and inserted sometime *after* the account's 1842 publication and (according to Mormon scholar Dean C. Jessee) on December 2, 1842. The *Times and Seasons* First Vision account of a vision of the Father and the Son was published in April 1842. Note B, which is included in the present printed account, concerned a conversation that he was

---

[35]Ibid., emphasis added.
[36]Dean C. Jessee, "The Early Accounts of Joseph Smith's First Vision," *BYU Studies* 9, no. 3 (Spring 1969): 291-92 n 27 (pp. 12-13 of internet version).

supposed to have had with his mother in the house after the vision in 1820.[37]

Why was that inconspicuous and awkwardly delayed post-publication amendment a matter of such concern? Joseph's mother, father and siblings didn't know about a vision of the Father and the Son in 1820. They also didn't know about a vision of the Son in 1821. Those events, recounted at different times in contradictory reports, were not described to them, or to anyone else, for many years. In the case of the vision of the Son without the Father (Joseph's 1832 Holographic Account), the document describing the vision was concealed and suppressed in the archives of the Church for more than one hundred thirty years. It is quite likely that Joseph's mother, father and siblings didn't ever know anything about the strange concealed account. That handwritten most intimate and first account of Joseph's first encounter with deity prepared in 1832 didn't surface until 1965.

Joseph Smith told his followers (but not until 1842, by which time his father was dead) that his "telling the story" of the canonized 1838-39 Account invited persecution, hatred and despair. Men of "high standing" took notice of him, an obscure boy of no particular consequence. Those prominent men then acted in unison to create "a bitter persecution" against him. For three-and-a-half years, he said, "all classes of men, both religious and irreligious," and "all the sects . . . united to persecute me" because "I continued to affirm that I had seen a vision." Can anyone suppose that Joseph's mother didn't know about those men of "high standing" who took notice of her fourteen-year-old son? Can anyone suppose that she, Joseph Sr., Alvin and Joseph's other siblings didn't know that all classes of men from all the sects had "united" to persecute him because he continued to affirm that he had seen a vision? It is absurd to think that they did not if what he said was true.

Lucy Mack Smith didn't know about that great First Vision of the Father and the Son in 1820, in 1823, in 1831, or any time before 1842, and maybe not even then. Alvin Smith didn't know about the First Vision of the Father and the Son when he died in 1823, and

---

[37]Ibid.

Joseph Smith Sr. didn't know about the vision when he died in 1840. Was Lucy supposed to say, after the vision, that Joseph didn't tell her and neither did anyone else? Was she supposed to say none of them knew about the vision, and none of them noticed the persecution? What Lucy didn't know, and had never known, was an issue to be addressed. Someone tried to defuse that not so tiny problem by adding a late to the table post-publication amendment, "Note B."[38]

By saying after the publication in 1842 that Joseph hadn't told his mother about the great event, the author of the note tried to protect her, Joseph and the message from criticism because of what Lucy should have known but didn't know. The revision in the note first said, not less than twenty-two years after the vision was supposed to have occurred, that Joseph went home after the vision exhausted, leaned up to the fireplace, and told his mother when she asked him what was wrong that nothing was ("Never mind, all is well . . ."[39]). Lucy Mack Smith's undeniable ignorance of the great event seems to have been on someone's mind after the final account had been publicly circulated. If some suitable explanation had been overlooked before the sanitized history was finally published in some better form, never mind. The problem could still be corrected, at least in part, even after publication, by means of yet another clever retroactive amendment.

Lucy Doesn't Follow the Script

In her 1845 "Preliminary Manuscript," Lucy Mack Smith said several things that seriously threatened the traditional (unfamiliar and late to the table) canonized Pearl of Great Price Fourth Account of the First Vision:

    1. *That on the evening of the vision of the Angel Moroni ("Nephi" according to Lucy and the manuscript), September 21, 1823, the Smiths were "sitting till quite late" discussing "the subject of the*

---

[38]The Pearl of Great Price, Joseph Smith – History 1:20. The contents of Note B were not found in the account published in the *Times and Seasons* in 1842. They have since been added to all editions and printings of the Pearl of Great Price.
    [39]Ibid.

diversity of churches" and "the many thousand opinions" about "the truths contained in scripture[.]"

2. That Joseph went to bed on September 21, 1823, "< and was pondering in his mind which of the churches were the true one>."

3. That when the angel appeared on September 21, 1823, he said, "I perceive that you are enquiring in your mind which is the true church[.]"

4. That the angel in charge of the plates told Joseph that "there is not a true church on Earth[,] No not one . . . ."[40]

According to his mother, Joseph Smith didn't know on September 21, 1823, or until the angel spoke, that none of the churches were true. He learned that there was "not a true church on Earth[,] No not one," according to her, not from Jesus in 1820 in some unannounced (or yet to be crafted) vision Lucy knew nothing about, but rather from "Nephi," the angel in charge of the golden plates in 1823, the vision she did know something about. What that meant was that Joseph hadn't gotten his "mind satisfied so far as the sectarian world was concerned – that it was not my duty to join with any of them, but to continue as I was until further directed."[41] As far as Lucy knew in September 1823, he had not until 1823 asked that question, gotten that answer, or received those instructions. And not until 1842 did he publicly say that he had asked that question, gotten that answer, and received those instructions, twenty-two years before in 1820, and from someone other than the angel in charge of the plates known to Lucy as Nephi.

Joseph's mother said that Alvin knew all about the golden plates when Alvin died on November 19, 1823. But Alvin didn't know about a vision of the Father and the Son in 1823, and neither did Lucy. After Alvin's death, sometime after November 19, 1823, Lucy visited the 1824-25 Palmyra revival in search of solace. Alvin was going to hell. A Puritan, Lucy was trying herself to decide

---

[40]Lucy Mack Smith, "Preliminary Manuscript" (1845), in the handwriting of Howard Coray, quoted in Dan Vogel, ed., *Early Mormon Documents*, 1:289-90, emphasis added.

[41]The Pearl of Great Price, Joseph Smith – History 1:26.

which of the churches to join. The comforting message that Joseph had seen the Father and the Son,[42] like the disturbing concern that he was then persecuted by almost everyone because he said that he had and refused to say that he had not, were not factors in Lucy Mack Smith's poorly informed equations, or in Alvin's contemplation of death concerns. Lucy announced that Alvin's death contributed to cause the religious excitement surrounding the revival that ultimately resulted in her conversion. Her ignorance of an 1820 First Vision after the deaths of Joseph and Hyrum presented a threat to the Church and subjected her 1845 manuscript to censorship. When Orson Pratt published Lucy's 1845 "Preliminary Manuscript" as Biographical Sketches in England in 1853, her account of the visit of the angel, the vision important to her, was omitted and replaced by "the account of Joseph Smith's First Vision printed in the 1842 "Times and Seasons.""[43]

"Join Any Church You Like": Joseph to Lucy After Alvin's Death

> ... *Mother, I do not wish to prevent you from going to meeting or joining any church you like or any of the Family who desire the like only do not ask me to go <do so> for I do not wish to go*[.][44]

Did he tell her then that all their creeds were an abomination in the sight of God? Did he say that those professors were all corrupt? That they taught for doctrine the commandments of men? Did Lucy say that Joseph told her, *"I have learned for myself that*

---

[42]Would a Joseph who had seen the Father and the Son, then parents and siblings who knew that he had, have failed to mention something so obviously comforting to a greatly beloved unaffiliated brother on his deathbed?

[43]LaMar Petersen, *The Creation of the Book of Mormon: A Historical Inquiry* (Salt Lake City: Freethinker Press, 2000), 15 n 32. When the book (Lucy's history) resurfaced as a "photomechanical reproduction" in 1965, it was postulated that the 1945 Preston Nibley edition, "then the current edition in use by the LDS Church," had been changed in one way or another – since 1853 – 2,751 times. (R. Vernon Ingleton, comp., Lucy Mack Smith, *History of Joseph Smith by His Mother, Lucy Mack Smith*, xxix). Ingleton used Jerald and Sandra Tanner's research.

[44]Lucy Mack Smith, *Preliminary* Manuscript (1845), quoted in Dan Vogel, ed., *Early Mormon Documents*, 1:307, emphasis added.

Presbyterianism is not true"? Or that God had told him not to join any of the sects "for they were all wrong"? Or that he had now gotten his "mind satisfied so far as the sectarian world" was concerned? Not according to Lucy. What she said he said, until what he said was changed in 1845, was this: *"Mother, I do not wish to prevent you from going to meeting or joining any church you like . . . ."* Does this sound like the message he would send to his family in 1824 or 1825 if he really had the 1820 vision he only many years later described? Would he say nothing more than this to those he loved? Shouldn't he have said that he had seen the Father and the Son? Shouldn't he have said that he was persecuted for saying so? Shouldn't he have said he had asked them which church he ought to join? That Lucy, Hyrum, Samuel and Sophronia shouldn't join the Presbyterian Church? Shouldn't he have told his mother and his siblings that they would offend God if they decided to join the Presbyterian Church?

The Smiths' Accounts Were Not Consistent

William Smith reported that Joseph told everyone in his family on September 22, 1823, about the visions he had by then received but not yet revealed to anyone else. According to William, the members of Joseph's family believed everything he said. But he didn't say anything about a vision of the Father and the Son. William and Lucy both then reported, very much later and in contradiction to the lessons of their lives, that the Smiths knew in September, two or three months before Alvin died, *that the angel told Joseph none of the sects were right.* The Smiths then also later reported that they knew what Joseph knew about the golden plates and the angel in 1823. So if that was true, if they really knew then what they said they knew later, what is Lucy doing against that background? If that was indeed the background? Why did she join the Presbyterian Church in 1824? So what are Hyrum, Samuel and Sophronia doing against that background? If that was the background? Why did Hyrum, Samuel and Sophronia join the Presbyterian Church in 1824? Why did Lucy say that Joseph said "join any church you like" after Alvin's death? If Joseph had actually gathered his family together on September 22, 1823, to tell them what the angel said? If he had then also described, as William said Joseph said that he would, all of the visions he had by then received? If he had never before described those visions to anyone? If all of them believed everything he said and they were Joseph's earliest converts?

Lucy told the world in 1845, many years after these discussions and after the death of her son, what Joseph was supposed to have told his family in 1823. But she didn't tell them about an 1820 vision of the Father and the Son. Joseph didn't talk about that vision in public until 1842, and neither did his mother, father or siblings. According to Lucy, the angel, Lucy's visitor, had been able to say what Joseph was thinking at the time:

> *I perceive that you are enquiring in your mind [in 1823] which is the true church[.] there is not a true church on Earth[,] No not one[,] nor <and> has not been since Peter took the Keys <of the Melchesidec priesthood after the order of God> into the Kingdom of Heaven[.]*[45]

What is wrong with this contradictory picture? Why did Lucy Mack Smith join the Western Presbyterian Church in Palmyra, New York, after the death of Alvin and remain there as an active member until 1828 if she already knew that "there is not a true church on Earth[,] No not one"? Joseph did not describe a vision of the Father and the Son to his mother or to his brothers and sisters *before* Alvin's death, *before* the revival in 1824, or *before* they joined the Western Presbyterian Church. He didn't tell his mother about the First Vision *before* Lucy wrote a letter explaining Joseph's new church to her brother Solomon Mack in 1831. In that letter, Lucy didn't mention Mormonism's most sacred event, a great First Vision of the Father and the Son. No one mentioned a vision of the Father and the Son in 1831. It is important to know that Joseph believed the Father was the Son in 1831.

Lucy Mack Smith's 1845 after-the-fact account of what the angel told Joseph Smith in 1823 is highly suspect. It is doubtful that an angel ever said that none of the churches were true. If Lucy Mack

---

[45]Ibid., 1:290, emphasis added.

Smith had known what she later said the angel had said, and Joseph had said, and what Joseph then later said the Savior had said, she would never have joined the Presbyterian Church.

Apostates

On March 3, 1830, and because the Smiths had been inactive for something close to two years, the Palmyra Western Presbyterian Church appointed a committee to visit the Smiths "to ask why they had been absent from church."[46]   The Smiths "had entirely neglected the ordinances of the church for the last eighteen months."[47]   They had been inactive "since about September 1828 when Lucy and Joseph Sr. had traveled to Harmony [Pennsylvania] to visit their son and daughter-in-law . . . ."[48] The visiting delegates, Reverend Alfred E. Campbell, Henry Jessup and a certain "Deacon [George] Beckwith," were, according to Lucy, mostly concerned about two things: (1) "the Smith's absence from public worship," and (2) "their connection to the Book of Mormon."[49]   Note that these visiting Presbyterians, like Lucy, Hyrum and Samuel, didn't know in 1830 that Joseph was supposed to have seen the Father and the Son in 1820. That wasn't an item on their Presbyterian agenda. It was in the context of Deacon Beckwith's Book of Mormon concern that Lucy was supposed to have spoken with a fiery tongue. *"Deacon Beckwith, if you should stick my flesh full of faggots, and even burn me at the stake, I would declare, as long as God should give me breath, that Joseph has got that Record [the Book of Mormon record], and that I know it to be true."*[50]

Hyrum and Samuel had been equally intransigent. Samuel, the third member of the Mormon Church, a quieter brother sometimes overlooked, wounded the Presbyterian committee with an image-

---

[46]Dan Vogel, *Joseph Smith: The Making of a Prophet*, 484.

[47]Ibid. (citing church records). The eighteen months quite closely correlates with the visit of the Smiths to the Hales in Pennsylvania in September of 1828, when they learned more of Joseph's mission.

[48]Ibid.

[49]Lucy Mack Smith, *Biographical Sketches of Joseph Smith*, 145-47 (Vogel, ed., *Early Mormon Documents*, 1:406-410), quoted in Vogel, *Joseph Smith: The Making of a Prophet*, 484.

[50]Dan Vogel, *Joseph Smith: The Making of a Prophet*, 485.

shattering scripture taken from Isaiah. In that scripture, Samuel
was reported to have said: "His watchmen are blind: they are all
ignorant, they are all dumb dogs, they cannot bark; sleeping, lying
down, loving to slumber; yea, they are greedy dogs, which can never
have enough, and they are shepherds that cannot understand: they
all look to their own way, every one for his gain, from his quarter."
"The three Presbyterian delegates felt insulted and departed."[51] A
trial, at which the Smiths failed to appear, "resulted in the family's
suspension from church worship"[52] on or after March 29, 1830.

---

[51]Ibid., emphasis added.
[52]Ibid., 484, quoting Isaiah 56:9-11.

CHAPTER THREE

Power, Glory, Message, Mission

About the year 1823, there was a revival of religion in that region [Palmyra], and Joseph was one of several hopeful converts.[1]

William Smith

I ["Nephi"] perceive that you ["Joseph"] are enquiring in your mind which is the true church . . . . [1823].

Lucy Mack Smith

Contemporary publications . . . illustrate the understanding of the early Mormons that their church dated from no earlier an event than the appearance of an angel to Joseph Smith in 1823.[2]

Dale Morgan

Why would anyone publish the report of an allegedly later event (the visit of the angel with the plates) eight years before one published the report of the allegedly

---

[1]Letter of Rev. James Murdock, who interviewed William Smith on 18 April 1841, statement reproduced at H. Michael Marquardt and Wesley P. Walters, *Inventing Mormonism: Tradition and the Historical Record* (n.p.: Smith Research Associates, 1998), 19.

[2]Dale Morgan, *Dale Morgan on Early Mormonism: Correspondence & A New History*, ed. John Phillip Walker, with a Biographical Introduction by John Phillip Walker and a Preface by William Mulder (Salt Lake City: Signature Books, 1986), 249.

earlier event (the visit of the Father and the Son)?
How is one to distinguish the lead-up to the alleged
earlier but later reported event from the lead-up to the
later but earlier reported event?

Joel M. Allred

SEPTEMBER 21, 1823

What Joseph Smith claimed to remember in 1838-1839 and
reported in 1842 was not what Lucy remembered in 1824, 1831, or
1845. Dale Morgan saw the forest for the trees: "That Lucy should
have failed to mention such a vision [the First Vision of the Father
and the Son in her letter to her brother] in 1831, and preserved no
independent recollection of it in 1845 when dictating her
autobiography does not make her the best of witnesses in her son's
behalf."[3]   Joseph's mother, like other early Mormons (and as
Joseph "originally gave the Saints to understand"), thought that the
First Vision – the vision that "led directly to the writing of the Book
of Mormon" and to the "founding of the Church"[4] – was the vision
of the angel in charge of the plates. "The prophet's younger
brother, William, never showed himself able to conceive of Joseph's
visions in any terms but a vision of the Angel Moroni."[5] The 1834-
35 History prepared by Oliver Cowdery and Joseph Smith and
published in installments in the *Messenger and Advocate*
unequivocally reported that the First Vision was the vision of the
angel in charge of the plates. *That can not be denied.*

The founders' first published account of the founding vision
described Joseph kneeling in his room on September 21, 1823,
seeking to know "in some way that his sins were forgiven."[6] In
consequence of what he described to have been a great revival in
1823, Joseph, "one of several hopeful converts," desired to converse

---

[3]Ibid., 250.
[4]Ibid.
[5]Ibid.
[6]Oliver Cowdery (and Joseph Smith), "Letter III To W.W. Phelps, Esq."
(Oliver Cowdery and Joseph Smith's 1834-35 History), *Messenger and Advocate*,
vol. 1 no. 3 (December 1834): 79.

"with some kind messenger who could communicate to him the desired information of his acceptance with God."[7] If Joseph Smith had actually seen the Father and the Son in 1820, he would not have had to ask three-and-a-half years later if the Father and the Son accepted him. If his sins had been forgiven in the sixteenth year of his age[8] – as the one hundred thirty year concealed and suppressed 1832 Handwritten (Holographic) Account of the First Vision said that they had – then why did some kind messenger need to tell him a year or two later that God had accepted him and that his sins had been forgiven again?

To credit this account (Oliver and Joseph's 1834-35 First Authorized History of the Church), one must wonder that a boy who had seen, conversed with and been forgiven by the Redeemer of the World in 1821 had so sufficiently sinned as to desperately require forgiveness in 1823. One *must* surmise when reading the 1834-35 History found in Joseph's journal, written at Joseph's request and published in the *Messenger and Advocate*, that Joseph Smith hadn't seen the Redeemer, or any other heavenly messenger, before 1823. One *must* also surmise that his sins had never been forgiven.[9]

In the 1834-35 History penned by Oliver Cowdery acting under the personal supervision of Joseph Smith, the angel who appeared to a seventeen-year-old Joseph in 1823 chose to describe Joseph's prophetic destiny. He would be "an instrument" in the hands of God to "cause the ears of men to tingle" and the "pure in heart" to rejoice.[10] This incredible event, the first actual reported visitation, was about a message, a book and a mission. The vision came as an answer to issues that Smith said had troubled him. This thoroughly remarkable encounter was about an ancient record of divine origin

---

[7]Oliver Cowdery (and Joseph Smith), "Letter IV To W.W. Phelps, Esq." (Oliver Cowdery and Joseph Smith's 1834-35 History), *Messenger and Advocate*, vol. 1 no. 5 (February 1835), 78.

[8]"I saw the Lord and he spake unto me saying [in 1821 in a vision not reported until 1965] Joseph <my son> thy sins are forgiven thee." (*The Personal Writings of Joseph Smith*, ed. Dean C. Jessee [Salt Lake City: Deseret Book, 1984], 6).

[9]In the *1832 Account* of the angel with the plates, Joseph said that the gold plates event occurred on September 21, *1822*.

[10]"Letter IV" (Cowdery and Smith's 1834-35 History), *Messenger and Advocate*, vol. 1 no. 5 (February 1835), 79-80.

that Smith had been selected to introduce to the world. He had been chosen when God unfolded a plan. This first vision (the first reported vision but not the vision of the Father and the Son), as Dale Morgan reports, "This second of his visions, as his autobiography [composed in 1838 and 1839] would have us believe, or his first, as he originally gave the Saints to understand, led directly to the writing of the Book of Mormon and so to the founding of his church."[11]

The 1833 *Book of Commandments*, a printed compilation of Joseph's revelations, reported that "the Book of Mormon – not the 1820 first vision known to the church today – . . . constituted Joseph's 'call . . . to his holy work.'"[12] For the first formative decade after the Church was organized, there was nothing to suggest that God himself had visited the earth to call an obscure boy to restore the primitive church. Evangelical conversion/forgiveness epiphanies were so relatively common as to render them of little account in preaching. In the early nineteenth century, they were expected Protestant evangelical occurrences.[13] Conversely, an angel delivering an ancient record of divine origin, something stunningly discernible, was to be considered greatly more impressive than one more unsupportable epiphany. The vision of the angel, a messenger in charge of an ancient record, the first reported visitation of any heavenly messenger to Smith, was more important at this time to the success of the early Church than one more suspicious epiphany (the First Vision of the Father and the Son) to be added to a thousand other epiphanies.

Nephi or Moroni?

After leading a treasure-digging expedition earlier in the evening on the night of a full moon at the time of the autumnal equinox (a

---

[11]Morgan, *Dale Morgan on Early Mormonism*, 250.

[12]Grant H. Palmer, *An Insider's View of Mormon Origins* (Salt Lake City: Signature Books, 2002), 239. Book of Commandments 24:7-11; Doctrine and Covenants 20:6-11. "Which book contained a record of a fallen people, and also the fulness of the gospel of Jesus Christ to the Gentiles." (Book of Commandments 24:8).

[13]Palmer, *An Insider's View of Mormon Origins*, 239.

propitious time for conjuration), Smith returned to his father's house where he said he received "a heavenly vision." In the unreported 1832 Holographic Account, this heavenly vision occurred "on the 22d day of Sept. AD 1822."[14] In the 1838-39 Pearl of Great Price Account (first publicly reported in 1842), this vision occurred on the evening of "the twenty-first of September, one thousand eight hundred and twenty-three,"[15] supposedly three and one-half years after the vision of the Father and the Son, which the 1838-39 Account was only then reporting. In this unexpurgated 1838-39 Account, *"A personage appeared at his bedside, announcing (according to the 1842 published 'History of Joseph Smith') that his name was Nephi, and that God had a great work for him to do."*[16] That was an astonishing error for which Joseph Smith should never have gotten a pass. This angel, in the beginning, according to Smith, wasn't *Moroni*, an historical figure who lived as late as 421 AD. This angel, in the beginning, according to Smith, was *Nephi*, an historical figure who inhabited the western hemisphere in about 600 BC. To mistake the one for the other is not inconsequential.

> *The name 'Nephi' appeared in reprints of the story for several years, including [and importantly] the Millennial Star, August 1842, the first edition of the Pearl of Great Price (1851), Lucy Mack Smith's Biographical Sketches of Joseph Smith the Prophet, and his Progenitors for Many Generations (Liverpool, England: Published for Orson Pratt by S.W. Richards, 1853), and the History of the [Reorganized] Church of Jesus Christ of Latter-day Saints (1897).*[17]

> *The first edition of the Doctrine and Covenants in 1835, Oliver Cowdery [and Joseph Smith] in the 1835 Messenger and Advocate, and the Elders' Journal in 1838 call him Moroni, but the 1839 manuscript 'History of Joseph Smith' [a highest value resource],*

---

[14]Joseph Smith Jr., *The Personal Writings of Joseph Smith*, ed. Dean C. Jessee (Salt Lake City: Deseret Book, 1984), 7.

[15]The Pearl of Great Price, Joseph Smith – History 1:27.

[16]LaMar Petersen, *The Creation of the Book of Mormon: A Historical Inquiry* (Salt Lake City: Freethinker Press, 2000), 10, emphasis added.

[17]Ibid., 10-11 n 21, emphasis added.

the 1842 Times and Seasons, the 1842 Millennial Star,
and the first edition of the Pearl of Great Price in
1851 refer to him as Nephi. "[18]

Joseph Smith was the editor of the *Times and Seasons* in 1842 and
the author of the article that described the heavenly messenger as
Nephi. He also dictated the manuscript *"History of Joseph Smith,"*
the historical document that first identified the angel as *Nephi.* "In
the Book of Mormon, Nephi and Moroni are distinctive characters
living a thousand years apart."[19] Petersen concludes:

> *To insist that the angel of western New York in the*
> *1820's was one or the other may seem of little*
> *consequence to the outsider – a distinction without a*
> *difference. But to the devout Mormon the angel is an*
> *historical figure of such stature and importance to the*
> *modern world that there can be no uncertainty as to*
> *his reality or identity. Moroni is . . . the link between*
> *Christ's two American churches – the Nephite and the*
> *Latter-day Saint, the one of whom John said, "And I*
> *saw another angel fly in the midst of heaven, having*
> *the everlasting gospel to preach unto them that dwell*
> *on the earth, and to every nation, and kindred, and*
> *tongue and people." (Rev. 14:6). Moroni, the lone*
> *survivor of the Nephite debacle, buried the record [the*
> *golden plates] in the Hill Cumorah, and as a*
> *resurrected being revealed them to Joseph Smith*
> *fourteen hundred years later.*[20]

So there is personage confusion, identity issues in the First Vision
accounts: First the Savior, no Father and no angels, next two
personages and many angels (in what was called a "first vision of
angels"), then only angels, then two personages and no angels. First
"the ['crucifyed'] Lord" appears in the sixteenth year of Joseph's
life (probably 1821), then "two Personages," one a Father and the
other a Son, appear in the fifteenth year of Joseph's life (1820). The

---

[18]Ibid., 18-19, emphasis added.
[19]Ibid., 19.
[20]Ibid., emphasis added. The image of Moroni (rather than Nephi) now
adorns Mormon temples all over the world.

angel *Nephi* or *Moroni* appears in 1822 (in the *1832 Account*) or in 1823 (in the *1838-39 Account*). In Oliver and Joseph's 1834-35 History, "*Nephi*" or "*Moroni*," one or the other (the issue is not at first resolved), actually comes before the Son, or the Father and the Son, or any of the personages and/or other angels. When do such incredible contradictions begin to spell deceit?[21]

How could the Prophet make a mistake of such incredible magnitude? The visit of the angel first assigned one or the other of two different names clearly concerned Joseph's call to the work.

---

[21]In 1854 in an Independence Day speech, Orson Hyde, the President of the Quorum of the Twelve Apostles, "declared that the same angel that revealed the Book of Mormon plates to Joseph Smith also accompanied Columbus on his voyage to the New World." (*Journal of Discourses*, 6: 368, cited by Petersen, *The Creation of the Book of Mormon*, 19). After the name Moroni was finally and firmly established by arbitrary fiat, other unlikely tasks were assigned to the miraculous messenger, including the dedication of the temple site at Manti, Utah.

> At a conference held in Ephraim, Sanpete County, June 25th, 1875, nearly all the speakers expressed their feelings to have a temple built in Sanpete County, and gave their views as to what point and where to build it, and to show the union that existed, Elder Daniel H. Wells said "Manti," George Q. Cannon, Brigham Young, Jr., John Taylor, Orson Hyde, Erastus Snow, Franklin D. Richards, Lorenzo Young, and A.M. Musser said "Manti stone quarry." I have given the names in the order in which they spoke. At 4 p.m. that day President Brigham Young said: "The Temple should be built on Manti stone quarry." Early on the morning of April 25, 1877, President Brigham Young asked Brother Warren S. Snow to go with him to the Temple hill. Brother Snow says: "We two were alone: President Young took me to the spot where the Temple was to stand; we went to the southeast corner, and President Young said: "Here is the spot where the prophet Moroni stood and dedicated this piece of land for a Temple site, and that is the reason why the location is made here, and we can't move it from this spot; and if you and I are the only persons that come here at high noon today, we will dedicate this ground." [Orson F. Whitney, *Life of Heber C. Kimball* (Salt Lake City: Bookcraft, 1967), 436, quoted by H. Donl Peterson (professor emeritus of ancient scripture at Brigham Young University), "Moroni, the Last of the Nephite Prophets" in *Fourth Nephi, From Zion to Destruction*, ed. Monte S. Nyman and Charles D. Tate Jr. (Provo, UT: Religious Studies Center, Brigham Young University, 1995), 235-49].

"That Moroni dedicated the Manti Temple site is one of the few statements the Brethren have made connecting a Book of Mormon figure with a specific current place and action." (Ibid.). At least in recent times.

Here were golden plates, magic spectacles, a breastplate and translation by the gift and power of God. The origins of the Americas are explained, the Gospel is explicated and the divinity of Christ is further confirmed. Those "translated" recitals provide the foundation for what was claimed to be the only true and living Church on the face of the earth today. For there is no extraordinary message of universal significance in the generic one-hundred-thirty year suppressed 1832 Holographic Account of a vision of the Son, a message of forgiveness and a promise of grace, the earliest dated presently known account, and the only presently known account in Joseph's own handwriting.

Getting Things Together

In the 1832 Gold Plates Part of the Holographic Account, although the angel "revealed unto me many things concerning the inhabitants of the earth,"[22] there is no Malachi, no Isaiah, no Acts of the Apostles and no prophet Joel, and the vision occurred on *September 22, 1822.* In the 1838-39 Gold Plates Part of the Pearl of Great Price Account, there is prophecy from Malachi, prophecy from Isaiah, interpretation and prophecy from Acts and poetry from Joel, side by side with "other passages of scripture" and "explanations which cannot be mentioned here,"[23] and the vision occurred on *September 21, 1823.* How different are the two accounts, separate drafts of the same event six years apart, how greatly more grand is the second, later and less contemporaneous account.

In the *History of Joseph Smith* (published in 1842):

> *Nephi [only later Moroni] quoted some of the prophesies of Malachi, but with variation from the Bible text. Although many [more than fifteen] years had now elapsed since his encounter with the angel, Joseph, in recording the interview, remembered the exact words that Nephi used on that memorable September night of 1823 (JS-H 1:37-39), noting*

---

[22]Jessee ed., *The Personal Writings of Joseph Smith*, 7.
[23]The Pearl of Great Price, Joseph Smith – History 1:35-41.

*perhaps as he wrote them that not only did they vary
from the King James Bible (Mal.4:1-6), but also from
his own Inspired Translation of the Scriptures (which
in 1842 was still a manuscript), as well as the Savior's
quotes from Malachi in the Book of Mormon (3 Ne.
25:1-6), and a revelation from God to Joseph dated 3
November 1831 (D&C 133:64).*[24]

What is one to think of Joseph's memory, Malachi, Malachi in the
Bible, Malachi in Smith's Inspired Translation, Malachi in the
Book of Mormon, Malachi in the Doctrine and Covenants and
correlation? If Malachi is ever to be read and understood, it will
not be in these multiple variant resources. The angel "Nephi" in
1823, according to Joseph in 1838-39, "spoke of the priesthood
which was soon to be restored by the hand of Elijah . . . ."[25]

*Behold, I will reveal unto you the Priesthood, by the
hand of Elijah the prophet, before the coming of the
great and dreadful day of the Lord.*

*And he shall plant in the hearts of the children the
promises made to the fathers, and the hearts of the
children shall turn to their fathers.*

*If it were not so, the whole earth would be utterly
wasted at his coming.*[26]

The 1876 revision of the Pearl of Great Price identified the angel as
"Moroni," rather than *"Nephi."*

Smith Family Accounts

William Smith and Lucy Mack Smith both described the visit of an
angel in the evening and early morning of September 21 and 22,
1823, and not some vision of the Father and the Son in 1820, as the
event that fixed in Joseph's mind the fact "that none of the sects

---

[24]Petersen, *The Creation of the Book of Mormon*, 10-11, emphasis added.
[25]Ibid., 11.
[26]Doctrine and Covenants 2:1-3, emphasis added.

was right." Lucy and William both believed that the 1823 vision of
the angel with the plates, and not some 1820 vision of the Father
and the Son, was the vision prohibitive of all other churches.[27] The
vision of the Father and the Son was not then part of the prophet's
original design.

Joseph's mother didn't know that Jesus told Joseph in the woods in
1820 that none of the churches were right. As far as she knew, that
was an open question in 1823. In her view, it was the angel in 1823
– *"I perceive that you are enquiring in your mind which is the true
church"* – who told Joseph in his father's house on September 21,
1823, and in the field on September 22, 1823, that none of the
churches were right (*"there is not a true church on Earth[,] No not
one . . ."*). She didn't know in 1823 that her son had ever had a
vision of the Father and the Son. And when Joseph gathered the

---

[27]Long after Lucy Mack Smith prepared her controversial autobiography in
1845 (with the assistance of Mormon tenders Howard and Martha Coray), the
book offended Brigham Young. Lucy's 1845 manuscript was initially published in
1853. In 1865, Young denounced Lucy's book "as a 'tissue of lies' from start to
finish." (Lucy Mack Smith, *History of Joseph Smith by His Mother, Lucy Mack
Smith: The Unabridged Original Version – An Up-To-Date Reprint of the Original
1853 Edition in Its Entirety, With Additional Information from the Rough-Draft
Manuscript and Corrections Resulting from Subsequent Research*, comp. R. Vernon
Ingleton, with a foreword by Richard Lloyd Dewey [Arlington, VA; Provo, UT:
Stratford Books, 2005], xxi, xxii). "Speaking to a congregation in Wellsville, Utah,
on May 18, 1865," Brigham (with his fingers crossed) warned his audience about
"the pernicious consequences of allowing false information to pollute the stream of
recorded history . . . ." Joseph's mother, like his wife Emma, according to
Brigham, was an author of lies. The Mormon leader conducted a campaign to
have the members of the Church turn in their copies in exchange for other books
or store goods so that all copies might be destroyed. (Ibid.). Young "indicted the
book" (Joseph's mother's book) on these grounds: It contained falsehoods and was
fictionalized. It portrayed William Smith, the prophet's younger brother,
positively. "Lucy's memory was shot." Then there was this: the project had been
stolen; Orson Pratt had published the book "out of greed" and without Brigham
Young's consent. (Ibid., xxi, xxii). After the book was later reworked, supposedly
made safe for consumption, it was repeatedly republished. All in all, before and
after revisions, it has been published in probably no less than fifteen editions over
151 years. Jerald and Sandra Tanner, Mormon historians, specifically challenged
the integrity of the 1945 edited edition. "Their analysis of the 1945 Preston Nibley
edition (then the current edition in use by the LDS church) reports that it had
2,751 changes from the original 1853 edition, that 2,135 words are deleted (only
756 of which are indicated to the reader), that it changes 220 words and adds 436."
(Ibid., xxix).

family together on September 22, 1823, to tell them "how the angel again appeared to him," William said, "The whole family were melted to tears, and believed all he said."[28] He had just made his first converts. Now, after everyone in his family "believed all [that] he said," Lucy, Hyrum, Samuel and Sophronia Smith joined the Presbyterian Church in 1824 *during* the great revival that started in 1824 and ended in 1825 and *after* the death of Alvin Smith on November 19, 1823. And Joseph Smith, who said that he received the golden plates in 1827, signed his name to a Methodist classbook in Harmony, Pennsylvania, in 1828 and tried to join the Methodist church.

In 1823 William Smith didn't know that his brother had ever had a vision of the Father and the Son. In 1823 Joseph Smith didn't know that he had ever had a vision of the Father and the Son. A careful reading of the 1823 vision described in Oliver and Joseph's 1834-35 first authorized History of the Church makes that point perfectly clear. In 1834-35 Joseph Smith told the Church in the *Messenger and Advocate* that he didn't know in 1823, the eighteenth year of his age, "*if a Supreme being did exist.*"

William Smith

"According to Joseph, his older brother Hyrum joined the Presbyterian church along with his mother *as a result of the revival.*"[29] William Smith agreed: "The consequence [of the revival] was that my mother, my brothers Hyrum and Samuel, older than I, joined the Presbyterian Church. *Joseph, then about seventeen years of age [about 1823],* [who] had become seriously inclined, though not 'brought out,' as the phrase was, *began to reflect and inquire, which of all these sects was right . . . .*"[30] William Smith, who described the revival and the conversions at different times in

---

[28]William Smith, *On Mormonism* (1883), Dan Vogel, ed., *Early Mormon Documents* (Salt Lake City: Signature Books, 1996), 1:496.

[29]Marquardt and Walters, *Inventing Mormonism*, 16, emphasis added. "In his 1838-39 account Joseph remembered that great multitudes joined the Baptist, Methodist and Presbyterian churches during the revival. Church membership rolls are carefully kept, and in most cases can still be traced." (Ibid., 17).

[30]William Smith, *On Mormonism* (1883), Vogel, ed., *Early Mormon Documents*, 1:495, emphasis added.

different terms, a family trait, provided this basic chronology: *"About the year 1823, there was a revival of religion in that region, and Joseph was one of several hopeful converts."*[31] William's homely account[32] more closely resembled Oliver and Joseph's 1834-35 History – published in the *Messenger and Advocate* in 1834-35, reproduced in Joseph's journal and republished "without any thought of correction" in the *Times and Seasons* – than it did Joseph's 1838-39 History (published in the *Times and Seasons* by its editor Joseph Smith in 1842). After being "stirred up" by the preaching of the Reverend Mr. Lane, who arrived in 1824, after beginning to *"reflect and inquire, which of all these sects was right,"* "He [Joseph] continued in secret to call upon the Lord for a full manifestation of his will, the assurance that he was accepted of him, and that he might have an understanding of the path of obedience."[33] William then described what he said happened next:

> *At length he determined to call upon the Lord until he should get a manifestation from him. He accordingly went out into the woods and falling upon his knees called for a long time upon the Lord for wisdom and knowledge. While engaged in prayer a light appeared in the heavens, and descended until it rested upon the trees where he was. It appeared like fire. But to his great astonishment, did not burn the trees. An angel then appeared to him and conversed with him upon many things. He told him that none of the sects were right . . . .*[34]

Here in the words of Joseph Smith's founding Apostle/Future Church Patriarch brother is an inside observer's personal account

---

[31]Letter of Rev. James Murdock dated New Haven, 19 June 1841, to the Hartford and New Haven, Connecticut, *Congressional Observer* 2 (3 July 1841):1, quoted in Marquardt and Walters, *Inventing Mormonism*, 19 n 14, 36 (citing William Smith), emphasis added.

[32]William Smith's comments about the revival, Joseph, Lucy, Hyrum, Samuel and Reverend Lane were made in an interview in June of 1841 with James Murdock. The minister "read back his notes for correction." (Ibid., 19).

[33]William Smith, *On Mormonism* (1883), Vogel, ed., *Early Mormon Documents*, 1:494-95, emphasis added.

[34]Ibid., 1:495-96, emphasis added.

of a first first vision[35] that failed to describe the Father and the Son. The long suppressed 1832 Holographic Account also failed to describe a vision of the Father and the Son. William and Lucy both describe, as do also others, the initial encounter as having been (as Joseph originally led his followers to believe) with the angel in charge of the golden plates. Later, in 1838-39, Joseph described an unfamiliar 1820 event in somewhat different terms: "I had now got my mind satisfied so far as the sectarian world was concerned – that it was not my duty to join with any of them, but to continue as I was until further directed." William told a different story, and so did Joseph's mother. What stirred the people in Palmyra in 1822 and 1823, including Joseph – then seventeen and *"one of several hopeful converts"* – according to William, was the "great revival preacher," "Mr. Lane, an Elder of the Methodist Church . . . ."[36] William was right about the inspiration, but not about the dates. Reverend Lane didn't preach in Palmyra until 1824 and 1825.

William Smith's dates, although more accurate than the dates furnished by his brother Joseph in that cynical 1838-39 revision of his earlier history, still got the date wrong by a year or two. The Palmyra revival, the spiritual architect of which was the Reverend George Lane, occurred as a verifiable historical fact in 1824-1825, not 1822–1823 (the dates reported by William). An 1822-23 revival would have preceded the death of Alvin Smith. William Smith said it was the angel who told Joseph that "none of the sects were right," forgave his sins and concluded that "the true way should be made known to him" if he was faithful in keeping the commandments.[37]

THE REAL FIRST VISION

William, who was close to those 1823 events, described the vision of the angel in charge of the plates, and its aftermath, in these terms:

---

[35]Mother Smith's "Preliminary Manuscript," dictated to Howard Coray in 1845, the year after Joseph's death, is yet a seventh inside account of the Mormon prophet's first vision.

[36]William Smith, *On Mormonism* (1883), Vogel, ed., *Early Mormon Documents*, 1:494.

[37]Ibid., 1:495-96.

The next day [September 22, 1823] I was at work in the field together with Joseph and my eldest brother Alvin. Joseph looked pale and unwell, so that Alvin told him if he was sick he need not work; he then went and sat down by the fence, when the angel again appeared to him, and told him to call his father's house together and communicate to them the visions he had received, which he had not yet told to any one; and promised him that if he would do so, they would believe it. He accordingly asked us to come to the house, as he had something to tell us. After we were all gathered, he arose and told us how the angel appeared to him; what he had told him as written above; and that the angel had also given him a short account of the inhabitants who formerly resided upon this continent, a full history of whom he said was engraved on some plates which were hidden, and which the angel promised to show him. . . . The whole family were melted to tears, and believed all he said.[38]

This was about the golden plates. It wasn't about the Father and the Son. No one in the family, either before or for a long time after this meeting, if ever at all, seemed to know anything about an 1820 vision of the Father and the Son. They knew nothing about those "men of high standing" from "among all the sects" who united to persecute their son and brother for three-and-a-half years after a vision in 1820, as Joseph claimed in and after 1838. When the angel told Joseph Smith to tell his family about "the visions he had received," Joseph failed to mention a vision of the Father and the Son. The angel told Joseph in 1823 to communicate to his family that "which he had not yet told to any one," then promised him that they would believe everything he said. Not yet told to anyone? This is 1823? In his later startling new 1838-39 Account of the previously unknown 1820 vision of the Father and the Son, first published in 1842, Joseph said he told everyone. He said that he suffered "severe persecution" at the hands of "all classes of men" because he "continued to affirm" that he had seen a vision and

---

[38]Ibid., 1:496, emphasis added.

refused to say that he had not. Within hours of the 1823 visitation, on-the-scene insider William Smith heard Joseph's angel-directed first-person disclosure. William proved in all of this that he, his father, mother and siblings knew nothing about a vision of the Father and the Son before or after that fateful family council in 1823.

Uncle Jesse Smith

Joseph's father was a Universalist, but his mother was a Puritan. While the Reverend Benjamin Stockton's sermon at Alvin Smith's funeral offended Joseph's father, it frightened Alvin's mother. Why else would Lucy say that "we could not be comforted because he was not"? The exercise of faith in a Bible-based society was more important to Lucy, who looked for solace in a community church, than it was to Joseph Sr. Joseph Sr. found less to like than Lucy in organized religion. The Presbyterian pastor's insensitive sermon at the unaffiliated Alvin's 1823 funeral provoked Joseph Sr.'s Universalist wrath.

On the other hand, Joseph Sr.'s Universalism and Joseph Jr.'s unsparing antagonism toward traditional Christianity were irritations not well received by Joseph Sr.'s brother, Jesse Smith. Jesse's anger came to a boil in 1829 at about the same time Hyrum left the Presbyterian Church[39] to join his charismatic brother Joseph in allegiance to a new and different kind of church. When Hyrum returned to Manchester in 1829, he received a curious letter from Oliver Cowdery, who was "feeling anxious" about Hyrum's "steadfastness in the great cause of which you have been called to advocate."[40]   Jesse Smith, who saw Hyrum as far too steadfast for his own good, had hard words for his nephews Joseph and Hyrum and for his erring brother, and he set them down in writing. Uncle Jesse was apoplectic. To Hyrum Smith from Uncle Jesse Smith, who was living in Stockholm, New York:

---

[39]Hyrum Smith left the Presbyterians in time to become the fourth member of the Mormon Church.

[40]Cowdery to Hyrum Smith, 14 June 1829, Joseph Smith's Letterbook 1:5, LDS Archives, quoted in Marquardt and Walters, *Inventing Mormonism*, 127, 145 n 53.

Again you say, if you are decieved [sic] God is your deciever [sic], Blasphemous wretch – how dare you utter such a sentence, how dare you harbor such a thot - aye, you never did think so, but being hardened in iniquity, you make use of the holy name of Jehovah! for what, why to cover your neferious [sic] designs & impose on the credulity of your Grandfather, one of the oldest men on the earth, Blackness of darkness! . . . You state your father cannot write by reason of a nervous affection this is a poor excuse, worse than none, he can dictate to others and they can write, If he knows not what to write, he can get your Brother's spectacles [the Urim and Thummim] he would then be as able to dictate a letter, as Joe is to decipher hieroglyphics, if more should be wanting he can employ the same scoundrel of a scribe, and then not only the matter but manner and style would be correct.[41]

Note that Uncle Jesse said nothing about a great First Vision of the Father and the Son.

The Angel and the Revival

The 1834-35 History, prepared and published by Oliver Cowdery and Joseph Smith, *unequivocally* reported that the Palmyra revival immediately preceded the vision of the Angel on September 21, 1823: "[W]hile this excitement continued [the "religious excitement, in Palmyra and vicinity"], he [Joseph] continued to call upon the Lord in secret for a full manifestation of divine approbation, and for, to him the all important information, *if a Supreme being did exist,* to have an assurance that he was accepted of him."[42] In the 1838-39 Pearl of Great Price Account dictated by Joseph in 1838 to a committee (penned by future apostate George W. Robinson, First

---

[41]Jesse Smith to Hyrum Smith, 17 June 1829, Joseph Smith's Letterbook, 2:59-61, LDS Archives, quoted in Marquardt and Walters, *Inventing Mormonism*, 127, 145 n 54, emphasis added.

[42]"Letter IV" (Cowdery and Smith's 1834-35 History), *Messenger and Advocate*, vol. 1 no. 5 (February 1835), 78, emphasis added.

Presidency Scribe), the Mormon prophet described an amended subordinate version of the vision of the Angel Moroni that wasn't associated with a Palmyra revival (with the "religious excitement in Palmyra and vicinity"). The removal of the revival events from the carefully crafted previously published vision of the angel in the altered account was abrupt and unsettling, disappointing and profoundly dishonest. In the Pearl of Great Price Account, which was changed to become a combined account of what were now supposed to have been two separate visions, the revival now had nothing to do with the vision of the angel in charge of the plates, and everything to do with the vision of the Father and the Son. As the Church's previous history was altered, the revival was backed out of the vision of the plates to then become the incredible precursor to a three-and-a-half year earlier previously unknown 1820 Account of a vision of the Father and the Son.[43]

> *[O]n the evening of the above mentioned twenty-first of September, after I had retired to my bed for the night, I betook myself to prayer and supplication to Almighty God for forgiveness of all my sins and follies, and also for a manifestation to me, that I might know of my state and standing before him; for I had full confidence in obtaining a divine manifestation, as I previously had one.*[44]

In Joseph's now dramatically altered recounting, setting reality at complete defiance (Cowdery has only now just recently been excommunicated), the Palmyra revival is no longer associated with the vision of the angel Joseph first called *"Nephi."* The revival, previously described as preliminary to Oliver and Joseph's 1834-35 Account of the vision of the angel in charge of the plates, is not

---

[43]The vision of the angel described by Oliver and Joseph in the 1834-35 History and preserved in Joseph's journal clearly described a great revival as preceding the vision of the angel in charge of the plates. The vision of the "crucifyed" Lord described by Joseph in the long suppressed 1832 Holographic Account of a Vision of the Son, on the other hand, didn't describe a revival. The 1838-39 Pearl of Great Price Account of the vision of the Father and the Son now suddenly claimed that it occurred as a consequence of the same revival that Oliver and Joseph had already described as preliminary to their 1834-35 History of the vision of the angel with the plates.

[44]The Pearl of Great Price, Joseph Smith – History 1:29, emphasis added.

preliminary to the *1838-39* golden plates retelling of that same event. This is a brazen, stunning, dishonest omission. It unsettles a previously settled equation. In the 1834-35 First Authorized History of the Church of the Latter Day Saints (published in the *Messenger and Advocate* in eight consecutive installments in 1834 and 1835), it was the "religious excitement, in Palmyra and vicinity" in 1823 that prompted a Joseph who hadn't seen the Lord, and wasn't sure there was a Lord, to fall to his knees and pray. It was in consequence of that prayer, and of the religious excitement that produced that event, that the angel first called Nephi then appeared. In the 1838-1839 Manuscript History (dictated by Smith to scribes), a different Joseph – one who had known in 1820 that there was a Supreme Being and expected to receive a divine manifestation because he had already had one – fell to his knees to pray, after which the angel then appeared. These contradictory accounts, both composed under the personal supervision of Joseph Smith, are supposed to describe the same event. What they do describe is an altered event.

The man who said in 1834-1835 that he desperately needed to know in September of 1823 *"if a Supreme being did exist"* was the same man who said in 1838-1839 that he already knew in September of 1823 that a Supreme being did exist, because *he had seen the Father and the Son in the spring of 1820* in a vision he didn't report until 1842. The 1834-35 History, described as a "full history of the rise of the church of the Latter Day Saints, and the most interesting parts of its progress to the present time,"[45] didn't mention an 1820 vision of the Father and the Son. Which Joseph shall the faithful then choose to believe? The 1823 Joseph who is desperately trying to determine *"if a Supreme being did exist,"* or the 1820 Joseph who "dared" not deny that he had seen a vision lest he "offend God, and come under condemnation"?[46] Joseph described one set of contradictory facts in 1834-35 and another set of facts in 1838-39. Future prophets and apostles have followed his lead. Revelations are used, truth be damned, to move the goalposts.

---

[45]Cowdery and Smith, *Messenger and Advocate* (September 1834), 13.
[46]The Pearl of Great Price, Joseph Smith – History 1:25.

The 1838-39 Pearl of Great Price Account

In the 1823 vision of the angel in charge of the plates (according to both Lucy and William), the angel told Joseph that none of the sects were true. In the 1838-39 Pearl of Great Price Account of a Great First Vision of the Father and the Son (according to Joseph, George W. Robinson, Sidney Rigdon and James Mulholland), Jesus told Joseph that none of the sects were true. Joseph asked and different messengers answered, with years between, but during two entirely different visions both inspired by the same great revival. In the 1838-39 Account, Joseph needed *"to know for himself"* in 1820 what in the 1834-35 History Joseph needed *"to know for himself"* in 1823. In 1820 he needed to know *"which of all the sects was right."*[47] In 1823 he needed to know *"of the certainty and reality of pure and holy religion."*[48] And in each case it was "in the midst" of a war of words "and tumult of opinions," meaning in the midst of the same great Palmyra revival, that the same probing inquiries came to be posed. Joseph was not the first visionary to frame the question and get the answer he said that he got.

> *[T]o Asa Wild, of Amsterdam, New York, the Lord God Jehovah had appeared to reveal the imminence of the Millennium and the great cataclysms which were at hand, including wars, massacres, famine, pestilence, and earthquakes. Every denomination of professing Christians, God had instructed Asa, had become extremely corrupt, many having never had any true faith at all, being guided only by depraved reason; the severest judgements were to be inflicted on the false and fallen professors of religion.*[49]

"Wild's vision was reprinted from the *Mohawk Herald* by the *Wayne Sentinel,* Oct. 22, 1823, one month to the day from the time when, as Joseph later asserted, the golden plates were first showed to him by the angel Moroni." A pamphlet setting forth Wild's

---

[47]Ibid., 1:18.

[48]"Letter IV" (Cowdery and Smith's 1834-35 History), *Messenger and Advocate*, vol. 1 no. 5 (February 1835), 78.

[49]Morgan, *Dale Morgan on Early Mormonism*, 261, emphasis added.

"views and visions" appeared at Amsterdam (New York) in 1824.[50]

The 1834-35 Account

There was an urgent necessity for an accurate account of the events associated with the early origins of the Mormon faith. The Saints were certain that they had been misrepresented by antagonistic elements, most particularly by a hostile press. E.D. Howe's nineteenth-century exposé (*Mormonism Unvailed*) was published in Painesville, Ohio, in 1834. In 1834-35, Oliver and Joseph chose to respond ("[W]e [Oliver and Joseph] have thought that a full history of the rise of the church . . ."). The 1834-35 History was intended to set the record straight. The two presidents (Cowdery had been ordained as one of "the presidents" of the Church in December 1834) confronted "*our opposers,*" those who "*cast a shade over the truth*" and decried the Church's progress. The 1834-35 History was Mormonism's post-Zion's Camp rebuttal to some of its most insistent critics, including E.D. Howe, Doctor Philastus Hurlbut, Ezra Booth, Isaac Hale, Willard Chase and a great many other New York, Ohio and Pennsylvania detractors. It was the founders' intention to see the truth "vindicated, by laying before the world a correct statement of events as they have transpired from time to time."[51] Lamar Petersen notes that:

> *In Cowdery's version [Cowdery and Joseph's version], thousands of words were used to relate the dramatic story of Joseph's early quest for guidance after partaking of the excitement of a religious revival, his prayer asking to know which church to join, the resultant visit of a personage – all of which occurred, it was said, in 1823 when Joseph was seventeen.*[52]

Cowdery had carefully corrected an earlier error in a later installment of the 1834-35 History:

---

[50]Ibid., 378 n 48.

[51]"Letter III" (Cowdery and Smith's 1834-35 History), *Messenger and Advocate*, vol. 1 no. 3 (December 1834), 42.

[52]Petersen, *The Creation of the Book of Mormon*, 12-13, emphasis added. "Cowdery has not a single word about a First Vision in 1820."

You will recollect that I mentioned the time of a religious excitement, in Palmyra and vicinity to have been in the 15ᵗʰ year of our brother J. Smith Jr's, age – that was an error in the type – it should have been in the 17ᵗʰ. – You will please remember this correction, as it will be necessary for the full understanding of what will follow in time. This would bring the date [of the revival] down to the year 1823.[53]

Why should this be debated today?   Oliver didn't know these things; Joseph knew these things. Here is an unequivocal admission from the founders that the Palmyra revival didn't occur in 1820. This is proof traceable to the man who knew, Joseph Smith, that the revival didn't occur in 1820.   The revival Oliver and Joseph described was supposed to have occurred in 1823. The being who appeared to Joseph Smith in the 1834-35 Account of the September 1823 vision of the angel in charge of the plates was not as glorious as the being who appeared to Joseph Smith in the 1838-39 Account of the same vision. The two versions show that the messenger and his message became more grandiose and important in the second telling.   The messenger in the earlier account, however, said something the messenger in the 1838-1839 Account did not. In the *1834-35 Account,* the messenger told Joseph Smith *"that his sins were forgiven."*[54]   The 1834-35 messenger ("The stature of this personage was a little above the common size of men in this age . . ."[55]), with a markedly less glorious message delivered in a markedly less impressive way to a markedly less impressive recipient, did not immediately identify himself. He would later be identified at various times and in unexpected places as the resurrected Nephi, but then still later, and now always, as the angel Moroni. Modern Mormons have never heard the name of Nephi connected with these early events. Nephi and Moroni were at opposite ends of the Book of Mormon's chronological spectrum.

In Joseph Smith's 1832 Holographic Account of a vision of Jesus, the first known account of his first (1821) encounter with deity, the

---

[53]"Letter IV" (Cowdery and Smith's 1834-35 History), *Messenger and Advocate*, vol. 1 no. 5 (February 1835), 78, emphasis added.

[54]Ibid., 79, emphasis added.

[55]Ibid.

"crucifyed" Lord told Joseph that "thy sins are forgiven thee."[56] Joseph's sins were likewise forgiven in the 1834-35 Account of the 1823 vision of the angel in charge of the plates. The 1823 Angel described in the 1834-35 Account "declare[d] himself to be a messenger sent by commandment of the Lord, to deliver a special message, and to witness to him that his sins were forgiven, and that his prayers were heard . . . ."[57] The forgiveness of sin was not even mentioned in the 1838-39 retelling, because by 1838-39 the priorities had changed. The 1834-35 messenger with the more sparing message quoted the Apostle Paul's demeaning letter to the Corinthians: God, the angel told Joseph, had chosen "the foolish things of the world to confound the things which are mighty; and base things of the world, and things wich [sic] are despised, has God chosen; yea, and things which are not, to bring to nought things which are, that no flesh should glory in his presence."[58] The 1834-35 Joseph (and various other Smiths) had just been badly maligned by more than eighty neighbors and acquaintances in several different communities in several different states (including Emma's relatives) in Howe's exposé *Mormonism Unvailed.* The 1838-39 version of the visit of the Angel Moroni (called Nephi in Manuscript History Book A-1) and the 1838-39 messenger would treat an emerging Joseph with a great deal more respect.

The encounter with the angel in charge of the golden plates was originally seen to have been Joseph's call to the work. The plates are ancient records containing "an account of the former inhabitants of this continent, and the source from whence they sprang."[59] The magic spectacles found in the box with the plates (which like the plates later disappeared), and not some stone found while digging a well, were connected to the original translation. In the modern Church, as we now know, the story was changed to admit that Smith translated the Book of Mormon with the help of a chocolate-colored stone concealed in an old white stovepipe hat. The messenger described in the 1834-35 History didn't say that Joseph's name "should be had for good and evil among all nations,

---

[56]Jessee ed., *The Personal Writings of Joseph Smith*, 6.
[57]"Letter IV" (Cowdery and Smith's 1834-35 History), *Messenger and Advocate*, vol. 1 no. 5 (February 1835), 79.
[58]Ibid.
[59]The Pearl of Great Price, Joseph Smith　History 1:34.

kindreds and tongues . . ."[60] (as the later messenger said). He said, "marvel not if your name is made a derision."[61] The Joseph Smith to whom this angel spoke, as described in Joseph's 1832 Account of a vision of the "crucifyed" Lord, had not seen the *Father*, but rather only the Son. Joseph held an essentially Trinitarian view of God in 1832. One god, the Father was the Son, was the gold standard in 1832. The amended Joseph, to whom the angel in the 1838-39 Account spoke, claimed to have seen the Father and heard him say, *"This is my Beloved Son. Hear Him!"* His view of the godhead had taken a turn since 1832.

> *The Book of Commandments, the earliest published compilation of Joseph Smith's revelations, contains nothing on such important events as Joseph's first vision, how the Book of Mormon came forth, the restoration of priesthood, or accounts by the witnesses to the Book of Mormon. As with the priesthood restoration accounts, current LDS interpretations of Joseph's first vision simplify and retrofit later accounts to provide a seemingly authoritative, unambiguous recital.*[62]

---

[60]Ibid., 1:33.

[61]"Letter IV" (Cowdery and Smith's 1834-35 History), *Messenger and Advocate*, vol. 1 no. 5 (February 1835), 80.

[62]Palmer, *An Insider's View of Mormon Origins*, 235, emphasis added.

CHAPTER FOUR

The Persecution Claims

. . . I had seen a vision; I knew it, and I knew that God knew it, and I could not deny it, neither dared I do it; at least I knew that by so doing I would offend God, and come under condemnation.

Joseph Smith, 1838-39

I continued to pursue my common vocations in life [from the morning of a beautiful, clear day, early in the spring of eighteen hundred and twenty] until the twenty-first of September one thousand eight hundred and twenty-three, all the time suffering severe persecution at the hands of all classes of men, both religious and irreligious, because I continued to affirm that I had seen a vision.

Joseph Smith, 1838-39

If he "exaggerated the reaction" to the vision, he did it as a mature adult with a lengthy religious resumé at the height of his prominence and after many years to reflect. Joseph Smith created the claims of persecution not as a boy, and not at the time, but as an adult and after the fact.

Joel M. Allred

SETTING THE STAGE

Joseph Smith didn't mention any persecution in the more than hundred-year-suppressed 1832 and 1835 First Vision accounts, including disclosures he made to Joshua the Jewish Minister and Erastus Holmes (Joshua 1:1835, Joshua 2:1835, Erastus Holmes: 1835).   But Joseph's 1838-39 Pearl of Great Price Account described an innocent boy who suffered "severe persecution at the hands of all classes of men" because he continued to affirm that he had seen a vision.[1] That "official" "canonized" account of the First Vision, the "hinge pin" upon which the whole cause turns, describes persecution that continued unabated from the spring of 1820 (when Joseph said he saw the Father and the Son) until September 21, 1823 (when Joseph said he saw the angel in charge of the plates). According to Joseph, that persecution was "the cause of great sorrow"[2] to himself. It was Smith the man who described Smith the boy when he composed his 1838-39 Pearl of Great Price Account. The prophet was thirty-six years old when he first publicly described the relentless persecution associated with the previously unknown 1820 vision of the Father and the Son as the editor of the *Times and Seasons*, a Mormon periodical in Nauvoo, Illinois, in 1842.[3]

> *It caused me serious reflection then, and often has since, how very strange it was that an obscure boy, of a little over fourteen years of age, and one, too, who was doomed to the necessity of obtaining a scanty maintenance by his daily labor, should be thought a character of sufficient importance to attract the*

---

[1]Joseph Smith, *The Pearl of Great Price: Being a Choice Selection from the Revelations, Translations, and Narrations of Joseph Smith, First Prophet, Seer and Revelator to the Church of Jesus Christ of Latter Day Saints* (Liverpool, UK: F.D. Richards, 1851), Joseph Smith – History 1:27.

[2]Ibid., 1:23.

[3]"After previous efforts at writing a personal history were thwarted by mobs, lawsuits, imprisonment, and getting the story straight, Joseph Smith wrote of his experiences with the divine.   Highlights include the First Vision (this time uncluttered by angels), the visit of Moroni, and persecution so intense that no one remembered it." (John K. Williams, "Concise Dictionary of Mormonism: Joseph Smith-History" [26 April 2012, accessed 13 September 2018], available from https://runtu.wordpress.com/?s=joseph+smith+thwarted+mob; Internet, p. 2 of 3).

attention of the great ones of the most popular sects of the day, and in a manner to create in them a spirit of the most bitter persecution and reviling. But strange or not, so it was, and it was often the cause of great sorrow to myself.[4]

Joseph offered contradictory accounts of his state of mind after the vision. He said, ". . . I was guilty of levity, and sometimes associated with jovial company, etc., not consistent with that character which ought to be maintained by one who was called of God as I had been. But this will not seem very strange to any one who recollects my youth, and is acquainted with my native cheery temperament."[5] On the one hand, "bitter persecution" was "often the cause of great sorrow to myself." On the other hand, those who knew him then will recall his "native cheery temperament," remember him as "guilty of levity" and recall his associations with "jovial company." Where is the place for "great sorrow," "persecution and reviling" in this light-hearted equation? Where does anyone in his family describe, at the time, the "bitter persecution" supposed to have been connected with a vision his mother, father and siblings knew nothing about?

In the 1838-39 Pearl of Great Price Account, Joseph Smith mournfully described the heavy burden associated with an 1820 Vision he just then first said that he had but didn't publicly announce until 1842.

However, it was nevertheless a fact that I had beheld a vision. I have thought since that I felt much like Paul, when he made his defense before King Agrippa, and related the account of the vision he had when he saw a light, and heard a voice; but still there were but few who believed him; some said he was dishonest, others said he was mad; and he was ridiculed and reviled. But all this did not destroy the reality of his vision. He had seen a vision, he knew he had, and all the persecution under heaven could not make it otherwise; and though they should persecute him unto

---

[4]The Pearl of Great Price, Joseph Smith-History, 1:23, emphasis added.
[5]Ibid., 1:28.

death, yet he knew, and would know to his latest breath, that he had both seen a light and heard a voice speaking unto him, and all the world could not make him think or believe otherwise.

So it was with me. I had actually seen a light, and in the midst of that light I saw two Personages, and they did in reality speak to me; and though I was hated and persecuted for saying that I had seen a vision, yet it was true; and while they were persecuting me, reviling me, and speaking all manner of evil against me falsely for so saying, I was led to say in my heart: Why persecute me for telling the truth? I have actually seen a vision; and who am I that I can withstand God, or why does the world think to make me deny what I have actually seen? For I had seen a vision; I knew it, and I knew that God knew it, and I could not deny it, neither dared I do it; at least I knew that by so doing I would offend God, and come under condemnation.[6]

Back-Tracking

Joseph's own mother was not included among those supposed to have known that Joseph had been a victim of bitter persecution starting in the spring of 1820. Or that he had seen a light in the midst of which there were "two Personages, whose brightness and glory" defied all description. Lucy Mack Smith, shockingly, knew nothing of any of this:

> *I soon found . . . that my telling the story had excited a great deal of prejudice against me among professors of religion, and was the cause of great persecution, which continued to increase; and though I was an obscure boy, only between fourteen and fifteen years of age, and my circumstances in life such as to make a boy of no consequence in the world, yet men of high*

---

[6]Ibid., 1:24, 25, emphasis added.

standing would take notice sufficient to excite the public mind against me, and create a bitter persecution; and this was common among all the sects – all united to persecute me.[7]

Richard L. Bushman, one of Joseph's sympathetic biographers, made this futile effort to describe why Lucy didn't know. Bushman describes an 1820 event Joseph Smith waited twenty-three or -four years to report:

> *When Joseph came to [after the disruption caused by the 1820 vision of the Father and the Son], he found himself lying on his back. Returning to the house, he spoke to his mother but said almost nothing about the vision. When she asked about his apparent weakness, Joseph said, "Never mind all is well – I am well enough off." All he would report was that he had learned for himself that Presbyterianism was not true. His refusal to say more may have been the natural reticence of a teenage boy keeping his own counsel, or he may have held back for fear of ridicule.*[8]

Does anyone really think she wouldn't have known if things had been the way Joseph said they were many years after the fact? Did Richard Bushman forget this?

> *I had actually seen a light, and in the midst of that light I saw two Personages, and they did in reality speak to me; and though I was hated and persecuted for saying that I had seen a vision, yet it was true . . . .*[9]

Or this?

> *I continued to pursue my common vocations in life until the twenty-first of September one thousand eight*

---

[7]Ibid., 1:22, emphasis added.

[8]Richard Lyman Bushman, with the assistance of Jed Woodworth, *Joseph Smith: Rough Stone Rolling* (New York: Alfred A. Knopf, 2005), 40, emphasis added.

[9]The Pearl of Great Price, Joseph Smith – History, 1:25, emphasis added.

*hundred and twenty-three, all the time suffering
severe persecution at the hands of all classes of men,
both religious and irreligious, because I continued to
affirm that I had seen a vision.*[10]

Joseph knew that he had seen a vision, and God knew, and Joseph knew that God knew, and "professors of religion" and "men of high standing" knew, but his mother, Lucy Mack Smith, did not. Men of "high standing" took notice of this "obscure boy," excited the "public mind" to unite against him and created a bitter persecution "common among all the sects."[11] The "public" knew, all of the "sects" knew, "all classes of men, both religious and irreligious" knew, but Lucy Mack Smith did not. Nor did Joseph Sr., Alvin, Hyrum, William, Samuel or Sophronia Smith. Nor did Willard Chase, Parley Chase, Orsamus Turner, Pomeroy Tucker, Joseph Capron, Roswell Nichols, Peter Ingersoll, Fayette Lapham, or any of the very many Staffords. Nor did the Josiah Stowells (Jr. or Sr.), the Joseph Knights (Jr. or Sr.), Martin Harris, Emma Smith, Isaac Hale, Oliver Cowdery, David Whitmer, John Whitmer, William E. McLellin, Sidney Rigdon, Alexander Campbell, Abner Cole, Doctor Philastus Hurlbut, E.D. Howe, J.B. Turner or Ezra Booth.

News of this terrible persecution of "an obscure boy, only between fourteen and fifteen years of age" (or of the vision) had not reached Mother Smith's ears eleven years later in January 1831, when she described her son Joseph and his new church to her brother Solomon Mack in an important letter calculated "to urge upon him the divinity of her son's claims." "Joseph," she said, "after repenting of his sins and humbling himself before God, was visited by an holy angel" who provided him with instruction and with the tools and means required "to translate the Book of Mormon."[12] To Lucy, the First Vision was the vision of the Angel Moroni. In the letter to her brother discussing "the divinity of her son's claims,"

---

[10]Ibid., 1:27, emphasis added.

[11]Ibid., 1:22.

[12]Lucy Mack Smith, letter to Solomon Mack, printed at Ben. E. Rich, *Scrapbook of Mormon Literature* (Chicago: 190-?), 1:543-45, quoted in Dale Morgan, *Dale Morgan on Early Mormonism: Correspondence & A New History*, ed. John Phillip Walker, with a Biographical Introduction by John Phillip Walker and a Preface by William Mulder (Salt Lake City: Signature Books, 1986), 249-50.

Joseph's mother failed to describe a vision of the Father and the Son or the persecution he said that he suffered because of it. That was significant, "all the more significant in view of the unrelenting persecution Joseph would have us understand came upon him in his youth . . . ." She still had no independent recollection of First Vision-related persecution when she wrote her autobiography in 1845, the year after Joseph's death. Orson Pratt, changing the narrative, incorporated Joseph's 1838-39 Pearl of Great Price Account of the vision into her heavily censored autobiography in 1853.[13]

Lucy Mack Smith knew nothing of a great 1820 First Vision of the Father and the Son in 1831, nor did any other member of Joseph's newly established Church of Christ. How could she not have known? How could anyone who knew Joseph Smith in that rural setting in those close quarters at that tender age not have known?

Credibility Issues

The Reverend Benjamin Stockton knew nothing about the severe persecution Joseph Smith only very much later described. Stockton was the pastor of the Western Presbyterian Church in Palmyra, New York, an important figure at the 1824-25 Palmyra revival, a speaker at Alvin Smith's funeral on November 19, 1823, and Lucy, Hyrum, Samuel and Sophronia Smith's spiritual leader. Despite Joseph's claims that "professors of religion" and "men of high standing" took notice of him, "excite[d] the public mind" against him, and "create[d] a bitter persecution" that "was common among all the sects," all of which "united to persecute" him,[14] Lucy,

---

[13]Morgan, *Dale Morgan on Early Mormonism*, 250. Lucy Mack Smith's 1845 *Preliminary Manuscript* account of the visit of the angel with the plates, in the handwriting of Howard Coray, was replaced by Joseph's 1842 *Times and Seasons* account of the vision of the Father and the Son when Orson Pratt published Lucy's manuscript as *Biographical Sketches* in 1853. (LaMar Petersen, *The Creation of the Book of Mormon: A Historical Inquiry* [Salt Lake City: Freethinker Press, 2000], 14-15 n 32). That was an incredible and thoroughly dishonest indiscretion. Four decades after these separate visionary events, "William [Smith] reaffirmed that his brother's First Vision was an unnamed angel in 1823." (William Smith, *William Smith on Mormonism* [Lamoni, 1A, 1883], quoted in Ibid., 16).

[14]Ibid., 1:22.

Hyrum, Samuel and Sophronia Smith didn't know about those persecution-related First Vision contentions. They knew nothing about the terrible persecution Joseph waited twenty years to describe. And they knew nothing about a great First Vision of the Father and the Son, which Joseph waited twenty years to describe. And neither did their Presbyterian pastor. How could the members of his family or anyone close to Joseph Smith in those tightly-knit communities not have known?

Richard L. Bushman softens the prophet's extraordinary deception by writing that *"Local people"* in those tiny communities *"seemed to have discussed his case, even though he had said nothing to his parents."*[15] He suffered "severe persecution at the hands of all classes of men" because he "continued to affirm" that he "had seen a vision," but he said nothing to his parents? Or to his siblings? No one else said anything to them? His parents and his siblings didn't know?

Not one of the more than eighty detractors whose affidavits and statements exploded upon the pages of *Mormonism Unvailed*, that remarkable exposé published in 1834, mentioned a vision of the Father and the Son or described any persecution suffered in consequence of such an event. Great ones of the most popular sects of the day? Those who *"seemed to have discussed his case"* did not include his mother, father or siblings, the Reverend Benjamin Stockton, uncle Jesse Smith, Solomon Mack (Lucy's brother), or any of his most fervent detractors. Where is any Smith family insider, any contemporary critic, any Manchester or Palmyra, New York, or Harmony, Pennsylvania, neighbor, friend or foe found to confirm those utterly dishonest allegations? Where is a witness prepared to corroborate in real time the alleged injustices supposed to have still rankled Joseph Smith when as a mature adult he published his twenty-two year after-the-fact official account of that previously unfamiliar 1820 vision in 1842? (Three earlier differing accounts were suppressed by prophets and apostles both early and late).

---

[15]Bushman, *Joseph Smith: Rough Stone Rolling*, 43, emphasis added.

The Smith family didn't know Joseph had a vision of the Father and the Son in 1820, and a fourteen-year-old Joseph didn't tell them. In the incredible words of Richard L. Bushman, a Mormon scholar of great renown (and Joseph Smith's twenty-first century biographer), "*[H]e had said nothing to his parents.*" Why would this brave and innocent boy tell everyone but the members of his own family? Why would he deny to them, his champions, what he so conspicuously said that he affirmed to everyone else? Did he not say with ringing conviction that he had suffered "severe persecution at the hands of all classes of men, both religious and irreligious" from the time of the vision of the Father and the Son in the spring of 1820 until the vision of the Angel Moroni in September of 1823? All of the sects, he said, "men of high standing," he said, "professors of religion," he said, united to "excite the public mind" against him, precisely because he stubbornly refused to be silent and "continued to affirm" that he "had seen a vision." How could anyone close to Joseph Smith not have known any of this if what he said was true? In any consideration of this remarkable quandary, one question separates itself from all others:

> "*Was Joseph Smith trustworthy?*"

Others: "Friend or Foe"

A prominent Mormon scholar (then later the Assistant Church Historian), writing in 1966 about the then newly released but never previously published 1832 Holographic Account of the First Vision, admitted that

> *[N]one of the available contemporary writings about Joseph Smith in the 1830's, none of the publications of the Church in that decade, and no contemporary journal or correspondence yet discovered mentions the story of the first vision . . . . The earliest anti-Mormon literature attacked the Book of Mormon and the character of Joseph Smith but never mentioned the first vision.*[16]

---

[16]James B. Allen, "The Significance of Joseph Smith's 'First Vision' in Mormon Thought," *Dialogue: A Journal of Mormon Thought*, vol. 1 no. 3, (Autumn

Of Mormonism's earliest detractors, no one ever mentioned the First Vision of the Father and the Son or described any persecution said to have been suffered because of it. In the years since 1966, when James B. Allen advanced those important insights, nothing seems to have changed.

Joseph Smith Jr. didn't mention the First Vision (or claims of persecution) (or the angel with the plates) at his Bainbridge trial in 1826, nor did his father, a witness in those proceedings. The First Vision wasn't mentioned in the Articles and Covenants of the Church of Christ in 1830, in the introductory material to the 1830 edition of the Book of Mormon, at any time before April 6, 1830 (when the Church was organized), on April 6, 1830 (when the Church was organized), in the 1833 Book of Commandments, in the 1835 first edition of the Doctrine and Covenants, or in the Lectures on Faith prepared and published in 1834-35. That vision was not described in *The Evening and the Morning Star* (Independence), in the *Evening and Morning Star* (Kirtland), in the *Latter Day Saints Messenger and Advocate* (Kirtland), or in the *Elders' Journal*. It wasn't described in print or in public until it was published in a rudimental form in Scotland by Orson Pratt in 1840, then officially published in the *Times and Seasons* in Nauvoo in 1842 (when Joseph Smith, the editor of the *Times and Seasons*, was about thirty-seven years old).[17]

The First Vision was not mentioned by the "Three Witnesses" to the Book of Mormon, or by the "Eight Witnesses" to the Book of Mormon. It was not described in Oliver Cowdery and Joseph Smith's 1834-35 First Authorized History of the "rise" of the Church, an account found in Joseph's journal and treated as Joseph's work. Nor was it mentioned in any of the more than a dozen religious publications known to have described 1816-17 and 1824-25 Palmyra revivals, publications where one might expect something to be found if Joseph was truly "thought [to be] a character of sufficient importance to attract the attention of the great ones of the most popular sects of the day."[18] As Professor

---

1966): 30-31, emphasis added. That, according to Allen, "is convincing evidence that at best it received only limited circulation in those early days."
    [17]Ibid., 33.
    [18]The Pearl of Great Price, Joseph Smith – History 1:23.

Allen further admits: *"Apparently not until 1843, when the New York Spectator printed a reporter's account of an interview with Joseph Smith, did a non-Mormon source publish any reference to the story of the first vision."*[19]

People who knew nothing about a vision of the Father and the Son could not have persecuted Joseph Smith because of it. When confronted with this irreconcilable dilemma, Bushman described "persecution light."

> *The talk with the [Methodist] minister [described in the 1838-39 Account], he remembered brought on ridicule by "all classes of men, both religious and irreligious because I continued to affirm that I had seen a vision." Local people seemed to have discussed his case, even though he had said nothing to his parents. Eighteen years later when he wrote his history [and twenty-two years later when it was published], the memories of the injustices still rankled. For whatever reason, his father's family suffered "many persicutions and afflicitions," he recalled, deepening a previous sense of alienation.*[20]

Shall we now believe that local people in those closely-knit rural communities, knowing something the Smith family did not, said nothing to the Smiths, or to their pastor, or to the *Wayne Sentinel,* or to the *Palmyra Reflector,* or to any of those more than a dozen religious publications? May we assume that they wrote nothing in their diaries and journals and said nothing in their declarations and affidavits? Shall we now believe that those people closest to the alleged victim knew nothing of any of this? That for some unknown reason Joseph's family suffered "many persicutions and afflicitions," none of them ascribed to the 1842 publication of Joseph's account of a vision no one, friend or foe, seemed to know anything at all about? Not one of the more than eighty Manchester, Palmyra, Kirtland and Harmony (New York, Ohio and Pennsylvania) neighbors identified by name in *Mormonism*

---

[19]Allen, "The Significance of Joseph Smith's 'First Vision' in Mormon Thought," 31, emphasis retained and supplied.

[20]Bushman, *Joseph Smith: Rough Stone Rolling*, 43, emphasis added.

Unvailed, the greatly larger number of whom were perfectly solid citizens, founders of their communities and personal acquaintances of the Smiths, knew that Joseph even claimed to have seen the Father and the Son. How could they possibly not have known if what Joseph so emphatically said had been remotely close to the truth? And if they knew, how could they not have said that they did? Not one of them knew, and none of them said that Joseph Smith was persecuted and reviled because he had seen a vision of the Father and the Son. But in and after 1838, Joseph emphatically said he knew that he had received a vision, knew that God knew that he had, and refused to say that he had not.

The Methodist Preacher

As a thirty-two and thirty-three year old man in 1838 and 1839, and in what later became an amended *fourth contradictory and then* only known account of the great event, Joseph Smith claimed that he told one of the Methodist preachers in 1820 something he didn't tell his father, mother or siblings. It was also something he had failed to discuss in any of what were four then unknown versions of three earlier accounts of that stirring vision of his precocious youth (Joseph Smith's 1832 Holographic Account of the Vision of the Son; Joshua 1 and 2: 1835; Erastus Holmes: 1835).

> *Some few days after I had this vision, I happened to be in company with one of the Methodist preachers, who was very active in the before mentioned religious excitement; and conversing with him [as a fourteen year old] on the subject of religion, I took occasion to give him an account of the vision which I had had. I was greatly surprised at his behavior; he treated my communication not only lightly, but with great contempt, saying it was all of the devil, that there were no such things as visions or revelations in these days; that all such things had ceased with the apostles, and that there would never be any more of them.*[21]

---

[21]The Pearl of Great Price, Joseph Smith – HIstory 1:21, emphasis added.

It was here with the minister, in a story no one else would hear for more than twenty years, that Bushman said that Joseph said the persecution started ("The preacher's contempt shocked Joseph"). Modern Latter-day Saints are mostly told that the problem Joseph described, rejection at the hands of a Methodist preacher, was to be expected in a society where clergymen held visionaries in "ill repute."[22] "[N]ot [and surprisingly] because of the [story's] strangeness," but rather "because of its familiarity."[23]

Personal epiphanies (like Joseph Smith's account of the First Vision) were a dime a hundred dozen. "The clergy of the mainline churches automatically suspected any visionary report, whatever its content," precisely because there were so very many. "The only acceptable message from heaven," according to Bushman, "was assurance of forgiveness and a promise of grace."[24] Over time, conversation with the deities has become steadily more sparing. The minister's rejection, to Mormon-toned modern minds, said more about those "corrupt" professors who insisted the day for visions had passed than it did about Joseph Smith whose God was alive and well. An honored historian who spent a lifetime thinking about Joseph Smith and his religion had this to say:

> *[I]t is significant, all the more significant in view of the unrelenting persecution Joseph would have us understand came upon him in his youth, that the folklore relative to his early life, an admirable index to the public mind if not a storehouse of exactly determinable event, at no time ever pictured Joseph as being, in the idiom of the day, "a miserable fanatic" given to delusions; he has always been, in Palmyra's collective memory, the moneydigger and seer in peepstones.*[25]

At first blush, the Methodist preacher's reported reaction seems odd and unlikely. Historian Dan Vogel writes:

---

[22]Bushman, *Joseph Smith: Rough Stone Rolling*, 40-41.
[23]Ibid.
[24]Ibid., 41.
[25]Morgan, *Dale Morgan on Early Mormonism*, 250, emphasis added.

> *Generally, nothing in the earliest recital of Smith's first vision, written in 1832, would have evoked this kind of reaction or the kind of persecution from the community that Smith described. Indeed, his claim to have seen Jesus was an expectation of revivalists. Even the premillenialist claim that the entire world was under sin and about to be destroyed was not unique.*[26]

It is highly unlikely that Reverend Lane, or any Methodist leader serving under his circuit-riding superintendence at the Palmyra revival, would have responded in the manner Joseph Smith twenty years later described. "It would have been unusual for a minister to promote spiritual manifestations in a revival and then denounce them to a potential convert – and not only denounce Joseph's own vision but all 'visions and revelations' since the apostolic dispensation."[27] It is probable that the Methodist preacher Joseph threw under the bus was the Reverend George Lane, the "great revival preacher" roundly praised by Oliver and Joseph in 1834 and then later by William Smith. Lane was Joseph's acknowledged mind-wakening mentor and the spiritual leader of the 1824-25 Palmyra revival.

In 1824 and then again in 1828 (in each case after some supposed but unreported 1820 vision), and after the supposed encounter with the Methodist minister, Joseph expressed some desire to join the Methodist Church, and in 1828 he actually put his name on a Harmony, Pennsylvania, classbook. Had the prophet forgotten this? "[H]e [the Methodist preacher] treated my communication ["an account of the vision"] not only lightly, but with great contempt, saying it was all of the devil . . . ." Had he forgotten this? "[T]hat there were no such things as visions or revelations in these days; that all such things had ceased with the apostles, and that there would never be any more of them." Had he forgotten this? "I had now got my mind satisfied so far as the sectarian world was concerned – that it was not my duty to join with any of them, but to continue as I was until further directed." What possible interest

---

[26]Dan Vogel, *Joseph Smith: The Making of a Prophet* (Salt Lake City: Signature Books, 2004), 64.
   [27]Ibid.

could Joseph Smith have had in the Methodist Church in 1824 and 1828, years after the vision, having been told what he later related, most particularly if what he said the minister said in 1820 was true? In resolving this incongruity, we should remember that Joseph didn't publicly say what the Methodist preacher said until 1842.

Does it seem likely that the Methodist elder who "awakened" Joseph's mind to religion[28] would treat the vision of a fourteen-year-old boy with "great contempt" or "lightly"? Would "a great revival preacher" be prompted to say that a youngster's sincerely stated epiphany "was all of the devil, that there were no such things as visions or revelations in those days; that all such things had ceased with the apostles, and that there would never be any more of them"?[29] This late ungracious literary construct unjustly seems to have described the visionary man who led Joseph Smith to the Epistle of James. It was the Reverend George Lane who invited seekers to pose that famous question, "which church shall I join?" to a God who "giveth to all men liberally and upbraideth not."

If the Methodist preacher Joseph described was not Presiding Elder Lane, the man so favorably described in Oliver and Joseph's 1834-35 History, what other Methodist preacher who was very active at the Ontario District Revival would so inexplicably contradict the principal architect of that compelling event, Presiding Elder Lane?[30] Modern Mormons are quick to assign Joseph's defamatory allegation to a myopic sectarian, to an unbiblical disrespect for a God who speaks today. Joseph's later in life claim that the minister treated his communication "lightly" and "with great contempt" is not unlike his late in life claim to have suffered persecution from

---

[28]Oliver Cowdery (and Joseph Smith), "Letter III To W.W. Phelps, Esq." (Oliver Cowdery and Joseph Smith's 1834-35 History), *Messenger and Advocate*, vol. 1 no. 3 (December 1834): 42.

[29]The Pearl of Great Price, Joseph Smith – History 1:21.

[30]Lucy Mack Smith described Willard Chase (the owner of Joseph Smith's chocolate-colored seerstone) as "a Methodist class leader." (Vogel, *Joseph Smith: The Making of a Prophet*, 64). It is unlikely that Chase – the brother of seeress Sally Chase (a woman with her own magic stone) and a man who had been associated with the Smith's moneydigging endeavors – would have discredited spiritual phenomena. Besides the Reverend George Lane, there would seem to be no other candidate for the Methodist minister Joseph Smith publicly chose to defame for the first time twenty-two years after the fact and in but one of six versions of five different First Vision accounts.

"the great ones of the most popular sects of the day" because he said he saw the Father and the Son. The conversation with the Methodist minister wasn't described in the 1832 Holographic Account, which was handwritten and early, or in any of the three other suppressed versions of two other more contemporaneous 1835 accounts. In sum it is highly doubtful that a fourteen-year-old Joseph Smith had a conversation about the vision of the deities with a Methodist minister in 1820. Nor did he have a conversation about the vision with his father in 1820, or with his mother, or with Hyrum, or with any of his other siblings.

In his 1832 Account, Joseph didn't ask "the Lord" which of all the sects was right and wasn't told that he should join none of them. In that first suppressed account of his first encounter with deity, Joseph Smith didn't have a conversation with a Methodist minister, nor did he describe a great revival. He was not confronted with the dark power of the underworld and didn't claim to have been persecuted. The question ("which of all the sects was right"), the answer ("they were all wrong"), the preacher, the underworld and issues of persecution were totally absent in Joseph Smith's 1832 first and only Holographic Account of a vision of the "crucifyed" Lord.

The Deities Were an Afterthought

If Joseph described the Vision to a Methodist elder some few days after it happened the way he described the vision in his *1832 Account* twelve years later, the minister's reaction – as described in private in 1838-39 and in public in 1842 – would be almost incomprehensible. Bushman softens the contradictions implicit in Joseph's *1832 Holographic Account of the First Vision* by saying that Joseph failed to comprehend the greater significance of that vision when he prepared his handwritten account "twelve years after the event"[31] allegedly occurred. (*"But twelve years after the event, the First Vision's personal significance for him still overshadowed its place in the divine plan for restoring a church."*[32]) If Smith didn't understand the greater significance of the 1820

---

[31]Bushman, *Joseph Smith: Rough Stone Rolling*, 39.
[32]Ibid., emphasis added.

event in 1832 (when he was twenty-six) because it was so personal, he likely wouldn't have understood the greater significance of the event in 1820 (when he was fourteen) because it was so personal.

Bushman explains Joseph's supposedly limited 1832 understanding of the 1820 event in these terms: "By 1832, when he first recorded the vision, Joseph knew that his experience was one step in 'the rise of the church of Christ in the eve of time,' along with Moroni's visits, the restoration of the Aaronic Priesthood, and the reception of the 'high Priesthood.'"[33] All of these great foundational events are supposed, by modern Mormon reckoning, to have occurred before Smith recorded his Holographic Account of the vision in 1832. Other than that, the 1832 epiphany, according to Bushman, was seen "in terms of the familiar" and as essentially personal. "He explained the vision as he must first have understood it, as a personal conversion." "It was the message of forgiveness and redemption he had wanted to hear."[34] But as the Mormon prophet matured, when twelve years (as in 1832) became eighteen or nineteen years (as in 1838-39), he seemed to have finally realized that the 1820 vision had meant a great deal more. If that is how it was, this is how it leaves us: What Joseph is supposed to have thought about the 1820 vision in 1832, as described by Joseph's biographer (it was essentially personal), if presented to a Methodist revival preacher in 1820, was what that Methodist preacher might have expected to hear from one who lacked wisdom and asked of God "that giveth to all men liberally and upbraideth not."

By 1832 Joseph Smith is supposed to have conversed with a trinitarian deity (only one god appeared), translated the Book of Mormon (the "vision of the angel who led him to the gold plates was not mentioned in the Preface to the first edition of the Book of Mormon"[35]), bestowed the gift of the Holy Ghost, received the Priesthood, seen the angel a dozen times, and welcomed other heavenly messengers, according to his status as *the* "Prophet, Seer and Revelator" of the kingdom of God. To Mormons, Joseph's words, when speaking while inspired (and since November 1831), are sacred scripture, the will of the Lord, the mind of the Lord, the

---

[33]Ibid.
[34]Ibid.
[35]Ibid.

word of the Lord, "the voice of the Lord, and the power of God unto salvation."[36]   He preached, baptized, conferred, confirmed, cursed, blessed, ordained, healed the sick and prophesied. He sent missionaries to the Lamanites, revised the Bible and received the larger part of some seventy revelations. And God said, "Thou shalt give heed unto all his words and commandments, which he shall give unto you, as he receiveth them . . . . For his word ye shall receive, as if from mine own mouth, in all patience and faith [April 6, 1830]."[37]

If the message Joseph conveyed to the Methodist minister was that all the churches were wrong, that their creeds were abominable, that their professors were corrupt, that their doctrines were uninspired and that they were led by wicked and calculating men, one might predict a harsh response. If Joseph had disclosed those details – all of them contained in his 1838-39 Pearl of Great Price Account, representations prohibitive of all of the churches, their creeds, leaders and doctrines – it would be easy to explain the minister's supposedly stern response. But if Joseph, like Bushman claimed, hadn't understood the deeper meaning of the 1820 event in 1832, twelve years later, and wouldn't understand the deeper meaning until 1838-39, eighteen or nineteen years later, there should have been no problem, because the 1832 Account, unlike the 1838-39 Account, did not include those ugly and offensive recitals. What minister actively involved in a great revival would treat a young seeker's forgiveness epiphany and a promise of grace "lightly" and with "great contempt"?

The 1834-35 History requested by Joseph Smith, penned by Oliver Cowdery and found in the prophet's journal, *unequivocally* described Joseph's first ever encounter with a heavenly messenger as the vision of the angel in charge of the golden plates, a vision supposed to have occurred on September 21 and 22 of 1823.[38] Had Joseph described this first vision, the vision of the angel with the plates, the only vision known to the early Mormons, to a Methodist

---

[36]Doctrine and Covenants 68:4.

[37]Book of Commandments 22:4-5.

[38]The vision of the angel who led Joseph Smith "to the golden plates was not mentioned in the first edition of the Book of Mormon." (Bushman, *Rough Stone Rolling*, 39).

preacher, there may have been a problem. Dan Vogel concluded as follows:

> *[P]lacing Smith's conversation with the minister in the context of the 1824-25 revival and the possibility that Smith actually related his 1823 and 1824 encounters with the heavenly messenger on the hill, the minister's reaction begins to make sense. While the preacher would have found little to condemn in Jesus forgiving a teenager of his sins, he certainly would have objected to an encounter with a treasure guardian and the promise of new canon to supplant the primacy of the Bible.[39]*

Youthful Sensitivity?

Speaking of the after-effects of the First Vision, Mormon historian Donna Hill reflected as follows:

> *Whether or not the scorn to which his youthful exuberance and faith were subjected by the local minister had as much social impact as he thought, the boy himself apparently felt deeply hurt and humiliated, and for years afterward would share his experience only with his family and a very few close friends. He neither included an account of it in the prefatory material published with The Book of Mormon nor told it publicly at the time of the organization of the church in 1830. It was not spoken of by missionaries then going out to preach and there was no reference to it in the Book of Commandments, published in 1833. Joseph's first known written account was made, as has been mentioned, in 1832, but it was not published. Joseph did not publish an account of his first vision until 1842, when he included it in the opening pages of his history, which he was induced to write, as he said, because of the*

---

[39]Vogel, *Joseph Smith: The Making of a Prophet*, 64, emphasis added.

*many false reports about the church then being
circulated.*[40]

Joseph's claims of persecution involved a great deal more than a
modest encounter with a Methodist minister. Bushman (like Donna
Hill) understates the imposing claims of persecution described by
Joseph Smith in the 1838-39 Pearl of Great Price Account ascribing
them to a "youthful sensitivity."[41] The minister's supposed abrupt
dismissal of Joseph's visionary claim "widened the gulf between
Joseph and the evangelical ministry."[42] Bushman is quite certain
that Joseph didn't really understand the 1820 vision or its meaning
for the world in 1832, when he first described the vision in writing,
and he diminishes the poignant persecution claims Smith described
as a mature adult in the canonized 1838-39 Account.

> *In the years after his First Vision, Joseph Jr. said little
> about his spiritual development. He had no sense of
> mission, no emerging prophetic identity unless a
> mysterious reference to "many other things did he say
> unto me which I cannot write at this time" is
> interpreted to mean religious instructions. What
> Joseph said explicitly was that the vision led to
> trouble, though his youthful sensitivity probably
> exaggerated the reaction.*[43]

And what a colossal exaggeration that was. The claims in the final
account of the vision are utterly grandiloquent. Joseph Smith
relates himself in a most personal way to the great Apostle Paul, the
architect of Christianity. To say that the "vision led to trouble" but
that Joseph's "youthful sensitivity probably exaggerated the

---

[40]Donna Hill, *Joseph Smith: The First Mormon* (Garden City, New York:
Doubleday & Company, Inc., 1977; reprint, Salt Lake City: Signature Books, 1982,
1999), 53, emphasis added.

[41]Bushman, *Joseph Smith: Rough Stone Rolling*, 43.

[42]Ibid., 41.

[43]Ibid., 42-43, emphasis added. What was true of the vision of the Father and
the Son, Bushman says, was also true of the vision of Moroni. "As late as 1831, he
was slow to say much about Moroni. He was not interested in notoriety." (Ibid.,
40). Lieutenant General Joseph Smith, Prophet, Seer and Revelator Joseph Smith,
had himself secretly ordained by the Council of Fifty to the office of King of the
Kingdom of Israel on earth.

reaction," to say that "local people seemed to have discussed his case even though he had said nothing to his parents," to say that "most early converts probably never heard about the 1820 vision" is to ignore Smith's self-aggrandizing deception. Mormon missionaries have taken egregious advantage of these thoroughly dishonest claims. No missionary ever says to Mormonism's investigators that Joseph's "youthful sensitivity probably exaggerated the reaction." In truth, there is no historical support for these outlandish persecution claims.

Before the Pearl of Great Price Account was published in the early 1840s, Joseph had discovered and obtained the breast plate, magic spectacles and golden plates, translated the Book of Mormon and revised the King James Bible. By 1838-39 Joseph had reported perhaps a dozen meetings with "Moroni" or "Nephi" (an ancient American prophet), and other meetings with John the Baptist (who baptized Jesus), with Peter, James and John (the leaders of the gospel church), and with various other religious figures, including Jesus again, Moses, Adam, Michael, Elias and Elijah. Before the *founding canonized account* was published in the early 1840s, Joseph claimed to have effectuated the restoration of the Aaronic and Melchizedek Priesthoods. John the Baptist had conferred the lower priesthood on Joseph Smith and Oliver Cowdery, and they had baptized and ordained each other and others. Peter, James and John had conferred the higher priesthood on Joseph Smith and Oliver Cowdery, and they had ordained each other and others. Elias had conferred the Abrahamic (Patriarchal) Priesthood on Joseph and Oliver, after which Joseph Jr., Joseph Sr. and Hyrum had been ordained one after the other to the office of Patriarch. Smith had established priesthood quorums and restored the emblems and offices of the gospel church. He had organized and officered the Church of the restoration, first as "The True Disciples of Christ," then as the "Church of Christ," then as the "Church of the Latter Day Saints" and finally as the "Church of Jesus Christ of Latter-day Saints."

In 1830 Joseph was ordained "Prophet, Seer and Revelator" of the Church of Christ by Oliver Cowdery. By 1838-39 Smith had identified the location of the Garden of Eden (in the state of Missouri). He had supervised the publication of the 1833 Book of

Commandments containing selections from the more than seventy revelations he had already received, and he had collaborated to prepare and publish the 1834-35 History. He had supervised the construction of a temple in Kirtland. He had published the revelations described in the 1835 Book of Doctrine and Covenants. He had "Prepared" the *Lectures on Faith*, and he had amended various provisions in the 1837 edition of the Book of Mormon to separate the Father from the Son. The Three Witnesses had selected and ordained twelve founding apostles.

Joseph Smith said, as a mature adult in the thirty-third and thirty-fourth years of his life in 1838-39 and after all of that history, that he suffered severe and unrelenting persecution at the hands of the "professors of religion," at the hands of "men of high standing," at the "hands of the great ones of the most popular sects of the day" because he repeatedly said and stubbornly refused to deny that he had had a vision. There was, he said, "a spirit of the most bitter persecution and reviling" sufficient "to excite the public mind against me" for "telling" the story of the vision. For three-and-a-half years he continued to suffer severe unrelenting persecution "at the hands of all classes of men, both religious and irreligious, because I continued to affirm that I had seen a vision."[44] That was true or it was not, and it may not now be dismissed by cavalierly suggesting that it was probably an exaggeration traceable to some "youthful sensitivity." "[Y]outhful sensitivity" it was not. It is a core fact at the heart of the mature prophet's incredible history, central to the First Vision founding story, a powerful claim prominently cited by Mormons to their great advantage for nearly two hundred years.

Something must be said to explain the contradictions between the one hundred thirty year suppressed 1832 Account – which emphasized personal conversion and forgiveness but failed to mention a revival, a dark power that bound the youngster's tongue, two glorious personages, a question about the churches, a conversation with a minister or claims of persecution – and the 1838-39 Account which mentions all of those details. To dismiss the fervent claims of widespread persecution described in the 1838-39

---

[44]The Pearl of Great Price, Joseph Smith – History 1:27.

Pearl of Great Price Account, but not in the 1832 or 1835 Accounts, Joshua 1:1835, Joshua 2:1835, Erastus Holmes: 1835, by saying that the 1838-39 recitals were the product of *"his youthful sensitivity,"* or that he *"probably exaggerated the reaction,"* or that those events didn't have *"as much social impact"* as he may have thought, is to starkly demonstrate the reason defeating depth and breadth of awkward apology.

When Joseph Smith first composed then published those claims of persecution in the late 1830s and early 1840s, following the path of other frontier pariahs, he was not some callow youth.   The harrowing *first* descriptions of what he called "severe persecution" were not crafted until 1838, when Joseph was thirty-two years old. They were further composed, recopied, revised and amplified in 1839, when he was thirty-three years old, and they were first published in the *Times and Seasons* in 1842, when he was thirty-six. If he "exaggerated the reaction" to the vision, he did it as a mature adult with a lengthy religious résumé at the height of his prominence and after many years to reflect. Joseph Smith created the claims of persecution not as a boy and not at the time, but as an adult and after the fact. No historian can hope to reconcile the incredible claims of persecution described in the Pearl of Great Price Account with anything that resembles historical fact and it is perfectly foolish to try.

CHAPTER FIVE

Contradictions and Discrepancies

[O]ur brother was urged forward and strengthened in the determination to know for himself of the certainty and reality of pure and holy religion. – And it is only necessary for me to say that while this excitement continued, he continued to call upon the Lord in secret for a full manifestation of divine approbation, and for, to him, the all important information, if a Supreme Being did exist, to have an assurance that he was accepted of him.

1834-35 History

THE REVIVAL

Joseph Smith's 1838-39 Pearl of Great Price Account of the 1820 vision of the Father and the Son was published in the *Times and Seasons* in 1842. Joseph Smith and Oliver Cowdery's 1834-35 History of the 1823 vision of the Angel in charge of the plates was published in the *Messenger and Advocate* in 1834-35. The two accounts described the same revival as preliminary to each of what were two completely separate visions supposed to have occurred three-and-a-half years apart. B.H. Roberts embraced the carefully crafted recitals of the 1834-35 History: "Joseph Smith's association with Cowdery in the production of these *Letters* make them, as to the facts involved, practically the personal narrative of Joseph Smith." Roberts did then further report that "The *Letters* have several times been reproduced in L.D.S. periodicals . . . ."[1] Joseph Fielding Smith also embraced the carefully crafted recitals of the

---

[1]Brigham H. Roberts, *A Comprehensive History of the Church of Jesus Christ of Latter-day Saints*, 6 vols. (Provo, UT: Brigham Young University Press, 1965), 1:77-8 n 8.

1834-35 History:

> *The quibbler might say that this statement from Oliver Cowdery [a statement excerpted from the 1834-35 History] is merely the opinion of Oliver Cowdery and not the expression of the Prophet Joseph Smith. It should be remembered that these letters in which these statements are made were written at the Prophet's request and under his personal supervision.*[2]

Joseph Fielding Smith noted that the History had been published and republished "under" Joseph Smith's "direction" in the *Messenger and Advocate*, then again later in the *Times and Seasons*, "without any thought of correction."

In this first authorized history of the rise of the Church – prepared by Oliver Cowdery and Joseph Smith, published in installments, posted in Joseph's journal and considered Joseph's work – Joseph Smith was determined "to know for himself of the certainty and reality of pure and holy religion."[3]   This personal concern, described in that important history, was said to have culminated on September 21, 1823.

In the 1834-35 History, familiar events associated with what was an 1824-25 Palmyra revival were said to have caused Joseph Smith to retire to his bedroom late in the evening on September 21, 1823, where he then received a vision of the angel in charge of the golden plates. In the 1838-39 Pearl of Great Price Account, however, the same 1824-25 Palmyra revival caused Joseph Smith to retire to the woods in the spring of 1820, where he then received a vision of the Father and the Son. That those two momentous events in Mormon history, different events years apart, should both be precipitated by the same great revival involving the same identifiable figures doing the same identifiable things presents a conflict logic cannot hope to

---

[2]"Where Is the Hill Cumorah?" in Joseph Fielding Smith, *Doctrines of Salvation*, comp. Bruce R. McConkie, vol. 3 (Bookcraft, 1956), 3:236, emphasis added.

[3]Oliver Cowdery (and Joseph Smith), "Letter IV To W.W. Phelps, Esq." (Oliver Cowdery and Joseph Smith's 1834-35 History), *Messenger and Advocate*, vol. 1 no. 5, February 1835, 78.

resolve. There was no Palmyra revival in 1820, and there was no Palmyra revival in 1823. The Palmyra revival spoken of in both accounts occurred as an historical event in 1824-25 *after* the death of Alvin Smith on November 19, 1823, *after* the arrival of the Reverend Benjamin Stockton in February 1824, and *after* the arrival of the Reverend George Lane in July of 1824.

Forgetting Father, Forgetting Son

The 1834-35 History describes a vision of the angel in charge of the plates while altogether neglecting to describe a vision of the Father and the Son. That first "authorized" history of the Church thus fails to mention what Latter-day Saints believe to have been the most important historical event since the resurrection. The 1834-35 History was promoted as "a correct statement of events" meant to counter the many spurious accounts then afloat and set the record straight.[4]

> *You will recollect that I informed you, in my letter published in the first No. of the Messenger and Advocate, that this history would necessarily embrace the life and character of our esteemed friend and brother, J. Smith Jr. one of the presidents of this church . . . .*[5]

However harmful those allegedly spurious accounts may have seemed at the time, none of them concerned allegations supposed to have been associated with an event that occurred "on the morning of a beautiful, clear day, early in the spring of eighteen hundred and twenty."[6] What might be said to explain that incredible omission from that important history described in meticulous detail fourteen years after the alleged event in 1820? When Oliver Cowdery and Joseph Smith collaborated to prepare and publish their first

---

[4]Oliver Cowdery (and Joseph Smith), "Letter III To W.W. Phelps, Esq." (Oliver Cowdery and Joseph Smith's 1834-35 History), *Messenger and Advocate*, vol. 1 no. 3, December 1834, 42.

[5]Ibid., 42, emphasis added. In December 1834 Oliver Cowdery was ordained to be "one of the presidents of this church . . . ."

[6]The Pearl of Great Price, Joseph Smith – History 1:14.

"authorized" 1834-35 *"full history of the rise of the church,"*[7] "one of the presidents of this church" didn't know that there had been an 1820 vision of the Father and the Son.[8] In 1834 and 1835, Joseph's father, mother and siblings were also unaware that there had been an 1820 vision of the Father and the Son. In the annals of a Church guilty of many historical discrepancies, where is one to match the failure to describe in the first official history of the rise of the church, an account of Joseph Smith's much earlier encounter with the deities?

An 1834-35 Description of an 1823 Joseph

Mormonism Unvailed, with all of its declarations and affidavits, was published in Painesville, Ohio (a city close to Kirtland) in 1834 by E.D. Howe. In this early exposé, Joseph Smith's reputation was utterly trashed by men and women of substance in no less than four different communities in three different states. The *1834-35 History* describes a pathetic Joseph dealing with a sense of his own precarious frailty. It was an effort to reconstruct the reputation of the man that Howe and many of the Smiths' New York, Ohio and Pennsylvania neighbors had vilified in print after Smith left New York and Pennsylvania and before he left Ohio. The line of defense suggested by the first heavenly messenger (the angel in charge of the golden plates) was patronizing: "God has chosen the foolish things of the world to confound the things which are mighty; and base things of the world, and things wich [*sic*, which] are despised, has God chosen, yea, and things which are not, to bring to nought

---

[7]Cowdery (and Smith), "Letter III To W.W. Phelps, Esq." (Oliver Cowdery and Joseph Smith's 1834-35 History), *Messenger and Advocate*, vol. 1 no. 3 (December 1834), 13.

[8]"In 1834, Oliver Cowdery became involved in a steamboat argument with a skeptic who would not believe that Christ had been seen upon the earth since his ascension, and though Cowdery published in the *Messenger and Advocate*, Oct. 1834, a lengthy account of his refutation, his argument did not include any reference to a visitation to the Mormon prophet, nor was there any editorial comment calling to the attention of the church membership, a circumstance of such striking interest to them." (Dale Morgan, *Dale Morgan on Early Mormonism: Correspondence & A New History*, ed. John Phillip Walker, with a Biographical Introduction by John Phillip Walker and a Preface by William Mulder [Salt Lake City, UT: Signature Books, 1986], 374 n 6).

things which are, that no flesh should glory in his presence."[9] Before an angel presented that scripture to Joseph Smith in 1823, the Apostle Paul presented that scripture to the Corinthians (". . . not many wise men after the flesh, not many mighty, not many noble, are called . . ."[10]).

Joseph was seventeen years old and thoroughly insecure. If there is a God – an open question in the 1834-35 History ("if a Supreme being did exist"[11]) – Joseph wonders out loud about some kind of a relationship. He doesn't know where to find the truth and has no sense of a religious mission. His mind is not "satisfied so far as the sectarian world is concerned," and no one has said continue as you are "until further directed,"[12] as he later claimed in 1838-39. Joseph doesn't begin to know if he has been forgiven. He hasn't seen a heavenly messenger and wonders about "the certainty and reality of pure and holy religion" (if any of the sects are true). These are stunning admissions from Joseph Smith in 1823. This unamended Joseph took solace from a scripture that said "that to him who knocks it shall be opened, & whosoever will, may come and partake of the waters of life freely."[13] *The 1823 Joseph described in his 1834-35 History has never communicated with a heavenly messenger, doesn't know if there is a God, has no sense of acceptance and hasn't been forgiven.*

These concerns should have been resolved long before 1823 if Joseph had seen the Father and the Son in 1820 when he was fourteen, as he claimed in the Pearl of Great Price Account published in the *Times and Seasons* in 1842. These concerns should have been resolved long before 1823 if Joseph had seen the "crucifyed" Lord in a "piller of firelight above the brightness of the sun at noon day" in 1821 in the sixteenth year of his age, as he

---

[9]From the Apostle Paul's letter to the Corinthians, 1 Cor. 1:27-29, quoted (paraphrased) in "Letter IV" (Cowdery and Smith's 1834-35 History), *Messenger and Advocate*, February 1835, 79.

[10]1 Corinthians 1:26.

[11]"Letter IV" (Cowdery and Smith's 1834-35 History), *Messenger and Advocate*, February 1835, 78.

[12]The Pearl of Great Price, Joseph Smith – History 1:26.

[13]"Letter IV" (Cowdery and Smith's 1834-35 History), *Messenger and Advocate*, February 1835, 78.

claimed in the one and only 1832 Holographic Account[14] published
in a Brigham Young University student's masters thesis in 1965. In
1834-35 Joseph Smith said that he was "endeavoring to exercise
faith in the scriptures" in 1823 at the age of seventeen.[15] Isn't this
the same person who said in 1838-39 that in 1820 "I had found the
testimony of James to be true – that a man who lacked wisdom
might ask of God, and obtain and not be upbraided"?[16] Isn't this
the person who said in 1832 that when he was about the age of
twelve he had

> *become seriously imprest [p. 1] with regard to the all*
> *importent concerns for the well=fare of my immortal*
> *Soul which led me to search=ing the scriptures*
> *believeing as I was taught, that they contained the*
> *word of God . . ."?*[17]

This 1823 Joseph seemed to have forgotten by 1834-35 what he had
already described in his unreported 1832 account of an 1821 vision:
"*Joseph <my son> thy sins are forgiven thee.*" "[B]ehold, I am the
Lord of glory I was crucifyed for the world that all those who
believe on my name may have Eternal life . . . ." "[A]nd my soul
was filled with love and for many days I could rejoice with great
Joy and the Lord was with me . . . ."[18] The seventeen-year-old
Joseph begging to communicate with "some kind messenger" at his
father's house in Manchester, Ontario County, New York, on
September 21, 1823, hadn't been to the Sacred Grove to see the
Father and the Son in 1820, hadn't seen the "crucifyed" Lord in a
"piller of firelight" in 1821 *and didn't know* in 1823 "*if a Supreme*
being did exist."

---

[14]Joseph Smith's 1832 Account, Joseph Smith Jr., *The Personal Writings of
Joseph Smith*, ed. Dean C. Jessee (Salt Lake City, UT: Deseret Book, 1984), 6.

[15]"Letter IV" (Cowdery and Smith's 1834-35 History), *Messenger and
Advocate*, February 1835, 79.

[16]The Pearl of Great Price, Joseph Smith – History 1:26.

[17]Jessee ed., *The Personal Writings of Joseph Smith*, 4-5, emphasis added.

[18]Ibid., 6.

The 1834-35 Description of the 1823 Vision

> *[O]n a sudden a light like that of day, only of a purer and far more glorious appearance and brightness, burst into the room. – Indeed, to use his own description, the first sight was as though the house was filled with consuming and unquenchable fire. This sudden appearance of a light so bright, as must naturally be expected, occasioned a shock or sensation, visible to the extremities of the body. It was, however, followed with a calmness and serenity of mind, and an overwhelming rapture of joy that surpassed understanding, and in a moment a personage stood before him.*[19]

Is it Jesus? No, but it is, according to this account, the first heavenly messenger to ever appear to Joseph Smith.[20] It is a treasure-guardian in charge of some golden plates and magical interpreters responding to the humble request of a treasure-seeking seer. It is a money-digging dream event. "Though fear was banished from his heart, yet his *surprise* was no less when he heard him declare himself to be a messenger sent by commandment of the Lord, to deliver a special message . . . ."[21]

---

[19]"Letter IV" (Cowdery and Smith's 1834-35 History), *Messenger and Advocate*, February 1835, 79, emphasis added.

[20]Dan Vogel, ed., *Early Mormon Documents* (Salt Lake City, UT: Signature Books, 1996), 1:496. William Smith, *On Mormonism* (1883). Before Joseph described these events to his family on September 22, 1823, William Smith said that Joseph said he had not yet told anyone about "the visions he had received." (Ibid.). *Before* that meeting, when Joseph told his family about the things he had not yet told to anyone else, no one knew about a vision of the Father and the Son. *After* that meeting on September 22 or 23, 1823, no one knew about a vision of the Father and the Son. "William said they were 'melted to tears, and believed all he said' after hearing the story of the angel and the plates. He had made his first converts." (Richard Lyman Bushman, with the assistance of Jed Woodworth, *Joseph Smith: Rough Stone Rolling* [New York: Alfred A. Knopf, 2005], 45-46). Those first converts didn't know about an earlier vision of the "crucifyed," "omnipotent," "omnipreasant" Lord that wouldn't be described until 1832 in an account that would be concealed and suppressed from the ordinary members of the Church until 1965.

[21]"Letter IV" (Cowdery and Smith's 1834-35 History), *Messenger and Advocate*, February 1835, 79, emphasis added.

THE 1834-35 HISTORY:
CONTRADICTIONS AND DISCREPANCIES

The 1834-35 History was prepared in meticulous detail in eight carefully crafted separate installments by Mormonism's founders (Joseph Smith and Oliver Cowdery) in the form of letters penned by Cowdery sent to W.W. Phelps. They were published one at a time in the *Messenger and Advocate* in Kirtland, Ohio, seven or eight years before the *Times and Seasons* published the 1838-39 Pearl of Great Price Account of the vision of the Father and the Son in 1842. Joseph's accounting in 1834-35 was created and expressed as if his own earlier handwritten (1832 Holographic) account didn't exist. In addition, it was as if his account of what happened in 1820 (written in 1838-39) never occurred. *The 1834-35 History described each of the following circumstances as having immediately preceded the vision of the angel in charge of the plates and interpreters on September 21, 1823, when Joseph Smith was seventeen years old.*

> "There was a great awakening, or excitement raised on the subject of religion, and much enquiry for the word of life."[22]

> There was "general strife for followers" among previously "harmonious" religionists. In the "general struggle" of "the different sects, for proselytes" the cry of "the old professors" became, "I am right – you are wrong – . . . ."[23]

> "All professed to be the true church," but none had satisfactory evidence to support their claims.[24]

> Proof as to the truthfulness of churches from some source was wanting. "'The Lord has said, long since . . . that to him who knocks, it shall be opened, & whosoever will, may come and partake of the waters of life freely."[25]

---

[22]"Letter III" (Cowdery and Smith's 1834-35 History), *Messenger and Advocate*, December 1834, 42.

[23]Ibid., 42.

[24]Ibid., 43.

[25]"Letter IV" (Cowdery and Smith's 1834-35 History), *Messenger and Advocate*, February 1835, 78.

Joseph's "mother, one sister, and two of his natural brothers, were persuaded to unite with the Presbyterians."[26]

The Reverend George Lane, "a presiding Elder of the Methodist Church, visited Palmyra, and vicinity" and "awakened" Joseph's mind ("[I]n common with others, our brother's mind became awakened"[27]).

"[O]ur brother was urged forward and strengthened in the determination to know for himself of the certainty and reality of pure and holy religion –. . . ."[28]

His "whole soul" was lost to "every thing of a temporal nature . . . ."[29]

"[H]is spirit was not at rest day or night."[30]

"On the evening of the 21st of September, 1823, previous to retiring to rest, our brother's mind was unusually wrought up on the subject which had so long agitated his mind [which of all the sects was right]. [H]is heart was drawn out in fervent prayer . . . ."[31]

While the "religious excitement in Palmyra and vicinity" continued, "*he continued to call upon the Lord in secret for a full manifestation of divine approbation, and for [what was], to him, the all important information, if a Supreme being did exist, to have an assurance that he was accepted of him.*"

He had but a single desire "to be prepared in heart to commune   with   some   kind   messenger   who   could

---

[26]"Letter III" (Cowdery and Smith's 1834-35 History), *Messenger and Advocate*, December 1834, 42.

[27]Ibid., 42.

[28]"Letter IV" (Cowdery and Smith's 1834-35 History), *Messenger and Advocate*, February 1835, 78.

[29]Ibid., 78.

[30]"Letter III" (Cowdery and Smith's 1834-35 History), *Messenger and Advocate*, December 1834, 43.

[31]"Letter IV" (Cowdery and Smith's 1834-35 History), *Messenger and Advocate*, February 1835, 78.

communicate to him the desired information of his acceptance with God."[32]

Do these 1823 observations preceding the vision of the angel in charge of the plates sound familiar? Do they sound like concerns one might expect to hear in 1823 from a boy who was yet to say that he had also seen the Father and the Son in 1820?

Let us pose some rhetorical questions to the seventeen-year-old 1823 boy described in that 1834-35 History who waited until 1842 to publicly say that he had also seen "two Personages whose brightness and glory defy all description" "on the morning of a beautiful, clear day, early in the spring" of 1820:[33]

> *Didn't you say before you later said you saw the Father and the Son in 1820 that in 1823 there was strife among what had been previously harmonious religionists? Didn't you then later say in 1842 that, as the various denominations struggled for proselytes in 1820 that the cry became, "I am right, you are wrong"?*
>
> *Didn't you say in 1842 that Jesus told you three-and-a-half years before September 1823 that all of the sects were "wrong"; that their creeds "were an abomination in his sight"; that their professors "were all corrupt," and that they taught "for doctrines the commandments of men"?[34]*
>
> *Didn't you say in 1842 that in 1820 you had "got" your mind satisfied "so far as the sectarian world was concerned?" Did you not say that in 1820 Jesus told you it was not your "duty to join" with any of those various denominations, but rather to continue as you were "until further directed?"[35] Hadn't Jesus told you in 1820 that you must not join any of them? Didn't he forbid you twice?*
>
> *If God and Jesus told you those things in 1820, then why was*

---

[32]Ibid., emphasis added.
[33]The Pearl of Great Price, Joseph Smith – History 1:14.
[34]Ibid., 1:19, emphasis added.
[35]Ibid., 1:26, emphasis added.

your mind "unusually wrought up" on that particular subject on September 21, 1823? What did it matter to you in 1823 that there was strife among what had been previously harmonious religionists?

Why did you care that some of those denominations said in 1823 that they were right and others were wrong? Had the Father and the Son not already settled that question by telling you in 1820 that none of them were right and that all of them were wrong?

Why was your mind "awakened" to religion in 1823 before you saw the angel with the plates when you were seventeen years old? Why was it not previously "awakened" to religion in 1820 when you said that you saw the Father and the Son when you were fourteen years old? And didn't you say in 1832 that "At about the age of twelve years my mind become seriously imprest [p. 1] with regard to the all important concerns for the well=fare of my immortal Soul . . ."?[36]

You know that you wrote in 1832 that in 1821 you "cried unto the Lord for mercy," that you were "filled with the spirit of God," that "the <Lord> opened the heavens" upon you, appeared and spoke to you and said "Joseph <my son> thy sins are forgiven thee. go thy <way> walk in my statutes and keep my commandments."[37] Why then was your "spirit" "not at rest day or night" in 1823? Didn't you say in 1832 that in 1821 "<in the 16th year . . ." of your age that your "soul was filled with love and for many days I could rejoice with great joy and the Lord was with me . . . "?[38]

Knowing what you said that you learned in 1820, or in 1821, why was your soul lost to every thing of a temporal nature in 1823?

If the Lord had already forgiven your sins in 1821 when you were in the sixteenth year of your age (as you said in 1832

---

[36]Jessee ed., *The Personal Writings of Joseph Smith*, 4, emphasis added.
[37]Ibid., 6, emphasis added.
[38]Ibid.

*that he did), why did you desperately need to have your sins
forgiven again in 1823, in the eighteenth year of your age (as
you said in 1834-35 that you did)?*

*If you had really seen the "crucifyed" Lord in 1821, as you
said in 1832 that you did,[39] how could you wonder "if a
Supreme Being did exist" in 1823, as you said in 1834-35 that
you did?*

*If you had really seen God the Father and Jesus Christ in
1820, as you said in 1838-39, how could you wonder "if a
Supreme Being did exist" in 1823, as you said in 1834-35?[40]*

*If you were told in 1820 to continue as you were "until further
directed," why did you desperately need a further
"manifestation of divine approbation" in 1823?*

*If the "crucifyed" Lord appeared to you in the sixteenth year
of your age (1821 or 1822), as you privately said in 1832, why
did you need to "have an assurance" that you were "accepted"
of God in 1823 in the eighteenth year of your age, as you said
in 1834-35?*

*If God the Father and Jesus Christ appeared to you in 1820,
as you privately said in 1838-39 and publicly said in 1842, why
did you need to "have an assurance" that you were "accepted"
of God in 1823?*

*If you had seen the Son in 1821, or the Father and the Son in
1820, why would you doubt the existence of heavenly
messengers in 1823? Knowing what you experienced earlier,
how could you have had but a single desire in 1823 – to
commune with some kind messenger who could satisfy what
you described as an urgent need for acceptance?*

*If God the Father and Jesus Christ told you in 1820 that none
of the sects were right, and that all of the sects were wrong, if*

---

[39]Ibid., emphasis added.
[40]"Letter IV" (Cowdery and Smith's 1834-35 History), *Messenger and
Advocate*, February 1835, 78, emphasis added.

you had then "got" your "mind satisfied so far as the sectarian world was concerned" in 1820, if you knew "it was not your duty to join with any of them," but rather to continue as you were "until further directed,"[41] why would you need to know for yourself in 1823 "of the certainty and reality of pure and holy religion"?

Why did it matter to you in 1823 that all of the sects professed to be the true church? Why did it matter to you in 1823 that none of the sects had satisfactory evidence to support their claims?

If you had had a vision of the Father and the Son in 1820, and if everything had happened in 1820 as you said in 1838 or 1839, or if you had had a vision of the "crucifyed" Lord in 1821, and if everything had happened in 1821, as you said in 1832:

You should have known that there was a Supreme Being in 1823.

You should have known that there were heavenly messengers in 1823.

You should have known that you were accepted of God in 1823.

You should not have needed a manifestation of divine approbation in 1823.

You should not have had to knock and God should not have needed to open in 1823.

Why did your mother, Lucy Mack Smith, your brothers Hyrum and Samuel, and your sister Sophronia join the Western Presbyterian Church in Palmyra, New York, some time after Alvin's death on November 19, 1823, if God the Father and Jesus Christ told you in 1820 that none of the

---

[41]The Pearl of Great Price, Joseph Smith – History 1:19, 26, emphasis added.

sects were right, that all of the sects were wrong, and that you "must join none of them"?

Why did your mother, Lucy, your brothers Hyrum and Samuel, and your sister Sophronia join the Western Presbyterian Church in Palmyra, New York, in about 1824 if you gathered your family together on September 22 or 23, 1823 (as your brother William said that you did), and told them that the angel who appeared to you on September 21 and 22, 1823, told you that "none of the sects were right" (as William and your mother said that you did), and the "whole family" believed everything you said? And why did they remain there as practicing Presbyterians until 1828? And why did they stay on the records of the Presbyterian Church until 1830? And why did you put your name on a class book and try to join the Methodist Church in Harmony, Pennsylvania, in 1828 after your marriage to Emma? And after you much later said that you and Emma had acquired the golden plates in 1827?

Did those family members really join the Presbyterian Church in the midst of an 1820 revival before the vision of the Father and the Son as your 1838-39 Pearl of Great Price account of the First Vision said that they did? If so, why did they join the Presbyterian Church in the midst of an 1823 revival before the vision of the Angel Moroni as the 1834-35 History said that they did? Did they join twice? Were there two separate revivals? How do you explain these conflicting accounts?

How do you explain the fact that all the evidence showed that there was no revival in Palmyra and vicinity in 1820, or in 1823, or until after Alvin's death, and then not until 1824 and 1825?

Do you really claim that your mother and siblings joined the Presbyterian Church before the death of Alvin Smith on November 19, 1823?

Wasn't your father, Joseph Smith Sr., angry, and didn't he refuse to attend the Presbyterian Church and to join the

Presbyterian Church, as your mother and your siblings did, because he was a Universalist and disliked the sermon that the Reverend Benjamin Stockton, an important figure at the Palmyra revival in 1824, preached at Alvin Smith's funeral in November 1823?

How do you explain the fact that the Reverend George Lane did not commence his ministry in Palmyra until July 1824? When you tied him to earlier revivals for which no evidence exists? Do you claim that your mother and siblings joined the Presbyterian Church before the Reverend Lane arrived?

How do you explain the fact that the Reverend Benjamin Stockton, Lucy, Hyrum, Samuel and Sophronia's pastor, did not commence his ministry in Palmyra until 1824?

How do you explain the fact that there were no "[l]arge additions" "made to the Methodist, Presbyterian, and Baptist churches" in Palmyra in 1823 as the 1834-35 History said that there were?[42] Or in 1820 as the 1838-39 Pearl of Great Price account said that there were?[43]

On September 21, 1823, Oliver and Joseph said that Joseph received a visit from a heavenly messenger so that all the wishes of his heart were granted. That radiant messenger came from the presence "of the Lord, to deliver a special message, and to witness to him *that his sins were forgiven,* and that his prayers were heard . . . ."[44] *What is wrong with that picture?* If Joseph's sins were forgiven in 1821, "<in the 16th year . . .>" of his age (as the one hundred thirty year suppressed 1832 Holographic Account said that they were), then why did he desperately need to have them forgiven again in 1823 when he was seventeen (as the 1834-35 History said that they were)? If Joseph saw God the Father and Jesus Christ in 1820 after he experienced the terrifying dark power of the

---

[42]"Letter III" (Cowdery and Smith's 1834-35 History), *Messenger and Advocate*, December 1834, 42, emphasis added.

[43]"[G]reat multitudes united themselves to the different religious parties." (The Pearl of Great Price, Joseph Smith – History 1:5, emphasis added).

[44]"Letter IV" (Cowdery and Smith's 1834-35 History), *Messenger and Advocate*, February 1835, 79, emphasis added.

underworld, why did he succumb to the "corruption" of his human nature and to the "gratification of many appetites" offensive in the sight of God, before September 21, 1823, when he went to his room to ask God "to forgive him for his sins and follies"?[45]

How are these contradictions supposed to be explained? In 1834 Joseph Smith and Oliver Cowdery described the first published account of Joseph Smith's first ever encounter with any heavenly messenger. Until that encounter occurred in 1823, that seventeen-year-old boy didn't know "*if a Supreme being did exist.*" In 1838-39 Joseph ignored that early report and changed his course to say that he had seen the Father and the Son, before he saw the angel with the plates. He did not report that amended account of a new and unfamiliar first 1820 encounter until 1842. In those awkward back-and-forth chronological revisions, the vision of the Angel Moroni and the vision of the Father and the Son were disconcertingly blurred. The elements of those two contradictory accounts were strangely altered. "The scene has ceased to be God the Father appearing in glory to Joseph in the woods but has become the Angel Moroni appearing to him in his bedchamber. The time is not the spring of 1820 but the early autum [*sic*] of 1823,"[46] three-and-a-half years later.

> *In fact, this is not Joseph's First Vision at all, but his Vision of the Angel Moroni, with Joseph not merely oblivious of the fact that he had once been visited of the Father and the Son, but, worse yet, concerned to know whether a supreme being ever existed.*[47]

---

[45]LaMar Petersen, *The Creation of the Book of Mormon: A Historical Inquiry* (Salt Lake City, UT: Freethinker Press, 2000), 10.

[46]Walker, ed., *Dale Morgan on Early Mormonism*, 249, emphasis added.

[47]Ibid., emphasis added. This stunning contradiction has defeated the best efforts of various Mormon scholars. Francis W. Kirkham physically separated Oliver and Joseph's unitary account of the 1823 "revival leading to the vision of an angel." He divided the account "into two separate parts . . . in order to make it appear to the reader that Cowdery describes an 1820 revival (1:443) as well as an 1823 vision of an angel." (Francis W. Kirkham, *A New Witness for Christ in America: The Book of Mormon*, enl. 3d ed. [Salt Lake City: Utah Printing Co., 1959] 1:85, 447-48, quoted in Petersen, *The Creation of the Book of Mormon*, 13 n 26).

The facts are the same in the two accounts, right down to their discordant result: A revival had occurred in the neighborhood of Palmyra which had begun among the Methodists and spread to the other denominations; the Smith family in general and Joseph in particular had been aroused; Joseph's mother and sister [and two of his brothers] had joined the Presbyterian church; and he himself, too much troubled by doubts about all of the denominations to join with any, had been led to seek in prayer the assurance and firm guidance that God alone could give. The discordance between the two accounts is not a mere matter of dates; it results from an enlargement of the original conception.[48]

No one seemed to know in 1834-35 that Joseph had been visited in his youth by the Father and the Son, and no one would know until "Joseph[,] having wrought further upon the divinity of his calling," allowed Orson Pratt to carry "the story to the world" (where it was first published in Scotland) in 1840.[49]   Morgan described the chronology in these terms:

Contemporary publications . . . illustrate the understanding of the early Mormons that their church dated from no earlier an event than the appearance of an angel to Joseph Smith in 1823.   The pronouncement by the Father and the Son that all churches before Mormonism were corrupt, which has yielded such aid and comfort to the modern church, is an argument so obviously useful that it is impossible to conceive that the early missionaries would not have employed it had they known of it.[50]

---

[48]Walker, ed., *Dale Morgan on Early Mormonism*, 249, emphasis added.

[49]Ibid.

[50]Excerpts from those important "Contemporary publications" are reprinted at Appendix B, 341-61, Walker, ed., *Dale Morgan on Early Mormonism*, 249, emphasis added.   The documents printed in whole or in part in Dale Morgan's unsparing Appendix share "two things in particular": 1) "their undoubted contemporaneity," and 2) "their lack of information that Joseph Smith had a visitation in 1820 from the Father and the Son." (Ibid., 341-61).

EVOLUTION: INVENTING AN UPGRADE

E.D. Howe's nineteenth-century expose painted early, excitable Mormonism, the Mormons, the Mormon Bible and the Smith family with a dark brush.[51] Mormonism had crossed the spunky journalist's path and divided his family, and he was admittedly angry. Joseph Smith's image was tarnished in *Mormonism Unvailed,* perhaps the most influential anti-Mormon book to be developed in the nineteenth century. Howe's eighty-some informants – real people, respected, valued citizens, neighbors of the Smiths and relatives of Emma – were founding members of different communities in at least two states. Howe's witnesses knew the Smiths well, often from years of personal interactions. They were wary of the Smiths and didn't like or trust them. The reputations of the Smiths in New York and Pennsylvania (where Joseph Smith Jr. and Joseph Smith Sr. practiced their juggling trade) would be identified with ritual magic, money digging, magic circles, magic daggers, magic talismans, treasure guardians, petulance and various things occult.[52] Joseph's own authorized 1834-35 History was an effort to tidy up the Mormon prophet's untidy image and a response to *Mormonism Unvailed.*

Joseph's God – seemingly sensitive to the prophet's somewhat less than stellar reputation and to his admissions of frailty – sent the following message: "'God has chosen the foolish things of the world to confound the things which are mighty . . . .'"[53] This curious condescension recognized that Joseph was incredibly flawed. This early demeaning conclusion would disappear when the 1838-39 Pearl of Great Price Account published in the *Times and Seasons* in 1842 achieved greater circulation.[54] The "foolish things" clause was

---

[51]Eber D. Howe, *Mormonism Unvailed: Or, A Faithful Account of That Singular Imposition and Delusion* (Painesville, OH: E.D. Howe, 1834; reprint, New York: AMS Press Inc., 1977).

[52]None of which are mentioned in the LDS manual *Teachings of Presidents of the Church – Joseph Smith* (Salt Lake City: The Church of Jesus Christ of Latter-day Saints, 2007).

[53]"Letter IV" (Cowdery and Smith's 1834-35 History), *Messenger and Advocate*, February 1835, 79.

[54]Dale Morgan described the reversal:

> Let us consider, in particular, the difference in mood between the legend of his life as Joseph delineated it in 1834-35 and that

not a ringing endorsement. One would think that the Lord had many choices when it came to deciding who should be the most important man on earth, his own divinely authorized oracle. The heavenly messenger who delivered a message to Joseph Smith in 1823 didn't exactly describe an unblemished prophet chosen to ring in the dispensation of the fullness of times.

The 1835 message to the 1823 Joseph, like so much else, would be forgotten by the time the prophet was finished recreating the past. An 1838-39 correction would retroactively ascribe to the then thirty-two year-old visionary the majesty he must have thought that he deserved. After several preliminary drafts and before the story was finished, Joseph would craft a vision sufficiently grand. That vision would not continue to describe a flawed, "foolish," "base," "despised" thing, but would rather describe the majestic prophet the boy by then had become. Paul's demeaning message to the Corinthians would not be repeated in the Pearl of Great Price Account.

Dale Morgan described an evolutionary process.

> *The First Vision itself is a conception investing him with an ineffable dignity, for in all recorded history, to what other men have the Father and the Son appeared? And how much more imposing the revised version of the words spoken to Joseph by Moroni than the version so thoughtlessly quoted to the church in*

---

legend as he refurbished it in 1838. The earlier version of the events which led to the founding of his church was written under the long shadow cast by his money-digging past, accounts of which were rife in the very country to which the Mormon missionary efforts were being most insistently addressed. Apology and explanation to set the facts at defiance color the whole of this first official history of the coming forth of the Book of Mormon.   By the time Joseph came to dictate his autobiography, he had survived not merely that small crisis but upheavals of proportions so seismic as to have all but destroyed him. The burden of his theme reflected both this change in his fortunes and the hardening of his spririt [sic]: now his theme was not apology but indictment. Not his own frailties but the stony heart of mankind stood arraigned.

(Walker, ed., *Dale Morgan on Early Mormonism*, 253).

1835! The autobiography pictures Moroni as telling a great prophet of his destiny, that prophet foretold by Malachi, Isaiah, and Joel, whose words men shall heed under penalty of being destroyed. Far more modest is the language of Moroni as recounted in 1835. The only scripture Moroni had thought to mention was, embarrassingly, the reminder given by Paul to the Corinthians, that God was wont to choose the foolish things of the world . . . to confound the things which were mighty. It is not surprising that Joseph, as time went on, searched the Bible for scripture less tactless in its application, more befitting the man he had become.[55]

Before 1842 and after 1834, the 1834-35 History was the gold standard. There wasn't anything else. For nearly a decade, as far as anyone knew, the vision of the angel in charge of the plates described the first public account of Joseph Smith's first encounter with a heavenly messenger.[56] Even so, the "vision of the angel who led him to the gold plates was not mentioned in the [Preface to the] first edition of the Book of Mormon."[57]

Is the Founding Story About the Gold Plates?

Joseph's multi-volume *History of the Church* – which started under his supervision but ended after his death as the post-mortem effort of a mysterious committee of equally undependable others – is partly autobiography and partly biography marketed as autobiography. The *"History of Joseph Smith, the Prophet by Himself"* presents a portrait of a prophet without warts painted by sycophants. It scrubs out incriminating evidence of ritual magic

---

[55]Walker, ed., *Dale Morgan on Early Mormonism*, 253-54, emphasis added.

[56]The messenger described in the 1834-35 account didn't mention the words of Malachi, Isaiah, the Acts of the Apostles or the "dread poetry" of Joel. The 1823 messenger described in the 1838-39 account, an angel of greater grandeur in a vision of greater grandeur, will mention all of those things but neglect to repeat Paul's mournful message to the Corinthians.

[57]Bushman, *Rough Stone Rolling*, 39.

and folklore and denies what is recognizably occult.[58]   Wisdom dictates that it should not now be quoted without access to its underlying resources.   Nevertheless, anyone who challenges these faith-promoting deceptions is immediately labeled "anti-Mormon." Ralph Waldo Emerson put that pathetic apologetic perception in this perspective: "Let me never fall into the vulgar mistake of dreaming that I am persecuted whenever I am contradicted."[59] The *History of the Church* falls apart when it is examined with the aid of uncorrelated resources.

The story of the angel in charge of the golden plates is the *real* founding story of the Church of Jesus Christ of Latter-day Saints; the vision of the Father and the Son is most decidedly not. The gold plates story (there are multiple accounts) has been principally told in what are two separate authorized histories. The first detailed report was included in the *1834-35 History* penned by Oliver Cowdery under the close personal supervision of the prophet Joseph Smith. Cowdery described the process: "With his labor [Joseph Smith's labor] and with authentic documents now in our possession [Joseph Smith's documents], *we hope* to render this a pleasing and agreeable narrative, well worth the examination and

---

[58]Joseph's *History of the Church*, seven volumes, was started by Smith and finished by others. This remarkable and miraculous story of the restoration was completed over a period of twenty-seven years by more than twenty scribes and four different editors. B.H. Roberts, "the defender of the faith," was commissioned to make extensive edits and footnotes. *"The History of Joseph Smith is now before the world, and we are satisfied that a history more correct in its details than this was never published."* (George A. Smith and Wilford Woodruff, quoted in Richard S. Van Wagoner, *Sidney Rigdon: A Portrait of Religious Excess* [Salt Lake City: Signature Books, 1994; paperback 2006], 311). Joseph Fielding Smith made this outsized claim during his tenure as the master of LDS theology: *"The most important history in the world is the history of our Church, . . . it is the most accurate history in all the world."* (Joseph Fielding Smith, *Doctrines of Salvation*, ed. Bruce R. McConkie, vol. 2 [Salt Lake City: Bookcraft, 1955], 199, quoted in Ibid., 198). Wilford Woodruff: *"We therefore, hereby bear our testimony to all the world unto whom these words shall come, that the History of Joseph Smith is true, and is one of the most authentic histories ever written."* (Wilford Woodruff, quoted in Roberts, ed., *History of The Church of Jesus Christ of Latter-day Saints*, Preface, v).

[59]Ralph Waldo Emerson, *Selected Writings of Ralph Waldo Emerson*, William H. Gilman ed. (New York, Toronto: The New American Library, 1965), 57.

perusal of the Saints . . . ."[60] Smith's 1838-39 Pearl of Great Price Account, including the authorized canonized official version of the gold plates story, was not published in the *Times and Seasons* until April 15, 1842.

THE FIRST VISION: "[A] LATE IMPROVISATION, NO PART AT ALL OF HIS ORIGINAL DESIGN."

During his lifetime (1914-1971), historian Dale Morgan did not have access to the earliest accounts of the First Vision, including an 1832 account written by Joseph Smith in his own hand. Discrepant accounts began to surface in and after 1965.[61] Morgan, who did his most meaningful work in the 1940s and 50s, offered these following thoughtful insights:

> *Strangely, although the discordances between Joseph's several versions of his visions [1834-35, 1838-39] have not gone unnoticed, no serious effort has ever been made to set his history of the visions within the framework of the religious history of his time. Although there is much subjective content in the visions, both of the Father and the Son and of the Angel Moroni, Joseph hinged them on reality, drawing upon the troubled memories of the revivals to give them the impact of truth. Thereby he also gave the visions an objective content by which they may be absolutely evaluated.*[62]

Morgan didn't fully describe how perfectly striking the "discordances" between the "several versions" of Smith's visions actually were. He couldn't possibly consider the impact of four different versions of three different missing accounts – the 1832 Holographic Account of a vision of the Son, Joshua 1:1835, Erastus Holmes:1835 or Joshua 2:1835 – the contents of which didn't

---

[60]Oliver Cowdery (and Joseph Smith), "Letter to W.W. Phelps, Esq." (Oliver Cowdery and Joseph Smith's 1834-35 History), *Messenger and Advocate*, vol. 1 no. 1 (October 1834), 13, emphasis added.

[61]Editor's note, Walker, ed., *Dale Morgan on Early Mormonism*, 374.

[62]Ibid., 255, emphasis added.

surface until 1965, 1966, 1969 and 1971, respectively. Even before those accounts gradually emerged from archival oblivion, Smith's reports were internally inconsistent. In 1838 and 1839, Smith ignored those previously unknown (to the laity) early discrepant accounts in order to create a new and "stirring legend of his youth." The contents of Smith's 1838-39 epiphany were not unique. "Visions of God, Jesus, and/or angels occurred to a number of religious believers in early nineteenth-century America. Some of those visionaries published accounts of their experiences. Richard L. Bushman, a professor of history at Columbia University, located thirty-two such pamphlets, and ten of them described visions of 'God or Christ or both.'"[63] Professor Bushman knew how common they were.

Dale Morgan, focusing on the Father, Son and Moroni, saw the forest for the trees:

> *Since Joseph placed his record of his visions before the world, the visions have been argued unceasingly. It is idle to argue over them any longer. His story of the visions is not a record of genuine event, objective or subjective, but a literary creation, of which we have both the [almost unrecognizable] trial draft [the 1834- 35 History] and the finished work [the 1838-39 Pearl of Great Price Account] . . . .*
>
> *It is impossible to grant them any standing, to accept them as an adequate accounting of Joseph Smith's youth, a history standing fierce in contradiction against what has been remembered about him by those who knew him so well.[64]*
>
> *If God had not appeared to Joseph in 1820, or the Angel Moroni in 1823, this was, Joseph could come to appreciate . . . an oversight which, after due*

---

[63]Richard L. Bushman, *"The Visionary World of Joseph Smith,"* Brigham Young University Studies 37, no.1 (1997-1998): 202 n 24, referenced in Petersen, *The Creation of the Book of Mormon*, 9.

[64]Walker, ed., *Dale Morgan on Early Mormonism*, 260, emphasis added.

consideration, he did not hesitate to amend.[65]

Dale Morgan dissects the contradictions implicit in these two great early tellings:

> *The "First Vision" depicts the appearance to Joseph Smith in his fifteenth year of no lesser personages than the Father and the Son to instruct him that the churches of his day were all corrupt and that he must hold himself apart from them. The "Vision of the Angel Moroni" is a companion piece delineating the appearance to Joseph three and a half years later of an angelic messenger sent to reveal to him his great calling as a prophet and rest upon him the responsibility for placing before the world an ancient record, the Book of Mormon.*[66]

Joseph's followers, Morgan firmly declares, "have brought the unconverted from afar" to admire his First Vision mural from the early 1840s, "and multiplied reproductions to scatter abroad to the world."[67]

Morgan was a great grandson of Orson Pratt, a colleague and friend of Joseph's biographer Fawn McKay Brodie, and a serious student of Mormonism. This remarkable historian described the painful evolution of Joseph's conceptions and "his progressive manipulation of reality in the service of his art."[68] As history recoiled, theology blossomed. It becomes apparent that Joseph's vision accounts were rendered on "two panels" (the First Vision of the Father and the Son and the vision of the Angel Moroni). Morgan concluded that the two panels

> *were originally to have been one, that elements from the original conception [the vision of the Angel] were altered and recombined to form a new design altogether [the vision of the Father and the Son], that*

---

[65]Ibid., 261, emphasis added.
[66]Ibid., 245, emphasis added.
[67]Ibid.
[68]Ibid.

it is indeed legend and not history with which we have
to deal in taking up Joseph's account of his youth.[69]

The official 1838-39 Pearl of Great Price Account, the founding
story of the Church of Jesus Christ of Latter-day Saints, is
Mormonism's "Night Watch." Morgan again: "Even iconoclasts,
impressed by the boldness of the conception and the glowing detail,
have so far accepted Joseph's masterpiece, placing upon it the
bizarre hypotheses as to the wellsprings of his personality."[70] After
measuring the First Vision of the Father and the Son, promoted by
the 1838-39 Pearl of Great Price Account, against the vision of the
Angel Moroni promoted by Smith and Cowdery's 1834-35 History,
Morgan offered these additional insights:

> *This [1838-39 Account], in bold outline, is Joseph's*
> *"First Vision." Before we leave it to inspect his*
> *"Vision of the Angel Moroni," let us rig some cross-*
> *lighting and take a penetrating second look, for the*
> *underpaint [of the "two panels"] is by no means*
> *obscured by the paint Joseph subsequently splashed*
> *on with so much assurance, for it readily becomes*
> *apparent that the idea of a visitation from the Father*
> *and the Son was a late improvisation, no part at all of*
> *his original design.*[71]

In that the stories fall apart. Joseph Smith "told two distinctly
different stories to account for his having become a prophet of
God." The first was the "Vision of the Angel Moroni." The second
story was the "Vision of the Father and the Son." These were
different stories told at different times. Initially, they were separate
and distinct, separated by time and contradictory content.

> *The First Vision is the last of these, entirely unknown*
> *to his followers before 1838, when he began to write a*
> *formal autobiography; and was not published in any*
> *form until late in 1840, and not by Joseph himself*
> *until the spring of 1842. Prior to that time, as early as*

---

[69]Ibid., 245-46, emphasis added.
[70]Ibid., 245.
[71]Ibid., 247, emphasis added.

> *1834-35, Joseph had published in the church*
> *periodical a history of his life having an astonishing*
> *different import, and that history [the 1834-35*
> *History] is the defiant underpaint of our metaphor.*[72]

The First Vision of the Father and the Son was supposed to have
been an 1820 event. Joseph did not draft the "official" account
until 1838 (eighteen years after the alleged fact), did not amplify
that account until 1839 (nineteen years after the alleged fact), nor
did he publish it in the *Times and Seasons* until 1842 (twenty-two
years later). The story was amended, after publication in 1843
and/or 1844, and then again in 1902. The second vision, the vision
of the angel in charge of the plates, was supposed to have been an
1823 event. Although it was the first vision to be reported (in 1834-
35), it is now considered to be the *second* vision. The first vision
reported became the second vision, and the second vision reported
became the First Vision.

> *This second of his visions, as his autobiography would*
> *have us believe, or his first, as he originally gave the*
> *Saints to understand, led directly to the writing of the*
> *Book of Mormon and so to the founding of his*
> *church.*[73]

> *Contemporary publications . . . illustrate the*
> *understanding of the early Mormons that their church*
> *dated from no earlier an event than the appearance of*
> *an angel to Joseph Smith in 1823.*[74]

A "CHRONOLOGICALLY IMPLAUSIBLE PICTURE"

The vision of the Angel Moroni preceded the Palmyra revival, the
death of Alvin Smith, the ministry of the Reverend Benjamin
Stockton, the ministry of the Reverend George Lane and the 1824
conversions of Lucy, Hyrum, Samuel and Sophronia Smith to the
Presbyterian faith. The vision also preceded all known reports of a

---

[72]Ibid., 247, emphasis added.
[73]Ibid., 250, emphasis added.
[74]Ibid., 249, emphasis added.

vision of the Father and the Son. The 1838-39 Pearl of Great Price First Vision Account describes an 1824-25 revival as the cause of an 1820 vision of the Father and the Son. The 1834-35 History describes the 1824-25 revival as the cause of an 1823 vision of the angel in charge of the plates. The visions occurred before the revival occurred. The reason for seeking the intercession of the deities followed the intercession of the deities; the effect preceded the cause.

> *From [the Reverend George] Lane's career only, and without reference to the abundant supporting evidence, it can be established that the revival which awakened Joseph to the importance of religion took place from four to five years after the Father and the Son appeared to him, and from a year to a year and a half after the Angel Moroni came to his bedside to reveal his momentous calling.*[75]

Moving the Goal Posts

> *The progressive enlargement of his story, climaxed finally in the breathtaking vision of the Father and the Son, involved him in difficulties that ended by setting reality at complete defiance. He committed himself very early to the thesis that he had been visited by an angel in 1823. When Joseph shifted his ground in 1834-35, drawing upon the troubled emotions of the revivals to give verisimilitude to his account of his visions, the revival of 1824-25 was wrenched out of its proper context and dated back to 1823, for it was logically impossible that Joseph's awakening to religion should have been delayed for months after the Angel Moroni appeared to him. From this position it was only a step to the final ground he occupied, the revival moved back in time three more years [dated back to 1820], and his sanction found in the Father and Son themselves.*[76]

---

[75]Ibid., 257, emphasis added.
[76]Ibid., 259-60, emphasis added.

The vision of the Angel Moroni was an established part of the Mormon firmament long before there was any public account of a vision of the Father and the Son. Oliver Cowdery, Joseph Smith, Lucy Mack Smith, William Smith and the declarations, affidavits, manuscripts, diaries, journals and newspaper accounts of Joseph Smith's contemporaries all support the proposition that the theological event in 1823 preceded the theological event in 1820, and that both of those literary constructs preceded the historical event in 1824-25. The historically irrefutable fact that the revival occurred in 1824-25 makes the 1820 vision of the Father and the Son and the 1823 vision of the Angel Moroni "chronologically implausible" events.

THE BOOK OF MORMON
A RECORD OF THE LAMANITES

Taken from the Plates of Nephi: *"Wherefore, it is an abridgment of the record of the people of Nephi, and also of the Lamanites. Written to the Lamanites, who are a remnant of the house of Israel; and also to Jew and Gentile – Written by way of commandment, and also by the spirit of prophecy and of revelation . . . sealed by the hand of Moroni, and hid up unto the Lord to come forth in due time by way of the gentile – The interpretation thereof by the gift of God."* The Book of Mormon was a record of the Lamanites written to the Lamanites.

BRIGHAM YOUNG AND THE LAMANITES

Brigham Young and the Failure of the Indian Initiative: *Brigham Young said that "he had approached the Lamanites with an open mind" when he joined the church, but that familiarity had bred contempt. In the end his "natural disposition and taste" came to loathe "the sight of those degraded Indians." His feelings of revulsion overwhelmed the expectation that he would convert them and co-exist. "Although he had initially responded to conflicts by calling for restraint, he eventually initiated military reprisals wholly disproportionate to alleged Indian crimes. Perhaps at moments of stress, Young's disgust at the Indians present condition made it easier for him to authorize their deaths." (John G. Turner, Brigham Young, Pioneer Prophet, 213). His conduct in the Great Basin, in the face of conditions on the ground, stood the prophecies of Joseph Smith and the teachings of the Book of Mormon on their head. The book's premise that Native American Hebrews (the "Lord's battle-axe") should reclaim their territories and their previous glory by the shedding of Gentile blood had been wildly misconceived and came to naught. So much for the notion that "converted Indians, thus would serve as God's foreordained vehicle of millennial judgment against the United States and its people." (Ibid., 209). Young concluded as early as 1850: "Let it be peace with them or extermination." (Ibid., 212).*

Brigham Young. Image source: Public domain, via Wikimedia Commons

MORMONISM UNVAILED

Mormonism Unvailed, by E.D. Howe, printed and published
by the author, 1834

This nineteenth-century investigative report has had a profound effect on Mormon studies.

Palmyra, Dec. 4, 1833.

We, the undersigned, have been acquainted with the Smith family, for a number of years, while they resided near this place, and we have no hesitation in saying, that we consider them destitute of that moral character, which ought to entitle them to the confidence of any community. They were particularly famous for visionary projects, spent much of their time in digging for money which they pretended was hid in the earth; and to this day, large excavations may be seen in the earth, not far from their residence, where they used to spend their time in digging for hidden treasures. Joseph Smith, Senior, and his son Joseph, were in particular, considered entirely destitute of *moral character, and addicted to vicious habits.*

Martin Harris was a man who had acquired a handsome property, and in matters of business his word was considered good; but on moral and religious subjects, he was perfectly visionary – sometimes advocating one sentiment, and sometimes another. And in reference to all with whom we were acquainted, that have embraced Mormonism from this neighborhood, we are compeled to say, were very visionary, and most of them destitute of moral character, and without influence in this community; and this may account why they were permitted to go on with their impositions undisturbed. It was not supposed that any of them were possessed of sufficient character or influence to make any one believe their book or their sentiments, and we know not of a single individual in this vicinity that puts the least confidence in their pretended revelations.

Geo. N. Williams,	H. Linnell,	Thos. Rogers, 2d.
Clark Robinson,	Jas. Jenner,	Wm. Parke,
Lemuel Durfee,	S. Ackley,	Josiah Francis,
E. S. Townsend,	Josiah Rice,	Ames Hollister,
Henry P. Alger,	Jesse Townsend,	G. A. Hathaway,
C. E. Thayer,	Rich'd. D. Clark,	David G. Ely,
G. W. Anderson,	Th. P. Baldwin,	H. K. Jerome,

H. P. Thayer,	John Sothington,	G. Beckwith,
L. Williams,	Durfey Chase,	Lewis Foster,
Geo. W. Crosby,	Wells Anderson,	Hiram Payne,
Levi Thayer,	N. H. Beckwith,	P. Grandin,
R. S. Williams,	Philo Durfee	L. Hurd,
P. Sexton,	Giles. S. Ely,	Joel Thayer,
M. Butterfield,	R. W. Smith,	E. D. Robinson,
S. P. Seymour,	Pelatiah West,	Asahel Millard,
D. S. Jackways,	Henry Jessup,	A. Ensworth,
John Hurlbut,	Linus North,	Israel F. Chilson,

Manchester, Nov. 3d, 1833.

We, the undersigned, being personally acquainted with the family of Joseph Smith, sen. with whom the celebrated Gold Bible, so called, originated, state: that they were not only a lazy, indolent set of men, but also intemperate; and their word was not to be depended upon; and that we are truly glad to dispense with their society.

Pardon Butts,	James Gee,	Joseph Fish,
Warden A. Reed,	Abel Chase,	Horace N. Barnes,
Hiram Smith,	A. H. Wentworth,	Silvester Worden.
Alfred Stafford,	Moses C. Smith,	

Note that not one of the witnesses who signed these statements in 1833 mentions an extraordinary event supposed to have occurred "on the morning of a beautiful clear day, early in the spring of eighteen hundred and twenty."

THE COPYRIGHT DEBACLE

William E. McLellin: *"When the Book [of Mormon] was translated, and at the printer's with the copy-right secured, Joseph delivered a long revelation for O. Cowdery and others to go to Kingston in Canada, and get a copy-right secured in that dominion, to the book, in order to sell it and make money out of its sale. They went, but did not succeed; and the revelation proved so false that Joseph never would have it printed . . . ."*

David Whitmer: *David Whitmer (and others) "asked Joseph how it was that he had received a revelation from the Lord"* directing some of the brethren (Hiram Page, Joseph Knight, Josiah Stowell, Oliver Cowdery) *"to go to Toronto and sell the copyright"* to the newly published Book of Mormon. *The issue concerned the fact that the brethren "had utterly failed in their undertaking."* Joseph, unable to explain why the mission didn't go as planned, *"enquired of the Lord"* and got yet another revelation *"through the stone: 'Some revelations are of God,' Joseph's Lord reported, 'some revelations are of men,'* he further said; *'and some revelations are from the devil.'"*

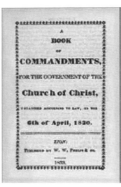

THE 1833 BOOK OF COMMANDMENTS

None of the sixty-five revelations described in the Book of Commandments published in 1833 refer to the conferral of priesthood authority on "May 15, 1829," by John the Baptist, or to the conferral of priesthood authority in "1829, May-June," by Peter, James, and John. Angelic ordination and dual priesthoods of different ranks were not part of the founders' original design.

THE 1835 DOCTRINE AND COVENANTS

William E. McLellin: *McLellin, who presided over the council that decided to print "Joseph's revelations," concluded that the many amendments to the Doctrine and Covenants caused that book to become "a relic of folly." "I have no use for that book . . . ." The first 1835 edition of the Doctrine and Covenants failed to mention an 1820 vision of the Father and the Son.*

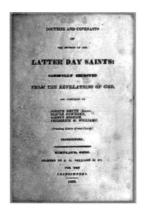

THE MOUNTAIN MEADOWS MASSACRE

"Confronted by two great virtues that had come into conflict – the good name of the church on the one hand and truth on the other, Juanita [Brooks] chose truth." (Wikipedia).

"In the last revision of her book . . . [s]he retained her original conclusion that the existing evidence did not prove that Brigham Young and George A. Smith specifically ordered the massacre, but it showed they 'set up social conditions that made it possible.' In a private letter to Roger B. Mathison of the University of Utah Library, she went much further: she had 'come to feel that Brigham Young was directly responsible for this tragedy.' John D. Lee, she believed, would make it to heaven before Brigham Young." (Bagley, 363)

ANGELIC ORDINATION, PRATT'S 1840 SCOTLAND ACCOUNT

"[I]n the year 1829, Mr. Smith and Mr. Cowdery, having learned the correct mode of baptism, as recorded in the 'Book of Mormon [3 Nephi 11],' had a desire to be baptized [immersed in a 'liquid grave']; but knowing that no one had authority to administer that sacred ordinance in any denomination, they were at a loss to know how the authority was to be restored, and while calling upon the Lord with a desire to be informed on the subject, a holy angel appeared and stood before them, and laid his hands upon their heads, and ordained them, and commanded them to baptize each other, which they accordingly did."

Although Pratt said the angel was supposed to have come in 1829, no ordinary member of the Church knew that for more than five years. Oliver Cowdery and Joseph Smith called the angelic ordination event to the attention of the unsuspecting Saints in the Messenger and Advocate, a Mormon publication, in October 1834.

PRIESTHOOD, PRATT'S 1840 SCOTLAND ACCOUNT

Although the word "priesthood" wasn't used to identify "authority" in the Church of Christ until 1831, and although the high priesthood was not bestowed upon lower authority elders until the Fourth Conference of the Church in Ohio on June 3, 1831, Pratt's 1840 account described how miraculous events identified with the authority of the higher priesthood were supposed to have occurred at Manchester, New York, on April 6, 1830, the day the Church was officially organized. Some few members, according to the 1840 version of the vision of the Father and the Son, were "called and ordained by the spirit of revelation and prophecy and began to preach and bear testimony, as the spirit gave them utterance." Many, according to Pratt, "were brought to repentance, . . . immersed in water confessing their sins," and "filled with the Holy Ghost by the laying on of hands." Many "saw visions and prophesied. Devils were cast out, and the sick were healed . . . ." All of those things were supposed to have occurred before the first lower authority elders received the Melchizedek Priesthood at the Fourth Conference of the Church held at Kirtland, Ohio, on June 3, 1831.

Messenger and Advocate, vol. 1 no. 5,
February 1835.

"Letter IV," Oliver Cowdery to W.W. Phelps, Esq.,
Messenger and Advocate, February 1835, p. 78.

MESSENGER AND ADVOCATE, 1834-1835

1834-35 History: *In this first authorized history of the Church of the Latter Day Saints, Cowdery and Smith meticulously dated the revival they described as having preceded the visit of the angel in charge of the plates. The following correction was made to that official history of the rise of the Church in the Messenger and Advocate in February 1835 by Oliver Cowdery.*

> *You will recollect that I mentioned the time of a religious excitement, in Palmyra and vicinity to have been in the 15th year of our brother J. Smith Jr.'s age – that was an error in the type – it should have been in the 17th. – You will please remember this correction, as it will be necessary for the full understanding of what will follow in time. This would bring the date [of the religious excitement that preceded the vision of the angel in charge of the plates] down to the year 1823.*

In 1834 and 1835, in the history Oliver Cowdery and Joseph Smith collaborated to prepare, the Palmyra revival that preceded the vision of the angel in charge of the golden plates occurred in 1823. In 1838-39, in the history Joseph Smith and others prepared, the Palmyra revival was removed from what was then a revised account of the visit of the angel in charge of the plates. The altered version of the vision of the angel found in the 1838-39 Pearl of Great Price Account was not preceded by the religious excitement associated with the Palmyra revival.

In 1838-39, Joseph Smith changed history to say that the Palmyra revival preceded a previously unfamiliar vision of the Father and the Son in 1820, ignoring his earlier report that the Palmyra revival preceded the vision of the angel in charge of the plates in 1823. The vision of the Father and the Son, he changed his mind to say, occurred during a great Palmyra revival that preceded that previously unreported event supposed to have occurred "on the morning of a beautiful clear day, early in the spring of eighteen hundred and twenty."

History demonstrates to a certainty that the Palmyra revival didn't precede the vision of the Father and the Son in 1820, or the vision of the angel in charge of the plates in 1823, or the death of Alvin Smith on November 19, 1823. The Palmyra revival occurred as a well-documented historical fact, and after all of those events, in 1824-25.

Pen and ink sketch of Joseph Smith by
Sutcliffe Maudsley, 1844.

RESTORATIONS

Restoration scholars (John Hamer, Steven L. Shields) estimate "that well over 400 groups are extant within the LDS restoration movement. From this perspective, the Church of Jesus Christ of Latter-day Saints [the Brigham Young remnant of the Restoration] is not a continuation of the original church Joseph Smith founded, but rather, its largest schism." (Steven L. Shields, Lindsay Hansen Park)

LYMAN WIGHT

In 1841 Lyman Wight, "The Wild Ram of the Mountains," became a member of the Quorum of the Twelve Apostles. After the death of Joseph Smith in 1844, he led a group of Latter-day Saints to Texas, created a settlement, broke with Brigham Young and became the President of a new Church of Christ. Still later, Wight sided with the claims of William Smith, Joseph's brother, and then eventually with those of Joseph Smith III, Joseph's son. After Wight's death, most of his followers joined the RLDS movement, the church of Joseph Smith III, a congregation that survived to become the Community of Christ. (Wikipedia, April 14, 2017).

Image source: Courtesy of Community of
Christ Archives, Independence, Missouri
[Public domain], via Wikimedia
Commons.

A CONSTITUTION FOR THE KINGDOM OF GOD

Willard Richards photo. By Likely, Lucian R. Foster
[Public domain], via Wikimedia Commons.

WILLARD RICHARDS

An early partial draft of a segment of a proposed Constitution for the Kingdom of God read by Richards to the Council of Fifty (110):

> *Art. 1ˢᵗ. I Am, the Lord thy God . . . to me alone belongs the right, the power, the majesty, the glory, and the dominion; I alone am King of Kings, and Lord of Lords; I alone am the rightful lawgiver to man; I alone have a right to judge the inhabitants of the earth, which is my footstool; [p. (153)] and I will acknowledge no other law, rule, power, Authority or dominion, than that which is instituted by me, the great I Am, And no other government, Kingdom, Dominion, authority, power, rule, or law, shall be acknowledged by my people.*

> *Art. 2ⁿᵈ. I the Lord will do nothing but what I have revealed or shall reveal unto my servants the prophets and I have appointed one man, holding the keys and authority, pertaining to my holy priesthood, to whom I will reveal my laws, my statutes, my ordinances, my Judgements, my will and pleasure concerning my kingdom on the earth. [p. (154)], (113).*

BERTRAND RUSSELL

"Even if the open windows of science at first make us shiver after the cozy indoor warmth of traditional humanizing myths, in the end the fresh air brings vigor, and the great spaces have a splendor of their own."

Image Source: Public domain,
via Wikimedia Commons.

CHAPTER SIX

"The City of Joseph"

[T]he doctrine of "sealing" for an eternal state was introduced, and the Saints were given to understand that their marriage relations with each other were not valid. That those who had solemnized the rites of matrimony had no authority of God to do so . . . . That they were married to each other only by their own covenants, and that if their marriage relations had not been productive of blessings and peace, and they felt it oppressive to remain together, they were at liberty to make their own choice, as much as if they had not been married.[1]

John D. Lee

I . . . entered into covenants to stand by my family, to cleave to them through time and eternity. I am proud to say I have kept my obligations sacred . . . . Others refused to enter into these obligations, but agreed to separate from each other, dividing their substance, and mutually dissolving their former relations on friendly terms. Some have mutually agreed to exchange wives and have been sealed to each other as husband and wife by virtue and authority of the holy priesthood.[2]

John D. Lee

---

[1]John D. Lee, *Mormonism Unveiled; Or; The Life and Confessions of the Late Mormon Bishop, John D. Lee* (St. Louis, MO: Bryan, Brand & Company; New York, NY: W.H. Stelle & Co., 1877; photomechanical reprint of the original 1877 edition, Salt Lake City: Modern Microfilm Co.), 146.

[2]Ibid., 165.

PROLOGUE

"Surely you jest" – A God of Trifles

Before July 12, 1843, before Joseph published the revelation that became (but not until 1876) Section 132 of the Doctrine and Covenants, there was no shortage of domestic anxiety in the city of the Saints (Nauvoo, Illinois). The Latter-day Saints were told that while they had solemnized their marriages in a secular forum, they were not married by the law of God for time and eternity. Those who were legally married by the civil sovereign, meaning almost everyone (including Joseph and Emma), were not spiritually married in heavenly terms.[3] They were bound only by their secular covenants which, if not satisfactory, were revocable. Thus anyone whose marriage relations "had not been productive of blessings and peace" was declared free to revisit his or her commitments. This controversial doctrine predicted chaotic domesticity.

In 1841 and 1842 (years that immediately preceded the final draft of a polygamic revelation) and in 1843 (up to the time the revelation was read to the Nauvoo High Council), Joseph was married many times. The revelation the prophet was supposed to have received on July 12, 1843, was not privately read to the High Council, in a meeting without minutes to men who could be trusted not to tell the

---

[3]Joseph Smith wasn't *sealed* to his legal wife Emma until 1843. After the doctrine of sealing for an eternal state (which nullified secular deputization and civil divorce) was introduced and prior to 1843, Joseph's marriage to Emma was a bargain of no eternal consequence made without the "authority of God to do so," because "the true priesthood was taken from the earth with the death of the Apostles and inspired men of God." (Ibid.). No conferral of sealing authority preceded Joseph's admitted intimacy with Fanny Alger, with whom he may have been involved as early as 1831 (when she was just fourteen years of age). "Joseph Smith did not claim the power to 'bind on earth and seal in the heavens' eternally, until Elijah appeared to himself and Oliver Cowdery in the Kirtland temple on 3 April 1836 . . . ." (Grant H. Palmer, "Sexual Allegations against Joseph Smith, 1829-35," pp. 3-4 of 6). Miss Alger left Kirtland as early as 1836. She left the state "and quickly rejected counsel by marrying a non-Mormon, something one would not expect from a Mormon plural wife." (Ibid., p. 4 of 6). Joseph was sealed to Fanny by proxy and posthumously on April 4, 1899, under the direction of President Lorenzo Snow. (Salt Lake Temple Sealing Records, Book D, 243, GS film 184, 590 [LDS Family History Library]).

truth, until August 12, 1843.[4]   The revelation described various invisible early generic unions in general terms and commanded Emma Smith to accept them. By July 12, 1843, Joseph had already married (in addition to Emma) about twenty-eight women.[5] And between July 12 and August 12, 1843, between the written receipt of the controversial revelation and the confidential report to the High Council, he would marry about four more. In his frenzied pursuit of partners, the prophet was like a man possessed. Preceding and following the secret declaration of "The Polygamous Principle" to some of his trusted colleagues, Mormon theology explored the endowment, deification, eternal marriage, sealing, polygyny, polyandry and adoption.

Now the Master of the Universe, the Creator of Heaven and Earth, the great last hope of insistent billions, whose voice by Mormon reckoning has gone essentially unheard no matter the crisis for more than 1600 years, concerns himself with the reordering of marital priorities in Nauvoo, Illinois. In 1842 and 1843, Joseph's God will tell Mrs. Henry Jacobs, Mrs. Norman Buell, Mrs. George Harris, Mrs. Orson Hyde, Mrs. Orson Pratt, Mrs. Hiram Kimball, Mrs. Robert D. Foster, Mrs. William Law, Mrs. Adam Lightner, Mrs. Windsor Lyon, Mrs. David Sessions, Mrs. John Cleveland, Mrs. Jabez Durfee, Mrs. Stephen Poulterer, Mrs. Edward Sayers, Mrs. Jonathon Holmes and Mrs. Lucien Woodworth that it was his holy will that they should also plurally marry their prophet. These women, with some few exceptions, would have two husbands for time, but only one for time and eternity.

Sometime later, William Smith, the prophet's brother who had been a founding Apostle and the Patriarch, told Isaac Sheen "that he [William Smith] had the right to raise up posterity from other

---

[4]Official Minutes, 1843: *"August 12, 1843; Saturday*. [At Hyrum Smith's Office.] No buisness [sic] before the Council. Teaching by Pres[iden]ts Hiram Smith & William Marks." Thomas Grover, attendee, 1869: "Hyrum Smith reasoned upon said Revelation for about an hour, clearly explaining the same, and then enjoined it upon said Council, to receive and acknowledge the same, or they would be damned." (Affidavit, Thomas Grover [6 July 1869], subscribed and sworn before James Jack). See *The Nauvoo City and High Council Minutes*, John S. Dinger, ed. (Salt Lake City: Signature Books, 2011), 467-68 n 61.

[5]George D. Smith, *Nauvoo Polygamy: "... but we called it celestial marriage"* (Salt Lake City: Signature Books, 2008), 621-23.

men's wives," that "it would be an honor conferred upon them and
their husbands, to allow him that privilege, and that they would
thereby be exalted to a high degree of glory in eternity."[6] William
didn't invent that concept, but rather gave voice to his brother's
doctrine. It suited William like it suited his older brother. God
would command previously married women to revisit their
spiritually barren commitments. He would tell them one at a time,
by means of special revelations, that they should share themselves
with their legal husbands and Joseph (as well as Brigham, Heber
and William) for time. They should then give themselves and their
biological children with their less-than-eternal civilly deputized
husbands to a time and eternity husband (exclusively and for
exaltation[7]) in a Mormon afterlife.[8]

---

[6]Isaac Sheen to Editor, *Cincinnati Daily Commercial*, 22 May 1850 (William's
take on Joseph's doctrine was that polyandry was sexual), quoted in Richard S.
Van Wagoner, *Mormon Polygamy: A History* (Salt Lake City: Signature Books,
1986), 245 n 7. "Sheen insisted that Smith offered his wife to him 'on the same
terms that he claimed a partnership in other men's wives.'" (Ibid.). From Brother
Joseph's mouth to Brother William's ears. Raising up "posterity" with the wives
of other men was the ultimate objective of these marriages and of the plurality wife
doctrine. Brigham Young proved when he had a child with Zina Huntington
(Jacobs) (Smith) (Young), but one case in point, that polyandry was sexual.

[7]When Zina Huntington (Jacobs) left her first husband, Henry Jacobs, to
become the (polyandrous) wife of Brigham Young, "President Young told Zina
D[iantha] if she would marry him she would be in a higher glory." (Mary
Firmage, "Recollections of Zina D.H. Young" [LDS Archives], quoted in Van
Wagoner, *Mormon Polygamy*, 43). On October 8, 1861, at General Conference,
Young explained divorce was not required. "There was," he said, "another way –
in which a woman could have a man – if the woman preferred – another man
higher in authority & he is willing to take her. & her husband gives her up – there
is no Bill of divorce required in the case it is right in the sight of God." (Ibid.).
Augusta Adams Cobb, a married woman with seven children, was secretly sealed
to Brigham Young before she was divorced from the father of her children (at the
request of the father). "Gentile law" (including civil marriage) "was publicly
denounced as early as 1847 by Orson Pratt [the Apostle of Polygamy] in a sermon
recorded by Wilford Woodruff . . . ." All the ordinances of the gospel administered
anywhere in the world "since the Aposticy of the [gospel] Church," including the
ordinance of marriage, "was illegal." According to Pratt, those "begotten through
. . . illegal marriage [meaning everyone, even Joseph] were bastards not Sons."
Until they were adopted (by the law of adoption) "into the Priesthood" they would
never become "sons & legal heirs to salvation." (Wilford Woodruff quoting Orson
Pratt, "27 August 1847," in Ibid., 43-44). Elenore McLean Pratt, Parley P. Pratt's
twelfth wife whose legal husband murdered her polyandrous husband, Parley,
dismissed her legal marriage: "The sectarian priests have no power from God to

Four of Joseph's nominees – Mrs. Orson Pratt, Mrs. William Law, Mrs. Robert D. Foster and Mrs. Hiram Kimball – declined to share "connubial bliss" with their prophet in this life or the next. They were seen to prefer the civil law to the spiritual law, the law of man to the law of God, the law of the state to the law of the theocracy. They will reject the "new and . . . everlasting covenant," meaning polygamy, and they will be "damned," because "all those who have this law revealed to them must obey the same," because "no one can reject this covenant and be permitted to enter into my glory."[9] And when Hyrum Smith presented the principle to the High Council in that meeting without minutes, to men who could be trusted not to tell the truth, that is exactly what he told them. Accept the principle or you will be damned.[10]

In a sense, most of the women approached by Joseph Smith from 1841 to 1843 were told that it was God's will that they, whether single or married, should give themselves to the prophet to be married or not. Every new alliance or marriage was supposed to be a reflection of the will of God. "It is his holy will," he told them, "that I should have you." That was the message given to the women

---

marry; and a so-called marriage ceremony performed by them is no marriage at all." (Elenore Pratt, quoted in Ibid., 44).

[8]William Law, a former counselor in the First Presidency, reported that Joseph Smith came to the Law home in the middle of the night when William was absent and told Jane Law, William's wife, that "the Lord had commanded that he should take spiritual wives to add to his glory." When asked to further explain, Mrs. Law reported that Joseph had "asked her to give him half her love; she was at liberty," he said, "to keep the other half for her husband . . . ." (Ann Eliza Young, *Wife no. 19*, cited in "William Law [Latter Day Saints]," [accessed 25 June 2018]; Internet, available from https://en.wikipedia.org/wiki/William_Law_%28Latter_Day_Saints%29#cite_note-wife 19-4, p. 2 of 4).

[9]Doctrine and Covenants 132:3-4.

[10]*On May 14, 1843*, Presiding Patriarch and Associate President Hyrum Smith assured "a citywide congregation that only the Devil would give a revelation approving 'wife's & concubines.'" (D. Michael Quinn, *The Mormon Hierarchy: Origins of Power* [Salt Lake City: Signature Books in association with Smith Research Associates, 1994], 638). *On August 12, 1843*, Hyrum Smith, who married Mercy Rachel Fielding (Thompson), Catharine Phillips, Lydia Dibble (Granger) and Louisa Sanger in August and September, before and after the meeting, informed the members of the Nauvoo High Council in a closed proceeding that if they didn't receive and acknowledge a revelation approving "wives and concubines" that "they would be damned." (Thomas Grover Affidavit, *The Nauvoo City and High Council Minutes* [ed., Dinger], 467-68 n 61).

who gave themselves and their biological children with their legal husbands to the Mormon prophet, to be shared for the short term but not for the long run. "This is the principle," according to Joseph, the situational principle "on which the government of heaven is conducted – by revelation adapted to the circumstances in which the children of the kingdom are placed." "Whatever God requires is right, no matter what it is . . . ."[11] Every new encounter was the subject in one way or another of a special revelation, whether written (Nancy Rigdon, Sarah Ann Whitney, Mrs. Vilate Kimball, Mrs. Marinda Nancy Hyde) or oral (Mrs. Sarah Pratt, Mrs. Melissa Schindle, Mrs. Lucinda Harris), blessing every new sacred arrangement (or rearrangement).

Joseph's God approached the children of the kingdom in these minuscule matters with a degree of specificity close to unparalleled in the long history of the Hebrews. God was always at the center of this confusing maelstrom, according to Joseph, and the deity's executor was a fearsome angel who threatened the Church and the life of the prophet with a drawn or flaming sword. The presence of the angel put the agency of the laity at risk. The angel and his terrible swift sword cost Henry Jacobs his wife and children, who left Henry after the death of Joseph Smith to become the wards of Brigham Young for time before being assigned to the prophet Joseph in a Mormon afterlife. When Joseph Smith secretly married Henry's Zina, she was seven months pregnant with Henry's child.

"[E]ven things which might be considered abominable to all who understand the order of heaven only in part" are right when known to be given of God "and sanctioned by special revelation."[12] Those approached by their prophet, who was said to be speaking the will of the Lord, found solace in God's meaningful personalized instructions. So much so that we could confidently lay "aside all our traditions and former notions in regard to marriage [Elizabeth Whitney],"[13] then surrender ourselves and those we loved (Sarah Ann Whitney) to the tender care of the messenger. The messenger was a man twice Sarah's age and the husband, when he married

---

[11]*History of the Church*, 5:134-36.
[12]Ibid.
[13]Elizabeth Whitney, quoted in Todd Compton, *In Sacred Loneliness: The Plural Wives of Joseph Smith* (Salt Lake City: Signature Books, 2001), 347.

her, of no less than fifteen other wives, including many women already married to other men. "Newel and Elizabeth [Whitney] received a revelatory witness concerning the principle. Elizabeth wrote, ' . . . our prayers were unceasing . . . the Lord was very merciful to us; He revealed unto us His power and glory.'" In the later words of Helen Mar Kimball, who was one of Joseph Smith's fourteen year old wives, "They [her friends the Whitneys] willingly gave to him [Joseph Smith] their daughter, which was the strongest proof that they could possibly give of their faith and confidence in him as a true Prophet of God."[14]

Sarah Ann Whitney could not have known that she had secretly just become the prophet's sixteenth wife. She did know, when she also married her recently widowed uncle in public in a pretended ceremony, that the cynical second marriage was intended to conceal the existence of the more important first marriage from the prying eyes of those outside of the faith and other less favored Saints. People who knew nothing about the prophet's private life. She wouldn't live with Emma and the children in the prophet's home, and she knew the prophet wouldn't acknowledge the marriage or provide for her support. Everything that happened to Sarah occurred under the revelatory supervision of a "merciful" God who "heard and approved" the Whitney's prayers ("a halo of light encircled us").

In 1842 many of Joseph's prominent men and women, more than thirty of them, signed fraudulent *Certificates* to be published in the *Times and Seasons*. In those *Certificates*, they told people who were uninformed, wherever they were, that nothing but conventional marriage (monogamous ceremonies open to the general public and dutifully recorded) was being practiced in the Mormon enclave. Many of those witnesses perjured themselves in declaratory support of traditional marriage and monogamy. Joseph's faithful signators were lying for their Lord, a duplicitous deity who understood "the order of heaven" and approved deception to achieve his "polygamic" objectives. Joseph Smith, the man who did know his history, the master of a harem, and the editor of the *Times and Seasons*, actually published the disingenuous *Certificates*.

---

[14]Helen Mar Kimball quoted in Ibid.

1842 EVENTS: SHOTS OVER THE BOW

Of all the rumors, the most contagious were the ones that originated in failed courtships. Nothing did more to alert the citizens than the story of a young woman who was cornered by a desperate Brigham Young in 1842; her story was closely followed by Nancy Rigdon's anger over Joseph Smith's importunate pleas, telling her that whatever God wanted was right.[15]

Martha [Brotherton] is remembered not only for refusing Young's suit but, more importantly, for making a public issue of it. This occurred as early as November 1841, but at least by April 1842, when Hyrum Smith publicly denounced reports of the incident.[16]

Brigham Young knew about sexual consent alliances, secret wives, polygyny and polyandry before Joseph's deceitful monogamous marriage *Certificates* were prepared and published in the *Times and Seasons* in October 1842. "[A]s early as February 1842, Senior Apostle Brigham Young began performing ceremonies that united Joseph Smith in some way with women who were already married to other men."[17] Young officiated at the January 6, 1842, marriage of Joseph Smith to Smith's sister-in-law, Agnes Coolbrith (Smith), the widow of Don Carlos Smith, five months after the death of Joseph's younger brother.[18]

Prior to April 1842, Brigham Young and Joseph Smith tried to force Miss Martha Brotherton, not yet of age and a recent English emigrant, to marry Young, an already married man more than twice her age. The Mormon leaders attempted to effectuate a secret

---

[15]George D. Smith, *Nauvoo Polygamy*, 264, emphasis added.

[16]Ibid., 265, emphasis added.

[17]Mary E.R. Lightner, "sealed to the said Joseph Smith by Pres Brigham Young," quoted in D. Michael Quinn, "Evidence for the Sexual Side of Joseph Smith's Polygamy," presented to the Mormon History Association's Annual Conference (Calgary, Alberta, Canada: 29 June 2012; expanded, finalized 31 December 2012; circulated mid-2013), 42.

[18]George D. Smith, *Nauvoo Polygamy*, 261.

marriage on the day of that request without her parents' consent. Until that unfortunate occurrence, Miss Brotherton didn't know and couldn't have known that the Church that brought her to America under false pretenses believed, taught or practiced polygamy. In 1870, many years later and following word of her death in England, Brigham Young (who failed to obtain the consent of the young convert to marry him in this life) had Martha Brotherton secretly sealed by proxy to him, still without her consent, for eternity in the life to come. Before that day in 1842, as was the case with all of the English Saints, and for the longest time, Miss Brotherton had not been told that the LDS Church had secretly embraced the doctrine of polygamy.

Brigham Young secretly married Lucy Ann Decker Seely, taking her as a plural wife, on June 14, 1842, shortly before those infamous monogamous *Marriage Certificates* were published in the *Times and Seasons* by the prophet Joseph Smith, the editor of the *Times and Seasons*. "[T]his was the first firmly dated polygamous marriage after Smith's initial twelve."[19] Polygamy was secret Mormon doctrine shared with a carefully selected few, and the domestically aggressive Brigham Young, a well-positioned insider, was the ranking Apostle. On October 1, 1842, Joseph Smith presented the name of Abigail Works (who would marry Brigham Young on January 28, 1846) as one of his thirty-one *Marriage Certificate Certificants*. Before Abigail Works became Brigham Young's thirtieth wife at the age of sixty-four, she was the mother of Brigham Young's first and legal wife, Miriam Works (who died in 1832), and Brigham Young's mother-in-law.

On April 7, 1842 (months before the publication of the controversial *Certificates* which fraudulently endorsed monogamous marriage as Mormon truth), Hyrum Smith explicitly repudiated "a report" that Brigham Young, Heber C. Kimball, Hyrum "and others of the Twelve" had shut a sister in a room for several days and tried to convince her that men should have two wives.[20] Although hard to believe, it was in the midst of just such incredible turmoil, shortly after the incident with Miss Brotherton and in April 1842, that Joseph Smith unsuccessfully approached Miss Rigdon. It was a

---

[19]Ibid., 262.
[20]Ibid., 269.

distasteful, poorly considered encounter supported by a document that has passed to posterity as unsettling.[21]

Mary Clift and Gustavus Hills

Gustavus Hills (sometimes Gustavius or Gustave Hills) joined a Missouri Danite, an oath-bound Ebenezer Robinson, as an editor of the *Times and Seasons* after the death of Joseph Smith's brother, *Times and Seasons* editor Don Carlos Smith, in August 1841. Robert B. Thompson, who had been Don Carlos' co-editor, died twenty days later. Robinson, who became an editor for the second time, was then joined by Gustavus Hills (author's spelling), and "Both served as editors until early 1842."[22] On October 23, 1841, two then well-regarded Latter Day Saints, Gustavus Hills and Orson Spencer, were appointed Aldermen and added to the Nauvoo City Council. At that same time, John Taylor, Orson Pratt, Hugh McFaul and Heber C. Kimball joined Hills and Spencer as "Co[uncil]l[o]rs" to the Nauvoo City Council.[23] Until early 1842, when the *Times and Seasons* was sold and the editors (by then Ebenezer Robinson and Gustavus Hills) were replaced, Hills walked (as a journalist, an editor and an Alderman) in rarefied circles privy to secrets.

Robinson, one of Smith's *Times and Seasons Certificants* in October 1842, would much later admit that he knew that polygamy had been talked about "in secret" for more than a year before the *Certificates* were published (and since 1841). Gustavus Hills, Robinson's co-editor at the *Times and Seasons* "until early 1842," knew or should have known about polygamy before October 1842, when Robinson and Robinson's wife signed *Joseph Smith's Monogamous Marriage Certificates*. Robinson could not but have known about Gustavus Hills' controversial case before the Nauvoo High Council.

---

[21]*History of the Church*, Roberts, ed., 5:134-36.

[22]Matthew Roper, Paul J. Fields and Atul Nepal, "Joseph Smith, the *Times and Seasons*, and Central American Ruins," *Journal of the Book of Mormon and Other Restoration Scripture*, vol. 22 no. 2 (2013), 88.

[23]Minutes (29 October 1841), *The Nauvoo City and High Council Minutes* (ed., Dinger), 30.

Both of the editors who guided the fortunes of the *Times and Seasons* until early 1842 (when the Church purchased the periodical and Joseph took control of the office as the publication's editor) knew that there was a secret system encompassing informal (sexual consent) alliances in Nauvoo. Robinson and his wife, who moved out of the Printing Office when the Church purchased the paper and the building (a home/office), knew that Willard Richards, the prophet's confidant, moved into the Printing Office with Apostle Orson Hyde's wife in 1842 while Orson was on a lengthy mission abroad. Robinson knew about the alleged relationship between Willard Richards and Marinda Nancy Johnson (Hyde) before Mrs. Hyde then later, and while Orson was still on his mission abroad, became one more polyandrous Mrs. Joseph Smith in April 1842, prior to the publication of the *Times and Seasons Certificates* in the fall of 1842. Editor Smith knew to a monstrous certainty that the *Certificates* were fraudulent before he ever published them.

Joseph Smith married about thirteen women in the nine months that immediately preceded the publication of the controversial *Certificates* (he had previously taken three other plural wives – including one set of already married sisters – in 1841). Including Emma, that then came to a total of not less than seventeen women, not including Fanny Alger.[24] He then secretly married at least twenty-one additional wives (at a frenetic pace) in the about thirteen months that immediately followed the publication of the disingenuous *Certificates*.[25] He actually married about thirty-four women in twenty-one months.

One can begin to recognize the ragged beginnings of Joseph's secret system in this report:

> *September 3, 1842: Saturday* [before twelve prominent Mormon men and nineteen prominent Mormon women certified and declared that traditional monogamous marriage – was the only rule or system of marriage practiced in Nauvoo]. [The Nauvoo Stake High] Council met according to

---

[24]George D. Smith, *Nauvoo Polygamy*, 621-23.
[25]Ibid.

> adjournment. A Charge was preferred against
> Gustavius Hills by Elisha Everett[,] one of the
> teachers of the Church[,] for illicit intercourse with
> a certain woman by the name of Mary Clift by
> which she is with child[,] and for teaching the said
> Mary Clift ~~that~~ that the heads of the Church
> practised such conduct & that the time would come
> when men would have more wives than one &c.[26]

Polygamy was in the air for Gustavus Hills, a Nauvoo insider. The
charges against Hills were raised with the High Council slightly less
than one month before the publication of the nothing but traditional
marriage *Certificates* in the *Times and Seasons*, Hills' former paper,
on October 1, 1842. Joseph Smith had by then taken the editorial
places of Hills and Ebenezer Robinson.

Gustavus Hills taught Mary Clift, who became pregnant with his
child, and in advance of the controversial *Certificates*, that
polygamy, or something like polygamy, was going to be the future
rule. Mary Clift to Gustavus Hills was not unlike Fanny Alger or
Lucinda (Morgan) (Harris) to Joseph Smith. She was involved in a
sexual consent relationship with a Nauvoo Alderman who, until
early that year when he was replaced by Joseph Smith, had been an
editor of the *Times and Seasons*. Gustavus Hills' message to Mary
was that the leaders of the Church had sexual consent relationships,
and that the time would come when men, including those men,
"would have more wives than one." He knew whereof he spoke.
The relationship between Gustavus Hills and Mary Clift, faithful
Mormon members, wasn't a marriage and didn't involve a
ceremony or a sealing. What Joseph had already allegedly had with
Fanny Alger and Lucinda Morgan Harris (sexual consent
relationships without a marriage or a sealing) was what he initially
proposed to have with Sarah Pratt and Nancy Rigdon, women
supposed to have denied the will of God when they both refused.

> Three months after Sarah Pratt turned Joseph
> Smith's proposition down in late 1840 or early 1841,
> he married Louisa Beaman on April 5, 1841. During

---

[26] *The Nauvoo City and High Council Minutes* (ed. Dinger), 424.

this short interval, Smith had streamlined his approach beyond mutual sexual consent. He had modified his sexual practice by requiring a marriage/sealing ceremony, requiring a witness, requiring that the ceremony be performed with his permission and by an authorized priesthood holder. In other words Smith's sexual practice became structured and religiously institutionalized.[27]

When Mary Clift was deposed on August 29 and September 4, 1842, just before the publication of Joseph Smith's *Times and Seasons Certificates* on October 1, Mary Clift, an unmarried woman, upon her oath averred:

> [T]hat she was pregnant with a child which, if born alive, may be a bastard and that Gustavus Hills was the father of such child. The Said Gustavus Hills[,] about 4 or 5 weeks since[,] requested deponent to remove to Columbus (Adams county) until after her confinement and [said that] he would assist her with support as far as his means would permit; and that such ilicit conduct was practiced by the heads of the Church and that the time would come when men would have more wives than one, and he wished that time would come.[28]

---

[27]Grant H. Palmer, "Sexual Allegations against Joseph Smith and the Beginnings of Polygamy in Nauvoo," 15. That notwithstanding, twelve of the thirty-three women "listed by Todd Compton as being plural wives of Joseph Smith" did not "have an officiator, ceremony or witness to their marriage/sealing." Those women included Fanny Alger and Mrs. Lucinda (Morgan) (Harris) in the 1830s, "Mrs. Sylvia Sessions, Mrs. Elizabeth Durfee, Mrs. Sarah Cleveland, and widow Delcena Johnson, in 1842; and single women, Flora Ann Woodworth, Sarah and Maria Lawrence, Hannah Ells, Olive Frost and Nancy Winchester, in 1843." Palmer wonders, "Is inadequate record keeping the problem or are some of these women – especially the married ones – sexual consent relationships?" Ibid., 16.

[28]Affidavits, Mary Clift, 29 August and 4 September 1842, reproduced at Minutes (4 September 1842), *The Nauvoo City and High Council Minutes* (ed. Dinger), 424-25 n 63. Mary Clift later became a plural wife (one of three Clift sisters – Mary, Eliza and Sarah Ellen – all married to Joseph Smith's trusted friend Elder Theodore Turley, who was destined to become the husband of five wives). (George D. Smith, *Nauvoo Polygamy*, 629). On "6 Feb[ruary] [1841] – [Joseph] Smith tells the Nauvoo high council not to excommunicate Theodore

On September 4, 1842, Mary Clift (names were redacted from the September affidavit read to the Council and retained with the Council's Minutes) again averred that "near the middle of the month" in January 1842, while "on the way between the House of [REDACTED] Br[other] [REDACTED] said [REDACTED] did hold illicit and carnal connexion with her [REDACTED]." He had, she said, "frequently used seducing efforts privious to that time." Miss Clift then further described what else the Alderman and former Editor reported to her. "Said [Gustavus Hills' (name redacted)] proposed several times to give [Mary Clift (name redacted)] some medicine or drug to carry it [the baby] off or cause an abortion. Said [Gustavus Hills (name redacted)] told Deponent [Mary Clift] that he was intimate with another woman in town besides his wife [Hills was married to Elizabeth Ann Mansfield] & that the authorities of the Church countenanced and practiced illicit connexion with women & said there was no harm in [such] things provided they kept it secret."[29]

Another woman by the name of Esther Victoria Smith, who married Amos Botsford Fuller in 1832, provided additional evidence at Hills' trial on September 4, 1842. Mrs. Fuller reported that the defendant

> told her it was lawful for people to have illicit intercourse if they only held their peac[e] & that ~~the time would~~ it was agreeable to the practice of some of the leading men or heads of the Church. It [presumably the seduction by Hills of Mrs. Fuller] took place the Thursday before the Choir was dismissed in the upper part of Town near the Bluff at 9 o'clock in the evening – She was going home &

Turley [one of the Lord's counterfeiters] for 'sleeping with two females . . . .'" (Quinn, *Origins of Power*, 632).

[29]Affidavit, Mary Clift, 4 September 1842, Minutes, *The Nauvoo City and High Council Minutes* (ed. Dinger), 424-25 n 63. On August 29 and September 4, 1842, when Mary Clift was deposed and when the proceedings occurred, Joseph Smith had already secretly "married" about sixteen women, not including Emma (or Fanny Alger), at least ten of whom were already previously married to, supported by and free to cohabit with their legal husbands. The marriage list is also seen to include two widows, including Joseph's sister-in-law. (George D. Smith, *Nauvoo Polygamy*, 621-23).

> he offered & went to accompany her and this took
> place upon the way – She further testified that Mary
> Clift joined the Choir at Br[other] Joseph Smiths.[30]

Gustavus Hills provided the Council with a document that contained his interrogation of Mary Clift. He then called several witnesses on his behalf, but was unable to prove "that he was inocent [sic]."[31] The Nauvoo Stake High Council, after due consideration, unanimously voted to disfellowship Gustavus Hills, a member of the Nauvoo City Council.

Joseph Noble

Joseph Bates Noble told a notary in June 1869 that "in the fall of the year A.D. 1840 [long before the publication of the controversial *Certificates*] Joseph Smith taught him the principle of Celestial marriage or a 'plurality of wives,' and that the said Joseph Smith declared that he had received a Revelation from God on the subject . . . ."[32] Before he became the Editor of the *Times and Seasons* (just after Gustavus Hills) and before he took the first of the sixteen wives (not counting Emma or Fanny Alger), whose *secret* marriages preceded the filing of the fraudulent *Times and Seasons Certificates*, Joseph informed his future brother-in-law, Joseph Bates Noble, that he had received a "Revelation from God" concerning a "plurality of wives" (polygamy). "Plural marriage had been in the air since the Book of Mormon was published, most especially since Smith began to teach it to such friends as Joseph Bates Noble in 1840-41. These clandestine instructions to one individual at a time grew into a community movement by 1842 as an increasing number of men brought 'celestial wives' into their homes."[33]

---

[30]Affidavit, Mary Clift, 4 September 1842, Minutes, *The Nauvoo City and High Council Minutes* (ed. Dinger), 425-26.

[31]Ibid. When Hills questioned Mary Clift on 4 September 1842, "He asked her when she stayed overnight at his house, to which she answered, 'Near the middle of Jan[uar]y.' She said she accompanied him home on three successive nights from the 'singing schools' he taught, where she must have been a student. 'The first two nights [she] slept [in bed] with [his] wife [and] the next night with [the] children.'" (Ibid., 426 n 65).

[32]Joseph Bates Noble quoted in George D. Smith, *Nauvoo Polygamy*, 260.

[33]Ibid., 242, emphasis added.

Joseph Smith and Joseph Noble performed marriages for each other, in the particular case of Smith on April 5, 1841 (Louisa Beaman), which was long before the publication of those *Monogamous Marriage Certificates* in the *Times and Seasons* on October 1, 1842. Noble officiated at the marriage of Joseph Smith to Louisa Beaman (a secret affair in a grove of trees with Miss Beaman dressed like a man and in disguise). Exactly two years later, on April 5, 1843, Smith officiated at the marriage of Joseph Nobel to Sarah B. Alley. Noble's legal wife, Mary Beaman, was Louisa Beaman's sister. Joseph Smith asked Joseph Noble to "step forward and assist him in carrying out the said principle" of plural marriage. The Mormon prophet begged Noble, like he later begged the Whitneys, not to "betray me to my enemies." "I have placed my life in your hands," he said. "This conversation predated by several months the marriage 'of Joseph Smith to Noble's sister-in-law, Louisa Beaman, over which Noble would officiate in [and perhaps even before] April 1841."[34] And it concerned events of an unusual and extraordinary nature a year-and-a-half or so before the Mormon prophet supervised the publication of the disingenuous *Times and Seasons Certificates* on October 1, 1842.

These witness statements (the *Times and Seasons Monogamous Marriage Certificates*) were the flip side of the witness statements attached to the Book of Mormon concerning the existence of the golden plates (those supported the notion that there were golden plates; these supported the notion that there was no plural marriage). With the passage of time and in retrospect, the accuracy of the Nauvoo statements can now be better measured. What time and study have disclosed is not a pretty picture. On the testimony of two or three witnesses, Church members had long been taught to depend. In this particular case, Joseph Smith, the editor of the *Times and Seasons*, presented thirty-one witnesses, every one of whom was wrong to the many times married Joseph Smith's certain knowledge. Many of those same witnesses are now known to have perjured themselves in declaratory support of traditional marriage and monogamy. It is a disconcerting but undeniable fact that Mormonism's nineteenth-century polygamists held traditional marriage and monogamy in utter contempt.

---

[34]Joseph B. Noble, Affidavit (26 June 1869), in "40 Affidavits on Celestial Marriage" (1869), quoted in George D. Smith, *Nauvoo Polygamy*, 261.

Plural Marriages

In 1841 or soon after, Smith spoke the language of plurality to a coterie of privileged insiders known to include Brigham Young, Heber C. Kimball and John Taylor. During that period, to those chosen ones (who together with others came to be called the "Quorum of the Anointed"), he presented what soon became Mormonism's most distinctive principle as a direct order from God, reinforced by an angel with a drawn or flaming sword. While it was the men, always the men, to whom the details of the doctrine were most insistently directed, it would be a serious mistake to forget the prophet's polygamous wives. Before the *Times and Seasons Marriage Certificates* were published in 1842, Joseph had taught the polygamous doctrine to more than a few women, no less than sixteen to be sure, meaning by that to say each of the sixteen women he had plurally married up to and until October 1, 1842 (and then also to an unknown number (not necessarily insignificant) of those who had rejected him).

Before Nauvoo was vacated in 1846, the number of privileged insiders and their dependents had grown to include "about 200 men and 700 women with children, amounting, all told, to perhaps ten percent of Nauvoo's estimated 1846 population of 12,000."[35] "After the westward migration, the 196 families who had practiced polygamy in Nauvoo came to account for a total of 1,134 wives and 3,171 children, an average incidence of 5.8 wives and 16.2 children per family."[36] The most important (and privileged) men in the Mormon Church became the most obvious and ardent advocates of what Joseph Smith proudly (but never publicly) described as "the most holy and important doctrine ever revealed to man on the earth."

Traditional monogamous marriage, according to Joseph (and Brigham Young), couldn't begin to get you where you needed to go. Joseph's God said this to the Saints: "For behold, I reveal unto you a new and an everlasting covenant ["the *principle* and *doctrine* of . . . many *wives* and *concubines*"[37]]; and if ye abide not that covenant,

---

[35]George D. Smith, *Nauvoo Polygamy*, 260.
[36]Ibid., 286.
[37]Doctrine and Covenants 132:1, emphasis added.

then are *ye* damned; for no one can reject this covenant and be permitted to enter into my glory."[38] That is exactly how Hyrum Smith presented the controversial doctrine to the Nauvoo High Council (an assembly of monogamous men) at that meeting without minutes on August 12, 1843. Polygamy wasn't policy and *a* principle; it was *doctrine* and *the principle*. The controversial doctrine preserved in Section 132 of the Doctrine and Covenants was then and is now inextricably tied to exaltation in a peculiar Mormon afterlife. Two members of the First Presidency, including the President of the Church, are sealed to more than one woman as this is written. They are celestial polygamists. Polygamy, the law of the Church, will govern their Mormon afterlife. The canonized doctrine, the most distinctive signature of the nineteenth-century Church, was suspended, not dismissed.

"Every one of Smith's Twelve Apostles who were present when he began marrying women in 1841 became a polygamist, as did brothers Hyrum and William, and his uncle John."[39] Before the Saints left Nauvoo in 1846, there had been at least 523 plural marriages entered into there (523 plural wives "married to 196 [polygamous] men"). "Adding the total number of first wives to plural wives produces a grand total of 717 wives (unadjusted for separation or unmarried widows) for an overall ratio of 3.7 wives per husband."[40] There were at least twenty plural marriages in Nauvoo in 1841 and 1842 – sixteen of which directly implicated Joseph Smith – and at least "four plural husbands" – Joseph Smith, Brigham Young, Heber C. Kimball and Reynolds Cahoon.[41] There were fifty-two more plural marriages in 1843, sixty-eight in 1844, and five hundred twenty-three by 1846.[42] From February to

---

[38]Ibid., 132:4, emphasis added.

[39]George D. Smith, *Nauvoo Polygamy*, 243. Joseph Jr., Joseph Sr., Joseph Jr.'s brothers Hyrum and William, and Joseph Sr.'s brother, Joseph Jr.'s uncle John, all became Presiding Patriarchs of the Church of Jesus Christ of Latter-day Saints. Every one of those first five Smith patriarchs was a polygamist.

[40]Ibid., 285.

[41]Ibid., 309. "[T]here would have been six [plural husbands] if John C. Bennett had not been expelled and Vinson Knight had not died." Brigham Young: "[N]o man can be perfect without the woman, so no woman can be perfect without a man to lead her . . . ." One man was capable of leading many women. (*Times and Seasons*, 1 July 1845, 955, quoted in Ibid., 277).

[42]Ibid.

November 2, 1843, Joseph Smith married about twenty-one additional women.[43]

In 1842 Joseph Smith invited the Presiding Bishop, Vinson Knight, to plurally marry Philinda Myrick. Knight's legal wife, Martha McBride (Knight), according to Knight family records, "is said" to have been "the first woman to give her consent for her husband to enter Plural Marriage."[44] Martha consented; Emma did not. Smith's legal wife (Emma) is not presently known to have given her consent (or to have been asked to give her consent) or even to have known about Smith's sixteen polygamous marriages in 1841 and 1842, with the possible exception of Eliza R. Snow. Or to have given sanction to his 1830s relationships with Elizabeth Winters, Marinda Nancy Johnson, Fanny Alger, Lucinda Morgan Harris, and/or with a number of less visible others. It is now known that not less than twenty-three women were sealed to Joseph Smith before Emma herself was sealed to him on May 28, 1843.[45] Martha McBride (Knight) appears to have been but one of them. Martha Knight was "resealed" to the then deceased Joseph Smith on October 12, 1844, "at which time she [also] became Heber C. Kimball's mortal wife [for time]." On January 26, 1846, "her life-marriage to Kimball was reconfirmed." Six months after Vinson Knight died, Philinda Myrick (Knight) married Daniel Hutchinson Keeler. Three years later "she was sealed to her first husband, Levi Myrick, with Keeler standing as proxy. Apparently, Knight was not expected to have a companion in the afterlife."[46]

Nauvoo's 1842 *Pre-Certificate* polygamous leaders included Joseph Smith (Mormonism's Prophet and Founder), Apostle Brigham Young (the Senior Apostle and Joseph's Utah Territory Successor), Apostle Heber C. Kimball (a future First Presidency First Counselor), Reynolds Cahoon (a Counselor to Bishop Newel K. Whitney and a member of the Council of Fifty), and Bishop Vinson Knight, a polygamous man who died before the *Times and Seasons Certificates* were published. Women already practicing *Pre-*

---

[43]Ibid., 621-23.
[44]Bella Belknap, "Martha McBride Knight," quoted by George D. Smith, *Nauvoo Polygamy*, 308.
[45]George D. Smith, *Nauvoo Polygamy*, 621-23.
[46]Ibid., 308-9.

Certificate polygamy included Joseph's *Times and Seasons* signators Emma Smith, Sarah M. Cleveland and Eliza R. Snow. Women who knew or should have known about polygamy included Joseph's signators Elizabeth Ann Whitney, Thirza Cahoon, Phoebe Woodruff, Leonora Taylor and Polly Johnson, then also sixteen plural wives married to Smith separate from and before the publication of the controversial *Certificates*. Then those who had refused his invitation to join him as a wife or concubine in some legally prohibited practice. That more undocumented listing should be amended to include Miss Nancy Rigdon and some unknown number of others, including at least some of the four married women who are known to have rejected Smith's proposals. In addition, every signator knew or soon would know that "the saints were given to understand that their marital relations with each other were not valid" because of "the doctrine of 'sealing' for an eternal state."[47] Traditional marriage be damned. Legal marriages (pursuant to Gentile covenants) were rudely dismissed by the plurally privileged class in the City of the Saints.

The "system of marriage" that was really "being practised in the church of Jesus Christ of Latter-day Saints" beginning in 1841 and 1842, and in a limited way in 1831, couldn't be described in the Book of Doctrine and Covenants, which defied the facts to say (from 1835 until 1876) that, "we declare that we believe, that one man should have one wife; and one woman, but one husband . . . ," and "that all marriages in this church of Christ of Latter Day Saints, should be solemnized in a public meeting, or feast . . . ."[48] On October 1, 1842, the day the infamous *Certificates* were published in the *Times and Seasons*, the editor Joseph Smith had seventeen wives, not including Fanny Alger; about ten of them were polyandrous women (married to more than one husband at the same time). Two of his plurally married women were sisters, and two others were widows. Smith married a mother and her daughter; another woman, Louisa Beaman, was married to the prophet in a grove of trees while dressed like a man. Sarah Ann Whitney was married to Joseph and then (in order to conceal that

---

[47]Lee, *Mormonism Unveiled; Or, The Life and Confessions of the Late Mormon Bishop, John D. Lee*, 146.
[48]"Marriage," Doctrine and Covenants (1835), 251; Doctrine and Covenants 101, after 1844, 109.

marriage) to her recently widowed uncle. Every polygamous marriage was secret, nothing was conventional, and no one said anything in public about the impact of an agency-defeating angel equipped with a flaming sword. Polygamy, when it was presented, wasn't an option. It was an ultimatum ("and if ye abide not that covenant, then are ye damned").

RAGGED BEGINNINGS
ILLICIT INTERCOURSE – 1841-1842:
THE ASSAULT ON TRADITIONAL MARRIAGE

Chauncey L. Higbee

On May 21, 1842, about four months before Joseph Smith presented thirty-one questionable witnesses in declaratory support of traditional marriage and monogamy, and before the trial of one of Joseph Smith's *Times and Seasons* predecessors, Gustavus Hills, the uncomfortable consequences of Mormonism's "secret informal alliances," those "sexual consent relationships" that both preceded and followed the advent of confidential polygamy, began to publicly surface. On May 21, 1842, George Miller, an obedience freak, presented a charge to the Nauvoo Stake High Council. Miller, a high-ranking Nauvoo Mason, was positively determined to discredit Joseph's former high ranking associate, another high ranking Nauvoo Mason, former Mayor and Assistant Church President, John C. Bennett.[49] Miller charged "Chancy L Higbee" (Major General Bennett's Nauvoo Legion *aide-de-camp*) with "unchaste and un-virtuous conduct with the widow [Sarah] Miller and others. [Higbee] plead [sic] not guilty." Two of Smith's future *Times and Seasons Monogamous Marriage Certificants*, Aaron Johnson and Newel Knight, members of the Nauvoo High Council, were among the four men selected to speak for and against "Chancy L Higbee" in a disciplinary proceeding, thus making the case for the Council to decide.[50]

---

[49]After the death of Joseph Smith, Miller and Bennett bit their tongues to become disciples in the society formed by James J. Strang. That society, another schism, also included many (if not most) of the Smiths.

[50]Minutes (21 May 1842), *The Nauvoo City and High Council Minutes* (ed. Dinger), 413-14.

The victim, widow Sarah Searcy Miller, just twenty-seven years old on May 21, 1842, was unlucky in love. In 1831 she married James J. Miller. "Sarah and James converted to Mormonism and in 1840 moved to Nauvoo where James died the next year at age 31." One year later, in December 1842, Sarah Miller married John Thorp. When the Nauvoo High Council discovered that Thorp had an estranged wife – a condition that wasn't always important – the Council "disallowed the marriage." The state didn't decide to end the marriage; the High Council did. Hyrum Smith didn't read the revelation on "wives and concubines" (Doctrine and Covenants, Section 132) to the Council until August 12, 1843. John C. Bennett had an estranged wife and abandoned children before he joined the Church and at the very moment the Lord praised him in 1841 in one of the prophet's revelations. In November 1843 Sarah Miller married John Bleazard. "Five years later, John Bleazard would marry Sarah's daughter, Mary Jane, as a plural wife." After the family immigrated to Utah in 1850, John took a third wife, and then much later a fourth. "After the family helped settle Las Vegas, Sarah divorced John and married George Pectol."[51]

But this is May 1842, and the issue on the Council's agenda is "Chancy [Chauncey] L[.] Higbee," "the widow [Sarah] Miller and others," and illicit intercourse. Three witnesses testified that Higbee "had seduced [several women], and at different times [had] been guilty of unchaste and unvirtuous conduct with them . . . ." On May 24, 1842, the testimony of Mrs. Sarah Miller (a widow), Miss Margaret (Nyman) and "Matilda Neyman" was taken against "Chancy Higbee." The witnesses testified that Higbee "taught the doctrine that it was right to have free intercourse with women if it was kept secret &c and also taught that Joseph Smith autherised him to practise these things &c."[52] The claim was that Joseph Smith authorized Chauncey Higbee's sexual consent relationships. "The sisters said Higbee had advised them that the prophet approved of 'spiritual wifery' but gave instructions to keep the matter a secret because 'there was no sin when there is no accuser.'"[53] Those contentions, which were raised over and over again, were central to these and other related proceedings. In an

---

[51]Ibid., 414, editor's note 36.
[52]Ibid., 414-15.
[53]Van Wagoner, *Mormon Polygamy*, 24, cmphasis added.

attempt to negate what the witnesses testified he had earlier said, in order to protect his prophet and in advance of his trial, Higbee "signed an affidavit saying 'he never knew said Smith to countenance any improper conduct whatever, either in public or in private, and that [Smith] never did teach [Higbee]' in private or public that an illicit intercourse with females was under any circumstances justifiable."[54] Higbee's Affidavit must be seen to have failed, for he was convicted as charged.

Over the lifetime of Mormon polygamy, men, women and children, including Joseph Smith, lied for the Lord and the cause. Difficult circumstances associated with the practice of plural marriage, a crime in the state of Illinois and almost everywhere else, made such duplicity inevitable. Smith never publicly admitted that he or the Church ever practiced polygamy, but he repeatedly denied that they did.

The testimony against Higbee (and of course the prophet) resembled the later testimony against Gustavus Hills on September 4, 1842, when the unmarried pregnant Mary Clift repeated the "it was right to have free intercourse" litany as having been presented to her by her equally prominent offender (Gustavus Hills). The modern editor of the Nauvoo High Council Minutes noted that Sarah Miller's case in May of 1842 was but "the first" of many. "This [the case of the widow Miller against Chauncey L. Higbee] is the first of over twenty cases the high council will adjudicate over the next few months stemming, in part, from Joseph Smith's introduction of plural marriage."[55] Those cases were unintended consequences of Joseph Smith's secret introduction of plural marriage, or of something like it (sexual consent relationships, "wives and concubines"), in 1840, 1841 and 1842. One must surmise that however many cases were brought to the council for adjudication, very many more, multipliers of more, were not. Joseph Smith had presented the ragged edges of this demanding doctrine to a burgeoning group of privileged insiders. It was a

---

[54]"Affidavits Contained in John C. Bennett's Letters," *The Wasp* (31 August 1842), quoted in *The Nauvoo City and High Council Minutes* (ed. Dinger), 415 n 37.
[55]Minutes (21 May 1842), *The Nauvoo City and High Council Minutes* (ed. Dinger), 415 n 37.

doctrine that he had first introduced, as it is well to remember, to the missionaries to the Lamanites as early as 1831.

John C. Bennett and William Smith

On and/or before May 25, 1842, Mrs. Catherine Fuller Warren alleged/confessed *to the members of the Nauvoo High Council* that she had shared intimacy (been "unchaste and unvirtuous") with John C. Bennett, Chauncey L. Higbee, Darwin Chase, Lyman O. Littlefield, Joel S. Miles and George W. Thatcher[56] – highly placed seemingly faithful Mormon men, friends of the prophet Joseph Smith. In another venue and even later, others alleged that she had also shared her bed with the prophet Joseph Smith. Mrs. Warren informed the Nauvoo High Council that "[N]early a year ago," somewhere close to the spring and summer of 1841, she began having sexual intercourse with John C. Bennett.[57] Then not only with Bennett, but with "Chauncy Higbee and the prophet's younger brother, Apostle William Smith."[58] Mrs. Warren and some other women had been persuaded to have "sexual intercourse" with anyone Assistant President John C. Bennett sent to them. Mrs. Warren's notorious encounters preceded the seduction of the widow Sarah Miller. Someone who wanted to hide these facts from the public tried to eradicate William's name (William Smith's name) from the manuscript of testimony that described William's visits to the newly married Mrs. Warren and to the widow Sarah Miller in 1841 and 1842 "for sexual intercourse."[59]

---

[56] *The Nauvoo City and High Council Minutes* (ed., Dinger), 417 n 45.

[57] Ibid., 417 n 46.

[58] Van Wagoner, *Mormon Polygamy*, 24. William Smith's first cousin, Apostle George A. Smith (a future Counselor in the First Presidency), "later complained about 'Wm Smith Commit[t]ing iniquity & we have to sustain him against our feelings." (Wilford Woodruff, *Wilford Woodruff's Journal, 1833-1898: Typescript*, ed. Scott G. Kenney [Signature Books, 1983], 4:157.

[59] Quinn, *Origins of Power*, 220. "Two women [Catherine Fuller Warren and Sarah Miller] identified William Smith as one of Bennett's friends who visited for sexual intercourse and said that William told them his brother approved of spiritual wifery. According to a later reminiscence [from Apostle Lorenzo Snow], Joseph Smith then asked Brigham Young to excommunicate his brother for 'adultery and many other sins.' As Young was about to act, however, the prophet changed his mind, accused the quorum's president of maligning the Smith family, and required Young to exonerate William. Then someone (probably Joseph) tried

The women's early paramours, elders in unison, "taught the doctrine that it was right to have free intercourse with women and that the heads of the Church also taught and practised it . . . ."[60] They were seen to support the efficacy of sexual consent relationships (meaning unembarrassed but confidential adultery). Mrs. Warren did not choose to ignore the teachings of the prophet's brother, Apostle William Smith, or those of Dr. John C. Bennett,[61] the Assistant President of the Church and Joseph's well-appointed confidant.[62] She did what she did, she said, because no less than seven prominent Latter-day Saints, including General Bennett and Apostle William Smith, all of them alleged sexual partners at one time or another, taught her that sex between consulting adults was not a sin, even among married people, if the parties kept their proceedings secret.

Mrs. Warren's Mormon men spoke to the efficacy of sexual consent relationships without the benefit of any kind of formal ceremony (that is to say free but secret love). For all intents and purposes, Mrs. Warren was a polyandrous consort, something less than a concubine. Her suitors are supposed (alleged) to have said that the highest leaders of the Church, Bennett was one, and William Smith was another, "practised" with others what her suitors proposed to practice with her. Those representations, she said, "caused her to be led away thinking it to be right . . . ." When she said she finally learned it wasn't right, she confessed her sins, repented, promised not to do it again and begged forgiveness. "[S]he was restored to fellowship by the unanimous vote of the Council."[63] Mrs. Warren famously reported that Dr. John C. Bennett told her that if she became pregnant, he would attend to that. That same point was

---

to eradicate William's name from the women's testimony [preserved in an 1842 manuscript]." (Ibid.).

[60]*The Nauvoo City and High Council Minutes* (ed. Dinger), 417.

[61]As a consequence of their various 1842 proceedings, Gustavus Hills, Chauncey Higbee and John C. Bennett were disfellowshipped or excommunicated after proof of the charges against them. "Despite Catherine Warren's testimony implicating William Smith along with Bennett and Higbee, instead of being excommunicated, he was sent on a mission to Tennessee. Retained in his apostleship, he became presiding church patriarch on 24 May 1845," after the death of Joseph Smith. (Van Wagoner, *Mormon Polygamy*, 24).

[62]William Law Interview with Dr. W. Wyl, 30 March 1887, published in *Daily Tribune* (*Salt Lake Tribune*) (Salt Lake City), 31 July 1887.

[63]*The Nauvoo City and High Council Minutes* (ed. Dinger), 417-18.

also made by several other women, including Mary Clift, and in a different way by Sarah Pratt. Mrs. Warren understood "that he [Dr. Bennett] would give medicine to prevent it [by that to say a pregnancy]."[64] Sarah Pratt, the wife of Apostle Orson Pratt, later reported that on one occasion Bennett showed her (and her husband) a metal tool.[65] Mrs. Warren said, "She learned from him [Bennett] that he was involved with 'Mrs. Shindle[,] now living beyond Ramus, and also with the two Miss Nymans."[66]   Mrs. Warren admitted that Chauncey L. Higbee, just one of a number of elders who had crossed her path, had "gained his object" with her "about five or six times."[67]

Sarah Miller, a vulnerable widow, one of not less than three women allegedly known to have been seduced by Higbee, had misgivings about Higbee's representations. Her apprehensions became less of a concern in a curious way: *"When he [Higbee] come again, [Apostle] William Smith come with him & told me that the doctrine which Chancy Higbee had taught me was true."*[68]

---

[64]Catherine Warren's statement published in the *Nauvoo Neighbor* (29 May 1844), quoted in *The Nauvoo City and High Council Minutes* (ed. Dinger), 417 n 46.

[65]Sarah Pratt interview by Dr. W. Wyl, *Mormon Portraits, or, The Truth About the Mormon Leaders From 1830 to 1866* (Tribune Printing and Publishing Company, 1886), 61. One day both Joseph Smith and John C. Bennett came on horseback to Sarah Pratt's house. "Bennett dismounted, Joseph remained outside. Bennett wanted me to return to him a [medical] book I had borrowed from him . . . . While giving Bennett his book, I observed that he held something in the left sleeve of his coat. Bennett smiled and said: '*Oh, a little job for Joseph; one of his women is in trouble.*' Saying this, he took the thing out of his sleeve. It was a pretty long instrument of a kind I had never seen before. It seemed to be of steel and was crooked at one end. I heard afterwards that the operation had been performed; that the woman was very sick, and that Joseph was very much afraid that she might die, but she recovered." (Ibid., 61-62, emphasis retained).

[66]Catherine Warren's statement published in the *Nauvoo Neighbor* (29 May 1844), quoted in *The Nauvoo City and High Council Minutes* (ed. Dinger), 417 n 46.

[67]*The Nauvoo City and High Council Minutes* (ed. Dinger), 417 n 46.

[68]Sarah Miller's Statement, 24 May 1842, quoted in Ibid., 415-16 n 40, emphasis added. These italicized words appear to have been omitted when the statement appeared in the *Nauvoo Neighbor* on May 29, 1844. They are preserved here from the unexcerpted original, "a photocopy of which exists in the Valeen Tippetts Avery Papers at Utah State University." "Like Sarah Miller, Matilda Nyman [one of two sisters (Margaret and Matilda) also involved with Chauncey L. Higbee]" said Chauncey brought someone with him "who affirmed that such intercourse was tolerated by the heads of the Church." (Editor's note, Ibid., 416 n 42). No doubt this too was the prophet's brother Apostle William Smith.

Melissa Schindle, Catherine Warren and Joseph Smith

Between two marriages in 1841 to Miss Louisa Beaman and Mrs. Zina Huntington (Jacobs), "[Joseph] Smith appears to have continued his sexual consent only approach on [Mrs.] Melissa Schindle and [Mrs.] Catherine Fuller Warren – suggesting he was practicing both adultery and polygamy simultaneously."[69] Neither of these women is known to have ever married Joseph Smith. Melissa Schindle, the wife of Colonel George Schindle, signed an affidavit on July 2, 1842. Her statement was published on July 15, 1842, in the *Sangamo Journal* in Springfield, Illinois. She said that Joseph Smith asked her "in the fall of 1841 . . . if he could have the privilege of sleeping with her . . . ." He told her it was "the will of the Lord" that he should and "that he never proceeded to do any thing of that kind with any woman without first having the will of the Lord on the subject."[70] She claimed she rejected the prophet's request. Mrs. Schindle described the event as having occurred on an evening when she had been overnighting with Catherine Fuller Warren. After she turned the prophet down, she said, "He then went to an adjoining bed where [Mrs. Warren] . . . was sleeping[,] got into bed with her and laid there until about 1 o'clock . . . ."[71] John C. Bennett claimed, in yet another affidavit, that he had "seen Joseph Smith in bed with Mrs. Fuller."[72]

Catherine Fuller Warren, a friendly faithful resource, was alleged to have been intimately involved with a quorum of elders, including (among others) Joseph and William Smith, the Mormon Founder and his Apostle brother. Bennett said that "Smith seduced women like Mrs. Fuller Warren 'by telling them that the Lord had granted [him] the blessing of Jacob," by that to say sex with him wasn't a sin. Smith told Bennett he had free access to "Mrs. _____, Mrs. _____, Mrs. _____, and various others."[73] As was the case with the initials used on another occasion to make it more difficult to

---

[69]Palmer, "Sexual Allegations against Joseph Smith and the Beginnings of Polygamy in Nauvoo," 16.

[70]Melissa Schindle Affidavit, 2 July 1842 (published in the *Sangamo Journal*, 15 July 1842), quoted in Ibid., 14.

[71]Ibid.

[72]John C. Bennett Affidavit, *Pittsburgh Morning Chronicle* (29 June 1842), quoted in Ibid., 14.

[73]Ibid.

identify some of Joseph's plural wives, Bennett protected the identities of these supposed victims by leaving them (in this particular case) without initials and totally anonymous, but treating them as married.   During Bennett's confederacy, spiritual wifery (adultery without remorse) eclipsed marriages to virgins, teens and polygamous plurality.

The Seduction of the Widow Miller

Sarah Miller told the Nauvoo High Council that,

> . . . I was pretty well persuaded, from Joseph's public teachings, that Chauncey had been telling falsehoods; but Chauncey said that Joseph now taught as he did through necessity, on account of the prejudices of the people . . . . Chauncey . . . wanted to know how long it had been since my husband died, and soon removed his seat near me [*"darwin chase was with him"*[74]]; and began his seducing insinuations by saying it was no harm to have sexual intercourse with women if they would keep it to themselves . . . . I told him I did not believe it, and had heard no such teaching from Joseph . . . but that it was wicked to commit adultery, &c. Chauncey said that did not mean single women, but married women . . . .

Sarah said when Chauncey came again, he brought the prophet's brother, who backed him up. William said *"the doctrine which Chancy Higby had taught me was true."*[75] Apostle William Smith told the young widow that, *"it was no harm to have sexual intercourse with women if they would keep it to themselves."* William supported Chauncey's earlier statement that Joseph "now taught as he did through necessity, on account of the prejudices of the people .

---

[74]These italicized words, like other words, were omitted from Sarah Miller's statement when it was published in the *Nauvoo Neighbor* on May 29, 1844.

[75]Sarah Miller, Statement (24 May 1842), from the Valeen Tippetts Avery Papers (Utah State University), reproduced at Minutes (25 March 1842), *The Nauvoo City and High Council Minutes* (ed. Dinger), 415-16 n 40.

..." That was what Chauncey taught, and William Smith said what Chauncey taught was true. What the prophet preached wasn't what the prophet practiced. Why shouldn't Sarah believe the brother of the prophet, a member of the Quorum of the Twelve Apostles? William said Joseph said what Chauncey said. The stories were tailored to the circumstances in which the children of the Kingdom found themselves. "I told him I understood he [Higbee], had recently been [re]baptized, and that Joseph, when he confirmed him, told him to quit all his iniquitous practices, – Chauncey said it was not for such things that he was [re]baptized . . . . Chauncey Higbee said it [a sexual encounter] would never be known. I told him it might be told in bringing forth [a child]. Chauncey said there was no danger, . . . that Dr. Bennett . . . would come and take it away."[76]

May 25, 1842, Before the Certificates

The modern editor of the Nauvoo High Council Minutes, John S. Dinger, reports that: "Excerpts from Catherine Warren's statement published in the *Nauvoo Neighbor* on May 29, 1844, emphasize Chauncey Higbee's venality and downplay Bennett's seduction."[77] Catherine Warren reported that: "I have had an unlawful connexion with Chauncey L. Higbee [who] taught the same doctrine as was taught by J[ohn] C. Bennet[t,] [saying] that Joseph Smith taught and practiced those things." Mrs. Warren (unlike Sarah Miller and Margaret J. Nyman, who implicated the prophet) said Higbee said he had his information directly from Dr. Bennett, with whom the Mormon prophet was known to be close, and with whom Mrs. Warren was alleged to be close. Joseph's friend, Dr. John C. Bennett, was the first Mayor of Nauvoo (February 1, 1841 – May 17, 1842), the Assistant President of the Church (April 8, 1841 – May 17, 1842), the Major General and Operational Officer of the Nauvoo Legion, the Quartermaster General of the State of Illinois,

---

[76]Ibid., 415-16 n 40.

[77]Editor's note, "Excerpts from Catherine Warren's statement published in the *Nauvoo Neighbor* on May 29, 1844," reproduced in Minutes (25 May 1842), *The Nauvoo City and High Council Minutes* (ed. Dinger), 417 n 46.

and the Chancellor of the University of Nauvoo.[78]   In her full
affidavit (not all of her testimony was published in the *Nauvoo
Neighbor*), Mrs. Warren amplified: "'Nearly a year ago I became
acquainted with John C. Bennett, [and] after visiting twice and on
the third time he proposed unlawful intercourse, being about one
week after [our] first acquaintance.'[79] If she became 'pregnant[,] he
said he would attend to that. I understood that he would give
medicine to prevent it.'"[80]

The Nauvoo High Council restored Mrs. Warren by a unanimous
vote to fellowship.[81]   Lyman O. Littlefield and Joel S. Miles were
disfellowshipped (but not excommunicated) for improper and
unvirtuous conduct, and for teaching false doctrine.[82] The charges
(allegations) against "Darwin Chace" were "not sustained."[83] Justis
Morse was disfellowshipped "for unchaste and unvirtuous" conduct
"with the daughter of Widow Neyman . . . ." Chauncey L. Higbee,
Darwin Chase, Lyman O. Littlefield, Joel S. Miles, George S.
Thatcher,[84] Gustavus Hills, and others told the same story about the

---

[78]After he had abandoned a wife and four children without a divorce and on
19 January 1841, just before Bennett took office as the Mayor of Nauvoo, and a
few months before he became the Assistant President of the Mormon Church,
Joseph's Lord took note of John C. Bennett, who was at that moment in time a
most important, highly respected servant. "[L]et my servant John C. Bennett help
you in your labor in sending my word to the kings and people of the earth, and
stand by you, even you my servant Joseph Smith, in the hour of affliction, and his
reward shall not fail if he receive counsel. And for his love he shall be great, for he
shall be mine if he do this, saith the Lord. *I have seen the work which he hath done,
which I accept if he continue, and will crown him with blessings and great glory.*"
(Doctrine and Covenants 124:16-17, emphasis added).

[79]*The Nauvoo City and High Council Minutes* (ed. Dinger), 417 n 46.

[80]Ibid.

[81]Minutes (25 May 1842), *The Nauvoo City and High Council Minutes* (ed.
Dinger), 417-18.

[82]Ibid., 418-19 n 48, 50.

[83]Ibid., 415-16 n 40.

[84]Chauncey L. Higbee later assisted Dr. William Law, Dr. Robert Foster, *et
al.*, with the publication of the *Nauvoo Expositor*. After he was excommunicated
for sexual promiscuity in 1842, "he went on to become a prominent lawyer, state
senator, banker, and judge in Pittsfield, Illinois, where in 1908 a high school was
named after him." (Minutes, *The Nauvoo City and High Council Minutes* [ed.
Dinger], 268 n 141). Darwin Chase was a Seventy. (Ibid., 418 n 49). Lyman D.
Littlefield (at age thirteen) was one of the youngest members of Zion's Camp.
(Ibid., 418 n 47). Joel S. Miles, a Missouri Danite, was a constable in Nauvoo and
onc of Joseph Smith's bodyguards in 1841. (Ibid., 419 n 50). Justis Morse was yet

teachings of the prophet Joseph Smith until such time as those representations, which were supposed to be secret, became toxic. They assigned the sexual-consent doctrine to their leaders (to President Joseph Smith, Assistant President John C. Bennett and Apostle William Smith). The testimony and statements of Sarah Miller, Margaret Nyman, Matilda Nyman, Catherine Fuller Warren, Esther Victoria Smith and Mary Clift – perceived as victims of those early elders – also attributed the sexual consent "doctrine" to the leaders of the Church.

Other Indiscretions: Words from Mrs. Sarah (Orson) Pratt

"You should bear in mind that Joseph did not think of a marriage or sealing ceremony for many years. He used to state to his intended victims, as he did to me: 'God does not care if we have a good time, if only other people do not know it.' He only introduced . . . [a] marriage ceremony when he had found out that he could not get certain women without it. I think Louisa Beemen [sic] was the first case of this kind."[85] Isn't what Sarah Pratt said the prophet said to her what Gustavus Hills, Chauncey L. Higbee, John C. Bennett, William Smith, Darwin Chase, Lyman O. Littlefield, Joel S. Miles, Justis Morse and George S. Thatcher said Joseph said to them? Isn't what the prophet is supposed to have said to Sarah what Margaret and Matilda Nyman, Sarah Miller, Catherine Fuller Warren, Esther Victoria Smith and Mary Clift said those faithful Mormon men also said to them?

John C. Bennett knew about the prophet's plans for Sarah Pratt, Apostle Orson Pratt's wife, while Pratt was out of the city on a mission. *"He [Bennett] knew that Joseph had his plans set on me; Joseph made no secret of them before Bennett, and went so far in his*

---

another Danite. (Ibid., 419 n 53). These men had access to Joseph Smith. They were often bound to the Church and to its leaders by the strongest oaths language could invent. Their representations were too similar in content, and too numerous to have been contrived. Joseph is alleged to have proved to be the man these good and faithful servants chose to describe across the board to their many different women.

[85]Sarah Pratt interview by Dr. W. Wyl, *Mormon Portraits* (1886), 62, emphasis retained and added. After Joseph Smith's death, Louisa Beaman (Smith) (Young) had five children with Brigham Young.

impudence as to make propositions to me in the presence of Bennett, his bosom friend."[86] Is it any wonder that John C. Bennett, a man who was in the confidence of the prophet, could tell the city's vulnerable women, as they said that he did, just exactly what the prophet is supposed to have said?

Many years later, Sarah Pratt had a conversation with Joseph Smith's son Joseph III, who grew to become another prophet in charge of yet another church.

> *Joseph Smith [III], the son of the prophet, and president of the re-organized Mormon church, paid me a visit, and I had a long talk with him. I saw that he was not inclined to believe the truth about his father, so I said to him: "You pretend to have revelations from the Lord. Why don't you ask the Lord what kind of man your father really was?" He answered: "If my father had so many connections with women, where is the progeny?" I said to him, "Your father had mostly intercourse with married women; and as to single ones, Dr. Bennett was always on hand, when anything happened."*[87]

Sarah Pratt told Dr. W. Wyl that, "Joseph did not content himself with his *spiritual* brides, who surrendered themselves to him 'for Christ's sake.' There lived on the Mississippi, near the steamboat landing, a certain young woman, a Mrs. White, very pretty and always very fashionably dressed. She was in the habit of being very hospitable to the captains of the steamboats . . . . Joseph was one of her customers and used to contribute [to] the expenses of her establishment."[88]

Sarah Pratt then further told Dr. Wyl in an interview near the end of her life, and conducted in her own name (no more "Mrs. P" – she wanted to be recognized and understood), that,

---

[86]Ibid., 61, emphasis added.
[87]Ibid., 60-61, emphasis retained and added.
[88]Ibid., 55, emphasis retained.

I have told you that the prophet Joseph used to frequent houses of ill-fame. Mrs. White . . . told me that Joseph had made her acquaintance very soon after his arrival in Nauvoo, and that he had visited her dozens of times. My husband (Orson Pratt) could not be induced to believe such things of his prophet. Seeing his obstinate incredulity, Mrs. White proposed to Mr. Pratt and myself to put us in a position where we could observe what was going on between herself and Joseph the prophet. We, however, declined this proposition.[89]

"Mrs. [G.W.] Harris [the remarried widow of the Masonic martyr William Morgan] was a married lady, a very great friend of mine [a very great friend of Sarah Pratt]. When Joseph had made his dastardly attempt on me, I went to Mrs. Harris to unbosom my grief to her. To my utter astonishment, she said, laughing heartily: 'How foolish you are! I don't see anything so wrong in it. Why I AM HIS MISTRESS SINCE FOUR YEARS!'"[90]

---

[89]Ibid., 60, emphasis added.
[90]Ibid., emphasis retained.

CHAPTER SEVEN

Miss Rigdon, The Prophet,
The Mayor and Polygamy

[N]o good thing will I withhold from them who walk uprightly before me, and do my will in all things – who will listen to my voice and to the voice of my servant whom I have sent; for I delight in those who seek diligently to know my precepts, and abide by the law of my kingdom; for all things shall be made known unto them in mine own due time and in the end they shall have joy.[1]

Joseph's Lord to Joseph
Smith for Miss Rigdon

Whatever God requires is right, no matter what it is, although we may not see the reason thereof till long after the events transpire.[2]

Joseph Smith

IN PURSUIT OF "MISS NANCY"

Willard Richards – the prophet's private secretary, an Apostle of Jesus Christ, Brigham Young's cousin and a future Second Counselor in the First Presidency of the Church of Jesus Christ of Latter-day Saints – hand delivered a letter from Joseph Smith to Nancy Rigdon to Miss Rigdon's home one day after a tumultuous

---

[1]"Happiness," Letter to Miss Nancy Rigdon, in *History of The Church of Jesus Christ of Latter-day Saints*, B.H. Roberts, ed., 7 vols., 2d ed., rev., (Salt Lake City: The Deseret Book Company, 1978), 5:136.
[2]Ibid., 5:135.

encounter between Smith and Miss Rigdon.[3] The encounter occurred in a private room at the Nauvoo Printing House (where Dr. Richards, a married man with a wife and son in Massachusetts, allegedly lived without the benefit of matrimony with the wife of another apostle, Orson Hyde[4]). Richards verbally requested that Miss Rigdon burn the prophet's message after she digested the contents. When John C. Bennett wrote *The History of the Saints*, his famous exposé, the prophet's original letter to Miss Rigdon "in the hand-writing of Dr. Richards" was in Bennett's possession. It hadn't been destroyed. "It was handed to me," Bennett said, "by Colonel F[rancis] M. Higbee, in the presence of General George W. Robinson."[5] These two important men were commanders of the military force known as the Nauvoo Legion. For all practical purposes, Bennett was the operational officer in charge of the day-to-day affairs of the Mormon militia. Higbee was a personal friend of Miss Rigdon, and George W. Robinson, the husband of Athalia Rigdon, was the young woman's brother-in-law.

Miss Rigdon, who was summoned by Smith to meet with him, had been forewarned of the prophet's probable intentions by John C. Bennett (through Bennett's intermediary, Higbee). "I . . . went to Colonel Higbee, and told him Joe's designs, and requested him to go immediately and see Miss Rigdon, and tell her the infernal plot – that Joe would approach her in the name of the Lord, by special revelation, &c., and to put her on her guard, but advise her to go and see for herself what Joe would do."[6]

Miss Rigdon waited for the prophet on two separate occasions. On the occasion of the first intended meeting, the prophet sent notice that other affairs had intervened and he would have to reschedule. "Miss Nancy," Richards said, "Joseph cannot be in today; please call again on Thursday."[7] The warning from Bennett (by way of

---

[3]The letter, like most of Joseph Smith's materials, was dictated to a scribe (in this case Richards).

[4]John C. Bennett, *The History of the Saints: Or, an Expose of Joe Smith and Mormonism* (Boston: Leland & Whiting, 1842; photomechanical reprint of 1842 original, Salt Lake City, UT: Modern Microfilm Company), 241-42. In 1841 and 1842, Orson Hyde was on a mission to the Holy Land.

[5]Ibid., 245.

[6]Ibid., 242.

[7]"Joe was busily engaged at his store." (Ibid., 241-42).

Higbee) preceded that second rescheduled visit to Smith. On that second occasion, an agitated Miss Rigdon had an unnerving confrontation with the prophet after he informed his young parishioner that he had asked the Lord for her. Joseph approached Nancy (as she had been told that he would) in the name of the Lord by means of a special revelation. Smith took her to a private room upstairs ("his favorite assignation room"), locked the door and swore her then to secrecy. There he proceeded to say "that she had long been the idol of his affections, and that he had asked the Lord for her . . . ." *He had asked the Lord for her! The married Mormon prophet had asked the Lord to give him the unmarried daughter of his counselor Sidney Rigdon!* The daughter of the man who said he guided the prophet's tottering steps till he could walk alone. On this particular occasion, the prophet had not been in the least reluctant to state his case. The infallible prophet, the "anointed" one, the voice of God and the most important man on earth, Nancy Rigdon's spiritual leader and her father's colleague and employer, had asked the Lord for her! And the Lord, answering the prophet's prayer, had said *"it was his holy will that he should have her as one of the Chambered Sisters of Charity."*[8] No compulsion needed. In this case there was no angel with a drawn sword. This proposition wasn't "more political than sentimental." It wasn't the language of government or very well regulated.

Joseph's first proposal wasn't marriage. Miss Rigdon was going to be a consort or a concubine. What Smith first proposed was a relationship blessed by the voice of God, cohabitation without a marriage, a lower lesser status in a class divided household. The prophet initially said "that it was his [the Lord's] holy will that he [Joseph Smith] should have her as one of the *Chambered Sisters of Charity* [by that to say as an unmarried consort]; but that if she had any scruples on the subject [unregulated domesticity], he would *consecrate her with the Cloistered Saints, AND MARRY HER IMMEDIATELY –*" with this important caveat: that her marriage to him (a man who already had a legal wife and secret plural wives) "would not prevent her from marrying any other person." Smith told her that "he had the blessings of Jacob granted to him – and that all was lawful and right before God. He then attempted to kiss

---

[8]Ibid., 242-43, emphasis added.

her, and desired her to kiss him . . . ."[9]   General George W. Robinson, Sidney Rigdon's son-in-law and a witness to a meeting between Miss Rigdon, her family and Smith, explained the circumstances of Miss Rigdon's meeting with Smith as she described them to her family in the presence of Smith:

> *Smith . . . stated to her that he had had an affection for her for several years, and wished that she should be his; that the Lord was well pleased with this matter, for he had got a REVELATION on the subject, and God had given him all the blessings of Jacob, &c. &c., and that there was no sin in it [something less than a marriage] whatever; but if she had any scruples of conscience about the matter [i.e., "that she should be his"] he would marry her PRIVATELY, and enjoined her to secrecy, &c, &c.*[10]

The Lord's intention for this accomplished young woman, according to Smith, putting a bold face on confusion and sin, was "happiness." This unusual proposal was not intended to make the principled Miss Rigdon feel morally insecure (any less faithful, any less holy, any less virtuous, any less upright); happiness is the prophet's offer. The path to this happiness includes keeping "*all the commandments of God*," which, Joseph now says and Nancy now learns, is intended to include plural wives, concubines, sexual consent relationships and polyandry. God's "holy will" is seen to embrace, in her case and for better or worse, each of these formidable (and previously forbidden) domestic perplexities.

To reject the Mormon prophet, who said he had spoken to God and that God had spoken to him, and then quoted his Lord, was to ignore God, deny the faith and so be damned.[11] Joseph had asked the Lord for Miss Rigdon, and the Lord had said "that he should

---

[9]Ibid., emphasis retained.

[10]Letter from General George W. Robinson to General James Arlington Bennet, LL.D, Nauvoo, July 27, 1842, reproduced at Bennett, *The History of the Saints*, 245-46, emphasis added and retained.

[11]"For behold, I reveal unto you a new and an everlasting covenant ["touching the principle and doctrine of . . . many wives and concubines –"]; and if ye abide not that covenant, then are ye damned; for no one can reject this covenant and be permitted to enter into my glory." (Doctrine and Covenants 132:1, 4).

have her." The message wasn't well received. "She told him she would alarm the neighbors if he did not open the door and let her out *immediately*."[12]

Not many faithful Mormon women could have rejected this proposal, supposedly God's very own sacred words soberly pronounced by the prophet of God. Had God not said that "his word ye shall receive, as if from mine own mouth, in all patience and faith"?[13] According to Joseph, God wanted him to have Miss Rigdon as a sexual consent partner and a concubine or mistress, or as a plural or polyandrous wife. Joseph's God, as the polygamous revelation (Doctrine and Covenants 132) reports, accepted both "wives and concubines" (Doctrine and Covenants 132:1). What Nancy Rigdon did by means of her refusal, other young women like Helen Mar Kimball and Sarah Ann Whitney didn't do. These impressionable young women, encouraged by their parents, didn't sell themselves for money; they sold themselves for exaltation in the afterlife (for them and those they loved). *This was, all things considered, the ultimate indulgence.*

When Miss Rigdon threatened to alarm the neighbors if the prophet did not immediately unlock the door and let her out, Joseph Smith reluctantly relented. Before taking his leave, he asked Mrs. Orson (Marinda Nancy) Hyde, an older and more experienced woman and a thoroughly flexible mentor, to further explain what he had just proposed.[14] "Mrs. Hyde told her that these things looked strange to

---

[12]Bennett, *The History of the Saints*, 242-43, emphasis Bennett.

[13]Doctrine and Covenants 21:5.

[14]Joseph Smith plurally married Mrs. Orson Hyde in April 1842 while her legal husband, Apostle Orson Hyde, was on a mission to the Holy Land. It is not clear when or if Orson knew that his wife was married to Joseph Smith or that she had lived with Willard Richards while he was away. When the prophet took control of the *Times and Seasons* in 1842, displacing Ebenezer Robinson (the printer and proprietor), Willard Richards (who had acted as the prophet's agent) "demanded that the Robinson family vacate [the printing office living space] immediately." That, although difficult, they then proceeded to do. Richards' family was residing at the time in Massachusetts, and Elder Orson Hyde was absent on his mission to Palestine.'" (Todd Compton, *In Sacred Loneliness: The Plural Wives of Joseph Smith* [Salt Lake City: Signature Books, 2001], 237). Mrs. Hyde had been living with the Robinsons before she lived with Willard Richards, which was before she married Joseph Smith while still the wife of Orson Hyde. Marinda Nancy Johnson was divorced from Orson Hyde at the age of fifty-five

her *at first*, but that she would become more reconciled on mature reflection. Miss Rigdon replied, 'I never shall,' left the house, and returned home."[15] If Nancy Rigdon had accepted either of Joseph Smith's proposals – 1) that she should be his, or 2) that they should be secretly married – she would have gone home to her father, Sidney Rigdon (Smith's First Counselor), sworn to secrecy, unable to tell even him that she now belonged to Joseph Smith.[16]

Bennett's Warning to Nancy Rigdon

John C. Bennett and Joseph Smith were rivals for the attentions of Nancy Rigdon, whom Bennett described as ". . . a beautiful girl, of irreproachable fame, great moral excellence, and superior intellectual endowments."[17] John W. Rigdon, Nancy Rigdon's brother, who as incredible as it may seem followed Brigham Young to Utah after his father lost his case to lead the Church, gave this version of the printing-office event, at the request of the Utah Church, in an affidavit prepared when he was over seventy-five years of age. The object of the affidavit was to prove to the Reorganized Church led by Joseph's son, Joseph III, that Joseph owned polygamy and that the plurality principle hadn't started its uneven course with his successor, Brigham Young.

---

after thirty-four years of marriage and ten children in 1870. She (and her biological children with Hyde) will belong to Joseph Smith, to whom she is sealed for time and eternity, in a Mormon afterlife.

[15]Bennett, *The History of the Saints*, 243, emphasis retained.

[16]Although Rigdon was an opponent of polygamy, he had been personally present – along with Frederick G. Williams and Oliver Cowdery – when Joseph, caught and confounded, confessed and humbly begged forgiveness for an in-the-barn-on-the-haymow encounter with Fanny Alger in the early days of the Church at Kirtland, Ohio. (George D. Smith, *Nauvoo Polygamy: " . . . but we called it celestial marriage"* [Salt Lake City: Signature Books, 2008], 40-41). It is doubtful that marriage or sealing was then discussed. Rigdon's subsequent conduct (he feigned ignorance about the doctrine of polygamy) suggested that he had no reason to believe (after the Fanny Alger incident) that Joseph Smith ever married Fanny Alger in the 1830s. There is in the archives of the Church no simultaneous record of such a marriage. Rigdon was, of course, familiar after 1842 with all of the circumstances concerning the propositions directed to Nancy Rigdon by the prophet Joseph Smith in person and in writing in 1842.

[17]Bennett, *The History of the Saints*, 241.

[S]ome time in the latter part of the year 1843, or the first part of the year 1844 [actually 1842], ["Joseph the Prophet"] made a proposition to my sister, Nancy Rigdon, to become his wife. It happened in this way: Nancy had gone to Church, meeting being held in a grove near the temple lot on which the "Mormons" were then erecting a temple, an old lady friend who lived alone invited her to go home with her, which Nancy did. When they got to the house and had taken their bonnets off, the old lady began to talk to her about the new doctrine of polygamy which was then being taught, telling Nancy, during the conversation, that it was a surprise to her when she first heard it, but that she had since come to believe it to be true. While they were talking Joseph Smith the Prophet came into the house, and joined them, and the old lady immediately left the room. It was then that Joseph made the proposal of marriage to my sister. Nancy flatly refused him, saying if she ever got married she would marry a single man or none at all, and thereupon took her bonnet and went home, leaving Joseph at the old lady's house. Nancy told father and mother of it. The story got out and it became the talk of the town that Joseph had made a proposition to Nancy Rigdon to become his wife, and that she refused him.[18]

A few days after the occurrence Joseph Smith came to my father's house and talked the matter over with the family, my sister, Mrs. Athalia Robinson also being present, who is now alive. The feelings manifested by our family on this occasion were anything but brotherly or sisterly, more especially

---

[18]Affidavit, John W. Rigdon, July 28, 1905, quoted in *Blood Atonement and the Origin of Plural Marriage – A Discussion*, Correspondence between Elder Joseph F. Smith, Jr., of the Church of Jesus Christ of Latter-day Saints, and Mr. Richard C. Evans, Second Counselor in the Presidency of the "Reorganized" Church (Salt Lake City: The Deseret News Press, 1905), 83-84.

on the part of Nancy, as she felt that she had been insulted.[19]

John C. Bennett claimed that Joseph asked him, because of his friendship with the Rigdons, to help him procure Nancy Rigdon as one of his spiritual wives. "Knowing that I had much influence with Mr. Rigdon's family, Joe Smith said to me, one day last summer, when riding together over the lawn in Nauvoo, 'If you will assist me in procuring Nancy as one of my spiritual wives, I will give you five hundred dollars, or the best lot on Main Street.'"[20] Bennett said that he declined the prophet's request because he "could not approach her on a subject of that kind." Bennett said that he thought that had been the end of it. But at the funeral of Ephraim R. Marks, Mrs. Hyde told Miss Rigdon that Joseph wanted to see her at the printing office, where Mrs. Hyde and Dr. Richards resided, "on special business." It was then that Miss Rigdon arrived to find that other concerns had made the prophet's appearance impossible. And it was then that Richards asked her to come back another day. Between these first and second appointments, Miss Rigdon spoke to Colonel Higbee "and asked his advice as to the second visit."[21]

Higbee then discussed that matter with Bennett. When Bennett came "to a knowledge of the facts," he said that he went to Smith and said to him, "Joseph you are a Master Mason, and Nancy is a Master Mason's daughter [and so is Mrs. Pratt, the daughter of Mr. Bates]; so stay your hand, or you will get into trouble – *remember your obligation*."[22] Joseph, who was offended, then sharply replied, "You are my enemy and wish to oppose me."[23] Bennett had failed to help him procure Miss Rigdon as one of his plural wives. Bennett then conferred with Francis M. Higbee, "told him Joe's designs," and suggested that Higbee should inform Miss Rigdon that Joseph planned to approach her in the name of the Lord by way of a "special revelation." Higbee then went to Miss Rigdon "to put her

---

[19]Ibid., 84.
[20]Bennett, *The History of the Saints*, 241.
[21]Ibid., 241-42.
[22]Ibid., 242, emphasis retained.
[23]Ibid.

on her guard" regarding "the infernal plot."[24]   When Nancy rejected Smith, he supposed that she had been forewarned about the nature of his proposal. That angered him yet again. That was Bennett's unforgivable offense, the betrayal that cut the cord.

George W. Robinson, who sided with Bennett (they were officers in the Nauvoo Legion), reported at the time as follows:

> Smith and Bennett have always been on very friendly terms, and were together a great deal, and I have no doubt but that Bennett was Smith's confidant in nearly all things . . . .[25]

> Smith sent for Miss Rigdon to come to the house of Mrs. Hyde, who lived in the under rooms of the printing-office. Miss Rigdon inquired of the messenger who came for her what was wanting, and the only reply was, that Smith wanted to see her. General Bennett [actually Francis M. Higbee] came to Miss Rigdon, and cautioned her, and advised her not to place too much reliance on revelation; but did not enlighten her on the object of Smith, but advised her to go down to Mrs. Hyde's, and see Smith. She accordingly went, and Smith took her into another room, and locked the door, and then stated to her that he had had an affection for her for several years, and wished that she should be his . . . .

> She repulsed him, and was about to raise the neighbors if he did not unlock the door and let her out; and she left him with disgust, and came home and told her father of the transaction; upon which Smith was sent for. He came.[26]

Nancy Rigdon defied the prophet's request to destroy the letter

---

[24]Ibid.

[25]Letter from General George W. Robinson to General James Arlington Bennet, LL.D, Nauvoo, July 27, 1842, reproduced at Bennett, *The History of the Saints*, 245-46.

[26]Ibid., 245-47, emphasis omitted.

delivered by Willard Richards and described the incriminating contents to her family. When she made so powerful a case in so sincere a manner that Joseph, who first boldly claimed that she had lied, "could not withstand the testimony," "he then and there acknowledged that every word of Miss Rigdon's testimony was true."[27] What else could he possibly say? The prophet had lied; she had not, and there was a letter.

> *She told the tale in the presence of all the family, and to Smith's face. I was present. Smith attempted to deny it at first, and face her down with the lie, but she told the facts with so much earnestness, and the fact of a letter being present, which he had caused to be written to her, on the same subject, the day after the attempt made on her virtue, breathing the same spirit, and which he had fondly hoped was destroyed – all came with such force that he could not withstand the testimony; and he then and there acknowledged that every word of Miss Rigdon's testimony was true.*
>
> *Now for his excuse, which he made for such a base attempt, and for using the name of the Lord in vain on that occasion. He wished to ascertain whether she was virtuous or not, and took that course to learn the facts . . . .*
>
> *I liked to have forgotten to state that the affair with Miss Rigdon was the cause of Smith's coming out so on Bennett, he having suspicions that Bennett had cautioned her on the matter – and he was further afraid that Bennett would make disclosures of other matters.*[28]

He told Miss Rigdon at the printing house that it was God's "holy will" that he should have her. At her home and with the Rigdons, he was forced to admit that he had invoked the name of God in vain in order to learn the facts about Miss Rigdon's virtue. Is it not also apparent that the well-appointed Bennett, Joseph's "bosom friend"

---

[27]Ibid., 246, emphasis omitted.
[28]Ibid., 246-47, emphasis author, original emphasis not retained.

(according to Sarah Pratt), knew a great deal about Joseph's "other matters" – private, personal, intimate "other matters"?   John C. Bennett was Joseph Smith's worst nightmare.

Consider the "Scamp"

For more than a year-and-a-half, John C. Bennett was closer to Joseph Smith than anyone else in the Church.   There were many who said so, among them Oliver Olney, George W. Robinson and William Law.   When the former Governor of Illinois, Thomas Ford, described Bennett as "probably the *greatest scamp* in the Western country . . ." and said that "he was everywhere accounted the same debauched, unprincipled and profligate character,"[29] one may pause to remember that particular rascal's extraordinarily close and highly confidential relationship with his great patron, Joseph Smith.   In 1841 and 1842 Dr. John C. Bennett ("that shining light"[30]) was the most visible man in the Mormon Church, next perhaps only to Joseph Smith.   Like Joseph, Bennett worked his way with women.   "Bennett's relations with the Prophet being of the most intimate character, it was easy for him to succeed in imposing upon silly women the 'spiritual-wife' doctrine as an emanation from Heaven; and this he is charged with doing with a success that is humiliating to confess."[31]

William Law described the rise and fall of John C. Bennett: "I believe now that John C. Bennett did know it [that Joseph was a polygamist], for he at that time was more in the secret confidence of Joseph than perhaps any other man in the city.   Bennett was a tool of Joseph for a time, but for some cause which I never knew, Joseph cast him off."[32]   General George W. Robinson knew exactly why Joseph cast him off.   *"[T]he affair with Miss Rigdon was the cause of*

---

[29]Thomas Ford, *A History of Illinois* (Chicago: 1854), 263, quoted in T.B.H. Stenhouse, *The Rocky Mountain Saints: A Full and Complete History of the Mormons, from the First Vision of Joseph Smith to the Last Courtship of Brigham Young* (New York: D. Appleton and Company, 1873), 184, emphasis added.

[30]Stenhouse, *The Rocky Mountain Saints*, 183.

[31]Ibid., 184.

[32]Letter from William Law ("the principal counsellor of Joseph") to T.B.H. Stenhouse, November 24, 1871, reproduced at Stenhouse, *The Rocky Mountain Saints*, 198.

Smith's coming out so on Bennett." Smith suspicioned "that Bennett had cautioned her" about the purpose for the meeting at the printing house.[33]

RIGDONS, RICHARDS, BENNETT: COMPLICATIONS, CONFUSION AND CHAOS

The Risky Letter

If Joseph's proposal to Nancy Rigdon had not proven to be as enticing as the stricken prophet may have liked, his follow-up, as reported in the letter, was reasoned and forceful. It was perhaps the prophet's only written explanation of the polygamous principle, if one excludes Section 132 of the Doctrine and Covenants, "the Polygamic revelation" which, while dated to 1843, wasn't actually published in the Doctrine and Covenants until 1876. Joseph had wanted the unusual letter, which was never intended for indiscriminate use, to be read and destroyed.

The day after the fateful meeting at the printing house, Apostle Willard Richards handed Miss Rigdon that most peculiar letter from Joseph Smith. Richards is (and rather abruptly) the prophet's new renaissance man, John C. Bennett's not-quite-so-busy replacement. He is not, like Bennett, the unanimously elected Mayor, or the Master in Chancery, a General in the Legion, the Chancellor of the University, or the Assistant President of the Church. He is, for now, mostly Joseph's private secretary, more literate than Clayton, and an Apostle. Bennett derisively described his capable successor, a man whose domesticity was complicated, as the "Pander-General for Lust."[34] Bennett "had long suspected," he

---

[33]Letter from General George W. Robinson to General James Arlington Bennet, LL.D, Nauvoo, July 27, 1842, reproduced in Bennett, *The History of the Saints*, 246-47, emphasis added to and omitted from original.

[34]Bennett, *The History of the Saints*, 241-42. After Sidney Rigdon "became estranged from Mormonism," very shortly after the death of the prophet, he wrote, "If R. [Willard Richards] should take a notion to H.'s [Orson Hyde's] wife in his absence [Hyde was away on a mission to Palestine], all that is necessary to be done is to be sealed. No harm done, no adultery committed, only taking a little . . . advantage of rights of priesthood. And after R. has gone the round of dissipation with H's wife, she is afterwards turned over to S. [Joseph Smith] and thus the poor

said (this pot will call the kettle black), that Richards was "up to his eyes in the business with Joe."[35]   Richards now enjoys Joseph's "most implicit confidence and trust" and quickly seems to take Bennett's place in Smith's affections. "Never did I have a greater intimacy with any man than him."[36] Willard Richards and Joseph Smith (like John C. Bennett and Joseph Smith) are seen to share conjugal secrets.

In the *History of the Church* (vol. 5, 134-36), there is something strangely called an "essay" on "Happiness" written by the prophet Joseph Smith. It is accompanied by this editorial comment: "It is not positively known what occasioned the writing of this essay . . . ."[37] The author of the editorial comment, like the late great P.T. Barnum, believed there was a fool born every minute and that many of them would be reading the *History of the Church*. For this document is not an "essay," but rather a letter unsigned and without a salutation. It is the letter Joseph Smith wrote to Nancy Rigdon after Miss Rigdon rejected his domestic proposals at that volatile meeting at the printing house. It was Nancy's cold response to Joseph's warm request that most certainly "occasioned the writing" of it. It is the document supposed to have been burned after Miss Rigdon had considered its contents. It is impossible that those who created *Joseph Smith's History of the Church* after his death, putting their own words in the dead prophet's mouth, didn't know what this document was or why it was written. The author of the incredible editorial comment, to his discredit, was the distinguished Mormon scholar and Seventy B.H. Roberts. He was then, in those days of his celebrity, known as the "defender of the faith."

This message from the prophet (a Master Mason) to the daughter of

---

silly woman becomes the actual dupe of two designing men, under the sanctimonious garb of rights of the royal priesthood." (Rigdon, quoted in Compton, *In Sacred Loneliness*, 237). If anyone knew the true facts of these encounters any better than Rigdon, it was probably John C. Bennett. In 1842, Bennett described "Dr. Richards" as one "who is so notorious for *Hyde*ing in these last days." (Ibid.).

[35]Ibid., 241-42.

[36]Joseph Smith, Letter to Jennetta Richards, 23 June 1842, *History of the Church*, 5:40-41.

[37]Smith, *History of the Church*, 5:134 (1842), footnote.

Rigdon (another Master Mason) was the prophet's first written defense of the doctrine of polygamy, the first published articulation of the theoretical elements of the controversial principle. It should be remembered that it was never intended to be made public. Joseph's pursuit of Nancy Rigdon was also described in *"The History of the Saints"* in another letter sent to James Arlington Bennet by Nancy Rigdon's brother-in-law, George W. Robinson. General George W. Robinson, a Mormon Danites' commander in Missouri and a veteran of the battle of Crooked River, was the first Secretary to the First Presidency and a scribe to the prophet Joseph Smith.[38] The letter from Joseph Smith to Nancy Rigdon came to rest as that generically misrepresented essay on "Happiness" in the *"History of the Church."*[39]

Testing Nancy's Virtue

In his letter, Joseph plied Miss Rigdon with what can only be called a threat. The prophet, like the master he said that he served, a God of vengeance, anger and ego, sold his vision with threats.

> *Our Heavenly Father is more liberal in His views, and boundless in his mercies and blessings, than we are ready to believe or receive; and, at the same time, is more terrible to the workers of iniquity, more awful in the executions of His punishments, and more ready to detect every false way, than we are apt to suppose Him to be ....*[40]

Now, in what he only later said was an effort "to ascertain whether she was virtuous or not," he spoke as a prophet, and in the words of God.

> *[H]e says, "Ask and ye shall receive, seek and ye shall find;" but if you will take that which is not your own, or which I have not given you, you shall be rewarded*

---

[38]After the death of the prophet, Robinson became a member of the Quorum of the Twelve Apostles in the Rigdonite Church.

[39]*History of the Church*, 5:134-36.

[40]Ibid., 5:136, emphasis added.

according to your deeds; but no good thing will I
withhold from them who walk uprightly before me,
and do my will in all things – who will listen to my
voice and to the voice of my servant whom I have sent;
for I delight in those who seek diligently to know my
precepts, and abide by the law of my kingdom; for all
things shall be made known unto them in mine own
due time, and in the end they shall have joy.[41]

So if an amended Joseph is to be trusted, this wasn't really about plural marriage, concubines or coupling, but rather Miss Rigdon's integrity. The creator of heaven and earth, the master of the universe, was merely conducting an interesting experiment supposed to determine whether Miss Rigdon, a nineteen-year-old resident of Nauvoo, Illinois, "was virtuous or not." Faced with that critical concern, the previously mostly silent Lord and the sexually aggressive holy man took the course just described "to learn the facts."

If Miss Rigdon, being confused, had believed that there was no sin whatever in what the prophet proposed; if she, being confused, had actually believed that Joseph "had had an affection for her for several years and wished that she should be his," and that the Lord wished that she "should be his"; if she had believed that he had received a revelation, and that those who ignored such revelations would discover that God was more terrible in his punishments than they were "apt to suppose"; and that it was her duty to listen to *"the voice of my servant whom I have sent,"* then, and somehow only then, would her lack of virtue have been seen to have been confirmed.

Only if she is quick to recognize the impropriety of the prophet's "course to learn the facts," and the deceitful nature of the representations uttered by "the voice of *my servant* whom I have sent," only if she is immune to such temptation and wise enough to know that this is all a trick, that God wasn't really speaking, that Joseph wasn't really sincere, can it be said that Miss Rigdon, virtue intact, had passed this formidable test. For she may have thought

---

[41]Ibid., emphasis added.

that it was God's "holy will" that God's "holy prophet" should have her. She may have thought that God "delights" in those who "diligently" seek to know his precepts. Had she said yes to him (God's "holy prophet"), and to that (God's "holy will"), she would then have failed the test to see if she "was virtuous or not."[42]

Thirty or forty other women faced with some variation of this particular theme, specific to their own circumstances, did say yes and did fail Joseph's in-the-name-of-God attempts to learn the facts about their virtue, and Joseph did nothing to interrupt them. Because they had taken him at his word when he said that God said they "should be his," and because they became his, their virtue, it must be said, must be seen to have been in doubt.

That the prophet of the restoration was a risk taker can not be doubted. Joseph Smith, imbued with passion and resolve, took many chances in his short but exciting life. He understood and cited the principle that without risk there is no reward. If the letter delivered by Richards had caused the excitable Miss Rigdon to reconsider, and had it been burned after it was read as Smith was seen to intend, it may have been worth the risk. Success meant claiming Miss Rigdon. It was unlikely, if nothing changed, that Smith would ever be able to speak to her again in a confidential way. Composing the incriminating letter and daring it delivered, although a process fraught with peril, was a risk the sometimes reckless prophet was willing to take.

The prophet will say in his letter what the agitated Miss Rigdon hadn't let him say at the printing shop. The master of the Mormons and the most important man on earth will explain to Nancy, a girl in her teens, why his strikingly unusual proposal passed theological

---

[42]"The 27 August 1842 *Wasp* . . . branded Martha H. Brotherton [a young woman approached by Brigham Young] a 'mean harlot,' and Nancy Rigdon suffered the same treatment after she opposed Smith's polygamous proposals [and was supposed to have passed the test of her virtue]. Stephen Markham, a close friend of Smith, certified in 31 August 1842 'Affidavits' that he saw Nancy Rigdon in a compromising situation with Bennett. He claimed 'many vulgar, unbecoming and indecent sayings and motions' passed between them and testified that he was convinced they were 'guilty of unlawful and illicit intercourse with each other.'" (Richard S. Van Wagoner, *Mormon Polygamy: A History* [Salt Lake City: Signature Books, 1986], 235-36).

muster.   In this letter Joseph Smith will offer a spirited but disguised defense of polygamy, a principle he never publicly chose to support. "Happiness is the object and design of our existence;" the letter initially said, and will be the end of our existence "if we pursue the path that leads to it." And this is the path: "[V]irtue, uprightness, faithfulness, holiness, and keeping all the commandments of God." Here in those few introductory words vice pays tribute to virtue. Now Joseph further reports, "But we cannot keep all the commandments without first knowing them, and we cannot expect to know all, or more than we now know, unless we comply with or keep those we have already received."[43]

Knowing the Commandments of God

Nancy Rigdon doesn't know all the commandments of God. How then shall she hope to keep them? And if she doesn't keep them because she doesn't know them, or doesn't want to, or doesn't keep the ones she knows, how shall she ever know more than she now knows? Practicing polygamy will help her climb this unpredictable precipice. As this dilemma sharpens, it seems that if she doesn't abide by all of the commandments, keeping those she has already received, she will not achieve that measure of happiness that is "the object and design of our existence." She must keep those commandments she has already received, including now the practice of plural marriage, or something like plural marriage, before she can keep those she doesn't know and hasn't yet received. Joseph will help "Miss Nancy" along.

> *That which is wrong under one circumstance, may be, and often is, right under another. God said, "Thou shalt not kill;" at another time He said, "Thou shalt utterly destroy." This is the principle on which the government of heaven is conducted – by revelation adapted to the circumstances in which the children of the kingdom are placed. Whatever God requires is right, no matter what it is, although we may not see the reason thereof till long after the events transpire.*[44]

---

[43]Smith, *History of the Church*, 5:134-135.
[44]Smith, Ibid., 5:135, emphasis added.

The government of heaven, the business of faith, is conducted by revelation "adapted to the circumstances in which the children of the kingdom are placed."[45] Now Joseph teaches Miss Rigdon that morality is relative, authoritarian and situational. What is wrong under one circumstance may be right under another, if God, the author of morality, says that it is. What "is right," what is moral, may be safely defined as whatever God requires. But deciding what is right and what is wrong and what it is that God requires is not her problem, or her prerogative. She need not decide if something is right or wrong; God will decide. And what he decides will be adapted to the circumstances in which she, a child of the kingdom, is placed, whatever she thinks. God's reasons are important and they are said to control. Her reasons are not important and they do not control. *She may not understand God's reasons "till long after the events transpire," or at all, or ever.* God's reasons, according to Joseph Smith, need not be explained and may not be understood, but it is not for her (or even him) to reason why. One must act when directed, even if confused. Obedience matters. While plural marriage to a Gentile is mortal sin, plural marriage to a prophet of God is lawful and right.   That which is wrong under one circumstance may be right under another.

Joseph Smith will tell Miss Rigdon what it is that God requires. Who is able to discern God's will in this as in all other matters? Joseph, Nancy's ardent but conflicted suitor, the man who has written this letter.

> *If we seek first the kingdom of God, all good things will be added. So with Solomon; first he asked wisdom, and God gave it him, and with it every desire of his heart, even things which might be considered abominable to all who understand the order of heaven only in part, but which in reality were right because God gave and sanctioned by special revelation.*[46]

If "Miss Nancy" considers Smith's proposal "abominable," at odds with the lessons of her life, it is because she understands the "order of heaven only in part." Whatever God requires is the order of

---

[45]Ibid.
[46]Smith, Ibid., 5:135, emphasis added.

heaven, and the rule of the earth, and either coupling with or plural marriage to Joseph is the order of heaven and the rule of the earth for her. It is God's "holy will," according to the prophet, that he should have her.

> *Everything that God gives us is lawful and right; and it is proper that we should enjoy His gifts and blessings whenever and wherever He is disposed to bestow; but if we should seize upon those same blessings and enjoyments without law, without revelation, without commandment, those blessings and enjoyments would prove cursings and vexations in the end, and we should have to lie down in sorrow and wailings of everlasting regret.*[47]

God gives us plural marriage (and "concubines"), and what he gives "is lawful and right," but not for everyone. The blessings of Jacob are reserved for those whom God selects and they are regulated by revelation and commandment. If someone should be so bold as to claim those blessings "without revelation, without commandment," he or she shall "lie down in sorrow" to "wailings of everlasting regret."

> *[W]ho will listen to my voice and to the voice of my servant whom I have sent; for I delight in those who seek diligently to know my precepts, and abide by the law of my kingdom; for all things shall be made known unto them in mine own due time, and in the end they shall have joy.*[48]

This is not Joseph speaking. These are the words of Joseph Smith's polygamous Lord. God himself is making the sale. "[L]isten to my voice and to the voice of my servant whom I have sent." Do what I require, "for I delight in those" who know and do my will. Those who do what I require will understand "all things" in "mine own due time," and "in the end they shall have joy." Or not. The Lord intervenes on behalf of the prophet to close the prophet's case. Nancy Rigdon, whose life has just been turned upside down, will

---

[47]Ibid., emphasis added.
[48]Smith, Ibid., 5:136, emphasis added.

CHAPTER EIGHT

"The Saintly Scoundrel"

*I have seen the work which he hath done, which I
accept if he continue, and will crown him with
blessings and great glory.*

Joseph's Lord to Joseph
January 19, 1841
(D&C 124:17)

*Dr. Bennett was wise in the ways of women and
wayward. His obvious access to the prophet (they
were often seen together), his remarkable position in
the Church (Assistant President), his prominence in
the community (Doctor, Mayor, Chancellor, Director,
Justice, General), his glib tongue, low morals and lack
of restraint made his objectives easily attainable.*

Joel M. Allred

"... THE GREATEST SCAMP" IN THE WESTERN COUNTRY

Convert

Dr. John Cook Bennett arrives in Nauvoo, Illinois, in August or
September 1840, before the city is chartered. After exchanges of
correspondence between Bennett and Smith, men of about the same
age, Bennett is baptized by Joseph Smith in August or September.
The impressive new convert temporarily quarters with Joseph and
Emma Smith at the Mansion House (thirty-nine weeks in 1840-41).
After he leaves he continues to take his meals there. This same
Bennett had at one time been a Campbellite preacher. He had met

Joseph Smith in Ohio in 1832, but Mormonism didn't interest him then. He had been known to Rigdon and some other Campbellite converts from as early as 1833. Bennett is smaller than the Smith men but impressive. He is highly intelligent and handsome, with dark features and eyes. He is knowledgeable and well spoken. He is polished, worldly, restless, educated and ambitious. He is well mannered, deferential, ingratiating and courtly. Joseph finds him interesting and likes him right away; Emma is more or less annoyed.[1]

Bennett is a physician. He is the Secretary of the Illinois Medical Society. He has been an instructor in midwifery at Willoughby University at Chagrin, Ohio, a small and rather undistinguished school. His training as a physician, coupled with unsatisfying scruples, makes him the kind of doctor careful women might choose to avoid. It will be reported that he had been an abortionist with a checkered background. In Nauvoo, elements of that accusation are made by friendly voices in the best of times. He has lived at many different places and done many different things.[2] He is described in early 1841 as "an adventurous malcontent." It doesn't matter. In no time at all Joseph Smith and John C. Bennett are joined at the hip.

This complex, richly flavored renaissance man comes to the emerging Mormon enclave with baggage he doesn't begin to describe. "After leaving Willoughby, Bennett wandered in the Midwest, living in six localities in three states before settling in Illinois."[3] He is self-trained at the law. He is a lobbyist with some previous legislative experience. He claims to be a thirty-third

---

[1]Linda King Newell and Valeen Tippetts Avery, *Mormon Enigma: Emma Hale Smith, Prophet's Wife, "Elect Lady," Polygamy's Foe – 1804-1879* (Garden City, N.Y.: Doubleday & Company, Inc., 1984), 91-92.

[2]At Christian College in New Albany, Indiana, a college he founded "without adequate funding or faculty," Bennett "peddled degrees in medicine, law, and theology to anyone who would pay." Willoughby University, where he opened a medical department, dismissed him "when reports of his diploma mill caught up with him." (Richard Lyman Bushman with the assistance of Jed Woodworth, *Joseph Smith: Rough Stone Rolling* [New York: Alfred A. Knopf, 2005], 411).

[3]Ibid., 411. Bishop George Miller will investigate Bennett's background at Joseph Smith's request. Miller concluded that a list of six localities in three states was probably incomplete.

degree Mason, a Brigadier General in the Illinois Invincible Light Dragoons, the Quartermaster General of the Illinois Militia and a student of military tactics. Although his military qualifications are more ceremonial than substantive, they are impressive to Joseph Smith and the Latter-day Saints. Converts like Master John C. Bennett are few and far between. Before this horse is out of the barn, Mormonism's brand new Patriarch predicted a magnificent future for the promising Bennett. *See* Appendix B, "Hyrum Smith Blesses Joab – General in Israel, John C. Bennett."

CONTRIBUTIONS

When the versatile Bennett appears in the budding Nauvoo (like an answer to a prophet's prayer), many of Mormonism's early stalwarts are out of the city and out of the country, away on missions preaching the gospel.[4] What can a man like Bennett do for a short-handed prophet, a fugitive only recently escaped from a Missouri jail? He can obtain charters for a new city, for a university and a Mormon militia from the Illinois legislature. As a skilled political operative, urbane and persuasive, he can use the burgeoning political power of the ever-gathering Saints and the details of their short but troubled history in clever ways to maximum advantage. Like Napoleon, the man he studies and most admires, Bennett is intensely ambitious. If Joseph controls the hearts and minds of the Latter-day Saints like the Pope in Rome, General John C. Bennett would like to control the Mormon militia like Napoleon in Paris.

A visionary man in a mostly secular sense, Bennett seems to understand the extraordinary vitality of the Mormon faith at this early stage better than most. He is prepared to show the prophet how to cleverly use and best protect his temporal power. Bennett is the not improbable friend of E.D. Howe, one of the first

---

[4]When the sky was falling in Kirtland, Ohio, in 1837-38, Joseph sent some of his best men on missions, thus saving them from being further infected by the dark spirit then evident there. Several seasoned apostles traveled to England to open a mission, where they would soon be joined by other prominent leaders. The English Mission, a brave endeavor, was destined to become the crowning glory of the restored Church.

investigative reporters to take the measure of the new religion.[5] Bennett has a silver tongue and influential friends. One of them, Stephen A. Douglas, is another small, brilliant, ambitious visionary. He is also interested in Mormonism and its nineteenth-century Mohammed. The Latter-day Saints, who vote in lockstep, vote for every Whig but one in the November 1840 election. They scratch their ballots to vote for James H. Ralston, a Democrat ("who had done the prophet some favors"), at the expense of the last name on the Whig list, that of an obscure young politician by the name of Abraham Lincoln.[6] Such were the fruits of the thirty-four year-old prophet's secular vision. So much for his civil discernment.

The Nauvoo Charter

It is a confident and politically astute Bennett who leads the charge to secure the passage of the Nauvoo Charter on a voice vote at the Illinois legislature. And it is a triumphant Bennett who returns to Nauvoo able to say that, "Every power we asked has been granted, every request gratified, every desire fulfilled."[7] This was a remarkable accomplishment. The charter improvidently allows the new "city-state" to pass ordinances on virtually any subject, provided they are "not repugnant to the Constitution of the United States" or to the Constitution of the State of Illinois.[8] This poorly considered grant of power to the Mormon theocracy virtually guarantees confusion, debate and delay on any questionable measure. Whether something is repugnant to the Constitution, no matter how repugnant it actually is, can always be debated. The Mormon prophet, a man with scant respect for the separation of

---

[5]Bennett could not but have heard from Howe, the publisher of *Mormonism Unvailed*, how perfectly fanatical some of the early Mormons actually were in Ohio in 1832. "When Bennett [before he joined the Church] . . . published an attack on the Mormons, he borrowed heavily from Howe's *Mormonism Unvailed*." (Bushman, *Joseph Smith: Rough Stone Rolling*, 411). His early exposure to such material may have turned a less ambitious more principled man around.

[6]*History of the Church*, 4:248, quoted in Fawn M. Brodie, *No Man Knows My History: The Life of Joseph Smith the Mormon Prophet*, 2d ed., rev. and enl. (New York: Alfred A. Knopf, 1972), 267.

[7]*History of the Church*, 4:248.

[8]Nauvoo Charter, An Act to Incorporate the City of Nauvoo, Section 11. (*History of the Church*, 4:241-42).

powers or Gentile law, will know what to do with this generous grant and is understandably thrilled. Who could have believed after the Mormon experience in Missouri that the citizens of the State of Illinois would be so welcoming? And who made all this possible? The bright "colorful newcomer,"[9] the "adventurous malcontent," the "shining light" who did what he said that he would.

Bennett's meteoric rise in the Mormon Church may be directly attributed to his remarkable work on the Nauvoo City Charter. The citizens of the State of Illinois will come to regret this hasty and unprecedented conferral of sovereignty on the Mormon enclave. But the Nauvoo Charter and *habeas corpus*, Bennett's gifts to his new best friend, will protect Joseph against extradition to the hated state of Missouri and provide the Mormon prophet with protection from the pressing claims of his Ohio creditors. Nauvoo was soon to become "the most notorious city in Illinois."[10] Illinois authorities will not be able to enter the city to apprehend and punish cattle thieves and counterfeiters. While outwardly sanctimonious, a jealously autonomous Nauvoo will soon be a place of peace, home base for unsavory frontier offenders.

During the April 7, 1841, General Conference in Nauvoo, John C. Bennett's remarkable efforts will be recognized for all to see at the "throne of grace." "*General Bennett* read the charters granted by the legislature of this state, for incorporating 'the City of Nauvoo,' 'the Nauvoo Legion,' 'the University of the City of Nauvoo,' 'the Agriculture and Manufacturing Association,' and 'the Nauvoo House Association.'"[11] After a motion, it is resolved that "the charters now read be received by the Church." The passage of these invaluable charters would be among the first services the resourceful Bennett would perform. These legislative accomplish-

---

[9]Richard Van Wagoner, *Mormon Polygamy: A History* (Salt Lake City: Signature Books, 1986), 15. "The absence of the missionary-apostles and the periodic illness of Sidney Rigdon may have contributed to a power vacuum in the church. . . . John C. Bennett filled this void by ingratiating himself into the inner circles of the church; his rapid rise to the hierarchical pinnacles of Mormonism remains virtually without precedent." (Ibid., 16).

[10]Brodie, *No Man Knows My History*, 268.

[11]*History of the Church*, 4:340, emphasis added.

ments represented Joseph's first political victory of any consequence.

All of this is recognized in the Report of the First Presidency to the Conference in April of 1841:

> *From the kind and generous feelings, manifested by the citizens of this state, since our sojourn among them, we may continue to expect the enjoyment of all the blessings of civil and religious liberty, guaranteed by the Constitution. The citizens of Illinois have done themselves honor, in throwing the mantle of the Constitution over a persecuted and afflicted people: and have given evident proof that they are not only in the enjoyment of the privileges of freemen themselves, but also that they willingly and cheerfully extend that invaluable blessing to others, and that they freely award to faithfulness and virtue their due.*[12]

The Nauvoo charters pass on a voice vote almost without discussion. Even the rejected Lincoln votes to approve them. They provide unprecedented powers to Smith's start-up theocracy. Bennett produces the Nauvoo City Charter in December 1840, about four months after his August or September baptism, and shortly after his September blessing.

Joseph, who has more ideas than a hundred men and far too few available elders to promote them, desperately needed a Talleyrand, a crafty, cynical, secular diplomat.[13] He gets one in Dr. John C.

---

[12]Ibid., 4:337-38, emphasis added.

[13]Bennett was not exactly without theological significance. "When Bennett was not practicing medicine, he served as an itinerant minister preaching in several Methodist Episcopal churches in Ohio. Chauncy Perkins predicted that Bennett's religious convictions would 'add a virtue to every act of his life.' An observer reported that when Bennett was not otherwise engaged, he gave practical demonstrations of his theological eloquence. He occasionally signed his name as the 'Rev. Doctor John Cook Bennett.' During December 1827 Bennett helped incorporate the Methodist Episcopal church, which required introducing and passing a bill in the Ohio legislature. This was his first known lobbying activity." (Andrew F. Smith, *The Saintly Scoundrel: The Life and Times of Dr. John Cook Bennett* [Urbana and Chicago: University of Illinois, 1997], 5). That newly incorporated church didn't thrive.

Bennett, next perhaps to Rigdon, the most distinguished and immediately useful convert in the relatively short history of the Mormon Church.

The Nauvoo Legion

As a physician, Bennett provides much needed service to suffering Latter-day Saints by offering them quinine for the treatment of malaria, a terrible problem at Nauvoo in the beginning. He then designs a highly successful plan to drain the swamps in order to eliminate the conditions that caused the malaria. Bennett soon becomes the Chancellor of the newly created University of Nauvoo, then a General in the Nauvoo Legion. Only Lieutenant General Joseph Smith outranks Major General John C. Bennett, the Legion's "effective commander."[14] In the months to follow, as Bennett multiplies accomplishments, no one will come close to presenting as impressive a portfolio built behind the prophet among the leaders and laity in the newly established Church.

In a measured way, the Mormons soon begin to look formidable to a new and darkening set of apprehensive neighbors as again they gather. Chastened by things that happened in Missouri, Mormon society becomes increasingly militaristic. An officer in the Nauvoo Legion (a new now visible Mormon army), Bennett refers to himself as General Bennett, and so does the General Conference report ("General John C. Bennett then spoke . . ."[15]). The citizens of Nauvoo, Illinois, will quickly be calling him "General Bennett," and once the militia is organized, he will be calling some of them "Colonel," "Major," "Captain" or "Guard." John C. Bennett was a "General" first[16] and a "Brother" second, more secular than spiritual. Joseph Smith, taken by his illustrious new colleague, will now indulge in the sincerest form of flattery and start to call himself "General Smith."

Bennett sends letters to General George W. Robinson, Colonel

---

[14]Bushman, *Joseph Smith: Rough Stone Rolling*, 459.
[15]*History of the Church*, 4:340.
[16]Bennett is identified to the Saints in code as "Joab, General in Israel." (Andrew F. Smith, *The Saintly Scoundrel*, 57).

Pratt, Colonel Higbee, Colonel Gove, Colonel Schindle and Captain Oliver Olney. Miss Brotherton and others will salute the under commander by addressing their correspondence to "General John C. Bennett." Joseph now rides his majestic stallion, Charlie, on Legion review while wearing "a blue coat, gold-colored epaulets, high black boots, and a sweeping hat topped with ostrich feathers," and he carries an impressive sword. "Only John C. Bennett outshone him, resplendent in gold braid, buttons, and tassels."[17]

The Nauvoo Legion seems capable of resolving knotty issues through the use of force, if that should ever prove to be necessary. These soldiers have sworn allegiance to the prophet, promising to defend him at the risk of their own lives. And they are far more visible than their earlier oath-bound Danite undercover precursors. Joseph's bodyguards – frontier tough Porter Rockwell, William Hickman, Hosea Stout, John D. Lee, and quite a number of others – wear smart white uniforms with red sash accents while surrounding the prophet on parade days.[18] There is a difference between an army of generic conscripts and a force composed of true believers. Oliver Cromwell, "God's Englishman," proved the power of disciples in England. Bennett sees in these obedient soldiers the foundation of an indomitable force.

This Nauvoo Legion is not typical Illinois militia. Mormon conscription applies to all able-bodied men between the ages of eighteen and forty-five. The Nauvoo citizen soldiers march and drill in ranks in earnest while Bennett creates a corps of riflemen. Other Illinois militias are sword and musket soldiers. The comparisons are striking. Only the United States Army outsizes the Nauvoo militia as a military force in antebellum America, and not by so very much. Then, too, there is a youth corps. The young Latter-day Saints who see the proud Legion and its exquisitely outfitted soldiers and leaders on ceremonial display on celebratory occasions develop the same martial spirit as their late-to-the-service fathers and brothers, and then some. They drill, like their role

---

[17]Newell and Avery, *Mormon Enigma: Emma Hale Smith*, 92.

[18]Years later, Mountain Meadows Massacre executor Lee – who guarded the prophet's home in Nauvoo, then Brigham Young's home in Nauvoo – would proudly wear his red sash to socials in southern Utah, where he was a Major in a militia commanded by Brigham Young.

models, until they too are old enough to serve. The youth brigades, like the Legion, also march in the Nauvoo parades.

Nauvoo's neighbors, watching legions of marching children following lines of well-drilled troops, and contemplating the supplementation of those threatening ranks both old and young by thousands, now begin to become alarmed. Nauvoo soon will have a population equal to or greater than that of Chicago. This army of the Lord makes Mormonism's Illinois neighbors uncomfortable. Some of them think the Mormons should be expelled before their burgeoning military power makes expulsion impossible.

The Nauvoo Mormons do what their prophet tells them to do. Because Joseph wants the then somewhat unfamiliar John C. Bennett to be elected as the first mayor of Nauvoo, Bennett will be elected by thousands of voters without a single negative vote. If Joseph wants the Mormons to vote for every Whig on the ballot but Abraham Lincoln, they will vote for every Whig but Lincoln. The Nauvoo Legion (Joseph's militia subject to Bennett's effective control) and the laws of the newly chartered city-state will combine to provide a nearly impenetrable barrier against the efforts of the Missouri authorities to extradite Joseph Smith, a fugitive from Missouri justice. The extradition of the prophet to Missouri is first on Joseph's list of things his formidable protectors should never allow.

Bennett, who is more politically astute than his philosophical client, curries favor with patrons in each of the parties. He regales Gentile politicians from both sides of the aisle, appearing to promise everyone Mormon support. He describes terrible persecutions suffered by the Latter-day Saints in the State of Missouri to sympathetic legislators in the State of Illinois. Sweet are the uses of such adversity then and forever after. His impact, like that of an earlier Rigdon, is immediate and pronounced. Bennett and Rigdon, renewing an earlier Campbellite acquaintance and bonding, will soon be fast friends. In retrospect, when viewed through history's unforgiving prism, Bennett may seem more swarthy than handsome, more facile than sincere, more ambitious than caring.

SMITH AND BENNETT: BROTHERS FOR TIME

For more than a year-and-a-half after the prophet baptized John C. Bennett, the two brothers are personally and professionally inseparable. Bennett quickly becomes the prophet's confidant. Joseph suddenly has no more intimate friend or trusted counselor. He sees in Bennett "a man of enterprize, extensive acquirements, and of independent mind" who is "calculated to be a great blessing to our community."[19] Bennett is now showered with favors by the grateful prophet. Joseph, already the General, now adopts some of the polished new convert's other personal idiosyncrasies, including his oratorical style, his military dress and bearing, "and his habit, no doubt enhanced by Smith's sometime-secretary W.W. Phelps own penchant for alliteration and Latinisms." Bennett uses "a wide variety of foreign phrases" to provide emphasis for his written communications.[20]

In all of this are a few striking facts that Joseph Smith has, at his risk, ignored. Joseph is informed as early as 1840 (shortly after the baptism of Bennett) that Bennett, who represented himself as a single man, actually has a wife and children.[21] Smith was told where Bennett's family lived, had he wanted to investigate the matter further. At that particular moment, he did not. It obviously didn't matter. After learning those then unannounced facts, Smith blessed the confidential Bennett with important postings and praise. And so did Joseph's Lord. Like the apostle Paul, Joseph said, Bennett "is active and diligent always employing himself in doing good to his fellow men."[22]

When the missionary apostles departed the English mission to repair to the land of their "nativity," they returned to find a new sheriff in Nauvoo. The unfamiliar face belongs to an ingratiating

---

[19]*Times and Seasons*, 15 January 1841, 275, quoted in Bushman, *Joseph Smith: Rough Stone Rolling*, 410.

[20]Van Wagoner, *Mormon Polygamy: A History*, 16.

[21]Bennett was married to Mary Barker, the daughter of Colonel Joseph Barker, a particularly prominent resident at Marietta, Ohio. (Andrew F. Smith, *The Saintly Scoundrel*, 1, 5.

[22]Andrew F. Ehat and Lyndon Cook, *The Words of Joseph Smith* (Provo, UT: Religious Studies Center, Brigham Young University, 1980), 59, quoted in Van Wagoner, *Mormon Polygamy: A History*, 16.

upstart, a dynamic man busy changing the landscape. The English (and other) missionaries return to find Bennett firmly ensconced in an ailing Sidney Rigdon's place. Rigdon did not leave his post as First Counselor in the First Presidency. Bennett assumed his duties but with a new title. Bennett is appointed to be the Assistant President of the Church of Jesus Christ of Latter-day Saints at General Conference on April 8, 1841. In that highly visible capacity he seems to stand between Joseph and the Quorum of the Twelve.[23] In 1841 and 1842, and until his fall from grace, next only to Smith, Bennett is the most powerful man in the Mormon Church. So said First Presidency Counselor William Law, so said Nauvoo Legion Captain Oliver Olney, so said Sarah Pratt, and so do the records appear to attest.

Joseph will debate John C. Bennett on the subject of "Lamanites and Negroes" in January 1842 (on the same day that he tries to persuade a young English convert by the name of Martha Brotherton, not yet of age and unfamiliar with "the Principle," to secretly become a plural wife of Brigham Young). Smith will praise his friendly adversary following that debate when he will say that Bennett's oratory is superior to that of the apostle Paul.[24] In 1841 and until April 1842, Bennett's influence is monumental, widely spread and broadly felt.

A complex man like Bennett, an ambitious and clever deceiver, could be a dangerous rival when and if he ever left the fold. And he will leave the fold. The issue that will divide these two powerful like-minded men and shake the kingdom will be a woman, Sidney's teenage daughter Nancy.

The Letter and the Dismissal

Soon after Bennett is baptized and before he achieves those various positions of spiritual and temporal prominence in the Church and in the community, aspersions are cast upon his character. "Soon after it was known that he had become a member of said Church, a

---

[23] *History of the Church*, 4:339. *See, e.g.,* Van Wagoner, *Mormon Polygamy: A History*, 16.

[24] Bushman, *Joseph Smith: Rough Stone Rolling*, 411.

communication was received at Nauvoo from a person of respectable character . . . residing in the vicinity where Bennett had lived."[25] "Bennett, it was said, had a respectable wife who had left him in the face of repeated infidelities."[26] This letter described Bennett as "a very mean man." It further said that his wife and two or three children were living in "McConnellsvill[e], Morgan county, Ohio."[27] Joseph does not credit those damning allegations, but rather acts in all the ways he later did in the face of them. He will excuse his disregard of that particular warning from a credible source, when the need for an explanation does arise, with a lame excuse. "[K]nowing that it is no uncommon thing for good men to be evil spoken against," he will only much later say, "the above letter was kept quiet, but held in reserve."[28] Joseph ignores those accusations and others when he then receives other even more incriminating allegations in the form of two additional letters from Bishop George Miller, and from Hyrum Smith (Bennett's Patriarch) and William Law, dated March 2, 1841, and June 1841, respectively. The letter from Hyrum and William "confirmed" what was then described as the earlier "speculation."[29] After the "speculation" is thus twice or thrice confirmed, Joseph leaves his valued associate in his various different postings for about a year.

After the 1840 letter, after the prophet received a seriously demeaning March 2, 1841, report from Bishop George Miller, whom he had sent to investigate, and just before the letter from Hyrum Smith and William Law (prepared in June 1841 but not delivered until July), the Church praised the character of John C. Bennett in the *Times and Seasons*, an official publication, in June 1841 in the following terms:

> *General Bennett's character as a gentleman, an officer, a scholar, and physician, stands too high to*

---

[25]Joseph Smith, "An Address to the Church of Jesus Christ of Latter-day Saints and to all the Honorable Part of the Community," *History of the Church*, 5:36.

[26]Bushman, *Joseph Smith: Rough Stone Rolling*, 460.

[27]Joseph Smith, "An Address to the Church of Jesus Christ of Latter-day Saints and to all the Honorable Part of the Community," *History of the Church*, 5:36.

[28]Ibid.

[29]Bushman, *Joseph Smith: Rough Stone Rolling*, 460.

need defending by us; suffice it to say, that he is in the confidence of the Executive, holds the office of Quarter-Master-General of this State, and is well known to a large number of persons of the first respectability throughout the state. He has, likewise, been favorably known for upwards of eight years by some of the authorities of the Church.[30]

Bennett's Character

Men and women of distinction, having attainments in civil society, seldom joined the Church. Bennett, who is a modest success in the State of Illinois, defied that convention. The Church doesn't capture him; he captures the Church. Not in 1832, when it is small and nondescript, but rather in 1840 when its prospects are rather improved. Bennett understands the dynamic possibilities of the new religion. While he claims to be a single man, Joseph knows almost immediately that he is not. That is a fact of some importance. It speaks to the character of the grantor of Bennett's postings, Joseph or Jesus, the prophet or his Lord. Only after the relationship between the two men is fractured in 1842 does Smith make this any kind of public issue.

Bennett had not been long in Nauvoo, Smith said after the rupture, before "he began to keep company with a young lady, one of our citizens," who, because she didn't know he had a wife, "became confident from his behavior towards her, that he intended to marry her; and this he gave her to understand he would do." Joseph, while not speaking of this until 1842, "seeing the folly of such an acquaintance," said that he had "persuaded him to desist." And when he did not, "and on account of his continuing his course," then "finally threatened to expose him if he did not desist." This strong request to all outward appearance, Joseph later reported, seemed to have had "the desired effect," and the acquaintance between Bennett and the vulnerable young woman was then seen to have

---

[30]*Times and Seasons* 2 (1 June 1841): 431-32, quoted in Van Wagoner, *Mormon Polygamy: A History*, 229 n 2, emphasis added.

broken off.[31]   These after-the-fact representations seem after-the-fact doubtful. Bennett blatantly courted other women in Nauvoo as a single man in 1840, 1841 and 1842, when the prophet well knew that he was not. And Bennett's greatest successes with the city's women, some of them documented in the Minutes of the Nauvoo High Council, then soon followed.

On March 2, 1841, Mormon second Bishop George Miller informed Joseph Smith that Bennett's "wife, Mary, had 'left him . . . .'"

> *The prophet sent Bishop George Miller to Ohio to investigate. Shortly after the January 1841 revelation [where the Lord is seen] praising Bennett's 'work,' Miller wrote Smith that Bennett appeared to be an adventurous malcontent who had lived in at least twenty different places and believed himself the "smartest man in the nation . . . always ready to fall in with whatever is popular." Miller added that the doctor's wife, Mary, had "left him under satisfactory evidence of his adulterous connections," and "it has been Dr. Bennett's wish that his wife should get a bill of divorcement, but as yet she has not."*[32]

He "at length . . . became," according to Miller, "so bold in his departures, that it was evident to all around that he was a sore offender." "[N]or," said Miller, "was this his only fault; he used her bad otherwise."[33] Miller's letter to Joseph, containing those recitals and others equally insistent, was dated *March 2, 1841*, just one month before John C. Bennett ascended the heights to become the Assistant President of the Church of Jesus Christ of Latter-day Saints. It hadn't mattered. Bishop Miller told Joseph, before that conference and prior to Bennett's impressive inspired appointment, that Bennett "was a superficial character, always uneasy," who

---

[31]Joseph Smith, "An Address to the Church of Jesus Christ of Latter-day Saints and to all the Honorable Part of the Community," *History of the Church*, 5:36.

[32]Letter, George Miller to Joseph Smith, 2 March 1841, *Times and Seasons* 3 (1 July 1842): 842, quoted in Van Wagoner, *Mormon Polygamy*, 17-18, emphasis added.

[33]Ibid.

"moved from place to place." "[I]t is not presumed that less than twenty towns has been his place of residence at different times . . . ." "[H]e has been able to push himself into places and situations entirely beyond his abilities . . . ." "[I]f he cannot at once be placed at the head of the heap, he soon seeks a situation . . . ." "[H]e is always ready to fall in with whatever is popular . . . ."[34] Joseph knew all of this and it didn't matter. In summary, the bishop told the prophet this:

> *During many years his poor, but confiding wife, followed him from place to place, with no suspicion of his unfaithfulness to her . . . . Mrs. Bennett now lives with her father; has two children living, and has buried one or two . . . ; in fine, he is an imposter, and unworthy of the confidence of all good men . . . . [W]e withhold the names of our informants, . . . but hold ourselves in readiness, at all times, to substantiate by abundant testimony, all that has been asserted, if required, as the documents are all on hand. George Miller.*[35]

For what Joseph knew, see Appendix C, "Timeline: John C. Bennett."

"PROMISCUOUS INTERCOURSE"

While the Bennett fissure was festering, and as some in Nauvoo heard about a controversial proposition made by Joseph Smith to Miss Rigdon, the *New York Herald* reported the rumor (on May 16, 1842) that men and women in Nauvoo "connected in promiscuous intercourse without regard to the holy bonds of matrimony."[36] The domestic climate in Nauvoo from 1841 and onward was well suited to the machinations of the clever Bennett, a knowledgeable physician ahead of the curve.

---

[34]*Times and Seasons* 3 (1 July 1842), 842.

[35]Ibid., emphasis added.

[36]*New York Herald,* 16 May 1842, quoted in Brodie, *No Man Knows My History,* 269.

When Joseph turned on Bennett in May and June of 1842, he then and for the first time reported "in a guarded public statement" that he had caught Bennett *"preaching promiscuous intercourse as early as December 1840 and had let him off with a severe rebuke."*[37] Every good thing that happened to John C. Bennett, his power and his postings, happened after December 1840. In a letter to Governor Thomas Carlin dated June 24, 1842, Joseph placed this date even closer to Bennett's baptism. "More than twenty months ago Bennett," according to Smith, "went to a lady in the city and began to teach her that promiscuous intercourse between the sexes was lawful . . . ."[38] Twenty months was October 1840, well before December 1840, and "[m]ore than twenty months" was earlier still. How bad is all of that? October 1840 was a month or two after Bennett was baptized by Joseph Smith in August or September, and a month or two before the legislature granted the Nauvoo charters. On January 19, 1841, hard on the heels of Joseph's supposed "severe" rebuke, and after the prophet's knowledge of everything already considered, Joseph's Lord spoke to Bennett in a revelation delivered to Smith in these terms: *"I have seen the work which he hath done, which I accept if he continue . . . ."*[39]

Bennett, the 1840s gynecologist ("instructor in midwifery"), was wise in the ways of women and wayward. His obvious access to the prophet (they were often seen together), his remarkable position in the Church (Assistant President), his prominence in the community, his glib tongue, low morals and lack of restraint made his objectives easily attainable. In principle, his pursuits did not markedly differ from those of church members William Smith, Chauncey L. Higbee, Darwin Chase, Justis Morse, Gustavus Hills, Joel S. Miles, Lyman D. Littlefield and various others.[40] Who could say that they had not

---

[37]Brodie, *No Man Knows My History,* 309, emphasis added.

[38]Letter, Joseph Smith to Governor Thomas Carlin, 24 June 1842, *History of the Church,* 5:42.

[39]Doctrine and Covenants 124:17, emphasis added.

[40]"6 Feb [1841] [Joseph] Smith tells the Nauvoo high council not to excommunicate Theodore Turley [later a member of the Council of Fifty arrested on a counterfeiting charge] for 'sleeping with two females,' requiring him only to confess 'that he had acted unwisely, unjustly, imprudently, and unbecoming.'" (D. Michael Quinn, *The Mormon Hierarchy: Origins of Power* [Salt Lake City, UT: Signature Books in association with Smith Research Associates, 1994], 632).

engaged in promiscuous intercourse or traded on their ties to the prophet in their relations with women?

Sex Without Commitment: Polygamous Beginnings

Like fraternity boys on some promiscuous campus, Apostle William Smith (the younger brother of Joseph Smith), John C. Bennett and Chauncey L. Higbee, important Mormons every one, are accused of contributing to the delinquency of some gullible Nauvoo women. Entries in the Minutes of the High Council dated "May 20th 1842" say that "Chancy L. Higbee," a special friend of Bennett, got charged by Bishop George Miller "[f]or unchaste and unvirtuous conduct *with the widow Miller and others.* Pled not guilty."[41] The High Council has not yet seen or heard about a revelation on polygamy, and marriage outside of the confines of the privileged few is still the union of one man and one woman as most particularly described in the carefully drafted (and canonized) Article on Marriage which remained in the Doctrine and Covenants (polygamy be damned) until 1876.

This early 1840s Nauvoo-centered promiscuity involving conjugal connections preceding the erection of the remarkable revelation soon to be put in place in support of Mormon polygamy is so relatively new in its strikingly attractive conception that the rules are undefined. The July 12, 1843, revelation (Section 132 of the Doctrine and Covenants since 1876), the revelation commanding polygamy, had not yet clarified the finer points of the doctrine for a small group of privileged insiders, and domestic relations in the City of Joseph thus left much to be desired. Such informal alliances –marriages by the civil authority remain unrecognized – are, to say the least, in a state of flux and very confused. William Smith, John C. Bennett, Chauncey L. Higbee, Theodore Turley, Gustavus Hills, Darwin Chase and a host of prominent other offenders, men almost invariably close to the prophet, did not concern themselves with the

---

Turley's crime? Getting caught. Turley did what others said the prophet said that they could do. His offence is seen to have called for contrition not a consequence.

[41]Fred C. Collier, comp., *The Nauvoo High Council Minute Books of the Church of Jesus Christ of Latter-day Saints,* 1 ed. (Hanna, UT: Collier's Publishing Co., 20 May 1842, additional copyright December 2005), 56, emphasis added.

doctrine of polygamy and its developing structures. They cut to the chase. More sparing in their own streamlined practices, they may seem to have settled for unembarrassed (but confidential) adultery.

Chauncey L. Higbee, in particular, cannot be ignored. "[T]hree witnesses testified" that Higbee "had seduced them, and at different times been guilty of unchaste and unvirtuous conduct with them, and *taught the doctrine* that it was right to have free intercourse with women if it was kept secret &c and also taught that Joseph Smith authorized them to practice these things &c."[42] Margaret and Matilda Nyman and Catherine Fuller Warren were all seduced by Higbee. Catherine Fuller Warren was also accused of "unchaste and unvirtuous conduct with John C. Bennett and others." She admitted to intercourse with Bennett. She confessed to having intercourse with Chauncey Higbee, "and [with] the prophet's younger brother, Apostle William Smith."[43]

So it was that Catherine Fuller Warren had been seduced by Bennett, the Assistant President of the Mormon Church, the Mayor of Nauvoo, the Chancellor of the University, the Master of Chancery, a Major General in the Nauvoo Legion, the Secretary of the Masonic Lodge, the doctor who cured malaria, an architect and the executor of the Nauvoo Charter. She had been seduced by William Smith, the prophet's brother, a member of the Founding Quorum of the Twelve Apostles and a future Patriarch, and by Chauncey L. Higbee, John C. Bennett's *aide-de-camp* in the Nauvoo Legion. The complaints implicating three highly placed and extremely visible Mormon men – John C. Bennett, William Smith and Chauncey L. Higbee – surfaced before the High Council at Nauvoo, Illinois, in 1842. The revelation on polygamy, Section 132 of the Doctrine and Covenants, did not surface there until August 12, 1843, and was not publicly proclaimed in Nauvoo or anywhere else until the Saints admitted the practice after relocating to the Utah Territory in 1847 in August 1852.

---

[42]Ibid., emphasis added.
[43]Van Wagoner, *Mormon Polygamy: A History*, 24.

Willard Richards: Polygamous Beginnings

On June 23, 1842, shortly after Joseph publicly denounced John C. Bennett (breaking a promise he made not to discard his notorious colleague), he found time to write a letter to Jennetta Richards, Willard Richards' wife, a woman then living away from her husband in Richmond, Massachusetts. After praising Richards, who had quickly become Bennett's replacement as confidant-in-chief ("Never did I have a greater intimacy with any man than with him"), Joseph now speaks for his new best friend. "We are about to send him in a few days after his dear family . . . ." Mrs. Richards seems to have said to Joseph at some earlier time that he had Willard and she had hardship. Joseph responded thus: "I want you, beloved sister, to be a general in this matter, in helping him along, which I know you will." "You say I have got him; so I have, in the which I rejoice, for he has done me a great good . . . ." "He will be able to teach you many things which you have never heard; you may have implicit confidence in the same."[44]

This is the supposedly unlettered Joseph speaking like Shakespeare to Willard Richards' wife. And maybe Willard helped. Joseph encourages Mrs. Richards to be stalwart. He wants her to return Willard promptly ("and may God speed his journey, and return him quickly to our society"). Prior to this letter, Willard, while away from his wife, is alleged to have been living with Orson Hyde's wife without the benefit of matrimony at the Printing Office. In 1842, this same Marinda Nancy Johnson (Hyde) will be secretly married for a second time and without a divorce to Joseph Smith, becoming Marinda Nancy Johnson (Hyde) (Smith). Hyde, an Apostle, is out of the country on a mission to the Holy Land, a place where Joseph Smith had sent him in the name of the Lord. Mrs. Orson Hyde, who now also became Mrs. Joseph Smith, the wife of two husbands, would be shared by both of her husbands for time, without the knowledge of one of them, but would, with her biological children fathered by Hyde (ten of them), belong to Joseph Smith in a Mormon afterlife.

What, besides abortion, has Bennett done that Willard has not? By

---

[44]*History of the Church*, 5:40-41.

what gospel principle can Willard's alleged cohabitation with Mrs. Hyde, the wife of a missing Apostle, be condoned? Forgotten and unpunished? Does Willard's alleged dalliance with the wife of Hyde while Hyde is on a mission to the Holy Land have anything to do with celestial marriage, kinship, social order or the eternal family?[45] Is his conduct more political than sentimental? Is this some acceptable manifestation of that vaunted New and Everlasting Covenant? Or is it adultery in your face? And is the prophet, the editor of the *Times and Seasons* and the master of the Printing Office, complicit?

Same Crime with Different Results

Bennett did almost nothing in principle that Apostle William Smith and others close to the faith, including Joseph Smith, did not. And it was not his conduct with women that caused the prophet to bring him down. Joseph's polyandrous marriages to thirteen or fourteen women who were already married to other husbands when they married him,[46] and his proposals to the married wives of other married men and to unmarried women[47] (who seem to have turned him down) could scarcely be considered different than John C. Bennett's and Willard Richards' simplified conjugal relations without the benefit of a ceremony in any important respect. Joseph Smith plurally married about thirteen women, including eight women who were already married to other men, in the first six months of 1842, the spring and summer of John C. Bennett's discontent. These women risked their marriages to non-Mormons,

---

[45]"Hyde married Marinda Nancy Johnson, in Kirtland, Ohio, on September 4, 1834. Joseph Smith also secretly married Marinda as a plural wife in Spring 1842 while Hyde was on his mission to Jerusalem. It is not clear when, or if, Hyde learned about his wife's marriage to Smith. However, three months after his return, Hyde had learned about plural marriage and married two additional wives. He ultimately took eight wives and fathered 32 children." ("Orson Hyde," [accessed 25 May 2018], available from https://en.wikipedia.org/wiki/Orson_Hyde; Internet, p. 4 of 6). Doctrine and Covenants 132:61-63 suggests that Joseph had zero business marrying Orson Hyde's wife while he was on a mission, or at any other time.

[46]George D. Smith, *Nauvoo Polygamy: "... but we called it celestial marriage"* (Salt Lake City: Signature Books, 2008), chapters 2 and 3, 53-239.

[47]Ibid., 229-35.

or to Church members of "low [or lower] ecclesiastical status," for secret marriages to the prophet who promised to take them to the head of the line in the afterlife.[48]

Joseph treated his brother, Apostle William Smith, an accomplished sinner, better than he did John C. Bennett or Chauncey L. Higbee, men guilty of the same crime. And he treated Bennett differently than he did Theodore Turley and Willard Richards.[49] Lorenzo Snow, a future President of the Mormon Church, described disciplinary proceedings against William Smith. Contrast this treatment with the humiliation of Bennett when it is further described.

> Brigham Young was once tried to the very utmost by the Prophet [Joseph Smith], and for a moment his standing in the Church seemed to tremble in the balance. Wm. Smith, one of the first quorum of apostles in this age had been guilty of adultery and many other sins. The Prophet Joseph instructed Brigham (then the Pres. of the Twelve) to prefer a charge against the sinner, which was done. Before the time set for the trial, however, Emma Smith talked to Joseph and said the charge preferred against William was with a view to injuring the Smith family. After the trial had began Joseph entered the room and was given a seat. The testimony of witnesses concerning the culprit's sins was then continued. *After a short time Joseph arose filed with wrath and said, "Bro. Brigham, I will not listen to this abuse of my family a minute longer. I will wade in blood up to my knees before I will do it."* This was a supreme moment. A rupture between the two greatest men on earth seemed imminent. But Brigham Young was equal to the danger, and he instantly said. "Bro. Joseph, I withdraw the

---

[48]Ibid., 229.

[49]Bennett's catastrophic issue wasn't about sin, women and sex; it was about Joseph and Nancy Rigdon, $500.00, or the best lot on Main Street.

charge." Thus the angry passions were instantly stilled.[50]

William Smith, a "sinner" and "culprit," an apostle "guilty of adultery and many other sins," had done what Bennett had done. Joseph, who will publicly excoriate the terrible Bennett, will threaten Brigham Young and say that he will "wade in blood" up to his knees to exonerate his "cadaverous" brother. Apostle William Smith's punishment? A brief mission to Tennessee. Bennett and Higbee were both excommunicated, but William Smith kept his protected place as a member of the Quorum of the Twelve Apostles. And on May 24, 1845, after the deaths of Joseph and Hyrum Smith, William Smith, like his prophet brother, father and Hyrum, briefly became the Presiding Patriarch of the Church of Jesus Christ of Latter-day Saints.[51] Unlike all of his predecessors, he was ordained by the authority of the Quorum of the Twelve Apostles.

While Joseph is supposed to be directing his rage at John C. Bennett for teaching Nauvoo women that promiscuous intercourse is acceptable if it is kept secret – because when there is no accuser there is no crime – and/or for seducing innocent women in Joseph's name with (or without) a promise of marriage, Joseph is sexually active. And so is his gregarious brother, an Apostle and a future Patriarch. Bennett's more private defense was simple, easy to say and hard to rebut: "I did what Joseph did." Joseph's spiritual wives, a number now suspected to include thirteen or fourteen women already married to and living with other men, but not including hundreds of posthumous sealings, many to the married wives of other men (the Empress Josephine, the former wife of Napoleon; St. Helena, the mother of Constantine; Queen Maude, the wife of Henry I), cannot be explained with reference to the revelation on celestial marriage. These deviant practices did not track the blessings of Jacob. The spiritual wife doctrine, then Mormon polyandry on earth as it is in heaven, is not doctrinal (and was) promiscuous intercourse.

---

[50]*Candid Insights of a Mormon Apostle: The Dairies of Abraham H. Cannon, 1889-1895,* ed. Edward Leo Lyman (Salt Lake City: Signature Books in association with the Smith-Pettit Foundation, 2010), 82-83, quoting Lorenzo Snow, emphasis added.

[51]Van Wagoner, *Mormon Polygamy: A History,* 24.

MASONIC DISCLOSURES

On June 16, 1842, about two months after Nancy Rigdon declined Joseph's offer to become one of his plural wives, an unusual Notice was published by Bishop George Miller, Bennett's fervent detractor and the Master of the Masonic Lodge.[52]

NOTICE

To all whom it may concern, greeting: -- Whereas, John Cook Bennett, in the organization of the Nauvoo Lodge, under dispensation palmed himself upon the fraternity as a regular mason, in good standing: and satisfactory testimony having been produced before said lodge, that he, said Bennett, was an expelled mason, we therefore publish to all the masonic world the above facts that he, the said Bennett, may not impose himself again upon the fraternity of masons . . . .

George Miller
Master of Nauvoo Lodge
under Dispensation[53]

General Bennett claimed to be a Mason in good standing. The Nauvoo Lodge now says that he is not. That information had to have surprised most of the Latter-day Saints. General Bennett had spoken at various times with what had seemed to be heartfelt sincerity about the obligations of Masonry. The Notice describes Bennett as a back-sliding "expelled mason" disgraced at the bar of

---

[52]Bishop George Miller, Mormon, Mason, Lodge Master, will become a follower of Lyman Wight and then of James J. Strang, after the death of Joseph Smith. He will become one of the King of Beaver Island's most dependable disciples. Some twelve thousand people will follow Strang, many of them formerly prominent Mormons, including many Smiths. Strang's community (a Mormon schism) will rival that of Brigham Young (another Mormon schism) in size. One of his members, besides Lodge Master Miller, will be John C. Bennett. George Miller and John C. Bennett, adversaries in the City of Joseph, will reunite as followers of Strang. Bennett will be excommunicated from the society of Strang in 1847. Miller will be loyal until the death of Strang.

[53]*History of the Church*, 5:32, 16 June 1842, emphasis added and retained.

some other lodge (exactly where the notice didn't say) for reasons not further explained.[54] The brief declaration says, in an inexplicit and guarded way, that "satisfactory testimony" had been produced before the lodge of Bennett's earlier expulsion. "Out of the Masons and into the Latter-day Saints?" The guarded way in which the message is framed, failing to describe the offended lodge or the alleged offense, leaves room for interpretation. Something would be needed to dampen the considerable excitement in what had somewhat abruptly become an unsettled community.

THE FALL OUT

Mine Fields: The Proposal and Disgrace

In 1842 insidious rumors surfaced concerning Joseph's alleged proposal of marriage to Miss Nancy Rigdon, her spirited refusal, and a confrontation that then rather quickly escalated between Joseph Smith, Bishop George Miller and the family of Sidney Rigdon. General John C. Bennett and General George W. Robinson (a former General Church Recorder and Clerk to the First Presidency[55]) are high ranking officers in the Nauvoo Legion and close personal friends.

When Bennett approached the prophet and said, "Joseph, you are a Master Mason, and Nancy is a Master Mason's daughter . . . – *remember your obligation*,"[56] Joseph replied and said, "You are my enemy, and wish to oppose me."[57] That was John C. Bennett's account. It wasn't about Bennett's women, or anything else just

---

[54]Joseph Smith Sr., Joseph Smith's father, was himself a "seceder" Mason, a covenant-breaker who left the craft after the death of William Morgan, the Masonic martyr. The precedent? Covenants (as in the case of Joseph's father, and as in the case of civil marriage), whether spiritual or temporal, may be dismissed upon a showing of good cause (examples: bad conduct, misrepresentations, lack of informed consent).

[55]Andrew Jenson, comp., *Church Chronology: A Record of Important Events Pertaining to the History of the Church of Jesus Christ of Latter-day Saints*, 2d ed., rev. and enlarged (Salt Lake City: Deseret News, 1914), 14 (1838).

[56]John C. Bennett, *The History of the Saints: Or, an Exposé of Joe Smith and Mormonism* (Boston: Leland & Whiting, 1842; photomechanical reprint of 1842 original, Salt Lake City: Modern Microfilm Company), 242, emphasis retained.

[57]Ibid.

discussed; it was about Miss Rigdon. The warning (from Bennett to Miss Rigdon) about the purpose for the meeting with Smith at the Printing Office had been presumed and was unwelcome. Joseph's energized *animus* was personal and more than merely fleeting. Bennett's indirect unexpected intervention, which had set Miss Rigdon on fire, had unmistakably threatened the charmed relationship between the "greatest scamp" and his locally powerful patron.

The Notice from the Masonic Lodge, on top of Joseph's malevolent reply, is a double whammy. Terrible news. Bennett, who had underestimated the inflammatory effects of his imposition, hopes to be restored, forgiven and reinstated. But what the Masonic Lodge has done, the Church will probably do. Bishop George Miller (the ambitious man who signed the Notice at the Lodge) is at that particular moment in time competing for Smith's favor, totally loyal and busy doing his bidding. Not in ten millennia would Miller have dared to publish that Notice publicly indicting Assistant President Bennett without the Prophet's consent. On tenterhooks at the home of Dr. Robert Foster, General John C. Bennett requests, and thinks that he has obtained, the ambivalent Prophet's promise of mercy. Anyone who saw the Notice at the Masonic Lodge probably knew that he had not.

John C. Bennett is larger than life in the City of Joseph. As the effective Commander of the Nauvoo Legion, he is its spit and polish organizer and military strategist. He is seen in resplendent military regalia at Legion reviews on ceremonial occasions, and he is seen conducting General Conference in Nauvoo. The thought that the well situated unanimously-elected Mayor John C. Bennett, one of the gods, might be excommunicated – consigned to the buffetings of Satan in the flesh – must have seemed almost inconceivable, but the Prophet was undecided and things were unsettled. Quite suddenly, and in remembrance of earlier tumultuous events at Kirtland, Nauvoo seems like a city possessed. "He said he was a Mason in good standing. Now they say he wasn't. They say he abandoned a wife and children in Ohio and isn't a single man. They say he tells women there's nothing wrong with adultery if you don't get caught." It had become a nightmare for Joseph, according to his biographer Bushman, to have his "carefully regulated celestial marriages debased into a device for seducing the unsuspecting."[58]

George W. Robinson, who was personally present when Joseph Smith met with "Miss Nancy" and the Rigdons, was an eyewitness to the turmoil that followed. Robinson opined that marriage had not been Joseph's first proposal.

> *Smith . . . stated to her that he had had an affection for her for several years, and wished that she should be his; that the Lord was well pleased with this matter, for he had got a revelation on the subject, and God had given him all the blessings of Jacob, &c., &c., and that there was no sin in it whatever; but if she had any scruples of conscience about the matter he would marry her privately, and enjoined her to secrecy, &c., &c.*[59]

"[C]arefully regulated celestial marriages"? Hardly. He would marry her privately if she failed to accept the proposition "that there was no sin in it whatever" (meaning in his wish "that she should be his" without a marriage), or if "she had any scruples of conscience about the matter," meaning about unregulated undeputized domesticity. In all of that, Smith's approach to Miss Rigdon was not unlike the propositions advanced by some of those other Mormon men to some of those other Mormon women. Sometimes marriage was promised, sometimes not.[60] Joseph's Lord allowed (in writing) both "wives and concubines." Many years later Sarah Pratt, a principled woman and reliable reporter, further confirmed the prophet's relaxed approach to intimacy. *"He used to state to his intended victims, as he did to me: 'God does not care if we*

---

[58]Bushman, *Rough Stone Rolling*, 460.

[59]Bennett, *The History of the Saints*, 246-47, emphasis omitted and added.

[60]Apostle William Smith's sexual relationship with Catherine Fuller Warren, whose favors he shared with John C. Bennett and Chauncey Higbee, and Higbee's other encounters, occurred without the benefit of a ceremony. As many as twelve of Smith's own marriages were not "carefully regulated," by that to say official, described, witnessed and properly recorded. Willard Richards' arrangement with Marinda Nancy Johnson, the wife of Orson Hyde, was not officially documented.

have a good time, if only other people do not know it."[61] That provided support for what Chauncey L. Higbee, John C. Bennett, William Smith, Gustavus Hills, Darwin Chase, Justis Morse, Joel S. Miles, Lyman D. Littlefield and others are supposed to have said to Sarah Miller, Catherine Fuller Warren, Margaret and Matilda Nyman, Esther Victoria Smith and various other women in 1842.

The first polygamous offenders in Nauvoo included Joseph Smith, Heber C. Kimball, Brigham Young, Reynolds Cahoon, Vinson Knight and William Clayton. Joseph would later offer William Law to Emma Smith, as recompense, if she would relent and allow him to practice polygamy with his girls in peace. It is hard to make a case for the proposition that these so-called celestial unions were "carefully regulated," and not merely formulas for the seduction of the "unsuspecting." Joseph's proposal to Nancy Rigdon and Brigham's proposal to Martha Brotherton are particular cases in point. Apostle Willard Richards alleged dalliance with the undivorced wife of Apostle Orson Hyde is a branch on the same tree. "By their fruits ye shall know them." Miss Rigdon, according to Smith, was at liberty to marry someone else even though she married him. Chauncey L. Higbee told women that illicit sexual intercourse was acceptable if kept secret. His victims said Higbee said Joseph said intimacy was acceptable if the parties kept their practice secret.[62] "Bennett told one woman after another that illicit sexual intercourse was acceptable if kept secret."[63] If they just didn't get caught. William Smith backed the sexually active Higbee up. William practiced what he told women his brother Joseph preached. Bennett did not deny his Nauvoo adulteries, but when he left the Church involuntarily, he didn't emphasize them.[64] After Bennett left the society, the records of his conquests are thought to have been scrubbed.

---

[61]Sarah M. Pratt interview with W. Wyl (21 May 1886), in Dr. W. Wyl (pen name, real name: Wilhelm Ritter von Wymetal), *Mormon Portraits 1 – Joseph Smith, The Prophet: His Family and Friends, A Study Based on Facts and Documents* (Salt Lake City, UT: Tribune Printing and Publishing Company, 1886), 62, emphasis retained and added.

[62]Bushman, *Joseph Smith: Rough Stone Rolling*, 460.

[63]Ibid.

[64]"Bennett never denied his Nauvoo adulteries, but he charged Joseph Smith with exactly the same wrongdoing." (Ibid.).

The Break Between Joseph and Bennett

The break between Smith and Bennett was initiated by Smith – at first hesitantly and with justified apprehension – in May of 1842, a few weeks after Nancy Rigdon refused Smith's proposal.   The Prophet approached Miss Rigdon in mid-April 1842, the same month he was plurally married and sealed to Mrs. Orson Hyde.

On June 18, 1842, Joseph denounces Bennett at a public meeting following the delivery of a notice disfellowshipping the now discredited Bennett. The certificate of disfellowshipment signed by Smith on May 11, 1842, wasn't delivered until May 25. In mid-June 1842, editor Joseph Smith publishes the notice of disfellowshipment in the *Times and Seasons,*[65] and on June 21, 1842, the disgraced Bennett leaves Nauvoo. Eight days later (on June 29, 1842), Joseph Smith recklessly takes a thirteenth plural wife, the thirty-eight year old poetess Eliza Roxcy Snow.   Smith's stated philosophical differences with Bennett included the fact that Bennett was teaching Nauvoo women, whether wedded or not, that sexual intercourse was acceptable to the leaders of the Church if the parties kept the practice secret.[66] Bennett seduced women in Smith's name. Other important Mormon men, including Apostle William Smith, soon faithfully followed Bennett's successful domestic model.   One of Bennett's victims "accused Bennett of teaching her that illicit sexual relations were innocent by claiming that Joseph was entering into such relationships."[67]

"[B]eware, be still, be prudent, repent, reform, but do it in a way not to destroy all around you"[68]

Nauvoo was a cesspool. On May 11, 1842, Joseph draws up a bull of excommunication for Bennett.   Bennett had seduced "innumerable women in Joseph's name quite without benefit of

---

[65]Ibid., 461.
[66]Ibid., 460.
[67]Ibid., 461.
[68]*History of the Church*, 5:20.

ceremony"[69] or the hint of a sealing. "Even worse he had promised abortion to those who became pregnant."[70] The promise was free but secret love with a correction in the event of a mistake. Zeruiah N. Goddard, repeating the gossip of Sarah Pratt, reported that, "Dr. Bennett told her he could cause abortion with perfect safety to the mother at any stage of pregnancy, and that he had frequently destroyed and removed infants before their time to prevent exposure of the parties and that he had instruments for that purpose."[71] Years after the fact, Sarah Pratt told Dr. W. Wyl that she had seen the long device Bennett used to perform abortions. She said it seemed to be of steel crooked at one end.[72] Joseph sharply interrogated some of Bennett's supposed victims and obtained their affidavits. When he had finished with them he demanded an affidavit from Bennett. Bennett's affidavit, which he later said had been coerced, was seen to report that Joseph had not been complicit in Bennett's crimes.

This is touchy stuff, and Joseph is playing with fire. Joseph initially concedes the privilege of a peaceable withdrawal with a public vote of thanks for Bennett's services as Mayor of Nauvoo.[73] In this dicey scenario, Bennett would be permitted to leave the carnage quietly. Brigham Young and Wilson Law, encouraged by Bennett, spoke in favor of a reconciliation. Salvaging the career of the dissolute Bennett did not offend a rough and ready Brigham Young. Bennett, for his part, made every effort to be at peace with Sidney Rigdon,[74] with whom he was known to have been close, the man whose position he had effectively (but temporarily) been asked to fill. The man whose daughter he was supposed to have tried to protect. On May 25, 1842, the Apostles and the High Council

---

[69]Brodie, *No Man Knows My History*, 311-12. "There can be no doubt that Bennett was an abortionist. Sarah Pratt told W. Wyl many years later that Bennett had showed her one of his instruments and indicated that he had performed illegal operations in the city." (Ibid., quoting Dr. W. Wyl, *Mormon Portraits, or, The Truth About the Mormon Leaders From 1830 to 1866* [Tribune Printing and Publishing Company, 1886], 61).

[70]Brodie, *No Man Knows My History*, 311.

[71]Ibid., 311-12.

[72]Sarah Pratt Interview with Dr. W. Wyl (21 May 1886), *Mormon Portraits 1 – Joseph Smith*, 61.

[73]Brodie, *No Man Knows My History*, 312.

[74]Ibid., 313.

excommunicated Bennett. Even now, Joseph remains conflicted. Is Bennett less dangerous in or out of the Church?[75] All of Nauvoo is in turmoil.[76]

A vacillating Smith now agrees to keep Bennett in fellowship if his former colleague will agree to make a public confession. Bennett makes his humiliating confession in a flood of tears at the Masonic Hall in front of a hundred brethren on May 26. The clever man, having absolved the prophet, confesses his sins, weeping in anguish and making every effort to stay. Now Joseph, to the surprise and indignation of his followers, pleads mercy for Bennett. "He wanted to recover the man in whom he had put so much trust."[77] There are many who do not like that craven message. The Relief Society, led by anti-polygamy crusader Emma Smith, is most particularly incensed. She didn't like the man. In her offended eyes, Bennett was a rascal who needed to be severely punished. Joseph made the case for mercy to a militant group of Relief Society sisters.

> *[A] little tale will set the world on fire. At this time, the truth on the guilty should not be told openly, strange as this may seem, yet this is policy . . . . It is necessary to hold an influence in the world, and thus spare ourselves an extermination . . . . I am advised by some of the heads of the Church to tell the Relief Society to be virtuous, but to save the Church from desolation and the sword; beware, be still, be prudent, repent, reform, but do it in a way not to destroy all around you.[78]*

---

[75]Ibid. "Stories of Bennett's depravity had seeped through the city, and if he was now restored to favor the prophet would be accused of countenancing abortion and prostitution."

[76]"The story got out and it became the talk of the town that Joseph had made a proposition to Nancy Rigdon to become his wife, and that she refused him." (Affidavit. John W. Rigdon [Nancy's brother], quoted in *Blood Atonement and the Origin of Plural Marriage – A Discussion*, correspondence between Elder Joseph F. Smith, Jr., of the Church of Jesus Christ of Latter-day Saints, and Mr. Richard C. Evans, Second Counselor in the Presidency of the "Reorganized" Church [Salt Lake City: The Deseret News Press, 1905], 81-84).

[77]Bushman, *Joseph Smith: Rough Stone Rolling*, 461.

[78]*History of the Church*, 5:20, emphasis added.

The truth is not always useful. For another month the Bennett issue actively festers. In facing this insidious challenge, Joseph looks circumstances fraught with peril squarely in the face. What had he previously had to experience that was the equal of this?

> *For four weeks more Bennett remained a sore on the church, foul-smelling and insistent on attention. Finally Joseph became convinced that it was better to cut him off and let him do his worst than to nurture the corruption he was breeding in Nauvoo. Bennett would damn him if he used the knife, but his own people would if he did not. On June 23, 1842 he publicly exposed him and issued the bull of excommunication which had been held in reserve since the 11th of May.*[79]

In that Joseph breaks his promise to keep Bennett in fellowship if Bennett makes a public confession. In this case it is not so much Joseph who changes his mind. Others change his mind for him. It is a prophet's prerogative to change his mind when speaking as a mortal. His word while speaking when inspired is the will of the Lord, the mind of the Lord, the word of the Lord, the voice of the Lord and the power of God unto salvation, and scripture.[80] What civil society can be morally and socially ordered on so undependable an axis?

PUBLIC DENUNCIATION

Bennett's close to unprecedented ascension started in August or September of 1840 (when he was baptized) and continued until the spring of 1842. Joseph's overtures to Miss Rigdon (the daughter of Sidney) occurred in mid-April, 1842, and the prophet's anger with Bennett played out in public in May and June. John C. Bennett was a powerful leader in the Mormon Church protected in his powerful postings long after the prophet knew that he was a sexual predator, a deadbeat dad with a wife and children, and undivorced.

---

[79]Brodie, *No Man Knows My History*, 313-14, emphasis added.
[80]Doctrine and Covenants 68:4.

Joseph's mounting irritation with Bennett surfaces on a day when there is to be a mock battle between divided elements of the Nauvoo Legion, one force to be commanded by the military novitiate, Lieutenant General Joseph Smith, the other force to be commanded by the "peerless strategist," Major General John C. Bennett. On this particular day, the prophet refuses to position himself and his security guard as General Bennett planned. Joseph's cohort ignores Bennett's elaborate choreography. Suspecting harm to his person for whatever reason, something that seems quite unlikely, Smith refuses Bennett's military direction. He positions himself and his protectors as he pleases, as opposed to the plan perfected by Bennett, and does not permit himself to be humiliated in the mock battle by the tactically superior Bennett. The military exercise is conducted in the presence of Stephen A. Douglas and other dignitaries from Carthage, Illinois, who are visiting Nauvoo as honored guests. On that field, and at that review, commences a public test of will that Bennett can not hope to surmount.

The Speech

On Saturday, June 18, 1842, Joseph publicly denounces John C. Bennett from the pulpit in what is called an "Address to the Church . . . and to all the Honorable Part of the Community." There is tension on the stand and in the congregation the atmosphere is electric. It must have seemed as if everyone in Nauvoo was there, excluding perhaps John C. Bennett, Nancy Rigdon, Sarah and Orson Pratt. The sober demeanor of the normally affable prophet indirectly indicates the great importance he attaches to this particular meeting. Perhaps every member of the immense congregation has seen General Bennett at one time or another leading the Latter-day Saints in places of honor and close to the prophet riding together across the green, or preening in front of the Legion. For Bennett (like God himself) is the Mormon prophet's "right-hand man." Joseph appears to hold no other earthly person in higher esteem. In addition to the "heavenly accolade" found in that revelation delivered to Bennett and the Church by the Mormon God in January 1841, Bennett has received earthly accolades, celebrity treatment from the Mormon press. He is one of the gods.

Other gods had fallen, and other gods would fall, but seldom so far and seldom so fast.

The stunning dismissal of Bennett, a shepherd introduced to the flock by Joseph Smith, is risky. If the flock knew everything that Bennett knew, how would it react? Joseph's prophetic *bona fides* had been vigorously challenged by angry dissenters in Kirtland. The prophet was driven from Kirtland, then later from the state of Missouri. Could it happen again in this City of Joseph? In this state of Illinois? Bennett is privy to classified information. He has had a secret security clearance. An aroused Bennett would have to be quickly neutered. Bennett posed as big a threat to the prophet and to the Mormon faith as any dissenter ever before. The denunciation of Bennett puts the confidential Joseph perilously close to the practice of polygamy, and ever so very much more. Bennett threatens to expose the dark underside of what the *New York Herald* scathingly called "a community of wives." General Bennett was not invited to respond. Or to attend. This is not a dialogue and there will be no debate. The man whose oratorical skills are superior to those of the Apostle Paul hasn't been asked to emote. This will be a monologue, guarded and tightly controlled. There will be no kind words for an embattled Bennett. It will be a test of authoritarian leadership.

Joseph will now say goodbye to General Bennett, the man who was previously joined at his hip. The question is how to approach this delicate task. How will Bennett react to this highly public censure? Wilford Woodruff said, "The citizens of Nauvoo, both male and female, assembled near the Temple for a general meeting; many thousands were assembled. Joseph the Seer arose and spoke his mind in great plainness concerning the inequity, hypocrisy, wickedness and corruption of General John Cook Bennett."[81] Speaking in a voice gathering momentum and ringing with conviction, Joseph explains that Bennett has been expelled from the Church. The honorable part of the community "may be aware of his proceedings," he says, and the honorable part of the community should be ready to treat him "as he ought to be regarded, viz., as an imposter and base adulterer." How could the prophet have spoken

---

[81]Minutes of a public meeting in Nauvoo, Wilford Woodruff Journal, quoted in *History of the Church*, 5:34-35.

his mind any more clearly?   Only if he had said something about Nancy Rigdon.

When Joseph Smith publicly denounces John C. Bennett in June 1842, he describes him as "an impostor"; as a "base adulterer"[82]; as "one of the most abominable and depraved beings which could possibly exist"[83]; as a purveyor of "willful and base falsehoods"; as a man with "a depraved heart"; as a man with "wicked lustful appetites" [84]; as a being "totally destitute of common decency"; as a man "without any government over his passions"; and as one guilty of "cruel and abominable deeds"[85] who committed adultery in "the most abominable and degraded" manner.[86]   Could this be the same man who received the prophet's praise as the Mayor of Nauvoo? The medical man who treated the sick with quinine, drained the swamp in the city of the Saints and cured malaria?   The healer, Joseph and Emma and Nancy Rigdon's physician?   The architect of the Nauvoo Charter?   The Chancellor of the University?   A Major General of the Nauvoo Legion?   The Chief Justice of the Nauvoo Municipal Court, a Director of the Nauvoo Agricultural and Manufacturing Association, the Secretary of the Masonic Lodge and the Assistant President of the Mormon Church?   The second most powerful man in the Mormon Church?   How terrible he has been, this man known to have been aligned with the prophet in "all of his windings."

What finally causes the Mormon prophet to break with the notorious Bennett?   None of those wicked acts.   Something rather more intensely personal.   Smith came to consider John C. Bennett either a rival for the affections of Miss Rigdon, or as an impediment to his own intentions.   Smith turns on Bennett, who is on cordial terms with Miss Rigdon and her family, when Bennett fails to plead his case to Sidney's promising daughter.

---

[82]Joseph Smith, "An Address to the Church of Jesus Christ of Latter-day Saints and to all the Honorable Part of the Community," *History of the Church*, 5:35.
        [83]Ibid., 5:36.
        [84]Ibid.
        [85]Ibid., 5:35-36.
        [86]Ibid., 5:37, 40.

Smith decided that Bennett had forewarned Miss Rigdon of the purpose for the meeting he had scheduled with her. Smith can ignore letters describing Bennett's abandoned wife, children and infidelities. He can forgive this "adventurous malcontent" for living everywhere, joining everything, craving personal prominence and "preaching promiscuous intercourse." He can forgive Dr. Bennett for his sordid adulterous connections, for representing himself as a single man, and for all the other things the prophet is heard to describe. But he can not forgive his flawed but always previously protected colleague for frustrating his efforts to secure a relationship with Sidney's daughter, a young woman for whom he "had had an affection . . . for several years."[87] Did Joseph's interest in Miss Rigdon appear to be platonic? Carefully regulated? More political than sentimental? Unemotional?

General George W. Robinson, Miss Rigdon's brother-in-law and a witness to a turbulent meeting between the principals at the Rigdon's home, saw the cause of the friction clearly.

> *[T]he affair with Miss Rigdon was the cause of Smith's coming out so on Bennett, he having suspicions that Bennett had cautioned her on the matter – and he was further afraid that Bennett would make disclosures of other matters.*[88]

---

[87]Letter, George W. Robinson to General James Arlington Bennet, LL.D, 27 July 1842, quoted in Bennett, *The History of the Saints*, 246.

[88]Ibid., 246-47, emphasis omitted and added. Dr. Wilhelm Ritter von Wymetal (W. Wyl), who interviewed Sarah Pratt and William Law, Chauncey Webb and others, thought he understood why John C. Bennett, Mormonism's renaissance man, abruptly fell from grace. The issue, according to Wyl, wasn't political; it was domestic. "He and Joseph wanted, it seems, 'to shower the blessings of Abraham and Jacob on the same beauties.'" (Wyl, *Mormon Portraits, or, The Truth About the Mormon Leaders From 1830 to 1866*, 128). In Dr. Wyl's view, John C. Bennett's deceptive exposé was more truthful than Joseph Smith's deceptive rebuttal. Bennett's tale ("theatrical pathos") was substantially true. "I had his tale confirmed by all my old witnesses." (Ibid., 128). History supports the proposition that "the greatest scamp in the western country" was more dependably truthful than "the voice of God on earth." Wyl noted that while Bennett told the truth "in all essential points," he didn't tell the *whole* truth. Bennett damned Smith, but reinvented himself. Had Bennett told the entire story, these previously confidential colleagues would have shared with their partisans their ignominious disrepute.

The prophet's preamble is harsh and unsparing. It has become his duty, Joseph says, to lay before the Saints and the public "some important facts relative to the conduct and character of Dr. John C. Bennett." These facts, he says, are not intended simply for the Saints, but for the honorable part of the community at large. There is no "goodnight, Sweet Prince" element in the prophet's dismissal of his previously most highly favored colleague. There is no "we shall not soon see such an one again." And this is no seventy-times-seven discourse. This is a bare-knuckle-knockdown. This is cut-and-burn march-to-the-sea burn-your-bridges kick-a-sleeping-dog rhetoric. It is a stunning indictment, and before the prophet is through, many terrible things are said. The prophet's excoriation of the notorious Bennett does not end there, but John C. Bennett's short and inglorious stint as an imposing Latter-day Saint does. Bennett, according to Joseph, is a scoundrel in full.

General Bennett will retaliate.

Bennett's Response

Bennett's first shot over the bow is printed in the *Sangamo Journal* in Springfield, Illinois.[89] From St. Louis Bennett published a letter that said that Joseph Smith had been complicit in an assassination attempt on the life of Missouri Governor Lilburn W. Boggs, an attack that terribly injured but didn't kill the prophet's most implacable enemy.[90] Bennett's book (*History of the Saints*) is supposed to have had a powerful impact. Bennett, although

---

[89]It was in Carthage, not Springfield, that the prophet would meet an ugly death at the hands of men with painted faces.

[90]Bushman, *Joseph Smith: Rough Stone Rolling*, 463. William Law, a former Counselor in the First Presidency, another man who had also been close to Smith, supported that allegation in an interview with W. Wyl in 1885. Law addressing Wyl: "You speak in your book of Joseph Smith having sent Rockwell to kill Governor Boggs. Let me tell you, that Joe Smith told me the fact himself. The words were substantially like this, 'I sent [Orrin Porter] Rockwell to kill Boggs, but he missed him; he wounded him instead of sending him to Hell.'" (Dr. W. Wyl, "Interview with Wm. Law, March 30, 1887," *Salt Lake Tribune* [1 July 1887]). Rockwell later admitted as much to General Patrick Connor in the Utah Territory. (Richard S. Van Wagoner, "Orrin Porter Rockwell: Lehi Yesteryears" [accessed 2 July 2018], available from https://www.lehi-ut.gov/wp-content/uploads/2014/03/PorterRockwellbyRIchardVanWagonerweb.pdf; Internet, p. 2 of 5).

thoroughly disgraced in Mormon Nauvoo, made his case in a yet larger forum.

Richard L. Bushman:

> *History of the Saints [Bennett's exposé] performed a notable cultural work in antebellum America: it dehumanized Joseph Smith. Bennett stripped Joseph of any human qualities, meaning that no sympathy or understanding had to be extended him. Joseph was a fanatic, not a person, a threat and a horror, not a human being with feelings and rights. There need be no compunctions about using force against him.*[91]

Had Brother Bushman never read Smith's "An Address to the Church of Jesus Christ of Latter-day Saints and to all the Honorable Part of the Community"?[92]   On balance, Joseph, who, like one of his heroes, Stephen Burroughs, was never above portraying himself as a persecuted victim, gave better than he got. His descriptions of Bennett as documented here were clearly over the top. Long before this rant claiming persecution, mother's milk to the Saints, Joseph hadn't exactly humanized John C. Bennett, or protected Boggs, and he had acted first. It was Smith who started the demoralizing dialogue in front of a cast of thousands. Bushman's claims of persecution here, as in the case of his discussion of the persecution supposed to have been associated with the canonized account of the First Vision, do not wash. Smith was the aggressor, the man in charge and the less truthful of these ugly antagonists.   The Mormons counter Bennett's allegations, which shock the country and confirm widely-held suspicions, with accusations and truth squads. Hyrum Smith obtains fraudulent affidavits that postulate an adulterous relationship between Sarah Pratt and John C. Bennett from Saints willing to lie for the Lord. The affiants later admit that the affidavits were falsifications. Latter-day Saint reporters also link Bennett's devious sexual predations to the upright Miss Rigdon. Miss Rigdon and Mrs. Pratt, one unmarried, the other married to a prominent apostle, come under attack because they are reluctant concubines or wives

---

[91]Bushman, *Joseph Smith: Rough Stone Rolling*, 465, emphasis added.

[92]*History of the Church*, 5:35-38.

and friends of Bennett. Joseph Smith had asked both women, at different times, to secretly join him, at first and in both cases without a proposal of marriage, and both of them had bravely refused. Their exercise of freedom and integrity was rewarded with venom and vitriol.

When Bennett published and lectured on Mormonism after his expulsion, he identified no less than seven of Smith's plural wives but protected their identities from outsiders by using their initials. Among them were women already married to and living with other men before and after they married Smith.[93] That Bennett knew who some of these women were, when others close to the prophet (including Emma and Hyrum Smith) did not, speaks to the level of trust that existed before the fracture between these two powerful like-minded men, Mormon *alpha* males.

For five months, Orson Pratt (who returned from a mission to find his wife offended by the prophet's nefarious proposals), refuses to leave Nauvoo and continues to call himself a Mormon, although he and Sarah are both out of the Mormon mix. Then Pratt unexpectedly sides with Smith against Bennett, who had thought that Pratt would come out and help him destroy the Church. When Pratt provides a letter he received from Bennett to a grateful Joseph, his excommunication is reconsidered. It is now ruled on the basis of a technicality that Pratt wasn't really excommunicated in August; that he is still a member of the Church, and he is reinstated to the office of apostle. After five unsettling months, Orson and Sarah are rebaptized in the Mississippi River. Some of the brilliant apostle's best and worst days are ahead of him. Orson now catches the plural marriage vision. He not only lives to reveal the practice of polygamy to the world in 1852, after more than twenty years of

---

[93]For a time, after Orson Pratt returned from his mission and learned that the prophet had requested "connubial bliss" with his wife during his absence, the apostle had seemed like a man possessed. Because of that, Pratt was dismissed as an apostle and excommunicated from the Church on August 20, 1842, some time after Bennett. During this period when the prophet was under attack and looking for dependable allies, "When William Law called upon the Saints in a public meeting to acknowledge Joseph as a 'good, moral virtuous, peaceable and patriotic man,' Pratt stood up, pale and lonely-looking among the thousands, to register the only negative vote." (*The Wasp*, extra, 27 July 1842, quoted in Brodie, *No Man Knows My History*, 319).

institutional dishonesty, he now marries nine additional women and fathers with them (and with Sarah) forty-five children. But Sarah, his first wife and some (perhaps even all) of his children with her, including his namesake son, will leave the Church.

Bennett Changes the Church

The controversy with Bennett would forever change the Mormon landscape.

> *Sidney Rigdon [after the death of Joseph Smith] in the 18 June 1845 Messenger and Advocate reported that Apostle Parley P. Pratt, in speaking of the means by which church leaders should sustain Joseph Smith, advised that "we must lie to support brother Joseph, it is our duty to do so." Not only were church leaders willing to violate the law to promote polygamy, they also did not hesitate to blacken the character of individuals who threatened to expose the secret practice of plural marriage. Sarah Pratt was not the only woman to suffer from this policy. The 27 August 1842 Wasp, for example, branded Martha H. Brotherton [who had declined a marriage proposal from Brigham Young] a "mean harlot,"[94] and Nancy Rigdon suffered the same treatment after she opposed Smith's polygamous proposals.[95]*

A brilliant English emigrant Elder who had been the President of the Southampton Conference of the British Mission, and an aide to both Lorenzo Snow and Brigham Young, described Mormonism's domestic dilemma at that time in these terms:

> *Many interesting affidavits were given to the public in denunciation of Bennett and in defence of the*

---

[94]Brigham Young had himself sealed to this "mean harlot," Martha Brotherton, in 1870 in Salt Lake City. Miss Brotherton died in England in 1864. Her sister, Elizabeth Brotherton Pratt, a plural wife (widow) of Parley P. Pratt, stood proxy for the deceased in the temple ceremony.

[95]Van Wagoner, *Mormon Polygamy: A History*, 235-36 n 12, emphasis added.

Prophet.   Everything that could be thought of was done to mislead the public as to the veritable teachings promulgated concerning marriage, and from the time of this outbreak with Bennett in 1842, until the announcement of the revelation [polygamy] by Brigham Young, in Salt Lake City, in 1852, it was the duty of the Mormon missionaries to prevaricate, and even positively deny, when necessary, that the Mormon Church was other than monogamic, and the extent of the demoralization growing out of these denials would be incredible were the facts not incontrovertible.[96]

Had this revelation [polygamy] been presented to the Mormons with the "first principles" taught by the elders, not one in ten thousand among them would have accepted it as an emanation from Jesus Christ. But educated by their priesthood to regard all questioning of a revelation through the Prophet as the subtile working of Satanic influence to darken the mind and to mislead the disciple into rebellion, and with the terrible consequences of "apostacy" pictured to them and ever present in their thoughts, the Mormons could do no other than try to believe the doctrine of polygamy.[97]

On the 1st of January 1853, it [the revelation on polygamy] was published in the Star.   It fell like a thunderbolt upon the Saints, and fearfully shattered the mission.   The British elders, who in their ignorance had been denying polygamy, and stigmatizing their opponents as calumniators, up to the very day of its publication, were confounded and paralyzed, and from that time to the present the avenues of preaching have closed, one after another,

---

[96]T.B.H. Stenhouse, *The Rocky Mountain Saints: A Full and Complete History of the Mormons, from the First Vision of Joseph Smith to the Last Courtship of Brigham Young* (New York, NY: D. Appleton and Company, 1873), 185, emphasis added.

[97]Ibid., 201, emphasis added.

*and the mission that was once the glory of the
Mormon Church has withered and shriveled into
comparative insignificance.*[98]

DECEIVERS

The Bennett scandal poisoned the atmosphere against the public
introduction of the plural marriage doctrine in Nauvoo. The after-
Bennett climate clearly didn't allow the outright teaching of the
doctrine. Brigham Young, Heber C. Kimball, William Clayton,
Reynolds Cahoon, Vinson Knight, Willard Richards and others will
soon be taking wives secretly. Joseph is also taking secret wives
helter skelter. When the prophet and Brigham Young jointly
attempted to impose Young on Miss Martha Brotherton in January
of 1842, Joseph and John C. Bennett (participants in a January
debate on the very day of the Brotherton debacle) were on the best
of terms. However,

> *Even before Martha left Nauvoo, rumors of the
> incident began to circulate. Hyrum Smith, believing
> Joseph's public posture that polygamy was not being
> practiced, publicly addressed the Saints on 7 April
> 1842*[99] *"in contradiction of a report in circulation
> about Elders Heber C. Kimball, Brigham Young,
> himself, and others of the Twelve, alleging that a
> sister had been shut in a room for several days, and
> that they had endeavored to induce her to believe in
> having two wives."*

> *Joseph, who addressed the group after Hyrum, added,
> "There is no person that is acquainted with our*

---

[98]Ibid., 201-2, emphasis added. "When it [the revelation] was first published
the British mission was in the highest prosperity; the elders were travelling all over
that island, meeting with great success, calls for preaching were everywhere heard,
and large numbers were being baptized into the new faith." (Ibid., 201).

[99]Joseph married Marinda Nancy Johnson (Hyde) in April 1842, seven other
women in January, February and March 1842, and thirteen women total in 1842.
(George D. Smith, *Nauvoo Polygamy* 621-22).

principles who would believe such lies."[100]

Joseph lied. This charismatic, clever, hypocritical Joseph lied then, there, everywhere else and repeatedly. And by their silence, and also overtly, Brigham Young and Heber C. Kimball acquiesced in the prophet's perjury. On this issue – plural wives or polygamy – Joseph was more confidential with the odious Bennett than with the odious Hyrum. When Bennett left Nauvoo, he could identify seven of Smith's about twelve plural wives. When Bennett left Nauvoo, Hyrum may not have known that Joseph had plural wives and publicly suggested that he considered the thought deplorable.

Perhaps the reports Joseph received and disregarded about the stunning new convert's abandoned family, about his 1840 preaching of promiscuous intercourse, and about the seductions of those innocent women, convinced the Mormon prophet that Bennett was less likely to be offended by the confidential introduction of "the most holy and important doctrine ever revealed to man on the earth" than his older brother was. Don Carlos Smith, the prophet's younger brother, while not entirely out of the loop, didn't seem to know what Bennett seemed to know when Don Carlos died in 1841.[101] In later 1842, Joseph importuned thirty-one prominent elders and sisters to sign affidavits swearing to the fact that none but the conventional order of marriage existed in Nauvoo, and that Bennett's system was "a creature of his own make." One person did know for sure that those affidavits were deceitful fabrications. One person knew without a shadow of a doubt that "our principles" did indeed allow for such reprehensible practices.

Now, after all of this in 1842 and until 1852, all Mormon elders

---

[100]*History of the Church*, 4:585-86, referenced in Van Wagoner, *Mormon Polygamy: A History*, 18-19, emphasis added.

[101]Don Carlos Smith, the prophet's younger brother, was reported to have disparaged polygamy before his death in 1841. "Any man, who will preach and practice spiritual wifery," he said, "will go to hell, no matter if it is my brother Joseph." (Reported by Ebenezer Robinson. Robinson and Don Carlos Smith were co-editors of the *Times and Seasons*. Robinson's reminiscences from *The Return* vol. III [February 1891], 28, are quoted in Brodie, *No Man Knows My History*, 303). Shortly after Don Carlos' premature death at the age of forty-one, Joseph Smith took Don Carlos' widow, Agnes Coolbrith Smith, as one of the thirteen women he married in 1842. (George D. Smith, *Nauvoo Polygamy*, 621-22).

everywhere continued to use the Book of Mormon, the Doctrine and Covenants and other Mormon scriptures in support of the proposition that nothing but the conventional order of marriage was practiced in the Mormon Church. A reckless Joseph Smith plurally married Eliza R. Snow on June 29, 1842, only eight days after John C. Bennett left Nauvoo, and eleven days after Joseph delivered his "Address to the Church . . . and to all the Honorable Part of the Community." It was a speech that described John C. Bennett as a purveyor of "willful and base falsehoods," and as a man with "wicked lustful appetites." Eliza, one of the signators to the *Times and Seasons Monogamous Marriage Certificates*, then perjured herself to say that only the conventional order of marriage was practiced by the Latter-day Saints. Newell and Elizabeth Whitney, also signators, had witnessed the marriage of their daughter, Sarah Ann, to the prophet before those *Certificates* were ever prepared. Newell had performed the ceremony that united his daughter with a man twice her age who by then already had fifteen other wives.

The words "mental reservation" took on new meaning after the Bennett expulsion. Lying for the Lord became an art form.

> *The denials of polygamy uttered by the Mormon leaders between 1835 and 1852, when it was finally admitted, are a remarkable series of evasions and circumlocutions involving all sorts of verbal gymnastics. When the brethren attacked spiritual wifism or polygamy, it was with the mental reservation that "the patriarchal order of marriage" or "celestial order of plurality of wives" was immeasurably different.*[102]
>
> *The demand for secrecy coupled with the need to warn others of unauthorized practices such as Bennett's led Joseph and the Twelve to develop a system of evasion. By employing "code words" the practitioners of the "new and everlasting covenant of marriage," as taught by Joseph, felt they could publicly deny one*

---

[102]Brodie, *No Man Knows My History*, 321-22, emphasis added.

*thing and privately live by another – and do it with a
clear conscience.*[103]

On October 19, 1843, William Clayton said Joseph privately told
him to keep his pregnant plural wife Margaret at home "and brook
it and if they raise trouble about it and bring you before me I will
give you a awful scourging & probably cut you off from the church
and then I will baptize you and set you ahead as good as ever."[104]
"[Joseph Smith]," according to Clayton, "informed me . . . 'It is
your privilege to have all the wives you want' . . . ."[105]

SO MUCH FOR BENNETT

When Joseph had finished the central part of his speech pertaining
to Bennett,

> He also prophesied in the name of the Lord,
> concerning the merchants in the city, that if they
> and the rich did not open their hearts and
> contribute to the poor, they would be cursed by the
> hand of God, and be cut off from the land of the
> living.
>
> The main part of the day was taken up upon the
> business of the Agricultural and Manufacturing
> Society . . . .
>
> Also Joseph commanded the Twelve to organize the
> Church more according to the law of God; that is to
> require of those that come in to be settled according
> to their counsel, and also to appoint a committee to
> wait upon all who arrive, make them welcome and

---

[103]Newell and Avery, *Mormon Enigma: Emma Hale Smith*, 112-13, emphasis added.

[104]William Clayton, *An Intimate Chronicle: The Journals of William Clayton*, ed. George D. Smith (Salt Lake City: Signature Books in association with Smith Research Associates, 1995), 122.

[105]George D. Smith, "William Clayton: Joseph Smith's 'Private Clerk' and Eyewitness to Mormon Polygamy in Nauvoo," *Sunstone* (December 1991), 33.

counsel them what to do. Brigham Young, Heber C. Kimball, George A. Smith and Hyrum Smith were the committee appointed to wait upon emigrants and settle them.[106]

It couldn't all be about the notorious Bennett. It also had to be about business as usual. It was important that Bennett be seen as but one item on a larger agenda. He needed to be portrayed as a problem requiring management, but not as a problem of sufficient gravity to interrupt the normal flow of events, agricultural and manufacturing planning, or issues of emigration. The subliminal message conveyed by the mixed agenda was that the Church remains in charge, despite the issue with Bennett, and that the growth of the Church will continue to require careful management.

Joseph didn't do for Bennett what he had earlier done for Orson Hyde and what he would later do for Orson Pratt. Nor did he paint Bennett and Apostle William Smith, equal opportunity offenders, with the same brush. Equal protection did not apply with equal force to men who were similarly situated in the City of Joseph. What the Masonic Lodge did on June 16, Joseph did on June 18 and again on the 23rd. The prophet had given the absent Bennett no forum for rebuttal. If Bennett was to disparage the Saints and their prophet, he would have to do it in the *Sangamo Journal*, or somewhere not Nauvoo.

Joseph would prove yet again, on June 18, that no Latter-day Saint could challenge his supremacy – not John C. Bennett, not Oliver Cowdery, David Whitmer, John Whitmer, Luke Johnson, Lyman Johnson, Martin Harris, William E. McLellin, Thomas B. Marsh, Orson Hyde, Frederick G. Williams, Warren Parrish, Warren Cowdery, John Corrill, Reed Peck, George Hinckle, Sampson Avard, or any combination of any or all of the above. One man controlled the Latter-day Saints. John C. Bennett would soon be seen as little more than a stink in the "norstrels" of an indignant community" – another lost and pathetic minion of the Father of lies. Joseph Smith, the Prophet of the Living God, was indestructible. Over the course of time and in retrospect, it has become obvious

---

[106]Minutes of a public meeting in Nauvoo, Wilford Woodruff's Journal, quoted in *History of the Church*, 5:34-35.

that John C. Bennett, "the greatest scamp in the western country," was more dependably truthful about those early issues of marriage and sex than his patron, Joseph Smith, the prophet of God.

CHAPTER NINE

Affairs to Remember

Well I shall leave it with Brother Joseph, whether it would be best for you to have time or not [time to decide if she would plurally marry Brigham Young].[1]

Brigham Young

I see no harm in her having time to think, if she will not fall into temptation.[2]

Joseph Smith

BRIGHAM YOUNG AND MARTHA BROTHERTON

The following solicitation directed to Miss Martha Brotherton by John C. Bennett appeared in the *Sangamo Journal* (a newspaper published at Springfield, Illinois) on July 15, 1842:

Now I call upon Miss Martha Brotherton, of Warsaw [Illinois], to come out and tell boldly the base attempt on her virtue when in Nauvoo – how she was locked up – and the proposals that were made to her.[3]

---

[1]Letter, Miss Martha Brotherton to "General John C. Bennett," quoting Brigham Young, reproduced at John C. Bennett, *The History of the Saints: Or, An Expose of Joe Smith and Mormonism* (Boston: Leland & Whiting, 1842; photomechanical reprint of 1842 original, Salt Lake City: Modern Microfilm Company), 239.

[2]Letter, Miss Martha Brotherton to "General John C. Bennett," quoting Joseph Smith, 13 July 1842, reproduced at Ibid., 239.

[3]"Further Mormon Developments!! 2d Letter from Gen. Bennett," *Sangamo Journal*, vol. 10 no. 47 (15 July 1842).

Following his reluctant dismissal, Bennett published elements of an exposé in several separate editions of the *Sangamo Journal*. Martha Brotherton – a young woman who lived in Nauvoo, then later in Warsaw, and finally in St. Louis – read one or more of Bennett's articles. She then proceeded to send a letter addressed to "Gen. John C. Bennett." "I left Warsaw a short time since for this city [St. Louis], and having been called upon by you, through the 'Sangamo Journal,' to come out and disclose to the world the facts of the case in relation to certain propositions made to me at Nauvoo, by some of the Mormon leaders, I now proceed to respond to the call . . . ."[4] Miss Brotherton, an "amiable, and accomplished" English convert new to the states,[5] described her experience, while still in her teens and underage, in these terms.

> I had been at Nauvoo near three weeks [it is January 1842], during which time my father's family received frequent visits from Elders Brigham Young and Heber C. Kimball, two of the Mormon Apostles, when early one morning, they both came to my brother-in-law's (John Mellwrick's) house, at which place I then was on a visit, and particularly requested me to go and spend a few days with them.[6]

Miss Brotherton told the apostles she could not go with them at that time because her brother-in-law was not at home. They then asked her to go the next day and spend one day with them, which she then agreed to do. When she arrived at the foot of the hill, the place of the meeting on the following day, Young and Kimball were standing conversing together. They both then came to her and offered several flattering compliments after which Kimball suggested they go to his house. Brigham Young then excused himself on a matter of business, after which Kimball turned to her and said,

> *"Martha, I want you to say to my wife, when you go to my house, that you want to buy some things at Joseph's store, . . . and I will say I am going with you, to show you the way. You know you want to see the*

---

[4]Ibid.

[5]Bennett, *The History of the Saints*, 236.

[6]Miss Brotherton's Statement, *Sangamo Journal*, vol. 10 no 47 (15 July 1842).

Prophet, and you will then have an opportunity." I made no reply. Young again made his appearance, and the subject was dropped.[7]

When they got to Kimball's house, Young excused himself, saying he would see her again. When they had been there for close to an hour, Kimball could see that Miss Brotherton did not intend to tell his wife what he had asked her to, so Kimball finally told his wife himself. Mrs. Kimball offered to go to the store with them, but Kimball declined that offer, saying he had "some business to do," but that he would return to take her to the debate between the prophet Joseph Smith and Dr. John C. Bennett scheduled to occur later that same day. So Heber C. Kimball and Miss Brotherton went to Joseph's store together. "As we were going along, he said, 'Sister Martha, are you willing to do all that the Prophet requires you to do?' I said I believed I was, thinking of course he would require nothing wrong." "'Then,' said he, 'are you ready to take counsel?' I answered in the affirmative, thinking of the great and glorious blessings that had been pronounced upon my head, if I adhered to the counsel of those placed over me in the Lord."[8]

Now Kimball said that there are many things revealed in these last days, "mysteries of the kingdom," at which "the world would laugh and scoff." He then said that she would need to learn to hold her tongue, after which he suggested that she would see the prophet, "and very likely have some conversation with him." When they reached the store, Kimball led Miss Brotherton up some stairs to a small room, the door of which was locked, and upon which there was a sign that said, "Positively no admittance." Thinking, he said, that "brother Joseph must be sick, for strange to say, he is not here," he then directed her back down the stairs to the tithing office, where two men were busy at work. She recognized one of the men as William Clayton, a person she had seen in England, but failed to recognize the second man. Now Brigham Young came in and seated himself in front of her "and asked where Kimball was." Miss Brotherton said that he had gone out. Soon after, Joseph then also came and said something to one of the clerks before climbing the stairs, followed by Young. Kimball then came back to say that

---

[7]Ibid.
[8]Ibid.

the prophet had come and invited Miss Brotherton back upstairs. When she got to the room, Brigham Young and Joseph Smith were both already there. She was introduced to Joseph Smith by Brigham Young. Then, to her "astonishment," Joseph offered her his seat, stood up and left the room with Kimball, leaving her there alone with Young, "who arose, locked the door, closed the window, and drew the curtain." "This," he said, "is our private room, Martha."[9]

Brigham wondered if he could ask her some questions. She said that he could. "And will you promise not to mention them to anyone?" "If it is your desire, sir," she said, "I will not." Would she think badly of him, he wondered, for asking her questions? She said that she would not. "'Well,' said he, 'what are your feelings toward me?'" And she replied, "My feelings are just the same towards you that they ever were, sir." Did she have such affection for him, he wondered, that "were it lawful and right," that she could accept him as her "husband and companion"? The blunt unexpected request to a woman who knew nothing about polygamy and little about the private Brigham Young startled the young English emigrant. *My feelings at that moment were indescribable. God only knows them.* "*What, thought I are these men, that I thought almost perfection itself, deceivers? and is all my fancied happiness but a dream? Twas even so.*"[10] Now she awkwardly thought how she should best deal with this. If she said, *no*, they may do as they think proper; and to say *yes*, "I never would." "So I considered it best to ask for time to think and pray about it. I therefore said, 'If it was lawful and right, perhaps I might; but you know, sir, it is not.'"[11]

Now Brigham told Martha Brotherton that Joseph had received a revelation from God. God told Joseph, Brigham said, that it was "lawful and right for a man to have two wives." As it was in the days of Abraham, he said, so shall it be "in these last days." He then further articulated his unexpected proposal in these terms: "*[I]f you will accept of me, I will take you straight to the celestial kingdom; and if you will have me in this world, I will have you in that*

---

[9]Ibid.
[10]Ibid., emphasis added.
[11]Ibid.

which is to come. . . . "[12] The offer embraced marriage and salvation
in the kingdom of God. Brother Joseph, Brigham said, will marry
us here today, the day she first learned that the leaders of the
Church were polygamists, "and you can go home this evening, and
your parents will not know anything about it." "Sir," she said, "I
should not like to do any thing of the kind without the permission of
my parents." "Well, but," Brigham then remarked, ". . . you are of
age, are you not?" She said that she was not, and would not be,
until the 24th of May. "'Well,' said he, 'that does not make any
difference. You will be of age before they know, and you need not
fear. If you will take my counsel, it will be well with you, for I know
it to be right before God, and if there is any sin in it, I will answer
for it.'"[13]

Perhaps sensing her reluctance, Brigham Young now proceeded to
tell Miss Brotherton that brother Joseph wanted to have some
words with her on this subject. "[H]e will explain things – will you
hear him?" She said she would. "Well, but I want you to say
something," said he. She then responded and said, "I want time to
think about it." "Well," he said, "I will have a kiss, any how, and
then rose and said he would bring Joseph,"[14] the man she had only
just met, to discuss a principle she knew nothing about. "He then
unlocked the door, and took the key, and locked me up alone." In
about ten minutes Brigham Young returned with Joseph Smith.
When they returned, Brigham told Joseph that Martha "would be
willing" to marry him if she knew that it was "lawful and right
before God."

> *"Well, Martha," said Joseph, "it is lawful and right*
> *before God – I know it is. Look here, sis; don't you*
> *believe in me?" I did not answer. "Well, Martha,"*
> *said Joseph, "just go ahead, and do as Brigham wants*
> *you to – he is the best man in the world, except me."*
> *"O!" said Brigham, "then you are as good." "Yes,"*
> *said Joseph.*
>
> *"Well," said Young, "we believe Joseph to be a*

---

[12]Ibid., emphasis added.
[13]Ibid.
[14]Ibid.

> *Prophet. I have known him near eight years, and always found him the same." "Yes," said Joseph, "and I know that this is lawful and right before God, and if there is any sin in it, I will answer for it before God; and I have the keys of the kingdom, and whatever I bind on earth is bound in heaven, and whatever I loose on earth is loosed in heaven, and if you will accept of Brigham, you shall be blessed – God shall bless you, and my blessing shall rest upon you; and if you will be led by him, you will do well; for I know Brigham will take care of you, and if he don't do his duty to you, come to me, and I will make him; and if you do not like it in a month or two, come to me, and I will make you free again; and if he turns you off, I will take you on."[15]*

Miss Brotherton answered, yet again, as she had before, that she would like to think first. The prophet then said, "Nothing ventured, nothing gained" and added that marriage to Brigham Young "would be the greatest blessing that was ever bestowed upon you."

> *"Yes," said Young, "and you will never have reason to repent it – that is, if I do not turn from righteousness, and that I trust I never shall; for I believe God, who has kept me so long, will continue to keep me faithful. Did you ever see me act in any way wrong in England, Martha?" "No, sir," said I. "No," said he; "neither can any one else lay anything to my charge."*

> *"Well, then," said Joseph, "what are you afraid of, sis? Come, let me do the business for you." "Sir," said I, "do let me have a little time to think about it, and I will promise not to mention it to any one." "Well, but look here," said he; "you know a fellow will never be damned for doing the best he knows how." "Well, then," said I, "the best way I know of, is to go home and think and pray about it." "Well," said Young, "I shall leave it with Brother Joseph, whether*

---

[15]Ibid., emphasis added.

it would be best for you to have time or not."[16]

She had had only a few minutes, absent any foreplay, to let the insidious doctrine and the prospect of marriage to an aggressive, already-married man more than twice her age and scarcely known to her settle in. Marriage, while underage, without her parents' knowledge or consent. Joseph responded and said, *"I see no harm in her having time to think, if she will not fall into temptation."* Desperate to escape, Martha said there was no chance of that.

> *"Well, but," said Brigham, "you must promise me you will never mention it to any one." "I do promise it," said I. "Well," said Joseph, "you must promise me the same." I promised him the same. "Upon your honor," said he, "you will not tell." "No, sir, I will lose my life first," said I. "Well, that will do," said he; "that is the principle we go upon . . . ."*[17]

When Miss Brotherton then rose to leave, Joseph gave Brigham's unsettling proposal one last try. "[H]e said it was the best opportunity they might have for months, for the room was often engaged." Nothing changed. Young then spoke to say that he would be preaching at the school-house close to her brother-in-law's home the following day and supposed that he would see her there. "Yes," she said, he would.

In the morning, on Sunday, instead of attending the morning meeting, Martha Brotherton sat down, while the events of the preceding day were fresh in her mind, and wrote a detailed accounting of her encounter with the Mormon leaders that she gave to her sister, "who was not a little surprised." Polygamy was a new and disturbing factor in a suddenly strange equation. Her sister said she thought it would be best for them to go to the meeting in the afternoon. They went and found Brigham Young administering the sacrament.

When the service was over and as Miss Brotherton stood up and started to leave, Young stopped her, saying, "'Wait, Martha, I am

---

[16]Ibid., emphasis added.
[17]Ibid., emphasis added.

coming.' I said, 'I cannot; my sister is waiting for me.' He then threw his coat over his shoulders, and followed me out, and whispered, 'Have you made up your mind, Martha?' 'Not exactly, sir,' said I; and we parted.'"[18] Martha Brotherton soon left the Mormon church and Nauvoo and never returned.

Brigham Young – who married more than fifty other women, including many wives of other men, undivorced polyandrous women, and had more than fifty children – never forgot Miss Brotherton. He was sealed to her by proxy in Salt Lake City, Utah, on August 1, 1870, some twenty-eight years after she left him standing with his coat over his shoulders at the schoolhouse. Elizabeth Brotherton Pratt, a plural wife of Parley P. Pratt, stood proxy for her sister, who died in England in 1864.[19] Martha, of course, knew nothing of her proxy marriage to a man who was by then the Mormon prophet, and once again did not consent. Brigham Young had promised the young English convert that, " . . . *if you will have me in this world, I will have you in that which is to come . . . .*" Now, it seemed, Brigham would relent; he would have her in the world to come, against the claims of anyone else, whether or not she would have him "*in this world.*"

Miss Brotherton to General Bennett:

> "*I shall proceed to a justice of the peace, and make oath to the truth of these statements . . . you are at liberty to make what use of them you may think best.*"

> "*Yours respectfully, Martha H. Brotherton.*"

> "*Sworn to and subscribed before me this 13th day of July, A.D. 1842. Du Bouffay Fremon, Justice of the Peace for St. Louis County.*"[20]

Joseph Smith never directly replied to Martha Brotherton's

---

[18]Ibid.

[19]George D. Smith, *Nauvoo Polygamy: " . . . but we called it celestial marriage"* (Salt Lake City: Signature Books, 2008), 271-72.

[20]Miss Brotherton's Statement, *Sangamo Journal*, vol. 10 no 47 (15 July 1842), emphasis in original.

charges, but Heber C. Kimball and Brigham Young did what Mormons do – they "called her story a base falsehood." Her two sisters and her brother-in-law, all of whom continued in the faith (Elizabeth Brotherton plurally married Parley P. Pratt), "were persuaded to swear that she was not only a liar but also a harlot." Their sworn statements were included with the materials published in *Affidavits and Certificates Disproving the Statements and Affidavits Contained in John C. Bennett's Letters*, a pamphlet published by the leaders of the Church on August 31, 1842.[21]

Joseph must be protected. To true believers there is no scenario by means of which the Mormon founder may be seen to fail. That is an unarticulated article of the Mormon faith. Nothing he did, however horrendous, can be said to support the proposition that he was a fallen prophet, or not a prophet at all. He can lie and cheat and fight and steal and kill. That Joseph Smith was a prophet of God is an untouchable principle. If he had sworn before a magistrate that he was not a prophet of God, it would have made no difference. The Mormon prophet, the role model for Mormon children, was above the law. No law was large enough to measure him, for Joseph Smith was a law unto himself. "[I]t is the strongest proof of the firm hold of a party, whether religious or political, upon the public mind, when it may offend with impunity against its own primary principles."[22]   To the uninitiated looking in from the offended outside, as opposed to the faithful looking out from the comforting inside, his life was a case study in contradictions.

"I Will Lose My Life First."

The ripple effects of the secret practice of polygamy were widespread. "Smith's revelation on polygamy opened floodgates of lies and hypocrisy. Hundreds of honest women and honorable men were forced to become liars" by their polygamous leaders.[23]

---

[21]Fawn M. Brodie, *No Man Knows My History: The Life of Joseph Smith the Mormon Prophet*, 2d ed., rev. and enl. (New York: Alfred A. Knopf, 1972), 307 n.

[22]Henry H. Milman, D.D., *The History of Christianity: From the Birth of Christ to the Abolition of Paganism in the Roman Empire*, vol. 2 (London: William Clowes and Sons, 1867), 206.

[23]Arza Evans, *The Keystone of Mormonism* (St. George, UT: Keystone Books

Polygamy was against the law in the state of Illinois. The state fined and provided prison terms for offenders. Every polygamist had to lie in order to avoid fines and prison terms. "Smith had to swear his new wives and also his friends and their plural wives to oaths of secrecy in order to stay out of prison."[24] Polygamy made every polygamist husband and each plural wife perjurers and outlaws in the state of Illinois. Arza Evans, a perceptive observer with polygamous roots, described how early Mormon polygamy actually worked:

> Let's consider a typical secret Mormon marriage in Nauvoo. A young woman, probably a convert from England who has been taught to almost worship the Prophet Joseph and other Church authorities, is taught "the principle" and then sworn to secrecy. What does she tell her parents when she comes home from this meeting with Smith? *She can't tell them the truth without violating her oath of secrecy. She is forced to deceive them. She must lie to her own parents.*[25]

Author Evans dedicated his book, *The Keystone of Mormonism*, to three noble women: Nancy Rigdon, Sarah Pratt and Martha Brotherton, whose reputations were uniformly trashed by Mormon tormentors.

HEBER C. KIMBALL AND VILATE

A God of trifles played tricks on Apostle Heber C. Kimball, a faithful Mormon leader and an early recipient of one of Joseph's special revelations. These private revelations proceeded to explain in tiny increments, early on and first, elements of the godfather doctrine behind modern Mormon polygamy (Doctrine and Covenants 132), the "thus saith the Lord" detailed explanation of the "great, sublime, beautiful, and glorious doctrine" of polygamy. Heber's revelation has never been published.

Inc., 2003), 139.
[24]Ibid.
[25]Ibid., emphasis added.

God approached Heber C. Kimball with a revelation adapted to the circumstances in which the children of the kingdom were placed. The Lord, the God of Abraham, Isaac and Jacob, spoke to Kimball by means of a secret message directed to him but delivered to Joseph Smith. Heber knew this was "the principle on which the government of heaven" was conducted. In 1842, the Lord of heaven and earth interrupted the business of heaven and earth to deliver this message: Heber C. Kimball, a special witness for Jesus Christ, would be required to surrender his legal wife, Vilate, and their biological children (ten during Vilate's lifetime), to the prophet Joseph Smith for time and eternity. This was not a joke or a request; it was a command. God wanted Joseph to privately have what Heber and Vilate had covenanted to have whatever the social cost. According to this, Vilate belonged to Heber's prophet. The civil union between the Apostle and his life partner would have to be fine-tuned and rearranged. What the Lord told Heber (and Vilate) was what the Lord told Zina, Presendia, Lucinda, Marinda, Patty, Sylvia and quite a number of others, and what the Lord tried to tell Sarah Pratt, Sarah Kimball, Jane Law and Mrs. Robert D. Foster.

Heber, who loved his Vilate dearly, was stunned by God's demand. His biographer grandson, Apostle Orson Whitney, wrote that Heber was paralyzed by this instruction. "Yet Joseph was solemnly in earnest." Joseph meant what Joseph said that God had said in a revelation to Heber. God commanded Heber C. Kimball to surrender Vilate to Joseph Smith in marriage.[26] Heber had doubts. He doubted Joseph's "motive and the divinity of the revelation," a revelation that isn't available to be weighed and measured. Orson Whitney:

> *For three days Heber endured agonies. Finally asked to choose between his loyalty to Mormonism and his intimacy with his wife, Mormonism and Smith won out. "Then, with a broken and bleeding heart, but with soul self-mastered for the sacrifice, he led his darling wife to the prophet's house and presented her to Joseph." "Joseph wept at this proof of devotion,*

---

[26]Orson Whitney, quoted in Todd Compton, *In Sacred Loneliness: The Plural Wives of Joseph Smith* (Salt Lake City: Signature Books, 2001), 495.

and embracing Heber, told him that was all that the
Lord required." It had been a test, said Joseph, to see
if Heber would give up everything he possessed.[27]

The Lord of heaven and earth was, of course, heavily invested in
this experiment. In other cases it was more than a test and in some
cases only the wife was consulted. This much can be safely said of
this curious set of early episodes: Joseph's God was always a third
party, the indisputable source, according to Joseph, of every one of
those revelations adapted to the circumstances in which the
children of the kingdom were placed. In Kimball's case, what God
really wanted to know, according to Joseph, was whether or not
Heber C. Kimball would willingly disregard his civil covenants and
surrender "his darling wife" to Joseph Smith in order to spiritually
test his faith. He would surrender her, and he would pass the test.
God had at first seemed determined to redirect Kimball's Vilate to
Joseph Smith, a more distinguished man who held a higher office in
the priesthood. In other cases involving similar issues, it was not a
test.   In those cases God required women to violate their civil
covenants, spiritually abandon their legal husbands and pledge
themselves and their biological children with their legal husbands to
Smith. In those cases they were to reject the laws of man and obey
the law of God as adapted to the circumstances in which they as the
children of the kingdom were placed. All of this was described in
specialized revelations delivered in increments by a conflicted
messenger. So what for Heber was a test was for others a lethal
command. In those cases, it wasn't Joseph who wept.

So it is that with such trifles the Mormon God concerned himself.
With subjects as numerous as grains of sand on a million earths, he
wonders if Heber will surrender Vilate to Joseph as a test of his
faith. God, who doesn't know Heber's heart, needs to test Heber's
heart. In the final analysis, and to be perfectly accurate, it is not
what Heber gives to God, but what Heber gives to Joseph that
counts. How can it be said that the surrender of one man's spouse
and children to another man for some better place in the life to
come is any kind of a decent thing? Or some sacred principle? God
didn't want Vilate for Joseph. He wanted Helen Mar Kimball,

---

[27]Ibid., emphasis added.

Heber and Vilate's daughter, for Joseph. Joseph got Helen Mar, a child of tender age, by promising salvation for her, and for her family, for as far out as the eye could see. To say that polyandrous plural marriage somehow serves to support the larger interests of a deity worthy of worship is to travel down a crooked path. The same can be said for those marriages to the children of congregants.

ORSON HYDE, WILLARD RICHARDS, JOSEPH SMITH AND MARINDA NANCY JOHNSON

T.B.H. Stenhouse, the father of Utah journalism, thought that Willard Richards was vastly superior to William Clayton as an amanuensis.

> *"The Lord's" style of revelation to Brigham is a great improvement upon "the Lord's" style of revelation to Joseph. It is just as much better English in Brigham's case than in that of Joseph, as Willard Richard's literary education was superior to that of William Clayton! "The Lord's" English in the Book of Mormon, while Oliver Cowdery was Joseph's scribe, and Joseph was tenacious in clinging to his unaltered inspirations, is a remarkable specimen of English composition; but as Joseph gathered around him better scribes, and concluded that "the Lord's" revelations could be somewhat improved, they became more readable.*[28]

Willard Richards, who held the line against all comers at Nauvoo after the prophet's death and until Richards' cousin Brigham Young returned to contest the succession, was a case study in complexity. Sidney Rigdon suggested Richards had been "*sealed*" to Marinda Nancy Johnson (Mrs. Orson Hyde), a married woman living with him in "the first floor suite of the *Times and Seasons* office on the corner of Bain and Water Streets" (the Nauvoo

---

[28]T.B.H. Stenhouse, *The Rocky Mountain Saints: A Full and Complete History of the Mormons, from the First Vision of Joseph Smith to the Last Courtship of Brigham Young* (New York: D. Appleton and Company, 1873), 255, emphasis added.

Printing House) while Marinda's husband, Apostle Orson Hyde, was away for the longest time on a mission to Palestine. There was no happy explanation for this alleged extraordinary liaison. Mrs. Hyde was sealed to Joseph Smith in April 1842, thus becoming "one of [the more than] several relationships contracted with married women during his lifetime (there were many more sealings to other married women after his death). Evidently Mrs. Hyde, although sealed to the prophet, was shared with Smith's scribe, Apostle Willard Richards, whose wife was in Massachusetts."[29]

In 1845, shortly after the death of Joseph Smith, an unleashed Rigdon excoriated Willard Richards and Joseph Smith for the laxity of their morals. In this we see Rigdon's sudden unexpected postmortem repudiation of his former leader. In this we see what Rigdon really thought about the character of the Mormon prophet.

> *If R[ichards] should take a notion to H[yde]'s wife in his absence, all that is necessary to be done is to be sealed. No harm done, no adultery committed; only taking a little advantage of rights of priesthood. And after R[ichards] has gone the round of dissipation with H[yde]'s wife, she is afterwards turned over to S[mith] and thus the poor silly woman becomes the actual dupe to two designing men, under the sanctimonious garb of rights of the royal priesthood.[30]*

Here Rigdon, a theoretician of the "royal priesthood," turns on Richards and Smith with venom and vitriol. Marinda Nancy Johnson (Hyde) (Richards) (Smith), somehow simultaneously tied to two prominent early apostles, then to Joseph Smith, had first known the Mormon prophet in Ohio when she was fifteen or sixteen years old. It is supposed by some scholars that it was because Smith took indecent liberties with Miss Johnson (while he briefly lived at the home of her father) that a Hiram, Ohio, mob was formed to

---

[29]Richard S. Van Wagoner, *Sidney Rigdon: A Portrait of Religious Excess* (Salt Lake City: Signature Books, 1994; paperback 2006), 294.

[30]Cited in Rigdon's letter, "TO THE SISTERS OF THE CHURCH OF JESUS CHRIST OF LATTER-DAY SAINTS," *Latter Day Saints Messenger and Advocate* (Pittsburgh), October 1845, cited at Van Wagoner, *Sidney Rigdon: A Portrait of Religious Excess*, 294.

punish him. Joseph and Sidney Rigdon were tarred and feathered, Sidney was injured and Joseph, these accounts further surmise, was threatened with castration. One or more of Marinda's brothers were supposed to have participated as members of an angry crowd. Joseph narrowly escaped disfigurement when a Dr. Dennison, who was brought to the scene to perform the gruesome procedure, had second thoughts and refused to proceed. Joseph and Sidney were allegedly tarred and feathered on March 24, 1832, by Simons Rider (*sic*, Symonds Ryder), Warren Waste, Eli Johnson (Nancy's brother), Edward Johnson and John Johnson.[31]

The Lord told the Latter-day Saints, before the Church was out of the box, to give heed unto Joseph's "words and commandments . . . as he receiveth them . . . as if from mine own mouth, in all patience and faith."[32] In 1841 God had delivered a special revelation to Joseph Smith for "Nancy Marinda Hyde," the legal wife of Orson Hyde. "[L]et my handmaid Nancy Marinda Hyde [Marinda Nancy Johnson (Hyde)] hearken to the counsel of my servant Joseph in all things whatsoever he shall teach unto her, and it shall be a blessing upon her and upon her children after her, unto her justification, *saith the Lord.*"[33] December 2, 1841:

> *Verily thus saith the Lord unto you my servant Joseph, that inasmuch as you have called upon me to know my will concerning my handmaid Nancy Marinda Hyde – behold it is my will that she should have a better place prepared for her, than that in which she now lives, . . . therefore go and say unto my servant, Ebenezer Robinson, and to my handmaid his wife [who live at the Nauvoo Printing Office] – Let them open their doors and take her and her children into their house and take care of them faithfully and kindly until my servant Orson Hyde returns from his mission, or until some other provision can be made for her welfare and safety.*[34]

---

[31]The uncorrelated source for this not quite certain assertion is "Mormon History – A Chronology" from http://www.exmormon. Org/mhistory.html.

[32]Doctrine and Covenants 21:4-5.

[33]*History of the Church*, 4:467, emphasis added.

[34]Ibid., emphasis added.

God took time to say that Marinda deserved better quarters. One month after that revelation, and in January 1842, Ebenezer Robinson (Marinda's caretaker) and his family were "forced to vacate the printing office" at the insistence of John C. Bennett's successor, Apostle Willard Richards. Ebenezer Robinson perceived that Richards was cohabiting with Marinda Nancy Hyde at the printing office while her husband, Apostle Orson Hyde, was on a mission to Palestine dedicating the land of Israel to the return of the Jews. According to Robinson, "Willard Richards" ("a nearly three hundred pound" nineteenth-century behemoth[35]) "nailed down the windows and fired off his revolver in the street after dark, and commenced living with Mrs. Nancy Marinda Hyde."[36] Sidney Rigdon, like Joseph Smith, had known Miss Johnson before her relationship for time to Hyde, and before her time and eternity marriage to Joseph. In April 1842, Marinda Nancy Johnson (Hyde) became Marinda Nancy Johnson (Hyde) (Smith), linked (with what became ten biological children with Hyde) to Smith, and not to Hyde or Richards, for eternity. She was a time and eternity polyandrous wife to Smith and a civilly deputized partner for time to her own out-of-sight Uriah.

The Affair and Marriages

John C. Bennett – like Willard Richards, Sidney Rigdon, Nancy Rigdon, Ebenezer Robinson, Joseph Smith and Joseph's God – thought he knew Apostle Richards and Mrs. Hyde had "special business" at the printing office.[37] Orson Hyde, a foreign missionary at a distant place, did not. Richards was supposed to have been practicing promiscuous intercourse in the absence of his own wife and child by trading on his unusually close association with Joseph Smith. Orson's wife had to think that cohabitation with Richards was acceptable to Smith as God was her witness.

If Willard and Marinda were not "sealed" – and she couldn't have

---

[35]Richard S. Van Wagoner and Steven C. Walker, *A Book of Mormons* (Salt Lake City: Signature Books, 1982), 231.

[36]Ebenezer Robinson, *The Return* (Davis City, IA), 2 October 1890, 347, cited at Van Wagoner, *Sidney Rigdon: A Portrait of Religious Excess*, 294.

[37]Bennett, *The History of the Saints*, 241.

been sealed to two men – then Willard Richards and Mrs. Hyde were living together with the consent of the prophet in the City of Joseph.[38] If there had been some kind of secret ceremony, say some marriage for time, Mrs. Hyde would have been in a polyandrous relationship with Richards, then also later with Smith. If Richards and Mrs. Hyde were married, then Marinda Nancy Johnson had two husbands for time, both historically important Apostles. If Willard and Nancy were "sealed," as Rigdon seemed to suppose, then Mrs. Hyde was the unlikely wife of three men for time and two men for eternity. That would suppose a polyandrous heaven, a premise not accepted in Mormonism's modern temples (where one man may be sealed in certain cases to multiple women but women may not be sealed to multiple men).[39]

Marinda Johnson was legally married to a man seen to become the President of the Quorum of the Twelve Apostles, Orson Hyde.[40] Rigdon thought that she was sealed to Willard Richards, a future counselor in Brigham Young's First Presidency. She was sealed to Joseph Smith, the Prophet of the Restoration. So for Marinda Nancy Johnson (Hyde) (possibly Richards) (certainly Smith), a place in eternity must have seemed secure. Marinda was legally married to Orson Hyde, somehow tied to Willard Richards, then married again and sealed to Joseph Smith. She and her ten children with Hyde belonged to Smith, and not to Hyde, in the life to come. All of those three men were fiduciaries holding positions of great authority in the Mormon Church.

---

[38]In early Mormon resources, gender equality is difficult if not impossible to find. There are more than two hundred men identified by name in the Book of Mormon, but only *three women*, whose roles were unimportant.

[39]Ebenezer Robinson, *The Return* (Davis City, IA), 2 October 1890, 347, cited at Van Wagoner, *Sidney Rigdon: A Portrait of Religious Excess*, 294.

[40]Orson Hyde would have stood ahead of Orson Pratt as senior to succeed to the Presidency when Brigham Young died, had Young not rearranged seniority in the Quorum to the disadvantage of both of those apostles late in his life. The purpose for Young's rearrangement was to insure that neither Hyde nor Orson Pratt, men Young held in low regard, would be able to succeed him. Willard Richards became the Second Counselor to his cousin Brigham Young in the First Presidency. John Willard Young, Brigham Young's son, long after the death of Richards became the First Counselor in Brigham Young's last First Presidency. John Willard Young, who was ordained to the office of Apostle at the age of eleven, was Brigham Young's most likely choice to succeed him.

Mrs. Hyde lived with Orson Hyde until 1841. She lived with Richards at the printing house, starting in January 1842, before being secretly married and sealed to Smith in April 1842.[41] Marinda separated from Richards in 1842, then lived again with Hyde, who was the father of her ten children, until 1870. She was divorced from Hyde, but not unsealed from Joseph Smith. She will be one of the prophet's wives, a queen in the Kingdom of Heaven. Marinda Nancy Johnson's notably complex domesticity advanced the concept of brotherhood. When Orson Hyde returned from his mission to Palestine, after some fits and starts, he and Marinda resumed their broken marriage. Their relationship, although "unsteady," lasted until 1870, when they were divorced.[42]

Shortly after the prophet was murdered and in October 1845, Sidney Rigdon criticized Richards' relationship with Marinda Nancy Hyde and turned on Joseph Smith.

H[yde] by and by finds out the trick which was played

---

[41]Richards would marry ten women, besides his legal wife, Jennetta, three of them Longstroth sisters (Sarah, age 16; Nanny, age 14; Alice, age 21), and at least one of them, Alice Longstroth, without the benefit of a religious or civil ceremony. In December 1845, Apostle Willard Richards, without deputization from the State, or any official religious formality, entered into what he seemed to consider a plural marriage with Alice Longstroth. "Without a formal ceremony, Alice and Willard 'mutually acknowledge[d] each other husband & wife, in a covenant not to be broken in time and Eternity . . . as though the seal of the covenant had been placed upon us." (Willard Richards Diary, quoted in George D. Smith, *Nauvoo Polygamy*, 649 n 315; *see, e.g.*, "Willard Richards," 615-16). Alice left Willard after the "self performed" sealing, one of early Mormonism's "informal arrangements," and was not then resealed to him in the Nauvoo Temple in 1846. She married Moses Whitaker, who died in 1851, then became a sister-wife to George D. Watt (a man who married and had children with his own biological half-sister). It is doubtful that she was ever divorced. The complex Richards, who always called himself Dr. Richards – after he paid twenty dollars to attend a six-week course in herbal medicine – to his credit will have a remarkable posterity. "Three of Richards's sons became prominent Utah physicians, and more than thirty of his grandsons and great grandsons earned M.D.'s or Ph.D.s" by 1982. (Van Wagoner and Walker, *A Book of Mormons*, 299). Richards' sister, Rhoda Richards, a plural wife, was sealed to Joseph Smith. "[O]n Jan. 31, 1846 [after the death of Smith], she married Brigham Young [her first cousin] for time, Brigham serving as proxy for her sealing to Joseph." (George D. Smith, *Nauvoo Polygamy*, 651 n 372). For Rhoda it was Brigham for time and Joseph for eternity.

[42]D. Michael Quinn, "Latter-day Prayer Circles," *BYU Studies*, 19 (Fall 1978), 98, quoted in Van Wagoner, *Mormon Polygamy*, 225.

*off upon him in his absence, by his two faithless
friends. His dignity becomes offended, (and well it
might) refuses to live with his wife, but to be even with
his companions in iniquity, takes to himself three
more wives.*[43]

WILLIAM, EMMA, JANE AND JOSEPH

On May 3, 1842, the *Latter Day Saints Millennial Star* described
Joseph's friend and disciple William Law, a "thirty-three year old
counselor in the church presidency," in glowing terms: *"No man
could be better fitted to his station – wise, discreet, just, prudent – a
man of great suavity of manner and amiability of character . . . ."*[44]
The Laws (William and Jane) and the Smiths (Joseph and Emma)
were at the top of the Church. Law believed Joseph Smith *was* a
prophet of God. When the John C. Bennett scandal rocked Nauvoo
(when Bennett was literally described as "a spoiler of character and
virtue, and a living pestilence walking in darkness to fester in his
own infamy"[45]), Wilson Law, William's valued brother, "called
upon the Saints in a public meeting to acknowledge Joseph as a
'good, moral, virtuous, peaceable and patriotic man . . . .'"[46] At
that time, neither Wilson nor William Law knew Joseph Smith was
a polygamist.

---

[43]Sidney Rigdon's *Latter Day Saints Messenger and Advocate* in an October
1845 letter "To The Sisters Of The Church Of Jesus Christ Of Latter-day
Saints," quoted in Van Wagoner, *Mormon Polygamy*, 224-25 n 4, emphasis added.

[44]*Latter Day Saints' Millennial Star* 3 (3 May 1842): 9, quoted in Linda King
Newell and Valeen Tippetts Avery, *Mormon Enigma: Emma Hale Smith, Prophet's
Wife, "Elect Lady," Polygamy's Foe – 1804-1879* (Garden City, N.Y.: Doubleday &
Company, Inc., 1984), 167, emphasis added. For so long as he was faithful, Law's
character was recognized to have been exemplary. After the revelation on
polygamy caused him to leave the Church, he was savagely reviled. This was then
(and is still now) a pattern in the Church. Willard Chase, who knew the Smiths up
close and personal, described this metamorphosis. "After they [the Smiths]
became thorough Mormons, . . . [t]hey did not hesitate to abuse any man, no
matter how fair his character, provided he did not embrace their creed. Their
tongues were continually employed in speaking scandal and abuse." (Willard
Chase Statement, 1833, Dan Vogel, ed., *Early Mormon Documents*, 5 vols. [Salt
Lake City: Signature Books, 1996-2003], 2:73).

[45]*Nauvoo Wasp Extra*, July 27, 1842, quoted in Brodie, *No Man Knows My
History*, 318.

[46]Ibid., 319.

Confiding to Joseph Jackson

Joseph H. Jackson, a man with a notorious past, approached Joseph Smith late in the prophet's life, confessed to *dark crimes* (not a disqualification) and quickly gained the prophet's confidence. A non-Mormon, Jackson became one of Nauvoo Legion Lieutenant General Joseph Smith's *aides-de-camp*. By Christmas 1843, after a period of fits and starts, Jackson supposed that "he was almost persuaded to be one" (meaning a Mormon) with his great good friend, whereupon Joseph graciously responded that "he was not only almost, but altogether" one. A supremely confident Jackson later reported, whether true or not, that he was "admitted into all of his [Joseph's] secret councils, and was confided in so far, that he disclosed to me every act of his life."[47] Until their relationship cooled, Jackson was close to Smith.

Jackson "claimed that Joseph confided to him that he had been attempting to get Mrs. William Law for a spiritual wife."[48] To that end, and "for the purpose of affecting his object [Joseph] got up a revelation that Law was to be sealed up to Emma, and that Law's wife was to be his; in other words there was to be a spiritual swop."[49] (This unpublished revelation may seem to be referenced in verse 51 of what became (after 1876) Section 132 of the Doctrine and Covenants, the canonized revelation on polygamy[50]). Jackson later reported that Joseph "had never before suffered his passion for any woman, to carry him so far as to be willing to sacrifice Emma for its gratification."[51] Jackson said Joseph said he had spent "some two months" "endeavoring . . . to get Mrs. William Law for a spiritual wife." Jackson said Joseph said "he had used every argument in his power, to convince her of the correctness of

---

[47]Joseph H. Jackson, *A Narrative of the Adventures and Experience of Joseph H. Jackson in Nauvoo, Disclosing the Depths of Mormon Villany [sic] practiced in Nauvoo* (Morrison, IL: K. Yost, 1844, reprint 1960), 20; *see* also Diary of Joseph Smith, 29 December 1842, *History of the Church*, 6:149, quoted in Newell and Avery, *Mormon Enigma: Emma Hale Smith, Prophet's Wife*, 176.

[48]Newell and Avery, *Mormon Enigma: Emma Hale Smith, Prophet's Wife*, 176.

[49]Ibid.

[50]Doctrine and Covenants 132:51.

[51]Jackson, *A Narrative of the Adventures and Experience of Joseph H. Jackson in Nauvoo*, 21.

the doctrine, but could not succeed."[52]   Jackson also said that
Joseph said that, "Emma wanted Law for a spiritual husband."[53]
John D. Lee, many years later when facing execution in the Utah
Territory for his crimes at Mountain Meadows, while busy writing
his confessions, also said that Joseph wanted the "amiable and
handsome" wife of William Law.[54] Ex-Illinois Governor Thomas
Ford reported in his *History of Illinois* "that Joseph Smith
attempted to win Jane Law for his wife.[55]

Giving and Taking

In 1877 as an old man, Law denied that Joseph offered a swap, but
acknowledged that word in the community had it he did. Because it
didn't come to pass, Law didn't have to know. The rumor was
"that Joseph offered to furnish his wife Emma with a *substitute* for
him, by way of *compensation* for his neglect of her, on condition that
she would stop her opposition to polygamy and permit him to enjoy

---

[52]Ibid., 19.

[53]Ibid., 20.

[54]John D. Lee, *Confessions of John D. Lee* (New York: Bryan, Brand &
Company: W.H. Stelle & Co., 1877; photomechanical reprint of 1877 original, Salt
Lake City, UT: Modern Microfilm), 147.

[55]Thomas A. Ford, *History of Illinois, From Its Commencement as a State in
1814 to 1847*, Applewood's Series Historiography (Applewood Books, 2010), 322;
see also Brodie, *No Man Knows My History*, 369. Alexander Neibaur, the Jewish
maternal great-grandfather of Professor Hugh Nibley, a particularly famous
Mormon apologist, put a different spin on Smith's relationship with Mrs. Law.

> Neibaur reported that William Law wished to be sealed to his
> wife for eternity, but Joseph "Answered no because Law was
> a[n] Adulterious person." Neibaur wrote in his journal on May
> 24, 1844: "Some days after Mr. Smith [was] going toward his
> office. Mrs. Law stood in the door [and] beakoned to him . . . as
> no one but herself [was] in the hous, she drawing her Arms
> around him [said] if you won't seal me to my husband Seal
> myself unto you, he Said stand away and pussing her Gently
> aside giving her a denial and going out, when Mr. Law came
> home to Inquire who had been [there] in his Absense, she said
> no one but Br. Joseph, he then demanded what had passed.
> Mrs. L[aw] then [said] Joseph wanted her to be married to
> him."

(Journal of Alexander Neibaur, 1841 to 1862, May 24, 1844, LDS Archives, quoted
in Newell and Avery, *Mormon Enigma: Emma Hale Smith*, 177).

his *young wives in peace* and keep some of them in the house."[56]

On July 12, 1843, the Creator of the Universe is supposed to have addressed Emma Smith in a revelation directed to Joseph: "Verily, I say unto you: A commandment I give unto mine handmaid, Emma Smith, your wife, whom I have given unto you, that she stay herself and partake not of that which I commanded you to offer unto her; for I did it, saith the Lord, to prove you all, as I did Abraham, and that I might require an offering at your hand, by covenant and sacrifice."[57]   Here we see the Mormon God looking beyond issues of war and peace, hardship, the poor and poverty, thrones, principalities and powers, salvation and immortality, to something rather more obscure.   A small domestic thing to measure the principles of the principals.   The Lord is now heard to retract an earlier commandment given from him to Joseph to Emma – *he is here to take back "that which I commanded you to offer unto her."* It had been yet another test, and not a real command, offered to prove Joseph and Emma, William and Jane.

Emma's brilliant biographers (Newell and Avery) describe Doctrine and Covenants 132:51 as "ambiguous."   "Its meaning remains a mystery," they say.[58]   That may be a bit too generous.   Let us look at what the Lord said with some amplification: *"Verily, I say unto you* [again I say, for I commanded you previously]: *A commandment* [a new and substituted commandment] *I give unto mine handmaid, Emma Smith, your wife, whom I have given unto you* [and not to William Law], *that she stay herself* [that she not give herself to William Law] *and partake not of that which I commanded you to offer unto her* [a spiritual marriage to William Law]; *for I did it* [offered William to Emma and Jane to Joseph], *saith the Lord, to prove you all* [William and Emma and Jane and Joseph], *as I did Abraham, and that I might require an offering at your hand* [this test

---

[56]William Law to Dr. W. Wyl, 7 January 1844, quoted in Newell and Avery, *Mormon Enigma: Emma Hale Smith*, 176, emphasis retained.

[57]Doctrine and Covenants 132:51.

[58]Newell and Avery, *Mormon Enigma: Emma Hale Smith, Prophet's Wife,* 177. It is a mystery in the same sense that Joseph Smith's famous letter to Miss Nancy Rigdon is published in the History of the Church disguised as an essay on "Happiness" with this comment: "It is not positively known what occasioned the writing of this essay . . . ." (*History of the Church,* 5:134).

of your virtue], *by covenant and sacrifice.*"[59]   God sets aside the weighty affairs of the universe to interrupt a *"spiritual swop"* that he had previously *"commanded"* occur (Joseph for William, Emma for Jane).

This provision as described by Joseph Smith to Joseph H. Jackson pertains to Joseph and Emma's plans for William Law and Emma, and to Joseph and Emma's plans for Joseph Smith and Jane, all as previously described saith the Lord in an earlier and still unpublished commandment ("that which I commanded you to offer unto" "mine handmaid, Emma Smith"). God has interrupted the urgent affairs of heavens and earths in order to reverse himself and say: I didn't really mean what I said when I commanded Joseph to offer William Law to Emma and Jane Law to Joseph. You belong to Joseph and not to William Law. This was only a test. In retrospect, is it not clear that what Joseph H. Jackson said that Joseph said was true? There was to be a "spiritual swop." Joseph would "sacrifice" Emma for Jane. Law was "to be sealed up to Emma," then Joseph to Jane.[60]

---

[59]Doctrine and Covenants 132:51, with author's insertions.

[60]Spiritual "swops" are known to have occurred in Nauvoo. Early informal arrangements (undeputized) did in fact occur. John D. Lee, while writing his confessions, described the spirit of the times and some of those early events:

> In the Winter of 1845 meetings were held all over the city of Nauvoo, and the spirit of Elijah [Elijah "conferred" the keys of the "sealing power" on Joseph Smith and Oliver Cowdery in the Kirtland Temple on April 3, 1836 (Doctrine and Covenants 110:13-16)] was taught in the different families as a foundation to the order of celestial marriage, as well as the law of adoption. Many families entered into covenants with each other – the man to stand by his wife and the woman to cleave unto her husband, and the children to be adopted to the parents. ... Others refused to enter into these obligations, but agreed to separate from each other, dividing their substance, and mutually dissolving their former relations on friendly terms. Some have mutually agreed to exchange wives and have been sealed to each other as husband and wife by virtue and authority of the holy priesthood. One of Brigham's brothers, Lorenzo Young, now a bishop, made an exchange of wives with Mr. Decker, the father of the Mr. Decker who now has an interest in the cars running to York. They both seemed happy in the exchange of wives."
> [Lee, *Confessions of John D. Lee*, 165].

William Law appealed to Emma (he was such "a 'sweet little man'"[61]), but Emma not so much to William ("Emma was a full accomplice of Joseph's crimes"). Dr. W. Wyl asked William Law this question: "Did Emma, *the elect lady*, come to your house and complain about Joseph?" Law told Wyl that she never came to the house to complain, but that when he met her sometimes on the street, she complained about "the girls" "Joseph kept in the house." "You have overrated her," Law then corrected Wyl. She was not "the elect lady" Dr. Wyl had chosen to describe. Law thought that "she was dishonest" all by herself and in her own right, "outside" of the sphere of Joseph's "influence."   When asked what he remembered about Emma and the revelation on plural marriage, Law remembered this: "Well, I told you that she used to complain about Joseph's escapades whenever she met me on the street. She spoke repeatedly about that *pretended* revelation. She said once: '*The revelation says I must submit or be destroyed. Well, I guess I have to submit.*' On another day she said, '*Joe and I have settled our troubles on the basis of equal rights.*'"[62] She would do what he had done.

"She [Emma Smith]," according to William Law, "was a large, coarse woman, as deep a woman as there was, always full of schemes and smooth as oil. They were worthy of each other, she was not a particle better than he."[63]

---

[61]Jackson, *A Narrative of the Adventures and Experience of Joseph H. Jackson in Nauvoo*, 20.

[62]William Law to Dr. W. Wyl, "Interview with Wm. Law, March 30, 1887," *Salt Lake Tribune* (1 July 1887), emphasis retained. On June 23, 1843, a Friday in the A.M., "President Joseph" took William Clayton aside "and conversed considerable concerning some delicate matters." He first told Clayton that Emma "wanted to lay a snare for me. He told me last night of this and said he had felt troubled. *He said [Emma] had treated him coldly and badly since I came . . . and he knew she was disposed to be revenged on him for some things. She thought that if he would indulge himself she would too.* He cautioned me very kindly for which I felt thankful." (William Clayton, *An Intimate Chronicle: The Journals of William Clayton*, ed. George D. Smith [Salt Lake City: Signature Books in association Smith Research Associates, 1995], 108), emphasis added. On May 29, 1843, Joseph had been somewhat more abrupt. "This A.M. President Joseph told me that he felt as though I was not treating him exactly right and asked if I had used any familiarity with E[mma]. I told him by no means and explained to his satisfaction. At the store office." (Ibid., 106).

[63]Wyl, "Interview with Wm. Law, March 30, 1887," *Salt Lake Tribune* (1 July 1887).

William Law on Polygamy

William Law took Hyrum Smith's place as a member of the First Presidency when Hyrum became the Patriarch. He was not a member of the Nauvoo High Council where the revelation on polygamy was read to the members, and a few selected others, on August 12, 1843. "Hyrum," according to Law, "gave it [the revelation] to me in his office, told me to take it home and read it . . . and bring it back again."[64] When William had digested the contents, he showed the revelation to Jane. It turned the two of them upside down, he said. That is how William Law described William and Jane's response to what later became the canonized revelation on polygamy (Doctrine and Covenants 132).

Law took the unusual document straight to Joseph. He didn't believe Joseph would acknowledge such a revelation and expressed that opinion to Jane before he approached the prophet. Mrs. Law did not share her husband's opinion, for reasons previously stated or implied, and said that Smith would acknowledge its authenticity. William Law: "When I came to Joseph and showed him the paper, he said, 'Yes, that is a genuine revelation.'" William found that a bitter pill to swallow. "I said to the prophet: 'But in the Book of Doctrine and Covenants there is a revelation just the contrary of this.'"[65] "'Oh,' said Joseph, 'that was given when the church was in

---

[64]Ibid.

[65]Section 101, the canonized article on monogamous marriage, preceded Section 132, the canonized revelation on polygamous marriage. After 1844 Section 101 became Section 109. That revelation, published in all editions and printings of the Doctrine and Covenants until 1876, contrary to Section 132 (which set it aside), provided as follows: "According to the custom of all civilized nations, marriage is regulated by laws and ceremonies: therefore we believe, that all marriages in this church of Christ of Latter Day Saints, should be solemnized in a public meeting, or feast, prepared for that purpose . . . . [A]nd at the solemnization, the persons to be married, standing together, the man on the right, and the woman on the left, shall be addressed, by the person officiating, ... [H]e shall say, calling each by their names: 'You both mutually agree to be each other's companion, husband and wife, observing the legal rights belonging to this condition; that is, keeping yourselves wholly for each other, and from all others, during your lives.' And when they have answered 'Yes,' he shall pronounce them 'husband and wife' in the name of the Lord Jesus Christ . . . . Inasmuch as this church of Christ has been reproached with the crime of fornication, and polygamy: we declare that we believe, that one man should have one wife; and one woman, but one husband, except in case of

its infancy, then it was all right to feed the people on milk, but now it is necessary to give them strong meat.'"[66]

The prophet lied to his people and to the world at large. He told them lies to rein them in so as not to interfere with their conversions, then told the truth – to a few carefully selected souls – later but privately. The unchangeable Lord is seen, in the case of polygamy, to have produced a changeable doctrine. In 1890, after the Lord changed his mind in 1843, he changed his mind again. *You won't, you will, you won't.* On just such uncertain terms did Joseph's malleable Lord order his affairs with a compliant people. After a long discussion that became heated, and before William Law left the Church and published the first and only edition of the ill-fated "Nauvoo Expositor" (a newspaper that offended because it threatened to tell the truth about polygamy), "the breach between us became more open and contentious every day . . . ." "[T]he revelation gave the finishing touch to my doubts . . .,"[67] Law would say to Dr. Wyl. From the moment William and Jane rejected the revelation, turning their backs on polygamy, Smith treated the Laws, William and Jane, as apostates. Law then later spoke his truth: "I've got a black spot on my life, which shall pain me to the very last minute of my existence."

BITTER BARGAINS

Religious Indulgences

Through the careful (and private) disclosure of the doctrine of plurality, nineteenth-century Mormonism's New and Everlasting Covenant, Joseph Smith bargained for wives (including other men's wives), and children (including other men's children) for *time* and *eternity*. In consequence of such transactions, some of Joseph's plural wives, purchased "immortality and eternal life" for themselves, their parents and their parents' posterity, "both old and

---

death, when either is at liberty to marry again." (Doctrine and Covenants [1835 ed.], Section 101).

[66]"Interview with Wm. Law, March 30, 1887," *Salt Lake Tribune* (1 July 1887), emphasis retained.

[67]Ibid., in Sullsburg, Wisconsin.

young" "from generation to generation."[68]   This dynastic notion
offended principled concepts of personal responsibility.   If
polygamy (or concubinage) was not the commandment Joseph said
that it was, and if Jesus Christ, Christianity's unmarried pastor,
was not the author of that principle, and had not authorized the
teaching of it, then it was quite certainly the abominable practice
the Book of Mormon described thus "saith the Lord."[69]

Catholic Indulgences -- Supererogation

Mormon scholars have long condemned in the strongest terms the
Catholic practice of granting indulgences. "Compare," they have
said, "this arrogant and tyrannical church of the world with the
Church of Christ."[70]   Indulgences began their march to acceptance
in the Catholic Church "as exemptions from temporal penalties."[71]
In the fourth century, Catholics promulgated the doctrine that
"errors in religion, when maintained and adhered to after proper
admonition, were punishable with civil penalties and corporeal
tortures" ("fine[s], imprisonment, bodily torture, and even death").
By the eleventh century, the Catholic Church was "providing for
mitigation or annulment of such sentences on payment of money."[72]
"This led to the shocking practice of selling *indulgences* or pardons,
which custom was afterward carried to the awful extreme of issuing

---

[68]The rewards for such obedience, "by virtue of the holy promise[s] which I
now make unto you, *saith the Lord*," were "immortality and eternal [lives]" for
themselves and their families. (Letter, Joseph Smith to Newel K. Whitney, 27 July
1842 [accessed 5 June 2018], available from https://www.reddit.com/r/exmormon/
comments/1ah2lw/here_is_joseph_smiths_letter_to_ newel_k_whitney/; Internet, p.
1 of 4).

[69]Book of Mormon, Jacob 2:24-30. "Wherefore, *thus saith the Lord* . . . I the
Lord God will not suffer that this people shall do like them of old . . . . For there
shall not any man among you have save it be one wife; and concubines he shall
have none."   "For I, the Lord God, delight in the chastity of women, and
whoredoms are an abomination before me; thus saith the Lord of Hosts."   Verse
30, however, states, "For if I will, saith the Lord of Hosts, raise up seed unto me I
will command my people; otherwise they shall hearken unto these things."

[70]James E. Talmage, *The Great Apostasy* (Salt Lake City: Deseret Book
Company, 1953), 134. Preface: "If the alleged apostasy of the primitive church
was not a reality, the Church of Jesus Christ of Latter-day Saints is not the divine
institution its name proclaims." (Ibid.).

[71]Ibid., 135.

[72]Ibid., 134.

such before the commission of the specific offense, thus literally offering for sale licenses to sin, with assurance of temporal and promise of spiritual immunity."[73] This evidence of how low the Christian (Catholic) Church had fallen has often been cited by Mormon scholars to support the proposition that the "Church of Christ" was lost from the earth by reason of apostasy and had to be restored by the prophet Joseph Smith.

The ("dreadful") *doctrine of supererogation* practiced by the Catholic Church and cited by Mormon scholars as evidence of the mother church's fall from grace presupposed the existence of "an immense treasure of *merit*, composed of the pious deeds and virtuous actions which the saints had performed *beyond what was necessary for their own salvation*, and which were therefore applicable to the benefit of others . . . ."[74] This was a resource reserved to infallible authority. "[T]he guardian and dispenser of this precious treasure was the Roman pontiff . . . ." The Pope "was empowered to assign to such as he thought proper a portion of this inexhaustible source of merit, suitable to their respective guilt, and sufficient to deliver them from the punishment due to their crimes."[75] Mormons consider the doctrine of *supererogation* as an offense against Christ, a monstrous distortion of the Christian faith. It is thought to be a concept devoid of logic and reason.

> *The doctrine of supererogation is as unreasonable as it is unscriptural and untrue. Man's individual responsibility for his acts is as surely a fact as is his agency to act for himself. He will be saved through the merits and by the atoning sacrifice of our Redeemer and Lord; and his claim upon the salvation provided is strictly dependent on his compliance with the principles and ordinances of the gospel as established by Jesus Christ.*[76]

---

[73]Ibid., 134-35, emphasis original.
[74]Ibid., 135, emphasis retained.
[75]Ibid.
[76]Ibid., 135-36, emphasis added.

The Great Reward

Joseph promised his plural wives that "they and their families would benefit spiritually from a close tie to the prophet. Joseph told a prospective wife that submitting to plural marriage would 'ensure your eternal salvation & exaltation and that of your father's household. & all your kindred.'"[77] Helen Mar Kimball: After her father had first explained the principle, Joseph Smith then visited her at the Kimball home where he "explained the 'principle of Celestial marriage' . . . ." "After which he said to me [to Helen Mar Kimball], 'If you will take this step [plural marriage to me], it will ensure your eternal salvation & exaltation and that of your father's household & all of your kindred . . . . [']" Joseph Smith promised fourteen-year-old Helen Mar Kimball, the daughter of Heber C. Kimball, that if she would marry him, it would mean salvation for her and for her family. She would obtain for herself, then also for them, exaltation and eternal life. *This promise was so great that I willingly gave myself to purchase so glorious a reward.*"[78]

Miss Kimball may have thought in the beginning that her marriage was dynastic, linking the families of Kimball and Smith, and for eternity only, if a fourteen-year-old could digest such complexity. She appeared to have only later learned that she had also married Joseph for *time*, which implied a more carnal course. Miss Kimball saw her marriage to the prophet "as limiting her freedom and isolating her from her friends."[79] Helen Kimball, Heber's "one Ewe Lamb," expressed her discontent after coming of age in verse:

---

[77]Richard Lyman Bushman with the assistance of Jed Woodworth, *Joseph Smith: Rough Stone Rolling* (New York: Alfred A. Knopf, 2005), 439. "The belief in salvation through connection to Joseph Smith and other leading figures led eventually to sealing of nonrelatives to these men." (Ibid., 645 n 12, citing Irving, "Law of Adoption," 291-314). This principle came to be known as the law of adoption. John D. Lee, who was executed for his crimes at Mountain Meadows in the Utah Territory, was the second adopted son of Brigham Young. "A father who gave his daughter to the Prophet as a plural wife was assured that the marriage 'shall be crowned upon your heads with honor and immortality and eternal life to all your house both old and young.' The relationship would bear fruit in the afterlife." (Ibid.).

[78]Helen Mar Kimball, cited at Todd Compton, *In Sacred Loneliness*, 499, emphasis retained and added.

[79]Ibid.

I thought through <u>this life</u> my time will be my own
  The step I now am taking's for eternity alone,
No one need be the wiser, through time I shall be free,
  And as the past hath been the future still will
  be.
To my guileless heart all free from worldly care
  And full of blissful hopes and youthful visions
  rare
The world seamed bright the thret'ning clouds were
kept
  From sight and all looked fair . . . .[80]

The conclusion is that Helen had expected her marriage to Joseph Smith to be for eternity only. "She had misunderstood the meaning of the marriage to Smith:"[81]

  . . . but pitying angels wept.
  They saw my youthful friends grow shy and
  cold.
And poisonous darts from sland'rous tongues were
hurled,
  Untutor'd heart in thy gen'rous sacrafise,
Thou dids't not weigh the cost nor know the bitter
price;
  Thy happy dreams all o'er thou'st doom'd
  alas to be
Bar'd out from social scenes by this thy destiny,
  And o'er thy sad'nd mem'ries of sweet
  departed joys
Thy sicken'd heart will brood and imagine future
woes,
  And like a fetter'd bird with wild and longing
  heart,
Thou'lt daily pine for freedom and murmor at thy lot;
. . . .[82]

---

[80]Ibid., 499-500, Poetry, Helen Mar Kimball, emphasis retained and added.
[81]Ibid., 500.
[82]Ibid., 500, Poetry, Helen Mar Kimball, emphasis added.

Helen Mar Kimball, who sold herself for what she thought to be a greater cause, suffered because of the principle of plurality. And what was brother "N.K. Whitney(s)" great reward for giving his daughter, Sarah Ann, Helen Mar's faithful friend, to the prophet Joseph? Joseph's God, in a revelation adapted to the circumstances in which the children of the kingdom were placed, chose to explain:

> *[T]he thing that my servant Joseph Smith has made known unto you and your family and which you have agreed upon is right in mine eyes and shall be rewarded upon your heads with honor and immortality and eternal life to all your house, both old and young because of the lineage of my Priesthood, <u>saith the Lord</u>, it shall be upon you and upon your children after you from generation to generation, by virtue of the holy promise which I now make unto you, <u>saith the Lord</u>.*[83]

---

[83]Compton, *In Sacred Loneliness*, 348, emphasis added. Here Newel K. Whitney, his predecessors and posterity, are "sealed up unto eternal life, by revelation and the spirit of prophecy, through the power of the Holy Priesthood." (Doctrine and Covenants 131:5). They are to be vicariously saved ("both old and young"), and from generation to generation, because Newel and Elizabeth Whitney had the faith and foresight to consign their daughter, Sarah Ann, to the care and keeping of the prophet, Joseph Smith, as a plural wife – in order *"to purchase so glorious a reward."* (Compton, *In Sacred Loneliness*, 499, citing Helen Mar Kimball).

> Though such persons [those "sealed up unto eternal life, by revelation and the spirit of prophecy"] "shall commit any sin or transgression of the new and everlasting covenant whatever, and all manner of blasphemies, and if they commit no murder wherein they shed innocent blood, yet they shall come forth in the first resurrection, and enter into their exaltation." [Doctrine and Covenants 132:26, cited at Bruce R. McConkie, *Mormon Doctrine*, 2d ed. (Salt Lake City: Bookcraft, 1966), 110].

> The Lord says to them: "Ye shall come forth in the first resurrection; and if it be after the first resurrection, in the next resurrection, and shall inherit thrones, kingdoms, principalities, and powers, dominions, all heights and depths." [Doctrine and Covenants 132:19].

Various Whitneys, because of these majestic promises, will get a pass – even those who sin or transgress. Newel and Elizabeth Whitney were said to have earned salvation for themselves, their progenitors and their posterity. But until then, until those promises come to pass, they will lie for the Lord and his prophet.

That is the Mormon God's incredible promise to Newel K. Whitney if he will give Sarah Ann to Joseph Smith as his sixteenth plural wife, as one of the thirty-four plural wives who pledged their troth to Smith in 1842 and 1843. That was how important the marriage of Joseph Smith to Sarah Ann Whitney – a teenager and one of thirteen secret brides in 1842, ten of them women already married to other men – was to Joseph's Lord, *saith the Lord*." The Whitneys were promised these great blessings as a result of the marriage. Newel K. Whitney "is told that he will be 'rewarded' 'with honor and immortality and eternal life to all your house.' By being linked to the prophet, the Whitneys' salvation was assured."[84]

The promises made to these long-suffering Mormon women, in order to obtain their consent to those plural marriage proposals endorsed by God himself, were nineteenth-century "indulgences." A fourth-century Pope offering forgiveness for currency would be hard pressed to match the quality of these incredible inducements.[85] Helen Mar Kimball described the magnitude of her friend Sarah's sacrifice. "No earthly inducement could be held forth to the women who entered this order. It was to be a life-sacrifice for the sake of an everlasting glory and exaltation. Sarah Ann took this step of her own free will."[86] Sarah Ann, a victim of improbable predictions, was under the management of others.

Mormon Indulgences

Young Mormon women, virgins, women of tender age, did not purchase immortality and eternal life for themselves and everyone

---

[84]Compton, *In Sacred Loneliness*, 348.

[85]After secretly marrying Joseph Smith on July 27, 1842, and publicly marrying her widowed Uncle Joseph C. Kingsbury on April 29, 1843 (in a pretended ceremony intended to conceal her secret marriage to Smith), Sarah Whitney (Smith) (Kingsbury), a nineteen year old, then later became the eighteenth wife of her third husband, Helen Mar Kimball's forty-three year old father, Heber C. Kimball. Sarah Whitney (Smith) (Kingsbury) (Kimball) had seven children with Kimball. Kimball's biological children with Sarah, and Sarah, will belong to Joseph Smith, to whom they are sealed, in the afterlife. Her marriage to Kimball was in the beginning secret and she "continued to be known as Sarah Kingsbury." (Ibid., 353).

[86]Ibid., 349, citing Helen Mar Kimball.

they loved – both old and young and from generation to generation – through the exchange of money. The *indulgences* purchased by those Mormon women were acquired with promises made for out-of-this-earth considerations, inducements greatly more dear but equally improbable. These Mormon women, frequently teens and in later years occasionally as young as twelve (John D. Lee), literally sold themselves.[87]

These promised rewards, indistinguishable in their remote intent from those early Catholic indulgences, and even more illogical, were also "licenses to sin, with assurance of temporal and promise of spiritual immunity." Listen to the definition of a peculiarly Mormon "indulgence." "Those so favored of the Lord [those "sealed up unto eternal life, by revelation and the spirit of prophesy through the power of the Holy Priesthood"] are sealed up against all manner of sin and blasphemy except the blasphemy against the Holy Ghost and the shedding of innocent blood."[88] Similar promises were made to persons who had received, and do still receive, Mormonism's vaunted second anointing, a secret ceremony virtually unknown to the laity. "Though such persons 'shall commit any sin or transgression of the new and everlasting covenant whatever, and all manner of blasphemies, and if they commit no murder wherein they shed innocent blood, yet they shall come forth in the first resurrection, and enter into their exaltation.'"[89] And, it is said, they shall "inherit thrones, kingdoms, principalities, and powers, dominions, all heights and depths."[90]

Were these promises to those future generations not bargained for? Was there not a consideration? Were they not both purchased and sold? Were they not issued before the commission of specific offenses? Were they not licenses to sin? These privileged recipients received assurances of spiritual immunity. Smith traded pardons,

---

[87]In the Utah Territory, the legislature, which did nothing without the consent of Brigham Young, allowed young men to marry at the age of fifteen, young women at twelve. John D. Lee, age forty-three, married Mary Ann Williams, age twelve, in 1856. (George D. Smith, *Nauvoo Polygamy*, 604, 605). They were later divorced after which she married John Alma Lee, one of his sons.

[88]Doctrine and Covenants 131:5, quoted in McConkie, *Mormon Doctrine*, 110.

[89]Doctrine and Covenants 132:26, quoted in McConkie, *Mormon Doctrine*, 110.

[90]Doctrine and Covenants, 132:19.

promises, exaltation and eternal life for intimacy,[91] and in the cases of women previously married to other men, for their earthly and eternal devotion, and that of their biological children. All at the expense of their civil covenants and traditional marriages. Non-consenting children were expected to follow their mothers and not their biological fathers to a life with Joseph Smith in the eternities.

Comparisons

The Pope, in the final analysis, *sold* forgiveness from punishment, eternal or otherwise, for money. Joseph Smith, in the final analysis, *sold* forgiveness from punishment, eternal or otherwise, for union. Both supposed that God allowed them to forgive sin, past, present or prospective, for an appropriate consideration. By marrying Joseph Smith, Joseph told Helen Mar Kimball that she had purchased her "eternal salvation & exaltation and that of your father's household & all of your kindred."[92] That was a promise of salvation and exaltation for Heber C. Kimball, his forty-three wives and his sixty-five children, and for his posterity, *nirvana* for the multitudes. Newel and Elizabeth Whitney purchased "honor and immortality and eternal life" for "all their house, both old and young," and for their children after them "from generation to generation."[93] The concept is abhorrent.

The Catholic Church, "in the days of its degeneracy," declared "that the merit of one may be bought by another and paid for in worldly coin. Can such a Church be in any measure the Church of Christ?"[94] The Mormon Church declared that one person, by

---

[91]"Joseph Smith wrote his teenage wife [Sarah Ann Whitney] a letter on March 23, 1843, and, once again, he emphasized the salvation that her marriage to him would bring to her and her family. If Sarah remained within the 'new and everlasting covenant' of marriage [faithful to polygamy] until the end, she and her father's house 'shall be saved in the same eternal glory,' and even if they should wander from the fold they could still repent and 'be crowned with a fullness of glory.' This is the same doctrine that is taught in Doctrine and Covenants 132: salvation, even despite 'wandering from the fold.'" (Compton, *In Sacred Loneliness*, 499).

[92]Ibid., 499.

[93]Compton, *In Sacred Loneliness*, 348.

[94]Talmage, *The Great Apostasy*, 136.

giving herself in marriage to some holy man, may buy the "immortality and eternal life" of untold others, including those unborn for as far out as the eye can see. Can such a Church be in any measure the Church of Christ? For four hundred years, the Catholic Church, according to Mormon scholar James E. Talmage, "claimed for its pope the power to remit all sins, and that the promise of remission had been sold and bought."[95] Joseph Smith claimed the power, through the Lord, Jesus Christ, to grant "immortality and eternal life" through the power of the priesthood to the houses of those who granted him intimacy and union, to those who pledged their earthly and eternal troth. Those who recognized him, and favored him here, would be recognized by him and favored for eternity. That was Brigham's promise to Martha Brotherton.

Joseph Smith, like James E. Talmage's officious Pope, "assumed to sit in judgment as God himself."[96]

"A SNAKE IN THE GRASS"

It is Friday, May 3, 1844; Joseph will die in June. Parley P. Pratt (the man who said, "we must lie to support the prophet") is tending to the affairs of the flock in Massachusetts. As part of his duties there, Pratt now writes Brother Joseph and Brother Orson Spencer a letter: "DEAR BROTHER JOSEPH AND BROTHER ORSON SPENCER, OR WHOM IT MAY CONCERN: This is to forewarn you that you have a snake in the grass – a base traitor and hypocrite in your midst, of whom perhaps you may not be fully aware." The offender, "Mr. Augustine Spencer," is Elder Orson Spencer's brother. Forget that Parley includes Orson in the salutation. Loyalty is more important than biology. Augustine Spencer has recklessly written a letter from Nauvoo to someone in Massachusetts "which is now going the rounds in this neighborhood."

According to Parley, the letter "is fraught with the most infamous slander." It "is calculated to embitter the minds of the people who read or hear [of] it [On May 3, 1844, Parley P. Pratt has two

---

[95] Ibid., 138.
[96] Ibid.

wives[97]]." "It [Spencer's letter] affirms that Joseph Smith is in the habit of drinking, swearing, carousing, dancing all night, &c., and that he keeps six or seven young females as wives, &c., and many other such like insinuations."[98]   On May 3, 1844, Joseph is really keeping about thirty-eight women, many of them young, more than a dozen of them the previously married civilly covenanted wives of other men.[99]   For the most part the husbands of Joseph's polyandrous women are faithful Latter-day Saints, a band of feckless brothers.

Parley, who is dignifying gossip and hearsay, has not seen the letter himself, but he has "carefully examined the testimony of those who have," and he has "seen and witnessed its baneful effect upon the people here."   Augustine Spencer is reported to have asked his communicants to keep the contents of the letter confidential from the people in Nauvoo, because he has a "confidential friendship with the 'Prophet Joe' and the Mormons."[100]   "[H]e hopes," he says, "to get into office by their means."   Drinking, swearing, carousing, dancing – that is fluff.   There are accredited persons who have seen the prophet drink and swear and carouse.   Consider the well informed McLellin.   At the heart of this betrayal is the inexcusable disclosure of polygamy to antiseptic saints who had accepted the gospel outside of the heartland, whether in distant England or Boston, Massachusetts, under false pretenses.   Disclosure to such innocent operatives in those pristine regions is strictly forbidden.

By May 3, 1844, Joseph Smith seems to have married most of the women he is now known to have married in mortality, including about nine teenagers (not including Fanny Alger), at least two of them just fourteen years of age.[101]   Augustine Spencer's representations about the numbers and ages of Joseph's wives were speculative and far from complete.   Like almost everyone he had seriously undercounted, because, as Joseph had famously said, "No man knows my history."

---

[97]George D. Smith, *Nauvoo Polygamy*, 613-14.

[98]*History of the Church*, 6:354, letter from Pratt to Smith and Spencer, 3 May 1844, Richmond, Mass., to Nauvoo, Ill.

[99]George D. Smith, *Nauvoo Polygamy*, 621-23.

[100]*History of the Church*, 6:355.

[101]George D. Smith, *Nauvoo Polygamy*, 621-23.

Pratt, an early thoroughly informed polygamous insider, would himself keep about eleven wives before his death at the age of fifty in 1857, not including his first wife, Thankful Halsey, who died in 1837. His wives would include Elizabeth Brotherton, the sister of Martha, the young woman who bolted, and Eleanor Jane McComb (McLean), the undivorced wife and mother of the children of Hector McLean, the enraged husband who would later find and murder him.[102] Parley had a few suggestions for the treatment of a man who couldn't be trusted not to tell the truth: "Now, I say to the Saints, Let such a man alone severely; shun him as they would the pestilence; be not deceived by a smooth tongue nor flattering words; neither accept of any excess or apology until he boldly contradicts and counteracts his lying words abroad; but rather expose and unmask him in your midst, ... *I remain, as ever, your friend and brother, in the love of truth.*"[103]

It would never do that members in Massachusetts should know that the Church was led by a man with close to forty wives, including many teenagers and as many as fourteen polyandrous women previously legally married to, supported by and cohabiting with other men. And Parley, "*as ever, your friend and brother, in the love of truth,*" is not afraid to say so.

---

[102]Ibid., 613-14.

[103]Parley P. Pratt, letter to Brother Joseph Smith and Brother Orson Spencer, 3 May 1844, *History of the Church*, 6:354-55, emphasis added.

CHAPTER TEN

Provocative Plurality

Wherefore, meaning the church, thou shalt give heed unto all his words, and commandments, which he shall give unto you, as he receiveth them, walking in all holiness before me: For his word ye shall receive, as if from my own mouth, in all patience and faith....[1]

Book of Commandments

From him I learned that the doctrine of plural and celestial marriage is the most holy and important doctrine ever revealed to man on the earth, and that without obedience to that principle, no man can ever attain to the fulness of exaltation in celestial glory.[2]

William Clayton

JOSEPH'S WITNESSES

In 1830 Joseph Smith produced eleven witnesses to say that he had the gold plates and the Book of Mormon was the word of God. In 1842 Joseph Smith produced thirty-one witnesses to say that monogamy was the only rule of marriage in the Mormon Church.

The Testimony of Three Witnesses, *1830*:

> *[W]e . . . have seen the plates which contain this record, . . . we . . . know that they have been translated*

---

[1]Book of Commandments 22:4-5.
[2]Statement, William Clayton, 16 February 1874 (sworn to before John C. Caine, a notary public in Salt Lake City), reprinted as "William Clayton's Testimony," *The Historical Record: A Monthly Periodical*, vol. 6 (May 1887), 224-26.

*by the gift and power of God, for his voice hath
declared it unto us; wherefore we know of a surety
that the work is true . . . we have seeen [sic] the
engravings which are upon the plates . . . we declare
with words of soberness that an Angel of God came
down from heaven, . . . brought and laid before our
eyes, that we beheld and saw the plates, and the
engravings thereon . . . the voice of the Lord
commanded us that we should bear record of it . . . .[3]*

Three Men

The Testimony of Eight Witnesses, *1830*:

*Be it known . . . that Joseph Smith, Jr., the Author
and Proprietor of this work, has shewn unto us the
plates of which hath been spoken, which have the
appearance of gold; and as many of the leaves as the
said Smith has translated, we did handle with our
hands; . . . we also saw the engravings thereon, all of
which has the appearance of ancient work, and of
curious workmanship . . . we . . . know of a surety that
the said Smith has got the plates of which we have
spoken . . . and we lie not, God bearing witness of it.[4]*

Eight Men

The Testimony of Twelve Witnesses, *1842*:

*We the undersigned members of the church of Jesus
Christ of Latter-Day Saints and residents of the City
of Nauvoo, persons of families do hereby certify and
declare that we know of no other rule or system of*

---

[3]The Testimony of Three Witnesses, Joseph Smith, Jr., trans., *The Book of
Mormon as it came from the mouth of the Prophet in its original unchanged
condition*, published in its first English edition (Palmyra, NY: E.B. Grandin, 1830;
New York, NY: reproduced [lithographed] by Wilford C. Wood, publisher,
Publishers Press, 1962), 589, witnesses statements at the back of the book. The
witnesses (except for Cowdery) did not prepare (or sign) these attestations, and
none of the men, including Cowdery, were notarized.

[4]Ibid., 590.

marriage than the one published from the Book of Doctrine and Covenants [unequivocal monogamy], and we give this certificate to show that Dr. J.C. Bennett's "secret wife system" is a creature of his own make as we know of no such society in this place nor never did.[5]

Twelve Men

The Testimony of Nineteen Witnesses, *1842*:

We the undersigned members of the ladies' relief society, and married females do certify and declare that we know of no system of marriage being practised in the church of Jesus Christ of Latter Day Saints save the one contained in the Book of Doctrine and Covenants [one man, one wife], and we give this certificate to the public to show that J.C. Bennett's "secret wife system" is a disclosure of his own make.[6]

Nineteen Women

PROLOGUE

The principles of plural marriage were revealed to Joseph Smith no later than 1831.[7] "The Prophet taught the doctrine of plural marriage, and a number of such marriages were performed during his lifetime."[8] On about July 17, 1831, an unpublished revelation

---

[5]*Times and Seasons*, 3 (1 October 1842), 939-40.

[6]Ibid., 940.

[7]*Blood Atonement and the Origin of Plural Marriage – A Discussion*, correspondence between Elder Joseph F. Smith, Jr., of the Church of Jesus Christ of Latter-day Saints, and Mr. Richard C. Evans, Second Counselor in the Presidency of the "Reorganized" Church (Salt Lake City: The Deseret News Press, 1905), 77 fn. *"[A]s early as 1831 the Lord revealed the principle of celestial marriage to him ["the Prophet Joseph Smith"] and he taught it to others."* (Ibid., emphasis added).

[8]*Teachings of Presidents of the Church – Joseph Smith* (Salt Lake City: The Church of Jesus Christ of Latter-day Saints, 2007), xii. Weasel words: "Over the next several decades, under the direction of the Church President who succeeded Joseph Smith, a significant number of Church members entered into plural

directed the elders "to form a matrimonial alliance with the natives," meaning Native Americans or "Lamanites." In the words of one early important observer, it would be "pleasing to the Lord, should they form a matrimonial alliance with the natives" by means of which they could "gain a residence in the Indian territory, independent of the [Indian] agent." The government's agents were determined to deny those elders access.[9] Joseph Smith privately taught "the principle of celestial and plural marriage" to some previously married missionaries sent to convert the Lamanites who had been relocated to places near the borders of the state of Missouri and encouraged them to marry Native American women so that the "posterity" of such women "through intermarriage" would "become white, delightsome, and Just."[10]

According to Ezra Booth, the Lord commissioned Cowdery "to proceed" to a "place where the foot of a white man had never trod." It was Cowdery's task "to rear up a pillar for a witness, where the temple of God" should be built "in the glorious new Jerusalem" on Indian land. Cowdery was disappointed by the Indian agents, and the missionaries' plans to erect the City of Zion on Indian land were quickly aborted. Cowdery was forced to wait upon the spirit and to improvise. As "every avenue leading to the Indians" unceremoniously closed, a new location for the city and the temple that had to be built needed to be found in some Gentile place. That

---

marriages." (Ibid.). "Several decades," when translated, should be interpreted to mean from about 1831 to about 1905 and even beyond. And under his own "direction," although he never publicly taught the doctrine, Joseph Smith married about thirty-eight women before his death on June 27, 1844. This widely distributed twenty-first century manual attempted to protect the true author of Mormon polygamy but threw his successor, Brigham Young, under the bus.

[9]Ezra Booth Letters, letter IX, Eber D. Howe, *Mormonism Unvailed: Or, A Faithful Account of That Singular Imposition and Delusion* (Painesville, OH: E.D. Howe, 1834; reprint, New York: AMS Press Inc., 1977), 220.

[10]W.W. Phelps to Brigham Young, 12 August 1861 (LDS Archives), quoted in George D. Smith, *Nauvoo Polygamy: "... but we called it celestial marriage"* (Salt Lake City: Signature Books, 2008), 14. The Book of Mormon prophesied that "the scales of darkness shall begin to fall from their [Indian] eyes; and many generations shall not pass away among them, save they shall be a white and delightsome people." (Book of Mormon [1830 edition], 2 Nephi 30:6). "The 1840 Book of Mormon substituted the word 'pure' for 'white,' although the wording reverted back to 'white' again in the English 1841 and later foreign editions, then became 'pure' again in 1981." (Ibid.).

meant adapting to circumstances directly opposed to the original plan and required a substitution plan foreign to the design "expressed" by Joseph's Lord "in several commandments." That awkward substitution befuddled the witness Booth. It was as if the directors of a project, say a courthouse in Ravenna, made a mistake and "built it in Trumbull County," a place where it served no particular purpose.[11]

The Book of Commandments published in *1833* reported that, "Thou shalt love thy wife with all thy heart, and shall cleave unto her and none else . . . ."[12] In 1833, the same year the Book of Commandments containing that monogamous commitment was published, it is said by some Mormon scholars (D. Michael Quinn and Todd Compton) that Joseph Smith plurally married Fanny Alger, with whom he was "reportedly involved" since "perhaps as early as 1831."[13] Fanny Alger, a housemaid in the Smith home, was born on September 20, 1816,[14] and until September 19, 1831, was fourteen years old. In March 1831, the Lord was supposed to have said, "[I]t is lawful that [a man] should have one wife, and they shall twain be one flesh . . . ."[15] The first edition of the Book of Doctrine and Covenants (published in 1835) reported that "we declare that we believe, that one man should have one wife; and one woman but one husband, except in case of death . . . when either is at liberty to marry again."[16]

---

[11]Ezra Booth in Howe, *Mormonism Unvailed*, 219.

[12]Book of Commandments 44:22, p. 91.

[13]Richard Lyman Bushman, with the assistance of Jed Woodworth, *Joseph Smith: Rough Stone Rolling* (New York: Alfred A. Knopf, 2005), 323.

[14]Todd Compton, *In Sacred Loneliness: The Plural Wives of Joseph Smith* (Salt Lake City: Signature Books, 2001), 26.

[15]Book of Commandments, 52:17, p. 117.

[16]Section 101, "Marriage," Doctrine and Covenants (*1835 edition*), 251. Section 101, the article on monogamy, was not replaced by Section 132, the revelation on polygamy, until 1876. The 1843 revelation on polygamy didn't become Section 132 of the Doctrine and Covenants (thus replacing the article "endorsing monogamous marriage") until "thirty-two years after Smith's death." In this twenty-first century, "Section 132 remains part of the LDS canon and continues to authorize a man to marry additional women" (George D. Smith, *Nauvoo Polygamy*, 43), meaning by that to say both plural partners and concubines. The 1835 statement, Section 101, endorsing monogamous marriage prohibited polygamy without qualification. There was no Book of Mormon exception that God might some day command his people to raise up seed to him in Section 101 of the Doctrine and Covenants. In defense of the claim that the

BREAKING BAD

In October 1842 Joseph Smith produced thirty-one witnesses, twelve prominent Mormon men ("residents of the City of Nauvoo" and "persons of families") and nineteen prominent Mormon women ("members of the ladies' relief society" and "married females"), to certify and declare that monogamy was the only rule of marriage "being practised" in the Mormon Church, that all marriages were solemnized in a public meeting or feast, and that the clerk was directed to keep a public record of every marriage. The twelve men likewise certified and declared that there was no "secret wife system" "in this place" (Nauvoo, Illinois), nor had there ever been.

On September 1, 1842, the provisions in the 1835 edition of the Doctrine and Covenants that "without qualification" endorsed monogamous marriage were published (without the attestation of witnesses) in the *Times and Seasons*, a Mormon periodical. The *Witness Certificates* for twelve men and nineteen women were then published in the *Times and Seasons* one month later on October 1, 1842. The October 1 publication included a preface written by Joseph Smith, the editor responsible for the contents of the Mormon publication. The revelations, compiled in the Doctrine and Covenants of the Church of the Latter Day Saints in 1835, as published in the *Times and Seasons* on September 1, 1842, included statements intended to reassure the public that the Church was not guilty of "the crime of fornication, and polygamy." Is it not clear that by 1835, even before 1835, the Church had been accused of "fornication and polygamy"?

Church was guilty of "fornication and polygamy," the Church explained "that the wording of the statement was 'selected from the revelations of God' and compiled by Oliver Cowdery and two other 'presiding Elders.'" The "presiding Elders" to whom the statement referred "were the same two men who had mediated Emma's complaint against Joseph and Fanny *in 1832*: Sidney Rigdon and Frederick G. Williams." (Ibid., emphasis added). Note that the incident in the barn and the contentious proceedings that followed occurred in 1832, one year before the Mormon scholars (Quinn and Compton) said that Smith married Fanny Alger. If anyone was in a position to provide evidence that Joseph Smith ever married Fanny Alger, it should have been those early founding fathers, Sidney Rigdon, Frederick G. Williams and Oliver Cowdery.

Book of Commandments, *1833 to 1835*: "Thou shalt love thy wife with all thy heart, and shall cleave unto her and none else . . . ."[17] Doctrine and Covenants, *1835 to 1876*: "Inasmuch as this church of Christ has been reproached with the crime of fornication and polygamy: we declare that we believe, that one man should have one wife; and one woman, but one husband, except in case of death, when either is at liberty to marry again."[18] "The Revelation" (1835 Doctrine and Covenants 101) was principally authored by Oliver Cowdery (one of the Three Witnesses to the Book of Mormon), with the assistance of Sidney Rigdon and Frederick G. Williams, and it was canonized.[19] Section 101, or Section 109 as it later became in 1844, was not replaced in the standard works by Section 132 ("the polygamic revelation") until 1876. The instructions delivered to the Saints *in 1835* as divinely approved (canonized) scripture were polar opposites of the instructions delivered to the Saints as divinely approved (canonized) scripture *in 1876*.

---

[17]Book of Commandments 44:22, p. 91, emphasis added.

[18]Doctrine and Covenants (1835), Section 101. "The Article on Marriage was printed in the 1835 [first edition of the] D&C [Doctrine and Covenants] as section 101 and in the 1844 D&C as section 109." ("1835 Doctrine and Covenants denies polygamy – D&C 101 (original)" [accessed 2014], available from https://www.fairmormon.org/answers/Mormonism_and_polygamy/1835_Doctrine_and_Covenants_denies_polygamy; Internet, p. 1 of 5. Doctrine and Covenants 101). The publication of the monogamous Section 109 in the 1844 second edition of the Doctrine and Covenants postdated the unpublished unreported revelation on polygamy which later became Section 132, which was written and received in its final form on July 12, 1843. The polygamous revelation was secretly presented to the Nauvoo High Council on August 12, 1843 (although the consideration of the revelation was not reflected in the Council's Minutes). By 1844, when the monogamy provision was reported in the second edition of the Doctrine and Covenants as Section 109 (and in fact by November 1843), Joseph Smith had personally married about thirty-eight women, without including Fanny Alger. (George D. Smith, *Nauvoo Polygamy*, 621-23).

[19]In January 1850, seven years after the final (1843) explication of the polygamous principle, the *Millennial Star* (an English publication edited by Apostle Orson Pratt) attributed this declaration (Section 109) to Joseph Smith and described the provisions endorsing monogamous marriage as a revelation in these following terms: "*The Revelation* given through Joseph Smith, states the following . . . 'We believe that one man . . . .'" (D. Michael Quinn, "LDS Church Authority and New Plural Marriages, 1890-1904," *Dialogue: A Journal of Mormon Thought*, vol. 18 no. 1, [Spring 1985], 19-20, emphasis added).

The 1844 Edition of the Doctrine and Covenants

The second edition of the Doctrine and Covenants was published in 1844. "Because the book had been stereotyped, keeping it in print was practical. A second printing of the [second edition of the] book was authorized the following year [1845] and a third in 1846 . . . ."[20] The precise date when this second edition became available is presently unknown. The book was unpublished but close to complete on June 27, 1844, the day the prophet died. "In a letter to his wife written from Carthage two days before the killings, John Taylor stated that '1,000 copies of the [1844 second edition of the] Book of Doctrine and Covenants' should be printed 'as quick as possible.'" Two days later, John Taylor, the publisher of the 1844 second edition of the Doctrine and Covenants, was shot at the Carthage jail and seriously injured. On 28 July 1844 (by which time the multi-year second edition project was substantially completed), W.W. Phelps invited subscriptions. The *Joseph Smith Papers* report that the first citation from the new volume is known to have occurred in the *Times and Seasons* on 2 September 1844. Parley P. Pratt quoted from the second edition at a meeting on 8 September 1844.[21]

The 1845 and 1846 printings of the second 1844 edition of the Doctrine and Covenants and all subsequent printings and/or editions, until in and including 1876, occurred on Brigham Young's watch. While the preparation of the 1844 second edition may be said to have preceded the death of Smith, the publications and printings for the next thirty-three years were conducted under the supervision and authority of Brigham Young.

In September 1844, when excerpts from the second edition of the Book of Doctrine and Covenants were first recited, in 1845 in association with the second printing of the second edition, and in 1846 in association with the third printing of the second edition and until 1876, a period that included the public announcement of

---

[20]Historical Introduction to Doctrine and Covenants, 1844, in *The Joseph Smith Papers: Revelations and Translations Volume 2: Published Revelations*, eds. Robin Scott Jensen, Richard E. Turley Jr., and Riley M. Lorimer (Salt Lake City: The Church Historian's Press, 2011), 641.

[21]Ibid., 641.

polygamy from the pulpit in the Utah Territory in 1852, the text of all editions or printings of the Doctrine and Covenants always continued to report as follows:

> *Inasmuch as this church of Christ has been reproached with the crime of fornication and polygamy: we declare that we believe, that one man should have one wife; and one woman, but one husband, except in case of death, when either is at liberty to marry again.*[22]

It should be remembered that the contents of the great revelation on polygamy (the recitals that became Section 132 but not until 1876) were secretly read to the High Council, men who could be trusted not to tell the truth, by Hyrum Smith in Nauvoo, Illinois, on August 12, 1843. The revelation read to the Council on August 12 was supposed to have been received on July 12, 1843.

When Joseph Smith died on June 27, 1844, about two months before the publication of Section 109 (a renumbered Section 101) of the second edition of the Book of Doctrine and Covenants, the "Revelation" that perpetuated the canonized provisions "endorsing monogamous marriage," he had about thirty-eight wives. By the time of the third printing of the second edition, and by 1846, Brigham Young had about forty-one wives.[23] By the time of the third printing of the second edition, and by 1846, Heber C. Kimball had about thirty-seven wives.[24] By the time the second edition of the 1844 Doctrine and Covenants was printed for the third time in 1846, to cynically report to anyone interested wherever the gospel was preached, that *"we believe, that one man should have one wife . . . ,"* Joseph Smith and Hyrum Smith (by then deceased), William Smith, Brigham Young and Heber C. Kimball, five early Mormon leaders, had already been married about one hundred twenty-eight times. By 1846, when the second edition was printed for the third

---

[22]Doctrine and Covenants (1844), 109, emphasis added. Second Edition, September 1844, Second Printing of Second Edition, 1845, Third Printing of Second Edition 1846.
[23]George D. Smith, *Nauvoo Polygamy*, 635-37.
[24]Ibid., 601-3.

time, there had been more than five hundred plural marriages in Nauvoo, Illinois.

"Teachings of the Presidents of the Church, Joseph Smith," 2007: "The doctrines and principles relating to plural marriage were revealed to Joseph Smith as early as 1831. The Prophet taught the doctrine of plural marriage, and a number of such marriages were performed during his lifetime."[25] *"Blood Atonement and the Origin of Plural Marriage," Joseph Fielding Smith, 1905*: "This [July 12, 1843] . . . was not the time this principle was first made known to the Prophet Joseph Smith, for as early as 1831 the Lord revealed the principle of celestial and plural marriage to him and he taught it to others."[26] *"Brigham Young: American Moses," Leonard Arrington, 1985*: "In 1831, while studying the Old Testament with Oliver Cowdery, Joseph Smith became persuaded that plural marriage was a biblical principle" and that "God required it for the Latter-day Saints."[27] In 1835, and again in 1844, 1845 and 1846, the Church published and republished Sections 101 and 109 of the 1835 and 1844 editions of the Doctrine and Covenants containing these disturbingly dishonest recitals: *"[W]e believe, that one man should have one wife; and one woman but one husband, except in case of death . . . ."*[28]

The Issue with Miss Alger

D. Michael Quinn, *"Selected Chronology,"* 1994: 1833: *"Winter. Smith's first polygamous marriage (Fanny Alger)."*[29] In this year Joseph Smith (by this particular scholar's twentieth-century reckoning) is supposed to have married Fanny Alger. That

---

[25] *Teachings of Presidents of the Church – Joseph Smith*, xii, emphasis added.

[26] *Blood Atonement and the Origin of Plural Marriage* (correspondence between Elder Joseph F. Smith, Jr., and Mr. Richard C. Evans) (1905), 77 fn, emphasis added.

[27] Leonard J. Arrington, *Brigham Young: American Moses* (New York: Knopf, 1985), 100, emphasis added.

[28] Section 101, "Marriage," Doctrine and Covenants (1835 edition), 251, emphasis added.

[29] D. Michael Quinn, *The Mormon Hierarchy: Origins of Power* (Salt Lake City: Signature Books in association with Smith Research Associates, 1994), 619, emphasis added.

marriage is said to have occurred about two years after God is supposed to have revealed the doctrine of polygamy (1831) to Joseph Smith (who then "directed" his already married missionaries to plurally marry Native American women). In 1833, the same year the scholar says that Smith took his first polygamous wife, the 1833 Book of Commandments was printed to report that, *"Thou shalt love thy wife with all thy heart, and shall cleave unto her and none else . . . ."*[30]

Richard L. Bushman, *"Joseph Smith, Rough Stone Rolling,"* 2005:

[Fanny] Alger was fourteen when her family joined the Church . . . in 1830. In 1836, after a time as a serving girl in the Smith household, she left Kirtland and soon married. Between those two dates, perhaps as early as 1831, she and Joseph were reportedly involved, but conflicting accounts make it difficult to establish the facts – much less to understand Joseph's thoughts. Was he a blackguard covering his lusts with religious pretensions, or a prophet doggedly adhering to instructions from heaven, or something in between?[31]

"[A] blackguard covering his lusts with religious pretensions"? "[S]omething in between"? *Fanny Alger was fourteen years old "as early as 1831" and until September 19, 1831.* Richard L. Bushman: *"There is evidence that Joseph Smith was a polygamist by 1835*[32]

---

[30]Book of Commandments 44:22, p. 91.

[31]Bushman, *Joseph Smith: Rough Stone Rolling*, 323, emphasis added.

[32]Ibid., emphasis added. On 13 June 1834 (*Evening and Morning Star* 2 [August 1834]: 181) and 21 August 1835 (*Messenger and Advocate*, 2 [October 1835]: 204-7), "Mormon Missionaries hold conference in the center of [the] polygamous sect of 'Cochranism,' converting many." "On August 21, 1835, nine of the Twelve met in conference at Saco, Maine." ("Polygamy Timeline" in Mithryn [anonymous contributor], Exploring Mormonism [accessed 13 November 1842, posted 2 September 2013], available from exploringmormonism.com/polygamy-timeline; Internet, p. 4 of 41; source – *Times and Seasons*, vol. 4 no 24]. W.W. Phelps presented the statement (a Chapter for Rules for Marriage among the Saints) endorsing monogamous marriage to the Church at the General Conference held on 17 August 1835 under the article titled "Marriage." On that occasion the following statement in that chapter was canonized: "Inasmuch as this church of Christ has been reproached with the crime of fornication, and polygamy [probably

[according to D. Michael Quinn and Todd Compton, both of whom contend that he married Miss Alger, he was a polygamist by 1833[33]]. Was he also an adulterer? In an angry letter written in 1838 [the year that he was excommunicated], Oliver Cowdery [Joseph Smith's scribe for the Book of Mormon and one of The Three Witnesses] referred to the 'dirty, nasty, filthy affair' of Joseph Smith and Fanny Alger."[34] Cowdery called brother Joseph an adulterer, and so did Emma Smith. Latter-day Saints believe with dogmatic certitude what Oliver said about the Book of Mormon. Why shouldn't they believe what Oliver said about Joseph and Emma's "serving girl"?

Emma's anger with Joseph threatened the Church. She had seen evidence of his infidelity with her own eyes. Cowdery, and two other persons who mediated the conflict between Joseph and Emma (Sidney Rigdon and Frederick G. Williams), didn't believe Joseph Smith married Miss Alger, and Cowdery, the ultimate insider, a fly on the Mormon wall, called their undeniably intimate relationship a "dirty, nasty, filthy *affair.*" He knew things those nineteenth and twentieth-century historians didn't know and never said that Joseph married her. "[A]t a meeting [with Cowdery] in November 1837. . . Joseph did not deny his relationship with Alger, but contended that he had never confessed to adultery," meaning sex outside of a marriage. *"On his part, Joseph never denied a relationship with Alger [part of which Emma witnessed on a hay mow in the barn], but insisted it was not adulterous. He wanted it on*

---

because of Joseph's problematic relationships: Elizabeth Winters, Fanny Alger, Marinda Nancy Johnson, et al.], we declare that we believe that one man should have one wife; and one woman, but one husband, except in case of death, when either is at liberty to marry again." "The assembled Saints voted to accept the statement as part of 'the faith and principle of this society as a body' by canonizing it in the official Doctrine and Covenants of the church." (Richard S. Van Wagoner, *Mormon Polygamy: A History* [Salt Lake City: Signature Books, 1986], 6). For further consideration of the efficacy of the canonized rules, the reader is referred to Ibid., 226-27.

[33]Joseph described the marriages as sealings. Mormon doctrine holds that the sealing power wasn't conferred upon Joseph Smith and Oliver Cowdery until April 3, 1836, in consequence of separate visitations by Elias and Elijah, separate identifiable figures, in the Kirtland Temple. (Doctrine and Covenants Section 110).

[34]Oliver Cowdery to Warren Cowdery, 21 January 1838, original in Huntington Library, copy in LDS Church History Library (Salt Lake City, UT), quoted in Bushman, *Joseph Smith: Rough Stone Rolling*, 323.

record that he had never confessed to such a sin. Presumably, he felt innocent because he had married Alger."[35]   This unlikely supposition, and the length of what may have been a very long relationship (1831-35), allows for the proposition that intimacy documented as having occurred as early as 1832 preceded a marriage.

Cowdery, the Book of Mormon witness, described an *"affair."* George D. Smith, the Nauvoo polygamy scholar, found no evidence in support of a marriage. He concluded that the prophet's first polygamous coupling involved his secret marriage to Louisa Beaman in 1841. Joseph B. Noble, Louisa Beaman's brother-in-law, also believed the marriage to Miss Beaman was Joseph's first plural marriage. Noble married Smith to Miss Beaman. Many years later, on April 14, 1899, Joseph was sealed to Fanny Alger by proxy in the temple in Utah under the direction of President Lorenzo Snow. It is fair to suppose, given that most untimely occurrence, that President Snow shared the views of George D. Smith and Joseph B. Noble. By Michael Quinn, Todd Compton and Richard Bushman's reckonings, and those of the twenty-first century Church,[36] anecdotal accounts, the *supposed* couplings were seen to have preceded the *supposed* restoration of the sealing power by those heavenly messengers (Elias and Elijah) in the Kirtland Temple on April 3, 1836.

If Joseph Smith didn't really marry Miss Alger, if God didn't really command polygamy, if the marriage preceded the restoration of the sealing power or occurred after the intimacy, then the relationship was what Oliver Cowdery and Emma Smith at different times chose to say that it was – not a marriage, but rather an "affair," a

---

[35]Ibid., 324-25, emphasis added.

[36]The modern Church has just now (2018) chosen to say that, "Following the Lord's command, Joseph proposed marriage to Fanny [Alger] with the help of Levi [Hancock] and the approval of her parents. Fanny accepted Joseph's teachings and his proposal, and her uncle [Levi] performed the ceremony. Since the time had not come to teach plural marriage in the church, Joseph and Fanny kept their marriage private, as the angel had instructed. But rumors spread among some people in Kirtland. By the fall of 1836, Fanny had moved away." (*Saints: The Story of the Church of Jesus Christ in the Latter Days, Volume I, The Standard of Truth, 1815-1846* [Salt Lake City: The Church of Jesus Christ of Latter-day Saints, 2018], 292).

"transaction" (presumably one of many) and "adultery."[37] Events
that surfaced with an encounter that occurred on a hay mow in the
barn *in 1832*. An event without the shade of divine consent. Oliver
Cowdery, one of the Three Witnesses to the Book of Mormon, said
that Joseph committed adultery with Fanny Alger; Emma Smith,
Joseph's wife and an eyewitness, described a tryst ("transaction")
outside of their marriage. No official contemporary record shows
that a marriage ever occurred. If Joseph Smith married Fanny
Alger in 1832 or 1833, or any time before 1836, as those three
scholars (Compton, Quinn, Bushman) and now the Church said or
say that he did, he was a bigamist by civil or spiritual reckoning (a
prophet without the sealing power). The marriages of two women
to one man violated the law of the land; thus Joseph, if so married,
committed a crime and lived outside of the law. "[I]t seems
possible," according to Bushman, "that he received the revelation

---

[37]In 1893 Wilford Woodruff (who had been called as a witness in the Temple
Lot Case, a man who learned about "The Principle" no later than 1841) perjured
himself when he testified under oath that when he signed the *Times and Seasons
Monogamous Marriage Certificate* in 1842, he "did not know of any other rule [of
marriage] at the time." Woodruff, a deputy editor of the *Times and Seasons*,
contended that he only knew "the *monogamy* standard" described in Section 101 of
the 1835 edition of the Doctrine and Covenants. (*Abstract of Evidence Temple Lot
Case* [Herald Publishing House, 1892], 303; Abstract and Woodruff quoted by
Rollo Tomasi, "FWIW: My Thoughts on 'Plural Marriage in Kirtland and
Nauvoo' Essay" [revised 13 November 2014], 14, emphasis retained). Lorenzo
Snow, yet another Mormon prophet, supported Wilford Woodruff's prevarication
in the same case in equally dishonorable terms:

> Q: Before the giving of that revelation in 1843 [which
> didn't become Section 132 of the Doctrine and Covenants until
> 1876,] if a man married more wives than one who were living at
> the same time, he would have been cut off from the church[?]
> A [Lorenzo Snow]: *It would have been adultery under the
> laws of the church and under the laws of the State, too*. [Abstract
> and Woodruff quoted in Ibid., essay, 30-31, emphasis added].

Snow's sworn testimony obliterated the modern claims that Joseph Smith could
have married Fanny Alger in 1832 or 1833, or any time before 1836, "under the
laws of the church" or those "of the State." By August 1843, when the revelation
was read to the High Council, Joseph Smith had already married about thirty-two
women, not including Emma, and not including Fanny Alger, but including
Lorenzo Snow's sister. By the early 1840s, no matter what the Doctrine and
Covenants said, "Smith had begun *requiring* that other men in the hierarchy
marry plural wives." (George D. Smith, *Nauvoo Polygamy*, 43, emphasis retained).
Wilford Woodruff and Lorenzo Snow were ultimate insiders. Snow's sister, Eliza
R. Snow, married Joseph Smith in1842.

on plural marriage in 1831 while working on the Old Testament."[38] That was eleven years before he published the fraudulent *Times and Seasons Certificates* over the names of thirty-one prominent early Mormon *Certificants* and ten years before the Church now says he married Fanny Alger in 1832 or 1833. Wilford Woodruff and Lorenzo Snow perjured themselves while under oath in the Temple Lot Case in 1893 (see footnote 37).

Brigham Young, a man to be trusted by Utah Mormons, famously reported that Joseph and Oliver learned about polygamy in 1829, even before the Church was officially formed, while they were translating the Book of Mormon. What faithful Latter-day Saint can challenge that finding by the Prophet Brigham Young, the man who said he knew Joseph Smith as well as or better than any man on earth? He was, he said, an Apostle of the Prophet Joseph Smith, a man in the perfect confidence of Mormonism's founder. This disclosure, if Brigham can be trusted, was from Joseph's mouth to Brigham's ear.

Smith and Cowdery claimed that Elias and Elijah, *two separate identifiable figures*, appeared to them behind the veil in the Kirtland Temple, one after the other, on April 3, 1836, to deliver the keys to the Patriarchal (Abrahamic) Priesthood and the power "to turn the hearts of the fathers to the children, and the children to the fathers." Until 1836, however Smith and Cowdery felt about polygamy, the keys to the power to effect a sealing didn't exist. Furthermore, until about 1841 Joseph "evidently viewed" all marriages, including his own, as "valid for 'time' only." It is known that "As late as 1840 he occasionally signed his letters to Emma with the benediction 'your husband until death.'"[39] Van Wagoner,

---

[38]Bushman, *Joseph Smith: Rough Stone Rolling*, 326. It would seem that a scholar with the credentials of Richard L. Bushman would have seen the 1831 revelation Mrs. Brodie described to Joseph Fielding Smith (and Joseph Fielding Smith described to Mrs. Brodie) in 1945 – a revelation that was in the archives but unavailable to Mrs. Brodie.

[39]"The Mormon concept of sealing and binding in both heaven and earth dates from 1831, but it seems not to have been connected with marriage until the 1840's . . . *the earliest references to plural unions confine explanation to imitation of the ancient patriarchs and refinement of the native race*." (B. Carmon Hardy, *Solemn Covenant: The Mormon Polygamous Passage* [Urbana, Chicago: University of Illinois Press, 1992], 51). When "the Principle" took hold and was seen as

another polygamy scholar in league with George D. Smith, finds it noteworthy that "a distinctly polygamous marriage ceremony was apparently not performed until Joseph Smith was 'sealed' to his plural wife Louisa Beaman on 6 April 1841."

Furthermore, and as a matter of some importance, Joseph wasn't sealed to Emma until more than twenty-some wives later on 28 May 1843.[40]   Without the sealing power, the controversial plurality doctrine was theoretically unfounded. Without the sealing power, Smith had no cover for an illicit sexual relationship.   Former Apostle William E. McLellin, on good terms with Emma Smith before and after the death of her husband, visited the prophet's widow in Nauvoo, Illinois, in 1847. *Mrs. Smith told me that she knew her husband practiced both adultery and Spiritual Wifery! And that she also knew that he had the Polygamic revelation* [after 1876, Doctrine and Covenants, Section 132, dated July 12, 1843]."[41]

If Joseph Smith became involved with a fourteen or fifteen year old Fanny Alger *"perhaps as early as 1831,"* as Richard L. Bushman reports, and if Joseph and Fanny didn't marry until 1832, 1833, 1835, or ever at all, and/or if the sealing power was not restored until 1836, then Joseph was guilty of everything Oliver and Emma said that he was. If he was involved with Miss Alger "perhaps as early as 1831," and if his conduct with her required mediation as early as 1832, he may have been a polygamist as early as 1832 or 1833.   Some scholars – fortified by decades-delayed anecdotal reports – are seen to assume that Joseph Smith married Fanny Alger before her uncle, Levi Hancock, married Clarissa Reed on March 29, 1833. Smith is known to have directed the Lamanite

---

"connected with marriage" in the City of Joseph, Nauvoo, Illinois, "it dominated nearly everything else."

    [40]Van Wagoner, *Mormon Polygamy: A History*, 7.

    [41]William E. McLellin letter to John L. Traughber, 14 Dec. 1878, in *The William E. McLellin Papers: 1854-1880*, eds. Stan Larson and Samuel J. Passey, foreword by George D. Smith (Salt Lake City: Signature Books, 2008), 515, emphasis added. Emma specifically referred to Section 132 of the Doctrine and Covenants, long before it ever became Section 132 of the Doctrine and Covenants, as "the Polygamic revelation." It was then, and is now, whatever the Church may choose to say that it is, a revelation about polygamy, a principle "without obedience" to which "no man can ever attain to the fulness of exaltation in celestial glory." (Affidavit, William Clayton, 16 February 1874, CHL, MS, 3423, reprinted as "William Clayton's Testimony," *Historical Record* [May 1887], 6: 225-26).

missionaries to plurally marry Native American (Lamanite) women in 1831.[42] That was many years before he and others fraudulently published monogamous marriage claims in the Book of Commandments in 1833, in Section 101 of the Doctrine and Covenants in 1835, in Section 109 of the Doctrine and Covenants in 1844, 1845, and 1846 (and in all further editions and/or printings of the Doctrine and Covenants until 1876). And in those *Times and Seasons Monogamous Marriage Certificates in 1842.*

Todd Compton, a Mormon scholar and biographer Richard L. Bushman's principal polygamy research resource, reported that: "As we trace the trajectory of Smith's marriages, we see that he apparently experimented with plural marriage in the 1830's in Ohio and Missouri."[43] There were some rough edges associated with that early reckless intemperate experimentation. "[O]f the thirty-three women listed by Todd Compton as being plural wives of Joseph Smith, twelve do not have an officiator, ceremony or witness to their marriage/sealing."[44] Grant H. Palmer was seen to inquire: "[A]re some of these women – especially the married ones – sexual consent relationships?"[45]

---

[42]An early Mormon convert named Ezra Booth, a man estranged from the Church, described a revelation that directed certain of the Mormon Elders to "form a matrimonial alliance with the natives" in the *Ohio Star* on 8 December 1831. "It is my will [Joseph's God's will] that in time, ye should take unto you wives of the Lamanites and Nephites [Native Americans] that their posterity may become white, delightsome, and Just . . . ." (Letter to Brigham Young from W.W. Phelps, 12 August 1861, [LDS Archives]), emphasis added. In that Joseph's God called Native Americans "Lamanites and Nephites." Joseph's God described the Native Americans as "Lamanites" at least a dozen times in the Doctrine and Covenants.

[43]Compton, *In Sacred Loneliness: The Plural Wives of Joseph Smith*, Prologue, 2.

[44]Ibid., 4-6, quoted in Grant H. Palmer, "Sexual Allegations against Joseph Smith and the Beginnings of Polygamy in Nauvoo," 16.

[45]Ibid. Don Carlos Smith, Oliver Cowdery, John C. Bennett, Austin Cowles, William Marks, Leonard Sobey, William, Jane and Wilson Law, Mrs. Hiram Kimball, Mrs. Orson Pratt, Mrs. George W. Harris, Mrs. Robert D. Foster, Nancy Rigdon, Martha Brotherton, Sidney Rigdon, William Smith, Gustavus Hills, Chauncey Higbee, Darwin Chase, Joel S. Miles, George Thatcher, Lyman D. Littlefield, Justis Morse, Catherine Fuller Warren, Esther Victoria Smith, Mary Clift, Melissa Schindle, Sarah Miller, several Ms. Nymans, Emma Smith and many others appeared, in one way or another and at different times, to acknowledge the proposition that there were "sexual consent relationships" in the City of Joseph.

Sarah Pratt (Mrs. Orson Pratt), one of the early objects of Joseph Smith's affection, told Dr. Wilhelm Wyl, as previously seen but important enough to be repeated here, that,

> . . . *Joseph did not think of a marriage or sealing ceremony for many years. He used to state to his intended victims, as he did to me: "God does not care if we have a good time, if only other people do not know it." He only introduced . . . ["a"] marriage ceremony when he had found out that he could not get certain women without it.*[46]

Mrs. Pratt thought that he incorporated marriage in his domestic equation in 1841. His representations to Emma until late in his married life (in 1840, "your husband until death") may suggest she had that right. "I think," Sarah said, that "Louisa Beeman [*sic*] was the first case of this kind." In that her assumption appears to have been accepted by George D. Smith,[47] Richard S. Van Wagoner and Joseph B. Noble. Michael Quinn, Todd Compton (with a question mark, "Mormonism's First Plural Wife?") and Richard L. Bushman (while drawing somewhat different conclusions among themselves) appear to cautiously accept anecdotal reports that Smith actually married Miss Alger, although he never publicly said that he did. Compton, like D. Michael Quinn, places the date of the possible marriage as "early 1833," when Fanny was sixteen and Joseph Smith was twenty-seven.[48] That was years before at least

---

[46]Wilhelm Wymetal, *Mormon Portraits or, The Truth About the Mormon Leaders From 1830 to 1866: Volume First: Joseph Smith, The Prophet, His Family and Friends, A Study Based on Facts and Documents* (Salt Lake City: Tribune Printing and Publishing Company, 1886), Interview with Sarah Pratt, 62, emphasis retained.

[47]George D. Smith decided against a marriage to Fanny Alger. "I hesitate to concur with Compton's interpretation of their relationship as a marriage," Smith said in his book. "In my view, Joseph Noble was correct when he said he had performed the first patriarchal marriage in this dispensation by sealing Louisa Beaman to Joseph Smith." (Joseph Bates Noble, Autobiography [typescript], 30, L. Tom Perry Special Collections [Provo, UT: Harold B. Lee Library, Brigham Young University], referenced in George D. Smith, *Nauvoo Polygamy*, 38-39 fn 81). Surely the source of Noble's claim was the prophet himself.

[48]Compton, *In Sacred Loneliness: The Plural Wives of Joseph Smith*, 4, describes the following anecdotal account of a marriage: "*According to Mosiah Hancock, Joseph Smith introduced his father Levi to polygamy in spring 1832 . . . .*"

two editions and many printings of the Doctrine and Covenants railed against polygamy, even after the teaching, preaching and practice of the doctrine was admitted from the pulpit in the isolated Utah Territory in 1852.

Between January 18, 1827, (Emma Hale) and November 2, 1843 (Fanny Young (Carr Murray)), Joseph Smith married what would seem to be about thirty-eight women, not including Fanny Alger.[49] Between October 8, 1824, and December 8, 1872, Brigham Young married what would seem to be no less than fifty-six women.[50] During the time that the Book of Commandments (from 1833 to 1835) and the Doctrine and Covenants (from 1835 to 1876) misled the uninformed by saying that the Mormon Church practiced

---

(Brigham Young, who joined the Church in 1832, didn't know about polygamy in the spring of 1832, and wouldn't know about polygamy until about 1841. Young took his first plural wife in 1842.) Joseph Smith loved Fanny Alger. Levi Hancock loved Clarissa Reed ("a hired girl [another hired girl] in Smith's home"). According to Mosiah, Mormonism's tremendously tardy source for this claim of a marriage never officially, even privately recognized, Joseph and Levi, in recognition of their respective feelings, made a grand bargain. "Therefore Brother Joseph said [']Brother Levi . . . – If you will get Fanny Alger for me for a wife you may have Clarissa Reed. I love Fanny' 'I will' Said Father . . . Father [Levi Hancock] goes to . . . [Fanny's father] Father Samuel Alger – his Father's Brother-in Law . . . ." and says, "Samuel[,] the Prophet Joseph loves your Daughter Fanny and wishes her for a wife what say you" – Uncle Samuel says, "talk to the Old woman . . . ." The Old woman (Mrs. Samuel Alger) says, "talk to Fanny." Fanny says "I will Levi." Father Levi Hancock then "gave her to Joseph repeating the Ceremony as Joseph repeated to him." (Mosiah Hancock's holographic autobiography, quoted in Ibid., 31-33, emphasis added). "Levi Hancock [is supposed to have] received his reward. Smith sanctioned his marriage to Clarissa Reed, which took place on March 29, 1833. Mosiah's narrative suggests that the Smith-Alger marriage occurred first, so Joseph [by this reckoning] probably married Fanny [if ever at all] in February or March 1833 . . . ." (Ibid., 32-33). The episode involving the prophet and Miss Alger on the hay mow in the barn and the mediation that followed occurred in 1832. If all of this is true, Levi Hancock, Clarissa Reed, Joseph Smith, Fanny Alger, Samuel Alger, Fanny Alger's mother, Oliver Cowdery, Sidney Rigdon and Frederick G. Williams all knew about polygamy in 1832, many years before the members of the Quorum of the Twelve Apostles did. In fact before there was a Quorum of the Twelve Apostles. That seems highly doubtful. That was more than ten years before Joseph Smith, Wilford Woodruff and John Taylor, the editor and his deputies, furnished those fraudulent *Monogamous Marriage Certificates* to the members of the Church, and to the public at large, in the *Times and Seasons* in 1842.

[49]George D. Smith, *Nauvoo Polygamy*, 621-23.

[50]Ibid., 635-37.

nothing but monogamous marriage, Joseph Smith and Brigham Young married, or otherwise encumbered, as between them, about ninety-four women.[51]   Those "marriages" included nearly thirty women (about thirteen or fourteen assigned to Smith, and about fifteen assigned to Young) who were already married to, supported by and cohabiting with their earlier and other less-than-eternal civilly deputized husbands.   Those married women and their biological children with their legal husbands were sealed to Joseph Smith and Brigham Young. They were bonded to their greater men not merely for time, but for *eternity* in a Mormon afterlife. Sealings, the eternal phase of those inexplicable relationships, were exclusive.   The sealing ordinance erased the claims of those legally married men and their biological children in favor of the claims of certain more spiritually entitled others.   Those biological husbands and their biological children will be separated from each other in a Mormon afterlife.

Celestial polygamy is routinely practiced in private rites in Mormon temples still today.   The prophet installed in 2018, Russell M. Nelson, is sealed to two women for eternity.   Twelve of Mormonism's seventeen prophets, including Joseph Fielding Smith, Harold B. Lee, Howard W. Hunter, Ezra Taft Benson and Russell M. Nelson (more modern prophets) have all been sealed in this life to more than one woman in rites to be honored in the life to come. Section 132 of the Doctrine and Covenants, though suspended until the order of heaven is restored, allows in celestial theory almost anything anyone needs for men.   Can you say "concubines"?   If Ezra Taft Benson can take a deceased plural wife, sixty years after the Manifesto, while he has a living legal wife willing to stand as proxy, what might be said to stop anyone else from anything at all? Who knows what goes on in the privacy of the temples?   How many Latter-day Saint civilians know anything about those Sunday empty temple twenty-first century second anointings?

---

[51]Brigham Young married no less than seven of Joseph Smith's widows. While practicing Joseph's doctrine, and when he became the Lord of Mormon marriage, he mostly did whatever he pleased for himself and others.

ABANDONING "MONOGAMY"

In addition to many pernicious hidden irregularities which littered the landscape, early Mormons took huge liberties with the laws of the land pertaining to marriage. People married and divorced (or didn't marry and didn't divorce) without civil superintendence. There were, particularly in the early stages of the developing doctrine and as already reported, "sexual consent relationships" ("informal alliances"). Formalities were ignored, enforcement was lax and rules were uncertain as the leaders "solemnized [cafeteria-style] relationships without deputization from the state." Even before Nauvoo, "The upheaveals that distracted the church in Kirtland, Ohio, nearly to foundering involved, over and again, charges of immorality."[52] Early Mormons were people largely governed independent of the state. They received Joseph's words as if they were from God's own mouth. They endeavored to "resacralize matrimony" on their own peculiar terms: "Beyond discomfort with secularization, the sense of withdrawal from an apostate world and belief that theirs was the authority of heaven allowed Mormons to believe their own performances as quite sufficient."[53] The particularly messy history of the proceedings before the Nauvoo councils would seem to suggest otherwise. "In the heated atmosphere at Kirtland [well in advance of the heated atmosphere at Nauvoo], it was inevitable that informal alliances would occasionally occur."[54]

Joseph Smith, a man who must be supposed to have had seventeen mothers-in-law (measured against the time of the preparation of those monogamous marriage *Certificates* on October 1, 1842), many brothers-in-law, sisters-in-law, fathers-in-law and non-biological children, disingenuously always publicly endorsed monogamous marriage. As many as five of the nineteen married females who dutifully signed Joseph Smith's *Times and Seasons Monogamous Marriage Certificates* appear to have been actually practicing polygamy on the day those *Certificates* were published, October 1,

---

[52]B. Carmon Hardy, *Solemn Covenant: The Mormon Polygamous Passage* (Urbana, Chicago: University of Illinois Press, 1992), 5-6.
[53]Ibid., 6. "Men remembered this early period as one when leaders sometimes behaved in ways that later made them blush."
[54]Ibid.

1842.   The list of probable polygamous wives who signed the
Certificates may be said to include Emma Smith, Sarah Cleveland,
Elizabeth Durfee, Eliza R. Snow and Thirza Cahoon.   Others were
aware of the doctrine.   Elizabeth Ann Whitney, a counselor to
Emma in the Relief Society Presidency, had just witnessed the
marriage of her seventeen-year-old daughter, Sarah Ann, to a
thirty-seven year-old prophet, the husband just then of fifteen other
wives.   The list of those likely to have been informed must be seen to
include the wives of men who were clearly informed (Leonora
Taylor, Phoebe Woodruff and Angeline Robinson[55]).   Their
husbands, men who absolutely knew the truth about polygamy on
October 1, 1842, didn't stop their wives from signing Smith's
fraudulent *Certificates*.   And Smith, the earthly architect of the
controversial doctrine of polygamy and the publisher of the
dishonest *Certificates*, knowing what he knew, didn't stop anyone
from putting their names on his list.   Women who probably knew
because their husbands certainly knew, certified and declared that
they did not.   No less than twelve of Joseph's nineteen female
witnesses – including those who were already committed partners
with other polygamous wives in existing polygamous unions when
they signed their names and allowed those *Certificates* to be
published – were actively practicing polygamy *by 1846* when the
third printing of the canonized second edition of the Doctrine and
Covenants said that they were not.

Joseph's Oneida Community Approach

John Humphrey Noye's "free love" Oneida community in New
York and Joseph Smith's early Mormon community in Illinois (as
reflected in the cases described in the Nauvoo City and Nauvoo
Stake High Council Minutes in the early 1840s) shared this simple
insight: "[S]ex between consenting adults was not a sin, even among
married people."   Former Mormon educator Grant H. Palmer
opines that "Smith's sexual behavior was very similar [to that

---

[55]Abigail Marks (Works), another *Certificant* who was married and sealed to
Brigham Young *in 1846*, was the mother of Brigham Young's deceased first legal
wife, Miriam Works.

espoused by the Oneida community] . . . ."[56] This free-love theme dominated many of the twenty-some contentions that crowded the Nauvoo High Council's minutes and agendas in 1841 and 1842 as Mormonism's early informal alliances began to unravel and begged to be further refined. The one small caveat that various early Mormon adventurers added to the Oneida community's unembarrassed approach to intimacy was that "it [sex] isn't a sin if it is secret." These early encounters generally described sexual consent relationships that for one reason or another (sometimes pregnancy) somehow went awry. It seems safe to say that only a small percentage of those secret encounters ever surfaced to encumber the Nauvoo Councils' efforts to hear and resolve those of them that did. The unlucky adventurers, those whose relationships foundered and then were publicized, were most often left to this oft repeated defense: Illicit "connexion[s]" are "authorized" and "countenanced" by the "heads of the church" if the participants "hold their peace."

Grant H. Palmer pointed to the "Perfectionists," another curious 1830s group of "Saints" who advanced the proposition that marriages performed on earth were "valid for eternity."[57] Joseph's mysterious visitor, Joshua the Jewish Minister, claimed the power "to dissolve" other people's marriages. Joseph Smith became, like Brigham Young later became, the Lord of Mormon marriage. Brigham Young dissolved hundreds of marriages, often for a fee and sometimes with the wave of an imperious hand. Because the "Perfectionists" were perfect, they felt they "could no longer sin." Section 132 of the Doctrine and Covenants applies some of their improbable tenets to Joseph Smith and those early polygamous men who followed him. The "Perfectionists" operated under the comforting assumption that "all arrangements for a life in heaven may be made on earth . . . spiritual friendships may be formed, and spiritual bonds contracted, valid for eternity."[58]

---

[56]Palmer, "Sexual Allegations against Joseph Smith and the Beginnings of Polygamy in Nauvoo," 2.

[57]The "Perfectionists" advocated "spiritual wifery," "a concept nearly identical to Mormon eternal marriage, wherein 'all arrangements for a life in heaven may be made on earth . . . .'" (Van Wagoner, *Mormon Polygamy: A History*, 9).

[58]Ibid.

Like the vision of the three degrees of glory, the concept of a spirit world, an improved perception of the natural man and other early insights, the celestial marriage concept didn't start with Joseph Smith. Robert Matthews, Joshua the Jewish Minister (the strange man to whom Joseph provided a hearing and an alternative account of the First Vision in 1835), was a spiritual wifery advocate. That may explain why that unusual man received the reception he did from Joseph Smith and various interested Mormon others. Spiritual wifery was an informal kind of alliance, some would say a less conspicuous more generous name for adultery.[59] Smith was exposed to the extravagant Matthews and his controversial doctrines before he reported having received the keys to the Patriarchal Priesthood, and to the sealing power, on April 3, 1836, behind the veil in the newly constructed Kirtland Temple. Matthews taught his followers that "all marriages not made by himself, and according to his doctrine, were of the devil . . . ."[60] Some of his ideas later applied to Joseph Smith and Brigham Young. No Latter-day Saint dedicated to the plurality principle married without the leaders' direct or delegated consent. It is a most surprising fact that this strange, peculiar unorthodox man (Matthews) seemed to have had Joseph Smith's ear on the occasion of his brief encounter with the Mormon prophet (to how many men, particularly Mormon men, did Joseph Smith give an account of the First Vision in 1835?).

Not long after Joseph's visit with "Joshua" (Robert Matthews) and in conjunction with the events that occurred on April 3, 1836, Joseph Smith and Oliver Cowdery "claimed the same privileges and powers as the 'Perfectionists' and Robert Matthews." A mid-1830s revelation with appearances by Elias and Elijah, Jesus and Moses defined the sealing power and opened "the eyes of our understanding." Elias and Elijah – different names (Hebrew and Greek names) for the same prophet – miraculously appeared as

---

[59]"*In 1832* Mormon missionary Orson Hyde, a former member of Sidney Rigdon's 'family,' visited a group he called 'Cochranites' and disdainfully described in his 11 October 1832 journal the groups 'Wonderful, lustful spirit, because they believe in a plurality of wives' which they call spiritual wives, knowing them not after the flesh but after the spirit, but by the *appearance they know one another after the flesh*." (Orson Hyde Journal, 11 October 1832, quoted in Van Wagoner, *Mormon Polygamy: A History*, 9, emphasis added and retained).

[60]Ibid.

separate identifiable entities bringing "the keys" to new and different powers. Like the Perfectionists and Matthews, "whatever Smith sealed or loosed on earth or in heaven" was approved by God – for the "keys . . . are committed into your hands."[61] "[B]y this ye may know that the great and dreadful day of the Lord is near even at the doors."[62] A most decent young woman by the name of Martha Brotherton described something Joseph Smith secretly said to her in 1842: "I have the keys of the kingdom, and whatever I bind on earth is bound in heaven, and whatever I loose on earth is loosed in heaven, and if you will accept of Brigham, you shall be blessed – God shall bless you, and my blessing shall rest upon you . . . ."[63]

"Wherever inspirationist religion thrives, spiritual license is easily converted to other entitlements. Early Mormonism displayed little of the closely bricked theological edifice it presents today. Many areas of ritual and belief were, if not inchoate, yet under construction."[64] "[T]he tendencies rooted in an abundance of new revelation and the conviction that old things were passing away, were clearly present. We should naturally expect that such a pentecost would find an outlet for some of its fires in sexual behavior." "Part of what alienated the prophet's disciple Oliver Cowdery was that the church's leadership had 'given loose to the enthusiastick.'"[65] Brigham H. Roberts, Mormonism's preeminent scholar, is counted among those who recognized that within a year of the publication of the Book of Mormon in 1830 (which was more than a decade before the publication of those fraudulent *Times and Seasons Certificates* in 1842), Joseph Smith became convinced that plural marriage was a correct principle.[66]

---

[61]Doctrine and Covenants 110:1, 13-16; Palmer, "Sexual Allegations against Joseph Smith and the Beginnings of Polygamy in Nauvoo," 3.

[62]Doctrine and Covenants 110:16

[63]Martha Brotherton letter to John C. Bennett, 13 July 1842, John C. Bennett, *The History of the Saints: Or, an Expose of Joe Smith and Mormonism* (Boston: Leland & Whiting, 1842; photomechanical reprint of 1842 original, Salt Lake City: Modern Microfilm Company), 239, emphasis added.

[64]Hardy, *Solemn Covenant: The Mormon Polygamous Passage*, 3.

[65]Oliver Cowdery to Warren Cowdery and Lyman Cowdery, 4 February 1838, Oliver Cowdery Letterbook (Henry Huntington Library, San Marino, California), quoted in Ibid.

[66]See Roberts' Introduction to Roberts, ed., *History of The Church of Jesus Christ of Latter-day Saints*, 5: xxix, xxxii.

Image source: Public domain, via Wikimedia Commons.

WILLIAM SMITH: JOSEPH'S BROTHER,
APOSTLE, PATRIARCH, LIBERTINE

Peter Ingersoll: *When Joseph went to Pennsylvania in the fall of 1827, Peter Ingersoll lost track of him. "[S]ince that time I have not been much in his society. While the Smiths were living at Waterloo, William visited my neighborhood, and upon my inquiry how they came on, he replied, 'we do better there than here; we were too well known here to do much.'" (Peter Ingersoll).*

Apostle: *In 1835, when Oliver Cowdery and David Whitmer chose Phineas Young to be a member of the Quorum of The Twelve Apostles, Joseph Smith made an "urgent request" that his brother William be selected instead. Joseph "insisted that his brother William Smith should be put in as it was the only way by which he could be saved." Cowdery and Whitmer later reported that William's selection as a member of the first Quorum of the Twelve Apostles was "contrary to our feelings and judgment, and to our deep mortification ever since."*

Accept It: *"3 November 1835 . . . Thus came the word of the Lord unto me . . . concerning the Twelve . . . verily I say unto you they must all humble themselves before me, before they will be accounted worthy to receive an endowment to go forth in my name unto all nations, as for my servant William let the Eleven humble themselves in prayer and in faith and wait on me in patience and my servant William shall return, and I will yet make him a polished shaft in my quiver, in bringing down the wickedness and abominations of men and their shall be none mightier than he in his day and generation, nevertheless if he repent not spedily he shall be brought low and shall be chastened sorely for all his iniquities . . . Verely thus saith the Lord Amen." (Jessee, PJS, 2:63-64).*

Bennett's Friend: *In 1841 "William became involved with the sexual practices of John C. Bennett. In 1842 the Nauvoo high council investigated Bennett's seductions of the previous year. Two women identified William Smith as one of Bennett's friends who visited for sexual intercourse and said that William told them his brother Joseph approved of spiritual wifery." Later on, "someone (probably Joseph) tried to eradicate William's name from the women's testimony." (Quinn, Origins, 220).*

Spiritual Wifery: *On May 14, 1845, after the deaths of his brothers, William Smith denied any knowledge of spiritual wifery. "I know," he said, "of no such doctrine in the Church of Christ, neither have I ever practiced or taught any such doctrine." (Quinn, 215).*

William's Women: *On June 22, 1845, Brigham Young performed a civil marriage for William Smith and a sixteen-year-old girl "exactly a month after the death of William's first wife." On August 8, 1845, Brigham Young plurally married William Smith to a fourteen-year-old identified in Young's diary as "Miss Rice." "At the citywide Sunday meeting on 17 August [1845] Smith stunned the congregation and his fellow apostles by giving 'a full declaration of his belief in the [still secret] doctrine of a plurality of wives &c.'" ("If a Sister gives me her hand upon the Spiritual Wife system to share with me the fate and destinies of time and eternity, I will not be ashamed of her before the public.") (Quinn, Origins, 220-22, 430 n 192). "John Taylor immediately repudiated Smith's talk." "William Clayton wrote that 'the people appeared disgusted and many left the ground.'" (Ibid., 222).*

Strang's Disciple: *After the deaths of his brothers and in January 1846, William Smith renewed his "association with his former 'spiritual wifery' accomplice John C. Bennett." Vouching for each other's virtue, Bennett and Smith negotiated with James J. Strang "to become leaders in his church [a separate schism]. Because of the two men's continued sexual liaisons, Strang repudiated Smith in April 1847 and Bennett the following October. In 1847 William organized his own church, which gained Lyman Wight's support only to collapse in 1850-51 due to Smith's polyandry." (Ibid., 223-24).*

William Meets "Aunt Peggy": *While contending for his claims to lead the Church as Patriarch after the deaths of his brothers, and after his citywide speech concerning the prohibited subject of polygamy, "the Twelve ordered him to discontinue his discourses," an order he refused to obey. With the help of his relatives, and in defiance of the order, wooden seats were built "to accommodate a large crowd near Lucy Mack Smith's house where he was living. On the first Sunday the new benches were to be used, the Smith family awoke to find 'every seat in the grove had been fouled with outhouse refuse.'" (Quinn, Origins, 222). Lucy, Joseph's mother, and Emma, Joseph's wife, denounced the Twelve for that "anointing of William Smith's stand and seats which he had fixed in his Mother's door yard."*

William Unveiled: *After the deaths of Joseph Smith and Hyrum, and then of Samuel in 1844, William Smith was the only surviving son of Joseph Sr., the original Presiding Patriarch. William, a founding Apostle who became the Presiding Patriarch in 1845, "never visited his brothers at Liberty Jail." And he said that Joseph "ought to have been hung up by the neck years ago . . . ." Accompanied by William Hickman, who protected him to a place of safety in northern Iowa, Smith left Nauvoo just as Brigham Young ordered the Nauvoo police not to let anyone leave. William left Brigham Young with a "Presiding Patriarch's parting vow: 'By God I'll let this people know who their ruler is.'" (D. Michael Quinn).*

Lucy Leaves Brigham Alone: *After she was "introduced" to "Queen Peggy's privy cabinet" by the Church's deacons (outhouse refuse on every seat in Lucy's grove), Lucy Mack Smith, Joseph's mother, took leave of the perpetrators of the odious anointing. She supported the Twelve "long enough to enter the Nauvoo temple for the endowment." Thereafter she "avoided further association with the Twelve." She "declined to receive from Brigham Young's hands the proxy sealing to her husband in the temple." (Quinn, Origins, 222).*

Lucy Mack Smith. Image Source: Public domain, via Wikimedia Commons.

William and Joseph III: *In 1847 the excommunicated William communicated with Orson Hyde. He wanted to be restored to his former position as a member of the Quorum of the Twelve. Hyde publicly mocked his former colleague. Years later, William wrote to Brigham Young, repeating that request. "Young never responded, and Smith wrote a letter in 1856 consigning him to hell." Without hope for the restoration of the apostleship, William looked to his nephew Joseph Smith III, who then became the President of the Reorganized Church of Jesus Christ of Latter Day Saints, to offer him an office in the Reorganization "in return for his support." William entered his nephew's church as a high priest in 1878, but bargained for higher office (Presiding Patriarch), a position that Joseph III assigned to one of his own brothers after his uncle William's death. In private correspondence surrounding those failed negotiations, Joseph III said that "William Smith's upcoming publication*

Joseph Smith III. Image Source: Public domain, via Wikimedia Commons.

of his reminiscences must 'fail to remember' anything that would challenge the RLDS president's effort to free the founding prophet [Joseph Smith] and pre-1844 Mormonism from the 'stigma and blame thrown upon them because of Polygamy.'" William honored his nephew's request. (Quinn, Origins, 224-26).

MORMON HYMN

"Now this advice I freely give,
If exalted you would be,

Remember that your husband must
Be blessed with more than thee.

Then, O, let us say,
God bless the wife that strives
And aids her husband all she can
T' obtain a dozen wives."

(Deseret News)

SARAH ANN WHITNEY

Married to Joseph Smith on July 27, 1842, when she was seventeen and he was thirty-six. Pretend married to Joseph C. Kingsbury on April 29, 1843, when he was thirty and she was eighteen. Her public marriage to her widowed uncle Kingsbury was intended to conceal her secret marriage to her time and eternity husband, Smith. Sarah was sealed to Joseph Smith on July 27, 1842, ten months before Joseph was sealed to Emma on May 28, 1843. No less than twenty-three women (including Sarah) were sealed to Joseph Smith before May 28, 1843. Sarah was married for time to Heber C. Kimball (after the death of Joseph Smith) when she was nineteen and Kimball was forty-three. Sarah Ann Whitney, Joseph Smith's sixteenth wife, later became Kimball's eighteenth wife, and he became her third husband while she was still in her teens. She continued to live with Kingsbury while pregnant with Heber C. Kimball's child. Her seven children with Kimball belong to the prophet Joseph Smith in the life to come.

Image source: Public domain, via Wikimedia Commons.

MARTHA BROTHERTON

George D. Smith, *Nauvoo Polygamy*

Joseph Smith: *"I know that this is lawful and right before God, and if there is any sin in it, I will answer for it . . . [Martha's consent to a polygamous marriage to Brigham Young]; . . . I have the keys to the kingdom, and whatever I bind on earth is bound in heaven, and whatever I loose on earth is loosed in heaven, . . . if you will accept of Brigham, you shall be blessed – God shall bless you, and my blessing shall rest upon you; . . . I know Brigham will take care of you, and if he don't do his duty to you, come to me and I will make him; and if you do not like it in a month or two, come to me, and I will make you free again; and if he turns you off, I will take you on." (Martha Brotherton Statement)*

The "wide circulation" of Miss Brotherton's notarized statement "brought Nauvoo's underground society into the light of day and formed the most lasting impression the public would have of Mormonism." (George D. Smith). Martha Brotherton "eventually returned to England where she died in 1864." After her death, and before his own, without her consent and on August 1, 1870, Brigham Young had this "mean harlot" "sealed to him for eternity. Her sister, Elizabeth Brotherton Pratt, plural wife of Apostle Parley P. Pratt, acted as proxy for the deceased."

THEY DRANK "FROM ANCIENT SPRINGS"

Joseph Smith

Brigham Young

John Taylor

Heber C. Kimball

William B. Smith

Wilford Woodruff

Orson Pratt

Orson Hyde

Parley P. Pratt

1844-1846 Doctrine and Covenants: *The second edition of the Doctrine and Covenants was published in 1844. The second printing of the second edition occurred in 1845 and the third printing of the second edition occurred in 1846. Section 109 in 1846, the third printing of the second edition, provided exactly as follows: "Inasmuch as this church of Christ has been reproached with the crime of fornication and polygamy: we declare that we believe, that one man should have one wife; and one woman but one husband, except in case of death when either is at liberty to marry again."*

1844-1846 Nauvoo Polygamy: *There were sixty-eight plural marriages in Nauvoo in 1844. In 1845, when it became clear that the Church was going to "leave the United States and members would be beyond the reach of the law," and after the Nauvoo Temple opened to endowments and sealings on December 10, "the inner circle of thirty-three polygamous men now broadened to nearly two hundred" There were eighty-six plural marriages in 1845, and two hundred seventy-five more in 1846, most of them in the months of January and February. "By the end of the Nauvoo period [in 1846], 196 men had married 717 women." (Smith, Nauvoo Polygamy, 406). In Nauvoo in 1844 to 1846, during the 1844, 1845 and 1846 first, second and third printings of the 1844 second edition of the Doctrine and Covenants, polygamy was on the march. Before the second edition promoted unequivocal monogamy in 1844, and again in 1845, and again in 1846, the great revelation on polygamy was read to the Nauvoo High Council on August 12, 1843.*

Marriages, Other than Mormon Marriages, Are for Time But Not Eternity: *"[E]verything that is in the world, whether it be ordained by men, by thrones, or principalities or powers . . . that are not by me or by my word saith the Lord, shall be thrown down, and shall not remain after men are dead . . . . Therefore, if a man marry him a wife in the world, and he marry her not by me nor by my word [ceremonies performed outside of a Mormon temple by persons who do not hold the Mormon Priesthood], and he covenant with her so long as he is in the world and she with him, their covenant and marriage are not of force when they are dead, and when they are out of the world . . . . Therefore, when they are out of the world they neither marry nor are given in marriage; but are appointed angels in heaven; which angels are ministering servants to minister for those who are worthy of a far more, and an exceeding, and an eternal weight of glory. For these angels did not abide my law; therefore they cannot be enlarged, but remain separately and singly [unmarried], without exaltation, in their saved condition, to all eternity; and from henceforth are not gods, but are angels of God forever and ever." (Doctrine and Covenants [1957], 132:13-17). Those who do not pay ten percent of their income to the Church can not enter the temple to be married there.*

Emma Smith, by Lee Greene Richards (July 27, 1878 – February 20, 1950).
Image source: Public domain, via Wikimedia Commons.

Joseph Owns Emma and Others: *"And I command mine handmaid, Emma Smith, to abide and cleave unto my servant Joseph, and to none else. But if she will not abide this commandment she shall be destroyed, saith the Lord; for I am the Lord thy God, and will destroy her if she abide not in my law." (Doctrine and Covenants [1957], 132:54). "[I]f any man espouse a virgin [thirteen or fourteen of Joseph's polyandrous wives, women already married to other men, were not virgins], and desire to espouse another, and the first give her consent, and if he espouse the second, and they are virgins, and have vowed to no other man, then he is justified; he cannot commit adultery for they are given unto him, for he cannot commit adultery with that that belongeth unto him and to no one else. And if he have ten virgins given unto him by this law, he cannot commit adultery, for they belong to him, and they are given unto him; therefore he is justified." (Ibid., 132:61-62).*

Joseph Smith, Jr. Image source:
Public Domain via Wikimedia Commons.

THE INFALLIBLE PROPHET WILL NEVER LEAD YOU ASTRAY

"[W]hatsoever you seal on earth shall be sealed in heaven; and whatsoever you bind on earth, in my name and by my word, saith the Lord, it shall be eternally bound in the heavens; and whatsoever sins you remit on earth shall be remitted eternally in the heavens; and whatsoever sins you retain on earth shall be retained in heaven . . . . [W]homsoever you bless I will bless, and whomsoever you curse I will curse, saith the Lord; for I, the Lord, am thy God." (Doctrine and Covenants [1957], 132:45-47).

THEOCRACY

"The Nauvoo city charter incorporated Joseph's theocratic ideas, including a government independent of the state with its own municipal court system and militia. Besides being prophet and president of the church, Smith became mayor, head of the city council, chief justice of the municipal court, and lieutenant general of the Nauvoo Legion." (Kingdom in the West)

A TALE OF TWO CANDIDATES

John C. Bennett engraving. Image source:
Public domain, via Wikimedia Commons

Image source: Alexander Gardner[Public domain],
via Wikimedia Commons.

ABRAHAM LINCOLN/DR. JOHN C. BENNETT

After Mormons once voted for every Whig but Lincoln, Lincoln voted for the "Nauvoo Charter." Smith used that conferral of extraordinary authority "to make the Mormon capital an independent theocracy." Dr. John C. Bennett, who carried the bill to the legislature, used that astonishing legislative success as a springboard to unequivocal acceptance in a community that worshipped its leaders. The Latter-day Saints unanimously elected Bennett to the office of Mayor, with thousands of votes cast, and Joseph Smith appointed him to be the Assistant President of the Mormon Church. While they elected Bennett to lead them, in one election, they rejected Abraham Lincoln to lead them in another election. It was a test of the leader's discernment.

LEAVING THE STATES

George Armstrong Hicks: *"It is my opinion that many dishonest men were among the Mormon people. I have heard many 'a good old saint' boast that he had stolen 'bear meet' and 'sweet oil' (honey & pork) from the Mosourians, and no doubt if the people belonging to the church had been strictly honest, we could have been living at our old homes in the States. I know that I have heard men boast here in Utah of their dishonest acts at Nauvoo. I heard one old man at Orderville in Kane Co., Utah, boast that he had killed a dozen head of cattle and that he knew they were all stolen from gentiles." (Kingdom in the West, vol. 13)*

WILLIAM LAW

Image Source: Public domain, via Wikimedia Commons.

Excommunication: *"According to his diary, William Law learned on 19 April 1844 that a council of church leaders had the night before 'cut off' or excommunicated him, his wife, his brother, and others: 'they said we were opposed to Joseph Smith and that was enough.'"*

Law Diary, April 15, 1844: *Almon Babbit, who baptized William Law, who was estranged from Smith and out of the First Presidency as a result of his opposition to plural marriage, wanted Law recovered. "Law's diary states that sometime in early April 'Almon Babbit came to me, and said, that Joseph Smith wished a reconsideration and that if I would let all drop and say nothing about it, and be friendly, he would restore me to my office of the first Presidency and raise me higher than ever, & would send me a writing to that effect. I told Mr. Babbit that I could not be bought, that if J. Smith wanted reconciliation with me he must make public acknowledgment and cease from his abominations &c.' (Law, Diary, Cook, "William Law," 50)."*

William Law to Dr. Wyl, January 7, 1887: *"Before reading your book . . . I had no personal knowledge of the swindling and other wicked doing in Kirtland, nor did I know anything about the Missouri trouble; [I] was told [converted by John Taylor and Almon Babbit] that their troubles in Ohio and Missouri all grew out of 'religious persecution.'" "I saw nothing wrong [in Nauvoo] until after the city charter was obtained. A change was soon apparent; the laws of the country were set at defiance and although outwardly everything was smooth, the under current was most vile and obnoxious." "The story [Smith and Law "swapping wives"] may have grown out of the fact that Joseph offered to furnish his wife, Emma, with a substitute for him, by way of compensation for his neglect of her, on condition that she would forever stop her opposition to polygamy and permit him to enjoy his young wives in peace and keep some of them in her house . . . ." "Mormon history is rather a mixed up affair." "Time revealed to me and many others much that we had not suspected." "The great mistake of my [life was my] having anything to do with Mormonism. I feel [it to] be a deep* *disgrace and never speak of it when I can avoid it; for over forty years I have been almost entirely silent on the subject and will so continue after this."*

William Law Remembers Sidney Rigdon: *Rigdon was "the originator of the fraud, the manipulator of Spalding's story into the 'Book of Mormon.'"* He *"aspired to be a church founder and a leader, as were the Campbells, and he used young Joseph Smith, the peepstone fellow, for that end . . . ."* *"Sidney now and then appeared as the 'head,' as when he washed Joe's feet in imitation of Jesus washing his followers' feet."*

William Law to Dr. Wyl, March 30, 1887: *"What position had Rockwell in Joseph's house? 'Rockwell was the lackey of the house. He used to comb and shave Joseph, blackened his boots and drove his carriage. He would have done anything Joe wanted him to do.'"* *"Have you had any knowledge of cases of poisoning in Nauvoo, ordered by the authorities? 'I know that several men, six or seven, died under very suspicious circumstances. Among them were two secretaries of the prophet, Mulholland and Blaskel Thompson. I saw Mulholland die and the symptoms looked very suspicious to me. Dr. Foster, who was a very good physician, believed firmly that those six or seven men had been poisoned, and told me so repeatedly.'"* *"Emma complained about Joseph's living with the L[awrence] girls, but not very violently. It is my conviction that she was his full accomplice, that she was not a bit better than he."*

William Law to Dr. Wyl, January 20, 1887: *"We committed a great error, but no crime. That is my consolation, that we only erred in judgment."*

A Black Spot on My Life: *"I got a black spot on my life, which will pain me to the very last minute of my existence." (Law Interview, March 30, 1887).*

SAMUEL H. SMITH

"In July 1844, Samuel H. Smith advanced a right to be church president because 'Joseph has said that if he and Hyrum were taken away Samuel H. Smith would be his successor.' In two weeks, Samuel was dead, possibly a murder victim of the succession crisis." (Quinn, 213). Members of his family thought that he had been poisoned.

Samuel H. Smith. Image source:
Public domain, via Wikimedia Commons.

A NINETEENTH-CENTURY PARADIGM:
"THE KINGDOM OR NOTHING"

Sterling M. McMurrin: *"The mainstream of the religion . . . was the watered-down Puritanism that informed the character of the foundation elements in American culture. Although Mormonism revolted against the traditional Christian absolutism, and . . . against the Calvinist doctrines of original sin, divine election, predestination, and salvation by grace only, it was well within the Puritan moral tradition that was grounded in the belief that the proper vocation of man is to create the Kingdom of God. Despite their bout with polygamy, their love of the theater, music, and dance, and their eudaemonistic moral philosophy, the Mormons have been from their beginning essentially Puritan in their morals, committed to the virtues that were built by the English colonists into the basic moral structure of American life."*

FOUNDING FATHERS

Wilford Woodruff: *"Two weeks before I left St. George [in 1877], the spirits of the dead gathered around me, wanting to know why we did not redeem them . . . ."* *"Everyone of those men that signed the Declaration of Independence, with General Washington, called upon me, as an Apostle of the Lord Jesus Christ, in the Temple at St. George, two consecutive nights, and demanded at my hands that I should go forth and attend to the ordinances of the House of God [baptism] for them. I straightway went into the baptismal font and called upon Brother McCallister to baptize me for the signers of the Declaration of Independence, and fifty other eminent men, making one hundred in all, including John Wesley, Columbus, and others. When Brother McCallister had baptized me for the 100 names I baptized him for 21, including General Washington and his forefathers and all the Presidents of the United States – except three."* *(Eminent Spirits Appear, April Conference Report, 1898, Wikipedia)*

James G. Bleak: *"I was also present in the St. George Temple and witnessed the appearance of the Spirits of the Signers of the Declaration of Independence. And also the spirits of the Presidents of the U.S. up to that time. And also others, such as Martin Luther and John Wesley, who came to [visited] Wilford Woodruff and demanded that their baptism and endowments be done."* *(Ibid.).*

Declaration of Indepdence (1819) by John Trumbull. Image source: Public domain via Wikimedia Commons.]

CHAPTER ELEVEN

Trysts and Transactions

Did the Lord ever tell any people that sleeping with their neighbors wives and daughters had anything to do with preparing the way of the Savior's coming[?][1]

Sidney Rigdon

The unusual secret marriages of Mormonism's founder to Sylvia Sessions and then to Sylvia's mother in 1842, preceding the Times and Seasons Certificates, were not traditional, monogamous, legal, reported, biblical or decent.

Joel M. Allred

DEVELOPMENTS

The Nauvoo Stake High Council

The doctrine described to some particularly vulnerable women by John C. Bennett, William Smith, Chauncey L. Higbee, Lyman O. Littlefield, Joel S. Miles, Darwin Chase, Justis Morse,[2] George

---

[1]Sidney Rigdon (Pittsburgh), *The Latter Day Saints Messenger and Advocate*, reproduced in Richard S. Van Wagoner, *Mormon Polygamy: A History* (Salt Lake City: Signature Books, 1986), 72.

[2]"In the year 1842, at Nauvoo, Illinois, Elder Amasa Lyman, taught me [Justis Morse] the doctrine of *sealing*, or marrying for eternity, called *spiritual wifery* . . . ." (Brian C. Hales, "A response to D. Michael Quinn's, 'Evidence for the Sexual Side of Joseph Smith's Polygamy,' Comments on a Session #2A, *Reconsidering Joseph Smith's Marital Practices*, Mormon History Association's Annual Conference, Calgary, Alberta, Canada, June 29, 2012, (unabbreviated version, revised during July)" [25 August 2012], 20, emphasis retained).

Thatcher, Gustavus Hills and others shared certain common themes.

> *The pattern of the female witnesses testifying before the Council was that these men taught: (1) "That any respectable female might indulge in sexual intercourse, and there was no sin in it [Joseph Smith: "What many people call sin is not sin . . ."], (2) providing the person so indulging, keep the same to herself [Joseph Smith: "If you will not accuse me, I will not accuse you . . . ."[3]]; (3) for there could be no sin where there was no accuser;" and (4) "using the name of Joseph Smith" they affirmed "that such intercourse was tolerated by the heads of the Church."[4]*

In the tumultuous proceedings before the Nauvoo Stake High Council as reflected in the Minutes of the Council in 1841 and 1842, these were consistent themes. Intercourse was allowed if it was kept secret. No report meant no offense. In the event of pregnancy, Dr. John C. Bennett had the chemical and surgical resources required to provide the parties with protection. Long before this dicey experimental period, Joseph Smith and Martin Harris were heard to say – at the home of the Hales in Pennsylvania in the presence of witnesses and before there was a book or a church – that adultery wasn't a crime.

INDISCRETIONS

"When Joseph and his wife Emma Hale Smith were living in Harmony [Pennsylvania] in 1827-1829, Emma's cousin, Levi Lewis, accused him of attempting 'to seduce Eliza Winters,' Emma's close

---

[3]Joseph Smith Jr., *History of The Church of Jesus Christ of Latter-day Saints*, B.H. Roberts, ed., 2d ed., rev., (Salt Lake City: The Deseret Book Company, 1978), 4:445.

[4]Gary James Bergera, "'Illicit Intercourse,' Plural Marriage and the Nauvoo Stake High Council, 1840-44," *The John Whitmer Historical Association Journal* 23 (2003), 68-69, quoted in Grant H. Palmer, "Sexual Allegations against Joseph Smith and the Beginnings of Polygamy in Nauvoo," 17, emphasis added and retained.

friend."[5]   "Lewis further said that he was well 'acquainted with Joseph Smith Jr. and Martin Harris and that he has heard them both say adultery was no crime. Harris said he did not blame Smith for his attempt to seduce Eliza Winters.'"[6] Fifty years later, "Levi's brother, Hiel Lewis, repeated these same sexual accusations against Smith . . . ."[7]

It is reported that Joseph and Emma's abrupt departure from Harmony, Pennsylvania, in May 1829 "may have been precipitated, in part, by Levi Lewis's accusations that Joseph had acted improperly toward Miss Winters."[8] Eliza Winters was just sixteen at the time. Beyond these awkward early beginnings, polygamy crossed the bar when Joseph Smith plurally married Louisa Beaman in a proceeding supposed to have occurred in or near Nauvoo on April 5, 1841.   "[T]he 'first authorized marriage sealing,' granting eternal marriage to a husband and wife, was not performed for 'two civilly [state deputized] married spouses' but [rather] for Smith and his first documented plural wife, Louisa Beaman." In this peculiar episode, the law of the land was ignored.

> *"In fact, plural marriage – known among early participants as celestial marriage – represented the highest order, the ne plus ultra, of Smith's teachings on eternal or patriarchal marriage, superceding civil marriage, an outdated marriage contract which, church members came to understand, was as inefficacious as an improper baptism.*[9]

---

[5]Affidavit of Levi Lewis, 20 March 1834, *Susquehanna Register and Northern Pennsylvanian* (1 May 1834), 1, quoted by Palmer, "Sexual Allegations against Joseph Smith and the Beginnings of Polygamy in Nauvoo," 6.

[6]Affidavit of Levi Lewis, Ibid., 3-4. See, *e.g.*, Eber D. Howe, *Mormonism Unvailed: Or, A Faithful Account of That Singular Imposition and Delusion* (Painesville, OH: E.D. Howe, 1834; reprint, New York: AMS Press Inc., 1977), 268.

[7]Hiel Lewis, "That Mormon History – Reply to Elder Cadwell," *Amboy (IL) Journal* (5 August 1879), 1, quoted in Palmer, "Sexual Allegations against Joseph Smith and the Beginnings of Polygamy in Nauvoo," 6.

[8]Ibid.

[9]Gary James Bergera, "The Earliest Eternal Sealings for Civilly Married Couples Living and Dead," *Dialogue: A Journal of Mormon Thought* 35 (Fall 2002): 41-42, quoted in George D. Smith, *Nauvoo Polygamy: ". . . but we called it celestial marriage"* (Salt Lake City: Signature Books, 2008), 45, emphasis added.

Other women later listed as wives in some quarters (Fanny Alger and Lucinda Pendleton [Morgan] [Harris]) were involved with Smith before 1840, in the case of Miss Alger in and/or after as early as 1831. Following the death of Smith and as an adult, Helen Mar Kimball – one of Smith's two fourteen-year-old wives, and one of his nine or ten teenagers – described conditions in the spring of 1841. Joseph addressed a group, she said, and "Astonished his hearers by preaching on the restoration of all things, and said that as it was anciently with Abraham, Isaac, and Jacob, so it would be again, etc."[10] It is important to know that Isaac, one of Smith's three designated patriarchs, was not a polygamist.[11]

Polygamy was not a religious "doctrine" by any reckoning, not in ancient Israel, and not in Old or New Testament times. It was strictly forbidden to commit adultery or to marry a mother and her daughter.[12] When was any ancient Patriarch or any early Christian

---

[10]Helen Mar Kimball (Smith) (Whitney), *Plural Marriage as Taught by the Prophet Joseph, a Reply to Joseph Smith [III], Editor of the Lamoni (Iowa) Herald* (Salt Lake City: Juvenile Instructor Office, 1882), 11, quoted in Palmer, "Sexual Allegations against Joseph Smith and the Beginnings of Polygamy in Nauvoo," 1. Isaac, though frequently cited by Smith, was not a polygamist. By Smith's nineteenth-century reckoning, Isaac, because disobedient "to that principle," could never "attain to the fullness of exaltation in the celestial glory." (Statement, William Clayton, 16 February 1874, reprinted as "William Clayton's Testimony," *Historical Record* [May 1887], 6:225-26). Is it not perfectly clear that Joseph, who referenced Abraham, *Isaac* and Jacob in support of the controversial practice, and for the longest time, didn't know that Isaac wasn't a polygamist?

[11]The revelation on polygamy, Section 132 of the Doctrine and Covenants, quotes Joseph's God: "Verily, thus saith the Lord unto you my servant Joseph, that inasmuch as you have inquired of my hand to know and understand wherein I, the Lord, justified my servants, Abraham, *Isaac* and Jacob, as also *Moses*, David and Solomon, my servants, as touching the principle and doctrine of their having many wives and concubines . . . ." (Doctrine and Covenants 132:1, emphasis added). In this accounting, Joseph's deity, like Joseph himself, was wrong because Isaac, the faithful husband of but one wife, wasn't a polygamist. Isaac was married to Rebekah. In addition, there is no reference to Moses having two wives at one time. His polygamy was unannounced and speculative. By this reckoning, if Moses was not a polygamist, and because Isaac was not a polygamist, neither of those two Patriarchs should have been able to hold high office in John Taylor's nineteenth-century Church. Nor either could Isaac, and/or maybe Moses "ever [hope to] attain to the fulness of exaltation in the celestial glory."

[12]Joseph married Mrs. Sylvia Porter Sessions (Lyon), the wife of Windsor Lyon, on February 8, 1842. He then married Mrs. Patty Bartlett (Sessions), the wife of David Sessions and the mother of Sylvia, on March 9, 1842. (George D.

apostle or leader ever heard to say that "the doctrine of plural and celestial marriage" was "the most holy and important doctrine ever revealed to man on the earth"?   When did any Christian foundational figure ever say that without obedience to the principle of polygamy no man can ever attain to the fulness of exaltation in the celestial glory?   How many of the Savior's Apostles ever had more than one wife at the same time?   Why didn't the Apostle Paul ever get married?   Why did he tell the members of the early church they were better off single than not?   Who did Jesus marry?   What did Jesus teach his followers about the practice of polygamy?   Why are Catholic priests celibate?   Who is able to say that Isaac, an Old Testament Patriarch and a monogamous man, could never attain to the fulness of exaltation in the celestial glory?   Adam, Brigham Young's "favorite deity," was not a polygamist, although Brigham Young said that he was.   Isaac, an important figure in Joseph Smith's polygamous equation ("Abraham, *Isaac* and Jacob"), was not a polygamist, although Smith said that he was.   The biblical

---

Smith, *Nauvoo Polygamy*, 621).   That was before Joseph published his *Times and Seasons Monogamous Marriage Certificates.*   Joseph married Flora Ann Woodworth on March 4, 1843, and then her mother, Mrs. Phebe Watrous (Woodworth), the wife of Lucien Woodworth, sometime before October 29, 1843.   (Ibid., 622-23).   "On January 17, 1846, Phebe would be sealed to [the deceased] Smith in preference to Lucien, and within a week Lucien would marry four additional wives himself."   (Ibid., 171).   Such confusion was not unusual during this season of domestic experimentation.   Michael Quinn was not so sure of those previously stated facts in the case of Phebe Woodworth.   Quinn, who may have recognized the Old Testament's abhorrence of such extraordinary unions, averred that it was "only a possibility" that Phebe married Joseph during his lifetime.   (Ibid., 652 note 376).   The Book of Leviticus, the third book of the Torah, consisting principally of God's speeches to Moses to be repeated to the Israelites, described the inevitable fate of a man who would commit adultery with another man's wife.   "And the man that commiteth adultery with another man's wife, even he that commiteth adultery with his neighbor's wife, the adulterer and the adulteress shall surely be put to death."   (Leviticus 20:10).   How did Joseph and his polyandrous wives escape that Old Testament injunction?   Leviticus went on to describe the fate of the principals when a man married a mother and a daughter, as Joseph did, and possibly twice.   "And if a man take a wife and her mother, it is wickedness; they shall be burnt with fire, both he and they; that there be no wickedness among you."   (Leviticus 20:14).   The restoration of all things, including Old Testament things (Leviticus is the third book of the Old Testament), must be seen to have ignored these prohibitions.   By Old Testament standards, Joseph Smith, because he took "a wife and her mother," was a candidate to be "burnt with fire."   Or, for committing adultery with another man's wife, he was a candidate to be "put to death."

Jesus never preached or practiced plural marriage, nor did any of his apostles. The unmarried Paul described marriage as an impediment to the spiritual production of the truly faithful. An architect of Christianity, the Apostle Paul taught those early Christians that if they did choose to marry, against his advice, that deacons, bishops and elders should be the husbands of one wife.[13]

In polygamy's nineteenth-century experimental period (infancy), after marrying Mrs. Zina Huntington Jacobs (while she was about seven months pregnant with her legal husband Henry Jacobs' child), Smith explained the importance of secrecy: "If you will throw a cloak of charity over my sins, I will over yours . . . ."[14] The unsettled order of those early things drove the decent but malleable Zina (the nineteenth-century victim of an angel with a drawn sword) to express dismay: "The thoughts of my heart or the emotions of my minde causes my very head to acke."[15]

Fanny Alger

In the course of a thoughtful conversation with William E. McLellin, a former Apostle and Secretary to the Founding Quorum of the Twelve, Emma agreed with a story McLellin said that he was told by another early Church leader, Dr. F.G. Williams. McLellin

---

[13]1 Timothy 3:2 – "A bishop then must be blameless, the husband of one wife . . . ." 1 Timothy 3:12 – "Let the deacons be the husbands of one wife . . . ." Titus 1:5-9 – "[O]rdain elders in every city, as I [Paul] had appointed thee: If any be blameless, the husband of one wife, having faithful children not accused of riot or unruly . . . ." (1 Corinthians 7:32-33). "He that is unmarried careth for the things that belong to the Lord, how he may please the Lord: But he that is married careth for the things that are of the world, how he may please his wife." (Ibid.). The marriage views of the Apostle Paul and those of Joseph Smith were diametrically opposed. Paul urged celibacy for the truly faithful, who would serve God and not the things of the world.

[14]Roberts, ed., *History of The Church of Jesus Christ of Latter-day Saints*, 4:445.

[15]Zina Huntington (Jacobs) (Smith) (Young), Diary entry, May 1845, quoted in John G. Turner, *Brigham Young: Pioneer Prophet* (Belknap Press of Harvard University Press, 2012), 136. Paul Toscano, a formidable scholar, provided this advice: "In each of us there is something with which we must never part: our identity, our free will, our heart, our mind, our power to choose, our soul." (Paul James Toscano, *The Sacrament of Doubt* [Salt Lake City: Signature Books, 2007], 33).

visited the prophet's widow in Nauvoo in 1847 after the death of Joseph Smith. Williams was one of the men who counseled Emma after Fanny Alger and Joseph Smith were found "in the barn together alone." *Emma acknowledged that on an evening when she missed her husband and Fanny Alger, she went and found them "in the barn together alone. She looked through a crack and saw the transaction!!!"*[16] What she said she saw when she found them on a hay mow "in the barn together alone" was not some kind of celestial encounter. Oliver Cowdery "said that he learned of this incident from Joseph Smith himself and that Joseph had confided to him that 'he had confessed to Emma,' seeking her forgiveness."[17] Cowdery would come to call Smith's dalliance with Emma's household helper sex and a sin. Joseph knew that it was, saw that he was caught and begged forgiveness. (Before anyone ever thought to call that *"transaction"* a marriage, it was sex and a sin, an act for which Smith, the voice of God on earth, begged to be forgiven).

Benjamin Johnson, a trusted friend (multiple times the brother-in-law) of the Mormon prophet who was known to have prized Benjamin's sisters, was heard to report that "the Alger incident was 'one of the Causes of Apostasy & disruption at Kirtland altho at the time there was little Said publickly upon the subject.'"[18] According to Johnson, Fanny Alger was "A varry nice & Comly young woman about my own age. towards whoom not only mySelf but every one Seemed *partial* for the ameability of her character and it was whispered even then that Joseph *Loved* her."[19]

---

[16]William E. McLellin letter to Joseph Smith III (3 July 1872), *The William E. McLellin Papers: 1854-1880*, eds. Stan Larson and Samuel J. Passey, foreword by George D. Smith (Salt Lake City: Signature Books, 2008), 489, emphasis added.

[17]Donald Q. Cannon and Lyndon W. Cook, eds., *Far West Record: Minutes of the Church of Jesus Christ of Latter-day Saints, 1830-1844* (Salt Lake City: Deseret Book Co., 1983), 167, quoted in Palmer, "Sexual Allegations against Joseph Smith and the Beginnings of Polygamy in Nauvoo," 11.

[18]Dean R. Zimmerman, "I knew the prophets: An analysis of the letter of Benjamin F. Johnson to George F. Gibb, reporting doctrinal views of Joseph Smith and Brigham Young" (Bountiful, UT: Horizon Publishing Co., 1976), 39, quoted in Palmer, "Sexual Allegations against Joseph Smith and the Beginnings of Polygamy in Nauvoo," 11.

[19]Zimmerman, "I knew the prophets," 38, quoted in Linda King Newell and Valeen Tippetts Avery, *Mormon Enigma: Emma Hale Smith, Prophet's Wife, "Elect Lady," Polygamy's Foe – 1804-1879* (Garden City, N.Y.: Doubleday & Company, Inc., 1984), 66, emphasis retained.

Although he was married to Emma, it was whispered that Joseph loved Fanny Alger. It wasn't platonic; Miss Alger wasn't a burden. An angel with a drawn or flaming sword didn't have to encourage Joseph to engage in forbidden intimacy with the teenage household helper. Joseph "*Loved* her."

One of Smith's biographers, while describing his motives as undefined, sets Mormon minds at ease and says that "Joseph did not explain plural marriage as a love match or even a companionship. Only slight hints of romance found their way into his proposals. He understood plural marriage," according to Richard Bushman, "as a religious principle."[20] Fanny Alger, Benjamin Johnson, Benjamin's sisters and quite a number of others (think of the Partridge girls) might have disagreed. Smith's encounters with Fanny didn't lack sentiment, and there was a love match. The holy man's performance in the barn did not advance "the millennial purpose of fashioning a righteous generation on the eve of the Second Coming."[21] Sidney Rigdon, the father of Miss Nancy and a man who knew Joseph better than that leader's twenty-first century biographer, threw Joseph under the bus shortly after the death of the prophet in 1845. Rigdon reported as follows: "Did the Lord ever tell any people that sleeping with their neighbors *wives and daughters* had anything to do with preparing the way of the Savior's coming?" Still other accounts, evidence of sexual encounters without progeny, further refute the biographer's temporizing view. The fact that some of the women's pregnancies were terminated by medical means (by Dr. Bennett and at remote locations) suggests that raising up seed unto the Lord was not the prophet's marital objective.

What Emma Smith knew about Joseph's intimate encounters with Fanny Alger caused turmoil in the house of the Smiths nearly ten years before Emma and eighteen other married females signed one of the *Monogamous Marriage Certificates* promoted by her sexually active husband for publication in the *Times and Seasons* on October 1, 1842.

---

[20]Bushman, *Rough Stone Rolling*, 326.
[21]Ibid.

The monogamous marriage "statement" published in the Doctrine and Covenants (1835, Section 101 and canonized) was compiled by Oliver Cowdery and two other "Presiding Elders."[22] It unequivocally described the Church's marital principle as "one wife . . . one husband." "[T]he statement tempered the Book of Mormon position that God might someday 'command' his people to 'raise up seed'" by failing to say as much. The canonized provision endorsed monogamy and dismissed polygamy without qualification. It is noteworthy that the two Presiding Elders (Sidney Rigdon and Frederick G. Williams), who were supposed to have assisted Cowdery in assembling Section 101 "from the revelations of God," were among those most familiar with the polygamous principle (Cowdery, 1829, 1831) and with Smith's reckless escapades with Fanny Alger in the early 1830s. The same three men who were called upon to pacify an angry Emma after she had personally witnessed that particularly disturbing "transaction" between her husband and her housemaid crafted the original monogamous marriage provision published in the Doctrine and Covenants as Section 101 in 1835.

No one was heard to suggest in real time that Emma, who learned about some few of Joseph's marriages after the fact, had reason to believe that he ever married Fanny Alger, or that Oliver Cowdery, Frederick G. Williams or Sidney Rigdon thought or said that he did. Cowdery called the sordid sexual encounter, something Emma called a "*transaction*," a "dirty, nasty, filthy *affair*." Not a marriage, just an "affair." The three presiding elders who attended the Smiths during the Fanny Alger episode, before they crafted the provisions endorsing monogamous marriage (Section 101 of the 1835 edition of the Doctrine and Covenants), knew as much about the Mormon prophet's doubtful morality as anyone in the Church. In the case of Emma and Fanny Alger, the law of Sarah (requiring the consent of the first wife in the event of a second marriage) wasn't applied. Sidney Rigdon knew that Smith had propositioned his daughter Nancy, then asked her to marry him, months before the *Times and Seasons Certificates* were published on October 1, 1842. Rigdon knew what he knew before Joseph published his *Times and Seasons Certificates*, but said nothing when he saw the

---

[22]"Marriage," Doctrine and Covenants (1835), Section CI (101).

prophet lead the people astray. If Joseph Smith had really married Fanny Alger (*as the Church in its official history published in 2018 has just now chosen to say*), then Section 101 of the first edition of the Doctrine and Covenants published in 1835 and the *Certificates* published over the names of thirty-one witnesses by Joseph Smith, the editor of the *Times and Seasons* in 1842, provided unmistakable evidence of unforgivable dishonesty on issues of great importance.

Sarah Marinda Bates (Pratt)

Joseph's Oneida Community approach to Mrs. Sarah Pratt was not an offer of conventional monogamous marriage (Doctrine and Covenants Section 101: "one man . . . one wife . . . one woman but one husband, except in case of death . . ."). The offer was not in compliance with the canonized statement described in the Doctrine and Covenants, or with the representations made in the prophet's *Times and Seasons Certificates.* It wasn't an offer supposed to serve "the millennial purpose of fashioning a righteous generation on the eve of the Second Coming."[23] "After the appropriate preliminaries, the prophet said: 'Sister Pratt, the Lord has given you to me as one of my *spiritual wives.* I have the blessings of Jacob granted me, as God granted holy men of old; and as I have long looked upon you with favor, and an earnest desire of connubial bliss, I hope you will not repulse or deny me.'"[24] This was not an offer conditioned upon the wonders of eternity or something to be officiated, or even a suggestion of a real marriage. It was a brazen request for "connubial bliss" outside of Mrs. Pratt's monogamous marriage, something greatly less encumbering. She would be undeputized and out of the nuptial loop. She proved she understood exactly what he meant.

Joseph said God gave Sarah to him! God put his prophet up to this. Sarah's legal husband, Smith's thoroughly devoted apostle Orson Pratt, was on a mission somewhere Smith had sent him for as long as Smith required, when his prophet approached his wife for sex.

---

[23]Bushman, *Rough Stone Rolling*, 326.

[24]Sarah Pratt, quoted in Fawn M. Brodie, *No Man Knows My History: The Life of Joseph Smith the Mormon Prophet*, 2d ed., rev. and enl. (New York, NY: Alfred A. Knopf, 1972), 316, emphasis retained.

The principle at the core of the prophet's strange proposal was that "sex between consenting adults was not a sin, even among married people," respectable married people, if there was no accuser. If such transactions were secret. Joseph did not intend to support Mrs. Pratt, or to take her and her children with Orson into his family, or to publicly acknowledge any kind of relationship. The leader of the Church and Mrs. Pratt understood the prophet's proposition in Oneida community terms, but with the added element of secrecy. Once again it seems important to say that Sarah Pratt described the prophet's approach in a late-in-life interview with Dr. W. Wyl. "*God does not care,*" Smith told Sarah Pratt, "*if we have a good time, if only other people do not know it.*"[25] If Sarah Pratt told the truth, and men of importance have praised her character, it is Katie bar the door.

Sarah Pratt spoke to her leader in these principled terms:

> *Am I called upon to break the marriage covenant, and prove recreant to my lawful husband? I never will. ... I care not for the blessings of Jacob, and I believe in no such revelations, neither will I consent, under any circumstance whatever. I have one good husband, and that is enough for me.*[26]

Much later in her life, following fits and starts, Sarah Pratt took herself and her children out of the Mormon Church.

Lucinda Pendleton (Morgan) (Harris)

Other women – including Lucinda Pendleton (Morgan) (Harris), the widow of the Masonic martyr William Morgan, the mother of his children and the most famous woman in the early Church – embraced the "*God does not care if we have a good time, if only other*

---

[25]Dr. W. Wyl, *Mormon Portraits or, The Truth About the Mormon Leaders From 1830 to 1866: Volume First: Joseph Smith, The Prophet, His Family and Friends, A Study Based on Facts and Documents* (Salt Lake City, UT: Tribune Printing and Publishing Company, 1886), 62, emphasis added and retained.

[26]Sarah Pratt, quoted in Brodie, *No Man Knows My History*, 316, emphasis retained and added.

people do not know it" principle. Mrs. Harris informed Mrs. Pratt in 1842 that she had been the prophet's *"mistress"* for four years. In making this stunning disclosure, the married woman didn't mention a marriage and wasn't embarrassed. Lucinda described consensual secret sex between married adults. William Morgan's widow, by then Mrs. George W. Harris, wasn't married to Joseph Smith in 1838, and they were not sealed. They had a sexual consent relationship. This *"mistress"* specifically told her friend Mrs. Pratt that married women as well as virgins ought be privileged to join his own circle of spiritual wives,[27] that is to say women pledged to the prophet in a life to come. Quite often this happened without the benefit of any kind of official proceeding. In time, but not really in time, Lucinda Pendleton (Morgan) (Harris) became Lucinda Pendleton (Morgan) (Harris) (Smith), one of Smith's many polyandrous partners. She and her children with Morgan were, because of her sealing to Smith, bonded to him for both time and eternity.

When Joseph Smith fled from Kirtland, Ohio, in the middle of the night in January 1838 to avoid violent internal unrest, angry constituents, doctrinal issues, double digit lawsuits and many formidable creditors, he and a pregnant Emma came to rest in the Far West, Missouri, home of George and Lucinda Harris (where they lived with Brother and Sister Harris for some few months before acquiring other more permanent lodgings). "When the Harris family moved to Nauvoo, they were given a lot directly across from the prophet and next door to that of Sarah Cleveland, another of Joseph's wives"[28] and one of Emma's counselors in the ladies' relief society. While Lucinda seemed to have taken sex between consenting adults, even married adults, in stride, she took the Mormon prophet's unexpected death with shock and sorrow. "B.W. Richmond, a stranger and guest in the Mansion House at the time of Joseph's death, noted 'a lady standing at the head of Joseph Smith's body, her face covered, and her whole frame convulsed with weeping. She was the widow," he said, "of William Morgan, of Masonic memory . . . ."[29]

---

[27]Brodie, *No Man Knows My History*, 252.
[28]Ibid., 460.
[29]Ibid.

Lucinda Pendleton (Morgan) (Harris), the undivorced legal wife of George W. Harris, took a third husband while her second husband still lived, this time for time and eternity, when she became Lucinda Pendleton (Morgan) (Harris) (Smith), after four years as the Mormon prophet's mistress, sometime before January 17, 1842.[30] Before Joseph Smith published the *Times and Seasons Certificates*. "George Harris either knew at the time – or learned later – of the relationship between his wife and the prophet, for he stood as proxy in the Nauvoo temple in January 1846 [after Smith's death] when Lucinda was sealed to Joseph Smith 'for eternity'"[31] (this sealing was likely reaffirmed). That sealing ordinance guaranteed that Joseph Smith and not George Harris or William Morgan would claim this adventurous woman and her biological children with William Morgan in the afterlife.[32]

Nancy Rigdon

When Joseph Smith approached Miss Nancy Rigdon, the daughter of Sidney Rigdon, in early 1842, he did not start the conversation with an offer of marriage. He "swore her to secrecy" before he offered anything at all. Joseph told "Miss Nancy" that God gave her to him. "[H]e had asked the Lord for her, and . . . it was his holy will that he should have her . . . ." After some posturing, which invited her anger, he made a case for an open marriage when he said that if she married him, "it would not prevent her from

---

[30]George D. Smith, *Nauvoo Polygamy*, 621.

[31]Brodie, *No Man Knows My History*, 460.

[32]A group of men destroyed a printing press and beat its owner in Batavia, New York, in September 1826. "In the press office were fresh proofs of a new book, an exposé of the secret rites and oaths of Freemasonry" written by Lucinda Pendleton's first husband, William Morgan. Morgan was abducted some few days later and carried to Canandaigua, just nine miles from Joseph Smith's home. Following a mock trial, he was secretly conveyed "to Fort Niagara on the Canadian border, where he disappeared." These events sparked massive anti-Masonry sentiments that "swelled to cover eight states." "In October 1827 a bloated corpse was washed up on the shore of Lake Ontario." Lucinda Morgan "had not a particle of doubt" about "the identity of the body." "Since an election was approaching [and because anti-Masonry was a national issue], the funeral show was delayed until shortly before the voting. Then hundreds of thousands of people poured into [rural] Batavia ['on the road to Buffalo'] to join in the obsequies of the great masonic martyr." (Ibid., 63-64).

marrying any other person."[33] This and other poorly-considered propositions opened a can of worms for Joseph Smith in the City of Joseph in 1842. In retrospect it was the event with Miss Rigdon and Smith's festering disagreement with Dr. John C. Bennett – which exploded because of it – that ultimately caused Joseph Smith to first acquire and then to publish the controversial *Times and Seasons Monogamous Marriage Certificates.* Joseph's own knowledge of the true facts, supplemented by the knowledge of certain important others, served to create a fraudulent process.

Thou Shalt Not Covet Thy Neighbor's Wife

On 15 October 1842, Joseph Smith (by this time a serial civil bigamist who had ignored the laws of the State of Illinois in order to illegally marry nine or ten already married women) published an incredibly inappropriate poorly-timed revelation in the *Times and Seasons.* Had God not said, "And again, I command thee, that thou shalt not covet thy neighbor's wife . . . ."[34] On 1 November 1842, Joseph Smith, adding one deception to another, "republishes in the *Times and Seasons* an earlier 1831 revelation condemning plural marriage."[35] "Thou shalt love thy wife with all thy heart, and shall cleave unto her and none else . . . ."

July 14, 1842: After Mrs. Sarah Pratt refused God and her prophet, Joseph Smith called Orson's wife "a w**** [whore] from her mother's breast."[36] On July 17, 1842, *The Wasp Extra*, a special edition of the Nauvoo newspaper, Apostle William Smith, Editor, accused John C. Bennett of "adultery, fornication, embryo infanticide and buggery . . . ."[37] On August 1, 1842, the *Times and*

---

[33]Bennett, *The History of the Saints* (photomechanical reprint of 1842 original), 242.

[34]Doctrine and Covenants 19:25; *Times and Seasons*, vol. 3 (15 October 1842), 944.

[35]*Times and Seasons*, vol. 4 no 24, 369, from "Polygamy Timeline" in Mithryn (anonymous contributor), "Exploring Mormonism" (accessed 13 November 1842, posted 2 September 2013), available from exploringmormonism.com/polygamy-timeline; Internet, p. 10 of 41.

[36]*Sangamo Journal*, vol. 10 no. 48 (Springfield, IL: 22 July 1842).

[37]Mithryn, "Joseph Smith, Orson and Sarah Pratt -- A timeline" (posted 31 January 2013, 2012, accessed 11 October 2018), available from

Seasons published affidavits that said that Sarah Pratt lied about her conversation with Joseph Smith and had an affair with John C. Bennett.[38] In August 1842 *The Wasp* described Martha Brotherton as a "mean harlot."[39] On "31 August 1842 – Stephen Markham signs 'Affidavits' [to say] that he saw Nancy Rigdon in a compromising situation with Bennett."[40] On April 27, 1845, after the death of Joseph Smith, Orson Hyde delivered a speech in which he said that Nancy Rigdon's conduct was notorious in this city, little better than a public prostitute.[41] It was no small thing to say no to the domestic requests of the Mormon prophet and to describe them.

Joseph Smith desperately wanted Zina Huntington before she married the smitten Henry Jacobs. She declined multiple proposals (having been apprised long before Smith published the *Times and Seasons Certificates* that God commanded her to marry Smith). When that ship seemed to have sailed because of her marriage to Jacobs, Smith sent Zina's trouble-shooting brother to further assert Smith's never-say-die continuing case. Dimick Huntington told his happily married sister that an angel with a drawn sword had come to earth in support of polygamy. That messenger had threatened Joseph's life and his ministry, and the future of the Church. All of that was then upon Zina, who until then had been a reluctant plural wife. Faced with that awkward dilemma, Zina changed course and complied. Smith "took her" as his first (and then only) polyandrous wife. When Zina married Henry, rather than Joseph, Joseph (who had been scheduled to officiate) failed to appear. Zina and Henry were married by the Mayor, Dr. John C. Bennett, before Joseph's "bosom friend" fell from grace.

---

https://www.reddit.com/r/ mormon/ comments/ xe69p/ orson _ pratt _ sarah _ pratt _ and _ joseph _smith_a/; Internet, p. 2 of 4.

[38]*Times and Seasons* (1 August 1842), 875-77.

[39]"Remarks," *The Wasp*, vol. 1 no. 19 (Nauvoo, IL: 27 August 1842).

[40]Mithryn, "Polygamy Timeline," Internet, p. 9 of 41.

[41]*Speech of Elder Orson Hyde, Delivered Before the High Priest's Quorum, in Nauvoo, April 27th, 1845* (City of Joseph: [Nauvoo], Ill., Printed by John Taylor, 1845), 27-29, quoted in Palmer, "Sexual Allegations against Joseph Smith and the Beginnings of Polygamy in Nauvoo."

Abnormalities

Joseph Noble said that he performed the first documented plural marriage for Joseph Smith and Louisa Beaman as early as 1840.[42] Agnes Coolbrith (Smith), Don Carlos Smith's widow, was plurally married to Joseph Smith in January 1842.[43] Bishop Vinson Knight died on July 31, 1842. It is believed that his widow, Martha McBride (Knight) was married and sealed to Joseph Smith on or sometime before August 5, 1842 with but little time to grieve.[44]

On 8 February 1842, Joseph Smith secretly married Sylvia Sessions (Lyon), another already married woman. Many years later, when she was on her deathbed, she told her daughter, Josephine Lyon (Fisher), that Joseph Smith was her biological father. If that had been true, it would have been undeniable evidence of Joseph's sexual polyandry. And even if it was not, it was subjective evidence of Joseph's sexual polyandry. Prior to that time Josephine thought she was Windsor Lyon's daughter. One month after he married Sylvia, Joseph violated the law of the Patriarchs[45] and secretly married Sylvia's mother, Patty Bartlett (Sessions), Nauvoo's honored midwife.[46] The unusual secret marriages of Mormonism's founder to Sylvia and then to Sylvia's mother in 1842, preceding the *Times and Seasons Certificates*, were not traditional, monogamous, legal, public, reported, biblical or decent. By Old Testament reckoning, Joseph Smith, then Sylvia and Patty Sessions, would have been "burnt with fire" because of their "wickedness."

---

[42]D. Michael Quinn, "Evidence for the Sexual Side of Joseph Smith's Polygamy," presented to the Mormon History Association's Annual Conference (Calgary, Alberta, Canada: 29 June 2012; expanded, finalized 31 December 2012; circulated mid-2013), 14. It has been assumed by some scholars that the marriage of Louisa Beaman to Joseph Smith occurred in 1841. (George D. Smith, *Nauvoo Polygamy* [5 April 1841], 21). In 1866 Apostle Wilford Woodruff, the officially appointed "Church Historian," recorded in his "Historian's Private Journal" that Joseph Smith and Louisa Beaman were sealed May 1840 by Joseph B. Noble. According to Quinn, Joseph Noble "also made statements that he performed the Smith-Beaman marriage in 1840." (Ibid.).

[43]Quinn, "Evidence for the Sexual Side of Joseph Smith's Polygamy," 8.

[44]George D. Smith, *Nauvoo Polygamy*, 621.

[45]"And if a man take a wife and her mother, it is wickedness: they shall be burnt with fire, both he and they; that there be no wickedness among you." (Leviticus 20:14). Polyandry, treated as adultery, was equally unacceptable.

[46]George D. Smith, *Nauvoo Polygamy*, 621.

Patty Bartlett (Sessions), a married woman, a polyandrous wife and the mother of another polyandrous wife, was married to Joseph Smith "by Willard Richards March 9, 1842, in Newel K Whitney's chamber [at] Nauvoo, *for time* [code for a license shared with her legal husband] *and all eternity* [meaning exclusively to Smith for the afterlife] .... Sylvia ... [Sylvia Sessions (Lyon)] was presant when I was sealed to Joseph Smith."[47] Sylvia was secretly sealed to Joseph Smith *for time and eternity* – before her mother (or Emma) – on February 8, 1842. It was in contemplation of death and as a devout disciple that Sylvia Porter Sessions (Lyon) (Smith) informed her married daughter *Josephine* Lyon (Fisher) that Joseph Smith was *Josephine's* biological father. That the Church thought that might be true was evidenced by the fact that Church officials, including Andrew Jenson (the Assistant Church Historian, the editor of the *Church Chronology* and a polygamy scholar) visited Josephine, intent upon documenting what others had long suspicioned regarding her paternity.[48] Modern DNA science seems to have proved in the year 2016 that Josephine Lyon (Fisher) was not the biological daughter of Joseph Smith, even though her mother thought and told her that she was. (DNA science has also been used to prove that Native Americans are not the descendants of Hebrews. The Church should find DNA science dependable for both purposes.)

To Zina D. Huntington (Jacobs): "Joseph sent [Zina's brother] Dimick to her with a message: an angel with a drawn sword had stood over Smith and told him if he did not establish polygamy he would lose 'his position and his life.'"[49] *To Marinda Nancy Johnson (Hyde)*: "[L]et my handmaid Nancy Marinda Hyde hearken to the counsel of my servant Joseph in all things whatsoever he shall teach

---

[47]Todd Compton, *In Sacred Loneliness: The Plural Wives of Joseph Smith* (Salt Lake City: Signature Books, 2001), 179, emphasis added and/or retained.

[48]Josephine told Andrew Jenson what her mother, Sylvia Sessions Lyon, told her: "She . . . told me that I was [t]he daughter of the Prophet Joseph Smith, she having been sealed to the Prophet at the time that her husband Mr. Lyon was out of fellowship with the Church." (Josephine Lyon Fisher, Statement to Andrew Jenson, 24 February 1915, cited in Brian C. Hales, "The Joseph Smith-Sylvia Sessions Plural Sealing: Polyandry or Polygyny?" in *Mormon Historical Studies* 9/1 [Spring 2008]).

[49]Compton, *In Sacred Loneliness: The Plural Wives of Joseph Smith*, 80-81.

unto her . . . ."[50] *To Helen Mar Kimball*: "If you will take this step, it will ensure your eternal salvation & exaltation and that of your father's household & all of your kindred . . . ."[51]

Joseph caused his witnesses to certify and declare that there was no "secret wife system" in Nauvoo precisely because John C. Bennett had so publicly said that there was. Bennett was right, there was; Smith knew there was. Bennett said something approaching the truth. While Mormons are supposed to obey the law of the land, nineteenth-century Mormons obeyed the law of the Lord. Joseph Smith was sixteen times a bigamist under the laws of the land when he published those *Times and Seasons Monogamous Marriage Certificates* on October 11, 1842. Sylvia Porter Sessions (Lyon) (Smith) was present on March 9, 1842, to see her biological mother and her children's biological grandmother also become her sister-in-law and her children's aunt. Joseph Smith was her husband and her mother's husband. Windsor Lyon's biological children with Sylvia Sessions, by Mormon polygamous reckoning, belonged to Joseph Smith – no matter who was the biological father – in the afterlife. These strange marriages were anything but conventional and definitely not public. On October 1, 1842, the critical date for the controversial *Certificates*, Smith had no less than sixteen polygamous wives, not including Fanny Alger, and he was just getting started.

---

[50]Revelation to Joseph Smith, 2 December 1841, Roberts, ed., *History of The Church of Jesus Christ of Latter-day Saints*, 4:467.

[51] Compton, *In Sacred Loneliness: The Plural Wives of Joseph Smith*, 499.

CHAPTER TWELVE

Thirty-one Witnesses Say:
"one man . . . one wife"

Disregard for truth. As early as the fourth century, certain pernicious doctrines embodying a disregard for truth gained currency in the [Catholic] Church. Thus, it was taught "that it was an act of virtue to deceive and lie, when by that means the interests of the church might be promoted." Needless to say, sins other than those of falsehood and deceit were justified when committed in the supposed interests of church advancement, and crime was condoned under the specious excuse that the end justifies the means. Many of the fables and fictitious stories relating to the lives of Christ and the apostles, as also the spurious accounts of supernatural visitations and wonderful miracles, in which the literature of the early centuries abound, are traceable to this infamous doctrine that lies are acceptable unto God if perpetrated in a cause that man calls good.[1]

James E. Talmage

I have already stated that I proved Mr. Caswell to have told one lie, and a man that will tell one falsehood to injure an innocent people, will tell five hundred, if necessary for the same object.

John Taylor[2]

---

[1]Mormon scholar James E. Talmage, *The Great Apostasy* (Salt Lake City: Deseret Book Company, 1953), 107. It is hard to imagine that a scholar familiar with the twists and turns of Mormon history and doctrine could produce such a recital.

[2]Mormon Apostle John Taylor in "Three Nights' Public Discussion between Revds. C.W. Cleeve, James Robertson, and Philip Cater and Elder John Taylor, of the Church of Jesus Christ of Latter-day Saints, at Boulogne-Sur-Mer, France"

How often these men and their accomplices stood up before the congregation, and called God and all the holy Angels to witness, that there was no such doctrine [polygamy] taught in the church; and it has now come to light . . . .[3]

Sidney Rigdon

PROTECTING "THE POLYGAMOUS PRINCIPLE": THE BEGUILING ORIGINS OF THE CELESTIAL FAMILY

In 2007 the LDS Church – under pressure to be more officially transparent – admitted in correlated materials (a lesson manual) that, "The doctrines and principles relating to plural marriage were revealed to Joseph Smith as early as 1831. The Prophet taught the doctrine of plural marriage, and a number of such marriages were performed during his lifetime."[4] The gravity of the admission wasn't further exposed. Brigham Young reported in an earlier era, before such things were obliterated from the minds and materials of believers,[5] and with somewhat less reserve, that Joseph Smith and

---

(Liverpool, UK: John Taylor, 1850), 7-8. When John Taylor said this about the Reverend Caswell while feigning indignation, he also said the Mormon Church didn't practice polygamy. When he told this story, he had already been the husband of about fifteen women.

[3]Sidney Rigdon letter to Br. J. Gregg, *The Latter Day Saint's Messenger and Advocate* (Pittsburgh, PA: 15 October 1844): 14.

[4]*Teachings of Presidents of the Church – Joseph Smith* (Salt Lake City: The Church of Jesus Christ of Latter-day Saints, 2007), xii. An earlier close-to-contemporaneous manual concerning Brigham Young allowed readers all over the world, wherever Mormonism was taught, to believe that the second Mormon prophet (who had 55 wives and 53-57 children [Wikipedia]) was a monogamist. Those particular correlated materials failed to mention Brigham's "wives," "children" or "polygamy."

[5]James E. Talmage, an important Mormon scholar and an Apostle, was implicated in the effort to obliterate evidence of Mormonism's checkered past from "the minds and materials of believers." In 1930, the Church published a "small volume" titled "Latter-day Revelations," edited by Apostle Talmage. It was a highly "selective version of the Doctrine and Covenants." Talmage described that incredible effort at suppression in these terms: It was intended "to make the strictly doctrinal parts of the Doctrine and Covenants of easy access and reduce its bulk" by choosing then to include "only the sections comprising scriptures of general and enduring value." "Ninety-five of the sections . . . were completely

Oliver Cowdery first learned about polygamy when they translated the Book of Mormon in 1829.[6] The first presently known written revelation on the subject of polygamy dated July 17, 1831, predated the fraudulent monogamous recitals described in Section 101 of the Doctrine and Covenants in 1835 by several years.[7] The 1831 revelation was not included in the Doctrine and Covenants and to this author's knowledge has never been officially published. Joseph Fielding Smith (who admitted the existence of such a revelation) refused to allow Fawn McKay Brodie, Joseph's biographer, to examine the manuscript in 1943.[8] Leonard Arrington, an LDS Church Historian, understood that the origins of the doctrine of

---

omitted – *most notably section 132 on plural and celestial marriage* – along with parts of" no less than twenty-one other sections. "Twenty complete sections were retained along with parts of 21 others." ("Doctrine and Covenants" [accessed 1 December 2015], available from https://en.wikipedia.org/wiki/ Doctrine_ and_Covenants; Internet, p. 3 of 36). These cynical omissions speaking to faith-defeating foundations angered the Fundamentalists (Fundamentalists were more important then). They were particularly offended by the exclusion of Section 132, the revelation on polygamy, and they accused the Church of "changing the scriptures." This particular effort, intended to scrub various less defensible narratives, failed because Church President Heber J. Grant (a polygamous prophet) "ordered the withdrawal of the book from sale with the remaining copies shredded in order to 'avoid further conflict with the fundamentalists.'" (Ibid.). Grant wanted this effort to be forgotten (blotted out of the minds and memories of those who knew of it).

[6]Brigham Young, Charles L. Walker Diary (Harold B. Lee Library, Brigham Young University, 1855-1902), 25-26.

[7]Doctrine and Covenants (1835), Section 101, "Marriage."

[8]"Joseph F. [Fielding] Smith, Jr., the present historian of the Utah Church, asserted to me [Fawn McKay Brodie] in 1943 that a revelation foreshadowing polygamy had been written in 1831, but that it had never been published. In conformity with church policy, however, he would not permit the manuscript, which he acknowledged to be in possession of the church library, to be examined." (Fawn M. Brodie, *No Man Knows My History: The Life of Joseph Smith the Mormon Prophet*, 2d ed., rev. and enl. [New York, NY: Alfred A. Knopf, 1972], 184 n *). What is known about the contents of the revelation is found in a letter sent to Brigham Young by W.W. Phelps. "Phelps reported that on 17 July 1831, the Lord told Joseph 'It is my will . . . ye should take unto you wives of the Lamanites and Nephites . . . .' Phelps then said that he asked Joseph three years later how this commandment could be fulfilled. Joseph replied, 'In the same manner that Abraham took Hagar and Keturah; and Jacob took Rachel, Bilhah and Zilpha, *by revelation*.'" (W.W. Phelps, *Letter to Brigham Young*, 1861, original in Church Archives, cited by B. Carmon Hardy, *Doing the Works of Abraham: Mormon Polygamy – Its Origin, Practice, and Demise*, vol. 9 of *Kingdom in the West: The Mormons and the American Frontier* [Norman, OK: The Arthur H. Clark Company, 2007], 36-37).

plural marriage were early and insistent. "In 1831, while studying the Old Testament with Oliver Cowdery, Joseph Smith became persuaded that plural marriage was a biblical principle" (and that "God required it for the Latter-day Saints").[9]

In July 1842 Joseph Smith received a private revelation ("Verily thus saith the Lord") that affected some confidential friends (Newel, Elizabeth and Sarah Ann Whitney). In this revelation the Creator gave specific instructions pertaining to the marriage of the Whitneys' seventeen-year-old daughter, Sarah Ann, to the thirty-six-year-old Joseph Smith. Smith was just then the husband of about fifteen other wives, many of them polyandrous women already legally married to other men. The revelation directed to "my servant, N[ewel] K. Whitney" by God himself provided as follows:

> *[T]hese are the words which you shall pronounce upon my servant Joseph and your Daughter S.A. [Sarah Ann] Whitney. They shall take each other by the hand and you shall say, 'You both mutually agree,' calling them by name to be each other's companion so long as you both shall live, preserving yourselves for each other and from all others and also through-out eternity, reserving only those rights which have been given to my servant Joseph by revelation and commandment and by legal authority in times passed....*[10]

---

[9]Leonard J. Arrington, *Brigham Young: American Moses* (New York: Knopf, 1985), 100.

[10]Joseph Smith, Revelation, 27 July 1842 (Nauvoo, IL), Archives, Historical Department, Church of Jesus Christ of Latter-day Saints (Salt Lake City, UT), reproduced with stylistic improvements at Todd Compton, *In Sacred Loneliness: The Plural Wives of Joseph Smith* (Salt Lake City: Signature Books, 2001), 348-49. "[T]he thing . . . which you have agreed upon is right in mine eyes and shall be rewarded upon your heads with honor and immortality and eternal life to all your house, both old and young because of the lineage of my Priesthood, saith the Lord, it shall be upon you and upon your children after you from generation to generation, by virtue of the holy promise which I now make unto you, saith the Lord." (Ibid., 348). "I [N.K. Whitney] . . . give you, S.A. [Sarah Ann] Whitney, my daughter, to Joseph Smith, to be his wife, to observe all the rights between you both that belong to that condition." (Ibid.). "The references to 'posterity' and the 'rights' of marriage suggest that the union would have a physical dimension,

Those rights reserved to Joseph (but not to Sarah) included the taking of other partners.

Joseph was sealed (bonded for eternity) to Sarah Ann Whitney, his sixteenth plural wife, long before he was sealed to Emma Hale Smith, his first and only legal wife. It is most unlikely that Sarah Ann Whitney and her malleable parents knew in July 1842 that the Mormon prophet was already married to fifteen other women not including Emma or Fanny Alger. Sarah, who agreed to preserve herself for Joseph and from all others, could not but have known that he was already married to Emma, that she wasn't going to be his only wife, or his legal wife. She knew the marriage would have to be kept secret; that he would not publicly acknowledge her; that she would not live in his home with Emma and the children; that she couldn't tell Emma or anyone else that she had married him and needn't expect support. She knew that her marriage to him was for both *time* and *eternity*, and that there was, in her particular case and whatever the *Times and Seasons* either then or later said, a "secret wife system" in the City of Joseph, Nauvoo, Illinois.

Joseph and Emma were not the first Nauvoo couple to be "sealed" in marriage for eternity. They were not sealed to each other until 28 May 1843. Sarah Ann Whitney, who was then only seventeen, was sealed to Joseph Smith on 27 July 1842, well ahead of Emma, as were more than twenty of his other wives. Jesus told Newel to say to Joseph and Sarah that, "You both mutually agree . . . to be each others companion so long as you both shall live . . . and also through [o]ut all eternity."[11]

THE TIMES AND SEASONS CERTIFICATES

In 1830 Joseph Smith published two different statements over the names of eleven different witnesses, three of whom said that they saw the golden plates and an angel, heard the voice of God and knew that the Book of Mormon was true. Eight others said they saw and handled some engraved plates which had "the appearance

---

consistent with the evidence for Joseph's other marriages." (Ibid., 349, editorial comment).

[11]Ibid.

of ancient work, and of curious workmanship."[12] The statements of Joseph's witnesses, despite the sound and fury that attended them, were not separately written, sworn, signed or notarized. And the gold plates, as seen in retrospect, proved to have been superfluous. The murder of Laban, a crime committed to secure the possession of the golden plates, is accordingly seen to have served no discernible purpose.

On September 1 and October 1, 1842, Joseph Smith produced and published – after receiving what were publicly unreported revelations on polygamy in 1829, 1831 and 1842 in each of three different decades – *Recitals* (September 1) and *"Certificates"* (October 1) that unequivocally endorsed monogamous marriage. Monogamous marriage had been described as Mormon truth in the Doctrine and Covenants in 1835 (Doctrine and Covenants 101). The October 1, 1842, *Certificates* published in the *Times and Seasons* included the statements of twelve prominent Mormon men and nineteen prominent Mormon women, plus an editorial note attributed to the prophet Joseph Smith. These witnesses (and their indispensable sponsor, *Times and Seasons* editor Smith) endorsed monogamy "without qualification" and rejected anything else. They certified and declared that all Mormon marriages were public and recorded by a clerk, that there were no secret wives, that there was no secret system, and that the "only" rule or system of marriage "practised in the Church" was that found in the book of Doctrine and Covenants. All of that was graphically described in an Article on Marriage prepared by Oliver Cowdery and two other prominent presiding elders. The carefully drafted article on marriage included the following important provision: *"Inasmuch as this church of Christ has been reproached with the crime of fornication, and polygamy: we declare that we believe, that one man should have one wife; and one woman, but one husband, except in case of death, when either is at liberty to marry again."*[13] "The Article on Marriage was printed [and canonized] in the 1835 D&C

---

[12]Book of Mormon, Testimony of Witnesses. Five of the eight witnesses, excluding Joseph Smith's father and two of his brothers, and all of the three special witnesses, those who said they heard the voice of God, left the Church. Two of the three didn't return until after the death of Joseph Smith. Five of the other eight didn't return at all.

[13]Doctrine and Covenants (1835), Section 101, emphasis added.

[Doctrine and Covenants] as section 101 and in the 1844 D&C [Doctrine and Covenants] as section 109."[14]

These recitals describing monogamous marriage in the Doctrine and Covenants were not removed when the practice of polygamy was publicly admitted in the isolated Utah Territory in 1852. They survived that remarkable admission to be retained, truth be damned, in the Doctrine and Covenants from 1835 to 1876. The provisions that endorsed monogamous marriage in 1835 in Section 101 were repeated verbatim in a second edition in 1844 in Section 109 (after the great revelation on polygamy in 1843 and the death of Joseph Smith in 1844) and in every edition and printing that occurred over the next thirty-two years under the supervision of President Brigham Young. Until 1876, when Section 132 (the Polygamic Revelation) replaced Section 109 (the Official Declaration on Monogamy), the Book of Doctrine and Covenants provided that a man should have one wife and a woman but one husband, that "all marriages in this church" "should be solemnized in a public meeting," and that couples should keep themselves "wholly for each other, and from all others" during their lives. The "clerk of every church" was then supposed to keep a public record of the marriages solemnized in his branch so nothing was secret. The principal author of those deceptive provisions, provisions deceptive *ab initio*, was Oliver Cowdery, Joseph Smith's prominent colleague and one of the Three Witnesses to the Book of Mormon.

Joseph Smith's Public Response to Dr. John C. Bennett

John C. Bennett got in the way of Joseph's sexual consent relationship approach, followed by Joseph's sacred plural marriage approach, to Sidney Rigdon's daughter, Miss Nancy Rigdon. The two men got at cross purposes when Bennett, a particular friend of the Rigdons, failed to produce (and in fact discouraged) the young woman's good offices in advance of an unusual meeting meant to discuss a plural marriage proposal tendered by the Mormon

---

[14]"1835 Doctrine and Covenants denies polygamy – D&C 101 (original)" (accessed 15 December 2015), available from https://www.fairmormon.org/answers /Mormonism_and_polygamy/1835_Doctrine_and_Covenants_denies_polygamy; Internet, p. 1.

prophet. Bennett had historically done what Joseph did at first, before Joseph determined that the consent of some of the women couldn't be gotten outside of a ceremony and without a marriage. "Bennett performed no ceremonies; neither did he teach that marriage vows were needed prior to conjugal relations."[15] Twelve of Joseph Smith's affiliations appear to have been unwitnessed and off the record unofficial.

On September 1, 1842, as a preface to the nothing-but-traditional-marriage *Certificates* published over the names of thirty-one witnesses in the *Times and Seasons* on October 1, 1842, it was announced that,

> *Inasmuch as the public mind has been unjustly abused through the fallacy of Dr. Bennett's letters, we make an extract on the subject of marriage, showing the rule of the church on this important matter. The extract is from the Book of Doctrine and Covenants, and is the only rule allowed by the church.*[16]

> *"All legal contracts of marriage made before a person is baptized into this church, should be held sacred and fulfilled. Inasmuch as this church of Christ has been reproached with the crime of fornication, and polygamy: we declare that we believe, that one man should have one wife; and one woman, but one husband, except in case of death, when either is at liberty to marry again.*[17]

---

[15]Brian Hales, *Joseph Smith's Polygamy, Volume 1: History* (Salt Lake City, UT: Greg Kofford Books, 2013), 189.

[16]*Times and Seasons*, vol. III no. 21 (1 September 1842), 909, emphasis added.

[17]Doctrine and Covenants (1835), quoted in *Times and Seasons*, vol. III no. 21 (1 September 1842), 909, emphasis added. As published in the *Elders' Journal* in July 1838, Joseph Smith reported as follows: "Do the Mormons believe in having more wives than one? No, not at the same time. But they believe that if their companion dies, they have a right to marry again." (*History of the Church*, 3:28). And to be sealed again. Mormon men in the twenty-first century may, in the event of the death of a wife, be married and sealed to another woman besides their deceased companion for time and eternity. If that next woman is not already sealed to someone else. Five modern Mormon prophets (since the suspension of polygamy) have been sealed (bonded for eternity) to another woman or women in rites intended to govern in a Mormon afterlife.

The clever *Certificates* soon to follow were in response to various allegations made and published in the secular press outside of Nauvoo by Joseph's greatly honored but suddenly estranged former confidant, Dr. John C. Bennett. William Law, who replaced Hyrum Smith in the First Presidency, believed that before their falling out John C. Bennett was more in the secret confidence of Joseph than perhaps any other man in the city. Bennett proved he was well informed when he correctly published the initials of some of Joseph's previously unknown plural wives in a newspaper in Springfield, Illinois, after he and Smith had quarreled. Smith denied Bennett's representations.

Ann Eliza Young – probably best known as Brigham Young's hell-hath-no-fury-take-no-prisoners-ex-wife, but in fact a decent, literate capable woman – described John C. Bennett as "one of the first persons to be initiated into the plural-wife doctrine, if not indeed Joseph's confederate in producing it . . . ." "[T]he pupil fairly outran the teacher, and his success as special pleader for the system of Celestial Marriage was so decided that he incurred the displeasure of the Prophet, and they quarrelled violently." Ann Eliza's father, Chauncey G. Webb, a tutor to Joseph and Emma's children, superintended the humiliating exit of Fanny Alger from the Kirtland community in the 1830s after what Oliver Cowdery described as a "dirty, nasty, filthy, affair" (which may have involved a pregnancy), and after a transaction (or transactions) Emma Smith described as adultery. Cowdery's inflammatory words, directed to the relationship between Smith and his teenage paramour, preceded Cowdery's unsettling excommunication. Bennett and Smith argued about Miss Nancy Rigdon. Cowdery and Smith argued about Miss Fanny Alger. Ann Eliza (Young) suggested that Bennett "taught the doctrine to some ladies whom Smith had intended to convert himself," causing "a rupture."[18] George D. Smith, an expert on Nauvoo Polygamy, opined "that Bennett's alliances were expunged from the record."[19] It would be interesting to review them now.

---

[18]Ann Eliza Webb (Dee) (Young), quoted in George D. Smith, *Nauvoo Polygamy: " . . . but we called it celestial marriage"* (Salt Lake City: Signature Books, 2008), 263.
    [19]Ibid.

The Certificates in Full

Measured against that daunting past, Joseph Smith, the Editor of the *Times and Seasons* (an official publication of the Church of Jesus Christ of Latter-day Saints), published this introduction to those controversial *Certificates* on October 1, 1842:

> *We have given the above rule of marriage [Section 101 of the 1835 Doctrine and Covenants published in the Times and Seasons on 1 September 1842] as the only one practiced in this church, to show that Dr. J.C. Bennett's "secret wife system" is a matter of his own manufacture; and further to disabuse the public ear and shew that the said Bennett and his misanthropic friend Origen Bachelor, are perpetrating a foul and infamous slander upon an innocent people, and need but be known to be hated and despised. In support of this position, we present the following certificates . . . .*[20]

FOR THE MEN: October 1, 1842

> *We the undersigned members of the church of Jesus Christ of Latter-Day Saints and residents of the city of Nauvoo, persons of families do hereby certify and declare that we know of no other rule or system of marriage than the one published from the Book of Doctrine and Covenants, and we give this certificate to show that Dr. J.C. Bennett's "secret wife system" is a creature of his own make as we know of no such society in this place nor never did.*

S. Bennett,	N.K. Whitney,
George Miller,	Albert Pettey,
Alpheus Cutler,	Elias Higbee,
Reynolds Cahoon,	John Taylor,
Wilson Law,	E. Robinson,
W. Woodruff,	Aaron Johnson

---

[20] *Times and Seasons*, vol. III no. 21 (1 October 1842), 939, emphasis added.

FOR THE WOMEN: October 1, 1842

We the undersigned members of the ladies' relief society, and married females do certify and declare that we know of no system of marriage being practised in the church of Jesus Christ of Latter Day Saints save the one contained in the Book of Doctrine and Covenants, and we give this certificate to the public to show that J.C. Bennett's "secret wife system" is a disclosure of his own make.

Emma Smith, President,
Elizabeth Ann Whitney, Counsellor,
Sarah M. Cleveland, Counsellor,
Eliza R. Snow, Secretary,

Mary C. Miller,	Catharine Pettey,
Lois Cutler,	Sarah Higbee,
Thirza Cahoon,	Phebe Woodruff,
Ann Hunter,	Leonora Taylor,
Jane Law,	Sarah Hillman,
Sophia R. Marks,	Rosannah Marks,
Polly Z. Johnson,	Angeline Robinson.
Abigail Works,[21]	

DOCTRINE AND COVENANTS, 1835-1876

The thirty-one witnesses sponsored by *Times and Seasons* Editor Joseph Smith "certify and declare" that the only rule of marriage in the LDS Church is the rule described in the Book of Doctrine and Covenants, the pertinent provisions of which may be stated as follows:

PRINCIPLE ONE: The Rule of Marriage in the Mormon Church Is Monogamy

Inasmuch as this church of Christ has been

---

[21] *Times and Seasons*, vol. 3 (1 October 1842), 940, emphasis added.

reproached with the crime of fornication, and polygamy: we declare that we believe, that one man should have one wife; and one woman, but one husband, except in case of death, when either is at liberty to marry again.

PRINCIPLE TWO: There Are No Secret Marriages; All Marriages in the Mormon Church Are Entered in Public

According to the custom of all civilized nations, . . . we believe, that all marriages in this church of Christ of Latter Day Saints, should be solemnized in a public meeting, or feast . . . at the solemnization, the persons to be married, standing together . . . shall be addressed, by the person officiating . . . he shall say, calling each by their names: "You both mutually agree to be each others' companion, husband and wife, observing the legal rights belonging to this condition; that is, keeping yourselves wholly for each other, and from all others, during your lives." And when they have answered "Yes," he shall pronounce them "husband and wife" in the name of the Lord Jesus Christ, and by virtue of the laws of the country and authority vested in him . . . ."[22]

We have given the above rule of marriage as the only one practised in this Church . . . .[23]

PRINCIPLE THREE: A Public Record Is Kept

The clerk of every church should keep a record of all marriages, solemnized in his branch.[24]

These unthreatening recitals remained in the Doctrine and Covenants from 1835 until 1876. That was through the reading of

---

[22]Doctrine and Covenants (1835), Section 101; Doctrine and Covenants (1844), Section 109, emphasis added.

[23]*Times and Seasons* enhancement, vol. III no. 23 (whole no. 59; 1 October 1842), 939, emphasis added.

[24]Doctrine and Covenants (1835), Section 101, emphasis added.

the polygamic revelation received on July 12, 1843, to the members of the High Council on August 12, 1843, through a new edition of the Doctrine and Covenants in 1844, and forty years of publications and printings, including one in 1845 and another in 1846. For twenty-four years after the Church publicly announced from the pulpit in the old tabernacle bowery in the isolated Utah Territory that it was practicing polygamy (the disclosure made in 1852), these disingenuous provisions held their station in Mormonism's most sacred scriptures in what was the larger world through every kind of contingency. According to Doctrine and Covenants 101 (until 1844), and Doctrine and Covenants 109 (until 1876), the written representations prescribed that all marriages were to be performed in a public place. In 1835 and for as long as Joseph Smith lived, and for a long time after he died, plural marriages were always entered in secret. T.B.H. Stenhouse, a recovering polygamist watching these developments,[25] reported how the failure to change the revelations to match the polygamous facts actually worked: "[T]he missionaries cited it [Section 109 after 1844 as reported above] in sermons and published it from the press in every country where Mormonism was taught." "[I]t [Section 101 in 1835, Section 109 in 1844] has been used by the apostles in the Mormon Church for many years . . . after they well knew that its use was a direct deception and falsehood."[26]

One particularly egregious example of the use of those provisions (in this case Section 109) for deception involved the Mormon Apostle John Taylor, who following Brigham Young became the

---

[25]Stenhouse was plurally married to Belinda Pratt, a daughter of Parley P. Pratt. He was sealed to Carrie Grant, the deceased sister of Heber J. Grant, and he was engaged for fifteen months to Zina Young, the daughter of Brigham Young and Zina Diantha Huntington (Jacobs) (Smith) (Young), one of four generational Zinas. Zina Young, Stenhouse's fiancé, the daughter of Zina Huntington (Jacobs) (Smith) (Young) and Brigham Young, was the product of a sexual polyandrous union.

[26]T.B.H. Stenhouse, *The Rocky Mountain Saints: A Full and Complete History of the Mormons, from the First Vision of Joseph Smith to the Last Courtship of Brigham Young* (New York, NY: D. Appleton and Company, 1873), 193. For nearly a quarter of a century Brigham "preserved that falsehood in the 'Book of Covenants,' notwithstanding the opportunities he had of removing it in the several editions of the book that have been published under his Presidency." "Unfortunately, it is now very clearly evident that those very passages upon marriage were written purposely for the deception of the public." (Ibid.).

third prophet. Taylor feigned indignation when a Protestant minister accused the Church of practicing polygamy in a public discussion at Boulogne-sur-mer, France, in a space Taylor had reserved for a public debate in *1850*. Joseph Smith had experimented with the rudiments of the controversial doctrine (and "this church of Christ" had been "reproached with the crime of fornication and polygamy") in Ohio and Missouri in the 1830s. Taylor was informed of the principle by Joseph Smith himself no later than *1841*.

Taylor started his practice of the principle (taking his first plural wife) in 1843. "We are accused here," Taylor said in 1850 in France, "of polygamy and actions the most indelicate, obscene, and disgusting, such as none but a corrupt and depraved heart could have contrived. These things," according to Taylor, a particularly accomplished deceiver, "were too outrageous to admit of belief . . . ."[27] Stretching hypocrisy to the stratosphere, Taylor then proceeded to read the "entire chapter upon [monogamous] marriage" as described in Section 109 of the Doctrine and Covenants. In that, by the indelicate use of outrage, he undoubtedly satisfied his innocent audience that "the Mormon Church had been vilely slandered by the accusation of polygamy."[28] When Taylor angrily reported to the audience in a hall he had rented that "one man should have one wife," and that all Mormon marriages were entered in public and recorded by a clerk, and that there was "no other rule or system of marriage" in the Church of Jesus Christ of Latter-day Saints, he had already secretly married (in addition to his legal wife, Leonora Agnes Cannon on January 28, 1833); Elizabeth Kaighan (December 12, 1843); Mary Cook (January 1, 1844); Ann Vowles (February 3, 1844); Jane Ballantyne (February 25, 1844); Annie Ballantyne (1844); Mercy Rachel Fielding (Thompson) (Smith) (1845); Mary Ann DeGroot Oakley (April 1845); Ann Hughlings (Pitchforth) (January 7, 1846); Mary Amanda Utley (January 17, 1846); Mary Ramsbottom (January 23, 1846); Lydia Dibble (Granger) (Smith) (January 30, 1846); Sarah Thornton (Coleman) (January 30, 1846); Sophia Whitaker (April 23, 1847); and Harriet Whitaker (December 4, 1847), a total of fifteen women who would bear him twenty-six children. In the

---

[27]Ibid., 194.
[28]Ibid., 195.

years that followed that utterly dishonest spectacle in France, Taylor married three more women who would ultimately produce nine additional children.[29]   John Taylor, a polygamous insider, a future prophet and one of the deputy editors of the *Times and Seasons*, personally (knowingly) signed the fraudulent *Certificates* published in the *Times and Seasons* on October 1, 1842, as did his legal wife, Leonora Taylor.

The disingenuous provisions Taylor described to his audience in 1850, recitals first authored by Oliver Cowdery and others in the 1835 edition of the Doctrine and Covenants, show Cowdery, the Book of Mormon scribe and one of the Three Witnesses, to have been – in collaboration with Smith – a sponsor of the monogamous marriage deceptions.

> The reader in re-perusing these short extracts from Cowdery's pen ["Inasmuch as this church of Christ has been reproached with the *crime* of fornication, and polygamy, we declare . . ."] will now perceive with greater force the double deceitfulness of their wording when it is observed that "crime" is only attached to the word fornication, but not to polygamy – "the *crime of fornication*, and polygamy." The Mormon apologist claims that the expression being "crime," and not "crimes," the condemnation is not attached to polygamy, but only to fornication. Grammatically, the apology is good; morally, it is very bad – a pious fraud, corrupting and degrading.
>
> The "witness," Cowdery, is further interesting. – "We declare," says he, "that one man should have one wife,["] and "one woman *but* one husband." The "*but*" is here cleverly put in. He designed to deceive under the guise of fairness. "One 'man should have one wife' (*at least 'one,'* is the after

---

[29]George D. Smith, *Nauvoo Polygamy*, 627-28.   When Taylor married Margaret Young (with whom he had nine children) in 1856, he was forty-seven and she was nineteen.   When Taylor married Josephine Elizabeth Roueche in 1886, he was seventy-eight and she was twenty-six.   Taylor's "Josephine" lived until 1943.

interpretation), and as many more as he should find it convenient to get, take, or acknowledge; and 'the woman *but* one husband.'" She, of course, was to be the monogamist of the family.[30]

The formerly faithful Stenhouse[31] – while considering Cowdery's clever deception – stated the obvious: "Mormonism was at this time a fearful tumult of contradiction and very doubtful morality."[32] Stenhouse recognized the invidious consequences of this institutionalized deception. "[T]he Mormon Church may never see the end of the denial of polygamy. It requires no profound study of human nature to comprehend to what that principle may extend. If once admitted to be justifiable, how frequently and to what other ends may it not be used? It is indeed a dangerous doctrine."[33]

JOSEPH SMITH, EDITOR-IN-CHARGE, TIMES AND SEASONS 19 FEBRUARY TO 15 NOVEMBER 1842

Three Latter-day Saint scholars associated with the Neil A. Maxwell Institute for Religious Scholarship at Brigham Young University in Provo, Utah, have examined the relationship of Joseph Smith to the *Times and Seasons* newspaper for the period of time directly concerned with this author's witness/signator/certificate analysis.[34]

---

[30]Stenhouse, *The Rocky Mountain Saints*, 194, emphasis retained.

[31]Thomas (T.B.H.) Stenhouse was a clerk in the Church Historian's office and a reporter for the *Deseret News.* "He became proprietor of Salt Lake's first newsstand, publisher of a short-lived literary magazine, university regent, Salt Lake postmaster, United States postal agent for the Intermountain West, patron of the Salt Lake Theatre, a cultural lecturer at the Seventies Hall, and eventually founder and publisher of the Salt Lake *Telegraph*, the city's first daily and at the time the most successful journal in the territory." (Ronald W. Walker, *Wayward Saints: The Godbeites and Brigham Young*, foreword by Jan Shipps [Urbana and Chicago: University of Illinois Press, 1998], 52). Stenhouse "often joined Brigham Young when he toured the outlying settlements and briefly exhorted the Saints during their meetings . . . ." (Ibid.). It was said of him that "his journalistic voice was undoubtedly the most powerful in the territory." (Ibid., 53). His daughter Clara became the fourth wife of Brigham Young's eldest son (Joseph A. Young).

[32]Stenhouse, *The Rocky Mountain Saints*, 198.

[33]Ibid., 192.

[34]Matthew Roper, Paul J. Fields and Atul Nepal, "Joseph Smith, the *Times and Seasons*, and Central American Ruins," *Journal of the Book of Mormon and Other Restoration Scripture*, vol. 22 no. 2 (2013), 85-97.

Their research, although applicable here, and while coincidental to the issues raised by this chapter, was not driven by these events.

While the Latter-day Saints lived in Nauvoo, Illinois, "John Stephens and Frederick Catherwood published *Incidents of Travel in Central America*, an illustrated report of the first discovery of ancient ruins in Central America by explorers. These discoveries caused great excitement among the Saints, and subsequently five editorials appeared in the *Times and Seasons* commenting on what these meant for the Church."[35] The authorship of those editorials (because they were not specifically signed) became an issue of interest ("historians have wondered if Joseph Smith penned them since he was the newspaper's editor at the time"). The authors of the report, seeking to address that question for reasons other than our own, offered "historical evidence" and "stylometric analysis" in support of their findings.

The possibilities assigned to the inquiry were limited to the names of three highly prominent early Mormon men: Joseph Smith, John Taylor and Wilford Woodruff (each of them a prophet in his time). The authors of the study chose to compare "the writing style in the editorials with the writing styles of Joseph Smith, John Taylor and Wilford Woodruff – the only men involved with the newspaper during the time the editorials were published." Since "the time the editorials were published" coincides with the time the *Times and Seasons Monogamous Marriage Certificates* (the issue of our concern) were also published, there is a kind of synchronization of simultaneous interests. The Abstract from the BYU report applies with equal force to the study here. "Both the historical and stylometric evidence point," the University's authors say, "toward Joseph Smith as the most likely author of the [unattributed] editorials."[36] (Taylor and Woodruff were the only other options). *"Even if he did not write them alone, he took full responsibility for the contents of the newspaper during his editorial tenure when he stated, 'I alone stand for it.'"*[37] What those authors have said in support of their findings applies to the publication of Joseph Smith's

---

[35]Ibid., Abstract.

[36]Two of the editorials were signed "Ed." "(presumably indicating editor) and three [were] left unsigned." (Ibid., 86).

[37]Ibid., Abstract, emphasis added.

fraudulent *Certificates*. "Matt Roper, Paul Fields and Atul Nepal have applied the latest iteration of computer analyses to the unsigned editorials that *appear in 1842* in the *Times and Seasons*." With the passage of time these analyses "have become more sophisticated and more accurate." While not entirely certain the accuracy of such findings is "still relegated to probability."[38]

1842 Findings Applicable to This Study

On June 15, 1841, when the Latter-day Saints in Nauvoo "became aware of Stephens and Catherwood's [Central American] discoveries, the *Times and Seasons* "was under the editorship of the Prophet's brother Don Carlos Smith and Robert B. Thompson . . . ."[39] "[T]he first issue of the *Times and Seasons* was printed in November 1839 under the editorship of Ebenezer Robinson and . . . Don Carlos Smith. On 1 December 1840, this partnership was dissolved and Don Carlos became the sole editor of the paper." Robert B. Thompson then joined Don Carlos as an editor. Don Carlos died in August 1841 after which Ebenezer Robinson joined Thompson, who then also died twenty days later. Robinson, who then again became the editor, was joined by Gustavus Hills. "Both served as editors until early 1842."[40]

Don Carlos Smith knew about "spiritual wifery" (an early iteration of celestial marriage) before his death in August 1841, which was before Joseph's *Certificates* were published, and so did Ebenezer Robinson. In 1841 Don Carlos Smith told Ebenezer Robinson that "Any man who will teach and practice the doctrine of spiritual wifery will go to hell; I don't care if he is my brother Joseph."[41]

---

[38]Ibid., 85.
[39]Ibid., 85-86.
[40]Ibid., 88.
[41]Ebenezer Robinson reporting, reproduced in Compton, *In Sacred Loneliness: The Plural Wives of Joseph Smith*, 152. Don Carlos Smith, according to Ebenezer Robinson, was bitterly opposed to "the 'spiritual wife' doctrine which was being talked quite freely, in private circles, in his lifetime." Ina Coolbrith, his daughter, whose informational resource appeared to have been her mother, said that her father planned to leave Illinois in protest. "He quietly made plans to go back to Kirtland in 1842, and was only prevented by his death." (Ibid.). Ina's representations as to her father's intent were challenged by others, including her

Don Carlos referred to the new and unusual "doctrine" as "spiritual wifery." That was a more charitable descriptor for what is sometimes more accurately described as "a sexual consent relationship." On October 1, 1842, more than one year later, Ebenezer Robinson and his wife Angeline Robinson signed Joseph Smith's *Monogamous Marriage Certificates*,[42] adding their own informed names to Joseph's deception. On January 6, 1842, before the *Certificates* were published (on October 1, 1842), Joseph Smith secretly married Agnes Moulton Coolbrith (Smith), his sister-in-law and Don Carlos Smith's only recently widowed wife.[43]

In the fall of 1841, Joseph Smith became concerned about Robinson and Hill's ownership and operation of the paper. On January 28, 1842, the Lord instructed Joseph to "go and say unto the Twelve, that it is my will to have them take in hand the editorial department of the *Times and Seasons* . . . ."[44] The Creator of the Universe wanted those underperforming editors out ("thus saith the Lord"). On that same day Brigham Young "bought the printing establishment" for the Church. On February 3, 1842, the Quorum of the Twelve appointed John Taylor and Wilford Woodruff to edit the *Times and Seasons,* and to "take charge of the whole esstablishment [*sic*] under the direction of Joseph the Secr." "On 19 February 1842, Woodruff indicated that Joseph Smith had become the *Times and Seasons* editor." While Taylor "assists" Smith "in writing," Woodruff took charge "of the Business."[45] On

---

first cousin, Joseph F. Smith.

[42]Ebenezer Robinson, who signed Joseph's *Times and Seasons Certificate*, made this admission later in life: "We knew it ["spiritual wifery" or "polygamy"] was talked of *in secret*, and had been for more than a year . . . . These secret rumors could not constitute a knowledge that certain persons taught such things when they had not been taught to us." (Ebenezer Robinson, "Items of Personal History of the Editor," *The Return*, vol. 3 no. 2 [Davis City, IA: February 1891], 28).

[43]George D. Smith, *Nauvoo Polygamy*, 621. Don Carlos Smith died in August 1841. Agnes Coolbrith (Smith) (Don Carlos), (Smith) (Joseph), (Smith) (George Albert) married three Smiths and at least one other person. John C. Bennett, who knew of her secret marriage to Smith, correctly published her initials in a secular resource after he left Nauvoo.

[44]Joseph Smith Jr., *History of The Church of Jesus Christ of Latter-day Saints*, B.H. Roberts, ed., 2d ed., rev., (Salt Lake City: The Deseret Book Company, 1978), 4:503.

[45]Roper, Fields and Nepal, "Joseph Smith, the *Times and Seasons*, and Central

March 1, 1842, the Mormon prophet publically announced his hands-on editorship: "This [issue of the] paper commences my editorial career. I alone stand for it, and shall do for all papers having my signature henceforward. I am not responsible for the publication, or arrangement of the former paper; the matter did not come under my supervision."[46]

On April 1, 1842, Editor Joseph Smith published what became the 1838-39 Pearl of Great Price Account of the vision of the Father and the Son. This was the first American publication of what later became the founding story of the Church of Jesus Christ of Latter-day Saints. When Joseph Smith announced the vision in the semi-monthly *Times and Seasons* ("a miniature newspaper devoted to the interests of the Mormon people") on Friday, April 1, 1842, the "thunderbolt" laid "obscurely on page 748: God, the Creator of the Universe had visited the earth and in company with his Son, Jesus Christ, the Redeemer of the World!" As one of his first official editorial acts, *Times and Seasons* Editor Smith published his visionary masterpiece, an 1838-39 account ("dictated in 1838 and recopied in 1839") of an 1820 event first publicly described when it was published on April 1, 1842, in the *Times and Seasons* by that paper's editor, Joseph Smith. "This plain announcement, set in lower case and without fanfare, was one of the most astounding items ever to appear in an American publication."[47] *Six months later, on October 1, 1842, Smith published his fraudulent Times and Seasons Monogamous Marriage Certificates. Why would the Pearl of Great Price account of the vision of the Father and the Son be any more reliable than the utterly dishonest recitals described in Joseph Smith's Monogamous Marriage Certificates?*

Joseph's editorial endorsement, in which he "declares his willingness to endorse 'all papers having my signature henceforward' . . . is more than an endorsement of individual articles, but rather of all content in all issues of the newspaper for

---

American Ruins," 89.

[46]*Times and Seasons* 3/9 (1 March 1842): 718, quoted in Roper, Fields and Nepal, "Joseph Smith, the *Times and Seasons*, and Central American Ruins," 89, 97 n 26.

[47]LaMar Petersen, *The Creation of the Book of Mormon: A Historical Inquiry* (Salt Lake City: Freethinker Press, 2000), 1.

which he is listed as editor.   The term *papers* does not mean 'documents' in this context; it means issues of the newspaper published with Joseph as editor."[48] Joseph was responsible for "all content in all issues" from March 1, 1842, from April 1, 1842, from October 1, 1842, to November 12, 1842. His editorship, supported by his signature, thus clearly covered all of the time periods associated with the publication of the controversial *Certificates* dated October 1, 1842, signed by twelve men and nineteen women in unambiguous support of monogamous marriage and the publication of the 1838-39 Pearl of Great Price account of the vision of the Father and the Son.   Smith transferred "editorial responsibilities for the paper to John Taylor and Wilford Woodruff around 12 November 1842."[49]   Don Carlos Smith, Ebenezer Robinson, Gustavus Hills, Joseph Smith, John Taylor and Wilford Woodruff, all *Times and Seasons* editors and leaders of the Church, knew about spiritual marriage and polygamy before Joseph Smith published his *Monogamous Marriage Certificates* over the names of more than thirty witnesses (including those of Robinson, Taylor, Woodruff and each of their wives) in the fall of 1842.

The Mormon authors make the case that Joseph's title as editor "was not an empty one." They note "that he read page proofs" and that he "sometimes collected and supplied content material to be used for the paper." They emphasized the obvious: "Regardless of who wrote the *Times and Seasons* editorials linking the Book of Mormon to Central America [their specific cherished objective], it is difficult to argue that Joseph Smith was unaware of or would have disapproved of the content of the editorials."[50] Or of the *First Vision*. Or of the *Monogamous Marriage Certificates*. Because of some untimely illness affecting John Taylor and Wilford Woodruff, it is suggested "that the Prophet must have had to bear alone the full editorial burdens during an extensive period of time" in August and September of 1842, dates that coincide more nearly simultaneously with the preparation and publication of the nefarious *Certificates*.[51]

---

[48]Roper, Fields and Nepal, "Joseph Smith, the *Times and Seasons*, and Central American Ruins," 89, emphasis retained.
[49]Ibid.
[50]Ibid.
[51]Ibid.

Among the various conclusions drawn by the Maxwell Institute's authors, these stand out:

> *Joseph Smith was the editor of the Times and Seasons from about 19 February to 15 November 1842, at which point he announced in the Times and Seasons that John Taylor was taking over as editor.*

> *Between February and November 1842, the only men said to be working in the printing office were Joseph Smith, John Taylor, and Wilford Woodruff. [All of those men were conversant for all of that time with the doctrine of polygamy, in the case of Joseph Smith for more than ten years.]*

> *While acting as editor, Joseph Smith took full responsibility for the content of the material published in the Times and Seasons. Although he may have received "assistance in writing" from John Taylor, Joseph Smith authored articles "with his pen."*[52]

After scientific stylometric analysis, the authors of this Mormon study concluded that "the evidence points to Joseph Smith as the author of the Central American editorials [and as the man in charge of the entirety of the content of the *Times and Seasons*]." "We conclude that Joseph was not editor in name only but was an active and conscientious participant in the work of writing as well as of editing the *Times and Seasons*, although he was influenced by his two apostolic brethren."[53]

> *Even if the Central America editorials were a collaborative work, that still does not reduce the authoritative nature of the statements in the articles since Joseph clearly stated that he took full responsibility for what was published in the paper under his editorship. So, whether he penned the words in their entirety or only partially or even not at all, he authorized the publication of the words and*

---

[52]Ibid., 91.
[53]Ibid., 94-96.

thereby made them his own, since he stated about the content of the paper, "I alone stand for it."[54]

"Joseph Smith was the Editor of the *Times and Seasons*" when it emphatically publicly denied *"everything* that he was privately revealing and practicing in 1842 regarding marriage."[55]

JANUARY 1844: THE LATTER-DAY SAINTS MILLENNIAL STAR

In *January 1844*, less than six months before the death of Joseph Smith and approximately six months after he received the revelation on polygamy on July 12, 1843, another Mormon periodical – the *Millennial Star* published in the English mission – reported that,

> *[W]e as a church believe that all legal contracts of marriage, made before a person is baptized into this church should be held sacred and be fulfilled. Inasmuch as this church of Christ has been reproached with the crime of fornication and polygamy we declare that we believe that one man should have but one wife and one woman but one husband except in case of death when either is at liberty to marry again . . . .*[56]

"The *Latter-day Saints Millennial Star* (usually shortened to *Millennial Star*) was the longest continuously published periodical of The Church of Jesus Christ of Latter-day Saints . . . ."[57] It was

---

[54]Ibid., 96, emphasis added.

[55]D. Michael Quinn, "Evidence for the Sexual Side of Joseph Smith's Polygamy," presented to the Mormon History Association's Annual Conference (Calgary, Alberta, Canada: 29 June 2012; expanded, finalized 31 December 2012; circulated mid-2013), 6, emphasis added.

[56]*Millennial Star*, vol. 4 no. 9 (January 1844), 144, emphasis added. "We wish these doctrines to be taught by all that are in the ministry, that the people may know our faith respecting them, and also to correct the public mind in respect to the church . . . ."

[57]"Millennial Star" (accessed 8 September 2014), available from https://en.wikipedia.org/wiki/Millennial_Star; Internet, p. 1 of 4.

circulated in England from 1840 until 1970. Its editors have included, among many others, such Mormon luminaries as Parley P. Pratt (a missionary to the Lamanites in 1831), Orson Hyde, Orson Spencer, Orson Pratt, Franklin D. Richards, Albert Carrington and George Reynolds. Every one of those men was, or would become, a practicing polygamist.

By January 1844, when these fraudulent statements were published for the instruction of the English Saints (who didn't learn about polygamy until 1852), Joseph Smith had "married" about thirteen or fourteen previously married women, legal wives of other husbands, most of them faithful Mormons, starting with Mrs. Zina Diantha Huntington (Jacobs) on October 27, 1841, and ending with a somewhat less than certain Mrs. Phebe Watrous (Woodworth) sometime before October 29, 1843.[58] By January 1844, Smith had tendered unsuccessful proposals of marriage, or something less official and encumbering than marriage, to no less than four other highly visible prominent married Mormon women (Mrs. Orson Pratt, Mrs. Hiram Kimball, Mrs. William Law, Mrs. Robert D. Foster). These marriages, sealings, relationships and rejections, adversely affecting all civil covenants (commitments and proposals antagonistic to "the laws of the country"), served to show just how *sacred* Joseph held "*all legal contracts of marriage, made before a person is baptized into this church*," and just how serious he was to see that "*all legal contracts of marriage*" were "*sacred*" and should "*be fulfilled.*"

By January 1844, when this monogamous marriage piece was deceitfully published in the *Millennial Star* addressed to the unsuspecting British, Joseph Smith had married no less than thirty-eight women, starting with Emma Hale (Smith), his legal wife, on January 18, 1827, and ending with Fanny Young (Carr Murray) on November 2, 1843.[59] These so-called marriages performed without civil deputization served to show just how closely Joseph followed the only rule or system of marriage allowed by the church, specifically that "one man should have *but* one wife and one woman *but* one husband except in case of death . . . ." The English publication corrected the unscrupulous "*buts*" by making them

---

[58]George D. Smith, *Nauvoo Polygamy*, 621-23.
[59]Ibid., 621-23.

gender neutral but no less dishonest. The depth and breadth of the disingenuous deception is stunning.

By January 1844, after the polygamous revelation in July 1843 and until the death of Joseph Smith in June 1844, the highest leaders of the Mormon Church conspired to continue to mislead the English Saints. While that practice continued across the board and through 1852, Joseph Smith, Hyrum Smith, William Smith, John Smith, Brigham Young, John Taylor, Joseph C. Kingsbury, Isaac Morley, Joseph B. Noble, Reynolds Cahoon, William Clayton, William D. Huntington, Orson Hyde, Benjamin F. Johnson, Heber C. Kimball, Vinson Knight, Parley P. Pratt, Willard Richards, Ebenezer C. Robinson, Edwin D. Woolley, Levi Hancock, Lorenzo D. Young and various carefully selected others *had all been secretly plurally married*. Every one of them, every one of their plural wives, every woman who rejected them, every one of the thirty-eight plural wives of Joseph Smith, every woman who rejected him, every member of the First Presidency, every Apostle, all fifteen members of the Nauvoo High Council, the presidents of the Nauvoo stake, and many legal wives knew that the "only rule allowed by the church" was not monogamy, that "all legal contracts of marriage" were not "sacred" and weren't "fulfilled," that one man didn't have but one wife, that some women didn't have but one husband, that the leaders married girls of tender age and the wives of other men, and that there was a "secret wife system" that heavily favored the prophet's most obedient, specially favored disciples. Secret alliances ("sexual consent relationships") were not uncommon as the Nauvoo Stake High Council records reflect. Not one of the members of this leadership "clique," this Quorum of the Anointed, stepped forward (whether early or late) to challenge the egregious deceptions published in the *Millennial Star* in January of 1844, or in the *Times and Seasons* in October of 1842. Everyone who knew gave those monumental deceptions a pass. *Not one faithful Latter-day Saint stepped forward to say this isn't the way Christians do business.*

DECEIVERS-IN-CHIEF

Times and Seasons Editor Joseph Smith

There was one particular person who knew better than anyone and beyond a shadow of a doubt that the *Times and Seasons* recitals published in the fall of 1842 were thoroughly fraudulent; that the rule of marriage wasn't monogamy; that one man wasn't limited to one wife; that one wife wasn't limited to one husband; that there was "a secret wife system"; that plural marriages were never public and clerks didn't report them. Joseph Smith, who published the fraudulent *Certificates* (after he added his own personal acidic preface), knew that Mormonism's polygamous marriages were performed by men who could be trusted not to tell the truth, and that the leaders of the Church were indeed guilty of "the crime[s] of fornication and polygamy" under "the laws of the country." The civil marriages of adherents, like "the laws of the country," were ignored and disrespected. "Polyandry," a word used to describe Joseph's indefensible "marriages" to the legal wives of other men, was a gentrified term for "adultery." As was that other term, "spiritual wifery." One must believe that God himself was the author of Joseph Smith's polyandry, that Joseph's Lord approved of his temporal/spiritual usurpation of the already married wives and biological children of other men. That was what Joseph told every one of his victims.

Polygamy developed as a conspiracy. The principal conspirator and the author of the alleged restoration of the unsettling practice was the managing editor of the *Times and Seasons*. Joseph Smith was personally responsible for the publication's content. He published those dishonest propositions and that angry preface in opposition to polygamy and in supposed support of traditional monogamous marriage. In 1830 Joseph Smith produced eleven witnesses willing to say that the Book of Mormon was the word of God. In 1842 Joseph Smith produced thirty-one witnesses willing to say that monogamy ("one man . . . one wife") was the only rule of marriage "practised" in the Mormon Church. In 1842 Joseph Smith produced himself to say that "the Creator of the Universe had visited . . . earth . . . in company with his Son . . . the Redeemer of the World!" In 1844, when Joseph had no less than thirty-eight wives, and after he had privately circulated "the Polygamic Revelation" in 1843, the *Millennial Star* continued to report that "we declare that we believe that one man should have but one wife, and one woman but one husband, except in case of death . . . ."

Joseph said Jesus said this to the Church: "[N]either shall anything be appointed unto any of this church contrary to the church covenants. For all things must be done in order, and by common consent in the church . . . (D&C 28:12-13). Smith's secret polygamous initiatives contradicted his own revelations . . . ." One anonymous detractor put that unsettling dichotomy in incontestible terms: "Smith's attempt to have one 'approved' standard of behavior for public consumption, and an opposite secret 'unapproved' standard of behavior for the benefit of a few elite leaders" approached what "[t]hose of us who live on Planet Sane" call "hypocricy."[60]

Joseph's association with polygamous theology was foundational, both early and fervent. "There is evidence," according to a respected B. Carmon Hardy (D. Michael Quinn, Todd Compton), "that during the 1830's Smith inaugurated the practice of taking plural wives in his own private life. Although he shared his views on the subject with only a small number, some spoke and behaved too freely." That this reputation preceded the publication of the thoroughly dishonest *Certificates* by many years can be easily documented. "The prophet said the Mormon reputation was such that, on his way from Kirtland to Missouri [in 1838], he was asked 'a thousand times over and over again' if, among other things, Mormons took more wives than one."[61] The answer was of course and always no.

Managing Scarce Resources

In the early 1840s, long before *he* published *his Certificates* in October of 1842, Joseph Smith "courted" no less than five different

---

[60]Randyj, "Recovery from Mormonism" (accessed 2 December 2014); Internet, available from http://www.exmormon.org; Internet, p. 3.

[61]B. Carmon Hardy, *Solemn Covenant: The Mormon Polygamous Passage* (Urbana, Chicago: University of Illinois Press, 1992), 6.

women, four of them already married (Zina Diantha Huntington [Jacobs], Presendia Lathrop Huntington [Buell], Sarah Marinda Bates [Pratt], and Marinda Nancy Johnson [Hyde]). In 1832 Joseph Smith was accused of taking indecent liberties with sixteen-year-old Marinda Nancy Johnson[62] (a woman he secretly "married" in 1842 without her legal husband's knowledge or consent). Marinda's husband, Apostle Orson Hyde, was on a mission abroad when Joseph secretly married his wife. In addition to Miss Louisa Beaman, his first documented plural wife, he secretly married two of the four already married women in 1841, and Marinda Nancy Johnson (Hyde) one year later. Two of the married women (including Sarah Pratt, who rejected him) were the wives of prominent apostles serving where Joseph had sent them. Orson Hyde was on a mission to Palestine from April 1841 to December 1842. "Near the end of the year [1841]" when many of the brethren who were out of the country on foreign missions returned, "the Twelve or a part of them spent the day with Joseph the Seer & he unfolded to them many glorious things of the kingdom of God[,] the privileges & blessings of the priesthood &c."[63] "These were coded terms for celestial [plural] marriage, confirming that Smith was beginning to unfold the privilege of more wives to his closest colleagues."[64] *In 1841.*

---

[62]"[R]umors may have been circulating already as early as 1832 that Smith had been familiar with *fifteen-year-old* Marinda Johnson, a member of the family with which Smith lived in Ohio . . . ." Marinda Nancy Johnson, who was later married to Apostle Orson Hyde, became "one of Smith's plural [polyandrous] wives in Illinois" in 1842. It is reported that when Marinda was fifteen and Smith lived with her parents, "Smith was dragged out of the house by, it was said, Marinda's brothers, who tarred and feathered him." (George D. Smith, *Nauvoo Polygamy*, 44). On December 31, 1864, one of Marinda's brothers (Luke Johnson) described what has come to be called "The tar and feather incident" (Smith was tarred and feathered) and an aborted castration (Smith wasn't castrated). "[T]hey tore off the few night clothes he had on, for the purpose of emasculating him, and had Dr. Dennison there to perform the operation; but when the Dr. saw the Prophet stripped and stretched on the plank, his heart failed and he refused to operate." (Luke Johnson, "The History of Luke Johnson (By Himself)," *Deseret News* 8 [May 26, 1858]). These events occurred on 24 March 1832. Emma Smith knew about this disturbing episode.

[63]Wilford Woodruff, *Wilford Woodruff's Journal, 1833-1898: Typescript*, ed. Scott G. Kenney (Signature Books, 1983), 2:144.

[64]See *e.g.*, George D. Smith, *Nauvoo Polygamy*, 84 n 71. Author Smith reports that similar terminology ("coded language") appears in other resources, examples of which he then describes. (Ibid.).

When *Times and Seasons Editor* Joseph Smith published his *Times and Seasons Certificates* on 1 October 1842, he had already married seventeen women (thirteen of them in the nine or ten month period immediately preceding the publication of those highly visible reports). "Between January and August 1842, Joseph Smith . . . would also experience an increasing number of rejections."[65] In his polygamy opus, *In Sacred Loneliness, The Plural Wives of Joseph Smith*, Todd Compton "lists, but does not discuss, nineteen possible rejections (*Sacred Loneliness*, 2, 633-34)."[66] "Among his successful [*Pre-Certificate*] courtships were three widows, ten married women, and three single women." Smith's early emphasis was directed toward married women and widows. During this same period, January to August 1842, "Smith continued to propound the doctrine to his apostles."[67] He is said to have requested John Taylor and Heber C. Kimball to surrender their legal wives (Leonora and Vilate) in marriage to him. Jedediah Grant, who became a Counselor in the First Presidency some years after the death of Smith and during the reign of Brigham Young, described those tumultuous days in these terms:

> . . . *Did the Prophet Joseph want every man's wife he asked for? He did not . . . . The grand object in view was to try the people of God, to see what was in them. If such a man of God should come to me and say, "I want your gold or silver, or your wives," I should say, "Here they are, I wish I had more to give you, take all I have got." A man who has got the spirit of God, and the light of eternity in him, has no trouble about such matters.*[68]

---

[65]George D. Smith, *Nauvoo Polygamy*, 85-86.

[66]Ibid., 86 n 74.

[67]Ibid., 86.

[68]Apostle Jedediah M. Grant, Counselor to Brigham Young, sermon (The Power of God and the Power of Satan) delivered 19 February 1854, in *Journal of Discourses* (Liverpool, England: F.D. Richards, 1855-1886), 2:13-14, emphasis added. Jedediah Grant's last wife, Rachel Ridgeway Ivins (Grant), was sealed first to the deceased Joseph Smith (by proxy) "for eternity" because Brigham Young reckoned that she had been fancied by Smith during his lifetime. Young allowed her marriage to Jedediah Grant, but only for time. (D. Michael Quinn, *The Mormon Hierarchy: Origins of Power* [Salt Lake City: Signature Books in association with Smith Research Associates, 1994], 549). Rachel Ridgeway Ivins (Grant) (Smith) was the mother and Jedediah Grant was the father of Heber J.

Joseph did want the wives of twelve or thirteen other men he didn't always ask their husbands for, and he also wanted the fourteen-year-old daughter of Heber C. Kimball.

Joseph Smith married four or five young women, some of them already married, in those eight or nine months (1 January to 30 August 1842) that he had first met when he was an adult and they were teens or children. Sarah Ann Whitney was five years old when she met Joseph Smith in 1831 and he was twenty-five. Louisa Beaman was twelve in about 1827; Mary Elizabeth Rollins was twelve in 1831; Zina Huntington was fifteen in 1836; and Miranda Johnson was sixteen in 1831. Fanny Alger was thirteen and fourteen the year her family joined the Church in 1830. Joseph Smith married eight or nine other young women in about nine months (February 1843 to November 2, 1843) that he had first met when he was old and they were young. Nancy Winchester was six years old when she met Joseph Smith in about 1834 and he was twenty-eight. She was fourteen when they were married in 1843. Helen Mar Kimball was eight when she met Joseph Smith by 1836 and he was thirty. She was fourteen when they were married in 1843. Emily Partridge was seven in 1831; Eliza Partridge was ten in 1831; Sarah Lawrence was eleven in 1837; Maria Lawrence was thirteen in 1837; Melissa Lott was twelve in 1836; Flora Ann Woodworth was fourteen by 1841; and Lucy Walker was fifteen in 1841.[69] "By the time the Latter-day Saints settled in Illinois, the young women Joseph once met [often] as pre-teenagers had become old enough for him to marry."[70]

Joseph Smith as a Family Man

Joseph Smith is the author of the Mormon system of marriage, the architect of the Mormon concept of the family, and the man supposed to have received the Patriarchal Priesthood and the keys

---

Grant, who became the President of the Mormon Church from 1918 to 1945. Thus, Heber J. Grant was sealed "for eternity" to Joseph Smith, a man other than his biological father. His mother, married to Grant for time, was bonded to Smith for eternity.

[69]George D. Smith, *Nauvoo Polygamy*, 36.
[70]Ibid., 51.

to the sealing power from Elias and Elijah in the Kirtland Temple on April 3, 1836. The Mormon concept of the eternal family is of necessity the lengthened shadow of Joseph Smith. Near the end of his life, the super secret Council of Fifty elected Smith to the super secret office of King of the Kingdom of Israel on Earth. Latter Day Saints are obliged to live their lives to something more than Smith's less than exacting personal standards. Brigham Young described every faithful Saint's manifest destiny: "Joseph Smith holds the keys of this last dispensation . . . ." "[N]o man or woman in this dispensation will ever enter into the celestial kingdom of God without the consent of Joseph Smith."[71] Billions of Christians will have to stand in this line.

In 1842 (when he married thirteen women in nine or ten months), and until his death in 1844 (by which time he had married twenty-one additional women), Smith was laser-like obsessed with highly provocative plurality (with cafeteria-style relationships, with secret matrimonial alliances, unofficiated matrimonial alliances, sexual consent relationships, spiritual wives, mistresses, sealings, concubines,[72] polygyny and polyandry). "William Clayton said that during the last year of Joseph's life they were seldom together alone when the prophet did not talk about the subject."[73] "From him," Clayton reported, "I learned that the doctrine of plural and celestial marriage [the two are one] is the most holy and important doctrine ever revealed to man on the earth and that without obedience to

---

[71]"Intelligence, Etc." A Sermon delivered by Brigham Young on 9 October 1859, from *Journal of Discourses* (Liverpool, England: F.D. Richards, 1855-1886), 7:282-291, reproduced at *The Essential Brigham Young*, with a foreword by Eugene E. Campbell (Salt Lake City: Signature Books, 1992), 130.

[72]In the Book of Mormon the Lord associated polygamy with concubinage, both were treated as wicked practices. (Book of Mormon, Jacob 1:15). In the 1843 revelation that commanded polygamy, the still canonized suspended sentinel, Doctrine and Covenants Section 132, wives *and* concubines are both allowed. "Section 132 establishes polygamy as a virtuous higher law that is forever 'true' – no longer a time-sensitive practice. According to the new message, Abraham received concubines 'for his righteousness.' This was also true for David and Moses because 'in nothing did they sin' except in taking some wives without prior authorization (D&C 132:37-38)." (George D. Smith, *Nauvoo Polygamy*, 49). In early Mormonism, such consent came from Joseph Smith and Brigham Young. What didn't Joseph Smith and Section 132 allow?

[73]William Clayton, quoted by Hardy, *Solemn Covenant: The Mormon Polygamous Passage*, 7.

that principle no man can ever attain to the fullness of exaltation in the Celestial glory."[74]   That domestic canopy, by no means forgotten, is in a protected place biding its time. Polygamy was unlawful under the laws of the state of Illinois. Every polygamous marriage was a criminal offense, an extralegal undeputized act of defiance against the laws and statutes of the commonwealth (supposed to include injunctions against pedophilia, fornication, adultery, bigamy, polyandry and polygyny).

If the Federal Government hadn't punitively forced the issue late in the nineteenth century by making the practice of the polygamous principle objectively unpalatable, the Church would still be practicing the principle today, like the Fundamentalists, the true defenders of Joseph's polygamous domestic legacy, still do. The suspension of polygamy was painful and involuntary, but the future of the practice (the law of heaven) is clear and unequivocal. Hundreds of women sealed by proxy in the privacy of the temple to a deceased Smith are expected to share their prophet for eternity.[75] That is the future for Joseph Smith and his extended family, and for those who expect to follow him.

---

[74]Affidavit, William Clayton, 16 February 1874, CHL, MS 3423, quoted in Andrew Jenson, "Plural Marriage," *Historical Record* (July 1887), 6:225-26.

[75]In 1870 Apostle and future Church President Joseph F. Smith (Hyrum Smith's son) performs the proxy sealing of Scotland's Queen Maude as an eternal wife to the deceased prophet Joseph Smith. This Queen Mother was related to William the Conqueror (her mother was the niece of William the Conqueror) and her second husband was David I, King of the Scots. On 5 September 1870, Apostle and future Church President Wilford Woodruff sealed eight historical women, including Charlotte Corday (who murdered the radical Marat during the French Revolution) and Empress Josephine (the former wife of the Emperor Napoleon) to the deceased prophet Joseph Smith. On September 15, 1870, First Presidency Second Counselor Daniel H. Wells sealed two Catholic Saints as wives to the prophet, Saint Helena (the mother of the Roman emperor Constantine) and Saint Theresa from sixteen-century Spain. "These are the first women of international prominence sealed as wives to Joseph Smith, but during fifty years after his death hundreds of deceased women are similarly joined to him, even though many had husbands during their lifetimes." (D. Michael Quinn, *The Mormon Hierarchy: Extensions of Power* [Salt Lake City: Signature Books in association with Smith Research Associates, 1997], Selected Chronology, date 26 July 1870, 766).

More Is Good

In 1843, the year following the publication of the fraudulent *Times and Seasons Monogamous Marriage Certificates*, Smith (the King of the Kingdom of Israel on Earth, the Grand Marshal of Mormon Marriage, the author and architect of the Mormon family) proceeded to marry twenty-one additional women in nine months, making a grand total of at least thirty-eight wives.[76] Smith married thirty-four women in twenty-one or -two months in 1842 and 1843. His plural intentions bulging at the seams simply couldn't be contained.   Before Editor Smith published his *Monogamous Marriage Certificates* in the *Times and Seasons* in October 1842 ("we know of no system of marriage being practised in the church of Jesus Christ of Latter Day Saints save the one contained in the Book of Doctrine and Covenants . . . "), he had illegally[77] (and secretly) dually married no less than nine women who were supported in all things by other men to whom they were legally married, most of them faithful Latter-day Saints. Their names and the dates of those indefensible polyandrous relationships were Mrs. Zina Diantha Huntington (Jacobs), October 27, 1841; Mrs. Presendia Lathrop Huntington (Buell), December 11, 1841; Mrs. Lucinda Pendleton (Morgan) (Harris), about January 17, 1842; Mrs. Mary Elizabeth Rollins (Lightner), February 1842; Mrs. Sylvia Porter Sessions (Lyon), March 9, 1842; Mrs. Sarah Kingsley (Howe Cleveland), about March 1842; Mrs. Elizabeth Davis (G. Brackenbury Durfee), about March 1842; Mrs. Marinda Nancy Johnson (Hyde), April 1842; and Mrs. Sarah Rapson (Poulterer), about July 1842. About three of his other women were widows.

---

[76]George D. Smith, *Nauvoo Polygamy*, 621-23.

[77]By October 1842 (the date of the publication of the *Certificates*), Joseph Smith was already plurally married to many different women. Emma Smith was "Never reconciled to her husband's polygamous marriages . . . ." Joseph's legal wife, who was mostly out of the polygamous loop (for her the law of Sarah didn't apply), "was the first to claim that they [those other marriages] were *all* for 'eternity only' . . . ," according to Quinn. (Quinn, "Evidence for the Sexual Side of Joseph Smith's Polygamy," for Session #2A, *Reconsidering Joseph Smith's Marital Practices* at Mormon History Association's Annual Conference, [Calgary, Alberta, Canada, 29 June 2012], 20). Joseph was a bigamist under the law. None of his many plural marriages were civilly recognized.   In Illinois it was a crime to perform a ceremony for an illegal marriage. Those who did were criminals under the law.

By 27 June 1844 Smith, a man who laid claim to the *time* and
eternity principle, had taken to himself nine teenagers, including
two fourteen year olds, three sets of sisters, one and possibly two
sets of mothers and daughters, thirteen or fourteen polyandrous
women (wives of two men at the same time), one of his wife's Relief
Society Counselors, the daughter of a second Relief Society
Counselor, the Relief Society Secretary, and his deceased brother's
widow. In addition he admitted to and begged forgiveness for his
intimate relationship with Miss Fanny Alger, a tenth teenager and a
household helper who had lived with Joseph, Emma and the
children in Kirtland. There is no official contemporaneous record
to suggest that Joseph ever married Miss Alger. The accounts of
such a marriage are late, secondary, anecdotal, dishonest and
unconvincing.

"05 October, 1842 [*sic*, 1843] – Concerning 'the doctrine of plurality
of wives,' Smith's manuscript diary reads: Joseph forbids it and the
practice thereof. No man shall have but one wife." But Joseph
actually has about thirty-four wives on October 5, 1843. "When
incorporating Joseph Smith's journal into the History of the
Church, Apostle George A. Smith, a cousin [of Joseph Smith],
altered this passage ["No man shall have but one wife"] to reverse
this prohibition on polygamy."[78] This alteration of Joseph Smith's
manuscript diary entry was but one of a great number of
unwarranted additions and revisions made to Joseph Smith's
undependable history by this undependable relative and various
undependable others following the death of the Mormon founder.

Joseph and Emma Smith lied to themselves and others in
tumultuous times. "In an effort to counter the Reorganized
Church's use of these Nauvoo denials [and because Emma Smith
taught Joseph Smith's children that the doctrine of polygamy
originated with Brigham Young]," Joseph Fielding Smith, an
Assistant in the Church Historian's Office since 1901, asserted in
1905, adding his dishonesty to that of uncountable others: "'I have
copied the following from the Prophet's manuscript record of Oct.

[78]Mithryn (anonymous contributor), "Exploring Mormonism" (accessed 13
November 2014, posted 2 September 2013); Internet, available from https://
exploringmormonism.com/greg-trimble-the-word-is-adultery/, quoting Joseph
Smith's Manuscript Diary, 05 October 1842 [*sic*, 1843].

5, 1843 [Joseph's revelation on polygamy (Doctrine and Covenants 132) was read to the Nauvoo High Council on August 12, 1843], and know it is genuine . . . .'" Joseph Fielding Smith then quoted the amended Joseph Smith as follows: "'[A]nd I have constantly said no man shall have but one wife at a time unless the Lord directs otherwise.' The handwritten Nauvoo diary of Joseph Smith for 5 October 1843 actually ends: 'No men shall have but one wife.'"[79]

"Duped"

William Law came to Joseph Smith's defense in 1842 when the scandals surrounding Nancy Rigdon, Martha Brotherton, Joseph Smith, Brigham Young, Heber C. Kimball and John C. Bennett erupted. Law reassured the Saints that the leaders of the Church didn't condone "'spiritual wifery' or any such behavior." The Mormon prophet looked the other way when the terribly mistaken Law filed an Affidavit in 1842 stating "that Bennett, rather than Smith, was the originator of 'spiritual wifery.'"[80] Because Joseph didn't attempt to correct his then faithful disciple, he became the fortunate beneficiary of the decent man's good reputation. Smith rewarded Law by including him as one member of "the first small group of male initiates to the endowment ceremony in May 1842." When Law later learned the unsettling truth about the prophet's

---

[79]Joseph Fielding Smith, quoted by Joel B. Groat, "Joseph Smith Statements Denying Polygamy" from "Mormons in Transition" (Institute for Religious Research), 1.

[80]Randyj, "Recovery from Mormonism" (accessed 2 December 2014); Internet, available from http://www.exmormon.org; Internet, 2. When Law became apprised of the true facts, he spoke in different terms as follows: "The great mistake of my [life was my] having anything to do with Mormonism. I feel [it to] be a deep disgrace and never speak of it when I can avoid it; for over forty years I have been almost entirely silent on the subject and will so continue after [t]his. Accept my kind regards." (Letter to Dr. Wyl from William Law, Letter I, "Three Letters from William Law on Mormonism: An Honest Man's View and Remorse," *The Daily Tribune*, 3 July 1887 [Salt Lake City] [accessed 12 June 2018], available from http://www.william-law.org/publications/the-mormons-in-nauvoo-three-letters-from-william-law-on-mormonism-an-honest-mans-view-and-remorse-the-daily-tribune-salt-lake-city-july-3-1887; Internet, p. 3 of 8). On another occasion, Law reported that, "I got a black spot on my life, which shall pain me to the very last minute of my existence." ("Interview with Wm. Law, March 30, 1887," *Salt Lake Tribune* [1 July 1887]).

secret alliances, he filed a complaint charging Smith with adultery in a Hancock County Circuit Court. He also joined with others to support the publication of the ill-fated *Nauvoo Expositor*, a dissident newspaper destroyed by a Mormon mob. Law was strongly opposed to polygamy and driven to despair by its unexpected secret spokesman. This Second Counselor in the First Presidency, William Law, was a community resource heavily invested in his Mormon faith. In the year 2014 in one of its undated and unsigned essays, the Church made it clear, without ever saying so, that Law and his colleagues told the truth in the *Nauvoo Expositor* in 1844. The admission was reluctant, guarded, unpublicized, more than a hundred and fifty years late and not an apology.

Hyrum Smith made a mistake when he showed William Law the "revelation on celestial marriage" in the fall of 1843. The "revelation on celestial marriage" (Doctrine and Covenants, Section 132) is the revelation on polygamous marriage. Celestial marriage was polygamous marriage by nineteenth-century reckoning; those are synonymous terms. In a private conversation with William E. McLellin, Emma innocently called Section 132 "the Polygamic revelation." In that the prophet's wife was spot on. Hyrum allowed William to take the revelation on polygamy home and read it. Law and his wife Jane didn't accept the *new* and *everlasting* covenant.[81]

After she had signed *Smith's Monogamous Marriage Certificate* which was published on October 1, 1842, Joseph Smith approached Jane Law, the wife of William Law, and asked her to become one of his plural wives. He actually told her that she could keep half of her love for her husband William Law. Whereas the two men might have agreed to share Jane for time on earth, that didn't hold for eternity. In the afterlife she and all of those other women (and their children with their real husbands), because of their sealings, were bonded to Smith for eternity. In 1842 Joseph Smith told Nancy Rigdon that her marrying him "would not prevent her from marrying any other person."[82]   On May 13, 1844, William Law

---

[81]Richard S. Van Wagoner, *Mormon Polygamy: A History* (Salt Lake City: Signature Books, 1986), 63.

[82]John C. Bennett, *The History of the Saints: Or, an Expose of Joe Smith and Mormonism* (Boston: Leland & Whiting, 1842; photomechanical reprint of 1842 original, Salt Lake City: Modern Microfilm Company), 242.

wrote in his journal that "[Joseph] ha[s] lately endeavored to seduce my wife and ha[s] found her a virtuous woman."[83]   On May 23, 1844, William Law (whose wife Jane and brother Wilson Law had innocently signed *Smith's Times and Seasons Certificates*) filed his adultery complaint against Joseph Smith. The offended Law, who fell from grace when he discovered polygamy, and because of his opposition to polygamy, charged Smith "with living with Maria Lawrence 'in an open state of adultery' from 12 October 1843 to 23 May 1844."[84]

In Sunday services the day that followed the filing of William Law's complaint, Joseph Smith – the husband at that moment of no less than thirty-eight women – seized the opportunity to comment upon Law's complaint. In a sermon delivered the month before his death, Smith publicly discussed William Law's legal contentions. "Another indictment has been got up against me," he said. "I had not been married scarcely five minutes, and made one proclamation of the gospel, before it was reported that I had seven wives . . . . What a thing it is for a man to be accused of committing adultery, and having seven wives when I can find only one."[85] "I am innocent of all these charges, and you can bear witness of my innocence, for you know me yourselves."[86] "This new holy prophet [William Law was building a congregation of members opposed to polygamy] has gone to Carthage and swore that I told him that I was guilty of adultery. This spiritual wifeism! Why, a man dares not speak or wink, for fear of being accused of this."[87] "I am the same man, and as innocent as I was fourteen years ago [when he founded the Church and denied polygamy]; and I can prove them [his critics and detractors] all perjurers."[88] In this incredibly brazen public utterance, Smith equated "having" multiple wives and practicing "spiritual wifeism" with "committing adultery."

---

[83]William Law Journal, quoted in Van Wagoner, *Mormon Polygamy: A History*, 65.

[84]Ibid., 64.

[85]Joseph Smith Jr., *History of The Church of Jesus Christ of Latter-day Saints*, B.H. Roberts, ed., 2d ed., rev., (Salt Lake City: The Deseret Book Company, 1978), 6:408-11, quoted in Van Wagoner, *Mormon Polygamy: A History*, 66.

[86]Roberts, ed., *History of The Church of Jesus Christ of Latter-day Saints*, 6:411.

[87]Ibid., 6:410.

[88]Ibid., 6:411.

In this fabricated report, Smith admits that the accusations of polygamy (meaning adultery) started as early as 1830 ("fourteen years ago") when the Church was barely out of the box. The Mormon prophet's unbecoming relationship with Miss Fanny Alger, according to Richard L. Bushman, may have started as early as 1831 when she was just fourteen years old. "[T]he later years of his journal – in which he wrote repeated denials of polygamy – are no less troublesome [than this dishonest speech], for after his death a dozen women proudly signed affidavits [to say] that he had taken them as wives."[89] He concealed his participation in these dubious doings in his private resources, protecting himself from those who read them.

Wilson Law, William Law's brother, later learned that he had also been betrayed. Joseph Smith wasn't a monogamist when Wilson Law and Jane Law signed a *Certificate* that said that he was. Both of the Laws later learned to their dismay that there was a secret "system of marriage" "practised" in Nauvoo. Someone, perhaps several someones, described Nauvoo Mayor Joseph Smith's perversity in verse:

> And 'tis so here, in this sad life –
>   Such ills you must endure –
> Some *priest* or *king*, may claim your wife
>   Because that you are poor.
> A *revelation* he may get –
>   Refuse it if you dare!
> And you'll be damned *perpetually*,
>   By our good *Lord* the *Mayor*.
> But if that you yield willingly,
>   Your daughters and your wives
> In *spiritual marriage* to our *Pope*,

---

[89]Brodie, *No Man Knows My History*, viii. The character of the Mormon leader was important to Mrs. Brodie, who described him in the preface to her book in these alternative terms: "[T]he story of Joseph Smith is more than the story of a new religion. If one were unscrupulously selective in choosing details, one could make him out to be not only a prophet, but also a political menace – a dictator complete with army, propaganda ministry, and secret police who created an authoritarian dominion on the American frontier." She presented a broader vision of the complicated man.

He'll bless you all your lives . . .[90]

The "official" doctrine of the Church, as stated in a canonized statement included in the Doctrine and Covenants in 1835, was unqualified monogamy. No exceptions were articulated in support of a demanding Lord who might sometime want to raise seed up unto himself. Thus Smith's secret polygamy, and the secret polygamy of the other leaders, lacked the common consent of the laity, people who were misinformed.[91] What was publicly preached and taught wasn't what was privately preached and practiced. Polygamy proceeded without the consent of the greater part of the members.

Bennett Accuses Smith, Future Prophets Respond

Before the wide-spread publication of "The Testimony of Thirty-One Witnesses" in October of 1842, the ubiquitous John C. Bennett correctly disclosed in his nineteenth-century exposé (*The History of the Saints*), the initials (gallantry demanded initials) of *L*ouisa *B*eaman, *P*rescindia *B*uell, *E*lizabeth *D*urfee, *S*ylvia *S*essions and *A*gnes *S*mith. Bennett identified these women whose identities were more or less protected by the initials "as a few of the concealed wives of the prophet." There was indeed a secret system of marriage being "practised" in Nauvoo when thirty-one witnesses and the prophet who gathered them said that there was not. John C. Bennett was more truthful about the marital turmoil in the City of Joseph than Joseph Smith, his former "bosom friend." His accurate insights emphasized Dr. Bennett's insiderness. His areas of concern were further discussed in a series of eight letters delivered by Bennett to the *Sangamo Journal* in Springfield, Illinois.

---

[90]Wilson Law or possibly Francis M. Higbee, "Buckeye's Lamentation for Want of More Wives," *Warsaw Message* (7 Feb. 1844), 1; *Warshaw Signal* (name change) (25 April 1844), 3, emphasis retained.

[91]There were two unseemly aspects to the publication of the *Certificates*. Some of Smith's witnesses knew about, believed in and/or practiced polygamy. In the case of those *Certificants* who didn't know, Joseph Smith requested they say what he knew not to be true. Some of Smith's witnesses didn't know about, believe in and/or practice polygamy. At least not then. Because Joseph knew and gathered those who didn't know to sign, he deceived not only the public but also some of the signators.

In those often exaggerated reports, he nevertheless proved, over and over again, how much he knew about the Mormon prophet's private life.

Smith's protected secret instructions conspired to create three other formidable enablers, Brigham Young, John Taylor and Wilford Woodruff, men destined to consecutively hold the highest office in the Mormon Church until close to the end of the nineteenth century – Young, then Taylor, then Woodruff – for more than fifty years. The three apostolic insiders, prophets, seers and revelators, all connected to the *Times and Seasons* in one way or another (Young purchased the paper for the Church), were thoroughly familiar with the particulars of "The Principle" (Mormon polygamy). Taylor and Woodruff, who were tutored by Smith before they signed their names (and had their wives sign their names), lent apostolic credibility to the disingenuous *Certificates* published by Smith in October of 1842. By publishing the monogamous marriage *Certificates*, Smith, Taylor, Woodruff and their wives orchestrated a great deception.

If Joseph Smith was capable of gathering a group of thirty-one people to swear to something he positively knew to be false, was he also capable of gathering a group of eleven people to swear to something else he positively knew to be false? Could such a man ever be trusted to tell the truth?

Witnesses for Christ: Apostles John Taylor and Wilford Woodruff

Of the twelve men who signed the *Marriage Certificate* presented to them in the interest of Joseph Smith in 1842, John Taylor and Wilford Woodruff were by far the most important. Brigham Young, the senior apostle who had officiated at Joseph's marriage to Agnes Coolbrith Smith before the *Certificates* were published, didn't sign but didn't object. Taylor and Woodruff knew about polygamy before each of them attached their signatures to Smith's fraudulent document. John Taylor was introduced to "The Principle" by Joseph Smith in July 1841, more than a year before he signed the controversial *Times and Seasons Certificates*. Wilford Woodruff received his polygamy tutorial in December 1841, approximately nine months before he signed the *Times and Seasons Monogamous Marriage Certificate*. "Nine of Smith's key men (Orson Hyde, Heber C. Kimball, brothers Parley and Orson Pratt, Willard Richards, George A. Smith, John Taylor, Wilford Woodruff, and Brigham Young) were away when he taught polygamy to Louisa Beaman and Joseph Noble." When those members of the Quorum returned, the prophet ratchetted the principle up. "When three of the apostles (Kimball, Taylor, and Young) returned on July 1, 1841, Smith introduced them to plural marriage. On December 27, he unfolded 'privileges' [code for polygamy] to the entire Twelve, according to Wilford Woodruff."[92] John Taylor, who embraced "The Principle" in 1841, took his first polygamous wife in 1843. Wilford Woodruff, who embraced "The Principle" in 1841, took his first polygamous wife in 1846. Taylor's legal wife, Leonora Taylor, and Woodruff's legal wife, "Phebe" (Phoebe) Woodruff, were also witnesses to *Joseph Smith's Certificates*.

On February 3, 1842, Woodruff became the Business Manager and a Deputy Editor of the *Times and Seasons*. On October 1, 1842, Woodruff did "certify and declare" in the *Times and Seasons* that he knew "of no other rule or system of marriage than the one published from the Book of Doctrine and Covenants" (meaning unequivocal restricted monogamy). On or shortly after July 1, 1841, the prophet Joseph Smith introduced Apostle John Taylor to the principle of plural marriage. On October 1, 1842, Taylor did "certify and declare" in the *Times and Seasons* that he knew "of no other rule or system of marriage than the one published from the Book of Doctrine and Covenants." In 1850, eight years and many wives later, he repeated those lies to a French audience in a public debate.

In the fall in 1842, three Mormon prophets – Joseph Smith, John Taylor and Wilford Woodruff, two of them (Taylor and Woodruff) signators, and one of them (Smith) the editor, publisher and sponsor in-chief – perjured themselves and suborned the perjury of others, including Taylor and Woodruff's wives. Joseph Smith's legal wife, Emma Smith, also signed in her official capacity as the

---

[92]Kenney, ed., *Wilford Woodruff's Journal*, 2:144; see *e.g.*, George D. Smith, *Nauvoo Polygamy*, 67 n 27.

president of "the ladies relief society." Brigham Young, who didn't sign, wasn't innocent. He read the *Times and Seasons* and didn't object. Furthermore, his mother-in-law, Abigail Marks (Works), the mother of his deceased legal wife, Miriam Works (Young), was one of Joseph's signators. Abigail Works was married and sealed to her son-in-law Brigham Young, becoming Abigail Marks (Works) (Young), on January 28, 1846.[93] Thus four present and future Mormon prophets were directly embroiled in these perfectly sordid affairs.

On March 15, 1843, the same year he took his first plural wife and became a full-fledged practicing polygamist, John Taylor, who had only just recently replaced Joseph Smith as the editor of the *Times and Seasons*, published his own piece in the official Mormon paper: "We [Latter-day Saints] are charged with advocating a plurality of wives, and common property. Now this is as false as the many other ridiculous charges which are brought against us. No sect has a greater reverence for the laws of matrimony, or the rights of private property."[94] Taylor demonstrated with his feigned outrage both then and later that he was a prolific liar, had no shame and couldn't be trusted. How could anyone ever hope to determine when he and other high-ranking Mormon officials, who lied about the practice of polygamy everywhere to everyone all of the time, were telling the truth about anything else? Like the Book of Mormon or the vision of the Father and the Son.

---

[93]George D. Smith, *Nauvoo Polygamy*, 636.
[94]Editorial, *Times and Seasons* (15 March 1843), quoted in George D. Smith, *Nauvoo Polygamy*, 418, emphasis added.

CHAPTER THIRTEEN

Snapshots:
"[B]y their fruits ye shall know them"

Church members' secrets set them apart from the world, sealed them up to one another through things arcane, and fortified them in their confidence that they were the special friends of God.[1]

B. Carmon Hardy

BUILDING SAINTS

The Strange Case of Miss Sarah Ann Whitney

Before N.K. Whitney signed *Joseph Smith's Times and Seasons Monogamous Marriage Certificate* in 1842, Whitney, the First Bishop of the Church and the father of Sarah Ann Whitney, became the recipient of an 1842 revelation that further authenticated the doctrine of polygamy. According to Joseph Smith, Joseph's God (Christianity's unmarried pastor) personally directed the smallest details of Miss Whitney's domestic proceedings. Newel K. Whitney officiated at the plural marriage and celestial sealing of his daughter, Sarah Ann, to Joseph Smith. Whitney's wife, Elizabeth Ann, was personally present and acted as a witness. Elizabeth Ann Whitney, who also signed Smith's *Times and Seasons Certificate*, was one of the two Counselors to President Emma Smith in the Ladies' Relief Society Presidency.

Joseph Smith, Newel K. Whitney, Elizabeth Ann and Sarah Ann Whitney were actors in an interesting drama that occurred on and

---

[1]"Lying for the Lord: An Essay," Appendix 1 in B. Carmon Hardy, *Solemn Covenant: The Mormon Polygamous Passage* (Urbana, Chicago: University of Illinois Press, 1992), 364.

after July 27, 1842. Smith plurally married and was sealed to Sarah Ann Whitney in secret proceedings two months before he published his *Times and Seasons Certificates* in unequivocal support of monogamous marriage. Those *Certificates* certified and declared that there was no plural marriage, or secret proceedings, in the City of the Saints. The fraudulent *Times and Seasons Certificates* were signed by both of Sarah's prominent parents on or before October 1, 1842. Both of them knew the *Certificates* were false and misleading and that their sponsor, *Times and Seasons* Editor Smith, wasn't telling the truth.

In July 1842 Joseph Smith's store was the headquarters of the Church of Jesus Christ of Latter-day Saints. It was in that store that Martha Brotherton met Brigham Young and Joseph Smith in a locked room located up some stairs ("our private room") (a room marked "positively no admittance"). Newel K. Whitney and his brother-in-law, Joseph C. Kingsbury, were both employed by their leader, Joseph Smith. They were clerks at the prophet's store.[2] On July 27, 1842, Joseph Smith, just then the thirty-six year-old husband of no less than fourteen other plural wives, plurally married Bishop Whitney's seventeen-year-old daughter.[3] Smith

---

[2]H. Michael Marquardt, *The Strange Marriages of Sarah Ann Whitney to Joseph Smith, the Mormon Prophet, Joseph C. Kingsbury and Heber C. Kimball* (first published 1973; revised 1982; web version © 2001), 1.

[3]In order to keep his marriage to Sarah Ann Whitney secret at this early stage of polygamous practice, Smith directed his young bride to live with her recently widowed uncle, Joseph C. Kingsbury, in a state of pretended matrimony. Kingsbury's wife, Caroline Whitney, died on October 16, 1842, some few months after Sarah Whitney was married to Joseph Smith. Sarah Ann Whitney (Smith), who later became Sarah Ann Whitney (Smith) (Kingsbury), knowingly "engaged in a sham marriage to Joseph Kingsbury to conceal her connection to Smith . . . . [H]e [Kingsbury] wrote in his autobiography that he 'agreed to stand by Sarah Ann Whitney as though I was supposed to be her husband [in] a pretended marriage.'" (George D. Smith, *Nauvoo Polygamy . . . But We Called It Celestial Marriage* [Salt Lake City: Signature Books, 2008], 400). After the death of Joseph Smith on June 27, 1844, Sarah Ann was sealed to Heber C. Kimball for mortality (meaning for "time"). Despite her marriage to Kimball, she continued to live with Kingsbury, "who was being groomed to begin choosing his own plural wives." "On March 4 [1845], Kingsbury married Dorcas Moore." That marriage was not "pretended." On March 17, 1845, after her marriage to Joseph Smith and her pretended marriage to Joseph Kingsbury, nineteen-year-old Sarah Ann secretly married Heber C. Kimball, the forty-three year-old father of her special friend, Helen Mar. "In all of this, her marriage to Kingsbury was ignored. There was no

first laid eyes upon Sarah Ann at Kirtland, Ohio, in February 1831 when she was almost six years old and he was twenty-five. She was married to him eleven years later, after he said that he received a revelation from God appointing her to him. It was a polygamous solicitation, from God to her father through Joseph, that she and her devoted parents chose to accept. "She was the first woman, in this dispensation, who was given in plural marriage by and with the consent of both parents."[4]   Joseph Smith *secretly* married Sarah Ann Whitney, his sixteenth wife (counting Emma), in Nauvoo, Illinois, in the presence of Newel K. and Elizabeth Ann Whitney, on July 27, 1842. Two months after Sarah's wedding, her parents signed Joseph Smith's fraudulent *October 1, 1842, Times and Seasons Monogamous Marriage Certificates.*

In the Whitney's revelation dated July 27, 1842, the God of Abraham, Isaac and Jacob told Newel K. Whitney what to say when he officiated at the secret marriage of his daughter to Joseph Smith. That *time* and *eternity* marriage occurred just before the busy prophet married more than twenty other women, including perhaps eight other teenagers, over the period from February to November 1843. Joseph Smith is known to have married about thirty-four women in about twenty-one or two months, on both sides of the publication of his *Monogamous Marriage Certificates* on October 1, 1842.

On October 1, 1842, Joseph Smith published Certificates that were not unlike other Certificates published over the names of other witnesses in support of the gold plates and the Book of Mormon in 1830. In these new *Certificates*, designed to support dishonest claims of

---

divorce – no sense of a need to grant the sham marriage any further legitimacy." When she then became pregnant with Kimball's child, it naturally appeared to be Kingsbury's child. Sarah Ann Whitney, one of Heber C. Kimball's "little heifers," had seven children with Kimball. Those children and their mother are bonded for eternity to Joseph Smith. They will belong to him, because of their sealings, not Kimball, in a Mormon afterlife. When Sarah married Kimball "for mortality . . . her sealing to Smith for eternity was re-confirmed." Kingsbury's marriage to Moore "was kept secret." (Ibid., 401).

[4]Orson F. Whitney, *The Contributor*, vol. 6 no. 4 (January 1885), 131, quoted in Marquardt, *The Strange Marriages of Sarah Ann Whitney,* 1. As of then: "The revelation commanding and consecrating this union, is in existence [and can be read], though it has never been [officially] published." (Ibid., revised edition, 1982).

traditional marriage, both of Sarah's parents certified and declared that the Mormon rule of marriage was that "one man should have one wife, and one woman, but one husband . . . ." *On June 19, 1869,* many years later, Sarah Ann Whitney (Smith) (Kingsbury) (Kimball) (by now the eighteenth wife of her third husband, Heber C. Kimball, a man many years her senior), in due form of law, and upon her oath testified that "she was married or sealed to Joseph Smith . . . by Newell [sic] K. Whitney . . . in the presence of Elizabeth Ann Whitney . . ." at Nauvoo, Illinois, on July 27, 1842. *On August 30, 1869,* her mother, Elizabeth Ann Whitney, upon her oath and in the presence of a notary, concurred and said that "she was present and witnessed the marrying or sealing of her daughter Sarah Ann Whitney to the Prophet Joseph Smith, for time and all eternity, by her husband Newel K. Whitney, then Presiding Bishop of the Church" on July 27, 1842.[5] Thus the Whitneys, at the risk of perjuring themselves in 1869, proved on the record and under oath that they perjured themselves in 1842.

On October 1, 1842, Newel K. Whitney and Elizabeth Ann Whitney did "certify and declare" in a fraudulent *Certificate* published by the Mormon prophet Joseph Smith, the Editor of the *Times and Seasons*, a publication of the Church of Jesus Christ of Latter-day Saints, that they knew of "no other rule or system of marriage than the one published from the Doctrine and Covenants . . . ." The Whitney witnesses stated that Dr. J.C. Bennett's "secret wife system" was a creature "of his own make as we know of no such society in this place nor never did [Bishop N.K. Whitney]," and as "a disclosure of his own make [Relief Society Counselor Elizabeth Ann Whitney]."

On October 1, 1842, Joseph Smith, just then the husband of about seventeen wives, published *Certificates* intended to show "that Dr. J.C. Bennett's 'secret wife system' is a matter of his own manufacture, and further to disabuse the public ear and shew that the said Bennett and his misanthropic friend Origen Bachelor, are

[5]Affidavits of Sarah A. Kimball and Elizabeth A. Whitney, reproduced in *Blood Atonement and the Origin of Plural Marriage – A Discussion*, correspondence between Elder Joseph F. Smith, Jr., of the Church of Jesus Christ of Latter-day Saints, and Mr. Richard C. Evans, Second Counselor in the Presidency of the "Reorganized" Church (Salt Lake City: The Deseret News Press, 1905), 73-74.

perpetrating a foul and infamous slander upon an innocent people, and need but be known to be hated and despise[d]." The knowledgeable Whitneys dishonestly attested to this ill-advised introduction on October 1, 1842. They knew about a secret wife system when they signed the disingenuous declaration because their daughter Sarah Ann was a party to one. On October 1, 1842, Sarah Ann Whitney was a member of a society of no less than sixteen secret sister wives.

On October 1, 1842, Newel K. Whitney and Elizabeth Ann Whitney, at the invitation of their leader, Joseph Smith, lied for the Lord and said that traditional monogamous marriage was the only "rule or system of marriage" practiced in the Mormon Church. They represented that every Mormon marriage was public and recorded by the clerk. There was, they said, no secret marriage system. Elizabeth Whitney much later explained the Whitneys' acceptance of polygamy (and their undeniable dishonesty) in these particular terms: "Our hearts were comforted, and our faith made so perfect that we were willing to give our eldest daughter, then seventeen years of age, to Joseph, in the order of plural marriage. Laying aside all our traditions and former notions in respect to marriage, we gave her with our mutual consent. ... Of course these things had to be kept an inviolate secret . . ."[6] at any cost. The Whitneys'

---

[6]Edward W. Tullidge, *The Women of Mormondom* (New York: 1877), 369. On August 18, 1842, twenty-two days after his marriage to Sarah Ann Whitney, Joseph Smith wrote the following letter to Newel K. Whitney, Elizabeth Ann Whitney and an anonymous Sarah in his own hand ("Dear, and Beloved, Brother and Sister, Whitney, *and & c.* –" [Sarah]). Joseph, who was avoiding arrest on the charge that he was an accessory to the attempted murder of ex- (Missouri) Governor Lilburn W. Boggs, was just then in hiding at the home of Carlos Granger, a friendly non-Mormon man. His instruction to the Whitneys, like his earlier instruction concerning his ill-advised letter to Miss Rigdon, was to "burn this letter as soon as you read it," something those trusted friends inexplicably failed to do. One must surmise that other letters of a similar sort to other followers of a similar sort had indeed been burned. "[M]y feelings," Joseph reports, "are so Strong for you Since what has pased lately between us" (a very untraditional secret marriage between two parties who were not equally yoked). "[I]f you Three would come and See me in this my lonely retreat, it would afford me great relief, of mind . . . ." "[N]ow is the time to afford me succour; in the days of exile . . . ." "I am now at Carlos Graingers, Just back of Brother Hyrums farm . . . let Brother Whitney come a little a head, and nock at the south East corner of the house att the window; . . . I have a room intirely by myself, the whole matter can be attended to with most perfect Safty, *I know it is the will of God that you should comfort me now in this time*

"crime was condoned under the specious excuse that the end justifies the means."[7] They, like hundreds and thousands of others, lied for the Lord; it was their duty to do so.

The Strange Case of Aaron Johnson

Aaron Johnson, who became a member of the Nauvoo City Council (taking the place of Orson Hyde) on April 29, 1844, had already been appointed to "The High Council" of the Church of Jesus Christ of Latter Day Saints "on February 6, 1841." With that High Council appointment, Aaron Johnson became a "General Authority." God specifically chose his servant Aaron Johnson to fill that important leadership position (the Nauvoo Stake High Council was in charge of the affairs of the Church at headquarters in Nauvoo, Illinois). Johnson's selection was made "in conformity to a revelation previously given to that effect . . . ."[8] "[V]erily I say unto you, let my servant Aaron Johnson be ordained unto this calling in his [Seymour Brunson's] stead . . . ." (Seymour Brunson was deceased; "Seymour Brunson I have taken unto myself . . ."). The Mormon God knew "Seymour Brunson," deceased, and "Aaron Johnson," Seymour's successor, by name.[9]

---

of affliction, or not at all, now is the time or never, . . . the only thing to be careful of, is to find out when Emma comes then you cannot be Safe, but when She is not here, there is the most perfect Safty: only be careful to escape observation, as much as possible, I know it is a heroick undertaking . . . burn this letter as soon as you read it; keep all locked up in your breasts, my life depends upon it . . . . I close my letter. I think Emma wont come tonight if she don't don't fail to come tonight, I subscribe myself your most obedient, and affectionate Companion, and friend. Joseph Smith." (Marquardt, *The Strange Marriages of Sarah Ann Whitney*, emphasis added). Almost immediately following this furtive communication, the Whitneys signed *Certificates* that said that the only Mormon rule of marriage was monogamy, that "one man should have one wife, and one woman but one husband," that there was no "secret wife system," and "that all marriages should be solemnized in a public meeting or feast . . . ." This First Bishop and his Relief Society Counselor wife, then and now, were and are considered to be exemplary Saints.

[7]James E. Talmage, *The Great Apostasy* (Salt Lake City: Deseret Book Company, 1953), 107.

[8]*The Nauvoo City and High Council Minutes*, ed. John S. Dinger (Salt Lake City: Signature Books, 2011), 6 February 1841, 387, cf. 236-37 (City Council, 29 April 1844).

[9]Doctrine and Covenants 124:132.

When George Miller presented a morals charge against Chauncey L. Higbee, on May 21, 1842, Aaron Johnson was one of the four members of the Council specifically appointed to speak at those important proceedings (others: George W. Harris, Thomas Grover, Newel Knight). Johnson heard the salacious testimony presented in that particular case, and in a rather large number of other similar cases, in 1841 and 1842. In the Higbee proceedings, three females testified that Chauncey L. Higbee "had seduced and at different times been guilty of unchaste and unvirtuous conduct with them and taught the doctrine that it was right to have free intercourse with women if it was kept secret &c and also taught that Joseph Smith autherised him to practise these things &c."[10] Sarah Miller, one of those three witnesses, was able to say that *"[Apostle] William Smith [Joseph Smith's brother] come with him & told me that the doctrine which Chancy Higbee had taught me was true."*[11]

Aaron Johnson heard (and weighed) those submissions, including those apostolic recitals, in the presence of and in consultation with George W. Harris,[12] Thomas Grover and Newel Knight, before Johnson (and his wife, Polly) signed *Joseph Smith's Times and Seasons Certificates.* Harris rendered this particular service as a member of the Nauvoo Stake High Council, which heard a large number of cases that served to show that traditional civil marriage and monogamy were under attack in the Mormon enclave. "This [George Miller's case against Chauncey L. Higbee on May 21, 1842] is the first of over twenty cases the high council will adjudicate over the next few months . . . ."[13] One would have to be truly derelict to miss all of these clues proclaiming the existence of Smith's new and emerging secret order, something Aaron Johnson is supposed to have publicly certified and declared that he had done.

Aaron Johnson, a High Council insider, a man known to God by name and one of Joseph's *Times and Seasons Signators,* took his

---

[10]Dinger, ed., *The Nauvoo City and High Council Minutes*, 21 May 1842, 414-15.

[11]Ibid., 415-16 n 40, emphasis retained.

[12]George W. Harris was the husband of Joseph Smith's mistress, Lucinda Pendleton (Morgan) Harris.

[13]Ibid., 415 n 37, cf. Gary James Bergera, "'Illicit Intercourse,' Plural Marriage, and the Nauvoo Stake High Council, 1830-1844," *John Whitmer Historical Association Journal* 23 (2003): 59-90.

first plural wife, his niece, Sarah Mariah Johnson, on December 22, 1844. He then took ten additional wives for a final total of twelve (including two fourteen year-olds, two fifteen year-olds, two seventeen year-olds, one eighteen year-old, and one nineteen year-old). Johnson's stable of eight teenagers included his eighteen year-old legal wife. He married teens when he was twenty-one, thirty-nine, forty-five, forty-six and fifty, including three teenagers (ages fourteen, fifteen and nineteen) at the age of fifty (on March 1, 1857).[14] According to Ann Eliza Webb (Dee) (Young), one of Brigham Young's ex-wives, Aaron Johnson's practice of polygamy was tasteless and vulgar. Can it be denied?[15] Besides the marriages, Aaron Johnson was embroiled in a number of things that were measurably worse.[16] Aaron Johnson married at least five

---

[14]George D. Smith, *Nauvoo Polygamy*, 598-99.

[15]In her exposé *Wife No. 19*, Ann Eliza alleged that, "Bishop Smith of Brigham City, married two of his own nieces." [Ann Eliza Young, *Wife No. 19* [Dustin, Gilman and Co., 1875; reprinted CreateSpace Independent Publishing Platform, 2014], 310). Joseph Smith, according to Joseph Jackson (Smith's *aide-de-camp*), was interested in his own niece, specifically Hyrum's daughter Lovina).

[16]Aaron Johnson later founded the town of Springville, Utah, according to instructions he received from Brigham Young with whom he was on good terms. Johnson, the Bishop of Springville, was implicated in the murders of two apostates who wanted to leave the church and the Utah Territory and live in California. In 1857 after a pair of non-Mormon horse thieves were released from a Utah penitentiary – "whereupon they headed for California" – Young instructed leaders in their path to monitor their journey should they "attempt to steal livestock on their way." "[W]e do not expect," he said that, "there would be any prosecutions for false imprisonment, or tale bearers left for witnesses." Author John G. Turner further described this authorization for "extra-legal violence" (and its effects) in his remarkable biography of Brigham Young. In that, he said, "Bishop Aaron Johnson of Springville used Young's directive as a justification for ordering an assassination." William Parrish, one of Johnson's parishioners and an apostate, had "decided to flee the territory." Johnson, stretching Brigham's directive, identified Parrish "as a potential horse thief" and "recruited spies to learn of Parrish's departure plans." "With the church's highest leaders advocating blood atonement for apostates, moreover, Johnson may have decided that Parrish's decision to leave the faith and the territory warranted death. The operation went awry. Assassins killed William Parrish and his son William, but they also fatally shot Gardiner ("Duff") Potter, one of Johnson's spies in the process," after mistaking him for one of the Parrish's sons. (John G. Turner, *Brigham Young: Pioneer Prophet* [Belknap Press of Harvard University Press, 2012], 259-60). The murders (like the vulgar marriages) did not affect Johnson's bishopric. Nothing is seen to suggest that Bishop Aaron Johnson was ever reprimanded for these disreputable crimes while serving as God's designated emissary in Springville, Utah.

of his nieces. Those sisters were the daughters of Aaron's brother Lorenzo. After he married Mary, who was fourteen at the time, Johnson arranged for the other nieces to be sealed to him when they grew up. "The youngest one was only two years old at the time that her father promised her to her uncle, and she was only about thirteen when she was sealed to him."[17]

On March 1, 1857, Aaron Johnson married fourteen year-old Julia Marie Johnson. He was fifty when he married Julia, his niece and ninth wife. Julia Marie Johnson is supposed to have been the fifth sister in her family to marry her Uncle Aaron. Aaron Johnson, a judge in Israel and a General Authority in Nauvoo – a man who certified and declared in 1842 that he and all others in that city believed in and "practised" nothing but traditional monogamous marriage – later married twenty-year-old Sarah Mariah Johnson on December 22, 1844. On May 18, 1846, at the age of thirty-nine, he married his second niece, fourteen-year-old Mary Ann Johnson. On December 16, 1852, and June 14, 1853, he married fifteen-year-old Harriett Fidelia Johnson and her seventeen-year-old sister Eunice Lucinda Johnson. On March 1, 1857, he married the last of the five nieces (fourteen year-old Julia Maria Johnson).[18]   On March 1, 1857, fifty year-old Aaron Johnson married Sarah James (nineteen), Cecelia Elmine Sanford (fifteen), and Julia Maria

---

[17]Ann Eliza Young, *Wife No. 19*, 310-11. Ann Eliza (Dee) (Young), Chapter 18, 578 n 66, quoted in Richard Abanes, *One Nation Under Gods: A History of the Mormon Church* (New York, NY: Thunder's Mouth Press, 2003), 293. Ann Eliza commented on Mormonism's peculiar kind of domestic confusion: "Uncles and nieces were married, one man would marry sisters [Heber C. Kimball married five sets of sisters]; and it was a very common thing for a mother and daughter to have the same husband [Joseph Smith: Mrs. Patty Bartlett (Sessions) and Mrs. Sylvia Porter Sessions (Lyon), then possibly also Flora Ann Woodworth and Mrs. Phebe Watrous (Woodworth)]." Although Flora's mother is known to have been sealed to Joseph Smith, scholars Compton and Quinn are not convinced that those facts implied a "temporal relationship." (George D. Smith, *Nauvoo Polygamy*, 652 n 376). In one family, at least three generations were represented as wives to the same husband – grandmother, mother and daughter; "and a case actually occurred in Salt Lake City where a man [George D. Watt, Mormonism's first English convert and Brigham Young's reporter] married [and had three children with] his half sister [they shared a common mother], and that, too, with the full knowledge and approval of Brigham Young." (Ann Eliza [Dee] [Young], *Wife No. 19*, 310).

[18]George D. Smith, *Nauvoo Polygamy*, 598-99.

Johnson (fourteen), all on the same day.[19]   Aaron Johnson had eleven children with his niece, Mary Ann, who was fourteen years old when she married him.

From their earliest days, Latter-day Saints have spoken of a Great Apostasy that enveloped the churches; priests weren't chaste, "Some had fallen into lust and incest," the "morals of the clergy" were "corrupt" and had become "an offense to laity." One Modern Mormon author, in a book entitled *The Inevitable Apostasy and the Promised Reformation*, concluded that sexual sins are markers of apostasy. Describing what were "tragic indictments of the church and its clergy [non-Mormon Christian churches]," he further said, "Does it seem plausible that God would allow men of this caliber, in these proportions to be the chosen vessels of his Church?   One cannot help," he says, "but recall the words of Peter concerning Church leaders, that they should be 'ensamples to the flock' (1 Peter 5:3)."[20]   Aaron Johnson, one of the men who signed Joseph Smith's *Times and Seasons Certificates*, like Joseph Smith himself, the Editor who promoted and published them, resembled those remarks. Bishop Johnson's wife, Polly, his legal wife, also signed Joseph Smith's *Times and Seasons Certificates*.

Other Deceivers

Some of Smith's witnesses didn't know about his "secret wife system," initially designed for the elite members of what came to be called the Quorum of the Anointed. Others, like the Whitneys, most certainly did. The two Apostles, Taylor and Woodruff (both of them future leaders of the Church), who recruited *Times and Seasons Certificants* and signed themselves, certainly did. They were fully implicated in the prophet's nefarious scheme. Those charged to collect and publish the statements, including Smith, knew which of the signators were uninformed and which of them were not. The three men who directed the affairs of the *Times and Seasons* (Joseph Smith, Editor, John Taylor and Wilford Woodruff, Deputy Editors), the only men on duty at the time, insiders, men

---

[19]Ibid.
[20]Tad R. Callister, *The Inevitable Apostasy and the Promised Restoration* (Salt Lake City: Deseret Book Company, 2006), 269, 275, 280.

who were not deceived, solicited other men and women who were not deceived to act as signators to Smith's fraudulent *Certificates*. Those who knew committed fraud; those who didn't know acted without knowledge of the facts to please their disingenuous leaders. John Taylor and Wilford Woodruff accepted the new and *everlasting* covenant of polygamy in 1841, before they and their wives signed the *Times and Seasons Certificates* more than a year later in 1842. The mother of Brigham Young's dead first wife (Abigail Works) also signed, and so did Emma Smith.

Before the publication of *Joseph Smith's Monogamous Marriage Certificates* in 1842, Apostle Heber C. Kimball married Sarah Peak (Noon). By the fall of 1842, when the *Certificates* were published, Vilate Kimball, the apostle's legal wife, and Sarah Peak (Noon), a plural polyandrous wife, were both "about seven month's pregnant." The undivorced Sarah's child would seem to have been the product of sexual polyandry. Sarah Noon and Kimball embraced "The Polygamous Principle" before the marriage. On September 9, 1869, in the presence of a notary, Sarah Peak (Noon) (Kimball) testified that "President Joseph Smith personally taught her the doctrine of a plurality of wives," after which she was "married or sealed for time and all eternity to Heber C. Kimball by President Joseph Smith in the presence of President Brigham Young."[21] In the presence of President Brigham Young, the third future prophet to be implicated in the then present prophet Joseph Smith's nefarious *Times and Seasons* proceedings. All of that, every bit, occurred before Smith published those fraudulent *Certificates* on October 1, 1842.

Heber C. Kimball, an important man in the early Church, had his first polygamous child with Sarah Peak (Noon) (Kimball) – a second wife in consequence of a secret marriage – just before or shortly after *Joseph's Times and Seasons Certificates* were officially published. Smith taught the principles of polygamy to the Lamanite missionaries in 1831, eleven years before he published his *Times and Seasons Certificates* over the names of thirty-one of his followers in 1842. Every knowledgeable Latter-day Saint, every Lamanite missionary, every legal wife of a plurally married man,

---

[21]Sarah Perry Peak (Noon), Affidavit (7 September 1869), in "40 Affidavits on Celestial Marriage" (1869), quoted in George D. Smith, *Nauvoo Polygamy*, 306.

every plural wife of a plurally married man, every woman any aspiring polygamist ever approached, Joseph Smith, Joseph Noble, Dimick Huntington, John Taylor, Wilford Woodruff, Brigham Young, Heber C. Kimball, Newel K. Whitney, Elizabeth Ann Whitney and all of the men and women who knew of the doctrine, before they either signed or read those *Certificates* in the *Times and Seasons,* could not but have known that those *Certificates* were intended to deceive. That there was a new order. That there was a secret marriage system.   That marriages weren't public or reported. By their unforgivable indifference in the face of Smith's unforgivable publication of such disingenuous facts, none of them true, prominent Mormon men and women, including the highest leaders of the Church, proved they couldn't be trusted to tell the truth.

Mormonism's *Pre-Certificate* polygamous pioneers included but were not limited to Dimick Huntington, who approached his married sister Zina Huntington (Jacobs) in 1841 for Joseph Smith after Smith said that his life and his ministry had been threatened by an angel with a drawn sword[22]; John C. Bennett, Joseph's physician confederate (a man with complicated potions, low morals, a difficult history and some nasty tools); Joseph Noble, who married Smith to Louisa Beaman in 1841; Emma Smith; Joseph Smith; seventeen women (including Emma but not Fanny Alger) who married Joseph Smith before October 1, 1842; other women (no less than four of them already married women) known to have rejected him; Brigham Young, John Taylor, Heber C. Kimball, Parley P. Pratt, Orson Pratt, Willard Richards, George A. Smith, Orson Hyde and Wilford Woodruff, all of whom were fully

---

[22]Joseph's Lord demanded Joseph's polyandrous marriage (and sealing) to the already married and pregnant wife of Henry Jacobs. Joseph told Dimick Huntington to tell his sister, Henry's wife, that the prophet's life and his ministry had been threatened by an angel with a drawn sword. According to Joseph, God sent an angel to enforce Joseph and Zina's compliance with the polyandrous principle. Zina had a child with Brigham Young, who took her away from Henry Jacobs after the death of Joseph Smith but during the life of Henry Jacobs. Her polyandrous marriage to Young was sexual, like Heber C. Kimball's polyandrous marriage to Sarah Peak (Noon), the mother of four of his children, appears to have also been. Dimick Huntington's sister, Presendia Huntington (Buell), another married woman, also married Joseph Smith, becoming still another polyandrous wife, in 1841.

informed.   None of these hall of fame founders, or their consorts, witnesses to this brazen deceit, addressed the duplicity of Smith's utterly dishonest *Certificates* as men and women of honor should have done.

Three of the twelve men who signed *Joseph's Certificate* became polygamists-in-fact just before or shortly after they signed.   They were: George Miller (1843), Aaron Johnson (1844), and Alpheus Cutler (1846).   Those three *signators* ultimately married about twenty-three women and had about sixty-eight children.[23]   Aaron Johnson, the Bishop of Springville, had eighteen children with his biological nieces.   Four of the twelve men who signed the *Certificates* (Taylor, Woodruff, Whitney and Reynolds Cahoon) accepted the New and Everlasting Covenant (polygamy) – "without obedience" to which "no man" could "attain to the fullness of exaltation in the celestial glory" – before October 1, 1842.   Eight of the twelve men who signed Joseph's *Certificates* were secretly practicing polygamy by 1846.   In 1842 at the age of fifty-two, Cahoon, whose legal wife was Thirza Stiles, married Lucina Roberts (Johnson), a widow. Reynolds and Thirza both signed the *Times and Seasons Certificates* in support of monogamy on or before October 1, 1842.

Vinson Knight took a polygamous wife in 1842 (". . . marrying Philinda Myrick").   Knight (Belnap) family history reports that Martha McBride (Knight), Vinson's legal wife, gave "consent for her husband to enter Plural Marriage, about May 1842"[24] before the publication of the *Certificates*.   Vinson Knight died on July 31, 1842.   His widow was married and sealed to Joseph Smith in yet another secret ceremony sometime before August 5, 1842,[25] before he published the *Times and Seasons Certificates*.[26]   On October 12, 1844, less than four months after the death of Joseph Smith, Martha McBride (Knight) (Smith) became Martha McBride (Knight) (Smith) (Kimball), the thirteenth of the more than forty wives of Heber C. Kimball.   One of Joseph's fourteen year-olds, Nancy Winchester, also came to rest with Kimball (after the death of Smith).   She and Kimball were later divorced.   Kimball married

---

[23]George D. Smith, *Nauvoo Polygamy*, 608, *see also* 598-99, 587.
[24]Ibid., 262.
[25]Ibid., 622.
[26]Ibid., 622, 644 n 179.

ten teenagers with whom he had about forty-one children.

All of these unconventional *Pre-Certificate* marriages – Joseph's (seventeen women, no less than ten of them legally married to other men and undivorced), Brigham Young's, Heber C. Kimball's, Reynolds Cahoon's, Vincent Knight's – occurred as unheralded elements of a "secret wife system." Emma, Thirza Cahoon, Phoebe Woodruff, Leonora Taylor, Elizabeth Whitney, Sarah Cleveland, Eliza R. Snow and various other women, young and old, married or not, and their husbands knew or should have known that there was a secret wife system in Nauvoo; that one man had more than one woman; that some women had more than one man; that there were sexual consent relationships and spiritual wives. Polygamous marriages weren't celebrated, legal, public, traditional or reported. Every plural alliance, whether formal or not (many were not), was unmistakably secret. Men and women arrived and departed without getting married or divorced.

Emma Smith Hated "The Principle"

Relief Society, "The Voice of Innocence," March 20, 1844:

> *Resolved unanimously, That . . . we raise our voices and hands against John C. Bennett's "spiritual wife system," as a grand scheme of profligates to seduce women; and they that harp upon it, wish to make it popular for the convenience of their own cupidity; . . . let polygamy, bigamy, fornication, adultery, and prostitution, be frowned out of the hearts of honest men to drop into the gulf of fallen nature, where the worm dieth not and the fire is not quenched! and let all the saints say, Amen!*
>
> EMMA SMITH, Prest.
> H.M. Ells, Sec. pro tem[27]

---

[27]"The Voice of Innocence from Nauvoo, A Denunciation of Polygamy" adopted by the Relief Society, published in the *Nauvoo Neighbor* (20 March 1844), "Book of Abraham Project," available at Archive.org; Internet, 2 col. 2 to 4, emphasis added. "Resolved unanimous, That Joseph Smith, the Mayor of the City

By their fruits ye shall know them. John C. Bennett's revenge when he lost place in the Kingdom was centered upon the disclosure of those secret alliances, including sexual consent relationships, unfettered by marriage and unofficiated, that cluttered the agendas of the governing councils in Nauvoo, Illinois, in 1841 and 1842. In this paragraph excerpted from a larger text, Emma admits that "polygamy, bigamy, fornication[,] adultery and prostitution" had taken root in "the hearts of honest men" and needed to be "frowned out," dropped "into the gulf of fallen nature." Whatever that means, it was a problem that the first President of the Relief Society desperately wanted addressed.

If on his way from Kirtland to Missouri in 1838 Joseph was asked "a thousand times over and over again" if, among other things, Mormons took more wives than one,[28] we may be sure that the reputation of the Mormons was known to Emma, who was seriously antagonized by Joseph's "dirty, nasty, filthy affair" with Fanny Alger on a hay mow in the barn in the early 1830s. Joseph's supposed reception of the sealing power in April 1836, authority to bind in heaven what is bound on earth (and essential to the principle and practice of polygamy), preceded by six years the publication of the *Monogamous Marriage Certificates* in 1842.

Building Memories; Joseph's Concept of the Eternal Family

In these events, as plurality advanced, one may hope to detect the prophet's personal prototype for the development of the Mormon concept of the eternal family.[29] Plural marriage is the sublime

---

be tendered our thanks for the able and manly manner in which he defended injured innocence in the late trial of O.F. Bostwick for slandering President Hyrum Smith, and almost all the women of the city." At the trial of Bostwick, Bostwick reported, to the dismay of the sisters, "that he could take a half bushel of meal, obtain his vile purpose, and get what accommodation he wanted with almost any women in the city." "H.M. [Hannah S.] Ells, Sec. pro tem" (as described in the *Certificates*) became the twenty-ninth wife of Joseph Smith in mid-1843. (George D. Smith, *Nauvoo Polygamy*, 622; see, e.g., 651-52 n 373).

[28]Hardy, *Solemn Covenant: The Mormon Polygamous Passage*, 6.

[29]The theology of plural marriage "was introduced as part of Smith's concept of an eternal family." His plan for his followers, what might be called extreme domesticity, was surrounded by formidable relational concepts, baptism for the dead, eternal plural marriage, eternal proxy marriage, and the law of adoption

centerpiece of the eternal Mormon family, like it or not. Joseph Smith is sealed for eternity to hundreds of women, including celebrated, historical, previously married and undivorced women. Secretly sealed previously married undivorced polyandrous women, consorts of kings and conquerors. What Mormons think they know (more than anyone else) about marriage, fidelity, virtue, consent, plurality, sealing and exaltation, they admit to have learned from the Mormon God speaking to Joseph Smith to whom all such sacred concepts were always first revealed.

Smith is the spiritual architect of the eternal family. Mormonism's concept of the eternal family cannot be captured without "crawling over . . . under or around" the lengthened shadow of the King of the Kingdom of Israel on Earth, the Mormon prophet Joseph Smith, Mormonism's domestic exemplar. Smith and his successors taught the Mormon people that the eternal Mormon family was to be constructed on earth as it is in heaven, one divinely ordained polygamous marriage and one divinely ordained posthumous sealing after another. The prophet's domestic example was unconventional and very complicated.

Emma Smith was witness to her husband's less than sanctified 1830s encounters with Eliza Winters, Fanny Alger, Marinda Nancy Johnson, and various less obvious others. She was further discomfitted to discover evidence of her husband's secret relationship with Eliza R. Snow, a tutor to the Smith children, in 1843. Emma is supposed to have violently cast Eliza out of the house after she learned Joseph had married her mostly thoughtful friend. Emma knew something about the plurality principle and the adulteries before she signed Joseph's *Certificate* on October 1, 1842. And she knew something about some of his other marriages (Emily and Eliza Partridge, Sarah and Maria Lawrence) by 1843. (Emma knew that five of these women, not including Miss Alger, whose circumstances were unexpected and poorly defined, had become plural wives to her husband). Emma didn't know and

---

("adoption sealings"), which added to "an expanding web of eternally procreative relationships." (Gary James Bergera, "The Earliest Eternal Sealings for Civilly Married Couples Living and Dead," *Dialogue: A Journal of Mormon Thought* 35 [Fall 2002]: 41-42, quoted in George D. Smith, *Nauvoo Polygamy*, 45). The law of adoption (like the early and important Patriarchal Priesthood) was later dismissed.

couldn't have known, because her husband didn't tell her, that he had taken very many other wives. He didn't ask Emma, his first and legal wife, to receive them – as divine protocol (the law of Sarah) was supposed to require – and he took them whether she liked it or not. Modern scholars now know better than Emma did then how this great experiment played out.

When Emma Smith signed *Joseph's Times and Seasons Monogamous Marriage Certificate*, in the face of every volatile thing associated with the expulsion of John C. Bennett, she could not but have known for many different reasons that polygamy was a fact, and that the *Certificate* she signed at Editor Joseph's request wasn't true. The *Certificate* was by way of response to a series of explosive allegations that surfaced because of Bennett in the City of Joseph to the knowledge of many in 1842. Those allegations published in the *Sangamo Journal* in 1843 exposed the prophet's polygamy for Emma and Sidney Rigdon, and various thoughtful others. From an Affidavit dated December 17, 1902, attested by Lucy Walker (Smith) (Kimball), the following recitals were brought to light:

> *I was a plural wife of the Prophet Joseph Smith, and was married for time and eternity in Nauvoo, State of Illinois, on the first day of May, 1843, by Elder William Clayton. The Prophet was then living with his first wife, Emma Smith, and I know that she gave her consent to the marriage of at least four women to her husband as plural wives, and she was well aware that he associated and cohabited with them as wives.*[30]

In a recent unsigned and undated essay (2014), one of a number of such essays, the Church reported that it is difficult to determine just exactly how Emma (and Joseph) felt about polygamy,[31] when in fact

---

[30]Affidavit of Lucy Walker, 17 December 1902 (Salt Lake County, State of Utah: LDS Archives, MS 3423, CHL); *Blood Atonement and the Origin of Plural Marriage* (correspondence, Elder Joseph F. Smith, Jr., and Mr. Richard C. Evans (1905), 68-69.

[31]"Plural Marriage in Kirtland and Nauvoo" (2014, accessed 15 March 2016), available from https://www.lds.org/topics/plural-marriage-in-kirtland-and-nauvoo ?lang=eng; Internet, 13-14. The exact quote is: "Because of Joseph's early death and Emma's decision to remain in Nauvoo and not discuss plural marriage after the Church moved west, many aspects of their story remain known only to the two

her opposition (consider the case of Eliza R. Snow) would seem to have sometimes been nothing less than violent. Consider the "voice of innocence" pronounced by the Relief Society, Emma Smith, President, on March 20, 1844.[32] Brigham Young, who claimed to know Joseph Smith as well or better than anyone else on earth, reported in General Conference, many years after the fact, that Emma actually poisoned Joseph. "On Sunday, November 5 [1843], Joseph became suddenly sick at dinner and vomited so hard that he dislocated his jaw and 'raised fresh blood.' His self diagnosis was that he had every symptom of poisoning . . . ." The prophet survived that dramatic incident to call foul. Twenty-two or three years later Brigham Young described how Joseph, in a secret council, told Emma "that she was a child of hell, and . . . the most wicked woman on this earth . . . ." "Joseph accused Emma of the poisoning." He spoke to her in "a very severe manner, and she never said one word in reply."[33]

Why would any faithful Latter-day Saint ignore the word of the "Lion of the Lord," a close personal friend of the Prophet, a self-

---

of them." William Clayton, who penned the canonized polygamous revelation (Doctrine and Covenants 132) as Joseph dictated, added this to that: "After the whole was written Joseph requested me to read it slowly and carefully which I did, and he then pronounced it correct. The same night a copy was taken by Bishop Whitney which copy is now here [in the Historian's office in Salt Lake City] and which I know and testify is correct. *The original was destroyed by Emma Smith.*" (William Clayton to Madison M. Scott, 11 November 1871, William Clayton Letterbooks [Salt Lake City, UT: Special Collections, J. Willard Marriott Library, University of Utah], quoted by George D. Smith, *Nauvoo Polygamy*, 48], emphasis added).

[32]"[L]et polygamy, bigamy, fornication, adultery, and prostitution, be frowned out of the hearts of honest men to drop into the gulf of fallen nature, where the worm dieth not and the fire is not quenched . . . ."

[33]Brigham Young Address, Semiannual Conference (7 October 1866), *Brigham Young Papers* (LDS Archives), quoted in Linda King Newell and Valeen Tippetts Avery, *Mormon Enigma: Emma Hale Smith, Prophet's Wife, "Elect Lady," Polygamy's Foe – 1804-1879* (Garden City, N.Y.: Doubleday & Company, Inc., 1984), 163-64. Emma's biographers, while recognizing an event, challenged Brigham Young's analysis. Joseph, they say, "was well enough in the evening to attend an Endowment Council meeting in the room over the red store." (Ibid., 164). No poison available in 1844, "they say," could do what Brigham said that Emma's did "and still be so ineffective as to allow the victim to pursue normal activities within a few hours." Perhaps, they say, "Joseph *believed* . . . that Emma poisoned him, but strong evidence suggests that his self diagnosis was mistaken . . . ." (Ibid.).

proclaimed witness to those events and the leader of the Utah Church for more than thirty years? Any student of Mormon history can easily determine, and surely must be able to figure, just exactly how Emma felt about polygamy. "Though evidence indicates that Emma possessed intimate knowledge of not only polygamy but also Endowment Council and Council of Fifty matters, she did not pass this information down to her children,"[34] or publicly incriminate her husband, who didn't incriminate himself. She was ashamed of the doctrine and angry with others who weren't. Think Brigham Young, think Joseph Smith, think poison.

"[T]he ladies relief society, and married females . . ."

By their fruits ye shall know them. When Emma Smith signed the monogamous nothing but traditional marriage, no secret wife, public ceremony marriage system *Certificate,* she was the legal wife of the Mormon prophet and the President of the Relief Society. Elizabeth Ann Whitney, who witnessed her daughter Sarah Ann's polygamous marriage to Joseph Smith on July 27, 1842, signed Joseph Smith's *Certificate* as one of Emma's Counselors on October 1, 1842. Mrs. Sarah M. Cleveland, Emma's other Counselor, secretly married Joseph Smith, although she already had a legal husband, some time before March of 1842. On October 1, 1842, Sarah Cleveland, one of Joseph's plural wives, certified and declared that monogamy was the only "system of marriage being practiced in the church of Jesus Christ of Latter Day Saints." Eliza R. Snow is shown to have done what Sarah Cleveland did. Eliza, Emma's Relief Society Secretary and a kind of confidante, secretly married Joseph Smith on June 29, 1842, some few days after John C. Bennett left Nauvoo and less than three months before she also signed the fraudulent *Certificate* published by the prophet and presented to the public on October 1, 1842.

Every one of these women, every member of the Presidency of the

---

[34]"Opposition to polygamy and other militant theocratic innovations attributed to his father" is said to have become "the hallmark of the leadership of Joseph Smith III" (Van Wagoner, *Mormon Polygamy: A History*, 75), the leader of the RLDS from 1860 to 1914.

Ladies' Relief Society, the most distinguished women in the Mormon Church, signed Joseph Smith's *Certificate* knowing it was false. Three of those four women were married to Joseph Smith when they signed the *Certificate*, and the fourth had been a witness to Smith's July 27, 1842, marriage to his sixteenth wife, her seventeen-year-old daughter. All four of these women certified and declared "that one man should have one wife; and one woman, but one husband, except in case of death . . . ." Each of them certified and declared that there was no secret wife system and that monogamy was the only rule of marriage "practised" in the Mormon Church.

Emma Smith, President; Elizabeth Ann Whitney, Counselor; Sarah M. Cleveland, Counselor; and Eliza R. Snow, Secretary; representing the Relief Society Presidency and the highest ranking women in the Mormon Church, all knew that Joseph Smith had more than one wife before they and fifteen other women signed a *Certificate* that unequivocally said that he did not.

After witnessing the marriage of her daughter, Sarah Ann, to Joseph Smith, Elizabeth Whitney witnessed the pretended marriage of her daughter, Sarah Ann, to Elizabeth's recently widowed brother-in-law, Joseph Kingsbury. That empty alliance was intended to protect the Mormon prophet from any possible claim that he had plurally married Sarah Ann Whitney. Joseph repeatedly demonstrated, by just such conduct, that he was ashamed to be recognized as a polygamist. During his lifetime, he never publicly admitted that he was a polygamist.

Every one of Smith's prominent Mormon signators certified and declared that they knew of "no system of marriage being practised in the Church of Jesus Christ of Latter Day Saints save the one contained in the Book of Doctrine and Covenants . . . ." None of the women who knew that wasn't true are seen to have told any of the women who didn't know that wasn't true, that it wasn't true, and neither did Editor Smith. And neither did Deputy Editors Taylor and Woodruff, nor either Brigham Young. Those circumstances put one in mind of a quote: "MORALITY: Doing what is right regardless of what you are told. OBEDIENCE: Doing what you are told regardless of what is right."[35]

Sarah M. Kingsley (Cleveland) served her *time* and *eternity* husband as an "intermediary," a word that is gentrified. In the spring of 1842, she introduced "the idea of polygamous marriage to 38-year-old Eliza R. Snow." She then "served as a witness for the *secret* ceremony that united Eliza as a *secret* sister in a *secret* system with Joseph Smith."[36] There was, she said in 1842, out loud and in print, no secret wife system in the Mormon Church. But Sarah Cleveland, Eliza R. Snow, Emma, Louisa, Zina, Presendia and nearly one dozen other women were secret sisters-in-law whether they knew it or not. They may not have known how many wives their prophet had, or just exactly who they were, but every one of them knew it was more than one.

Eliza R. Snow, like Smith's other *Pre-Monogamous Certificate* brides, was sworn to secrecy. The initiated women were bound by their covenants not to describe the doctrine to anyone, a prohibition seen to include family and friends. Despite the intense concern with secrecy, the polygamous principle was hard to protect. What the initiated knew (their secrets set them apart), those who were not initiated had cause to suspect. As rumors circulated, many of those who nurtured suspicions were able to discern the truth from the cryptic comments Smith repeatedly made about the restoration of ancient practices.[37] Eliza R. Snow's dishonesty was traceable to the "infamous doctrine that lies are acceptable unto God if perpetrated in a cause that man calls good." Everything Eliza R. Snow is thought to have ever accomplished is tarnished by her dishonesty as a member of Joseph Smith's family. The poetess in residence is seen to have lacked at this particular time of her life, the most important element of her delicate craft, the attribute of honesty.

If some of the signators among the women didn't know about Mormonism's secret marriage system in October of 1842, many of

---

[35]Attributed to H.L. Mencken.

[36]D. Michael Quinn, "Evidence for the Sexual Side of Joseph Smith's Polygamy," presented to the Mormon History Association's Annual Conference (Calgary, Alberta, Canada: 29 June 2012; expanded, finalized 31 December 2012; circulated mid-2013), 24, emphasis added.

[37]George D. Smith, *Nauvoo Polygamy*, 264.

them knew ever so quickly after. All of them should have known before another set of disingenuous denials of a similar sort were officially published in the *Millennial Star* in the United Kingdom two years later in 1844. With one or two notable exceptions, none of the previously innocent believers moved to retract their misleading testimony. Those who knew, like those who came to know, did nothing to correct the dubious record. Joseph and his witnesses misled a majority of the members and the world at large[38] under the apprehension that "it was an act of virtue to deceive and lie, when by that means the interests of the Church might be promoted." Some who may not have known the whole truth on October 1, 1842, did know in a matter of minutes: Thirza Cahoon was Reynolds Cahoon's first wife. He took a second wife in 1842.[39] Mary C. Miller was George Miller's first wife. He took a second wife on July 20, 1843.[40] Leonora Taylor was John Taylor's first wife. He took a second wife on December 12, 1843.[41] Ann Hunter was Edward Hunter's first wife. He took a second wife on December 15, 1845.[42] Polly Z. Johnson was Aaron Johnson's first wife. He took a second wife on December 22, 1844.[43] On 8 July 1869, Martha McBride (Knight) (Smith) (Kimball), the first and legal wife of Vinson Knight, a man who died on July 31, 1842, upon her oath personally appeared and said "that sometime in the summer of the year 1842, at the city of Nauvoo . . . she was married or sealed to Joseph Smith . . . by Heber C. Kimball, one of the Twelve Apostles . . . ."[44]

Three Hundred and Eighty Other Witnesses: August 1842

On 29 August 1842 (two days before *Times and Seasons* Editor Joseph Smith published the monogamous marriage provisions from

---

[38]"[S]o that the world might understand the abusive conduct of our enemies [ex-Governor Boggs of Missouri is mentioned by name] and stamp it with indignation." (Jessee, ed., *The Papers of Joseph Smith: Journal, 1832-1842*, 443).

[39]George D. Smith, *Nauvoo Polygamy*, 581.

[40]Ibid., 608.

[41]Ibid., 627.

[42]Ibid., 597.

[43]Ibid., 598.

[44]*Blood Atonement and the Origin of Plural Marriage* (correspondence, Elder Joseph F. Smith, Jr., and Mr. Richard C. Evans (1905), 72.

Section 101 of the 1835 edition of the Doctrine and Covenants in the *Times and Seasons* on September 1, 1842), three hundred and eighty elders agreed to travel statewide to distribute a broadside filled with affidavits and certificates in a massive effort to convince the unwitting public that Joseph Smith was not the person John C. Bennett said that he was.[45]   The central thrust of John C. Bennett's provocative criticism of Joseph Smith concerned various highly charged and controversial domestic issues.   It was in order to combat those particular allegations, and some less provocative others, that Joseph's "volunteers" were asked to step up, spread out, travel and defend.   *"[It] was wisdom in God that the Elders should go forth and deluge the States with the flood of truth . . . ."*[46]

What did *"wisdom in God"* and *"the flood of truth"* require? What were those nearly *four hundred* elders recruited by Joseph Smith charged to *go forth* to report? That the leaders of the Church had been falsely accused of the crimes of fornication and polygamy; that the Mormons believed that one man should have one wife and one woman but one husband; that all marriages should be solemnized in a public meeting or feast; that men and women should keep themselves wholly for each other, and from all others during their lives; that monogamy was the only system of marriage practiced in the Church; that there was no secret wife system; and that the clerk kept a public record of all marriages solemnized in his branch. The problem was that none of that was true.

Other Stunning Deceptions

Millennial Star, August 1842:

> *But, for the information of those who might be assailed by those foolish tales about two wives, we would say that no such principle ever existed among*

---

[45]Joseph Smith Jr., *History of The Church of Jesus Christ of Latter-day Saints*, B.H. Roberts, ed., 2d ed., rev., (Salt Lake City: The Deseret Book Company, 1978), 5:131-32; Joseph Smith Jr., *The Papers of Joseph Smith: Journal, 1832-1842*, ed. Dean C. Jessee (Salt Lake City: Deseret Book Company, 1989-1992), 443-47.

[46]Jessee, ed., *The Papers of Joseph Smith: Journal, 1832-1842*, 443, emphasis added.

> *the Latter Day Saints, and ever will . . . .*[47]

Four weeks after the October 1, 1842, denunciation of polygamy in the *Times and Seasons*, Mr. Joseph Smith, the editor and proprietor of the *Times and Seasons*, improvidently published a lengthy defense of polygamy in a booklet entitled *The Peace Maker*, a document of considerable sophistication.   The timing of the publication of the piece could not have been worse. This particular misstep may have precipitated Smith's leaving the editorship on November 15, 1842. "The *Peace Maker's* call for a restoration of polygamy caused a stir [among the uninformed] in Nauvoo."[48] After sending up this trial balloon in supposed support of a doctrine he was privately keen to promote, "Smith responded to the uproar" awkwardly. The booklet had been published, he said, "without my knowledge" (at that particular time that was impossible). What he said, in response to those who challenged the piece, those who were not in the polygamous loop, was just another prevarication. "[H]ad I been apprised of it, I should not have printed it[,] . . . I do not wish to have my name associated with the authors, in such an unmeaning rigmarole of nonsense, folly and trash."[49]

In this craven hypocritical retreat from his secretly cherished initiative, men to gods and glory, an eternally essential precept at the heart and soul of the Mormon concept of the eternal family, and in the face of furor, Joseph publicly derided what he privately called "the most holy and important doctrine ever revealed to man on the earth." Polygamy was a doctrine without obedience to which "a fullness of exaltation" could never be obtained. At that moment, and for public consumption, "The Principle" was described by the same editor who recklessly published the then controversial piece, meaning Smith himself, as "an unmeaning rigmarole of nonsense, folly and trash."

On August 12, 1843, Hyrum Smith presented the definitive revelation on polygamy (the canonized Section 132 of the modern Doctrine and Covenants dated July 12, 1843) to the Nauvoo High

---

[47]*Millennial Star*, vol. 3 no. 4 (Liverpool, Great Britain), 74, emphasis added.
[48]Van Wagoner, *Mormon Polygamy: A History*, 47.
[49]*Times and Seasons*, vol. 4 (1 December 1842): 32, quoted in Van Wagoner, *Mormon Polygamy: A History*, 47.

Council. "[T]he year 1843 was when the doctrine officially [though not yet publicly] arrived for a small elite group of followers."[50] The new document said: "For behold, I reveal unto you a new and an everlasting covenant [celestial/plural sealing]; and if ye abide not that covenant, then are ye damned; for no one can reject this covenant and be permitted to enter into my glory."[51]

In March 1844, after Hyrum had delivered the confidential revelation to the members of the High Council to be secretly read and accepted in August 1843, Hyrum published a statement in the *Times and Seasons* in which he unequivocally denied the teaching of "plural wives or polygamy," reporting to the paper's faithful clientele "that all such teaching is false doctrine."[52] When Hyrum – who succeeded Joseph Sr. as the Presiding Patriarch – published those misrepresentations, he had, in addition to his dead legal wife Jerusha Barden (date of death: October 13, 1837) and his living second legal wife, Mary Fielding (date of marriage: December 24, 1837), just recently married Mercy Rachel Fielding (Thompson) (August 11, 1843), Catharine Phillips (August 1843), Lydia Dibble (Granger) (ca. August 1843), and Louisa Sanger (before September 17, 1843).[53]

---

[50]"Four of Smith's Nauvoo associates – James Allred, David Fullmer, Thomas Grover and Aaron Johnson – testified that on August 12, 1843 'Hyrum Smith presented to the [Nauvoo Stake] High Council in his brick office at Nauvoo Assembled, the Revelation on Celestial Marriage, given to Joseph Smith and written on the 12th day of July 1843.'" (David Fullmer et al, Affidavit, 10 October 1869, quoted by George D. Smith, *Nauvoo Polygamy*, 47). One of the members of the Nauvoo High Council, and one of those testators, was this author's third great-grandfather and first Mormon ancestor, James Allred.

[51]Doctrine and Covenants 132:4.

[52]Joel B. Groat, "Joseph Smith Statements Denying Polygamy: WWCB Series (Why We Can't Believe) (Institute for Religious Research, accessed December 2015), available from mit.irr.org/joseph-smith-statements-denying-polygamy); Internet, 1.

[53]George D. Smith, *Nauvoo Polygamy*, 620-21. Hyrum's marriage to Mercy Rachel Fielding (Thompson) was supposed to have been decreed "by direct revelation from Heaven through Brother Joseph the Prophet." (Mercy Fielding [Thompson] [Smith] [Taylor, Mrs. John, divorced], Autobiographical Sketch). "This was a marriage for time, Hyrum serving as proxy for Mercy's sealing to her deceased husband, Robert B. Thompson." Mercy declared that they were married "a few weeks before" Hyrum read the revelation on marriage to the High Council on August 12, 1843. Catharine Phillips said that "the prophet Joseph Smith himself" performed her marriage to Hyrum in Hyrum's "brick office building."

Hyrum's unfortunate publication then further reported that, "[S]ome of your elders say [a brother by the name of Richard Hewitt is mentioned as having made this allegation], that a man *having a certain priesthood*, may have as many wives as he pleases, and that doctrince [*sic*] is taught here: I say unto you that that man teaches *false doctrine*, for there is no such doctrine taught here; neither is there any such thing practised here."[54]   Hyrum, like his brother Joseph, was ashamed to publicly embrace a doctrine God is supposed to have required.   It is now 1844, and Hyrum, like his brother Joseph, could be trusted not to tell the truth.

In the *Times and Seasons* in 1844, after the revelation on polygamy was read to the Nauvoo High Council on August 12, 1843, but before it was publicly reported in 1852, the Mormon publication then further reported that the spiritual wife system merely allows a man to be married to another wife if his first wife dies."[55]   In other words, it wasn't polygamy (until the afterlife), and what it was was not against the law of man or God or offensive, but rather only something quite benign.   About two years prior to that 1844 declaration, and on May 11, 1842, the leaders had to decide what to do with Dr. John C. Bennett.   Those who concurred with the decision to "withdraw the hand of fellowship" from Bennett for

---

Joseph Jackson was apparently referring to Louisa Sanger in his *Narrative of the Adventures and Experience*, 30, when he wrote "that Joseph Smith offered his brother 'one of his spiritual girls, whom Hyrum loved dearly, a Miss S,' in consideration for Joseph's alleged interest in Hyrum's daughter, Lovina." (Joseph H. Jackson, *A Narrative of the Adventures and Experience of Joseph H. Jackson in Nauvoo, Disclosing the Depths of Mormon Villainy* [Warsaw, IL: Signal Office, August 1844], quoted in George D. Smith, *Nauvoo Polygamy*, 650, footnotes and cites 347-50).   Lovina was Joseph Smith's niece.   Hyrum married Louisa Sanger sometime before September 17, 1843 (Louisa received her patriarchal blessing coincident with these events on Sept 17.)   She was Hyrum's fourth plural wife. (George D. Smith, *Nauvoo Polygamy*, 650).

[54]*Times and Seasons*, vol. 5 (March 1844), 474, emphasis retained.

[55]*Times and Seasons*, vol. 5 (15 November 1844), 715.   "The law of the land and the rules of the church do not allow one man to have more than one wife *alive at once*, but if any man's wife die, he has a right to marry another, and to be sealed to both for eternity; . . . there is no law of man or God against it!   This is all the spiritual wife system that ever was tolerated in the church . . . ."   This *Times and Seasons* report followed the death of Joseph Smith by nearly five months.   Before Joseph Smith died, and until November 2, 1843, he had about thirty-eight wives "*alive at once*," not counting Fanny Alger. (George D. Smith, *Nauvoo Polygamy*, 621-23, emphasis added).

practicing *spiritual wifery* (Bennett didn't marry his women) included Joseph Smith, Hyrum Smith, Brigham Young, William Law and Newel K. Whitney, among others.[56] In Bennett's case, as in other cases, spiritual wifery came to mean permissible conjugal relations without any temporal commitment, free love, secret adultery without remorse. Bennett was excommunicated for practicing secret spiritual wifery on June 18, 1842.

On February 1, 1844, the *Times and Seasons* publicly announced the excommunication of elder Hiram Brown for "preaching polygamy, and other false and corrupt doctrines" in the state of Michigan. "This is to notify him and the church in general, that he has been cut off from the Church, for his iniquity, and he is further notified to appear at the special conference, on the 6th of April next, to make answer to these charges." This particular announcement was signed by "JOSEPH SMITH, HYRUM SMITH, Presidents of said Church,"[57] in unmistakable recognition of the supreme importance of what was then called the Patriarchal Priesthood. Hyrum, the Presiding Patriarch and elder brother, had come to be treated as Joseph's equal because of that Smith family patriarchal priesthood inheritance. By February 1, 1844, the date of this publication, Joseph Smith had married nearly forty women. And in the six months prior to this announcement, Hyrum Smith had taken about three polygamous wives.[58] Elder Brown's offense was that he had preached what Joseph and Hyrum had both already practiced, without the consent of the prophet and outside of Nauvoo. This nondescript elder preaching doctrines above his pay grade in some forbidden place was not a highly privileged confidential insider.

More than six years after the revelation dated July 12, 1843, and as but part of a rhetorical reply to some detractors published for the British Saints in the *Millennial Star*, the Church reported as follows:

---

[56] *Times and Seasons*, vol. III no. 16 (15 June 1842), 830.
[57] *Times and Seasons*, vol. V no. 3 (1 February 1844), 423.
[58] George D. Smith, *Nauvoo Polygamy*, 620-21.

Millennial Star, January 1850:

> *12TH LIE – Joseph Smith taught a system of polygamy.*
>
> *12TH REFUTATION – The Revelations[59] given through Joseph Smith, state the following . . . "Thou shalt love thy wife, and shalt cleave unto her, and none else." Page 124 [Doctrine and Covenants] – "We believe that one man should have one wife. 'Doctrine and Covenants,' page 331."[60]*

By their fruits ye shall know them. Joseph first "taught a system of polygamy" in *1831*, nineteen years before *January 1850*. Todd Compton and D. Michael Quinn both say that the prophet probably married Fanny Alger in 1833. The editor of the *Millennial Star*, and the publisher of this incredible piece, was Apostle Orson Pratt, the man who ate crow to rather become the "Apostle of Polygamy." By January 1850, when this report was published, Pratt was plurally married to Sarah Marinda Bates, Charlotte Bishop, Adelia Ann Bishop, Mary Ann Merrill and Louisa Chandler, women with whom he ultimately had twenty-three children. After 1850, Pratt married Marian Ross, Sarah Louisa Lewis, Juliet Ann Phelps, Eliza Crooks and Margaret Graham, women with whom he had twenty-two more children.[61]

By January 1850, the date of the *Millennial Star* submission, the practice of polygamy was full blown in Mormonism's isolated Utah Territory. Lieutenant John Gunnison 1852: "That many have a large number of wives in Deseret [Utah], is perfectly manifest to any

---

[59]The Mormon publication describes the monogamous provisions in the Doctrine and Covenants – which defend traditional marriage, a public ceremony and a written record in 1850 – as *"Revelations given through Joseph Smith."* Section 132, the *true doctrine* of the Church in January 1850, as secretly presented to the Nauvoo High Council on August 12, 1843, was not added to the second edition of the Doctrine and Covenants in 1844. (Emphasis added).

[60]*The Latter-day Saints' Millennial Star*, 12 no. 2 (15 January 1850), 29-30, emphasis added and retained. While this refutation quoted Section 101 (dated 1835) or Section 109 (dated 1844), it ignored the unpublished revelation (today's Doctrine and Covenants 132) dated July 12, 1843.

[61]George D. Smith, *Nauvoo Polygamy*, 612-13.

one residing long among them . . . ."[62] Yet converts who joined the Church in the British Isles from 1837 to 1852 – as in the case of Joseph Morris, the martyred future leader of the ill-fated Morrisites – were ignorant of the fact that Joseph Smith and the Utah Church taught and secretly practiced polygamy. That was an affront to people who wanted to be honest, an omission of enormous magnitude. English Saints who joined the Church before 1852 or 1853 were never properly founded. Their consent to the deliberately deceptive doctrine of the unprincipled new society was incomplete and uninformed. They were misled. Every United Kingdom conversion from 1837 to 1852 (number them in the thousands) was tainted by this incredible impropriety.

POLYGAMY VERSUS ADULTERY – ILLEGAL BY ANY NAME

The subject of polygamy is historically troublesome. In this case, as in so many others, the Church "that asks its members to be honest in their dealings with their fellow men" hasn't been honest with them. Mormon apologists, when faced with this moral dilemma, are forced to call adultery sacred and dishonesty justified. For the faithful this is a slippery slope. An anonymous contributor to the internet put the issue in these terms: "Let's get one thing straight, polygamy is the nice word."

Members (every member an apologist) are asked to awkwardly defend what is morally indefensible – meaningless civil covenants, undeputized marriage, wife swaps, sexual consent relationships, plural wives, concubines, pre-pubescent and polyandrous wives. The doctrine allowed for husbands sharing wives for time, nieces as wives, mothers and daughters and sisters as wives, and children wrested from their biological fathers to share the wonders of eternity with strangers in a peculiarly plural kind of Mormon afterlife. In Illinois, from 1833 forward, polygamous marriages were always illegal. Performed outside of the law by someone other

---

[62]Lieut. John W. Gunnison, *The Mormons, or Latter-day Saints, in the Valley of The Great Salt Lake: A history of their rise and progress, peculiar doctrines, present condition, and prospects, derived from personal observation, during a residence among them* (Freeport, NY: Books for Libraries Press, 1852, 1972), 67.

than a justice of the peace or any other figure of authority, they were not marriages under the law.[63]

Polygamy was illegal in Illinois, the Utah Territory, Mexico and Canada. The Church didn't publicly admit that it was practicing polygamy until 1852. Prior to that disclosure, the leaders lied to each other and everyone else. Before the Church came out of the closet in 1852, the revelation and the doctrine wasn't presented to the membership for a favorable vote in any public proceeding. And in 1852, when the secret practice was admitted and disclosed, it wasn't voted on or consented to. "[A]ll polygamy practiced before that date was [by Mormon reckoning] illicit and unapproved."[64] In the early days of the Church, from the beginning and until the day he died, Joseph Smith, who promoted what might be called extreme domesticity, secretly tested society's "moral boundaries" in his freewheeling encounters with underage females, sisters, mothers and daughters, and with the previously married and undivorced wives of other men.

MORMON BELIEF IN POLYGAMY TODAY

The LDS Church was led by polygamous men from the 1830s until 1945. "Mormons still practice polygamy. They are called the FLDS, . . . they believe in the Book of Mormon and Joseph Smith" and say that Adam is God. "[Y]ou shouldn't leave them [those Mormon Fundamentalists] out of your definition of Mormon, unless you're fine with Christians calling you non-Christian even though you believe in Christ."[65] The leaders of the FLDS, people who refused to "suspend" their polygamous practice, still follow the distinctive teachings of Joseph Smith, Brigham Young, John Taylor, Wilford Woodruff, Lorenzo Snow, Joseph F. Smith and Heber J. Grant. Those are the first seven polygamous prophets,

---

[63]Mithryn (anonymous contributor), "Greg Trimble, the word is 'Adultery,'" Exploring Mormonism (accessed 25 November 2014), available from https://exploringmormonism.com/greg-trimble-the-word-is-adultery/; Internet.

[64]Randyj, "Recovery from Mormonism" (accessed 2 December 2014); Internet, available from http://www.exmormon.org; Internet.

[65]Mithryn, "Greg Trimble, the word is 'Adultery,'" Exploring Mormonism (accessed 25 November 2014); Internet.

every one of whom actively practiced polygamy during their lifetimes, then lived to lead the Mormon Church. The practice of polygamy has been suspended, but the canonized doctrine has never been dismissed. Make no mistake; the battered Manifesto was never intended to be the last gasp of Mormon polygamy.

The leaders of the FLDS (Fundamentalists) faithfully follow (and indeed revere) Section 132 of the Doctrine and Covenants (the polygamic revelation on celestial/plural marriage). They are light years closer to practicing the true teachings of Joseph Smith and of those other plural prophets than the modern prophets and the present Quorum of the Twelve. Furthermore, they claim lineal apostolic authority from early Church leaders by the laying on of hands. These beleaguered Fundamentalist Mormons continue to practice "The Principle," polygamy, under conditions of extreme adversity. They believe "there are three heavens or degrees." They believe that "in order to obtain the highest [heaven or degree], a man must enter into this order of the priesthood [plural marriage]; and if he does not, he cannot obtain it, He may enter into the other, but that is the end of his kingdom; he cannot have an increase."[66]

Those true advocates of the true teachings of Joseph Smith know that if they do not "abide" the new and everlasting covenant (plural marriage), they are "damned, for no one can reject this covenant and be permitted to enter into my glory."[67]   Today's Fundamentalists believe that everyone to whom this law is revealed must obey the same. They believe that Christ told them (and everyone else) that this new and everlasting covenant would not be taken from the earth until he returned, and that compliance with the dictates of the everlasting covenant is essential to a fullness of exaltation in the kingdom of God.

1833 (OR 1841) TO 1852

On or before April 5, 1841, Smith married Louisa Beaman, an attractive woman, in a secret ceremony officiated by her brother-in-law, Joseph Bates Noble. In 1841 Smith married two sisters, both of

---

[66]Doctrine and Covenants 131:1-4.
[67]Doctrine and Covenants 132:4.

whom were already married to other men. Zina Jacobs, one of them, was seven months pregnant by her legal husband, Henry Jacobs, and undivorced, when she then also married Smith. Mrs. Zina Diantha Huntington (Jacobs), a future General President of the Relief Society, a position Emma Smith initially held, and Zina's sister, Presendia Lathrop Huntington (Buell) both joined Smith (with their children) *for time and eternity.*

In 1842, before he published those ill-considered *Certificates* in the *Times and Seasons*, and before he sent four hundred elders out to support "*wisdom in God*," "*the flood of truth*" and "*the character*" of their prevaricating prophet, Joseph Smith married thirteen women in eight or nine months. One of them was the widow of his dead brother Don Carlos Smith. Eight of those 1842 women (ten if one includes two 1841 wives, Zina Huntington (Jacobs) and Presendia Huntington (Buell)), were women already married to, supported by, living and cohabiting with other men and undivorced. This polyandrous formula should be weighed and measured against Joseph Smith's personal prototype for the celestial family. The prophet's marital life is Mormonism's domestic example. "Follow the prophet" is just as apt here, under these unusually formidable circumstances, as it is for any other principle, practice, time or place.

Joseph knew before he personally published the *1842 Times and Seasons Certificates* on October 1, 1842, how many wives that he then had (at least seventeen), how secret the rituals had been (invariably secret), and that some of his signators were polyandrous women (Sarah M. Cleveland) and polygamous women (Eliza R. Snow), and plural wives to him. One of the witnesses (Newel K. Whitney) was one of the prophet's fathers-in-law after July of 1842. One of the witnesses (Elizabeth Ann Whitney) was one of the prophet's mothers-in-law after July of 1842. Two apostle witnesses, John Taylor and Wilford Woodruff, both future Presidents of the Church, and an unsigned Brigham Young knew all about the remarkable "privileges and blessings of the priesthood" when they solemnly "certified and declared" in those fraudulent *Certificates* that they did not. Leonora Taylor and Phoebe ("Phebe") Woodruff, the wives of those apostles knew then, or very soon after, that their

knowledgeable husbands had promoted their participation in a fraudulent scheme.

If Joseph Smith didn't tell the truth about polygamy from 1829 or 1831, or 1833 to 1844, in public, not even once, how could he have been trusted to tell the truth about anything else? If the Mormon Church didn't tell the truth about polygamy from 1829 or 1831 to 1852, not even once, how could it be trusted to tell the truth about anything else? If the truth could be so easily sacrificed in defense of the doctrine of polygamy, could it not be equally easily sacrificed in support or defense of anything else?   If thirty-one witnesses couldn't be trusted to tell the truth about the practice of marriage, if four hundred elders couldn't be trusted to tell the truth about the practice of marriage, why should anyone trust the testimony of the witnesses to the Book of Mormon.

"[T]he story of the gold plates could not be fanciful mythology and the Book of Mormon still be scripture."

"All of the Book of Mormon's historically defined functions would be disabled in the presence of fraudulent origins."[68]

---

[68]Terryl L. Givens, *By the Hand of Mormon: The American Scripture that Launched a New World Religion* (*n.p.*: Oxford University Press, Inc., 2002; reprint, New York, NY: Oxford University Press paperback, 2003), 178, emphasis added.

CHAPTER FOURTEEN

The Elders to the Rescue

But, for the information of those who might be assailed by those foolish tales about two wives, we would say that no such principle ever existed among the Latter Day Saints, and ever will . . . .[1]

Millennial Star, August 1842

. . . Doctor! [Joseph Smith to John C. Bennett in 1842] why are you using my name to carry on your hellish wickedness? Have I ever taught you that fornication and adultery was right, or polygamy, or any such practices?[2]

Joseph Smith, Reported Under Oath by Hyrum Smith

Bro. James Sloan [General Clerk and Recorder] – You will be so good as to permit Gen. Bennett to withdraw his name from the Church Record, if he desires to do so, and this with the best of feelings towards you and General Bennett.[3]

Joseph Smith, May 17, 1842

---

[1] *Millennial Star*, vol. 3 no 4 (Liverpool, Great Britain: August 1842), 73, emphasis added.

[2] *Millennial Star*, vol. 3 no 6 (Liverpool, Great Britain: October 1842), 105, emphasis added.

[3] For more than one hundred years, excommunication was the only way a living person could leave the Church. Bennett was an exception. "[A]s you have now withdrawn from the Church in an honorable manner, over my own signature, a privilege never granted to any other person, you must and shall, place it out of your power to injure me or the Church, – do it or the Mississippi is your portion . . . ." (Bennett's Second Letter, *Sangamo Journal*, vol. 10 no 47 [15 July 1842]).

JOSEPH'S DEFENSE

Smith's Reaction to Bennett's Letters

The defenses promoted by Smith and his associates in "Affidavits and Certificates" abused the concept of civilized discourse. If Bennett's hard-bitten exposé was the disease, and if Smith's "Affidavits" were the cure, the cure was worse than the disease. After Smith had savaged Bennett and various other alleged conspirators, Nauvoo looked like a cesspool.

In combating the allegations of John C. Bennett, Sarah Pratt, Nancy Rigdon, George W. Robinson, Francis M. Higbee, Martha Brotherton, Melissa Schindle, J.F. Olney, Carlos Gove, Henry Marks and others, Smith and his supporters attacked the integrity of his accusers with reckless impunity, truth be damned. Character assassination, *ad hominem* accusations, ascended the heights. However accursed Smith's accusers were, however tarnished he made them seem to be, Smith's allegations did nothing to change the fact that by August 29, 1842, he had secretly married about sixteen women (not including Emma Smith or Fanny Alger), ten of whom were women already legally married to other men who fathered their children and supported them. After all those accusations back and forth, Smith proceeded to marry about twenty-one additional women before he died on June 27, 1844.

On July 22, 1842, Wilson Law (William Law's brother, an innocent follower late to the table on polygamy) presented a resolution to a meeting of Saints after "having heard that John C. Bennett was circulating many base falsehoods" about some of the Saints "and especially against our worthy and respected Mayor, Joseph Smith." "[S]o far as we are acquainted with Joseph Smith," and for Wilson Law that wasn't as far it might have been, "we know him to be a good, moral, virtuous, peaceable and patriotic man . . . ." This reassuring resolution "was signed by over eight hundred men," lemmings in lockstep, but not by Orson Pratt. "The Ladies Relief Society also drew up a petition to Illinois Governor Carlin defending Joseph Smith's virtue." The Relief Society petition "was signed by a thousand women,"[4] other lemmings in lockstep. More than eighteen hundred Latter-day Saints, many of them uninformed but some of them not, defended Smith in general terms against the specific allegations circulated against him by their previous worthy, respected, unanimously elected mayor, the now suddenly notorious John C. Bennett.

Wilson Law, who later left the Church after concluding that Joseph wasn't a good, moral, virtuous, peaceable and patriotic man, didn't know on the date of the resolution that Joseph Smith had married about fourteen women in addition to Emma, perhaps ten or eleven of them in the first six or seven months of that particularly memorable year. Most of the eight hundred men and thousand women who signed those two resolutions didn't know that their leader was a polygamist. But Joseph knew and let them sign. He allowed those petitions to be delivered with his own personal letter to Governor Carlin in Quincy on July 26.[5] Wilson Law delivered the resolutions and the prophet's letter.

By the end of the month in which a thousand women presented a Relief Society resolution "defending Joseph Smith's virtue," he was married to Louisa Beaman, Mrs. Zina Diantha Huntington (Jacobs), Mrs. Prescindia Lathrop Huntington (Buell), Agnes Moulton Coolbrith (Smith), Mrs. Lucinda Pendleton (Morgan) (Harris), Mrs. Mary Elizabeth Rollins (Lightner), Mrs. Sylvia Porter Sessions (Lyon), Mrs. Patty Bartlett (Sessions), Mrs. Sarah M. Kingsley (Howe Cleveland), Mrs. Elizabeth Davis (G. Brackenbury Durfee), Mrs. Marinda Nancy Johnson (Hyde), Delcena Diadamia Johnson (Sherman), Eliza Roxcy Snow, Sarah Rapson (Poulterer) and Sarah Ann Whitney. Smith recklessly married Eliza R. Snow on June 29, 1842, slightly more than one week after John C. Bennett left Nauvoo. He married Sarah Ann Whitney on July 27, 1842.[6] In the scheme of things, about one-third of Smith's many plural marriages were unofficial, not recorded or

---

[4]Andrew F. Smith, *The Saintly Scoundrel: The Life and Times of Dr. John Cook Bennett* (Urbana and Chicago: University of Illinois, 1997), 110.

[5]Ibid.

[6]George D. Smith, *Nauvoo Polygamy: "... but we called it celestial marriage"* (Salt Lake City: Signature Books, 2008), 621-22, 651 n 365.

witnessed.   There is nothing to suggest they were anything more than sexual consent arrangements.[7]

Four of the women in the Relief Society leadership, Emma Smith, Sarah Cleveland, Elizabeth Durfee and Eliza R. Snow, were plural wives of Joseph Smith when the Relief Society resolution was signed.   Hannah S. Ells (a "Sec. Pro Tem" of the Relief Society on October 1, 1842) married Smith sometime shortly after that petition in 1843.   "[A] good, moral, virtuous, peaceable and patriotic man" would not have secretly married the already married wives of other men, most of them faithful Mormon men, then say that he did not. Or have his followers, including those twice married women, say that he did not.   A good, moral, virtuous man would not have married a mother (Patty Bartlett [Sessions]) and her daughter (Sylvia Porter Sessions [Lyon]), both of them legal wives of other men.   Such a man would not have concealed morally indefensible scripturally prohibited polyandrous marriages from his legal wife, the mother of his children and the President of the Relief Society. Smith publicly denied to his uninformed, insufficiently favored followers that he and some other highly favored, better informed followers were actively preaching and practicing the "*doctrine*" of polygamy.   At that early time, that doctrine was just then reserved for the benefit of a carefully selected few of his especially favored friends.

A blissfully ignorant Wilson Law, a man empowered by the principle of plausible deniability, hand-delivered that personal letter from Joseph Smith at the same time he delivered the two resolutions signed by eight hundred men and a thousand women to

---

[7]"[O]f the thirty-three women listed by Todd Compton as being plural wives of Joseph Smith [a list that is likely incomplete], twelve do not have an officiator, ceremony or witness to their marriage/sealing."   These women were Fanny Alger, Mrs. Lucinda Harris, Mrs. Sylvia Sessons, Mrs. Elizabeth Durfee, Mrs. Sarah Cleveland and widow Delcena Johnson.   Those who were single were seen to include Flora Ann Woodworth, Sarah and Maria Lawrence, Hannah Ells, Olive Frost and Nancy Winchester.   Grant H. Palmer asks, "Is inadequate record keeping the problem, or are some of these women – especially the married ones – sexual consent relationships?"   (Grant H. Palmer, Sexual Allegations against Joseph Smith and the Beginnings of Polygamy in Nauvoo," typescript, n.a. [after 1999], UU_Accn 0900, H. Michael Marquardt Collection, Marriott Library, photocopy in possession of Joel M. Allred).

Governor Carlin in Quincy, Illinois, on July 26, 1842. One day
after those petitions were delivered and on July 27, 1842, Joseph
Smith plurally married (was bonded for eternity to) seventeen-year-
old Sarah Ann Whitney, a woman less than half his age who then
became his sixteenth wife.

*The Down and Dirty Details: Joseph Defends Himself from John C.
Bennett's "Falsehoods"*

When John C. Bennett was expelled from the Nauvoo Masonic
Lodge on August 8, 1842, the first charge was seduction.
"Seduction. For seducing certain previously respectable females of
our city by using Joseph Smith's name as one who sanctioned such
conduct." The second charge was adultery. "Adultery. For illicit
intercourse with various females frequently." The third charge was
lying. "Lying. In using Joseph Smith's name . . . saying that said
Smith taught and practiced illicit intercourse with women, he
knowing it to be false."[8] On August 27, 1842, editor William
Smith's *Wasp*, a Mormon publication, condemned Bennett as "the
pimp and . . . leader of such mean harlots as Martha H. Brotherton
and her predecessors from old Jezebel."[9]

Before August 29 and for the extensive use of hundreds of elders,
Joseph Smith published a collection of statements and quotes,
including previously published materials, in a notorious broadside
cumbrously titled "Affidavits and Certificates Disproving the

---

[8]Charges, reproduced in Andrew F. Smith, *The Saintly Scoundrel*, 111.

[9]Ibid., 111. In 1845, after the death of his father and brothers, also patriarchs,
and in the year that he briefly became the Presiding Patriarch, William Smith
married Mary Jane Rollins, Henriette Rice, Priscilla Mogridge, Mary Jones and
Elizabeth Weston. William and Mary Jane Rollins "separated within two months
and formally divorced in 1847." Henriette Rice was fourteen years old when she
married Smith. "Henriette separated from William the same year they were
married." William and Elizabeth Weston married and separated the same year.
In 1846 William married Abeanade E. Archer. They "separated in 1847." William
Smith married sisters Sarah Ann Libby and Hanna Mariah Libby in 1844. Both
were separated from him in 1845. Mary Ann Covington (Sheffield) married
William Smith in 1843. They separated in 1845. Susan M. Cooney (Clark)
married William Smith in 1844, and they were separated in 1844. (George D.
Smith, *Nauvoo Polygamy*, 623, 652 n 380-388). The prophet's apostle/patriarch
brother was a well-traveled somewhat shopworn consort.

Statements and Affidavits Contained in John C. Bennett's Letters."
Among the Affidavits and Certificates was one that had not been
previously published, a statement prepared by Joseph's friend,
Stephen Markham. Markham said that he saw Nancy Rigdon in
bed, and that John C. Bennett was "sitting by the side of the bed"
("near the foot"), engaged "in close conversation with her."
Markham said that "vulgar, unbecoming and indecent sayings and
motions passed between them." He was "satisfied," he said, because
of what he said that he had seen, "that they were 'guilty of unlawful
and illicit intercourse, with each other.'"[10]

Sidney Rigdon, Nancy's prominent father, attacked Markham, his
daughter's tormentor, as a person who had "previously lied under
oath."   Lying under oath was standard procedure in Nauvoo,
Illinois, and in the Utah Territory (and in the mission field) in the
nineteenth and twentieth centuries. George W. Robinson, Nancy's
brother-in-law, was present "during the incident that Markham
had witnessed." Robinson said that Nancy "was ill and Bennett was
her attending physician" and denied that any such conversations
ever occurred. He said that Markham invented the story "to injure
the character of Miss Rigdon," and more particularly for "the use
of the Elders" sent "to rebut Dr. Bennett's statements." Robinson
hired an attorney to sue Markham, followed by affidavits filed in
support of Miss Rigdon's character, "by Oliver Olney, Carlos Gove
and Henry Marks."[11]

William Smith's *Wasp*, the lengthened shadow of its cadaverous
editor, accused Bennett of "buggery," but offered no proof. Some
sources seem to suggest that Bennett was bisexual.[12] Higbee, who
had forewarned Miss Rigdon of Joseph Smith's polygamous
intentions in advance of their scandalous meeting, had charged
Joseph Smith with slander. By way of response, Smith appeared
before the Nauvoo municipal court, a friendly forum, and requested
a writ of *habeas corpus*, "presenting evidence against [Nauvoo
Legion Colonel Francis] Higbee who was not present." Brigham
Young appeared in those empty proceedings as a witness in support
of Smith. Young testified that John C. Bennett told Joseph Smith in

---

[10]Andrew F. Smith, *The Saintly Scoundrel*, 111-12.
[11]Ibid., 112.
[12]Ibid., 112-13.

Brigham Young's presence "that Francis Higbee had contracted a venereal disease from a 'woman on the hill,'" "a 'French girl' from Warshaw. Bennett had supposedly cured Higbee of the disease." Higbee admitted but then later denied that the allegation was true.[13] "Before Bennett left Nauvoo, Smith visited Higbee and found him in a bed on the floor. The editor of the *Times and Seasons* refused to print the next part of Joseph Smith's testimony, stating that it was 'too indelicate for the public eye or ear'" and was "'revolting, corrupt, and disgusting.'"[14]

There were no winners in these slime-ridden exchanges. The allegations on both sides were "revolting," "indelicate," "corrupt" and "disgusting." The social and domestic environment required to produce such appalling revelations left much to be desired.

> *Bennett was also charged with performing abortions, or "embryo infanticide," a charge that was likely true. Hyrum Smith alleged Bennett seduced women with the promise "that he could give them medicine to produce abortions, providing they should become pregnant." Zeruiah Goddard claimed Bennett told Sarah Pratt "that he could cause abortion with perfect safety to the mother at any stage of pregnancy, and that he had frequently destroyed and removed infants before their time to prevent exposure of the parties, and that he had instruments for that purpose."[15]*

Many years later, after she had left the Church, Sarah Pratt placed that talent squarely at the disposal of Joseph Smith. In her interview with Dr. Wilhelm Ritter von Wymetal ("Dr. W. Wyl"), "Pratt related that when Joseph Smith had intercourse with women, 'Dr. Bennett was always on hand, when anything happened.' Bennett had a long instrument that was made 'of steel and was crooked at one end' that he used for inducing abortions."[16]

---

[13]A claim made by Samuel W. Taylor, author of *Nightfall at Nauvoo*. (Ibid., 112).

[14]Ibid., 112-13.

[15]Ibid., 113, emphasis added.

[16]Ibid.

Mormonism's hundreds of missionary elders, while on their missions to support the character of their prophet, "tried to encourage editors to insert Joseph's 'Affidavits and Certificates' into their newspapers. Few succeeded, but many newspapers mentioned that these anti-Bennett certificates had been published in the Mormon press."[17]

The Break Between Joseph and Bennett

There was more truth in Bennett's claims than there was in Joseph Smith's denials. Smith's thoroughly dishonest approach to the secret practice of polygamy supported the society's elaborate prevarication concerning that most difficult issue. That problem involved broadly-based institutional deception with missionaries, foreign and domestic, citing monogamic materials from the Book of Mormon, iterating principles that were canonized in the Doctrine and Covenants.

If celestial marriage was a celestial principle, what eternal dominion could those forgotten husbands already married to women and bound by their civil covenants (whose wives were bonded for eternity to the Mormon prophet) be said to have? Those marriage-destructive sealings were far more important than any earthly covenant. Those legally married men lost their legal wives and their biological children as against the claims of the prophet for eternity. And their biological children lost their biological fathers for eternity. These crazy families and their eternally forgotten fathers were destined to be fractured forever.

There could be no meaningful justification for secretly marrying another man's wife and inheriting his biological children in the afterlife, as is supposed to have occurred in the cases of Zina Huntington Jacobs, Lucinda Morgan Harris, Marinda Nancy Johnson Hyde and Presendia Huntington Buell. Or for soliciting the wives of other men like Mrs. Robert D. Foster, Mrs. Orson Pratt, Mrs. William Law and Mrs. Hiram Kimball. That is unless God, who Joseph put at the head of the class, intended to undo all

---

[17]Ibid.

existing marital arrangements to the earthly and eternal advantage of the Mormon prophet and some privileged few of his most highly favored followers. When Joseph Smith married the wives of other men in those polyandrous couplings, and sealed them to himself, he claimed them and their biological children, against the claims and covenants of those less important others, for both time and eternity.

Four Hundred Elders Say: "[W]e Believe That One Man Should Have One Wife, and One Woman But One Husband . . ." (August 29, 1842)

After leaving Nauvoo and the Church he had done so much in so little time to lead, John C. Bennett impugned the character of Joseph Smith. He accused the Mormon prophet of practicing polygamy ("freelove," "spiritual wifery"). Joseph said he wasn't practicing polygamy; Bennett said he was and identified (but only with initials) seven of Smith's polygamous wives. Bennett's initials correctly matched those of the wives when the fact of Joseph's polygamy and the names of some of the wives were only very much later exposed. Bennett was specific in his description of Joseph's domestic depredations. His exposé put the world in touch with Sarah Pratt, Nancy Rigdon, Martha Brotherton, Emeline White and Melissa Schindle. Smith attempted to counter Bennett's sexually weighted allegations and his claims of intimidation (the Mississippi would be his "portion") with the assistance of an army of elders. In response to Bennett's allegations, Smith collected his outlandish "Affidavits and Certificates."

A SPECIAL CONFERENCE

On August 29, 1842, the elders assembled for a special conference "in the grove near the Temple." Hyrum Smith may not just then have known about "wifes and concubines," or about those clandestine sealings, or about the earthy practices of some other elite men who were particularly close to the prophet. Hyrum reported that the excitement over "John C. Bennett's false statements"[18] required that every able elder "should now go forth to every part of the United States and take proper documents with them setting forth the truth . . ." and preaching the gospel.[19]

Many months later, on May 14, 1843,

> *Hyrum Smith addressed the people [citywide] . . . . He said there were many that had a great deal to say about the ancient order of things as Solomon and David having many wives and concubines, but it is an abomination in the sight of God. If an angel from heaven should come and preach such doctrine, some would be sure to see his cloven foot and cloud of darkness over head, though his garments might shine as white as snow. A man might have one wife but concubines he should have none.*[20]

A revelation preaching "wifes and concubines" (his actual expression), according to this May 1843 Hyrum, was from the devil. At that special conference sending the elders out to counter Bennett, Joseph also took the stand. "During the whole of this address, the feelings of the brethren was indiscribable and the greatest joy and good feeling imaginable was manifest . . . . About Three hundred and eighty of the brethren volunteered to go out immediately and it is probable they will nearly all be gone in two weeks."[21] Their

---

[18]By June 26, 1842, "Bennett had begun a vigorous campaign to disparage those who had exposed his immoral schemes. On 8 July the *Sangamon Journal* at Springfield began publication of a series of Bennett letters attacking Joseph Smith and the Church." ("Illinois Journal, 1841-1842," Joseph Smith, Jr., *The Papers of Joseph Smith: Volume 1, Autobiographical and Historical Writings*, ed. Dean C. Jessee [Salt Lake City: Deseret Book Company, 1989], 393 n 2). It was these letters that were to be addressed by Joseph's collection of "Affidavits and Certificates, Disproving the Statements and Affidavits Contained in John C. Bennett's Letters." That collection was published in the *Times and Seasons* under the date of 31 August 1842 (*see also* August 1, 1842), 869-78. (Ibid., 444 n 1).

[19]"Illinois Journal, 1841-1842," *The Papers of Joseph Smith* (ed. Jessee), 444.

[20]Levi Richards, Journal, May 14, 1843, Church History Library, emphasis added, quoted in Brian C. Hales, "Encouraging Joseph Smith to Practice Plural Marriage: The Accounts of the Angel with a Drawn Sword," *Mormon Historical Studies*, vol. 11 no. 2 (Fall 2010), 59, emphasis added.

[21]"Illinois Journal, 1841-1842," Jessee, ed., *The Papers of Joseph Smith: Journal, 1832-1842*, 447.

principal errand? To spin the facts. To say what wasn't true.

THE BENNETT LETTERS

Before he was excommunicated and while he was still revered –
protected against any contingency by his powerful patron – John C.
Bennett (who left Nauvoo on June 21, 1842) knew a great deal about
a doctrine Joseph Smith publicly denied from 1829 or 1831 to the
day of his death on June 27, 1844. When Bennett retreated from
Nauvoo, fearful for his life, he made the most of the many things he
knew about the Mormon prophet by putting them in print. Dean C.
Jessee (Mormonism's Joseph scholar) described Bennett's
exposures in just these terms:

> *After Bennett's treachery was discovered, which
> resulted in excommunication and his leaving the
> community in disgrace, he lashed out at Joseph Smith
> and the Church with a scandalous exposé. In a letter
> published in the Sangamo Journal on 15 July, 1842,
> Bennett charged Joseph Smith with improprieties
> toward Orson Pratt's wife, Sarah.*[22]

Joseph Smith's domestic concerns, as Jessee was quick to surmise,
were front and center in Bennett's exposé, which took the form of a
series of letters to a Springfield, Illinois, newspaper. (It seems quite
likely that a young Illinois politician by the name of Abraham
Lincoln would have been familiar with the contents of the *Sangamo
Journal* in 1842). On July 8, 1842, Bennett denounced Joseph Smith
"as the seducer of single and married females."[23] The only recently
released former Assistant President of the Mormon Church
chanced to describe, in addition to Mrs. Pratt, the supreme leader's
"attempts on the virtue of Miss Nancy Rigdon," and then the
peculiar case of Miss Martha Brotherton.[24] Two of those women
were daughters of oath-bound Masonic men. Bennett asserted that

---

[22]Editorial Note, "Illinois Journal, 1841-1842," Jessee, ed., *The Papers of
Joseph Smith: Journal, 1832-1842*, 398 n 1, emphasis added.
 [23]John C. Bennett, "Astounding Disclosures! Letters from Gen. Bennett,"
Sangamo Journal, vol. 10 no. 46, July 8, 1842, emphasis added.
 [24]Ibid.

"Joe Smith had violated his obligations as a mason and has established 'a new order' himself."[25]

Joseph, Bennett reported, "attempted to seduce Miss Nancy Rigdon . . . [to] become one of his clandestine wives under the new dispensation." Smith had, according to Bennett, established polygamy in a new lodge by inspiration. The obligation for this new order was supposed to read in part as follows: "I furthermore promise and swear that I will never touch a daughter of Adam unless she is given me of the Lord." That particular oath was intended to accord with what was a new dispensation based upon the ancient order of things. Smith's establishment of Old Testament polygamy in Nauvoo, something he always publicly denied, is what he wanted hundreds of elders to also publicly deny, whatever the truth would seem to require. "A good, moral, virtuous, peacable and patriotic man" would not have dispatched hundreds of his followers to support his character at the expense of the truth. Bennett's first letter to the *Sangamo Journal*, written on June 27, 1842, was published on July 8, 1842.

Bennett Speaks of Sarah Pratt

In a second letter in a fourth allegation, Bennett was specific:

> *Mrs. Sarah M. Pratt, wife of Professor Orson Pratt, of the University of the city of Nauvoo. Joe Smith stated to me at an early day in the history of that city, that he intended to make that amiable and accomplished lady one of his spiritual wives, for the Lord had given her to him . . . .*[26]

Bennett warned Sarah Pratt, in advance of a meeting, what the prophet had in mind. Mrs. Pratt doubted what Bennett had said: "Joseph can not be such a man," to which Bennett said, "[Y]ou will see."

---

[25]John C. Bennett, "Astounding Disclosures! Letters from Gen. Bennett," *Sangamo Journal*, vol. 10 no. 46, July 8, 1842.

[26]John C. Bennett, Second Letter, *Sangamo Journal*, vol. 10 no. 47, July 15, 1842, emphasis added and retained.

Bennett was personally present when Joseph Smith approached Sarah Pratt in the name of the Lord. He described to the *Sangamo Journal* what he said occurred. The two men traveled to the Pratts' home by way of a circuitous route. "[I]n a few days Joe proposed to me to go to Ramus with him. I consented to go, and we started from his house about 4 o'clock P.M., rode into the prairie a few miles, and returned to the house of Captain John T. Barnett, in Nauvoo . . . ."[27] The two friends arrived at the Captain's house "about dusk, where we put up the horse with Barnett's permission. He, Joe, pretended we were looking for thieves." The two of them then proceeded on foot to the home of Sarah Pratt, whose husband Orson, an apostle, was away on a mission. "Sister Pratt," Joseph said, "the Lord has given you to me as one of my spiritual wives. I have the blessings of Jacob granted to me, as he granted holy men of old, and I have long looked upon you with favor, and hope you will not deny me." Her reply, according to Bennett, was both brave and succinct. "*I care not for the blessings of Jacob, and I believe in no such revelations . . . . I have one good husband, and that is enough for me.*"[28] Faced with Sarah's rejection, Joseph "went off to see Miss _____[29] at the house of Mrs. Sherman.[30] He remained with her an hour or two and then returned to Barnett's harnessed our horse, started for Ramus, and arrived at Carthage at early breakfast."

> Three times afterwards he tried to convince Mrs. Pratt of the propriety of his doctrine, and she at last told him: "Joseph, if you ever attempt any thing of the kind with me again, I will tell Mr. Pratt on his

---

[27]Ibid.

[28]Ibid., emphasis added.

[29]The *Sangamo Journal* omitted several names from the letter as it was printed, "being unwilling to injure the feelings" of anyone "unnecessarily." The omitted names, the editor said, "can be seen in the original manuscript" by any person inclined to so further proceed. (Ibid.).

[30]Delcena Diademia Johnson (Sherman), a widow, became one of Joseph's wives (circa June 1842). She was one of the more than twenty women sealed to Smith before Emma was (Emma: May 28, 1843). Delcena's sister, Almera, became yet another sister wife of Joseph Smith. Almera, like Delcena, was also sealed to the prophet before Emma was (Almera: "<[before] Aug 5 1842"). (George D. Smith, *Nauvoo Polygamy*, 622). After the death of Joseph Smith, Delcena married Almon W. Babbitt, "who acted as proxy for her eternal sealing to Lyman Sherman." (Ibid., 651 n 363).

return home. I will certainly do it." Joe replied,
"Sister Pratt, I hope you will not expose me; if I am
to suffer, all suffer; so do not expose me. Will you
agree *not* to do so?" "If," said she, "you will never
insult me again, I will not expose you unless strong
circumstances require it."[31]

Times passed on in apparent friendship until Joe
grossly insulted Mrs. Pratt again, after her husband
had returned, by approaching and kissing her. This
highly offended her, and she told Mr. Pratt, who was
much enraged and went and told Joe never to offer
an insult of the like again.[32]

After detailing those other attempts to convince Mrs. Pratt that the
Lord had given her to Joseph, followed by the insulting kiss,
Bennett then asked Mrs. Pratt in his *Sangamo Journal* exposé to
confirm for publication the accuracy of what he had just reported.
"I now appeal to Mrs. Pratt if this is not true to the very letter. Just
speak out boldly."[33] She did not. Sarah Pratt, disappointing the
expectant Bennett, did not then choose to respond. (And although
the Pratts were excommunicated at about that time, they later
returned to the Church).

Sarah Pratt Does Respond

Many years later, Sarah Pratt (again out of the Church) confirmed
that Bennett did know "that Joseph had his plans set on me." In a
May 21, 1886, interview with the intrepid Dr. W. Wyl, Mrs. Pratt
reported just how bound to Bennett the prophet was seen to have
been. "Joseph made no secret of . . . [his plans] before Bennett, and
went so far in his impudence as to make propositions to me in the
presence of Bennett, his bosom friend."[34] The two, John C. Bennett

---

[31]John C. Bennett, Second Letter, *Sangamo Journal*, vol. 10 no. 47, July 15,
1842, emphasis in the original.
[32]Ibid.
[33]Ibid.
[34]Sarah Pratt, Interview with W. Wyl, May 21, 1886, *Mormon Portraits or, The
Truth About the Mormon Leaders From 1830 to 1866: Volume First: Joseph Smith,*

and Joseph Smith, according to Sarah Pratt, had been partners in depravity. Sarah Pratt recognized, and told Dr. Wyl, that "Bennett was the most intimate friend of Joseph for a time." What Bennett reported to the *Sangamo Journal* in July 1842, Sarah Pratt reported to Dr. Wyl in 1886. She recounted what was raised in an earlier chapter and is repeated here: *"You should bear in mind that Joseph did not think of a marriage or sealing ceremony for many years. He used to state to his intended victims, as he did to me: 'God does not care if we have a good time, if only other people do not know it.' He only introduced . . . ["a"] marriage ceremony when he had found out that he could not get certain women without it."*[35] Like Louisa Beaman. Considering what Mrs. Pratt said concerning Smith before his sealing to Louisa Beaman, it would seem to appear that he did not marry Miss Fanny Alger (before he got the sealing power in April 1836). Several Mormon scholars said that he did. George D. Smith in his important book, *Nauvoo Polygamy*, thought that he did not.[36]

In a letter interview with Dr. Wyl in 1886, Mrs. Pratt provided an addendum to her earlier interviews with Wyl in the spring of 1885, following which he had protected her privacy by quoting only her initial (addressing her as "Mrs. P."). Sarah Pratt stated her revised intent in that 1886 addendum in these terms: "I want you to have all my statements correct in your book and put my name to them; I want the truth, the full truth to be known, and [I want to] bear the responsibility of it." Now she changed her report from that of "Mrs. P" in her earlier disclosure to that of "Mrs. Pratt" in the 1886 addendum. She then again supported this astounding disclosure, which bears repeating here: *"I have told you,"* she said, *"that the prophet Joseph used to frequent houses of ill-fame."* Mrs. White, "a very pretty and attractive woman," confessed to Sarah, that "she made a business of it to be hospitable to the captains of the Mississippi steamboats." According to Mrs. White, Joseph "had made her acquaintance very soon after his arrival in Nauvoo," and he "had visited her dozens of times." Now Sarah Pratt invited Dr. Wyl to revisit an error in an earlier segment of one of his reviews.

The Prophet, His Family and Friends, A Study Based on Facts and Documents (Salt Lake City, UT: Tribune Printing and Publishing Company, 1886), 61.

[35]Ibid., 62, emphasis retained.

[36]George D. Smith, *Nauvoo Polygamy* (2008).

"You have made a mistake in the table of contents of your book in calling this woman [Mrs. White] 'Mrs. Harris.' Mrs. [George W.] Harris was a married lady, a very great friend of mine."[37] That particular woman, Mrs. Pratt's friend, was the Masonic Martyr William Morgan's widow. Mrs. White, on the other hand, the person Dr. Wyl incorrectly named in his table of contents, was the woman who was hospitable to the captains of the Mississippi steamboats and, she said, to Joseph Smith.

In her earlier interview with Dr. Wyl in 1885, "Mrs. P" had added this allegation to her list of recitals: *"Abortion was practiced on a large scale in Nauvoo."* Bennett, "the evil genius of Joseph," showed us the instruments "he used to 'operate for Joseph.'" There was a house across the flat about a mile and a-half from town. It was a kind of hospital used for that purpose. "They sent the women there, when they showed signs of celestial consequences. Abortion was practiced regularly in this house."[38] So said Sarah Pratt.

What Bennett reported in the *Sangamo Journal* in July 1842 (Bennett left Nauvoo in June), and what Sarah Pratt reported to Dr. Wyl in 1885 and 1886 was what Sarah Pratt told Orson Pratt when he returned from his mission to England. Pratt, like John C. Bennett and others, thought that Sarah told the truth. In the Utah Territory, Chief Justice Charles S. Zane, Territorial Secretary Arthur L. Thomas and the Fort Douglas Chaplain, Reverend J.W. Jackson, believed that Sarah Pratt was a woman whose word was to be depended upon, and said so in support of her character in 1886. "We, the undersigned cordially bear witness to the excellent reputation of Mrs. Sarah M. Pratt. We feel well assured that Mrs. Pratt is a lady whose statements are absolutely to be depended upon."[39]

---

[37]Interview with Sarah M. Pratt, May 21, 1886, quoted in Dr. W. Wyl, *Mormon Portraits*, emphasis added.

[38]Wyl, *Mormon Portraits*, 59, emphasis Wyl.

[39]Charles S. Zane, Chief Justice, Utah Territory; Arthur L. Thomas, Secretary (and future Governor), Utah Territory; Rev. J.W. Jackson, Chaplain, Ft. Douglas, Sarah Pratt, Interview with W. Wyl, May 21, 1886, *Mormon Portraits*, 63.

The Sorry Saga of Orson Pratt

Mormon scholar Dean C. Jessee described Bennett's report in apologetic terms:

> *In a letter published in the Sangamo Journal on 15 July 1842, Bennett charged Joseph Smith with improprieties toward Orson Pratt's wife, Sarah. Faced with statements of his wife and Bennett on one hand, and the Prophet's denial on the other, Orson sided for a time with his wife and Bennett, and, in a moment of despondence, left Nauvoo on 15 July amid rumors of possible suicide, setting off a community alert to find him. Five weeks later he was excommunicated from the Church but by January 1843, learned he had made a faulty judgment and was reinstated in his apostolic calling.*[40]

When did Joseph Smith ever publicly tell the truth about polygamy? Who wouldn't side with Sarah Pratt? Is it not apparent that Orson dismissed the "Prophet's denial" and sided with Sarah when he crafted a suicide note and left the city? He bet his life on words Sarah had said. Joseph's treatment of the wife of his most faithful subordinate – while Orson was far from home at a place the prophet selected (for as long as the prophet said) – was an inexcusable betrayal of trust. He approached his follower's wife for sex ("connubial bliss"). Had Joseph succeeded in his plans for Mrs. Pratt, as he succeeded with his plans for more than a dozen other previously married women (think Orson Hyde), the Old Testament described the consequence: "If a man be found lying with a woman married to an husband, then they shall both of them die, both the man that lay with the woman, and the woman: so shalt thou put away evil from Israel."[41] Where did Israel's God make an exception for Joseph's polyandrous women? And if sanction is found in the Old Testament for polygamy, then restrictions found in the Old Testament for "a man . . . found lying with a woman married to an husband" must also be seen to apply.

---

[40]Editor's Note, "Illinois Journal, 1841-1842," *The Papers of Joseph Smith* (ed. Jessee), 398 n 1, emphasis added.

[41]Deutoronomy 22:22.

In despair and suicidal, Orson Pratt's extraordinary life of service to the Church became ashes in his mouth. With his life an apparent failure, Pratt "wandered about Nauvoo like a man bereft of sense, proclaiming the innocence of his wife to every passer-by. When William [Wilson] Law called upon the saints in a public meeting to acknowledge Joseph as 'a good, moral, virtuous, peaceable and patriotic man,' Pratt stood up, pale and lonely looking among the thousands, to register the only negative vote."[42] When the First Presidency and nine of the Twelve Apostles gave "Notice" that the Church had withdrawn "the hand of fellowship from Gen. John C. Bennett, as a Christian," after it was reported that they had labored for his rehabilitation, Orson Pratt "refused to sign." When the backdated "Notice" was "presented to Orson Pratt, one of the twelve, . . . after I [Bennett] showed him my [earlier] official withdrawal," Mr. Pratt refused to sign.[43]

Smith turned Orson Pratt around after the apostle's apostasy (and excommunication), back to the Church *and then, and surprisingly, on to the doctrine of polygamy.* Orson and Sarah were rebaptized, the excommunication was reversed on a technicality and Orson recovered his membership and his office as an apostle in the Quorum of the Twelve. When Orson Pratt caught the polygamous vision, to the chagrin of his monogamous wife, he became that principle's most articulate advocate. In what was a shocking reversal of fortune, the beleaguered Pratt would live to become the *"Apostle of Polygamy."* It was Orson Pratt who would present the "great," "beautiful," "sublime" and "glorious" doctrine to the world when the Church took "The Polygamous Principle" public, after decades of deceit, at the Tabernacle in the Utah Territory in 1852.

> *We further learn from other sources that Smith, finding his attempts on Mrs. Pratt were matters of notoriety, went to her husband with a manufactured story that his wife was a base woman, and that the fact was well known to him. This communication had*

---

[42]Fawn M. Brodie, *No Man Knows My History: The Life of Joseph Smith the Mormon Prophet*, 2d ed., rev. and enl. (New York: Alfred A. Knopf, 1972), 319.

[43]John C. Bennett, Second Letter, *Sangamo Journal*, vol. 10 no. 46, July 8, 1842, emphasis omitted.

*such an effect upon Mr. Pratt -- at once blasting his
happiness and the reputation of a virtuous woman --
that the wretched husband left the city.*[44]

He did, however, recover.

Nancy Rigdon

On August 19, 1842, ten days before Hyrum Smith presided over
that special conference in Nauvoo asking elders to travel nationwide
to dispute the "charges" made by John C. Bennett against the
Mormon prophet, the *Sangamo Journal* published a "6th Letter
From Gen. Bennett." This submission reproduced an "exact copy"
of a letter Nancy Rigdon received from Joseph Smith in Willard
Richards' handwriting, a message hand delivered by Richards to
Miss Rigdon after she refused the Prophet's proposal to become one
of his spiritual wives.[45]

Bennett described the prophet's proposal to Miss Nancy Rigdon.
He had also publicly called upon Miss Martha Brotherton of
Warsaw to describe "the base attempt on her virtue when in
Nauvoo" (an event involving Joseph Smith, Brigham Young and
Heber C. Kimball). On July 13, 1842, Miss Brotherton responded
to Dr. Bennett's request in particularly poignant detail. Miss
Brotherton did what Mrs. Pratt didn't do then, but did do many
years later at the request of Dr. Wyl.

Nancy Rigdon was introduced to a larger audience when Joseph
Smith's letter, a kind of revelation, was published in the *Sangamo
Journal* at John C. Bennett's request – not at her request and not at
her father's request, and followed by their objections. Smith's
letter to Miss Rigdon was then also published in the August 31,
1842, issue of the *New York Herald*. The representations contained
in Smith's letter to Nancy Rigdon, the representations contained in
Martha Brotherton's letter to John C. Bennett and the *Sangamo
Journal*, the representations made by Smith to Sarah Pratt,
together with various other allegations associating Joseph with

---

[44]*Sangamo Journal*, vol. 10 no. 48, July 22, 1842, emphasis added.
[45]Ibid., vol. 10 no 52, 19 August 1842.

extreme domesticity were prominent among those with which the elders convened at the conference on August 29, 1842, would be asked to contend.

Similarities

"The cases of Mrs. Pratt, Miss Rigdon, and Miss Brotherton, all ladies of the first order of talents, and the highest respectability, are precisely similar."[46]   Notwithstanding the fact that Bennett's allegations against the prophet covered more than polygamy, the claims that Joseph was a polygamist, a man with spiritual wives, a sponsor of spiritual marriage, an adulterer and promiscuous, were always front and center. "Why does not Nauvoo Lodge, U.D., deal with Joe for the attempted seduction of Nancy Rigdon, a Master Mason's daughter, and for the actual seductions of several Master Masons' wives and sisters and daughters[?]"[47]   Bennett discussed the circumstances of his departure from Nauvoo, positing a claim of duress.   His statement to the *Sangamo Journal* contradicted Hyrum's affidavit.

> *1ˢᵗ. THE DURESSE. – – On the 17ᵗʰ day of May, A.D. 1842, Joe Smith requested to see me alone in the preparation room of the Nauvoo Lodge, U.D., on some important business. We entered, and he locked the door, put the key in his pocket, and drew a pistol on me and said - - "The peace of my family requires that you should sign an affidavit, and make a statement before the next City Council, on the 19ᵗʰ, exonerating me from all participation whatever, either directly or indirectly, in word or deed, in the spiritual wife doctrine, or private intercourse with females in general; and if you do not do it with apparent cheerfulness, I will make catfish bait of you or deliver you to the Danites for execution tonight – for my dignity and purity must and shall be maintained before the public, even at the expense of life, – – will you do it or die?" I replied that he had better procure*

[46]General Bennett's 4ᵗʰ Letter, *Sangamo Journal*, vol. 10 no. 48, July 22, 1842.
[47]Bennett Third Letter, *Sangamo Journal*, vol. 10 no. 47, July 15, 1842.

some other person or persons to do so, as there were a
plenty who could do it in truth. "No," said he, "that
will not do – for it is known that you are well
acquainted with all my private acts, better than any
other man, and it is in your power to save me or damn
me; and as you have now withdrawn from the church
in an honorable manner, over my own signature, a
privilege never granted to any other person, you must
and shall, place it out of your power to injure me or
the church, – – do it or the Mississippi is your portion
. . . ."[48]

Bennett said that he relented ("under the circumstances") and Smith unlocked the door. The former colleagues then proceeded downstairs, where Bennett gave an affidavit to Alderman Daniel H. Wells, after which he made the statement required before the City Council on the 19th. On June 30, 1842, Francis M. Higbee, one of Joseph's Missouri Danites, and a leader of the Nauvoo Legion, appeared before Hiram Kimball, another Alderman, "being duly sworn according to law," to corroborate Bennett's earlier claim of duress. Higbee reported "that Joseph Smith told him that John C. Bennett could be easily put aside or drowned, and no person would be the wiser for it." Higbee said Smith said "it ought to be attended to . . . the sooner this was done the better for the Church." Smith feared, Higbee recounted, "that Bennett would make some disclosures prejudicial to said Smith."[49]

The allegations of duress were strongly denied in the elders' documents, as were the allegations of polygamy in all of its early permutations. It is likely that with the claim of duress that can not be objectively measured, as with the claims of polygamy that can be objectively measured, that Bennett was more dependably truthful than Smith. This much was certain: When Bennett exonerated Joseph in an Affidavit (he said he was coerced to sign) from all participation, directly or indirectly, in word or in deed, in the spiritual wife doctrine and "poligamy," and/or in respect to

---

[48]Bennett's Second Letter, *Sangamo Journal*, vol. 10 no. 47, July 15, 1842, emphasis added.

[49]Francis H. Higbee Affidavit, reproduced at *Sangamo Journal*, vol. 10 no. 47, July 15, 1842.

promiscuous intercourse with females in general, Joseph was up to his neck in wives, women and transactions. Smith got an affidavit from Bennett, that he then transmitted to about four hundred elders, that said what Smith (and Bennett) positively knew not to be true. Smith had married approximately twelve women in the first six or seven months of 1842 (and three others in 1841), before the elders even started to march, with more than twenty other wives still to come.

BENNETT'S ALLEGATIONS

Bennett asserts in a series of letters that Joseph is taking various women, whether single or married, at warp speed as spiritual wives. To Sarah Pratt: Joseph says, according to Bennett, that he has the blessings of Jacob. ("Sister Pratt, the Lord has given you to me as one of my spiritual wives"). ("I have the blessings of Jacob granted to me, as he granted holy men of old, and I have long looked upon you with favor, and hope you will not deny me"). To Nancy Rigdon Joseph said that what he proposed was "lawful and right before God." ("Joseph . . . swore her to secrecy, and told her that she had long been the idol of his affections, . . . that he had asked the Lord for her, and that it was his holy will that he should have her . . ."). To Martha Brotherton (and in support of Brigham Young) Joseph said that she would be blessed. ("'Yes,' said Joseph, '. . . I know that this is lawful and right before God, and if there is any sin in it, I will answer for it before God . . . I have the keys of the kingdom, and whatever I bind on earth is bound in heaven, and whatever I loose on earth is loosed in heaven . . .").

Bennett made other accusations.

To the Editor of the Journal:

... Joe Smith stands indicted for murder, treason, burglary, and arson in Missouri, and he defies the laws and the legally constituted authorities to deliver him over for trial.[50]

---

[50]John C. Bennett, "Astounding Disclosures! Letters from Gen. Bennett," *Sangamo Journal*, vol. 10 no. 46, July 8, 1842, emphasis added.

That was true, and those were facts that couldn't be denied. The Mormon leader was a fugitive who had escaped from a Missouri jail. In order to meet and rebut what Smith called Bennett's "false statements" and charges, including those just described, Joseph and his elders had much else with which to contend. In addition to the inflammatory social proposals, seductions and spiritual wives, polyandry, polygyny and promiscuity, adultery, abortion and sexual consent, there was his alleged complicity in the attempted assassination of Missouri Governor Lilburn W. Boggs. Bennett accused the Prophet of cheating his creditors in bankruptcy, fraudulently speculating in real estate, and of creating a secret society to threaten and murder apostates. Joseph Smith did encourage the assassination of Governor Boggs and publicly predicted or prophesied his violent death. He did discharge his debts in bankruptcy. He speculated in real estate and supervised the activities of a secret society designed to threaten and injure apostates and Gentiles. That dreaded society ethnically cleansed Caldwell and Daviess Counties (in Missouri) by forcing Gentiles out. Sampson Avard testified as to the success of those efforts in criminal proceedings at Richmond, Missouri.

REPERCUSSIONS

Joe Smith, in a speech in Nauvoo on Thursday the 14th last, (and which was heard by two gentlemen of our city,) said -- "He wished Bennett was in Hell! -- he had given him more trouble than any man he ever had to do with." Joe was undoubtedly sincere in this expression of his wishes.

In the same speech he declared that Mrs. Pratt, the wife of Mr. O. Pratt, "had been a w**** from her mother's breast." This was the lady whom Bennett says Joe attempted to seduce, and who resisted all his efforts with the heroism of insulted virtue.[51]

---

[51]*Sangamo Journal*, vol. 10 no. 48 (whole no. 568), July 22, 1842, emphasis retained and added.

CONCLUSION

This Bennett, "an adder in the path, and a viper in the bosom,"[52] since leaving us has said, "that we believed in and practiced polygamy – that we believed in secret murders, and aimed to destroy the government &c. &c."[53] Since the Church withdrew their fellowship from him,

> *[H]e has published that the conduct of the Saints was bad – that Joseph Smith and many others were adulterers, murderers, &c., – that there was a secret band of men that would kill people, &c., called Danites – that he was in duress when he gave his affidavit, and testified that Joseph Smith was a virtuous man – . . . ."*[54]

The *Sangamo Journal* disclosures by John C. Bennett caused turmoil in Nauvoo and at various places abroad. The purpose of the special conference held in the grove near the Temple on August 29, 1842, was to enlist every able bodied elder to "now go forth to every part of the United States" with Affidavits and Certificates, "setting forth the truth as it is" for the benefit of the "people abroad." The massive undertaking that threatened the resources of the community was directed at those who had been "excited by John C. Bennett's false statements." Joseph's emissaries were to also "preach the gospel, repentance, baptism & salvation and tarry preaching untill they shall be called home."[55] "They must go wisely, humbly, setting forth the truth as it is in God" to counter the allegations of General John C. Bennett, Nauvoo Legion General George W. Robinson, Nancy Rigdon, Martha Brotherton, Melissa Schindle, the *Sangamo Journal*, *The New York Herald*, and a host of other individuals and publications.

On that day, and upon those who had allegedly betrayed his trust, the prophet heaped particular scorn. "I will live to trample on their ashes with the soles of my feet." That did not occur. "I prophecy in

---

[52] *Times and Seasons*, Joseph Smith ed. (1 August 1842), 868.
[53] Ibid., 869.
[54] Ibid., emphasis added.
[55] "Illinois Journal, 1841-1842," *The Papers of Joseph Smith* (ed. Jessee), 444.

the name of Jesus Christ, that such shall not prosper, they shall be cast down in their plans."[56] That did not occur.

> *Let the Twelve send all, who will support the character*
> *of the Prophet – the Lords anointed. And if all who*
> *go will support my character I prophecy in the name*
> *of the Lord Jesus whose servant I am, that you will*
> *prosper in your missions.*[57]

Let the elders support "The character of the Prophet." Thus on August 29, 1842, about "three hundred and eighty of the brethren" volunteered to leave Nauvoo to tell the world that Joseph Smith was not a polygamist; that he didn't believe in plural marriage and had no spiritual wives; that he had not been complicit in the attempted assassination of Governor Boggs; that he had not cheated his creditors in bankruptcy proceedings, speculated in real estate or created a secret society to terrorize dissenters. They were to say that John C. Bennett, Sarah Pratt, George W. Robinson, Nancy Rigdon, Martha Brotherton, Melissa Schindle, Francis M. Higbee, Governors Lilburn W. Boggs and Thomas Carlin were liars; that Bennett and his correspondents hadn't told the truth about assault, assassination, bankruptcy, fraud, counterfeiting, failed banks and secret societies. The details of the Affidavits and Certificates, and the credentials of the affiants intended to support them, are enumerated in an attached Appendix D, entitled "Joseph's Response to Dr. John C. Bennett."

The central thrust of this massive unprincipled endeavor was to ask four hundred elders to defend the indefensible; to say that Joseph Smith didn't have and had never had any spiritual wives; that he hadn't encouraged fornication or promiscuous intercourse; hadn't committed adultery; didn't practice and had never practiced polygamy. *What shall these disciples say when moved upon by the spirit?* That "we know of no other rule or system of marriage than the one published in the Book of Doctrine and Covenants." *And what is the rule or system of marriage published in the Doctrine and Covenants?* That our Church, like your churches, preaches and practices monogamy; that "Inasmuch as this Church of Christ has

---

[56]Ibid., 446.
[57]Ibid., 447, emphasis added.

been reproached with the crime of fornication and polygamy, we declare that we believe that one man should have one wife, and one woman but one husband, except in case of death, when either is at liberty to marry again."[58] In all of this, as Wilford Woodruff duly noted, "about 400 elders left to carry out the mission designated by the conference." Those elders, every one, were fortified with falsified talking points. "[T]heir has never at any time been," Woodruff reported, "as great a turn out into the vineyard since the foundation of the Church."[59]

---

[58]Doctrine and Covenants (1835 edition), 101, emphasis added.
[59]"Illinois Journal, 1841-1842," *The Papers of Joseph Smith* (ed. Jessee), 447 n 2.

CHAPTER FIFTEEN

Lying for the Lord

Children were instructed to deny knowledge of family relationships, of their parents whereabouts, and even of their own last names.[1]

B. Carmon Hardy

[T]he endless subterfuges and prevarications which our present conditions impose . . . threaten to make our rising generation a race of deceivers.[2]

Charles W. Penrose

Mormon scholars deliberate behind (official) untenable conclusions lacking the freedom to follow the facts wherever they lead.

Joel M. Allred

PROLOGUE

What Did They Say?

Mormonism has never been transparent. Consent has always been uninformed. "The field of Mormon history is a hall of mirrors, full

---

[1]"Lying for the Lord: An Essay," Appendix 1 in B. Carmon Hardy, *Solemn Covenant: The Mormon Polygamous Passage* (Urbana, Chicago: University of Illinois Press, 1992), 368.

[2]Correspondence, Charles W. Penrose to President John Taylor, 16 February 1887, John Taylor Letter File, transcriptions by Raymond Taylor (Salt Lake City, UT: University of Utah Library). *See* Hardy, *Solemn Covenant: The Mormon Polygamous Passage*, 368.

of distorted and incomplete reflections of nearly any event."[3] "[B]ecause the Church of Jesus Christ of Latter-day Saints would not give scholars access to documents that peered behind ecclesiastically sanctioned [correlated] narratives of Mormon history," one historian (Philip Taylor) predicted more than half a century ago that "Brigham Young's life was a 'biography which will not be written.'"[4] Despite "greater access to church-controlled primary resources" in this twenty-first century, the great polygamist's recent and most accomplished biographer, John G. Turner, recognizing the limitations of Mormon transparency, concluded the preface to his "elegantly written biography"[5] with these important words: "When it was impossible to transcend the limitations of the historical record, I have preserved a sense of ambiguity."[6]

Mormonism still has chickens that haven't come home to roost. What you might assume from the official narratives can't be sustained when more closely examined. The secret society has concealed and suppressed stubborn facts, visions, documents, diaries, revelations, minutes and magical stones.[7] Deception was embraced by men and women trapped in polygamy who lived outside of the law. Nauvoo women sometimes said they didn't know who the fathers of their children were, or that their husbands were away on missions. And some of them traveled to remote locations, safe houses, in order to better publicly manage the reality of inconvenient celestial encounters.

Charles W. Penrose, who later became an Apostle and a Counselor in the First Presidency, "was so concerned about the pervasiveness of intentional falsehood that he feared for its effect on the moral

---

[3]John G. Turner, *Brigham Young: Pioneer Prophet* (Belknap Press of Harvard University Press, 2012), preface, viii.

[4]Philip Taylor, quoted in Ibid., vii.

[5]Richard L. Bushman, dust jacket endorsement, John G. Turner, *Brigham Young: Pioneer Prophet*.

[6]Turner, *Brigham Young: Pioneer Prophet*, preface, viii.

[7]Paranoia, persecution and a sense of mystery associated with "oath protected" secrets not to be shared have "strengthened the Mormon sense of community." What infuriated their enemies empowered them. (Appendix 1 in Hardy, *Solemn Covenant*, 364).

fiber of Mormon society."[8] *Penrose* was one of the authors of the 1890 Manifesto, the edict that involuntarily (and temporarily) *suspended* the practice without abrogating the doctrine of polygamy. In a letter to John Taylor in 1887, crafted before he helped to draft this disingenuous Manifesto, a cynical policy that wasn't at first enforced, Penrose referred to "the endless subterfuges and prevarications" that "threaten to make our rising generation a race of deceivers."[9] By then, by 1887, such concerns were obsolete because the horse was out of the barn. They were already "a race of deceivers." Mormonism's striking duplicity started during the reign of the prophet Joseph Smith and didn't end with the Manifesto.[10]

In 1903, Wiley Nebeker of Afton, Wyoming, wrote a letter to Apostle John Henry Smith. Troubled by the fact that the church had made official statements that plural marriages were no longer condoned (it was now thirteen years after the Manifesto), he said that he frequently heard of men and women, some from his own area, who had entered the principle and said they were called by apostles to continue the practice. While he believed in polygamy, he didn't believe in dishonesty ("a duplicitous policy that said one thing while doing another"). While Nebeker was fully converted to the belief that polygamy was a true principle, he was not converted to the idea that the Lord justifies deceit and falsehood. Surely, Nebeker declared, if God wanted the practice carried on, it would be better to openly admit as much, "even if it brings persecution upon us, because then there can be no reproach – we will not be under the necessity of apologizing to our own consciences."[11]

Problems that surfaced in Nauvoo over polygamy's secrecy – before perhaps close to half of the members left the city to follow Brigham Young – resurfaced when Young and those who considered him to

---

[8]Hardy, *Solemn Covenant*, 368.

[9]Ibid., Appendix 1, 368.

[10]Latter-day Saints predated post-1890 marriages to make it appear that they occurred before the Manifesto. (D. Michael Quinn, "LDS Church Authority and New Plural Marriages, 1890-1904," *Dialogue: A Journal of Mormon Thought*, vol. 18 no. 1 (Spring 1985), 9-105.

[11]Wiley Nebeker to Apostle John Henry Smith, 27 May 1903, "John Henry Smith Letterbooks" (Church Archives), quoted in Hardy, *Solemn Covenant*, 370-71.

be their leader began to raise the children of the "new and everlasting" polygamous covenant. Decades after allegations of the practice of polygamy divided the Church and enraged the citizens of the state of Illinois, and after Brigham Young's constituents left the United States to settle the Great Basin, Mormon children, the products of plurality, were "instructed to deny knowledge of family relationships, of their parents' whereabouts, and even of their last names."[12]

Because everyone who was trapped in the unlawful practice of polygamy learned to lie about polygamy, they also knew how to lie about everything else. Men, women and children, who used fictitious names and told tall tales at home and school and abroad, practiced this dishonesty in their interactions with strangers. Mormonism's polygamy-based deception was institutional. It started with the founders. Only the uninformed, a diminishing class among the faithful, could deny the practice of polygamy without being intentionally deceptive.

In respect to all issues related to polygamy – and in the case of all those who practiced polygamy – dishonesty was not the exception, but rather the rule. Those people lied for the Lord at the behest of their polygamous leaders. Their Mormon God expected them to, and their Mormon leaders showed them how it was to be done. In the words of Parley P. Pratt, a smart but unprincipled man, it was "their duty to do so," and not just in support of polygamy.[13] Honesty wasn't an option then. In the beginning, many dishonest and unsettling things were concealed by some of the "informed" Saints from most of the other Saints. When those less privileged other Saints joined the ranks of the better informed, they, like everyone else, surrendered their freedom and integrity to the dictates of lawbreakers, people who didn't tell the truth. In the beginning, uninformed Latter-day Saints – oblivious to what was really going on – trusted their leaders. They failed to learn the facts, and their leaders failed to teach the facts, before they joined the less than transparent Church.

---

[12]Ibid., 368.

[13]"[W]e must lie to support brother Joseph, it is our duty to do so." (Sidney Rigdon quoting Pratt, *Messenger and Advocate*, 18 June 1845).

B. Carmon Hardy, a recognized scholar and meticulous researcher, wrote ground-breaking works on Mormon polygamy. His award-winning 1992 book, published by the University of Illinois Press, includes an important essay in which Professor Hardy praised the Mormon Church. "Modern Mormonism's reputation for sobriety and honesty," he said, "is proverbial."[14] Hardy cited statements from some prominent early Mormons. "Those trafficking in deceit, warned George Q. Cannon, lost the spirit of God as well as the trust of man."[15] That seems like something a Christian ought to say. Long before Hardy ever wrote that insightful essay and published it as an Appendix[16] to his book, the Church validated that laudable principle of honesty, at least in theory. "In early 1907 the First Presidency issued a major address in which they specifically denied the use of duplicity in any of their dealings. 'Enlightened investigation,' they said, had always been the goal of the church."[17] Other such endorsements are included in Hardy's seminal work. "[A] member of the First Presidency, enlarging on the same theme, warned that when one resorts to falsehood and deception, even in behalf of a worthy cause, there is danger such practice will spread to other employments 'like a disease that is endemic.'"[18] Truer words were never spoken.

Yet all of those expressions of high praise are challenged by Mormonism's undeniable duplicity concerning the difficult subject of polygamy. Hardy, a friendly voice, recognized the importance of what he could only then describe as a strange dichotomy. "Professions of this sort ["We Believe in Being Honest"] call into question the behavior we have seen attending Mormonism's contest with the world over polygamy. It is as if the church read from differing scripts."[19] This is how that sounds in retrospect: "We didn't tell the truth about polygamy. We always deceived everyone everywhere about polygamy. But we always tell the truth about everything else."[20] There have been many attempts to put the best

---

[14]Hardy, *Solemn Covenant*, 363.

[15]Ibid.

[16]"Lying for the Lord: An Essay," Appendix 1 in Ibid., 363-88.

[17]Ibid., 363.

[18]Gordon B. Hinckley, "We Believe in Being Honest," *Ensign* (October 1990): 5, quoted in Ibid., 363-64.

[19]Ibid., 364.

[20]"Justus Morse told how, as a Danite in Missouri in 1838, he and others were

possible face on decades of institutional dishonesty.

Speaking of protecting polygamy by the use of deceit, T.B.H. Stenhouse, an early convert who later became a dissenting voice, put an obvious issue in these terms: "[I]f once admitted to be justifiable [deception and fraud in the service of polygamy], how frequently and to what other ends may [such resorts] . . . not be used?"[21]

B. Carmon Hardy, at a loss to explain these glaring discrepancies, put that issue in these terms: "Mormon authorities," he said, "seemed to shift between registers of opposing values." While perpetuating one standard for polygamy (unrepentant dishonesty), they were then supposed to perpetuate another standard for everything else (proverbial sobriety). "So dramatic an inconsistency," he said, "cannot fail to provoke inquiry. It fairly begs the scholar's attention."[22] Since those words were spoken in and/or before 1992, modern scholarship has devastated the "proverbial sobriety" side of that innocent equation. Astonishing modern disclosures of other disingenuous discrepancies, both old and new, matters of great importance, show that the truth divide between the Mormon approach to polygamy and the Mormon approach to various other issues of many different kinds was never really so pronounced.

The ascendancy of the Internet as an agent of information has blown the whistle on decades of previously concealed broadly based deceit. The dissimulation associated with nineteenth-century polygamy is now seen to have carried over to other issues "like a disease that is endemic." In this era of information overload, the same issues that attended "Mormonism's contest with the outside world over polygamy" are now seen to have attended Mormonism's contests with the world over almost everything else. The supposed

---

directed to assist each other when in difficulty by lying, 'and to do it with such positiveness and assurance that no one would question our testimony.'" (Justus Morse Affidavit, 23 March 1887, quoted in Hardy, *Solemn Covenant*, 366).

[21]T.B.H. Stenhouse, *The Rocky Mountain Saints: A Full and Complete History of the Mormons, from the First Vision of Joseph Smith to the Last Courtship of Brigham Young* (New York, NY: D. Appleton and Company, 1873), 192.

[22]Hardy, *Solemn Covenant*, 364.

divide "between registers of opposing values" is not now seen as so well defined as B. Carmon Hardy once supposed. Now it can be said that other claims of equivalent importance have been equally duplicitous. It is not now safe to continue to say that, "It is as if the church read from differing scripts." Whereas in 1992 the scholar could say, "Depending on circumstances [polygamous/non-polygamous], Mormon authorities seemed to shift between registers of opposing values,"[23] that dichotomy has disappeared. The claims of the past, burdened by the disclosures of the present, should no longer be viewed as more or less unexplainable polarities. Whereas in 1992 B. Carmon Hardy felt it safe to say that, "So dramatic an inconsistency [between separate sets of opposing values, everything concerning polygamy and everything not] cannot fail to provoke inquiry," in this twenty-first century, that now outdated equation has changed because the "registers of opposing values" are not so markedly disparate. They were and are everywhere the same.

The messiness of Mormonism's actual history, as opposed to the faith-promoting discourse presented by the Church, has become disturbingly apparent. The challenge of the Internet has been to unsettle the dishonest sanitized version of Mormonism's history promoted by generations of more or less deceitful stewards. Mormonism's true history – in all of its sordid particulars – is becoming available to any person committed to the pursuit of the truth. By concealing the facts, the leaders of the Church set at naught their sacred trust. Such stewards do not deserve the generous treatment they receive at the adoring hands of those who have been deceived, of those Church-broken Saints who have learned to "love their servitude." Mormons are the unfortunate victims of cult-like manipulation from the cradle to the grave. They are the hapless victims of uninformed consent. In all of that, and oh so very much more, Latter-day Saints have been betrayed. They have, knowingly or unknowingly, lived inauthentic lives.

"[T]he fact of plurality on the part of Joseph and his associates and the coloring of truth in connection with it has been reported by almost every student of the period."[24] It is now apparent that

---

[23]Ibid.
[24]Ibid., 365.

Mormonism has deep roots in duplicity and that "Enlightened investigation" was never the fact or the goal.

The devil is in the details.

JOSEPH SMITH SPEAKS TO THE SAINTS

The Legacy of Deception

As William Law – Joseph Smith's former highly respected Counselor in the First Presidency (he took the place of Hyrum Smith) – left Joseph and the Church with several hundred other disenchanted Saints, Smith counter-attacked. Law's unwelcome dissent surrounded that decent man's rejection of polygamy (and Joseph's uncommon interest in President Law's wife). One day William was "wise, discreet, just, prudent"; the next day he was the Prince of Darkness. No decent right-thinking man ever left the Mormon Church or criticized the Mormon prophet. Or Sidney Rigdon. The transformation from Saint to sinner was often abrupt.

> *This new holy prophet [Joseph Smith speaking of William Law] has gone to Carthage and swore that I had told him that I was guilty of adultery. This spiritual wifeism! Why a man dares not speak or wink, for fear of being accused of this."* [25]
>
> *I am innocent of all these charges, and you can bear witness of my innocence, for you know me yourselves.* [26]
>
> *What a thing it is for a man to be accused of committing adultery, and having seven wives, when I can only find one.* [27]

When Joseph Smith turned on his detractors in this boastful sermon delivered one month before his date with doom and said, *"I*

---

[25]*History of the Church*, 6:410, emphasis added.
[26]*History of the Church*, 6:411, emphasis added.
[27]Ibid., emphasis added.

can prove them all perjurers," because he said he only had one wife, he actually had nearly forty wives. *"What a thing it is,"* he said, *"for a man to be accused of committing adultery, and having seven wives, when I can only find one."* When Joseph Smith told his followers that he was a monogamist in May 1844, the month before he died in June, he told a whopper, for between January 6, 1842 and November 2, 1843, just before his death on June 27, 1844, he married about thirty-four women in twenty-two months.[28] The greater number of the legal husbands of his more than a dozen undivorced polyandrous wives were the prophet's priesthood brothers. How shallow do these bytes sound, considering that, in retrospect:

> *"[D]on't forsake me. I want the friendship of my brethren – Let us teach the things of Jesus Christ."*[29]

> *"I am innocent of all these charges, and you can bear witness of my innocence, for you know me yourselves."*[30]

> *"God is in the still small voice. In all these affidavits, indictments, it is all of the devil – all corruption. Come on! ye prosecutors! ye false swearers! All hell, boil over! Ye burning mountains, roll down your lava! for I will come out on the top at last."*[31]

Nineteenth-century polygamous Mormons, inside society Saints, confidential privileged covenant friends of Joseph Smith, those who knew the truth, were men and women who could be trusted not to tell the truth. "Brigham Young remembered that . . . the prophet told him that if he was open about what he had received from heaven, 'not a man or woman would stay with me.' And Levi Hancock recalled that Joseph once remarked to him that if he were to reveal all God had shown him, his own followers would seek his

---

[28]George D. Smith, *Nauvoo Polygamy: " . . . but we called it celestial marriage"* (Salt Lake City: Signature Books, 2008), 621-23.
[29]*History of the Church*, 6:411, emphasis added.
[30]Ibid., emphasis added.
[31]Ibid., 6:408, emphasis added.

life."[32]　One modern detractor descended from a family deeply rooted in polygamy identified the problem with a term that snugly fit.　There was with them, he said, *"A Legacy of Deception."*[33]　This culture of deception, this poisonous polygamous legacy, started squarely with Smith, the person directly responsible for Mormon polygamy, and for everything that since has followed, including present day (modern) polygamy.

Mormons assume that leaders bound by covenants made to each other to lie about polygamy, the signature principle of the nineteenth-century Church, could be trusted to tell the truth about everything else.　From polygamy's early beginnings in 1829 (so said Brigham Young) or 1831 (so said Joseph Fielding Smith) until Orson Pratt publicly announced the practice of polygamy in 1852, Mormons lied to their investigators and converts wherever they preached.　"[C]hurch leaders at the time of Joseph Smith withheld knowledge concerning polygamy not only from the general public but from many of their own followers."[34]　To the discredit of those early Mormon leaders, and to the shame of their supposed God, "deceit" (most particularly in the mission field) was considered necessary to shelter them.　Because polygamy was denied in Europe, when converts arrived in Utah they got a rude awakening.

Joseph Smith led the duplicitous charge.　To people taught to lie about polygamy in order *to protect the faith*, it is a small thing to lie about other things *to protect the faith* – doctrinal things; spiritual things; embarrassing provocative things.　Protecting the faith, both then and now, even to those who are beautifully educated, is more important than telling the truth.　The truth isn't always useful and may not always matter.　History must be made to seem inspiring. Mormon scholars deliberate[35] behind preconceived untenable conclusions, lacking the freedom to follow the facts wherever they lead.　The process is institutionalized and intellectually dishonest.

---

[32]Hardy, *Solemn Covenant*, 366.
[33]Arza Evans, *The Keystone of Mormonism* (St. George, UT: Keystone Books Inc., 2003), 134.
[34]Appendix 1 in Hardy, *Solemn Covenant*, 364.
[35]"Deliberations and accounts by the church's highest leaders remain unavailable to the public to the present day." (Ibid.).

Denials

Joseph Smith protected "the church's polygamous affairs" by lying for the Lord for nearly fifteen years, from 1829 or 1831 to 1844. Brigham Young protected "the church's polygamous affairs" by lying for the Lord from 1841 until 1852. Smith equated failure to lie to protect the leaders to "sinning against the Holy Ghost and proving a traitor to the brethren." Failure of a member to do this duty, truth be damned, was considered a violation of loyalty and friendship. Above all else, Smith told the Quorum in 1839, "[D]o not betray your *Friend*."[36] The Mormon Church found its footings in this morally confusing maelstrom.

"The greatest of evils, Joseph said in his 1839 address to the apostles, were 'sinning against the Holy Ghost and proving a traitor to the brethren.'"[37] Who dared dispute the prophet? Did God not say, "Thou shalt give heed unto all his words, and commandments, which he shall give unto you, as he receiveth them, walking in all holiness before me: For his word ye shall receive, as if from mine own mouth, in all patience and faith . . ."?[38] That notwithstanding, true Christians must be able to assume that God is not the Father of lies.

Joseph Smith and those who followed him into the legally prohibited practice of polygamy offered "repeated denials that they were engaging in the practice under any name." "[T]he term *spiritual wife*," assigned to John C. Bennett's secret wife system, and sometimes condemned as different from "plural" or "celestial" marriage, "was, in fact, employed by Mormons both before and after their exodus to the Great Basin."[39] "Outright denial was but

---

[36]Hardy, *Solemn Covenant*, 365-66, emphasis retained. Anthony W. Ivins, an authority on the Book of Mormon, an Apostle and later a member of the First Presidency, heard President Joseph F. Smith say at a meeting of apostles that he "would lie any day to save [his] . . . brother." (Ibid., 371-72). That was something Joseph F. Smith, a witness, would prove to the nation at the Senate hearings that attended the difficulties associated with the seating of Senator Reed Smoot in the early 1900s. Ivins' daughter Florence "believed her father troubled over President Smith's statement for the rest of his life." (Ibid.).

[37]Hardy, *Solemn Covenant*, 366.
[38]Book of Commandments, 22:4-5.
[39]Hardy, *Solemn Covenant*, 365.

one of several strategies employed"[40] to conceal the practice of polygamy. "[E]xpressions of outrage when accused of departures from traditional morality" were commonly employed by those who were guilty of "departures from traditional morality" before the practice of polygamy was finally admitted by Brigham Young and Orson Pratt in 1852.

From the time Joseph Smith first privately revealed the controversial principle to several of the missionaries proselyting the Indians ("Lamanites") on the border of Missouri in 1831 until the day he died (June 27, 1844), Joseph Smith never publicly admitted and always publicly denied practicing the principle he privately called "the most holy and important doctrine ever revealed to man on the earth." It was the signature principle of the nineteenth-century Church. Those detractors who said that he had taken plural wives were roundly defamed, most particularly women who escaped. Critics were described by the prophet as "persecutors," "perjurers" and "false swearers." For more than thirteen years, from 1829 or 1831 to 1844, Smith's inner circle of about thirty Nauvoo men – brothers in plurality, "members of the so-called Quorum of the Anointed"[41] – never publicly admitted and always publicly denied the truth about the new and everlasting covenant, "the most holy and important doctrine ever revealed to man on the earth." For more than twenty years, from 1829 or 1831 to 1852, his increasingly knowledgeable followers – burgeoning to become thousands of men, women and children – never publicly admitted and always publicly denied the truth about polygamy.

During the months just before he died, the prophet's polygamy became increasingly difficult to continue to conceal. During this unsettling period, his duplicity as an offender of enormity threatened to bring the prophet down. What the editors of the *Nauvoo Expositor* reported in June of 1844 about life in the City of Joseph was true. What Joseph Smith reported in a boastful sermon delivered on May 26, 1844, the month before he died, was most decidedly not. Joseph Smith was the "perjurer." It was William Law who told the truth.

---

[40]Ibid.

[41]These men and their women are identified by George D. Smith in *Nauvoo Polygamy*, 573-639; *see, e.g.*, 573.

EMMA SMITH SPEAKS TO THE SAINTS

"Last Testimony of Sister Emma"

At the end of her life in the year of her death, Emma Smith was interviewed by her sons Joseph III and Alexander. Joseph III grew to become the prophet of the patriarchal branch (the Joseph as opposed to the Brigham schism) of the Mormon Church after the death of his father.[42] The interview was conducted over the period from February 4 to February 10, 1879, at Nauvoo, Illinois. The results were published, but not until after Emma's death, in *The Saints Herald* – the official paper of the Reorganized Church of Jesus Christ of Latter Day Saints – at Plano, Illinois, on October 1, 1879.

In this last important interview, Emma told her sons that she had lost her marriage certificate "many years ago" but thought a marriage date of January 18, 1827, had been correct. Speaking further Emma said: "My folks were bitterly opposed to him," but that "being importuned by your father, aided by Mr. Stowell . . . and preferring him to any other man I know, I consented." She then proceeded to marry the man she had come to know as the indispensable shaman of a group of money-digging men assembled under the patronage of Mr. Stowell who boarded at the home of her parents.

When asked "about the revelation on Polygamy," "spiritual wifery," by Joseph III in the presence of her then husband, "Major Bidamon," a non-Mormon man, Emma now testified that, "There was no revelation on either polygamy, or spiritual wives."[43]   In

---

[42]Emma Smith told William Clayton, "[I]t was secret things which had cost Joseph and Hyrum their lives." (Hardy, *Solemn Covenant*, 367).

[43]William E. McLellin (an Apostle, a former Secretary to the Founding Quorum of the Twelve Apostles and a trusted, respected friend to Emma Smith) contradicted that assertion in 1875 (before it was made) in these terms: "I visited Mrs. Emma Smith in Nauvoo, in 1847. She told me plainly and frankly that her husband did receive and deliver the Polyamic revelation [Doctrine and Covenants 132] himself, *and she knew he practiced its provisions.* And she said she knew that he had committed adultery with girls previous to that." (Letter to John L. Traughber in *The William E. McLellin Papers: 1854-1880,* eds. Stan Larson and Samuel J. Passey, foreword by George D. Smith [Salt Lake City: Signature Books,

describing her late husband to her son, and to posterity, she said that, "There were some rumors of something of the sort, of which I asked my husband. He assured me that all there was of it was, that, in a chat about plural wives, he had said, 'Well, such a system might possibly be, if everybody was agreed to it, and would behave as they should; but they would not; and, besides, it was contrary to the will of heaven.'"[44] In the later years of his private journal, Joseph Smith Jr. "wrote repeated denials of polygamy."[45] So Emma said, as she said Joseph said, that he didn't practice polygamy.

In this last testament, Emma Smith described to her children, and to the Reorganized Church of Jesus Christ of Latter Day Saints, what had come to be her bottom line: "No such thing as polygamy, or spiritual wifery, was taught, publicly or privately, before my husband's death, that I have now, or ever had any knowledge of."[46] Her oldest son, Joseph's duly ordained successor, Joseph III, proceeded to ask the following questions: Joseph III: *"Did he not have other wives than yourself?"* The purpose for the interview was "to present to her a few prominent questions . . . the answers to which might, so far as she was concerned, settle these differences of opinion [differences as to how and on whose authority polygamy started]." "[I]t had been frequently stated to us [the sons of Joseph Smith – Joseph III, Alexander, Frederick and David]: 'Ask your mother, she knows.' ... 'You do not dare to ask your mother!'" "Our thought [in so proceeding] was, that if we had lacked courage to ask her, because we feared the answers she might give, we would put aside that fear; and, whatever the worst might be, we would hear it."

So the question was: *"Did he not have other wives than yourself?"* And the answer was: "He had no other wife but me; nor did he to my knowledge ever have." So the next question was: *"Did he not hold marital relation with women other than yourself?"* And the

---

2008], 501, emphasis added).

[44]*The Saints Herald* (Plano, IL: Reorganized Church of Jesus Christ of Latter-day Saints, 1 October 1879).

[45]Fawn McKay Brodie, *No Man Knows My History: The Life of Joseph Smith the Mormon Prophet*, 2d ed., rev. and enl. (New York, NY: Alfred A. Knopf, 1972), viii.

[46]*The Saints Herald* (Plano, IL: Reorganized Church of Jesus Christ of Latter-day Saints, 1 October 1879).

answer was: "He did not have improper relations with any woman that ever came to my knowledge."

> Q.   *Was there nothing about spiritual wives that you recollect?*

> A.   *At one time my husband came to me and asked if I had heard certain rumors about spiritual marriages, or anything of the kind; and assured me that if I had, that they were without foundation; that there was no such doctrine, and never should be with his knowledge or consent. I know that he had no other wife or wives than myself, in any sense, either spiritual or otherwise.*

Joseph III asked his mother this:

> Q.   *It has been stated sometimes that you apostatized at father's death, and joined the Methodist Church. What do you say to this?*

> A.   *I have been called apostate; but I have never apostatized, nor forsaken the faith I at first accepted; but was called so because I would not accept their new fangled notion [Brigham Young's polygamy].*

Emma's interview "accurately portrayed the public posture of both Emma and Joseph Smith."[47]   Both of them lied to the Latter-day Saints, and to everyone else, wherever they were for as long as they lived.

---

[47]1879 Interview with Joseph III and Alexander Smith, Last Testimony, 289-90, reproduced at Richard S. Van Wagoner, *Mormon Polygamy: A History* (Salt Lake City: Signature Books, 1986), 75-77. *See, e.g.,* "Last Testimony of Sister Emma," *The Saints Herald*, vol. 26 no. 19 (Plano, IL: 1 October 1879).

JOHN TAYLOR

A favorite trick of Mormonism's early polygamists was to employ "expressions of outrage when accused of departures from traditional morality." (Hardy, 365). Hear that in this: "We [John Taylor and colleagues] are accused here [at a debate in a hall rented by Taylor in France in 1850] of polygamy, and actions the most indelicate, obscene and disgusting, such that none but a corrupt and depraved heart could have contrived. These things are too outrageous to admit of belief . . . ." (Discussion, Boulogne-sur-mer, 1850). When he uttered these prevarications, Taylor (who would succeed Brigham Young to become Mormonism's third prophet) had already been the husband of fifteen wives. The names of Taylor's pre-Discussion women were Leonora Agnes Cannon, Elizabeth Kaigan, Mary Cook, Ann Vowles, Jane Ballantyne, Annie Ballantyne, Mercy Rachel Fielding (Thompson) (Smith), Mary Ann DeGroot Oakley, Ann Hughlings (Pitchforth), Mary Amanda Utley, Mary Ramsbottom, Lydia Dibble (Granger Smith), Sarah Thornton (Coleman), Sophia Whitaker and Harriet Whitaker. He would have twenty-six children with them. After the French episode he would take three additional wives with whom he would have nine more children. On December 19, 1886, at the age of seventy-eight, Taylor married a twenty-six year old woman, Josephine Elizabeth Roueche. He had nine children with Margaret Young, a woman he married when he was forty-seven and she was nineteen. (George D. Smith). Lorenzo Snow, another future prophet, married a fifteen year old when he was fifty-seven. They had five children. Snow's last polygamous child was delivered when he was eighty-two years old.

On the first day of the French discussion, Taylor turned his attention to one of his earlier tormentors. "I have already stated that I proved [the Reverend] Mr. Caswell to have told one lie, and a man that will tell one falsehood to injure an innocent people, will tell five hundred, if necessary, for the same object." (Discussion). What Apostle Taylor said of the reverend gentleman, Mr. Caswell, should have been said of Taylor. From December 12, 1843, when Taylor took his first plural wife, and until August 1852, Taylor, like all of the other apostles, denied that the Church taught, preached or practiced polygamy.

POST-MANIFESTO PATRIARCHS

"[Apostle Cowley] told my dad that there was still a way to live polygamy and there were a few select people that he was able to choose to give this opportunity to." (Elna Mary Palmer)

"Alexander Finlay MacDonald, 1825-1903. As a patriarch in the Mormon colonies in Mexico, Macdonald performed numerous polygamous marriages between the time of the Manifesto in 1890 and his death in 1903." (Hardy, Solemn Covenant).

Alexander Finlay MacDonald. Image Source: Mesa Historical (https://www.azcentral.com/story/news/local/history/2015/05/14/125-republic-anniversary-people-helped-shape-east-valley/70949758/)

"Anthony Woodward Ivins, 1852-1934, leading authority in the Mormon colonies in Mexico, 1895-1907. By permission of the First Presidency in Salt Lake City, Ivins performed more than forty polygamous marriages during the years from 1897 to 1904. Ivins was made an apostle [after the 1890 Manifesto and on October 6, 1907] upon the death of George Teasdale and later [May 25, 1925] became a member of the First Presidency itself." (Ibid.).

JOSEPH SMITH III

The leader of the patriarchal branch of his father's church from 1860 to 1914. "Known as 'Josephites' in Utah, members of the Reorganized Church of Jesus Christ of Latter Day Saints ("RLDS") rejected polygamy and temple rituals. They believed church authority passed to the descendants of Joseph Smith." The Josephites, because of the Book of Mormon, are Trinitarians. William Marks, the President of the Nauvoo High Council, was in the room when Hyrum Smith read the revelation on polygamy (Section 132) on August 12, 1843. He became a Counselor in the First Presidency of the Reorganized Church ("RLDS") on April 6, 1863, and was the First Counselor in the First Presidency when he died in Plano, Illinois, on May 22, 1872. President Marks knew everything Joseph III, Frederick, Alexander and David Smith needed to know about Nauvoo polygamy.

Image source: Photo by Heman Conoman Smith [Public domain], via Wikimedia Commons.

CLAYTON REBUKES THE SONS OF JOSEPH SMITH

William Clayton. Image source: Public domain, via Wikimedia Commons.

In a letter to one Madison Scott dated November 11, 1871, the principal topic of which "is what is commonly called polygamy, but which I prefer to call celestial marriage," William Clayton challenged the views of Joseph Smith's sons in apocalyptic terms. "As to young Joseph [Joseph III], saying that the Church here have apostatized; that we have introduced polygamy, denying bitterly that his father ever had a revelation on the subject, that is . . . bosh! I believe he knows better, and I have often felt sorry to learn that the sons of the Prophet should spend their time in contending against a pure and holy principle which their father's blood was shed to establish. They will have a heavy atonement to make when they meet their father in the next world. They are in the hands of God, and my respect for their father will not permit me to say much about the wicked course of his sons."

CLAYTON SUPPORTS "A PURE AND HOLY PRINCIPLE"

"I did write the revelations on celestial marriage given through the Prophet Joseph Smith, on the 12th of July, 1843." "I . . . testify . . . that the Prophet Joseph both taught and practiced polygamy . . . . In April, 1843 [which was before Joseph received the revelation on polygamy], he sealed me to my second wife, my first wife being then living. By my said second wife I had two sons born in Nauvoo. The first died; the second is here now and is married."

"I had the honor to seal one woman [Lucy Walker] to Joseph under his direction. I could name ten or a dozen of his wives who are now living in this [Utah] territory so that for any man to tell me that Joseph did not teach polygamy, he is losing his time . . . . I positively know of what I speak . . . ."

"President Young and his associates . . . have been doing everything they can to carry out the plans and instructions of the Prophet Joseph, and so eternity will prove to the condemnation and confusion of all their enemies." (Clayton, "Blood Atonement and the Origin of Plural Marriage," 1905, Elder Joseph F. Smith, Jr.)

Clayton "was unique among Joseph Smith's scribes in that he actually seemed part of Smith's household and was with him almost every day of the last two years of the Prophet's life." (George D. Smith). Clayton married ten women, three of whom later left him. With those ten wives he fathered forty-seven children.

SUPPRESSION

William Clayton recorded Joseph Smith's "casual conversations and controversial doctrines which dealt with plural gods, God as a man, God as Adam, and resurrection by literal rebirth through a woman." He was an important member of the Council of Fifty. "Clayton's writings, although scattered among various articles, books, and library collections, have for years been generally inaccessible to all but a few favored scholars." (George D. Smith)

Clayton began keeping minutes for the mysterious Council of Fifty on March 10, 1844. On June 23, 1844, after being called to the prophet's home in the middle of the night, Joseph "whispered and told me either to put the r[ecords] of k[ingdom] into the hands of some faithful man and send them away, or burn them or bury them." Clayton "returned home and immediately put the records in a small box and buried them." Several days later, on June 27, 1844, Joseph Smith was murdered. No ordinary Latter-day Saint saw Joseph Smith's Council of Fifty Minutes from 1844, when they were prepared, until 2016, when they were published in "The Joseph Smith Papers."

WILLIAM MARKS

"As the president of the Nauvoo Stake, Marks was the presiding local authority in Nauvoo." William Marks married Rosannah Robinson on May 2, 1813. When he died on May 22, 1872, after rejecting Brigham Young as his leader, this First Counselor in the First Presidency of the Reorganized Church, a "Josephite" and a monogamous man, was the father of five children. He married a second woman in 1866 after his first wife died in 1862. Joseph Smith spoke at the funeral of William Mark's son where he confessed his mortality.

After Marks was appointed President of the Nauvoo Stake of Zion, he was elected as an alderman. He was one of the regents of the University and a founder of the Nauvoo Agricultural and Manufacturing Association. He was the landlord of the Mansion House.

He assisted in the laying of the cornerstones of the Nauvoo temple. He was initiated into Masonry and on May 4, 1842, became a member of the secret Council of Fifty. Marks was the agent of the Messenger and Advocate. He received "his endowments and anointings before any other successor claimants (including every member of the Quorum of Twelve) . . . ." (William Marks, Wikipedia).

On August 12, 1843, while he was the President of the Nauvoo Stake High Council, at a meeting held at Hyrum Smith's office, there was an inquiry made "in relation to the subject of plurality of wives . . . ." Marks was present at the time. In the absence of Joseph (who was ill), Hyrum took the query, briefly adjourned the meeting, and walked home to get a copy of the revelation. Upon his return, in a meeting without minutes, Hyrum read the revelation on plural marriage dated July 12, 1843. "After reading the document to the High Council, he admonished those who believed the words of the revelation to 'go forth and obey the same' and 'be saved.' Those who rejected it would be 'damned.'" (George D. Smith, Nauvoo Polygamy, 419; "Thomas Grover's Testimony," Historical Record 6 [May 1887]).

William Marks, who heard the prophet's brother read the prophet's revelation, wasn't on board. His opposition to plural marriage was immediate and pronounced. (William Marks, Wikipedia). Marks chose damnation over polygamy.

William Marks later claimed that Joseph Smith approached him just weeks before the prophet's death "and told him that plural marriage had proved a curse rather than a blessing to the church. Smith," according to Marks, "wanted to take decisive steps to end the practice, but time ran out . . . ." (Ibid.). Marks said Joseph said "that the 'doctrine of polygamy or Spiritual Wife System . . . will prove our destruction and overthrow . . . it is wrong; it is a curse to mankind, and we shall have to leave the United States, unless it can be put down." (Marks, George D. Smith, Nauvoo

Polygamy, 442-43). Other evidence, such as Joseph's burning of the polygamy revelation and destroying his temple garments, seems to support Marks' story. One more compelling fact adds veracity to the claim of William Marks, and to the speculations of D. Michael Quinn. From February 1843 to November 2, 1843, Joseph Smith married about twenty-one women. From November 2, 1843, to June 27, 1844, the date of his death, and over the last eight months of his life, Smith neglected to take a plural wife, even one. (George D. Smith, 621-23). Brigham Young himself would say that Smith had wearied of polygamous marriage by the time of his death. (Quinn, Origins of Power, 146-47).

When Joseph Smith died, the issue of church succession "revolved around one central issue: plural marriage." As the President of the High Council, Marks was well positioned to succeed the prophet Joseph Smith. His intransigence on the question of plural marriage endeared him to Emma Smith but doomed his chances to become the prophet himself, and more than that to continue as a faithful member of the Brigham branch of what became a divided Church. "Young and the majority of the Quorum of the Twelve . . . feared that Marks would end plural marriage and other ordinances that they saw as crucial to exaltation in the afterlife." (Ibid.). Marks was removed from the High Council and dismissed as the President of the Nauvoo Stake of Zion. Brigham Young, not yet all powerful, wanted Marks to be excommunicated but the Nauvoo High Council "refused his request." (Wikipedia).

William Clayton's diary noted that Emma Smith "supported Marks [although he did not support himself] as the successor to her husband . . . ." For Emma, the issue of succession did not revolve around the preservation of plural marriage. The emergence of such a concern, even privately, may serve to explain why she so disliked the Senior Apostle, Brigham Young. The High Council, under the direction of Marks, was important at the headquarters of the Church in Nauvoo, Illinois, until Marks rejected polygamy. "According to Emma, Marks had a right to church succession as the High Council President, a Council which she asserted was equal in authority to the Quorum of the Twelve and the First Presidency. Furthermore, she felt that while apostles had authority in unorganized parts of the church, they did not have authority at headquarters in the stake of Zion, Nauvoo." (Ibid.). There was historical support for that proposition.

After Young's followers followed him to Utah, Marks (and many important others) joined James J. Strang, where Marks became a counselor "in the Strangite First Presidency." Leaving Strang sometime later, Marks and others convinced "that succession in the Presidency of the Church must be lineal, descending from father to son," promoted the idea that the Church of Jesus Christ of Latter-day Saints should be "reorganized." (Ibid.). The unexcommunicated Marks helped to form the new church, which he served as the First Counselor in the First Presidency of Joseph Smith III from April 6, 1863, until the date of his death, May 22, 1872. In 1866 Marks helped the Josephite Branch of Joseph's Church to print Joseph Smith's Inspired Translation of the King James Bible. It is quite certain that William Marks didn't know about the extraordinary contribution of a Methodist theologian, Adam Clarke, to Smith's Inspired Translation.

THE INCIDENCE OF THE PRINCIPLE

As a missionary to Norway, this author was taught to respond to investigators with questions about Mormonism's polygamy (and there were many) that no more than three percent of the Saints ever practiced the polygamous principle. No particular emphasis was placed upon the extensive incidence of the practice among the principal leaders and founders of the faith. "The question of how many Mormons accepted the call and entered the principle has been debated for more than a century." When successfully sequestered in the vast and empty American West, and before the unusual practice met the kind of opposition that became intense, leaders and Saints admitted that the number involved could have been ten percent or more. "After the national crusade against" this second relic of barbarism (the first was slavery), and when the "Mormon leaders decided to mute their polygamous image, they began insisting that few of their number ever had more wives than one. By counting only polygamous husbands or using other devices, it was said that the number of pluralists amounted to no more than 2 or 3 percent of the church's membership." The First Presidency, the highest leaders of the Church, encouraged what then became yet another more than hundred-year deception. "These low figures continued to be cited well into the present century [the twentieth century]." (Hardy, "Solemn Covenant," 16-17, 37 n 111).

Recent studies obliterated the Presidency's calculated deception. "Mormons living in polygamous families between 1850 and 1890, while varying from community to community and year to year, averaged between 20 and 30 percent. In some cases the proportion was higher. The practice was especially extensive with Mormon leaders, both locally and those presiding over the entire church." Over the active life of the pernicious doctrine, "the number of men, women, and children living in polygamous households amounted to tens of thousands." This "awesome phalanx" presented Western society "with what was, perhaps, the most serious challenge to traditional family life in centuries." (Ibid., Hardy, 17).

UNDISCERNED DECEPTION

Image Source: The Salt Lake Tribune, April 22, 1980.

Mark W. Hofmann, left (who forged Mormon documents and sold them to the Church, some to be concealed and suppressed) was convicted of murder. In this photo, LDS Church leaders N. Eldon Tanner, Spencer W. Kimball, Marion G. Romney, Boyd K. Packer and Gordon B. Hinckley examine the Anthon transcript.

ADDRESSING DECEPTION

George Q. Cannon. Used by permission, Utah State Historical Society. All rights reserved.

Charles Penrose. Image source: Andrew Jenson [Public domain], via Wikimedia Commons.

Gordon B. Hinckley. Image source: Public domain, via Wikimedia Commons.

"Those trafficking in deceit, warned George Q. Cannon, lost the spirit of God as well as the trust of men." (Cannon in Hardy, "Solemn Covenant," 363). Gordon B. Hinckley, another Mormon prophet, "warned that when one resorts to falsehood and deception, even in behalf of a worthy cause, there is danger such practice will spread to other employments 'like a disease that is endemic.'" (Ibid., 363-64). When one learns to lie, even in support of the good, it becomes easy to apply deception and artifice in support of anything else or evil. Charles Penrose, an author of the Manifesto and a future member of the First Presidency, told President John Taylor that: "[T]he endless subterfuges and prevarications which our present condition [the need to conceal the unlawful practice of polygamy] impose . . . threaten to make our rising generation a race of deceivers." (Letter, Penrose to John Taylor, 1887).

The reluctant and unexpected late twentieth and early twenty-first century digital disclosure of the many notorious elements of the society's difficult past tend to support that nineteenth-century concern. Dishonesty by important leaders presents a slippery slope to the people at large. The Latter-day Saints must ignore burgeoning evidence of the fraudulent declarations and acts of leaders whose words they must then also accept in patience and faith as the words of God. It is no easy task to determine when men, speaking as prophets, are thought to be telling the truth. The Church's truth claims are under attack because its leaders and scholars haven't been honest. The leaders of the less than transparent Church have had a problem telling the truth.

WILFORD WOODRUFF

Plural Marriage and the Manifesto: *On October 6, 1890, President Wilford Woodruff spoke to the Latter-day Saints, and to the world, about Mormon polygamy. Noting that the Utah Commission had reported to the Secretary of the Interior that plural marriages were "still being solemnized," and that "forty or more such marriages" had been "contracted in Utah since last June or during the past year," and that "the leaders of the Church have taught, encouraged and urged the continuance of the practice of polygamy," Woodruff said this:*

> *I therefore, as President of the Church of Jesus Christ of Latter-day Saints, do hereby, in the most solemn manner, declare that these charges are false. We are not teaching polygamy or plural marriage, nor permitting any person to enter into its practice, and I deny that either forty or any other number of plural marriages have during that period been solemnized in our Temples or in any other place in the Territory. ["Official Declaration (Manifesto)," 1890].*

When those representations proved to be false, when the performances of new plural marriages by various leaders of the Church became known to people outside of the Church, those marriages and the Mormon leaders' unrepentant duplicity troubled many Americans. Woodruff's Manifesto, which emerged as "a tactic to preserve polygamy"– after fits and starts – was seen to become a revelation "now used to prohibit" earth-centered polygamy.

MANIFESTO, 1890

"I hereby declare my intention to submit to . . . [laws forbidding plural marriage] and to use my influence with the members of the Church over which I preside to have them do likewise." (President Wilford Woodruff, "Official Declaration [Manifesto]," 1890).

The Salt Lake Tribune compiled a list of two hundred and thirty-nine men who had taken plural wives since the Manifesto. A tentative accounting of the names and circumstances surrounding post-Manifesto polygamous marriages may be found in Appendix II to B. Carmon Hardy's book entitled "Solemn Covenant: The Mormon Polygamous Passage" (pp. 389-426). One conspicuous name on that imposing list is that of the prophet Wilford Woodruff, who married Lydia Mountford in a covert proceeding outside of the state of Utah, in 1897, the year before his death in 1898 at the age of ninety-one. Hardy's list alleged that "a sizable number of church members were given permission to enter polygamous unions after 1890." (Ibid., 389). Hardy's study found 262 plural marriages involving 220 different men between October 1890 (the date of the Manifesto) and December 1910. "[M]ore than half [of those men] served their church as missionaries, or [as] other high officers [branch presidents, bishops, stake presidents or apostles]." George Q. Cannon's son (United States Senator, Frank Cannon) "said that the Salt Lake Tribune's list of two hundred or so was probably only one tenth of the actual number." (Ibid., 392-93).

GEORGE Q. CANNON

"My [unmarried] son David died without seed, and his brothers cannot do a [levirate] work for him in rearing children to bear his name because of the Manifesto. I believe in concubinage, or some plan whereby men and women can live together under sacred ordinances and vows until they can be married." Noting that such relationships would have to be kept secret, he then further said that concubinage would allow the Saints to take care of "our surplus girls" and to keep faith with the commandment to multiply and replenish the earth. President Wilford Woodruff agreed with Cannon, his First Counselor in the First Presidency. It (concubinage) was, Woodruff said, an acceptable resort until men were again able to openly embrace plural marriage. (Abraham H. Cannon Diaries, 5 April 1894).

Image Source: The Goates Notes, available from thegoateskids.blogspot.com.

George Q. Cannon with his older sons. L-R (Standing): Brigham T., Hugh J., Frank J., Willard T., William T., Joseph J., Sylvester Q., David H. (Seated): Lewis T., John Q., Angus J., George Q. Cannon, Read T., Abram H., Mark Y. Image source: http://www.georgeqcannon.com/ImageThumbs/GQC/Thumbnails.html.

STEPHEN C. LeSUEUR

"The expulsion of these men [dissident founders and leaders] from Far West [which preceded the 1838 forced expulsion of everyone else from Far West] reflected a growing militant spirit among the Mormons, revealed a rigid intolerance for those who opposed their practices and teachings, and demonstrated their willingness to circumvent the law to protect their interests."

"The Danites bound themselves with secret oaths and signs and pledged to support each other and the leaders of the Church – whether right or wrong – in all conflicts with their enemies. They prohibited excessive criticism of the First Presidency, demanded adherence to the communitarian practices of the Church, and served as an arm of the Church leadership in controlling local politics. The Danites sought by these activities to purge the Church of evil and to help build a righteous city of Zion."

DANITES

"THE TESTIMONY GIVEN BEFORE THE JUDGE OF THE FIFTH JUDICIAL CIRCUIT OF THE STATE OF MISSOURI, ON THE TRIAL OF JOSEPH SMITH, JR., AND OTHERS, FOR HIGH TREASON, AND OTHER CRIMES AGAINST THAT STATE."

"Sampson Avard, a witness produced, sworn and examined on behalf of the State, deposeth and saith: That about four months since [the Richmond, Missouri, "criminal court of inquiry begun November 12, 1838"], a band, called the Daughters of Zion, (since called the Danite band) was formed of the members of the Mormon Church, the original object of which was to drive from the county of Caldwell all those who dissented from the Mormon Church; in which they succeeded admirably, and to the satisfaction of those concerned. I [Danite Commander Avard] consider Joseph Smith, jr., as the prime mover and organizer of this Danite band . . . . Joseph Smith, jr., blessed them ["The officers of the band"], and prophesied over them: declaring that they should be the means, in the hands of God, of bringing forth the millenial kingdom. It was stated by Joseph Smith, jr., that it was necessary this band should be bound together by a covenant, that those who revealed the secrets of the society should be put to death." (Senate Document 189, 26th Congress)

Danite Band, Public Domain, https://en.wikipedia.org/wiki/File:Danites_Charge.jpg#filelinks

POLITICS AND THE PRINCIPLE

"After the election of B.H. Roberts, a member of the First Council of the Seventy, to the U.S. Congress, it became known that Roberts had three wives, one of whom he married after the Manifesto. A petition of seven million signatures demanded that Roberts not be seated. Congress complied, and Roberts was barred from his office. [Davis Bitton, The Exclusion of B.H. Roberts from Congress]." The illegal marriages continued during the administration of President Lorenzo Snow, and with even greater (deceitful and cynical) impunity after the problematic Joseph F. Smith became Church President in 1901.

WILFORD WOODRUFF,
SHOCK AND AWE

1894: *"I hurl defiance at the world to prove that the manifesto forbidding plural marriage has not been observed."* **1897:** *"Circumstantial evidence indicates that Wilford Woodruff married Madame [Lydia Mary Mamreoff von Finkelstein] Mountford as a plural wife in 1897 [when he was ninety years old and the year before his death]. President Woodruff recorded attending her lecture [in Salt Lake City] on 7 February 1897, the first of ninety references to her in his diary during the next eighteen months." With his confidential secretary L. John Nuttall, Woodruff traveled to San Francisco to see Mrs. Mountford. The trip proceeded from Salt Lake City to Portland [where the two "avoided the usual visits with Mormon officials and non-Mormon friends"]. They "made all their hotel and travel arrangements under 'assumed names.'" They traveled from Portland to San Francisco, after which Mrs. Mountford joined them on a steamship for a return trip to Portland, and then by train to Ogden, Utah, where the prophet, brother Nuttall and Madame Mountford then parted company. (D. Michael Quinn)*

The evidence appears to support the proposition that L. John Nuttall "performed a polygamous marriage for Wilford Woodruff and Madame Lydia Mary Mountford aboard ship on the Pacific Ocean on 20 September 1897 [seven years after the Manifesto]." (D. Michael Quinn).

Six of Woodruff's ten or eleven wives were teenagers. He married Eudora Lovina Young in 1877 when he was seventy and she was twenty-four. He had eight children with Sarah Brown, a woman he married when he was forty-six and she was nineteen. He had eight children with Emma Smoot Smith, a woman he married when he was forty-six and she was fifteen. He had nine children with Sarah Delight Stocking, a woman he married when he was fifty and she was nineteen. (George D. Smith)

Image source: Public domain, via Wikimedia Commons.

JOSEPH F. SMITH

*"**Under oath before the [United States] Senate [in 1904]**, Joseph F. Smith [Joseph Smith's nephew and then Prophet] led future witnesses by example. He volunteered that he had cohabited with his wives and that they had borne him eleven children since the Manifesto [in 1890], even though he said that the Manifesto 'was a revelation to me.'" Upon this point the following exchange then occurred:*

> **SENATOR OVERMAN.** *If that is a revelation [requiring an end to unlawful cohabitation], are you not violating the laws of God?*

> **MR. SMITH.** *I have admitted that, Mr. Senator, a great many times here. (D. Michael Quinn)*

The Prophet Testifies: *"I understand the law of celestial [plural] marriage to mean that every man in this Church, who has the ability to obey and practice it in righteousness and will not, shall be damned, I say I understand it to mean this and nothing less, and I testify in the name of Jesus that it does mean that."*

CHAPTER SIXTEEN

"You can't start with a rock in your hat and finish with a flurry of logic."[1]

To tell the truth as God has revealed it, and commend it to the acceptance of those who need to conform their opinions thereto, is the sole purpose of this presentation [the first man was not a development "from lower orders of the animal creation"].

First Presidency, 1909 and 2002[2]

Seekers no more, those who believed now belonged to God's Kingdom. ... They were here to fulfill God's divine purpose and follow His revealed word and His inspired prophet in all things. Released from the burden of uncertainty that life's choices impose, they now knew the true meaning of free will. They were free to choose: either to obey Him and gain the promise or defy Him and suffer His judgment.

The Mormon Rebellion[3]

More and more I come to a condition of astonishment at the parallelism in methods between Utah in the early days, and any totalitarian state today . . . – private army, secret police, encirclement myth, territorial dynamism, self sufficiency, chosen people,

---

[1]thingsithink (Anonymous informant), "Re: The Morg's lawyers dodging the issues," *Recovery from Mormonism* (posted and accessed 15 March 2014), available from exmormon.org/phorum/read.php?2,1204555, 1204663,quote=1; Internet, 1.

[2]Joseph F. Smith, John R. Winder, Anthon H. Lund, "The Origin of Man: 1909 First Presidency Message," *Improvement Era* (November 1909), 75-81, reaffirmed in the *Ensign* (February 2002), 75.

[3]David L. Bigler and Will Bagley, *The Mormon Rebellion: America's First Civil War, 1857-58* (University of Oklahoma Press: Norman, 2011), Introduction, 8.

absolute dictatorship operating through party rule, group psychology, esoteric symbols and distinguishing uniforms (garments), New Order and all.

Wallace Stegner[4]

"SEEKERS NO MORE . . ."

Many faithful Latter-day Saints struggle to say that Mormonism, this tiny blip on a gigantic screen, is the only true church. Yet that non-negotiable postulate lies at the bottom of its theology. The pathetic proposition that the Mormon Church is the only true Church and that every other denomination is "wrong" has been promulgated by a sales force that can now be counted as more than a million missionaries for nearly two hundred years. It started with Joseph Smith, who is supposed to have asked the Father and the Son "on the morning of a beautiful, clear day, early in the spring of eighteen hundred and twenty" "which of all the sects was right," that he might know which of them to join. According to Smith, the Lord answered him and said that he "must join none of them, for they were all wrong," "that all their creeds were an abomination," that their "professors were all corrupt," that "they draw near to me with their lips" but not their hearts, and "teach for doctrines the commandments of men."[5] Those are the founding words and that is the founding story – the canonized First Vision of the Father and the Son. It is upon those ethnocentric words in that ethnocentric story that the whole cause rests.

Mormon prophets talk to God; his words are their commands. "Whatever God requires [racism, slavery, polygyny, polyandry, misogyny, concubinage, incest,[6] homophobia, blood oaths, blood

---

[4]Wallace Stegner to Dale Morgan, 24 November 1941, in P. Stegner, *Selected Letters of Wallace Stegner*, 326, quoted in John Gary Maxwell, *Robert Newton Baskin and the Making of Modern Utah* (Norman, OK: The Arthur H. Clark Co., 2013), 80.

[5]The Pearl of Great Price, Joseph Smith – History 1: 14, 18, 19.

[6]Brigham Young announced: "I believe in Sisters marrying brothers, and brothers haveing their sisters for Wives." (Brigham Young, General Conference, 8 October 1854, LDS Church Archives, *Brigham Young Papers* [Ms d 1234, ff marked: Addresses-1854, July - Oct.], 20).

"You can't start with a rock in your hat
and finish with a flurry of logic."

453

atonement[7]] is right, no matter what it is, although we may not see the reason thereof till long after the events transpire."[8] The words of the prophet are more important than the law of the land. God commanded this tiny theocratic flock to follow the dictates of one infallible man: "Wherefore, meaning the church, thou shalt give heed unto all his words, and commandments, which he shall give unto you, as he receiveth them, walking in all holiness before me: For his word ye shall receive, as if from my own mouth, in all patience and faith . . . ."[9] That is what the Mormon God requires. The Mormon leader tells the Mormon people what God requires.

Since its founding in 1830, the Church has perfected the rhetoric of polarization, softening the *public* message but not the *private* belief. There are hard unspoken truths at the heart and soul of the uncompromising, less than transparent faith. Mormonism's divisive message destroys families in and out of the Church. Latter-day Saints solicit men, women and children to leave their biological families and their traditional faiths in order to embrace Mormonism's unconventional authoritarian theology, but those who leave their Mormon families and their Mormon faith are pariahs to be shunned and disrespected. By twenty-first century Mormon reckoning, those disconnected from the spirit are to be disconnected from those who are not.[10] For Mormonism's converts, victims of uninformed consent one hundred percent of the time, it is kindness in but daggers out. For more than a century and until about 1989, those caught in the gospel net by birth or conversion could orchestrate their exits only by means of the humiliating process of excommunication. It is publicly reported that, "[I]t's

---

[7]Brigham Young informed his bishops in 1846 that, "When a man is found to be a thief, he will be a thief no longer, cut his throat, & thro' him in the River." (D. Michael Quinn, *The Mormon Hierarchy: Origins of Power* [Salt Lake City: Signature Books, 1994], Selected Chronology, 657).

[8]Joseph Smith Jr., *History of The Church of Jesus Christ of Latter-day Saints*, B.H. Roberts, ed., 2d ed., rev., (Salt Lake City: The Deseret Book Company, 1978), 5:134-36. Designated "Happiness" in the *History of the Church*, this statement made by Joseph Smith is part of a one-of-a-kind letter defending polygamy delivered by Willard Richards, Smith's emissary and scribe (the "Pander General for lust"), to Miss Nancy Rigdon, after she rejected the prophet's proposals.

[9]Book of Commandments (1833), 22:4-5.

[10]L. Whitney Clayton, "Getting and Staying Connected," BYU Commencement Speech (21 April 2016, accessed 16 March 2018), available from https://speeches.byu.edu; Internet, 3 pages.

wrong to criticize the leaders of the Church, even if the criticism is true . . . ."[11] In the LDS Church the truth is not always useful, the whole truth need not always be spoken, the leaders don't apologize and can't be criticized, and the members "persistently disdain the comfortable fraternity of ecumenical Christianity."[12]

The Mormon Church is under unprecedented attack. The skeletons in its historical closet are on digital display and "the tempest is raging."   Having lost control of its message, the authoritarian society   fears   subversive,   revolutionary,   destructive   and uncorrelated thought as it does "nothing else on earth."

> *[T]hought is merciless to privilege, established institutions, and comfortable habits; [it] is anarchic and lawless, indifferent to authority, careless of the well-tried wisdom of the ages. Thought looks into the pit of hell and is not afraid. It sees man, a feeble speck, surrounded by unfathomable depths of silence; yet it bears itself proudly, as unmoved as if it were lord of the universe. Thought is great and swift and free, the light of the world, and the chief glory of man.*[13]

> *No man can be a great thinker who does not recognize that as a thinker it is his first duty to follow his intellect to whatever conclusions it may lead.*[14]

> *The free mind recognizes that the question of truth – the determination of truth – is prior to the obligation to believe. The insistence upon faith begs the question of truth. The local [Utah Mormon] culture penalizes the reluctant believer by holding him suspect as to*

---

[11]Dallin H. Oaks, Interview, *LDS Newsroom*, PBS documentary (20 July 2007).
[12]Dallin H. Oaks, *Salt Lake Tribune*, 18 August 1985.
[13]Bertrand Russell, *Why Men Fight* (New York: The Century Co., 1917; reprint 1920), 178-79, emphasis added. "Even if the open windows of science at first make us shiver after the cozy indoor warmth of traditional humanizing myths, in the end the fresh air brings vigour, and the great spaces have a splendour of their own." (Bertrand Russell, *What I Believe*, [New York: E.P. Dutton & Co., 1925], in Bertrand Russell, *The Basic Writings of Bertrand Russell*, Robert E. Egner and Lester E. Denonn, ed. [London: George Allen & Unwin Ltd., 1961], 348).
[14]John Stuart Mill, *On Liberty* (London, England: J.W. Parker, 1859), 28.

"You can't start with a rock in your hat
and finish with a flurry of logic."

455

*character. … For too many, the idea that an
unbeliever may be a good man is quite unthinkable.*[15]

"THE WHORE OF ALL THE EARTH"

Six hundred years before the birth of the Savior, before Jesus lived
his extraordinary life and taught his remarkable disciples, before
there was a gospel church ("upon this rock I will build my church;
and the gates of hell shall not prevail against it"[16]), a prophet by the
name of Nephi living somewhere in the Western Hemisphere
related words spoken to him by an angel of God. Nephi's visitor
described the fate of the Catholic Church still far from formed.
"Behold," he said, looking to some incredibly distant future, "there
are save two churches only; the one is the church of the Lamb of
God, and the other is the church of the devil; wherefore, whoso
belongeth not to the church of the Lamb of God belongeth to that
great church, which is the mother of abominations; and she is the
whore of all the earth."[17] So declares the most correct of any book
on earth, Mormonism's most sacred scripture.

The message of the angel's peculiar prophecy, and of its
refinements in the text of Mormonism's Golden Bible (The Book of
Mormon), was that the society founded by the Son of God was
designed to fail, that failure was a foreseeable part of some founding
plan. This incredible prolepsis vision is supposed to have predicted,
hundreds of years before the unincarnated Savior visited earth, the
decline of the Lord's primitive society, the flight of his followers and
the formation of a new and more perfect society, one that would
never fail. What shall mankind make of so dire a forecast? Nephi's
vision predicted that the gospel society founded by the Creator of
Heaven and Earth was going to be replaced by "the church of the
devil" and "the mother of abominations." That was destined to
occur as some incomprehensible consequence of some great eternal
plan. The end result of something discernible to a Western

---

[15]Waldemer P. Read, "What Freedom is Found in the Local Culture," *Great
Issues Concerning Freedom* (Salt Lake City, UT: University of Utah Press, 1962),
125-26, emphasis added.

[16]Bible, Matthew 16:18.

[17]Book of Mormon, 1 Nephi 14:9-12.

Hemisphere holy man six hundred years before the birth of Christ. According to this ancient accountant, after centuries of barren spiritual neglect baked into some inexplicable process, some new and better society led by some new and lesser soul was going to become some new and better version of a church first formed by the Lamb of God. What wasn't going to work for a Book of Mormon Father, who clothed in flesh revealed himself as Jesus Christ in the meridian of time, was going to work for some late-to-the-table disciple in the state of New York, a new and more durable kind of Christian and a better manager, in the dispensation of the fullness of times. How may anyone hope to make sense of so improbable a conception? This is one more supposed reality at the heart and soul of the less than transparent uncompromising faith. For this is the tale of "The Great Apostasy," a falling away at the heart of a plan.

The Book of Mormon – a book supposed to have been translated by the "gift and power of God," a book supposed to contain the "fulness of the everlasting Gospel" as delivered by a new and different kind of Savior, a god of vengeance, anger and ego, appearing to the ancient inhabitants of the North American continent – slanders the natural man, every other Christian leader and congregation, every dark skinned human and the kinder, gentler God who lived and died in Palestine. Nephi's messenger described the "great and abominable church" as "the church of the devil." Nephi's messenger reported that the "dominions" of "the church of the Lamb of God," the restored church, a "restoration" at the heart of a plan, would be small and its numbers would be few.[18] The historical Jesus, conversely, is supposed to have predicted that the "gates of hell" would not prevail against what he is supposed to have described as the gospel church.

To many Latter-day Saints and to their leaders, whatever they may choose to say in public, the Catholic Church (which claims to date from the Apostle Peter) *is* "the whore of all the earth," the "mother of abominations," the "church of the devil" and "satanic." Those are not reckless calculations, but rather canonized verities. To the prophet Joseph Smith, the Protestant "sects" and their sectarian priests were the spiritual offspring of that "mother of abominations,

---

[18] 1 Nephi, 14:9-17.

"You can't start with a rock in your hat
and finish with a flurry of logic."

457

whose founder is the devil."[19] Bruce R. McConkie – a twentieth-
century Mormon theologian and a greatly honored Mormon
Apostle after 1972 – was the son-in-law of Joseph Fielding Smith
(Mormonism's tenth prophet) and the author of the 1981
Introduction to the Book of Mormon. Until 2006 or 2007 that
Introduction said that "the Lamanites . . . are the *principal*
ancestors of the American Indians." McConkie wrote in the 1958
first edition of his encyclopedic opus "Mormon Doctrine" – an
imposing doctrinal resource published in three editions and dozens
of printings, selling tens of thousands of copies over a period of
more than fifty years (1958 to 2010) – that,

> **Harlots: See Church of the Devil, Sex Immorality.**
> *Literally an harlot is a prostitute; figuratively it is any*
> *apostate church. Nephi, speaking of harlots in the*
> *literal sense and while giving a prophetic description*
> *of the Catholic Church, recorded that he "saw the*
> *devil that he was the foundation of it;" that he "saw*
> *many harlots," and that among other things, "the*
> *harlots," were "the desires of this great and*
> *abominable church" (1 Ne. 13:6-8). Then, speaking*
> *of harlots in the figurative sense, he designated the*
> *Catholic Church as "the mother of harlots" (1 Nephi*
> *13:34; 14:15-17), a title which means that the*
> *protestant churches, the harlot daughters which broke*
> *off from the great and abominable church would*
> *themselves be apostate churches.*[20]

> *Iniquitous conditions in the various branches of the*
> *great and abominable church in the last days are*
> *powerfully described in the Book of Mormon. ... It is*
> *also [there] . . . to which we turn for the plainest*
> *description of the Catholic Church as the great and*
> *abominable church. Nephi saw this "church which is*

---

[19]Ibid., 14:9.
   [20]Book of Mormon, 1 Nephi 13:6-8 and 1 Nephi 13:34; 14:15-17, quoted in
Bruce R. McConkie, *Mormon Doctrine*, 1ˢᵗ ed. (1958), 314-15, reproduced in *Where
Does it Say That? Photo Reprints of Hard-To-Get Mormon Documents,* Bob Witte,
comp. (Michigan: Institute for Religious Research) 7.5, emphasis retained and
added.

most abominable above all other churches" in vision.
He "saw the devil that he was the foundation of it"
and also the murders, wealth, harlotry, persecutions,
and evil desires that historically have been a part of
this satanic organization.[21]

He saw that this most abominable of all churches was
founded after the day of Christ and his apostles; that it
took away from the gospel of the Lamb many
covenants and many plain and precious parts; that it
perverted the right ways of the Lord; that it deleted
many teachings from the Bible; that this church was
"the mother of harlots;" and finally that the Lord
would again restore the gospel of salvation.[22]

Nephi beheld further that this church was the "mother
of abominations," and "the whore of all the earth"
who "sat upon many waters; and she had dominion
over all the earth, among all nations, kindreds,
tongues and people." In contrast the dominions of the
true Church were small upon the earth.[23]

The dominions of the *"true Church,"* the church that restored "the gospel of salvation," when first compared to those of the church of the devil, were not imposing. The "true Church," a beacon of light in a dark and dreary world, was not deterred by this temporary embarrassment. To the Latter-day Saints, the "true Church," which was predestined to fill the earth, already reigns supreme. Faithful Mormons do not pretend to surmise but rather *know* that this is true. Other churches are corrupt, satanic, confused, unenlightened, misled, incomplete or depraved. Mormonism's

---

[21]Book of Mormon, 2 Nephi 28; Mormon 8:28, 32-33, 36-38; Doctrine and Covenants 10:56; and 1 Nephi 13:1-10, quoted in McConkie, *Mormon Doctrine* (1st ed., 1958), 130, reproduced in *Where Does it Say That?* (Bob Witte, comp.), 7.5, emphasis retained and added.

[22]Book of Mormon, 1 Nephi 13:24-42, quoted in McConkie, *Mormon Doctrine* (1st ed., 1958), 130, reproduced in *Where Does it Say That?* (Bob Witte, comp.), 7.5, emphasis retained and added.

[23]Book of Mormon, 1 Nephi 14:9-17; 2 Thess. 2:1-12, quoted in McConkie, *Mormon Doctrine* (1st ed., 1958), 130, reproduced in *Where Does it Say That?* (Bob Witte, comp.), 7.5, emphasis retained and added.

"You can't start with a rock in your hat
and finish with a flurry of logic."

459

halting modern institutional outreach to the rest of organized humanity is superficial and insincere, contradicted by the "restored" "canonized" doctrine.

DEMOGRAPHICS

While the Mormon Church presently claims more than sixteen million members, less than one-third of them actively practice their religion. The rolls of the Church are bloated with the records of inactive (often bitterly hostile) members who never attend and can't be found. It has been loosely reported (and not denied) that the Church can not produce addresses for up to fifty percent of its members. In 2010 Latter-day Saints claimed 1,138,740 members in Brazil. But in the 2010 Brazilian census, only 225,695 registrants – less than twenty percent of the supposed membership – identified themselves as Latter-day Saints. Those few self-identified Saints had no way to report whether or not they were active. That huge disparity, despite repeated admonitions from Mormon pulpits directing the members to declare themselves, is close to a million people in Brazil alone. In these numbers the integrity of the Church – a society that doesn't pretend to be transparent – is put at risk. Nearly a million Brazilians, claimed to be members of the Mormon Church, failed to declare that they were on the Brazilian census. Over the ten-year period from 2000 to 2010, the Church claimed to have enrolled 362,918 new members in Brazil. The 2000 census showed that 196,645 Brazilians identified as Mormons. The 2010 census showed that 225,695 Brazilians identified as Mormons. While the Church claimed 362,918 new members from 2000 to 2010, the census registered the increase at "only 7 percent of the membership increase reported by the church."[24]

The statistics for Brazil seemingly apply to other countries all around the world, in spite of what the Church reports. "About 30 percent of Mormons worldwide – or [as this is written] 4.5 million – regularly attend church meetings." The activity rate in the United States is 40 percent; in Mexico, 20 to 25 percent; Brazil, 25 percent; Chile, 12 percent; New Zealand, 40 to 45 percent; Tonga, 30 to 35

---

[24]Peggy Fletcher Stack, "Brazil Mystery: Case of the missing Mormons (913,045 of them, to be exact)," *Salt Lake Tribune* (Salt Lake City, 16 July 2012).

percent; Germany, 25 percent; Ireland, 35 percent; Japan, 15 to 20 percent; and Nigeria, 50 to 55 percent. "There are at least seven countries or dependencies with member activity rates of 15 percent or less – Chile, Portugal, South Korea, Panama, Hong Kong, Croatia and Palau." For the last three years "the lowest convert retention rates have appeared to occur within Latin America" where "many nations have experienced no noticeable increase."[25]

Unidentified members are not removed from what are wildly inflated and thoroughly dishonest membership claims, representing years of cumulated misrepresentation. They are only removed when they are statistically one hundred and ten years old.[26] There are countries where as few as 12 percent of the baptized members are actually active (Chile).[27] There are countries where no more than 25 percent of the members are actually active (Japan, Italy, Russia, Mexico, Brazil). In those difficult outposts, despite the Church's inflated contentions, inactive Saints outnumber active Saints three or four (and sometimes seven or eight) to one. Many newly baptized converts – victims of high pressure missionary tactics – do not even return to the Church to be confirmed. One measure of the integrity of the institution might be the distorted statistical factors it routinely promotes in support of its growth.[28]

---

[25]Based on statistics produced by David Stewart and Matt Martinich, *Reaching the Nations: International Church Growth Almanac 2014 Edition* (David Stewart, 2013), quoted in "Counting Mormons," *Salt Lake Tribune*, 11 January 2014.

[26]The names of people born in 1908 are only now being removed.

[27]The author's former bishop who presided over a congregation in a Mormon rich environment situated on the affluent east bench in Salt Lake City, Utah, claimed an activity rate of close to 50 percent. More recently a clerk serving the same congregation reported that in that ward of about four hundred members, the average attendance at the weekly sacrament service is about one hundred and seventy or slightly over 40 percent. A former Scottish Mission President couple told this author and others that only about 3,500 of Scotland's supposed 35,000 Mormons attend Church on Sunday. More recent figures may make even that speculation seem inflated. Some of the Scotch inactives were baptized as children by unscrupulous missionaries under false pretexts without the consent of their parents. A former Mission President's wife has reported more than once that 60 percent of all returned missionaries eventually leave the Church. These insights are of necessity anecdotal because the Church is not forthcoming.

[28]When this author was the Secretary of the Norwegian Mission and then the District President of the Oslo District in various stints between 1958-1960 – according to his now present memory – there were about 5,000 members in

Mormon-friendly Brigham Young University demographer Tim Heaton, "seeking to better understand the dynamics of growth and retention" with some yet earlier figures, postulated activity rates "ranging from 45 percent in North America and the South Pacific, to 35 percent in Europe and Africa, to 25 percent in Asia and Latin America."[29] Even those pitiful numbers appear to be inflated. In one revealing demographic, it is said "that as many as 80 percent of . . . single Mormon women between 18 and 30 are no longer active . . . ."[30] An independent researcher, California physician David G. Stewart, Jr., estimates worldwide activity at about 35 percent, "which would give the church about four million active members" at the time of his posting.[31] Those figures would seem to be inflated because the names of those who cannot be located are believed to have been removed from the congregational records before the congregational records are used to determine percentages of activity. The true percentage of those seen to attend services across the board on Sunday all over the world is estimated at no more than 30 percent, and more probably in the high twenties. These numbers, it may be supposed, are not stagnant. Attendance and resignation numbers are affected by the exposure to the internet.

It is reported (without official confirmation) that many thousands of members request the removal of their names from the membership records of the Church every year. The Church does not expose the size of its resignation staff, the numbers of its evacuees, or even its deaths. Mormonism's conversion and retention rates are not keeping pace with world population growth, with Mormonism's earlier growth, or with the growth of some of

---

Norway (perhaps 1,800 of them active), and about one hundred thirty or forty missionaries. More than fifty years later, as this is written, there are about 4,000 members (perhaps 1,500 active) and less than half as many missionaries.

[29]Tim Heaton in "Series of Articles Challenges LDS Claim to Be 'Fastest Growing Religion,'" *Sunstone*, issue 138 (September 2005), 74.

[30]Peggy Fletcher Stack, "Wayward LDS Invited Home," *Salt Lake Tribune*, 7 April 2008.

[31]David G. Stewart, Jr., Tim Heaton in "Series of Articles Challenges LDS Claim to Be 'Fastest Growing Religion,'" *Sunstone*, issue 138 (September 2005), 74. As of January 2014, "about 30 percent of Mormons world-wide – or 4.5 million – regularly attend church meetings." (Based on statistics produced by David Stewart and Matt Martinich, *Reaching the Nations: International Church Growth Almanac 2014 Edition* [David Stewart, 2013], 12 fn 36, quoted in "Counting Mormons," *Salt Lake Tribune*, 11 January 2014).

the other churches. The intensity of the faith of the members is a matter of increased concern. In 2015 the net growth rate of the Church was reported at 1.7 percent, the lowest rate since 1937. The 2016 figures were worse, and in 2018 the Church didn't report the 2017 numbers at General Conference, interrupting a practice that had continued during better times for many years.[32]

Faithful Mormon sociologist Armand Mauss opines that 50 percent of American converts and 75 percent of foreign converts are inactive within a year of their conversions. Although they are gone, their names are not.[33] In an oral report to this author from a close personal friend and a recent president of an important mission, the figure for the retention of new converts in a particularly diverse enclave was reported to be close to one-third. While about two-thirds of the newly baptized members leave, their names remain on the rolls until they reach the age of one hundred ten. If any of these facts are incorrect because the Church refuses to report them, those in charge of the suppression of such facts should step forward with the evidence required to rebut them. The institution has a solemn but neglected duty to present accurate facts to its members and to the public at large concerning its growth. The accumulation of many years of misrepresentations cries out to be corrected. The image the Church presents in respect to its population and growth is thoroughly dishonest.

---

[32]The growth rate in 2016 was 1.59 percent. The growth rate in 2017 was 1.47 percent, and in the United States in 2017 it was 0.75 percent, down from 0.93 percent in 2016. American growth has not been this low "in approximately 100 years or longer." California lost "50 or 60" wards and branches in 2017 as smaller and smaller congregations were consolidated. In 2016 and 2017 "there was no net increase of congregations in the United States." (Jana Riess, "Mormon growth continues to slow, especially in the US" [13 April 2018, accessed 30 July 2019], available from https://religionnews.com/2018/04/13/mormon-growth-continues-to-slow-especially-in-the-u-s/; Internet, p. 2 of 4).

[33]Stacey A. Willis, *Las Vegas Sun* (4 May 2001). Cumorah.com: "This postbaptismal attrition is heavily front-loaded. Elder Dallin H. Oaks concluded that 'among those converts who fall away, attrition is sharpest in the two months after baptism,' and missionaries report being told in the MTC [Missionary Training Center] that up to 80% of inactivity occurs within two months of baptism. In some parts of Latin America, 30 to 40 percent of new converts do not even return to church after baptism to be confirmed." ("LDS Church Growth, Member Activity, and Convert Retention: Review and Analysis: Chapter IV-06: Member Activity and Convert Retention").

It is estimated that there are currently about seven-and-a-half billion people on earth. After what is approaching two centuries of Mormonism, after the distribution of one hundred fifty million Books of Mormon (2011) by more than a million missionaries, there appears to be as this is written less than five million active members.[34] Five million practicing Mormons represent something less than one-fifteenth of one percent of the world's population.[35] More optimistic assumptions in the event these figures should be disputed by the less than transparent Church (which clearly knows but fails to report the truth about its financial records, operating policies, growth, death, withdrawal, retention and activity rates), would only ever so slightly alter that insignificant percentage. Some record keeping questions are included in this text at Appendix E.

---

[34]"Greece . . . has seen little Mormon growth notwithstanding proselytizing missionaries serving in the country for more than two decades." There are more non-Greeks than ethnic Greeks who are active LDS in Greece, where nominal membership remains at less than a thousand people. (Based on statistics produced by David Stewart and Matt Martinich, *Reaching the Nations: International Church Growth Almanac 2014 Edition* [David Stewart, 2013], quoted in "Counting Mormons," *Salt Lake Tribune* [Salt Lake City], 11 January 2014). The LDS Church when that was written had only about one-third the number of missionaries in Belgium that it had "in the 1980's and 90's." "Belgium remains reliant on foreign missionaries because few locals serve Mormon missions." (Ibid.). Russia, where the missionary effort has been extensive, has only 21,709 members. The Jehovah's Witnesses have more than 144,000 members in Russia, greater growth and markedly higher retention. There are ten Jehovah's witnesses for every Latter-day Saint in Italy.

[35]The percentage of Mormons in Utah "has been declining steadily in the last fifteen years, from 70 percent to 62.4 percent. One study suggests that if current trends continue, 'LDS residents no longer will constitute a majority by 2030.'" (Matt Canham, *Salt Lake Tribune* [copyright 2005, updated 22 June 2006], quoted in *Sunstone*, issue 138 [September 2005], 74 [from membership data provided to Utah's Office of Planning and Budget]). ("While continuing to grow in actual numbers, the LDS share of the state population showed a slow but constant decline every year from 1989 to 2004." [Matt Canham, "Mormon Portion of Utah Population Steadily Shrinking," *Salt Lake Tribune* (2005)]). "The LDS Church said its count comprises 'all members' – including children in LDS families under age 8, when most Mormons are baptized, and nonpracticing members." (Ibid.). Such figures, although subject to slight variations up or down with time, suggest that church-going Latter-day Saints are already a minority in the State of Utah. "Fewer than half the people living in Salt Lake County are on the rolls of The Church of Jesus Christ of Latter-day Saints." (Matt Canham, "Salt Lake County is now minority Mormon, and the impacts are far reaching," *Salt Lake Tribune*, 9 December 2018).

Mormonism is a bit player, a tiny part of a gigantic cast on an enormous stage. Mormonism's leaders are big fish in a tiny pond. The "stone . . . cut out of the mountain without hands," the kingdom set up by "the God of heaven . . . which shall never be destroyed," the movement that shall consume all other movements and "stand for ever,"[36] is proceeding at a glacial pace.

MANAGING THOUGHT

Latter-day Saints tolerate contention poorly. Those who rock the boat are ostracized. "Too frequently, it is assumed that an attitude of skepticism or of unbelief is a sign of moral turpitude and of spiritual rebellion."[37] To the willfully uninformed, the foundational narratives are impervious to criticism. "Perhaps no theme is more popular with Conference speakers than the importance of deferring to the authorities in matters of judgment – not only with respect to doctrinal interpretation, the reading of the scriptures, but with respect to matters of policy and practice." It has been said that, "When those who are in authority have decided, the thinking has been done." For the faithful, "The *virtue* of deference to authority is thought to be one of the strongest assurances of salvation."[38] In fact, such deference, whether early or late, is not a "virtue" at all. It is rather instead "an abnegation of individual responsibility in thought. When carried to extreme," the philosopher says, "it is the antithesis of freedom of the mind."[39]

Well-intentioned scholars have been excommunicated for speaking truth to power. In the one true Church, history must be inspiring, faith promoting, inoffensive but not necessarily thoughtful. Truth is the first casualty of correlated constraints. Offending scholars examining sensitive subjects have been denied access to historical resources, precluded from speaking in church and excluded from attendance at the temple. True believers are churchbroken; they have learned to hold matters of doubt concerning the faith close to

---

[36]Bible, Daniel 2:44-45.
[37]Read, "What Freedom is Found in the Local Culture," *Great Issues Concerning Freedom*, 126.
[38]Ibid., emphasis added.
[39]Ibid.

"You can't start with a rock in your hat
and finish with a flurry of logic."

465

the vest. Mormonism has a siege mentality – cross the line, feel the pain. Many who suffer the faith's stunning contradictions conceal their feelings and soldier on whatever the cost. Others leave the difficult faith in fact or in spirit.

For multigenerational Mormons making their lives in the Mormon corridor, leaving the Church (and then often their families) can be an agonizing experience. Failing to suppress their errant opinions may result in the loss of their membership. In matters pertaining to faith, Mormonism is death to the inquiring mind. "Dogmatism ["I know Joseph Smith was a prophet of God"], adoration of faith ["I know the gospel is true"], and deference to authority ["When the leaders have spoken the thinking has been done"]: all three conditioned beliefs tend to solidify and perpetuate uniformity of belief."[40] The society is better designed for those who flee from the necessity to think for themselves – for those who desperately need fixed ideas and comforting dogmas. Members are "Released from the burden of uncertainty that life's choices impose . . . ." "Our lives," according to Martin Luther King, "begin to end the day we become silent about things that matter."[41]

No question has been any more prevalent in the history of the Church both early or late than this: *"What do we believe?"* The issue more fully framed is this: *"What do the prophets say? For what we believe is what the prophets say."* Many more now than in the past see folly in that. The process of sublimating critical thinking to the dictates of fallible men is intellectually dishonest. Mormonism's dogmatic certainty denies the need to further inquire. It ignores logic and reason and science and inhibits healthy intellectual growth. The true believers' conclusions on all matters of faith are stunningly predictable. The facts must be seen to conform to a set of preconceived conclusions often drawn in rudimentary form by indoctrinated children, or by investigators encouraged to embrace the Kingdom of God by uninformed missionaries who *never* obtain *informed* consent.

---

[40]Read, "What Freedom Is Found in the Local Culture," *Great Issues Concerning Freedom* (Salt Lake City: University of Utah Press, 1962), 126.

[41]Martin Luther King Jr. (accessed 1 January 2016), available from http://www.brainyquote.com/ quotes/quotes/m/martinluth103526.html; Internet, 1.

Mormons may aggressively challenge almost anything temporal, other religions, and their leaders and communicants, but the laity may not challenge their own prophets, leaders or faith. Mormon reformers are always unwelcome. Those who find themselves at odds with their leaders and doctrines may be disfellowshipped, excommunicated,[42] alienated from families and friends, fired from their jobs, shunned and disrespected. A modern prophet, Gordon B. Hinckley, described protocol for critics: "They [those who have problems with doctrine] can carry all the opinion they wish within their heads . . . but if they begin to try to persuade others, then they may be called in to a disciplinary council (Hinckley 1998)."[43] That ominous threat carries considerable weight with the unerringly faithful. One particularly prominent excommunicated former Mormon bishop, a well credentialed Australian scholar, described that formidable landscape: "[T]here are many bright and faithful Mormons who have chosen to keep their intellectual struggles between their own two ears. Increasingly, these Saints occupy the ranks of the less active or the back rows of LDS congregations." They assemble in what might be rudely called the demilitarized zone. All of this is seen to have become desperately complicated. "Many in Utah choose this option because to do otherwise risks alienation from community, work environment, and families. In communities where workmates, closest friends, and most relatives are multi-generational Latter-day Saints, Mormonism is a part of

---

[42]Excommunication has consequences Latter-day Saints regard as eternal. Between 1850 and 1854, over a period that preceded and followed Apostle Orson Pratt's stunning 1852 disclosure that the Mormons – in spite of everything they for so long so solemnly said – were practicing polygamy, the Mormon Church is supposed to have excommunicated more than 15,000 members in the English Mission. (Eugene E. Campbell, *Establishing Zion: The Mormon Church in the American West, 1847-1869* [Salt Lake City: Signature Books, 1988], 165 fn 4). "T.B.H. Stenhouse, in *The Rocky Mountain Saints*, asserts that many excommunications followed the [polygamy] announcement, but B.H. Roberts more careful study indicates that there were about as many excommunications in the six months prior to the announcement as in the six months after. Nevertheless, from 1850-1854, some 15,000 excommunications took place in England, evidence of significant unrest, whatever the reason." (Ibid., 165 fn 4). Eugene E. Campbell, the scholar who reported those figures, was a professor of history at Brigham Young University until his retirement in 1980.

[43]Gordon B. Hinckley, quoted in Simon G. Southerton, *Losing a Lost Tribe – Native Americans, DNA, and the Mormon Church* (Salt Lake City: Signature Books, 2004), 200.

"You can't start with a rock in your hat
and finish with a flurry of logic."

467

one's cultural heritage and identity."[44]

One conspicuous Latter-day Saint who didn't keep her intellectual misgivings between her own two ears was Joseph Smith's brave biographer Fawn McKay Brodie.[45]   Mrs. Brodie wrote her remarkable biography of Joseph Smith before she reached the age of thirty. It was published in 1945 under the title *No Man Knows My History: The Life of Joseph Smith, the Mormon Prophet* by Alfred Knopf in New York, and she was excommunicated in 1946.[46] She was "persecuted by those who ought to have been [her] friends and to have treated [her] kindly, and if they supposed [her] to be deluded to have endeavored in a proper and affectionate manner to have reclaimed [her] . . . ."[47] She was excoriated by the Church's leaders, historians, publications, committees and critics; dismissed as a novelist, challenged as a historian ("No ma'am, that's not history"); then last of all cruelly consigned to the buffetings of

---

[44]Ibid.

[45]Miss McKay (Mrs. Brodie) was the daughter of an Assistant to the Quorum of the Twelve Apostles. Her father, Thomas E. McKay, also served as the President of the Utah State Senate. She was the niece of a future President of the Church of Jesus Christ of Latter-day Saints, David O. McKay; the granddaughter of George H. Brimhall, a President of Brigham Young University; and the wife of a prominent American national defense diplomat, a Jewish scholar by the name of Bernard Brodie. Miss McKay graduated as salutatorian from Weber High School in Ogden, Utah, at the age of fourteen, from the University of Utah with a B.A. in English literature at the age of eighteen, and from the University of Chicago (with an advanced degree, M.A.) at the age of twenty-one. Her mother, a "closet skeptic" troubled by issues of faith (a "thoroughgoing heretic"), and her grandfather, George H. Brimhall, both committed suicide. After two unsuccessful attempts ("the second by cutting herself with a Catholic crucifix"), Brodie's mother finally succeeded by setting herself on fire. ("Fawn M. Brodie" [accessed 13 July 2014], available from wikipedia.com; Internet). As this is written Utah has the highest incidence of mental illness in any of the fifty states. What is true of mental illness is also true of the use of antidepressant drugs. (Julie Cart, "Study Finds Utah Leads Nation in Antidepressant Use," *Los Angeles Times* [20 February 2002]). A website titled "Recovery from Mormonism" founded in 1995 claims more than two million posts as of December 4, 2018, articles on more than one hundred fifty thousand topics and a thousand posts a day. (As of 15 September 2010; available from www. exmormon.org). Another website, Exmormon Reddit, claims (as this is written) more than one hundred thirty-one thousand members.

[46]Fawn McKay Brodie, *No man Knows My History: The Life of Joseph Smith the Mormon Prophet*, 2d ed., rev. and enl. (New York, NY: Alfred A. Knopf, 1972).

[47]Words essentially spoken by Joseph Smith concerning his claims of persecution. (Joseph Smith, *Pearl of Great Price*, Joseph Smith – History 1:28).

Satan in the flesh.   This courageous young woman changed a particularly barren landscape.   After Fawn McKay Brodie's intelligent groundbreaking biography – *"Newsweek* called Brodie's book 'a definitive biography in the finest sense of the word,'" and *Time* praised the author for her "skill and scholarship and admirable detachment"[48] – Mormonism would never be the same.

SELDOM SPOKEN THINGS

Polygamy

A correlated manual dated 2007 reluctantly reported as follows: "The doctrines and principles relating to plural marriage were revealed to Joseph Smith as early as 1831.   The Prophet taught the doctrine of plural marriage, and a number of marriages were performed during his lifetime."[49]   The carefully drafted manual failed the public by omitting this: "The Prophet [secretly] taught the doctrine of plural marriage" to several small groups of privileged insiders.   And in this: From sometime in the 1830s until 1844 (the year of his death), he not only taught but actually practiced plural marriage.   And in this: Smith, by himself, married about thirty-four women in about twenty-two months (January 6, 1842, to November 2, 1843).[50]

Some Latter-day Saints don't know, even today, that Joseph Smith secretly married about forty women before he died, more than a dozen of whom were the undivorced wives of other living husbands, most of them legally married faithful Mormon men.   They don't know that Joseph Smith was a polygamist because, until the day of his death and without the least regard for the truth, he always *publicly* said that he was not.   Emma Smith, Joseph's legal wife, who also *publicly* said he hadn't taken plural wives, *privately* told a special friend after the death of Smith that she knew he had

---

[48]"Fawn M. Brodie" (accessed 13 July 2014), available from wikipedia.com; Internet.
[49]*Teachings of Presidents of the Church – Joseph Smith* (Salt Lake City: The Church of Jesus Christ of Latter-day Saints, 2007), xii.
[50]George D. Smith, *Nauvoo Polygamy: " . . . but we called it celestial marriage"* (Salt Lake City: Signature Books, 2008), 621-23.

"You can't start with a rock in your hat
and finish with a flurry of logic."

469

committed adultery *and* taken plural wives.[51]   Emma Smith married her second husband, a non-Mormon man by the name of Lewis Bidamon, after Joseph Smith died and on Joseph Smith's birthday, December 23, 1847.   Joseph and Emma's four sons – Joseph III, Alexander, Frederick and David – grew up proclaiming their father's innocence, denying as adults that their father practiced polygamy, because their mother always told them he did not. In effect, Joseph lied, Emma lied, and when they could not but have known better, so did Joseph III, Alexander, Frederick and David Smith. These highly visible celebrity Smiths, big fish in a tiny pond, didn't tell the truth.

Joseph Smith shared his polyandrous women (women already legally married to other men) and their polyandrous children (the biological children of the legal husbands of those multiply married women) with their polyandrous and biological husbands and fathers *for time* (meaning for the period of this life). But he claimed and sealed them to himself *for eternity*. By virtue of the sealing power and the way it was used, bonding women to men for eternity, Smith's morally indefensible eternal claims to his polyandrous wives and their children, the legal wives and biological children of other men, were and are exclusive.[52]

This author, in common with most other Latter-day Saints, didn't know that Joseph Smith practiced polyandry (a particularly tender subject) until Richard L. Bushman published his biography of the prophet Joseph Smith, *Rough Stone Rolling*, in 2005. Nor did he know that Church leaders, including Brigham Young and Heber C. Kimball, also married and sexually cohabited with the undivorced

[51]William E. McLellin to John L. Traughber, 6 December 1875, *The William E. McLellin Papers: 1854-1880,* eds. Stan Larson and Samuel J. Passey, foreword by George D. Smith (Salt Lake City: Signature Books, 2008), 501. Emma discussed these issues, adultery and polygamy, privately with William E. McLellin.

[52]Some of the spiritually abandoned husbands, as Brigham Young informed the hapless Henry Jacobs, needed to find other eternal mates. Jacobs was forced to surrender his biological children and his legal wife, Zina Huntington (Jacobs) (Smith), to Brigham Young for *time* and Joseph Smith for *eternity*. Brigham Young, unlike his mentor Joseph Smith, didn't choose to share the beleaguered Jacobs' life estate and didn't let Zina continue to live with her first and legal husband. Thus Zina had two husbands for time, Henry Jacobs and Brigham Young, and one husband for eternity, Joseph Smith. After Henry was ruthlessly dismissed, she lived with Brigham Young.

wives of other men. In the case of Brigham Young that meant as
many as fifteen previously committed legally married women.
Young, like Smith, practiced morally incoherent polyandry. Zina
Young (Card), Brigham and Zina Huntington's daughter, was a
biological product of sexual polyandry.[53] Proof positive that this
polyandry was sexual.[54]

Most Latter-day Saints do not know, because they have never been
told, that Joseph Smith struck the guard who attempted to protect
the *Nauvoo Expositor's* printing press as Smith, the Mayor of
Nauvoo, led a Mormon mob on a reckless rampage on the evening
of the day the press was destroyed. The type was pied and the
publishers were threatened with the loss of their lives.[55] The
dissenters' terrible crime? Trying to tell the members of the
Church *the truth* about the prophet and polygamy. Joseph Smith's
crimes: Denying freedom of speech, destroying an American
newspaper, confiscating the property of the publisher, damaging
the publishers' premises, leading a Mormon mob and assaulting a

[53]Her great-granddaughter, Zola Brown (Jeffs) (Hodson), the daughter of
LDS First Presidency Counselor Hugh B. Brown, was, until her divorce in 1941,
the first and legal wife of Rulon Jeffs, who lived to become the husband of many
wives, the father of many children, and the "Beloved Prophet" of the modern
Fundamentalists. Zola had two sons with Jeffs.

[54]Doctrine and Covenants, Section 132.

[55]Samuel W. Taylor, *Nightfall at Nauvoo* (New York, NY: Avon Books, 1971),
244. *"To the Marshall of said City, greeting.* You are here commanded to destroy
the printing press from whence issues the *Nauvoo Expositor*, and pi the type of said
printing establishment in the street, and burn all the *Expositors* and libelous
handbills found in said establishment; and if resistance be offered to your
execution of this order by the owners or others, demolish the house . . . . By order
of the City Council, Joseph Smith, Mayor." (Ibid.). This happened in America. In
the Utah Territory in 1870, according to John Beadle, "Gentiles are subjected to all
the annoyances of petty tyranny . . . . [I]n their business and social life they are
constantly subjected to the secret espionage of the Church." Further, "[non-
Mormons] are hampered in business by church hostility and the imposition of
excessive taxes . . . . [F]riends and fellow countrymen have been secretly
murdered, and the Church prevents them from obtaining justice; in short, they are
exposed to the tyranny of an unopposed majority . . . controlled by a small and
compact hierarchy, working out its Star-chamber decrees against liberty by secret
and . . . irresponsible agents." (John Hansen Beadle, *Life in Utah; or the Mysteries
and Crimes of Mormonism* [National Publishing Company, 1870], 400, reproduced
at John Gary Maxwell, *Robert Newton Baskin and the Making of Modern Utah*
[Norman, OK: The Arthur H. Clark Company, 2013], 84).

"You can't start with a rock in your hat
and finish with a flurry of logic."

471

security guard.[56] It was a nasty errand that led to an unfortunate
consequence.

The Death of Joseph Smith

No Mormon missionary pauses to report that someone smuggled a
gun to Joseph Smith in his cell at Carthage, or that Joseph, a
fugitive from Missouri justice, and his brother Hyrum both had
pistols on their persons while in jail on the day they died. No
Mormon missionary ever reports that Joseph may have shot
(and/or killed) several of his attackers and might have shot (and/or
killed) several more if the weapon hadn't misfired.[57] After Hyrum
was shot directly in the face by a bullet that passed through a panel
on the door, "Joseph crouched over his dead brother," after which
"he sprang to the door, pulled it open a crack and fired into the
mob on the landing, pulling the trigger as fast as he could. Three
chambers misfired, but the other three sent bullets into the mob."
"The mob fell back as Joseph emptied his pistol . . . ." When the
men at the doorway returned and were now turned toward Joseph,
he "flung his empty pistol at the mob" before leaping to the window
to try and escape. "Is there no help for the widow's son?" he said.
In that he cried for mercy. In that the prophet, a Mason, gave the
Masonic order's "signal of distress." But there was no help for this
widow's son on June 27, 1844.[58] Yet another report described those
events in these terms: "Joseph defends himself with a pistol, jumps
out the window, and begins to shout the Masonic cry of distress:
'Oh, Lord, my God, is there no help for the widow's son?'"[59] "Two
balls hit him from behind and one from below" before he toppled

---

[56]"The big guard [John Eagle] tumbled off the steps [after Joseph Smith
"smashed a blow below Eagle's ear"], groggy. Willing men – Porter Rockwell one
of them – grabbed up the sledges and smashed the door from its hinges. Soon the
printing press crashed into the street. Men dumped type cases upside down atop it,
copies of the *Expositor*, papers from desks. A policeman emptied a can of cleaning
fluid onto the heap. Somebody struck a sulphur match." (Taylor, *Nightfall at
Nauvoo*, 244). It is well to remember that the printing office in Kirtland, Ohio, had
burned to the ground in 1838, within days of Smith and Rigdon's middle-of-the-
night departure. In the hands of the dissenters it threatened to expose the facts
that gave rise to the prophet's precipitous leave-taking.
[57]Ibid., 281-83.
[58]Ibid.
[59]Quinn, *Origins of Power*, 646.

forward and fell from the second-floor window.[60]

First Vision Accounts and God in Mormon Scripture

Most Mormon missionaries don't know or even begin to attempt to teach their investigators that there are at least six versions of five presently known strikingly different primary accounts of the First Vision. At least four of the six versions of those five accounts were concealed and suppressed in the highly prominent archives of the Mormon Church – *to be seen only by men who could be trusted not to tell the truth* – for more than one hundred thirty years. Those complicating accounts, which crossed the plains in the 1840s with the Church's leaders, were not "brought to light" until in and after 1965. Until 1965 the members of the Church were told that Joseph Smith told his story only once. In 1965, sixth and seventh generation Latter-day Saints were finally allowed to begin to hear what the prophet actually said in those concealed and suppressed accounts of Mormonism's most ever important event.[61]

Who knew for one hundred thirty years that the canonized 1838-39 Pearl of Great Price Account of the First Vision of the Father and the Son – "the hinge pin upon which the whole cause turns" – wasn't the first, second or even third account of that supposedly great event? How many missionaries tell their investigators that the canonized "First Vision" version of the fourteen-year-old boy's 1820 vision wasn't ever publicly reported until 1842, twenty-two years later, when Joseph Smith was thirty-six years old? Or that the governing version, the fourth of six versions of five different primary accounts, didn't begin to be composed until 1838? Who

---

[60]Taylor, *Nightfall at Nauvoo*, 281-83. Not many Latter-day Saints know that the prophet wasn't wearing his ceremonial undergarments at the time of his death. "Willard Richards . . . is the only one not killed or severely wounded. Mormons immediately attribute this to the fact that he alone wore the undergarment given to endowed persons." (Quinn, *Origins of Power*, 646). In fact, not many investigators are ever informed (before they join the Church) that Mormons wear ceremonial undergarments. Wallace Stegner called the Mormon underwear "distinguishing uniforms," one of the elements of an authoritarian order.

[61]For a complete discussion of the issues surrounding these different accounts, see Chapters 2 to 4 of Volume II, *Mormonism Under the Microscope: "Breaking Bad."*

"You can't start with a rock in your hat
and finish with a flurry of logic."

473

knew it was revised and recomposed in 1839? Who knew that
Joseph Smith was assisted in the drafting of that official account by
a committee that included Rigdon (thought by some to be the *Iago*
of the Mormonite movement[62]), Rigdon's son-in-law General
George W. Robinson, a First Presidency clerk as scribe, and still
later James Mulholland as scribe? Who knew that the vision,
supposed to have caused "men of high standing" to "excite the
public mind" against a fourteen-year-old Joseph Smith, went
unnoticed at the time by his mother, father and siblings (and then
and later by all of his New York, Pennsylvania and Ohio critics)?

No one has been able to find and authenticate any public reference,
prior to 1835, to a great First Vision of the Father and the Son, or to
claims of persecution, because of an event supposed to have
occurred in 1820. *No non-Mormon source is known to have
mentioned the First Vision in print until 1843.*[63] *"As far as Mormon
literature is concerned, there was apparently no reference to Joseph
Smith's first vision in any published material in the 1830's."*[64] Those
are shocking facts. They should give pause to those who have
misrepresented that First Vision Account millions of times to
millions of people all over the world.

Mormon missionaries never tell their investigators that Joseph
Smith initially taught his followers that the Father and the Son were
"one God" – one "omnipotant," "omnipreasant," "crucifyed"
"essentially Trinitarian" Spirit. That unfamiliar teaching is found
in the Articles and Covenants of the Church of Christ, the
Testimony of the Three Witnesses, the Book of Mormon, the Book
of Commandments, and Joseph Smith's Inspired Translation of the
King James Bible.[65] And in the teachings of the Reorganized
Church. This undeniable fact (evidence from authoritative
resources that the deities were not initially separate) is a dagger in

---

[62]"*Iago*," the villain of Shakespeare's tragedy *Othello*.

[63]"Apparently not until 1843 when the *New York Spectator* printed a
reporter's account of an interview with Joseph Smith, did a *non-Mormon* source
publish any reference to the story of the first vision." (James B. Allen, "The
Significance of Joseph Smith's 'First Vision' in Mormon Thought," *Dialogue*, Vol.
I, No. 3 [Autumn 1966]: 31), emphasis added.

[64]Ibid., emphasis added.

[65]See Chapter 1, *Mormonism Under the Microscope: "Breaking Bad,"* Volume
II.

the heart to the 1842 proposition that there was a great First Vision of *two separate personages* in 1820. Joseph Smith didn't separate the Father from the Son in Mormon theology until some time in and/or after 1834, and even then the details of such a separation were cloaked in ambiguity.

Adam/God Doctrine

How many missionaries or investigators know (or think to report) that Brigham Young taught the Latter-day Saints from the pulpit at general conferences, when speaking while inspired, that Adam was God, a less-than-eternal transplanted previously resurrected deity come to occupy this planet from some other planet with Eve (one of his wives) and with all of this verdant earth's plant and animal life? Brigham's honored Adam, when considered in Brigham's terms, was a kind of intergalactic Noah. Brigham was teaching the Latter-day Saints that Adam was God until the day he died. Wilford Woodruff, the fourth President of the Church, believed that Adam was God until the day he died. George Q. Cannon, a powerful figure in the nineteenth-century church (the *de facto* leader of the Church under two different prophets), instructed the Saints that that doctrine (the doctrine that Adam was God) was revealed to Joseph Smith and Brigham Young by the Lord himself.[66]

In a nasty letter to a nice man, Apostle Bruce R. McConkie referred to a speech that he (McConkie) had delivered to an audience at a Mormon devotional.

> *I said: "there are those who believe or say they believe that Adam is our Father and our God, that he is the father of our spirits and our bodies and that he is the one we worship." I, of course, indicated the utter absurdity of this doctrine and said it was totally false. Since then I have received violent reactions from Ogden Kraut and other cultists in which they have*

---

[66]George Q. Cannon in Wilford Woodruff's Journal of 4 September 1860, quoted in Fred C. Collier, *President Brigham Young's Doctrine of Deity, Volume 1* (Hanna, UT: Collier's Publishing Co., 1999), 360.

"You can't start with a rock in your hat and finish with a flurry of logic."

475

expounded upon the views of Brigham Young and others of the early Brethren relative to Adam.

McConkie castigated Ogden Kraut, a Fundamentalist leader who believed Adam was God. McConkie called Brother Kraut a *"cultist"* for having faithfully followed the teachings of Joseph Smith and Brigham Young, something McConkie did not. Kraut and McConkie's *"other cultists"* took the measure of McConkie, finally forcing the important Mormon scholar to admit the obvious:

> *They [the maligned Fundamentalists] have plain and clear quotations [from multiple early Mormon leaders, not just Brigham] saying all of the things about Adam which I say are false. The quotations are in our literature and form the basis of a worship system followed by many of the cultists who have been excommunicated from the Church.*[67]

McConkie's denigrated *"cultists"* were excommunicated. They became pariahs because they faithfully followed the teachings of Joseph Smith, Brigham Young, Wilford Woodruff, George Q. Cannon, Daniel H. Wells and very many other early and important Mormon leaders. Joseph Smith and Brigham Young were *"cultists"* by McConkie's modern Mormon reckoning. They led Ogden Kraut astray. Every Utah Mormon's roots run through Joseph Smith and Brigham Young. Ogden Kraut and others became heretics and disrespected outcasts because they drank from "ancient springs." Their problems multiplied because they faithfully followed the most distinctive teachings of the nineteenth-century Church, *Joseph Smith* and *Brigham Young* (including Adam/God and polygamy).

Ezra Booth, a Methodist clergyman before becoming a "Mormonite" and thinking he had made a mistake (*it was "a delusion to which I had fallen a victim"*[68]), described something like

---

[67]"Bruce R. McConkie's Letter of Rebuke to [BYU] Professor Eugene England" (19 February 1981, accessed 8 September 2009), available from http://www. myplanet.net/mike/LDS/McConkie_England_letter.html; Internet, 4, emphasis added.

[68]Booth letter reproduced at Eber D. Howe, *Mormonism Unvailed* (Painesville, OH: E.D. Howe, 1834; reprint, NY: AMS Press Inc., 1977), 176, emphasis added.

Bruce R. McConkie's theological dilemma. In 1831:

> *Mormonism has in part changed its character, and assumed a different dress, from that under which it made its first appearance on the Western Reserve. Many extraordinary circumstances which then existed, have vanished out of sight; and the Mormonites desire, not only to forget them, but wish them blotted out of the memory of others . . . .*[69]

The modern Church and its scholars, including the rigid McConkie, had liked to forget that Brigham Young *publicly* taught what Joseph Smith *privately* taught (that Adam was God), in the case of Young in sacred venues on important occasions while claiming to be inspired.

After professing to be an admirer of Brigham Young, "a mighty prophet" "called of God" who "led Israel the way the Lord wanted his people led," a man who "built on the foundation laid by the Prophet Joseph," McConkie contradicted Young, who had been the voice of God to the members of the Church for more than thirty years: "Nonetheless," according to McConkie, "as Joseph Smith so pointedly taught, a prophet is not always a prophet, only when he is acting as such." Prophets are men and they make mistakes. Sometimes they err in doctrine. This is one of the reasons the Lord has given us the Standard Works." Brigham Young and Wilford Woodruff both asserted in positive terms at different times that Mormon prophets never lead people astray.[70] Adam was Brigham's God until the day of his death. In all of that, Apostle McConkie was forced to admit what Brigham Young and Wilford Woodruff both denied, that prophets lead people astray. From all of that, the Mormon theologian McConkie drew these indefensible conclusions:

> *Yes, President Young did teach that Adam was the father of our spirits, and all the related things that the cultists ascribe to him. This, however, is not true. He*

---

[69]Ibid., 183.

[70]"You may go home and sleep as sweetly as a babe in its mother's arms, as to any danger of your leaders leading you astray, for if they should do so the Lord would quickly sweep them from the earth." (Brigham Young, *Teachings of the Presidents of the Church: Brigham Young* [1997], 138).

"You can't start with a rock in your hat
and finish with a flurry of logic."

477

*expressed views that are out of harmony with the
gospel. But, be it known, Brigham Young also taught
accurately and correctly, the status and position of
Adam in the eternal scheme of things. What I am
saying is that Brigham Young contradicted Brigham
Young, and the issue becomes one of which Brigham
Young we will believe. The answer is we will believe
the expressions that accord with the teachings in the
Standard Works.*[71]

**If Brigham Young, who greatly outranked McConkie (modern
Mormonism's Wizard of Oz), had been able to respond, he would
have made short work of the arrogant scholar.**

*"Some years ago I advanced a doctrine with regard to
Adam being our Father and God, that will be a curse
to many of the Elders of Israel because of their folly.
With regard to it they yet grovel in darkness . . . . It is
one of the most glorious revealments of the economy
of heaven . . . ."*[72]

*"What I know concerning God . . . I have received
from the heavens."*[73] *"I believe our God to be so near
to us as Father Adam."*[74]

*"How much unbelief exists in the minds of the Latter-
day Saints in regard to one particular doctrine which I
revealed to them, and which God revealed to me –
namely that Adam is our father and God . . . ."*

*". . . I could not find any man on earth who could tell
me this, although it is one of the simplest things in the
world, until I met and talked with Joseph Smith."*[75]

---

[71]McConkie Letter to Mr. Eugene England (19 February 1981), 5-6 emphasis
added.

[72]"Adam-God Doctrine," Manuscript Addresses of Brigham Young, G.D.
Watt transcriber, 8 October 1861, "with minor misspelling corrected," (accessed 16
July 2014), available from wikipedia.com.

[73]Brigham Young, *Discourses of Brigham Young*, selected and arranged by
John A. Widtsoe (Salt Lake City: Deseret Book Company, 1925), 433.

[74]*Journal of Discourses*, 5:331.

In the final analysis, after all is said and done, Joseph Smith and Brigham Young described a less than eternal Savior, the progeny of Father Adam, in Christian theory a finite deity constitutionally incapable of superintending an infinite atonement.[76]

The "Lecture at the Veil"

"Shortly after the dedication of the lower portion of the [St. George] temple, Young decided it was necessary to commit the endowment ceremony to written form." "The St. George endowment included a revised thirty-minute 'lecture at the veil' first delivered by Young. This summarized important theological concepts taught in the endowment and contained references to Young's Adam-God doctrine."[77] "The copy of the veil lecture . . . is not presently available,"[78] for reasons that must seem to be obvious, but on February 7, 1877, L. John Nuttall "summarized in his diary

---

[75]Brigham Young, *Deseret News*, vol. 22 no. 308 (18 June 1873), just four years before he died. "Our Father Adam is the man who stands at the gate and holds the keys of everlasting life and salvation to all his children who have or who ever will come upon the earth. I have been found fault with by the ministers of religion because I have said that they were ignorant." (Ibid.). Brigham Young taught "one particular doctrine" from 1852 to the date of his death, and he said that what he knew about the deity he had learned from the deity and from his mentor, Joseph Smith.

[76]Brigham Young spent the last months of his life preparing the Lecture at the Veil for the St. George Temple (Utah's only temple then), a lecture that recognized and applied the Adam-God doctrine.

[77]David John Buerger, *The Mysteries of Godliness: A History of Mormon Temple Worship* (San Francisco, CA: Smith Research Associates, 1994, 2002), 110. While standardizing the endowment in written form and before, Brigham operated under the apprehension that, "we can seal women to men, but not men to men, without a Temple." Women were not as important as men. Women could be excommunicated by the bishop; men required a disciplinary counsel. In 1873, Young explained that, "This [women to men sealing] we can do in the Endowment House; but when we come to other sealing ordinances, ordinances pertaining to the holy Priesthood, to connect the chain of the Priesthood from father Adam until now, by sealing children to their parents, being sealed for our forefathers, etc., they cannot be done without a Temple." (*Journal of Discourses*, 16:186, quoted in Buerger, *The Mysteries of Godliness*, 105). With the completion of the St. George temple on the horizon, when the Temple ordinances could be performed, "*men* will be sealed to their fathers, and those who have slept clear up to father Adam." (Ibid., emphasis added).

[78]Buerger, *The Mysteries of Godliness*, 111.

"You can't start with a rock in your hat
and finish with a flurry of logic."

479

additions which Young made . . . in Nuttall's presence . . . ."

We may be certain that Brigham Young's meticulous formulation of the "Lecture at the Veil," as one of the last acts of his life, is not "presently available" because of "its Adam-God teaching." "[O]ne of the most glorious revealments of the economy of heaven"[79] has vanished from the temple ceremony because Brigham and Joseph's God didn't survive to become the modern Mormon God. The unchangeable God changed in unacceptable ways. (Brigham's *"glorious revealment"* became McConkie's *"utter absurdity."*) To conceal and suppress the mistakes of the prophetic past has always been the Mormon way. Nothing is forever. That is one of the evils of an open canon. In these contradictory reports about the name and nature of God, early and late leaders proved they didn't really know "the only true God and Jesus Christ whom He hath sent."

Other Secrets

How many members and missionaries know that more than forty percent of the Latter-day Saints, including all of the living witnesses to the Book of Mormon, most of the Smiths, six members of the founding Quorum of the Twelve Apostles, and many important officers of the Illinois Church failed to follow Brigham Young to the Utah Territory in 1846 and 1847? How many young Mormon missionaries know that all of the living Whitmer witnesses, plus Martin Harris, William and Warren Cowdery,[80] Emma Smith, Lucy Mack Smith and William Smith (the prophet's widow, mother and only surviving brother) initially accepted James J. Strang, the King of Beaver Island, as their interim post-Mormon leader, recognizing him as the prophet Joseph Smith's designated successor?[81] Who knows that Joseph Smith III (Joseph's anointed

---

[79]Discourse, October 8, 1861, (unpublished) manuscript entitled "A Few Words of Doctrine," Brigham Young Collection (LDS Archives), as cited in David John Buerger, "The Adam-God Doctrine," *Dialogue: A Journal of Mormon Thought*, vol. 15 no. 1 (Spring 1982): 29.

[80]In January 1844, only months before the death of Joseph Smith, Oliver Cowdery, the Second Elder, became "a charter member of the Methodist church in his town." (Quinn, *Origins of Power*, 642).

[81]On 1 March 1846, after ample time to reflect, "Lucy Mack Smith signs a published statement in support of the succession claim of James J. Strang." (Ibid.,

heir, a boy whose patriarchal claims Brigham Young ignored) became the prophet of the Reorganized Church of Jesus Christ of Latter-day Saints, Mormonism's second largest schism (call them "Josephites") for fifty-four years (from 1860-1914)?

Who knew that Brigham Young secretly ordained four of his sons, including an eleven year-old (John Willard Young) to the office of apostle? Or that Martin Harris, who joined something remarkably close to ten different churches (a man baptized as a Mormon three or four different times) upon becoming a Shaker reported that his faith in the Shaker society and its resources was greater than his faith in the Book of Mormon. Who knows that Harris traveled to England and served a mission for Strang? Who knows that William Marks, the Stake President in Nauvoo, Emma's choice as Joseph's successor and the President of the Nauvoo High Council, ultimately became the First Counselor in the First Presidency of the "Josephites," that Mormon schism led by Joseph III, another set of apostles and three of Joseph and Emma's other sons?

What the missionaries don't know, they are unable to teach. The missionary lessons are incomplete, deceptive and misleading. Missionaries never tell their investigators that there are six versions of five discrepant accounts of the First Vision, or that more than twenty women were sealed to Joseph Smith before he was sealed to his legal wife. Or that Smith plurally married children of tender age and the undivorced legal wives of other faithful Mormon men. Investigators who join the Church, upon becoming better informed, may choose to leave feeling bitter and betrayed. The leaders of the Church strongly caution the members not to examine uncorrelated resources. What others call "history" they call "antimormon." The society that professes to value truth has concealed and suppressed hurtful facts. Mormon missionaries, who cheerfully undermine the foundations of all other societies, are expected to avoid exposure to unofficial resources that might be seen to undermine their own. While science *invites testing*, experimentation, competition, doubts and critical thinking, elements of freedom of thought, Mormonism *demands strict obedience* to the transient teachings of ethnocentric

---

656). "23 Dec. [1847]. Emma Hale Smith marries non-Mormon Lewis Bidamon on the birthday of her deceased husband, and begins attending the Methodist church with her children." (Ibid., 660).

"You can't start with a rock in your hat
and finish with a flurry of logic."

481

holy men. **Faithful Mormons draw their conclusions before they gather their facts. Their reactions to almost anything can be predicted with a high degree of assurance; the truth isn't always useful, needn't always be told and doesn't always matter.**

Science is the best method men and women have for discriminating what is and isn't empirically true about the natural world. Margaret Mead, a cultural anthropologist who served as the President of the American Association for the Advancement of Science nearly fifty years ago, spoke these words which every parent might do well to consider: *"Children must be taught how to think, not what to think."* **Considering all of the forces at work in Mormon culture, that is, simply said, impossible. It is a forbidden objective. Everyone knows that there are legitimate concerns that cannot be discussed in a public way in any Mormon forum.**

Mormons sacrifice freedom and integrity for the warmth and comfort of a community that worships its leaders and releases them "from the burden of uncertainty that life's choices impose." In the rough and tumble of the real world, unembarrassed uncertainty is scientific method. Science allows skeptics freedom to move from hypothesis to theory to cautious truth. In scientific jargon a theory isn't a hunch; it is an explanation.[82] "When an honest man discovers he is mistaken, he will either cease to be mistaken, or cease to be honest."[83] Science invites propositions to present their credentials. Scientists are charged to arrive at their conclusions after first considering facts. They seek to understand before they presume to explain.

THE PROPHET'S WORDS AS SCRIPTURE

Brigham Young taught the members of the Church that the penalty for mixing the blood of blacks and whites was (and would forever

---

[82]Gregory A. Clark, "Commentary: Students must be taught what science is. And is not." *The Salt Lake Tribune* (Salt Lake City: 20 January 2019), emphasis added.

[83]Anonymous.

be) death on the spot. Young despised the federal government,[84] wanted the South to win the Civil War, believed in slavery, codified slavery in the Utah Territory and promoted a slave owner (William H. Hooper) to political office.[85] He assigned slave-owners with notorious pasts to act as local spiritual authorities in Utah's Dixie and received a slave as tithing. Young attributed his racial doctrine to his spiritual mentor Joseph Smith. A statement issued by the First Presidency reported that Mormonism's discriminatory *doctrine* was taught to Joseph Smith by God himself. That was emphasized in the Book of Mormon and in further detail in the canonized books of Abraham and Moses.[86]

---

[84]*"I have a proposition to make to [senators Aaron] Cragan [sic], Wade and all such men,"* Young wrote to William H. Hooper, Utah's congressional delegate, in 1868, *"when my old niger has been dead one year, if they will wash their faces clean they may kiss his ass."* (Brigham Young to William H. Hooper, quoted in John G. Turner, *Brigham Young: Pioneer Prophet* [Belknap Press of Harvard University Press, 2012], 362). Today some thirty thousand students privy to his correlated teachings attend but one of the several universities actually named for the poorly educated perpetually angry Brigham Young. *"We will rid ourselves,"* Young raged, *"of as many such white livered, blackhearted, sycophantic Demagogues, as the Administration shall send."* By that he meant federal emissaries sent to the Utah Territory to administer the nation's affairs. Under threat some of them left the Territory fearful for their lives. (Correspondence, Brigham Young to John Bernhisel, quoted by Turner at Ibid., 244).

[85]Brigham Young's grandson, the son of the once-ordained eleven-year-old Apostle and former First Presidency First Counselor John Willard Young, a young man honored to bear the name of Young's slave-holding delegate to Congress, "William Hooper Young," is supposed to have murdered a woman in John Willard Young's apartment in New York City. Brigham's grandson wrote the words "blood atonement" in a notebook, with references to several biblical verses that described the meaning of blood atonement for those who were guilty of committing unatonable crimes. (William Hooper Young [accessed 15 July 2014], available from wikipedia.com). Police found blood on a carving knife, on the bedsheets, in a closet, under the kitchen sink, and on the floor and walls. It was "determined" that the victim, Anna Pulitzer, "had died of a drug overdose from chloral poisoning and that the head bruising and abdomen stabbing occurred after her death." ("Slayer of Mrs. Anna Pulitzer Is Known," *The New York Times* [20 September 1902], cited in Ibid.). Brigham's grandson and the slave-holding William Hooper's namesake appeared to have applied, or attempted to apply, Joseph and Brigham's doctrine to a Gentile whose sins weren't covered by the atonement. William Hooper Young, a returned missionary, pleaded guilty to second degree murder in 1903. Paroled in 1924, he was living with his father, the unquorumed apostle John Willard Young, in New York City when his father died in February 1924.

[86]First Presidency Statement (by Hugh B. Brown and N. Eldon Tanner), 15 December 1969 (accessed 18 February 2019); available from https://www.fair mormon.org/answers/Mormonism_and_racial_issues/Blacks_and_the_priesthood/

"You can't start with a rock in your hat
and finish with a flurry of logic."

483

Eleven consecutive Mormon prophets perpetuated Joseph and
Brigham's racial doctrines for more than one hundred thirty years.
Young said he was an apostle of the prophet Joseph Smith. And he
told the Church that Joseph Smith was the gatekeeper of the spirit
world. According to Young, no one could enter that interim state
without the founding prophet's express consent.

According to Young, some crimes were too heinous for the
atonement of Christ to cover. By Mormon reckoning, apostasy
(leaving the faith), an offense next to murder, was one of them.
Christian charity required good Saints to help bad Saints shed their
blood as "incense" to the Almighty. Besides blood atonement,
Brigham Young endorsed (and practiced) the demeaning law of
adoption and promoted a hateful reformation in the Utah Territory
in 1856 and 1857. Mormons knew that what Brigham Young said,
as the oracle of the Almighty whose servant he said that he was,
would be treated as scripture.

Mormon scholars say that "Mormon doctrine subordinates its own
canon to the principle of living revelation [the "church assigns more
weight to living oracles than textual ones"] . . . any opposition
between living oracles and printed scripture is always subject to
renegotiation."[87] What that seems to mean, in the scheme of things,
is that the current word of the current prophet is more important
than the earlier word of some earlier prophet, and/or in either case
than the law of the land. The "Standard Works" meant less to
Brigham Young and Joseph Smith than they did to the confounded
Bruce R. McConkie. Brigham supposed and said that his sermons
and words were scripture, and the members of the Church, falling
in line, agreed. "No book presides over this Church and no books
lie at its foundation."[88] "[T]oday's inspired utterances may become
part of tomorrow's standard works."[89] Brigham Young's prophetic

---

Statements; Internet, p. 3 of 5; *See also* First Presidency Statement (President
George Albert Smith), 17 August 1949 (Ibid., 2).

[87]Terryl L. Givens, *By the Hand of Mormon: The American Scripture that
Launched a New World Religion* (*n.p.*: Oxford University Press, Inc., 2002; reprint,
New York, NY: Oxford University Press paperback, 2003), 195.

[88]Orson Whitney, *Conference Reports of the General Conference of the Church
of Jesus Christ of Latter-day Saints* (October 1916), 55, quoted in Givens, *By the
Hand of Mormon*, 195.

[89]Ibid.

voice, accepted by the Saints, trumped the teachings of McConkie's "Standard Works."[90]

"THERE IS THE NEED NOW TO BE UNITED WITH EVERYONE FACING THE SAME WAY."

Latter-day Saints commit to do what their prophets say that God requires. "We Thank Thee, O God, for a Prophet." "Praise to the Man." "Follow the Prophet." Mormon hymns and songs describe Mormon concepts recklessly instilled in the smallest and most vulnerable children to their life-long disadvantage. Joseph Smith described the sealing doctrine to an English convert he unsuccessfully encouraged to plurally marry Brigham Young (a man nearly twice her age). Smith told his shell-shocked disciple, ". . . I know that this is lawful and right before God . . . . [W]hatever I bind on earth is bound in heaven . . . ."[91] Latter-day Saints surrender the dictates of conscience to just that smothering kind of authority. They sacrifice precious autonomy, freedom, the consolations of science, the wonders of a large and exciting world, truth and integrity for the warmth and comfort of their community. They subordinate their personal judgments to the will of their leader. The obedience required of the true believers is complete and entire. According to Apostle Boyd K. Packer: "There is the need now to be united with everyone facing the same way. Then the sunlight of truth, coming over our shoulders, will mark the path ahead. If we perchance turn the wrong way, we will shade our eyes from that light and we will fail in our ministries."[92]

---

[90]"The Latter-day Saints do not do things because they happen to be printed in a book. They do not do things because God told the Jews to do them: nor do they do or leave undone anything because of instructions that Christ gave to the Nephites. Whatever is done by this Church is because God speaking from Heaven in our day has commanded the Church to do it." (Ibid.).

[91]Joseph Smith, quoted in Martha Brotherton's Letter to General John C. Bennett, 13 July 1842, a copy of which is reproduced at John C. Bennett, *The History of the Saints: Or, an Expose of Joe Smith and Mormonism* (Boston: Leland & Whiting, 1842; photomechanical reprint of 1842 original, Salt Lake City: Modern Microfilm Company), 239. Her letter was also published in *The American Bulletin*, a newspaper in St. Louis, Missouri, on July 16, 1842 (vol. 1 no. 145).

[92]Boyd K. Packer, Talk to the All Church Coordinating Council (18 May 1993). Kurt Cobain: "They laugh at me because I'm different. I laugh at them because they're all the same."

"You can't start with a rock in your hat
and finish with a flurry of logic."

485

Latter-day Saints accepted the strange and unfamiliar doctrine of polygamy after an angel was supposed to have threatened their prophet with a drawn sword. Those nineteenth-century Saints were told that the practice of the polygamous principle was as essential to their spiritual progression as the ordinance of baptism. ("For behold," we may repeat, "I reveal unto you a new and an everlasting covenant; and if ye abide not that covenant, then are ye damned; for no one can reject this covenant and be permitted to enter into my glory."[93]) That covenant was not monogamy – not then, not now, not ever. Brigham Young said that, "The only men who become Gods, even the Sons of God, are those who enter into polygamy."[94] "In 1873, Brigham Young . . . said that if a man refused to take a second wife, in the eternities he would lose the wife he had."[95] Joseph Smith said, but only in private, that polygamy was "the most holy and important doctrine ever revealed to man on earth."[96] John Taylor wanted monogamous men out of the leadership, and George Q. Cannon tied the doctrine of polygamy to Eugenics. He described the principle as one of the natural laws that governed the propagation of humankind. In an important essay in an official Mormon publication, Cannon, a powerful Saint, argued that polygamy should be implemented through the careful management of all sexual relationships by the state.[97] *See* George Q. Cannon, "Mormon Eugenics: 1857," at Appendix A.

---

[93]Doctrine and Covenants 132:4.

[94]Brigham Young, *Journal of Discourses*, 11:269.

[95]Carol Lynn Pearson, *The Ghost of Eternal Polygamy: Haunting the Hearts and Heaven of Mormon Women and Men* (United States: Pivot Point Books, 2016), 122.

[96]Richard S. Van Wagoner, *Mormon Polygamy: A History* (Salt Lake City: Signature Books, 1986), Introduction, iii, cf. William Clayton in *The Historical Record*, vol. 6 nos. 3-5, Andrew Jenson, ed. (May 1887): 226.

[97]Cannon and the nineteenth-century Church took a dark view of monogamy. This is what they really thought: "[A]s long as monogamy is the law, bastardy, whoredom, and degeneracy will exist; and also their concomitants, irreligion, intemperance, licentiousness and vice of every kind and degree." (George Q. Cannon, "The Improvement of Our Species," *The Western Standard,* a Mormon newspaper [7 August 1857 (2/4-6)], 2:22). In this twenty-first century society, because of the Manifesto, monogamy is all that the twenty-first century leaders are at liberty to continue to propose. Monogamous celestial marriage is not, however, the ultimate objective. Mormonism's highest leaders have proved that polygamy, the first principle of the truly faithful, is the rule to be observed in a Mormon afterlife, where men are gods, kings and priests of the Kingdom of God, and women are their matrons, fertile queens and princesses, obedient consorts.

How did that work?   Of seventy-two general authorities who actively embraced Joseph's "most holy and important doctrine," thirty-nine were divorced or separated more than eighty times.[98] Brigham Young personally granted 1,645 divorces "during the period of his presidency," many of which "were obtained by prominent pioneer leaders involved in the practice of plural marriage."[99]   The heartbreak those mournful facts engendered cannot be measured. It is projected "that there were well in excess of 2,000 divorces granted prior to the 1890 Manifesto."[100] The first seven Mormon prophets – *those who practiced polygamy in this life and led the Church from 1830 to 1945, from Joseph Smith to Heber J. Grant*[101] – had, as between them, about one hundred forty wives.[102]

---

[98]D. Michael Quinn discovered "that of the 72 General Authorities who entered into plural marriage, 39 were involved in broken marriages, including 54 divorces, 26 separations, and 1 annulment." (D. Michael Quinn, "Organization Development and Social Origins of the Mormon Hierarchy, 1832-1932: A Prosopographical Study" [M.A. thesis, University of Utah, 1973], 248-91, quoted in Eugene E. Campbell and Bruce L. Campbell, "Divorce among Mormon Polygamists: Extent and Explanations" [paper read at the Annual Meeting of the Utah State Historical Society, September 17, 1977, Salt Lake City], *Utah Historical Quarterly*, vol. 46 no. 1 [winter 1978], 6).

[99]Ibid., 5.

[100]Ibid.

[101]Heber J. Grant's uncle George D. Grant "was divorced from three wives on the same day and a fourth within five weeks." (Campbell and Campbell, "Divorce among Mormon Polygamists: Extent and Explanations," 5). One of his victims was Heber J. Grant's mother, who (although sealed to Joseph Smith) married her brother-in-law for time after Heber's father, Jedediah (another husband for time) died only days after Heber's birth.

[102]Mrs. Brodie's biography, *No Man Knows My History,* was initially published in 1945, the year Heber J. Grant died. Grant, the Prophet of the Mormon Church from 1918 to 1945, was the last of the first seven Mormon prophets known to actually live the principle of polygamy. There was never a time from 1830 to 1945 when the Mormon Church was not actually led by a polygamist. Grant, who had twelve children, married Lucy Stringham (1877, six children), Hilda Augusta Winters (1884, one child) and Emily Harris Wells (1884, five children). In perilous polygamous times (1889) he established his wife Emily Harris Wells in exile in Manassa, Colorado. That was done to avoid her being forced to testify against him in a cohabitation proceeding. As the husband of three wives, he did plead guilty to a charge of unlawful cohabitation in 1899, nine years after the Manifesto. Two of Grant's wives, Lucy and Emily, died before he became the President of the Church. Heber J. Grant never lost faith in "The Principle." "Despite the fact that Grant had violated his 1891 amnesty agreement with the government, [and] had attempted unsuccessfully to take Fanny Woolley as a post-Manifesto plural wife," he agreed to "obey the law." In 1937, nineteen years into his presidency, he

"You can't start with a rock in your hat
and finish with a flurry of logic."

487

"Happiness," according to Joseph Smith, speaking in code and privately of his most highly favored polygamous doctrine, "is *the* object and design of our existence." Men were happy; women not so much.[103] What did Joseph Smith publicly teach the Latter-day Saints about the doctrine of polygamy during his lifetime? *Nothing at all.* He told everyone willing to listen that he (and his church) didn't practice polygamy. *"Inasmuch as this church of Christ has been reproached with the crime of fornication, and polygamy, we declare that we believe, that one man should have one wife; and one woman but one husband, except in case of death, when either is at liberty to marry again."*[104] That was what he told them, and what he told them was canonized, granted the stamp of divine approval. What was known to have been untrue was canonized. That dishonest statement graced the pages of the Doctrine and Covenants (all editions and printings) from 1835 to 1876. Smith *publicly*

---

announced that, "We never believed polygamy was wrong, and never will." (*Salt Lake Tribune*, 26 July 1937, quoted in Van Wagoner, *Mormon Polygamy: A History*, 192). One prominent apostle Richard R. Lyman cohabited with two women, one of them his legal wife, from 1925 to 1943 when he was excommunicated for his violation of the law of chastity. For all of those years, and in fact from 1918-1943, the well-connected Lyman was an active member of the Quorum of the Twelve Apostles. He was "caught with his 71-year-old plural wife in [a] late-night, smashed-door raid by [the] Salt Lake City police chief, [accompanied by] Apostles JFS-2 [Joseph Fielding Smith] and Harold B. Lee 11 November 1943 . . . ." His legal wife, Amy Brown Lyman, was the President of the Relief Society, the ranking woman in the Mormon Church, at the time of the raid. His father and grandfather were both important Apostles. Amasa Lyman, Richard Lyman's grandfather, was a Counselor in Joseph Smith's last First Presidency. (D. Michael Quinn, *The Mormon Hierarchy: Extensions of Power* [Salt Lake City: Signature Books in association with Smith Research Associates, 1997], 669-70). Apostle Richard R. Lyman was excommunicated on November 12, 1943. No criminal charges were filed.

[103]In August 1854, Lieutenant Colonel Edward Steptoe entered the Salt Lake Valley with three hundred and twenty-five U.S. soldiers and wintered there. (Turner, *Brigham Young: Pioneer Prophet*, 244). Although faced with "threats of violence . . . from the highest level," when Colonel Steptoe left the Territory for California in 1855, he took as many "as one hundred single and married Utah women" who wanted to leave under his protection. (John Gary Maxwell, *Robert Newton Baskin and the Making of Modern Utah* [Norman, OK: The Arthur H. Clark Co., 2013], 86). Brigham's thundering retort to this confiscation was, "Let the women be ever so bad, so help me God, we will slay them." (Charles Kelly and Hoffman Birney, *Holy Murder* [New York: Minton, Balch and Company, 1934], 119, quoted in Baskin, Ibid.). "Leaving the Saints" was never (is never) an easy task.

[104]Doctrine and Covenants 101 (1835 edition), emphasis added.

denied that he and his followers believed, taught or practiced polygamy until the day of his death (June 27, 1844). The *Nauvoo Expositor*, a local newspaper, had to be destroyed because it told (and/or promised to further tell) the truth about the polygamous principle. What did Joseph Smith *privately* teach some few specially selected highly favored insiders about the doctrine of polygamy during his lifetime? (1) That it was "the most holy and important doctrine ever revealed to man on the earth." (2) That "[i]f ye abide not that covenant then are ye damned." (3) That no one could reject that covenant and enter into God's glory. (4) That God is "more awful in the executions of His punishments . . . than we are apt to suppose him to be."

Joseph's account of his adolescent life was written, not as a child and not at the time, but "at the height of his career." In his journal "he wrote repeated denials of polygamy." He didn't tell the truth, not in public or even to himself. He was ashamed to be *publicly* identified with the most "*holy and important doctrine*" ever revealed to man on earth. Joseph's nineteenth-century successors would come to consider Old Testament polygamy as "the most distinctive signature" of the nineteenth-century Church. Without proof, Brigham Young described Jesus as a polygamist. His resurrected Adam came to this earth with Eve, "one" of his "wives."

Polygamy is countenanced in Mormonism's many temples in this twenty-first century. No less than twelve Mormon prophets – including seven who actively practiced polygamy with about one hundred forty women – are sealed to more than one woman in temples. During this interim earthly period, while the "doctrine" ("the law of heaven") is not practiced but held in a state of suspense, Mormon men can be sealed to more than one woman in the event of the death of a wife. Those plural marriages (sealings), like any earlier marriage to a deceased spouse, are equally eternal by modern Mormon reckoning. While that is true for Mormon men, it isn't true for Mormon women. The women are monogamists in the plural marriage equation. In the immortal words of Ogden Nash and/or possibly others, "Hogamous, Higamous, Man is polygamous. Higamous, Hogamous, Woman is Monogamous."[105]

---

[105]Poem of unknown authorship, attributed to Ogden Nash as well as Mrs. Amos Pinchot, William James, Dorothy Parker, and others. (*See* "Hogamous,

"You can't start with a rock in your hat
and finish with a flurry of logic."

489

In Missouri, Ohio, Iowa, Illinois, and in the Utah Territory, Latter-day Saints conducted their secular affairs in lockstep, acting like their leaders said they should. John C. Bennett was elected to office as the Mayor of Nauvoo by thousands of members without a single dissenting vote. Ambitious Gentile politicans disgraced themselves by courting the monolithic Mormon vote, until the entire exercise became so utterly distasteful that the Mormons found themselves – in their desperate search for theocratic sovereignty and despite their votes – without dependable allies in any of the parties.

In this twenty-first century, Latter-day Saints are at liberty to vote their conservative consciences in public elections, but not in their local wards and stakes, where every member raises his or her arm to the square to support every proposition all of the time. Against the authority of the prophet, there can be no loyal dissent, however well-intended. For his words are those of a surrogate God. Obedience is Alpha and Omega. While fifteen Mormon men rule the world, not everyone knows it yet. Fawn McKay Brodie, who started but didn't finish life as a Mormon princess, understood the theocracy; misogyny was inevitable. In the autocratic Church, "only the trappings were democratic." George Orwell would have grasped the subliminal meaning of what the Latter-day Saints call "agency" with their fingers crossed. Mormonism's agency is a laughable concept (double talk), meaning to obey or suffer.

> *The membership voted on the church officers twice a year. But there was only one slate of candidates, and it was selected by the first presidency, comprised of Joseph himself and his two counselors. Approval or disapproval was indicated by a standing vote in the general conference. Dissenting votes quickly became so rare that the elections came to be called – and the irony was unconscious – "the sustaining of the authorities."*[106]

Higamous, Man is Polygamous, Higamous, Hogamous, Woman is Monogamous" [8 March 2012, accessed 28 December 2018], available from https://quote investigator.com/ 2012/03/28/hogamous/; Internet, page 1 of 9).
[106]Brodie, *No Man Knows My History*, 162, emphasis added.

PROPHECY FAILS

What Joseph said God promised the Zion's Camp militia never happened. Specific prophecies concerning the urgent gathering of Israel in the state of Missouri, the location and return of the ten lost tribes, the building of a temple at Independence, Missouri, the building of the city of the New Jerusalem at Independence, Missouri, and the second coming didn't come to pass.

> *Verily this is the word of the Lord, that the city New Jerusalem shall be built by the gathering of the saints, beginning at this place, even the place of the temple, which temple shall be reared in this generation. For verily this generation shall not all pass away until an house shall be built unto the Lord . . . which house shall be built . . . unto the Lord in this generation, upon the consecrated spot as I have appointed . . . .*[107]

Those unredeemed (and irredeemable) promises are seldom (if ever) mentioned by the modern Church. Like the Book of Abraham and the Inspired Translation of the King James Bible, there are sensitive subjects still under review. Mormons couldn't retain title to their properties in Missouri as the Lord in a revelation said that they should, because when the republic rose up and ousted their theocracy,[108] God didn't lift a hand to help them. The gathering of the Saints wasn't as urgent as Joseph and the missionaries said that it was. The Savior didn't come as Joseph and the missionaries said that he would, and the Mormons were rudely evicted from the land of their inheritance in Jackson County, Missouri. The great promise made by Smith to the Mormons – that the Saints must leave wherever they were to urgently gather to Zion in the State of Missouri because the Second Coming was imminent – proved to be utterly false. The Ten Tribes didn't return; the temple

---

[107]Doctrine and Covenants 84:1-5, 31, emphasis added.

[108]Joseph Smith, 16 August 1834: "I shall now proceed to give you such counsel as the Spirit of the Lord may dictate . . . [B]e in readiness to move into Jackson County in two years from the eleventh of September next, which is the appointed time for the redemption of Zion . . . ." (Roberts, ed., *History of The Church of Jesus Christ of Latter-day Saints*, 2: 144-45). This deadline, like every other deadline, was never met.

"You can't start with a rock in your hat
and finish with a flurry of logic."

491

wasn't built and Jesus didn't come. The revelations and prophecies
that caused well-intentioned nineteenth-century Saints to leave
everything and follow utterly failed. It is not saving to say that it is
not yet "the last syllable of recorded time." The "revelations"
Joseph Smith delivered to his nineteenth-century disciples in the
name of God with apocalyptic urgency – revelations that forever
changed the course of so many lives – were not the word of God.

When Joseph Smith died, Nauvoo was beginning to look more and
more like failed Kirtland. When the Church abandoned all hope of
creating its consecrated sanctuary in the state of Missouri and then
in Illinois, and when those who *chose to follow* an indicted
counterfeiter *chose to leave* Nauvoo under terrible conditions in the
wintertime (before the U.S. Marshal could arrest their leader
Brigham Young), many Saints failed to follow the usurper to yet
another remote place of refuge in the early American west.

The Real Reason the Saints Went West in the Winter

"A Federal grand jury at Springfield had indicted twelve prominent
Saints, including Brigham Young and four others of the Twelve, on
the charge of making bogus [counterfeiting]."[109] Everyone knew
that a counterfeiting ring was operating in the Mormon city
(Nauvoo). In December 1845 Theodore Turley, a man close to the
prophet Joseph Smith and an important man in the early Church,
was imprisoned at Springfield, Illinois, for counterfeiting. It was at
about that same time that the federal grand jury indicted five of the
Twelve Apostles for counterfeiting.[110]

The issue of enforcement was federal. When the U.S. Marshal
asked Illinois Governor Ford to provide the support required to
arrest the alleged offenders, including Brigham Young, no small
task, Ford responded and said, "that was entirely an affair of the
U.S. Government, in which this state took no official part." On one
occasion, after the Marshal was seen "waiting at the temple steps [to
arrest him], Brigham had exchanged coats with William Miller."
The Marshal took Miller to Carthage "before discovering that the

---

[109]Taylor, *Nightfall at Nauvoo*, 365.
[110]Quinn, *Origins of Power*, Selected Chronology, 654.

man he was arresting on a bogus charge was himself a bogus Brigham."

Willard Richards read a letter that Governor Ford had sent to Sheriff Backenstos, to the Quorum of the Twelve, to the Nauvoo High Council, and to the members of the Council of Fifty. The threat of prosecution was getting altogether too close for comfort. Ford to Backenstos: "This indictment in the U.S. court against the leading Mormons puts a new face on the matter. It will bring them and the United States for the first time into collision." Ford supposed ("I think it likely that . . .") President Polk "will order up a regiment or two of the regular army and perhaps call on me for the militia." If requested by President Polk, Ford thought that he would be "compelled to comply." Ford then added this to the militant Saints' anxiety: "I also think that it is very likely that the government at Washington will interfere to prevent the Mormons from going west of the Rocky Mountains."[111] "U.S. Army troops were stationed at New Orleans, Brigham had been warned, waiting only the breakup of the river ice to take ship up the Mississippi and occupy the city."[112]

Why did the Mormons leave "in mid-winter without waiting until grass grew and water ran," something no one then required? So that Brigham Young, four other apostles and more than half a dozen other prominent men wouldn't be arrested on the counterfeiting indictments. So that the government couldn't interfere with their departure. So that they could cross the river before the ice melted and the troops arrived to arrest their leaders. Brigham "hoped the Lord would temper the wind to his flock."[113] The move couldn't wait for the more normal conditions their oppressors had promised. The early departure that caused so much suffering, and about which there has been so much historical fuss, was all about Brigham Young. Would he leave the United States to show them the Rocky Mountains, or live to inhabit a Government jail?

---

[111]Taylor, *Nightfall at Nauvoo*, 365-66.
[112]Ibid., 365.
[113]Ibid.

"You can't start with a rock in your hat
and finish with a flurry of logic."

493

More Failures

Many of the forty to fifty percent of the colony who refused to enlist
followed other schismatic Mormon leaders (all of whom, like Smith,
owned the truth, spoke to the Lord and claimed Pentecostal
credentials). As it turned out, Brigham Young didn't need to keep a
wagon in his Utah Territory barn, ready at a moment's notice to
carry him back to Zion in Independence, Missouri. He would never
be relocated there.[114] Nor will any prophet ever be.

Jesus didn't come when Joseph Smith said that he would, and
Joseph wasn't there to meet him as he said that he would be. The
city of Independence in Jackson County, Missouri, hadn't really
been the Garden of Eden. Spring Creek, Missouri, was not Adam-
ondi-Ahman, and Adam didn't leave the visible remnants of an
ancient altar somewhere close to Daviess County. Cain didn't kill
Abel in Far West, Missouri; Noah didn't build the ark in South
Carolina; there was no Tower of Babel, there were no Jaredites,
and the Book of Mormon, not the Constitution, is hanging by a
thread.

The Book of Mormon was not transcribed from reformed Egyptian.
The "Caractors" in the Anthon manuscript were not recovered
from ancient plates, and Abraham, Moses, Aaron and Egyptian
Joseph didn't write on the Egyptian papyri as Joseph Smith said
that they did. Reverend Caswall's Greek Psalter wasn't an
Egyptian dictionary. Joseph didn't translate a fragment from a
parchment buried by John the Beloved, and the Lord "didn't
gather His elect to build the New Jerusalem, to which the city of
Enoch would one day descend from heaven in millennial
greeting."[115] The Mormon prophet's purported partial translation
of the Kinderhook Plates was foolishness. The Kinderhook plates
were created as a hoax in order to confound the gullible prophet.

---

[114]"In 1900, [Wilford] Woodruff's successor, Lorenzo Snow, affirmed at a
special priesthood meeting in [the] Salt Lake Temple that 'there are many here
now under the sound of my voice, probably a majority who will live to go back to
Jackson County and assist in building that temple.'" (Klaus J. Hansen, "The
Metamorphosis of the Kingdom of God: Toward a Reinterpretation of Mormon
History," *Dialogue: A Journal of Mormon Thought*, vol. 1 no. 3 [Autumn 1966], 74).

[115]Brodie, *No Man Knows My History*, 96.

The Egyptian papyri, artifacts kept safe in a secret vault, are common funerary documents having nothing to do with the age of Abraham. Joseph's mother didn't purchase them for the sum of $6,000, or ever at all, and the "translation" of that perfectly incredible book was a colossal fraud.

Joseph did not reveal a conversation between God and Moses that was omitted from the Old Testament because of the wickedness of the Hebrews (the book of Moses).[116]   Joseph Smith's Inspired Translation of the King James Bible involved the unannounced borrowing of hundreds of passages from Methodist Adam Clarke's famous Bible commentary. "Zelph" wasn't nine feet tall, or white, or a Lamanite. "Darkies" have inherited the priesthood, the sun isn't inhabited, and there are no very tall men who look like Quakers on the moon. The Book of Mormon has no geography, and the temple ritual was stolen from less than ancient Masons.

The caption "Latter-day Saints," an apocalyptic term cheapened by the passage of time and threatened by hundreds of broken promises, describes a failed millennial expectation. The promises God supposedly made to the early Mormons more than a hundred years ago never came to pass. If God makes a promise he doesn't keep, faithful Latter-day Saints look to the next great promise. Heaven forbid that anyone should ever say, "God didn't make that promise; or we did everything that God required; or our leaders failed us."   Joseph Smith described in more revelations than modern Latter-day Saints are allowed to read, promises God didn't make and hasn't kept. Because God didn't say what Joseph said that He did, God didn't do what Joseph said that He would.

---

[116]Ibid.

Epilogue

Epilogue

"The Prophet Will Never Mislead You"

The Lord Almighty leads this Church, and he will never suffer you to be led astray if you are found doing your duty. You may go home and sleep as sweetly as a babe in its mother's arms, as to any danger of your leaders leading you astray, for if they should try to do so the Lord would quickly sweep them from the earth.

Brigham Young

I say to Israel, the Lord will never permit me or any other man who stands as President of this Church to lead you astray. It is not in the programme. It is not in the mind of God. If I were to attempt that, the Lord would remove me out of my place, and so He will any other man who attempts to lead the children of men astray from the oracles of God and from their duty."

Wilford Woodruff

Astrayals: Joseph Smith

"Astrayals"[1]: Joseph Smith

GOD ISSUES

For more than one hundred years – during the administrations of eight consecutive Mormon prophets and until 1965 – Latter-day Saints were repeatedly informed that Joseph Smith told his story only once.[2] It is now known (but only since 1965, 1966, 1969, 1971) that there are no less than six different primary versions of five strikingly different accounts of Joseph Smith's First Vision, "the hinge pin upon which the whole cause turns." Before 1965 no Mormon missionary taught any Mormon investigator that there were multiple accounts of the First Vision. Those omissions have affected all First Vision scholarship. Investigators and converts have never been told the truth about the founding story of the Mormon Church.

Joseph Smith taught his earliest followers (including the Three Witnesses to the Book of Mormon) that the Father, Son and Holy Ghost "*is*" one God. ("*And the honor be to the Father, and to the Son, and to the Holy Ghost, which is one God.*"[3]) Smith was a monotheist (a believer in "one God") from the time he started to spiritually organize the Church until about 1834 or so. King James Bible, 1611, Luke 10:22: "*[N]o man knoweth who the Son is, but the Father; and who the Father is, but the Son, and he to whom the Son will reveal him.*" Joseph Smith Inspired Translation, 1831-32, Luke

---

[1]This Epilogue details "Astrayals," incidences where past prophets have taught doctrine and practiced principles that did lead the Saints astray. Some of the prophets' practices were concealed and suppressed. Some of the issues to be described have surfaced as the Church has tried to clean up its history with the passage of time.

[2]"Whenever new historical information is published [like the emergence of a previously unknown handwritten account of the First Vision], a host of questions demand answers, and the disclosure [in 1965] that Joseph Smith told his story more than once has been no exception." (James B. Allen, "Eight Contemporary Accounts of Joseph Smith's First Vision," *Improvement Era* [April 1970], 6).

[3]Book of Mormon, The Testimony of Three Witnesses, emphasis added.

10:23: *"[N]o man knoweth that the Son is the Father, and the Father is the Son, but him to whom the Son will reveal it."*[4] Mormonism's founder didn't separate an essentially Trinitarian Father from an essentially Trinitarian Son, creating "two Personages, whose brightness and glory defy all description," or abandon his early and extreme monotheistic theology, until he was about thirty years old in 1834, and maybe until sometime even later. Those incredible facts are a dagger in the heart of the 1838-39 canonized fourth Pearl of Great Price Account of an 1820 vision supposed to have separated the Father from the Son. That 1820 event wasn't publicly reported until 1842.

In about 1835, in the thirtieth year of his life and in his *Lectures on Faith*,[5] Joseph Smith (who was only then changing his mind and his doctrine by separating the deities) taught his followers that the Father was a personage of the spirit, "omnipotent, omnipresent and omniscient," that the Son was a personage of tabernacle, and anthropomorphic, and that there were "only two personages" in the godhead.[6] The canonized *Lectures on Faith* (the *"Doctrine"* part of the Book of *Doctrine* and Covenants) were removed from that book without sufficient formality in 1921, seventy-seven years after the death of Joseph Smith, after being part of the Doctrine and Covenants since 1835, because of these and other doctrinal discrepancies.

After 1835 (and the publication of the canonized *Lectures on Faith*), Joseph Smith sometimes referred to the names Jehovah and Elohim as interchangeable epithets for the same indivisible Spirit. Hear that in the prophet's prayer as it is recorded in the History of the

---

[4]Joseph Smith created "The Inspired Translation of the King James Bible" by borrowing from Methodist theologian Adam Clarke's Trinitarian Bible Commentary (a project seen to describe plagiarism beyond the possibility of "coincidental overlap"). (Haley Wilson and Thomas Wayment, "A Recently Recovered Source: Rethinking Joseph Smith's Bible Translation" [Brigham Young University Journal of Undergraduate Research, Department of Ancient Scripture, *16 March 2017*]).

[5]Rigdon assisted with the drafting of the *Lectures on Faith*, but the *Lectures* were credited to and published by Joseph Smith (*Lectures on Faith: Prepared by the Prophet Joseph Smith, Delivered to the School of the Prophets in Kirtland, Ohio, 1834-35* [Salt Lake City: Deseret Book Company, 1985]).

[6]*Lectures on Faith*, Lecture Fifth.

Church in August 1842, the same year that the 1838-39 Pearl of Great Price account *publicly* separated the Father from the Son.

> *O Thou, who seest and knoweth the hearts of all men*
> *– Thou eternal, omnipotent, omniscient, and*
> *omnipresent Jehovah – God – Thou Eloheim, that*
> *sittest, as saith the Psalmist, "enthroned in heaven,"*
> *look down upon Thy servant Joseph at this time; and*
> *let faith on the name of Thy Son Jesus Christ, to a*
> *greater degree than Thy servant ever yet has enjoyed,*
> *be conferred upon him . . . .*[7]

"Jehovah – God – Thou Eloheim," one indivisible person described as a spirit ("omnipotent, omniscient, and omnipresent"), is reported to be the Father of Jesus (and not Jesus) according to Joseph Smith in this prayer composed and uttered less than two years before he died. The Proclamation to the World, issued by the Quorum of the Twelve Apostles in 1845 after the death of Joseph Smith, repeated these Jehovah/Eloheim discrepancies ("*The great* Eloheim Jehovah has been pleased once more to speak from the heavens; and also to commune with man upon the earth by means of open visions, and by the ministration of HOLY MESSENGERS."). See Appendix F (Proclamation, April 6, 1845). Jehovah God, also called "Eloheim," interchangeable and indivisible, was not Jesus to Joseph Smith in this important prayer in 1842, or to Brigham Young and the Quorum of the Twelve in the Proclamation to the World in 1845.

In 1834-35 in his canonized *Lectures on Faith*, Joseph Smith described the Holy Spirit *as the common mind* of the Father and the Son, but not as a separate *personage*. Only two "personages" – the

---

[7]Joseph Smith Jr., *History of The Church of Jesus Christ of Latter-day Saints*, B.H. Roberts, ed., 2d ed., rev., (Salt Lake City: The Deseret Book Company, 1978), 5:127-28, emphasis added. Section 110:1-4 of the Doctrine and Covenants, a vision that reflected "Personal manifestations of the Lord Jesus Christ [in the Kirtland Temple on April 3, 1836]," identified Jesus with "the voice of Jehovah saying: I am the first and the last; . . . I am he who was slain; I am your advocate with the Father." (Doctrine and Covenants 110:3-4). As evidence of further confusion, on that earlier occasion and in that same revelation, Smith identified Elijah and Elias, two names for one person (Elijah, Hebrew; Elias, Greek) as separate persons. Smith said that Elijah *and* Elias visited the Kirtland Temple on that same day at separate times for different reasons.

Father, a spirit, and an anthropomorphic Son – were described in the *Lectures on Faith* "Prepared by the Prophet Joseph Smith" in 1834-35. The Holy Spirit, a mysterious designated noncorporeal component of the godhead, wasn't one of them. On April 9, 1852, Brigham Young declared that, "The Holy Ghost is the Spirit of the Lord, and issues forth from Himself . . . . The Lord," he said, "fills the immensity of space."[8]   The Holy Spirit became a third *"personage"* in Mormon theology many years after the death of Joseph Smith, and some time after the death of Brigham Young, with some assistance from First Presidency Counselor George Q. Cannon, who told the members of the Church in 1899 *"that he had heard [the] audible voice of [the] Holy Ghost as [a] separate personage."*[9]

While the Holy Spirit as an influence was (in the beginning) a member of the Godhead by some mystical reckoning,[10] it unequivocally became a "personage" of spirit in the form of a man early in the twentieth-century after the death of Joseph Smith. The Father was a spirit personage in the form of a man when the *Lectures on Faith* were published in 1834-35. What the Father was in the *Lectures on Faith* in 1834-35 was what the Holy Spirit became after the deaths of Joseph Smith and Brigham Young. In the *Lectures on Faith*, the Holy Spirit was not a *"personage,"* and the Father wasn't *anthropomorphic*. Some time after those doctrines were published, the Spirit is supposed to have become a personage, and the Father is supposed to have become anthropomorphic. What the Father had been the Spirit became. What the Son had been the Father became.

After Joseph Smith studied Hebrew, he separated "Gods" from "God" upon learning that Elohim, one of the Hebrew words for God, was a plural term in Hebrew usage. "Instead of saying: God created the earth," as he had previously said, the Mormon prophet changed his mind in order to accept the idea of a plurality of Gods,

---

[8]D. Michael Quinn, *The Mormon Hierarchy: Extensions of Power* (Salt Lake City, UT: Signature Books in association with Smith Research Associates, 1997), 750.

[9]Ibid., 647, emphasis added.

[10]"Do the Father, Son and Holy Spirit constitute the Godhead?   They do. (Lecture 5:2)." (*Lectures on Faith*, Lecture Fifth, 65).

which represented a significant reordering of what had been a "slowly evolving metaphysical system." Now he said, that "The Gods organized the earth" and that the Bible, when speaking of "God" rather than "Gods," had been "carelessly translated." When he read Thomas Dick's "Philosophy of a Future State" after much water under the Mormon bridge, Smith concluded that the earth had been "organized" from existing matter rather than created *ex nihilo* from nothing.[11] After taking classes in Hebrew from an instructor, Smith changed his mind about the nature of God and governance. This later Joseph, in contrast to that earlier Joseph, abandoned monotheism ("one God") and embraced polytheism ("Gods") with puritanical fervor.

After this reordering occurred, an 1832 first and only Holographic (handwritten) Account of a First Vision of one God in 1821, the Son who was the Father, was superceded by an account of a great First Vision of two glorious personages, a Father and a Son, a retroactive account of an 1820 event composed in 1838-39. The existence of the earlier holographic account was concealed and suppressed in the archives of the Church for more than one hundred thirty years. That account was not "brought to light" until 1965.

In a vision of the Celestial Kingdom received on January 21, 1836, and described in Joseph Smith's Diary, Smith reported that, "The heavens were opened upon us and I beheld the celestial kingdom of God . . . . I saw *father Adam*, and Abraham *and Michael* and my father and mother, *my brother Alvin*."[12] In a family "of goodly parents who spared no pains . . . instructing me [Joseph Smith] in <the> Christian religion,"[13] Alvin Smith (who is now in the celestial kingdom) had not been baptized, nor had the two brothers' other siblings. Thus it would appear that a person didn't have to be baptized to be admitted to "the celestial kingdom of God." Alvin was not. And it would also appear that the Smiths weren't much on church. On April 3, 1976, the Church canonized the 1836 vision of

---

[11]Fawn M. Brodie, *No man knows my history: The Life of Joseph Smith the Mormon Prophet*, 2d ed., rev. and enl. (New York, NY: Alfred A. Knopf, 1972), 171.

[12]Joseph Smith's Diary, 21 January 1836 (original in LDS Church History Library), 136, emphasis added.

[13]*The Personal Writings of Joseph Smith*, ed. Dean C. Jessee (Salt Lake City: Deseret Book, 1984), 4.

the Celestial Kingdom, an event seen to have occurred one hundred forty years after that revelation was supposed to have been received. The words of the vision were then amended to read as follows: "I saw *Father Adam* and Abraham; and my father and my mother; and *my brother Alvin* . . . ." In the twentieth-century version of the revelation, and in the History of the Church where the 1836 vision is also misdescribed,[14] the words "*and Michael*" have been omitted.[15] Joseph Smith first reported that he supposed he saw "*father Adam*" and also "*Michael*," two different persons, despite the fact that he initially taught that Michael was Adam's name in the preexistence. Michael and Adam were, according to Joseph Smith, actually two different names for the same person.[16] The Church moved to correct the prophet's foundational error by means of these unannounced nineteenth and twentieth-century omissions. The altered passage conflicted with the more contemporaneous provisions that described the revelation in Joseph Smith's diary.

Joseph Smith ultimately taught his followers that God, who had been a spirit in the canonized *Lectures on Faith* in 1834-35 and in the Doctrine and Covenants until 1921, did in altered fact become an exalted anthropomorphic man. At some point the Father changed to become a personage of tabernacle like the Son had been in those *Lectures on Faith* published in 1834-35.

In the Kirtland Temple Dedication Prayer (preamble 1957: "According to the Prophet's written statement, this prayer was given to him by revelation"), Joseph clearly identified Jehovah as God the Father. "And now we ask thee, holy Father ["O Jehovah"], in the name of Jesus Christ, the Son of thy bosom . . . to accept of this house . . . ." "[W]e have given of our substance to build a house

---

[14]Roberts, ed., *History of The Church of Jesus Christ of Latter-day Saints,* 2:380-81.

[15]Jerald Tanner and Sandra Tanner, *The Changing World of Mormonism: A Behind-the-Scenes Look at Changes in Mormon Doctrine and Practice* (Moody Press, 1979), 62-63, emphasis added.

[16]*Adam* and *Michael* as one: "And the Lord appeared unto them, *and they rose up and blessed Adam and called him Michael, the prince, the archangel.*" (Doctrine and Covenants [1835], 107:54, emphasis added). "And also with *Michael or Adam, the father of all, the prince of all, the ancient of days.*" (Ibid., 27:11, emphasis added).

to thy name ["O Jehovah," "O Lord God of Israel"], that the Son of Man might have a place to manifest himself to his people."[17]   In Joseph's Church, even after the deities were separated, Jehovah wasn't Jesus. In this canonized revelation, Jehovah was the "holy Father," the Father of Jesus, the Son of His "bosom."

The Old Testament and Joseph Smith's revelations do not support Jehovah as the preincarnated Christ. That doctrine didn't become definitive and wasn't canonized until 1915. Joseph identified Jehovah as the Father, and "Jehovah – God – Thou Eloheim" as the Father, during his lifetime, but then sometimes only spoke of Elohim. Brigham Young described Adam as both Michael and "Yahovah."

In Joseph's now expanded view, "God himself was once as we are now, and is an exalted man, and sits enthroned in yonder heavens! ... It is the first principle of the gospel," he now said, "to know for a certainty the Character of God, and to know that we may converse with Him as one man converses with another, and that he was once a man like us . . . ."[18] So much for those *Lectures*, and for a Father who was "omnipotent, omniscient, and omnipresent," an absolute personage of the spirit. Like that amended Joseph who changed his mind about the nature of God, Lorenzo Snow taught that God was an exalted man: "As man now is, God once was; as God now is, man may be." "The prophet Joseph Smith confirmed the validity of the revelation Elder Snow had received: . . . 'Brother Snow, that is a true gospel doctrine, and it is a revelation from God to you.'"[19]

---

[17]Doctrine and Covenants, 109.

[18]Joseph Smith, The King Follett Sermon (7 April 1844), Roberts, ed., *History of The Church of Jesus Christ of Latter-day Saints*, 6:305.

[19]Eliza R. Snow Diary, 22 December 1846 (LDS Archives), quoted in LeRoi C. Snow, "Devotion to a Divine Inspiration," *Improvement Era* (June 1919), 656. Eliza R. Snow, like her plural husband, Joseph Smith, believed that Adam was God. "Adam is our father and God. He is the god of the earth." In a poem entitled "We Believe In Our God," included in the LDS collection of hymns, Snow wrote:

> We believe in our God, the Prince of his race,
> The archangel Michael, the Ancient of Days
> Our own Father Adam, earth's Lord as is plain,
> Who'll counsel and fight for His children again.
> We believe in His Son, Jesus Christ . . . .

(Eliza R. Snow, "We Believe In Our God" in *Sacred Hymns and Spiritual Songs for the Church of Jesus Christ of Latter-day Saints*, 11th ed. [Liverpool, England:

In 1997 Gordon B. Hinckley publicly dismissed the teachings of Joseph Smith and Lorenzo Snow, two of the prophets who preceded him: "Question: Is this the teaching of the church today, that God the Father was once a man like we are? Hinckley: 'I don't know that we teach it. I don't know that we emphasize it. I haven't heard it discussed for a long time in public discourse, I don't know . . . .'"[20] Again in 1997 Hinckley said this in response to yet another request: "Question: 'Don't Mormons believe that God was once a man?' Hinckley: 'I wouldn't say that. There was a little couplet coined, As man is, God once was. As God is, man may become. Now that's more of a couplet than anything else.'"[21] Joseph Smith, as Hinckley well knew, ultimately taught his followers that baptized members of "the church of the Firstborn" would become "gods, even the sons of God." As such, and because exalted, they would dwell with God in a "celestial kingdom."[22]

> *[I]f a man marry a wife by my word, which is my law, and by the new and everlasting covenant [polygamy], . . . and if ye abide in my covenant, and commit no murder whereby to shed innocent blood . . . Then shall they be gods because they have no end; therefore shall they be from everlasting to everlasting, because they continue; then shall they be above all, because all things are subject unto them. Then shall they be gods, because they have all power, and the angels are*

Franklin D. Richards, 1856], 375). The term "ancient of days" is reserved in scripture for the Father of all. "Adam is the great Archangel of this creation. He is Michael. He is the Ancient of Days. *He is the father of our elder brother, Jesus Christ* – the father of him who shall come as Messiah to reign. He is the father of the spirits as well as the tabernacles of the sons and daughters of man. Adam!" (Edward W. Tullidge, *The Women of Mormondom* [New York: 1877], 179, emphasis added). Like her next plural husband, Brigham Young, Eliza taught that "Adam and Eve are the names of the fathers and mothers of worlds." Every first man is Adam and every first woman is Eve. (Ibid., 180).

[20]David Van Biema, "Kingdom Come," *Time Magazine*, vol. 150 no. 5 (4 August 1997), 51-57.

[21]Don Lattin, "Sunday Interview – Musings of the Main Mormon/Gordon B. Hinckley, 'president, prophet, seer and revelator' of the Church of Jesus Christ of Latter-day Saints, sits at the top of one of the world's fastest-growing religions," *The San Francisco Chronicle* (13 April 1997), 3/Z1.

[22]John G. Turner, *Brigham Young: Pioneer Prophet* (Belknap Press of Harvard University Press, 2012), 33.

subject unto them.[23]

Joseph Smith was the first Latter-day Saint to articulate the doctrine that Adam was God. Brigham Young: *"Adam ["the Ancient of Days"] . . . holds the keys of everlasting life . . . . I could not find any man on the earth who could tell me this . . . until I met and talked with Joseph Smith."*[24] In 1860, the Minutes of the Quorum of the Twelve Apostles reported that, *"It was Joseph's doctrine that Adam was God . . ."*[25] "[T]hat Adam was at once the spiritual as well as the physical father of all persons born in this world, including Jesus Christ,"[26] was Joseph's doctrine. It then later became Brigham's doctrine as enumerated in various discourses and in the Lecture at the Veil, which was part of the temple ritual for many years. Until it was dismissed, after the deaths of Joseph Smith and Brigham Young, because it said that Adam was God. In Joseph and Brigham's Church, Adam was God and Jehovah, and Jehovah wasn't Jesus. George Q. Cannon, a vastly influential figure in the nineteenth-century Church, praised Joseph and Brigham's *"doctrine."* *"[T]hat Adam is our Father is a true doctrine revealed from God to Joseph to Brigham."*[27] During his presidency, Wilford Woodruff concurred with them when he also

---

[23]Doctrine and Covenants 132:19-20, emphasis added.

[24]*Deseret News*, 18 June 1873, emphasis added. *Young attributed the Adam-God doctrine to Joseph Smith at the Salt Lake School of the Prophets on April 4, 1860, December 16, 1867, and May 14, 1876.* Adam was God in 1877, the year that Brigham Young died.

[25]Minutes, 4 April 1860, Quorum of the Twelve Apostles (LDS Church History Library), emphasis added.

[26]Gary James Bergera, "The Orson Pratt-Brigham Young Controversies: Conflict Within the Quorums, 1853 to 1864," *Dialogue: A Journal of Mormon Thought*, 13(2) (1980): 41. Bergera aptly described the doctrine without assigning it to Smith.

[27]George Q. Cannon quoted in Wilford Woodruff's Journal, 4 September 1860, quoted in Fred C. Collier, *President Brigham Young's Doctrine of Deity, Volume 1* (Hanna, UT: Collier's Publishing Co., 1999), 360, emphasis added. George Q. Cannon, next to Joseph Smith and Brigham Young perhaps the most important Mormon leader of the nineteenth century, shared Brigham's view (Adam was God, and Joseph said so), and the Quorum's view (Adam was God and Joseph said so). Cannon fully endorsed the doctrine that Father Adam was God at the School of the Prophets in the Utah Territory in 1870. (Remarks given on 15 October 1870, *Salt Lake School of the Prophets Minute Book*, LDS Archives, as cited in David John Buerger, "The Adam-God Doctrine," *Dialogue: A Journal of Mormon Thought*, vol. 15 no. 1, [Spring 1982], 31).

said that Adam was God. Woodruff's allegiance to Adam as the Father was reaffirmed shortly before his own death just prior to the end of the nineteenth century.

JOSEPH SMITH AND A FINITE GOD

"On April 7 [1844], Joseph Smith gave his most famous sermon, namely the King Follett Sermon, announcing that the eternal and unchanging God of the Bible and *Book of Mormon* does not exist, rather, 'he would refute the idea that God was God from all eternity. God that sits enthroned is a man like one of yourselves.'"[28] *He was a man; he is now a god.* A finite deity, by this reckoning, an anthropomorphic god in a grove, was then supposed to have orchestrated an infinite atonement. Traditional Christians found that incomprehensible.

THE SUPERNATURAL

Joseph Smith and Sidney Rigdon embraced doctrines promulgated by the Swedish mystic Emanuel Swedenborg, including concepts of the afterlife (three tiers of glory, realms likened to the sun, the moon and the stars), elements of marriage (required to reach the highest degree in the celestial division), and the concept of the spirit world (a transitional stage between heaven and earth). Swedenborg, who lived and died before Smith and Rigdon were born, described "the pure heavenly speech of angels" and a multiplicity of "visions and wonders." His own literary masterpiece *Heaven and Hell* "became an American bestseller in the 1820s." Joseph Smith and Sidney Rigdon went to school on the teachings of the Swedish cleric Emanuel Swedenborg.

Early Mormons accepted the supernatural in some of its most extreme manifestations. "Prophets appeared, men and women filled with the Holy Ghost spoke in tongues, and believers told of angelic visitors."[29] Dead husbands visited living wives and dead mothers visited living sons. Visions, spirit possession, spiritual

---

[28]Melonakos, *Secret Combinations*, 388.
[29]Turner, *Brigham Young: Pioneer Prophet*, 29.

tongues and gifts and healings and visitations, although not so common now, were early Mormon staples. Joseph Smith gave instructions to his followers about how to encounter angels and devils. According to Smith, the devil could transform "himself nigh unto an Angel of Light." Smith directed his followers "to verify angelic encounters by shaking hands with purported angels. If 'the man takes hold of his hand . . . and feels no substance he may know it is Satan.' In Smith's heaven, an angel was a 'Saint with a resurrected body,' and thus today's Saints on earth were tomorrow's angels in heaven and already could greet their angelic brethren as equals.'"[30]

Joseph Smith solemnly informed his followers that, "There are those of the rising generation who shall not taste death till Christ comes." The Doctrine and Covenants, where Jesus supposedly speaks, says repeatedly that "I come quickly," etc. Apparently "quickly" didn't mean any time in the following one hundred eighty years. "I was once praying earnestly upon this subject, and a voice said unto me, 'My son, if thou livest until thou art eighty-five years of age, thou shalt see the face of the Son of Man.' ... I prophesy in the name of the Lord God, and let it be written – the Son of Man will not come in the clouds of heaven till I am eighty-five years old [1890]."[31] "He clarified that this meant '48 years hence or about 1890' and said he had received this communication on April 2, 1843, at Ramus, Illinois"[32] (where he was courting Almera Johnson,

---

[30]Ibid., 64. "Key to detect Satan: As there are many Keys to the Kingdom of God the following one will detect Satan when he transforms himself nigh unto an Angel of Light. When Satan appears in the form of a personage unto man &— reaches out his hand unto him & the man takes hold of his hand & feels no substance he may know it is satan. for an angel of God (which is an angel of light) is a saint with his resurrected body & when he appears unto man and offers him his hand & the man feels a substance when he takes hold of it as he would in shaking hands with his neighbor he may know it is an Angel of God, & should a Saint appear unto man whose body is not resurrected he will never offer him his hand for it would be against the law by which they are governed & by observing this Key we may detect Satan that he deceive us not." ("Discourse, 27 June 1839, as Reported by Willard Richards," *The Joseph Smith Papers*, 9-10).

[31]Roberts, ed., *History of The Church of Jesus Christ of Latter-day Saints*, 5:336-37 (April 1843).

[32]Scott H. Faulring, *An American Prophet's Record: The Diaries and Journals of Joseph Smith* (Salt Lake City, UT: Signature Books and Smith Research Associates, 1987), 349, quoted in George D. Smith, *Nauvoo Polygamy: "... but we*

who would soon become his twenty-first plural wife).   With the restoration of the ancient order of things, the second coming of Christ was "at hand."[33]   Smith didn't live to the age of eighty-five, and the promised Second Coming never occurred.

THIS IS THE PLACE

Joseph Smith informed his followers with apocalyptic urgency that Zion in Jackson County, Missouri, was their consecrated place of refuge, the place of the city of the New Jerusalem, the place of the gathering, and the place where Christ would come to his temple. It was the place where the Latter-day Saints would avoid the harsh consequences of the day of desolation, inherit the wealth of the Gentiles and rule the world when Christ literally came and Babylon literally fell before the end of the nineteenth century.[34]

Joseph Smith unriddled "the mystery of the Lost Ten Tribes" when he told his faithful followers that Israel's missing tribes lived in a land "contiguous to the north pole, separated from the rest of the world by impassable mountains of ice and snow."[35]   While the world wondered about the Ten Lost Tribes, Mormonism's visionaries informed their disciples that they had "discovered their place of residence."   In their "sequestered" isolation, the Lost

---

called it celestial marriage" (Salt Lake City: Signature Books, 2008), 6. See also Doctrine and Covenants 130:14-16.

[33]"[T]he keys of this dispensation are committed into your hands [Elijah had come to fulfill Malachi's prophecy that he "should be sent, before the great and dreadful day of the Lord . . ."]; and by this ye may know that the great and dreadful day of the Lord is near, even at the doors." (Doctrine and Covenants 110:13-16).

[34]"The plan is . . . ingeniously contrived, having for its aim one principal point, viz: the establishment of a society in Missouri, over which the contrivers of this delusive system, are to possess unlimited and despotic sway." (Eber D. Howe, *Mormonism Unvailed: Or, A Faithful Account of That Singular Imposition and Delusion* [Painesville, OH: E.D. Howe, 1834; reprint, New York: AMS Press Inc., 1977], Ezra Booth Letters, 178). Joseph Smith told Brigham Young in Kirtland, Ohio, to "[n]ever do another day's work to build up a Gentile [non-Mormon] city." (Turner, *Brigham Young: Pioneer Prophet*, 34). In 1843 he said that, "The sectarian world are going to hell by hundreds, by thousands, and by millions." (Roberts, ed., *History of The Church of Jesus Christ of Latter-day Saints*, 5:554).

[35]Brodie, *No man knows my history*, 111.

Tribes "enjoy the society of Elijah the Prophet, and John the Revelator and perhaps the three immortalized Nephites. By and by, the mountains of ice and snow are to give way, and open a passage for the return of these tribes, to the land of Palestine."[36]

Joseph Smith taught his faithful followers that Zion, revealed by revelation to be located at or near the city of Independence in Jackson County, Missouri, was and would always be the Saints' earthly and eternal inheritance. Smith told the Saints that the temple Christ would visit when he returned again would be built at that place in that generation. "18 Nov. [1860], Brigham Young: 'right where the Prophet Joseph laid the Foundation of the Temple, in the Center Stake of Zion [near Independence, Missouri], was where God commenced the Garden of Eden, & there He will end or Consummate his work.'"[37]

POLYGAMY

While Joseph Smith publicly (and in his private journal) denied he was a polygamist, he was privately and secretly practicing polygamy with close to forty women, many of whom were legally married and civilly covenanted to other men (and undivorced) when they also married him.[38] In one frenetic stretch, the Mormon prophet married about thirty-four women in about twenty-two months.[39] His polyandrous women often had biological children with their legal husbands. Most of the husbands were faithful Latter-day Saints when Joseph also married their wives. Two of his non-polyandrous wives were fourteen years old,[40] about nine of

---

[36]Howe, *Mormonism Unvailed*, Ezra Booth Letters, 185-86.

[37]Quinn, *The Mormon Hierarchy: Extensions of Power*, 760.

[38]George D. Smith, *Nauvoo Polygamy*, 621-23. Mrs. Zina Diantha Huntington (Jacobs); Mrs. Presendia Lathrop Huntington (Buell); Mrs. Lucinda Pendleton (Morgan) (Harris); Mrs. Mary Elizabeth Rollins (Lightner); Mrs. Sylvia Porter Sessions (Lyon); Mrs. Patty Barlett (Sessions); Mrs. Sarah M. Kingsley (Howe) (Cleveland); Mrs. Elizabeth Davis (G. Brackenbury) (Durfee); Mrs. Marinda Nancy Johnson (Hyde); Mrs. Sarah Rapson (Poulterer); Mrs. Ruth Daggett Vose (Sayers); Mrs. Elvira Anna Cowles (Holmes); Mrs. Phebe Watrous (Woodworth).

[39]6 January 1842 to 2 November 1843. George D. Smith, *Nauvoo Polygamy*, 621-23.

[40]Helen Mar Kimball and Nancy Winchester. (Ibid.).

them (including the fourteen-year-olds, but not the problematic Miss Fanny Alger) were teenagers.[41]   He married three sets of sisters and at least one and possibly two sets of mothers and daughters.[42] In addition to his already legally married women – women who were supported by and continued to live and cohabit with their legal husbands, and to raise their biological children – he directed propositions or polyandrous proposals to no less than four other married women (Mrs. Orson Pratt, Mrs. William Law, Mrs. Hiram Kimball, Mrs. Robert D. Foster), all of whom rejected him. The Mormon leader told Miss Nancy Rigdon that her marrying him "would not prevent her from marrying any other person."[43]   He informed Miss Martha Brotherton, a seventeen-year-old English convert whom he tried to persuade to marry Brigham Young, that if Brigham Young "turns you off, I will take you on."[44] If the four already married women who received but rejected his overtures had accepted them, if Miss Rigdon had agreed to the prophet's proposal and taken another husband, if Miss Southerton had married Brigham Young and he had turned her off and Smith had

---

[41]Sarah Ann Whitney; Flora Ann Woodworth; Emily Dow Partridge; Lucy Walker; Sarah Lawrence; Maria Lawrence; Helen Mar Kimball; Nancy Maria Winchester; Melissa Lott. (Ibid.). If Smith had married Fanny Alger, who was fourteen years old in 1831, the number of the prophet's teenage wives would have increased to ten. In this twenty-first century, the Church contends that he did marry Fanny Alger. ("After marrying Fanny Alger sometime before 1836, Joseph, it appears, married no one else until . . . 1841 . . . ." [Bushman, *Rough Stone Rolling*, 437]. "Several Latter-day Saints who lived in Kirtland in the 1830s later reported that Fanny Alger married Joseph Smith, becoming his first plural wife." ["Fanny Alger" (n.d., accessed 19 February 2019), available from https://www.lds.org/study/history/topics/fanny-alger?lang=eng; Internet, p. 1 of 2]).

[42]*Sisters*: Zina Diantha Huntington (Jacobs) and Presendia Lathrop Huntington (Buell); Emily Dow Partridge and Eliza Maria Partridge; Sarah Lawrence and Maria Lawrence. *Mothers and Daughters*: Patty Bartlett (Sessions) and Sylvia Porter Sessions (Lyon), Phebe Watrous Woodworth and Flora Ann Woodworth. (George D. Smith, *Nauvoo Polygamy*, 621-23). Phebe Woodworth was a member of Joseph's privileged anointed, "and was sealed to him instead of her civil husband, himself a polygamist, after Joseph's death." Two scholars, Compton and Quinn, are unconvinced (or doubtful) that the facts surrounding the Woodworths implied "a temporal relationship." (Ibid., 653 n 376, cf. 651 n 367).

[43]John C. Bennett, *The History of the Saints: Or, an Expose of Joe Smith and Mormonism* (Boston: Leland & Whiting, 1842; photomechanical reprint of 1842 original, Salt Lake City, UT: Modern Microfilm Company), 242.

[44]Martha Brotherton to John C. Bennett, 13 July 1842, correspondence reproduced at Bennett, *The History of the Saints*, 236-40, 239.

taken her on, Smith's total would have risen to nineteen or twenty polyandrous wives. He has since been sealed posthumously to many married women, including women of distinction, some of whom preceded him in life, and some of whom followed him in death.

According to his daughter Ina Coolbrith, Don Carlos Smith (Joseph Smith's younger brother) caught a violent cold and suffered a fever, preceded by "a severe pain in his side." "[W]ith all our exertions, we were unable to arrest the disease, which I have no doubt was consumption, brought on by working in a damp room [the "printing cellar" of the *Times and Seasons*]." "Don Carlos died on August 7 [1841] at the age of twenty-five. On his deathbed, according to Ina Coolbrith . . . when Joseph Smith asked him if he had a last request, he replied, 'Yes, I have, Joseph Smith, I want you for the rest of your life to be an honest man.'"[45] On January 6, 1842, Don Carlos Smith's widow, Agnes Moulton Coolbrith (Smith), plurally married Joseph Smith. When Agnes married her dead husband's brother, she became the fifth of his nearly forty wives. After a checkered course and much travail, and after the death of Joseph Smith, Agnes married George A. Smith, the prophet's cousin, another important early Mormon leader. In 1847, feeling abandoned by George A. Smith, she married William Pickett. Agnes Moulton Coolbrith (Smith) (Smith) (Smith) (Pickett) died out of the Church in California on December 26, 1876. Ina Coolbrith, Joseph Smith's niece and a literary figure in Oakland (who didn't take the name of the Smiths), reported these as her mother's last words[46]: "O! what a dupe I have been; what a dupe I have been!"[47]

On May 14, 1843, almost a year after John C. Bennett's departure, Presiding Patriarch and Associate President Hyrum Smith (Joseph Smith's older brother) "assures a [Nauvoo] citywide congregation that only the Devil would give a revelation approving 'wife's &

---

[45]Todd Compton, *In Sacred Loneliness: The Plural Wives of Joseph Smith* (Salt Lake City: Signature Books, 2001), 153.

[46]Ina's report is preserved for posterity in a 1918 letter (quoting her) sent by Joseph F. Smith, her cousin (although her mother married three of them, Ina wasn't known as a Smith). Joseph F. Smith challenged Ina's report. (Ibid., 169).

[47]Ibid.

concubines.'"[48]   On August 12, 1843, Hyrum Smith, who took his first plural wife on August 11, 1843 (in a ceremony officiated by his brother Joseph Smith), presented a revelation (Section 132 of the Doctrine and Covenants) that approved wives and concubines to the Nauvoo Stake High Council for its consideration. At that meeting (a meeting without written minutes), he said that members who did not accept a revelation that required them to practice polygamy would be damned. In 1841 Don Carlos Smith, the husband of Agnes Coolbrith, told Ebenezer Robinson (they were co-editors of the *Times and Seasons*) that "any man who will teach and practice the doctrine of spiritual wifery will go to hell; I don't care if it is my brother Joseph."[49]

SEALINGS

Joseph Smith was sealed to Louisa Beaman, said by some to have been the first plural wife in this dispensation, on April 5, 1841 (and perhaps even earlier) by Joseph Noble. They were married in a grove of trees in Nauvoo, Illinois. Miss Beaman concealed her identity for a clandestine service by disguising herself as a man. Joseph Smith wasn't sealed to Emma Smith until May 28, 1843, meaning until about twenty-six months after he was sealed to Louisa Beaman.[50] To be sealed was to be bonded for time on earth

---

[48]D. Michael Quinn, *The Mormon Hierarchy: Origins of Power* (Salt Lake City: Signature Books in association with Smith Research Associates, 1994), 638.

[49]Compton, *In Sacred Loneliness: The Plural Wives of Joseph Smith*, 152.

[50]After he was sealed to Miss Beaman and before he was sealed to Emma Smith, his legal wife, Joseph Smith would seem to have been sealed to no less than twenty-four other women. Their names, and the likely dates of their sealings, may be stated as follows: Louisa Beaman, April 5, 1841; Mrs. Zina Diantha Huntington (Jacobs), October 27, 1841; Mrs. Presendia Lathrop Huntington (Buell), December 11, 1841; Agnes Moulton Coolbrith (Smith), January 6, 1842; Mrs. Lucinda Pendleton (Morgan) (Harris), before January 17, 1842; Mrs. Mary Elizabeth Rollins (Lightner), February 1842; Mrs. Sylvia Porter Sessions (Lyon), February 8, 1842; Mrs. Patty Bartlett (Sessions), March 9, 1842; Mrs. Sarah M. Kingsley (Howe Cleveland), before March 1842; Mrs. Elizabeth Davis (G. Brackenbury Durfee), March 1842; Mrs. Marinda Nancy Johnson (Hyde), April 1842; Delcena Diadamia Johnson (Sherman), ca. June 1842; Eliza Roxcy Snow, June 29, 1842; Mrs. Sarah Rapson (Poulterer), before July 1842; Sarah Ann Whitney, July 27, 1842; Martha McBride (Knight), before August 5, 1842; Mrs. Ruth Daggett Vose (Sayers), February 1843; Flora Ann Woodworth, March 4, 1843; Emily Dow Partridge, March 4, 1843; Eliza Maria Partridge, March 8, 1843; Almera

and in the life to come.

IDIOSYNCRACIES (MAGIC AND POWER)

Encouraged by his father, his money-digging mentor, Joseph Smith convinced his early followers that he could tell fortunes, locate lost things, interpret ancient plates and receive revelations with an unusual stone found while digging a well for "Mr. Chase." Smith used the same stone that he used as a money-digging treasure-seeking seer in search of "filthy lucre" (Joseph Sr.'s term) to receive some of his early revelations, but then and most importantly to translate the Book of Mormon. The magic stone, an artifact in the possession of the modern Church (it was concealed and suppressed), was photographed (but not publicly displayed) in 2015, nearly one hundred ninety years after it was observed by others in Smith's money-digging criminal proceedings heard by Judge Albert Neely in Bainbridge, New York, on March 20, 1826.[51]

On May 27, 1843, Joseph reported that, "The patriarchal office [the

---

Woodward Johnson, before April 25, 1843; Lucy Walker, May 1, 1843; Sarah Lawrence, May 11, 1843; Maria Lawrence, ca. May 1843; and Helen Mar Kimball, ca. May 1843. *Emma Hale, May 28, 1843.*

[51]On March 20, 1843, James C. Brewster published "his claim that as part of an 1836 Ohio treasure-quest, Presiding Patriarch Joseph Smith, Sr., 'anointed the mineral rods and seeing stones with consecrated oil, and prayed over them in the house of the Lord in Kirtland." (Quinn, *Origins of Power*, 637). The prophet's father did that in the temple while serving as the Presiding Patriarch. On June 6, 1844, just before the death of Joseph Smith on June 27, 1844, Apostle Heber C. Kimball "clothes himself in endowment robes and prays in the 'true order,' while holding a divining 'rod' . . . ." Kimball asks for answers to "yes-no questions." The movement of the rod means "yes," the failure of the rod to move, means "no." (Ibid., 645). An 1829 revelation "commended Cowdery's use of his 'rod of nature' . . . behold it has told you things." (Ibid.). Some years later and on July 28, 1847, Brigham Young selected the site of the Salt Lake Temple by using Oliver Cowdery's divining rod. (Ibid., 659). In March of 1826, Peter Bridgman, a nephew of Joseph's patron Josiah Stowell, issued a warrant that accused Smith of being "a disorderly person and an impostor." Those issues are more fully described by Wesley P. Walters in "Joseph Smith's Bainbridge, N.Y., Court Trials," reprinted by permission from the *Westminster Theological Journal* 36, no. 2 (Winter 1974) (Salt Lake City: Utah Lighthouse Ministry, 1974 and 1977), 123-55; Marvin S. Hill, "Joseph Smith and the 1826 Trial: New Evidence and New Difficulties," *BYU Studies*, 12 (Winter 1972).

office of the Presiding Patriarch] is the highest in the church, and father Smith conferred this office, on Hyrum Smith, on his death bed."[52]   On July 16, 1843, Joseph Smith said he "would not prophesy any more, and proposed Hyrum to hold the office of prophet to the Church, as it was his birthright" as the Presiding Patriarch.[53] On February 1, 1844, a few months before they died, Joseph and Hyrum jointly signed a "Notice," directed to one Hiram Brown as "Presidents of said Church."[54] On June 15, 1844, "The Presiding Patriarch publishes an announcement signed as 'HYRUM SMITH, President of the Church.'"[55] In 1979, long after the death of Joseph Smith, the previously heralded "highest" office of the Presiding Patriarch was discontinued, allowed (designed) to disappear.[56]

A COUNCIL OF FIFTY

Joseph Smith created, then others perpetuated, maintained and administered the Council of Fifty, a reveal your membership and your agenda at the risk of your life secret society. (This publicly silent Council secretly ordained Joseph Smith, Brigham Young and John Taylor to be Kings, Priests, and Rulers over the kingdom of Israel on Earth). The Council of Fifty was a shadow government created to rule the world when Mormons took control during the lifetimes of some of the members before the end of the nineteenth century. Included among the Mormon luminaries on this less than sacred super secret council were two allegedly notorious killers,

---

[52]Quinn, *Origins of Power*, 638.

[53]Ibid., 639.

[54]*Times and Seasons* 5 (1 February 1844): 423.

[55]Quinn, *Origins of Power*, 645.

[56]Almost no one now speaks of a separate patriarchal third order of the priesthood.   Joseph Smith described three grand orders of priesthood and is supposed to have said that the "second Priesthood, Abraham's Patriarchal power, was the greatest yet experienced in the Church." (Roberts, ed., *History of The Church of Jesus Christ of Latter-day Saints*, 5:554-55. Andrew F. Ehat and Lyndon W. Cook, *The Words of Joseph Smith: The Contemporary Accounts of the Nauvoo Discourses of the Prophet Joseph Smith* [Provo, UT: Religious Studies Center, Brigham Young University, 1980], 245, quoted in Quinn, *Origins of Power*, 34). Joseph's fawning flirtation with Abraham – the power of Abraham, the Egyptian papyri and the Book of Abraham – created a monumental problem for the Church and its apologists.

Orrin Porter Rockwell and Hosea Stout. Both of those particularly violent men died with all of their priesthood and temple blessings intact. Their callings and elections have been made sure by leaders who claimed the authority to confer salvation and glory upon allegedly notorious criminals,[57] including John D. Lee, another member of the Council of Fifty.

Before his death, Joseph Smith instructed his scribe William Clayton to destroy the controversial Minutes of the Council of Fifty, or put them in some perfectly safe place in some totally dependable hands. They were not intended to see the light of day, and some of them were burned. Clayton buried them in his garden. The Church, which concealed and suppressed those indelicate resources for more than one hundred fifty years, has only recently (in the year 2016) in the face of incessant clamor finally released them in turbulent times for better or worse.

> *[A]mong the first forty members that joined Joseph's Council of Fifty by March 19, 1844, at least fourteen were known or suspected counterfeiters. This count includes the members of the Quorum of the Twelve who would be federally indicted for counterfeiting in 1845 (Brigham Young, John Taylor, Parley P. Pratt, Willard Richards, and Orson Hyde) as well as several members whose main association with Smith appears to be counterfeiting, such as non-Mormons Edward*

---

[57]The fabled second anointing, selling escape from sins (and by implication license to sin) for service and high standing in the Church, is supposed to make the callings and elections of its recipients, a tiny group of the truly elite (with some exceptions made for scoundrels), eternally secure. This earthly assurance of salvation and glory for those who have committed sins *not supposed to include* the shedding of innocent blood or the denial of the Holy Ghost is still administered in the twenty-first century by those who continue to say they have the power to act in pursuance of such pursuits in the sacred name of God. Mormonism's second anointing is the ultimate indulgence, a twenty-first century sin. Two estranged Mormon leaders, men of stature whose faiths collapsed, Tom Phillips, a Stake president in the United Kingdom, and Hans Mattsson, a General Authority Area Leader from Sweden, have described having received (with their wives) the secret second anointing in the twenty-first century. ("Episode #985: Truth Seeking with Hans and Birgitta Mattsson, Pt. 2," Mormon Stories, hosted by Dr. John Dehlin [published 27 September 2018]. "Tom Phillips, The Second Anointing, and LDS Apostle Jeffrey R. Holland," Mormon Stories, by John Dehlin [27 April 2015].)

Bonney and Marinus G. Eaton, and Mormons Peter Haws, Theodore Turley and John Bernhisel.[58]

SCRIPTURES AND TRANSLATION

Joseph Smith included Isaiah passages supposed to have been excerpted from the brass plates of Laban – parts of which were actually written long after Lehi and his family left Jerusalem by persons other than the original Isaiah – as ancient elements of the Book of Mormon. After nearly two centuries claiming translation from the gold plates with the aid of Urim and Thummim interpreters, Smith is now resupposed to have translated the Book of Mormon by looking at a peepstone in a stovepipe hat. All of this is now resupposed to have occurred while the golden plates were covered with cloth or hidden in the woods. Pomeroy Tucker, a Palmyra resident, described Joseph's "insignificant little stone," a magic artifact, as "the acorn of the Mormon oak."[59] It was the same stone the money-digging treasure-seeking seer had much earlier used to tell fortunes and locate lost things.

Joseph Smith demonstrated his translation skills when he copied discretionary italicized words added to the 1611 and 1769 editions of the King James Bible by seventeenth and eighteenth-century translators in his nineteenth-century "translation" of the Book of Mormon. He then also reproduced translation errors found in the 1769 edition of the King James Bible. Those errors (anachronisms like the Isaiah passages) infected the Mormon Bible– a history of the hemisphere covering events supposed to have occurred from 2200 B.C. to 421 A.D. – a work the "translation of which" the

---

[58]Kathleen Kimball Melonakos, *Secret Combinations: Evidence of Early Mormon Counterfeiting 1800-1847* (Lyrical Productions, 2016), 386, emphasis added and retained. "[John C.] Bennett [Joseph Smith's one-time "bosom" friend] may or may not have dealt in counterfeit money, yet he certainly lived the life of a nineteenth century con-man: claiming titles and degrees he did not earn, pocketing money on false pretenses, forging names on public documents, acting out different identities in different places, and constantly relocating to avoid detection." (Ibid., 347. *See, e.g.,* Andrew F. Smith, *The Saintly Scoundrel: The Life and Times of Dr. John Cook Bennett* [Urbana and Chicago: University of Illinois, 1997]).

[59]Pomeroy Tucker Account (1867), Dan Vogel, ed., *Early Mormon Documents* (Salt Lake City: Signature Books, 2000), 3:99.

Mormon leader chose to call "the most correct of any book on earth."

Smith and those who succeeded him claimed (contrary to everything we now know and for close to one hundred and seventy-five years) that he translated the Book of Mormon from the golden plates with the aid of the Urim and Thummim by the gift and power of God. His scribes faithfully described his method of translation, no matter the interpreters, as word for word correct. The translation – according to the early reports of important witnesses Martin Harris, Emma Smith, Oliver Cowdery, and David Whitmer – was not discretionary. According to them, it was produced in its first edition in final form by the gift and power of God. Others who were not witnesses to the translation, but rather inspired to know of it – Joseph F. Smith (and his reporter Oliver Huntington) – repeated those contemporaneous claims.

Joseph Smith informed his followers ("the eyes of our understanding were opened"[60]) that Elijah and Elias – Hebrew and Greek names for the same Old Testament prophet – were actually two different prophets. He then compounded that colossal error when he reported that both of them appeared to him and to Oliver Cowdery behind a veil in the Kirtland Temple on April 3, 1836.[61] On that day Mormonism's founders said they saw Jesus Christ "standing upon the breastwork of the pulpit" in the Kirtland Temple. After that they said they saw Moses, who came to confer "the keys of the gathering of Israel" and the return "of the ten tribes from the land to the north." Then Elias came to commit "the dispensation of the gospel of Abraham" (the Patriarchal Priesthood). After all of that and finally, still on April 3, Elijah came to "turn the hearts of the fathers to the children, and the children to the fathers, lest the whole earth be smitten with a curse (D&C 110)." Joseph and Oliver's Elias and Joseph and Oliver's Elijah are the same person in the Bible, but in the Doctrine and Covenants, they are described as two different persons. In Section 27 of the Doctrine and Covenants, *Joseph's God* identifies Elijah

---

[60]Doctrine and Covenants 110:1.

[61]*In that same year in that same temple*, Joseph Smith Sr., the then Presiding Patriarch, anointed mineral rods and a seeing stone with consecrated oil, before praying over them prior to a treasure-seeking adventure.

and Elias as separate persons supposed to have come at different times to deliver different authorities. The Ten Lost Tribes didn't ever appear, and the hereditary Patriarchal Priesthood, after the deaths of the Smiths and the passage of time, became inconvenient, a threat to the un-Smiths. In this modern age there is no Presiding Patriarch, and the separate Priesthood that said that there was has been dismissed.

Joseph Smith said that Abraham, Moses and Aaron, three ancient patriarchs, actually wrote upon the ancient Egyptian papyri, which he acquired at Kirtland. He then translated part of one of the rolls prepared by and at the direction of those patriarchs to become the Book of Abraham. He told two important early American visitors that Abraham's papyri, now known to have been dated approximately 2000 years after the era of Abraham, included the autographs of Abraham and Moses and lines written by Aaron. He further represented that "one of the rolls" contained "the writings of Joseph of Egypt."

Forty-three days before his death in 1844, Joseph Smith was visited at Nauvoo, Illinois, by Charles Francis Adams (the son of former American President John Quincy Adams) and by Charles' cousin Josiah Quincy. Both of those distinguished visitors ("Boston Brahmins") kept journals recording the details of their visit. "Ten closely written pages of my journal [Quincy] describe my impressions of Nauvoo, and of its prophet, mayor, general and judge . . . ." After a discussion about theology, the Mormon leader showed his guests "the curiosities" (Egyptian mummies and papyri preserved under glass) and introduced them to his mother who had, he said, purchased them "with her own money, at a cost of six thousand dollars." He first showed them "four human bodies, shrunken and black with age" preserved in "some pine presses fixed against the wall of the room." "These are mummies," he said. "I want you to look at that little runt of a fellow over there. He was a great man in his day. Why, that was Pharaoh Necho, King of Egypt."

Next he directed their attention to some "parchments inscribed with hieroglyphics." They were not spread out or lengthy. "They were preserved under glass and handled with great respect." *"That is the handwriting of Abraham, the Father of the Faithful,"* Smith said. *"This is the autograph of Moses, and these lines were written by his brother Aaron. Here we have the earliest account of the Creation, from which Moses composed the First Book of Genesis."*[62] (Modern scholars now mostly concede that Moses did not compose "the First Book of Genesis.") At yet another place, the Mormon leader described those same papyri in these terms:

> *I commenced the translation of some of the characters or hieroglyphics, and much to our joy found that one of the rolls contained the writings of Abraham, another the writings of Joseph of Egypt etc., – a more full account of which will appear in its place, as I proceed to examine or unfold them.*[63]

The papyri were not purchased by the prophet's mother for six thousand dollars or at all, but rather by some citizens in Kirtland for twenty-four hundred dollars, no small sum at the time. What the Mormon prophet told his visitors about the papyri and their purchase wasn't true. The manuscripts had nothing to do with Abraham and did not contain the autograph of Moses or lines "written by his brother Aaron."

Joseph Smith informed another visitor, Reverend Henry Caswall, that Caswall's Greek Psalter was an Egyptian dictionary. Caswall visited Joseph Smith at Nauvoo, Illinois, on April 19, 1842. Professor Caswall, an Episcopal Clergyman, carried an ancient Greek Psalter[64] written on parchment. The manuscript was hundreds of years old but of discernible identity. Reverend Caswall asked Smith to examine the ancient manuscript and tell him what it was. After he had examined the document, Joseph told his visitor it was an Egyptian dictionary (A Dictionary of Ancient Egyptian Hieroglyphics). When Caswall made it clear that the prophet had

---

[62]"Two Boston Brahmins Call on the Prophet," in William Mulder and A. Russell Mortensen, eds., *Among the Mormons: Historic Accounts by Contemporary Observers* (New York: Alfred A. Knopf, 1958), 131-42, emphasis added.

[63]Roberts, ed., *History of The Church of Jesus Christ of Latter-day Saints*, 2:236, emphasis added.

[64]A Psalter is a volume containing the Book of Psalms that may be supplemented with other devotional material.

misrepresented the contents of the ancient document, the prophet abruptly left his visitor and the room in which they met and didn't return. This small but meaningful event cast doubt upon Smith's ability as a translator. One may presume that Joseph Smith applied the same set of skills that he applied to the identification of Caswall's Greek Psalter to the Book of Mormon, the Anthon Manuscript, the Inspired Translation of the King James Bible, St. John's Parchment, the Kinderhook Plates, the Egyptian Papyri, the Grammar and Alphabet of the Egyptian Language, and the now notorious Book of Abraham.

In May 1843, Joseph Smith claimed he had partially translated fraudulent Kinderhook plates.

> *I [Joseph] insert fac-similes of the six brass plates found near Kinderhook, in Pike County, Illinois, on April 23, by Mr. Robert Wiley and others, while excavating a large mound. They found a skeleton about six feet from the surface of the earth, which must have stood nine feet high. The plates were found on the breast of the skeleton and were covered on both sides with ancient characters. I have translated a portion of them, and find that they contain the history of the person with whom they were found. He was a descendant of Ham, through the loins of Pharaoh, king of Egypt, and [I concluded] that he received his kingdom from the Ruler of heaven and earth.*[65]

The Kinderhook Plates have since proved to be nineteenth-century fraudulent productions created by rascals determined to test the prophet's translation integrity. The Church treated the plates as authentic for one hundred thirty-seven years, and until 1980. In 1920 one of the plates came into the possession of the Chicago Historical Society (now the Chicago History Museum). In 1980 that remaining plate was scientifically examined by experts at Northwestern University. Their testing concluded, because of the plates' composition, that it was not of ancient origin. It was further

---

[65]Roberts, ed., *History of The Church of Jesus Christ of Latter-day Saints* (1978), 5:372, emphasis added.

determined that it had been etched with acid and not engraved.[66] Facsimiles of the plates were reproduced by the Church and described as authentic in this author's 1978 edition of the History of the Church.[67] In 1981 the Church admitted the plates were a hoax but denied they had fooled the prophet Joseph Smith.

THE INSPIRED TRANSLATION OF THE KING JAMES BIBLE

Joseph Smith told the members of the Church in the Articles of Faith that, "We believe the Bible to be the word of God as far as it is translated correctly." In the *History of the Church* the Mormon founder added this: "I believe the Bible as it read when it came from the pen of the original writers. Ignorant translators, careless transcribers, or designing and corrupt priests have committed many errors."[68]

On March 7, 1831, Joseph's God instructed Joseph to begin to more correctly "translate" the New Testament (Doctrine and Covenants 45:60-61), and on March 8, 1833, Joseph's God directed him to finish the "translation" of the Old Testament (Doctrine and Covenants 90:13). In consequence of those supposed commandments, and from June 1830 to on and after July 1833, the Prophet corrected the King James Version of the English Bible to form what since has importantly come to be called "Joseph Smith's Inspired Translation." "During this time he and his scribes . . . produced nearly 500 pages of manuscript, containing thousands of variant readings and new passages." Mormonism's Inspired Translation scholar, Robert J. Matthews, reported having "observed 3,400 verses in which it ['Joseph Smith's Inspired Translation'] differs from the King James Version . . . ." Those revisions, that faithful scholar said, "clarify and enhance the message of the Bible."[69]

---

[66]"Kinderhook Plates" (accessed 14 February 2019), available from Wikipedia.com.

[67]Roberts, ed., *History of The Church of Jesus Christ of Latter-day Saints* (1978), 5:374-78.

[68]*History of the Church*, Roberts, ed., 6:57.

[69]Robert J. Matthews (Assistant Professor of Ancient Scripture), "Joseph Smith's Inspired Translation of the Bible," Brigham Young University (accessed

Apostle Bruce R. McConkie's Review of Joseph Smith's Inspired Translation

The King James Bible, according to Apostle Bruce R. McConkie, 2004:

> *As far as the Bibles of the world are concerned the King James version is so far ahead of all others that there is little comparison. It rates as an item of five or six on our scale. It is the Bible that came into being to prepare the way for the translation of the Book of Mormon and to set a literary pattern and standard for the revelations in the Doctrine and Covenants. It is the official Bible of the Church.*[70]

Joseph Smith's Inspired Translation of the King James Bible, according to Apostle Bruce R. McConkie, 2004:

> *It can scarcely be stated with too great an emphasis. The Joseph Smith Translation, or Inspired Version, is a thousand times over the best Bible now existing on earth. It contains all that the King James Version does, plus pages of additions and corrections and an occasional deletion. It was made by the spirit of revelation, and the changes and additions are the equivalent of the revealed word in the Book of Mormon and the Doctrine and Covenants.*[71]

"The Latter-day Saint edition of the Bible footnotes many of the major changes made in the Inspired Version and has a seventeen-page section that sets forth excerpts that are too lengthy for inclusion in the footnotes." According to McConkie,

---

March 2018), available from htpps://www.lds.org/ensign/1972/12/Joseph-Smiths-Inspired-Translation-of-the-Bible?/lang=eng; Internet, p. 4 of 9.

[70]Bruce R. McConkie in "The Bible, a Sealed Book," *Teaching Seminary: Preservice Readings* (2004), 123-32 (accessed March 2018), available from https://www.lds.org/manual/teaching-seminary-preservice-readings-religion-370-471-and-475/the-bible-a-sealed-book?lang=eng; Internet, p. 10 of 17, emphasis added.

[71]Ibid., p. 11 of 17, emphasis added. "Use and Rely On the Joseph Smith Translation," the Apostle reports. This Bible rates an eight or nine on our scale.

Reference to this section and to the footnotes themselves will give anyone who has spiritual insight a deep appreciation of this revelatory work of the prophet Joseph Smith. It is one of the great evidences of his prophetic call.[72]

The author of *Mormon Doctrine* gives unequivocal praise to Joseph Smith's Inspired Translation of the King James Version of the English Bible, the work of a prophet inspired by the gift and power of God.

"Rethinking Joseph Smith's Bible Translation" (March 16, 2017), Brigham Young University, Journal of Undergraduate Research[73]:

"In 2017, scholars at Brigham Young University published research suggesting Smith borrowed heavily from Methodist theologian Adam Clarke's famous Bible commentary"[74] when he produced his "Inspired Translation of the King James Version of the English Bible." That stunning discovery, many decades after the fact, was an unwelcome occurrence for the University's researchers.

[I]n conducting new research into the origins of [Joseph] Smith's Bible translation, we uncovered evidence that Smith and his associates used a readily available Bible commentary while compiling a new Bible translation, or more properly a revision of the King James Bible. The commentary, Adam Clarke's famous Holy Bible, Containing the Old and New Testaments, was a mainstay for Methodist theologians and biblical scholars alike, and was one of the most widely available commentaries in the mid-1820's and 1830's in America.[75]

---

[72]Ibid.

[73]Haley Wilson and Thomas Wayment, "A Recently Recovered Source: Rethinking Joseph Smith's Bible Translation" (Brigham Young University Journal of Undergraduate Research, Department of Ancient Scripture, 16 March 2017).

[74]"Joseph Smith Translation of the Bible" (accessed March 2018), available from Wikipedia.com; Internet, 7 pages.

[75]Wilson and Wayment, "A Recently Recovered Source: Rethinking Joseph Smith's Bible Translation," p. 1 of 5, emphasis added.

Direct evidence of *"borrowing* from this source has not previously been connected to Smith's translation efforts . . . ."

> *Our research has revealed that the number of direct parallels between Smith's translation and Adam Clarke's biblical commentary are simply too numerous and explicit to posit happenstance or coincidental overlap. The parallels between the two texts [Adam Clarke's Bible Commentary and Joseph Smith's Inspired Translation of the King James Bible] number into the hundreds, a number that is well beyond the limits of this paper to discuss.*[76]

Because "Adam Clarke's textual emendations came through Smith's translation as inspired changes to the text" (from Adam Clarke to Joseph Smith to Mormon scripture), they show that Smith plagiarized the work of Adam Clarke. He called those unannounced but extensive borrowings "inspired," then used and abused, as he had done with other early and important resources, the meaning of the term "translation." The previously undiscovered borrowings from the work of the Methodist scholar are described by Brigham Young University's Department of Ancient Scripture researchers as "obvious," "numerous" and "explicit."

"The authors [Brigham Young University scholars Wilson and Wayment] further posit that this evidence is sufficient to 'demonstrate Smith's open reliance upon Clarke . . .' before suggesting Sidney Rigdon was likely responsible for urging the use of Clarke's source material."[77] Why that is suggested to have been something important provides food for thought. The speculative claim that Rigdon was somehow implicated in the misuse of Adam Clarke's commentary is made in an offhanded way in the absence of proof and does nothing to assuage the ultimate guilt of the plagiarist-in-chief. This buck stops squarely with the Mormon

---

[76]Ibid., pp. 1, 2 of 5, emphasis added.
[77]"Joseph Smith Translation of the Bible" (accessed March 2018), available from Wikipedia.com; Internet, p. 3 of 7.

prophet, Joseph Smith.[78] No one ever described Sidney Rigdon's Inspired Translation of the King James Version of the English Bible. Brigham Young University's ancient scripture researchers have just now discovered the scholarly resources Joseph Smith used to create that heralded "Inspired Translation of the King James Version of the English Bible."

A revelation dated January 10, 1832, commanded Smith "to continue the work of translation until it be finished." (Doctrine and Covenants 73:4). One busy year-and-a-half later and on July 2, 1833, Joseph Smith announced the work was done. "We this day finished the translating of the Scriptures, for which we return gratitude to our Heavenly Father."[79]

The twenty-first century discovery of the use of Adam Clarke's "famous" biblical commentary, represented as the word of the Lord in the work of Joseph Smith, is exposed by hundreds of exemplars reflected in Joseph Smith's "Inspired Translation." *That unexpected shock has created a synthesis with no plane of dissection, "parallels . . . simply too numerous and explicit to posit happenstance or coincidental overlap."* Joseph Smith's "Inspired Translation" is toast. Adam Clarke was inspired to make those interpretations, and Joseph Smith was inspired to copy them.

A PROPHET IN TRAINING: JOSEPH SMITH MEET STEPHEN BURROUGHS

Pomeroy Tucker, a Palmyra newspaper man who knew the Smiths,[80] said that as a youth Joseph Smith Jr. loved reading the "stories of Stephen Burroughs." Burroughs, who is known to have called himself "Preacher" and sometimes "Prophet," was widely known in that early era in the Northeast as the "Emperor of the

---

[78]Bruce R. McConkie offered none of the credit to Rigdon when he assayed the indelible value of Joseph's revelatory masterpiece in 2004. Now that it is known (and because it is shown) to have been incredibly flawed, fraudulent, borrowed, "obvious," "numerous," "explicit" and ill advised, let us not assign the blame to Rigdon.

[79]*History of the Church,* Roberts, ed., 1:368.

[80]Tucker was the man who called Joseph Smith's chocolate colored stone ". . . the acorn of the Mormon oak."

Counterfeiters." A skillful writer, he, like Joseph Smith (and before Joseph Smith) (and as a model to Smith), also presented himself as the "injured innocent."[81] He was, he said repeatedly, a victim of persecution. "Sweet are the uses of adversity." Persecution was a recurring theme particularly favored in his then famous "memoirs," where he "entertainingly defended his life of crime."

> *There are parallels between the lives of Joseph Smith Jr. and Stephen Burroughs. They both acted as "seers" of lost or stolen goods in their youths. They were designated "disorderly persons" upon arrest, with Smith prosecuted in 1826 for being an "imposter" and Burroughs for counterfeiting.[82] They used sophisticated language skills to mesmerize and charm people. They wrote books that became best sellers. They engaged in land speculation. They led groups into the wilderness where legal jurisdiction was ambiguous in order to evade law enforcement.[83]*

> *They claimed to be "persecuted" victims when authorities attempted to call them to account. They involved their family members in their schemes. They both womanized and had complicated marital histories. People said they mocked traditional Christianity with both their words and their actions, while claiming to be traditionally pious Christian preachers. Finally, both Burroughs and Smith were continually at odds with the legal authorities and were the objects of numerous lawsuits and indictments,*

---

[81]Melonakos, *Secret Combinations*, 45-48.

[82]In March 1826, Joseph Smith, not yet twenty-one years of age, was arrested and charged in the court of Judge Albert Neely in Bainbridge, New York, accused of being a "disorderly person" and an "impostor." It was said that he had defrauded people by claiming to be a glass-looker who used magic stones to seek for buried treasure, tell peoples' fortunes and locate lost property. The court record reported as follows: "[T]he Court find(s) the Defendant guilty." Several years later, subsequent to those earlier findings, the defendant founded Mormonism by translating the golden plates, which came to him by magical means, with one of those magical stones.

[83]Pomeroy Tucker, *Origin, Rise and Progress of Mormonism: Biography of the Founders and History of Its Church* (New York: Appleton and Company, 1867), 17, cited in Melonakos, *Secret Combinations*, emphasis added.

spending considerable periods of time in hiding, courtrooms or jails.[84]

Both Smith and Burroughs were alleged to have been counterfeiters. Both of them were antinomians, people who did not need conventional morality to guide them in life.[85] Both of them rejected socially established morality.

COUNTERFEITING

Joseph H. Jackson, an *aide-de-camp* and Nauvoo confidant of Joseph Smith before they argued and went their different ways, published a pamphlet in 1844 in which he said "that Smith had revealed to him that Mormon leaders had been involved in counterfeiting in Kirtland." According to Jackson, "Joe told me that in Ohio, he, Dr. Boynton, Lyman Wight, Oliver Cowdry and Hyrum were engaged with others in a Bogus establishment at Licking Creek . . . ." Joseph further said that their operations were interrupted by the failure "of the Kirtland Bank."[86]

Smith testified in a Far West meeting that a Mr. Sapham (a non-Mormon) "told him that Cowdery was about to be arrested for counterfeiting, so he [Smith] had warned him to escape if he were guilty." An historian of that period, Mrs. Melonakos reports that Joseph had reason to believe his Book of Mormon scribe (and witness) "was involved in counterfeiting" before he aided and abetted Cowdery's escape (from Kirtland, Ohio, to Far West,

---

[84]Melonakos, *Secret Combinations*, 50, emphasis added.

[85]Ibid., 24, 51. Burroughs "ended up changing his occupation thirteen times, defended against twenty criminal prosecutions (eleven of which were initiated by Canadian authorities), endured seven imprisonments, three escapes, two or three exposures in the pillory, and the infliction of approximately 300 lashes." (Ibid., 49). Burroughs' father, Reverend Eden Burroughs, was a first cousin of Asael Smith, Joseph and Hyrum's grandfather. He was a trustee on the Dartmouth College Board when Hyrum (a Masonic "Hiram" then), Joseph Smith's brother, "attended Moor's Academy, the prep school for Dartmouth, between 1811 and 1815." Joseph Smith's father, Joseph Sr., "had ties to Stephen Burrough's father . . . ." (Ibid.).

[86]Joseph H. Jackson, *A Narrative of the Adventures and Experience of Joseph H. Jackson in Nauvoo* (Warshaw, IL: 1846), 15, quoted in Ibid., 293-94.

Missouri).[87] **Shortly after the out of favor counterfeiter Cowdery's ignominious departure, Smith and Rigdon effectuated their own dramatic escape from Kirtland, Ohio, to Far West, Missouri,[88] some few days before the Kirtland printing office burned to the ground. The fire deprived the Kirtland dissenters the chance to further sully the prophet's already damaged reputation.[89]**

In Missouri "Joseph, Hyrum and Sidney Rigdon formed the Danite secret society, holding clandestine meetings and requiring members to swear blood oaths to support the First Presidency as God, as well as each other 'right or wrong.'"[90] Gruesome oaths, examples of which were staples in the Church both then and later (and in the temples until 1990), contained the strongest terms language could invent. "Their first official act was to present the 'Danite Manifesto' signed by Hyrum Smith, Sidney Rigdon and eighty-four Danites, addressed to . . . [men among them perceived to be] dissenters with the ultimatum that *they leave Missouri or die . . . .*"[91] **The Danite Manifesto, over the signatures of the highest leaders of the Church, described the crimes of the dissenters, Mormon founders, most particularly counterfeiting:**

> *Oliver Cowdery, David Whitmer, and Lyman E. Johnson united with a gang of counterfeiters, thieves, liars and blacklegs of the deepest dye, to deceive, cheat*

---

[87]Ibid., 295. "Why," Mrs. Melonakos avers, "was this Mr. Sapham warning Smith about his partner getting arrested, unless all three of them were in the counterfeiting network?" (Ibid., 294).

[88]Smith and Rigdon, according to the scholar, left Kirtland "on the fastest horses they could find," pursued by a posse.

[89]Warren Parrish disparaged "The recent outrage committed here [Kirtland], viz: the burning of the Printing establishment . . . – the printing establishment, book bindery &c., was formerly the property of Smith and Rigdon; it had been sold the day previous to its being set on fire, by virtue of two executions obtained against them of one thousand dollars each, for issuing banking paper contrary to law. The establishment had fallen into the hands of those who have of late remonstrated against the wickedness of the above named individuals . . . ." According to Parrish, that Press from the standpoint of the fugitives (Smith and Rigdon) "must not at all hazards be suffered to be put into requisition against them . . . ." (Warren Parrish, "To the Editor of the Painesville Republican," *Painesville Republican 2* [15 February 1838]:3).

[90]Melonakos, *Secret Combinations*, 296.

[91]Ibid., emphasis retained.

*and defraud the saints out of their property by every
art and stratagem wickedness could invent . . .
encouraging them ["your gang of marauders in
Kirtland"] to go on with their iniquity . . . ; stealing,
cheating, lying; instituting vexatious lawsuits, selling
bogus money, and also stones and sand for bogus; in
which nefarious business [all as just described], Oliver
Cowdery, David Whitmer, and Lyman Johnson, were
engaged while you were there . . . ."*[92]

The Danite Manifesto went further to say that, "We have evidence
of a very strong character that you are at this very time engaged
with a gang of counterfeiters, coiners, and blacklegs, as some of
those characters have lately visited our city [Far West, Missouri]
from Kirtland, and told what they had come for . . . ."[93] Thus the
Far West Mormons, by then the most prominent members of the
Church, were in communication with the dissenters' counterfeiters
and claimed to know the details of their operations.[94]

Guilt by Association

"Reed Peck, a Danite dissenter, said he believed [both] the Mormon
leaders and the dissenters were guilty of 'purchasing and
circulating Bogus money . . .' because they accused each other of it."
John Corrill, "who succeeded Cowdery and [John] Whitmer as
church historian, reported that the leaders of the church 'accused
the dissenters with dishonesty, want of faith, stealing, lying,
encouraging the making of counterfeit money, &c.'"[95] Before what
might be called a final reckoning of the counterfeiting issue, Smith
is known to have walked in tandem with many marginal people,
some of whom emerged to become numbered among the most
important people in the early Church – men and women alleged to

---

[92]"Document Showing The Testimony Given Before the Judge of the Fifth
Judicial District of the State of Missouri, on the Trial of Joseph Smith, Jr., and
others, for High Treason and Other Crimes Against that State," Senate Document
No. 189 (Washington D.C.: Blair & Rives; photomechanical reprint of 15 February
1841, Salt Lake City: Utah Lighthouse Ministry), 8, emphasis added.

[93]Ibid., 9.

[94]Melonakos, *Secret Combinations*, 296-97.

[95]Ibid., 298.

have trafficked in "Bogus" (counterfeiting), including but far from limited to Oliver Cowdery, David Whitmer, Lyman Johnson, John Boynton, Lyman Wight and Hyrum Smith.

The author of the book *Secret Combinations: Evidence for Early Mormon Counterfeiting*, Kathleen Kimball Melonakos, a generational granddaughter of Heber C. Kimball (an early and important Mormon leader), identified the persons described in a footnote to follow to have been *"associated with Joseph Smith Jr. who are known to have [had] bench warrants, indictments, arrest records, jail sentences, or testimony (including by Smith himself) that they trafficked in counterfeit money."*[96]

---

[96]Ibid., 299. *Smith Associates:* Joseph Smith Sr., the father of the prophet, a Mason, the Presiding Patriarch of the Church and a money-digging expert; Stephen Burroughs, the "Emperor of the Counterfeiters," who through others in his network is alleged to have "passed counterfeits to Joseph Smith, Sr."; Warren Cowdery Jr., a Woodscrape principal, the father of Oliver Cowdery and a friend of Justus Winchell; Justus Winchell aka Paine Wingate, a money-digger and a counterfeiter; Luman Walters, who went to jail in Palmyra but was "a fast friend of the Smiths" (Walters appeared to have invited Joseph Jr. to look for things invisible to the natural eye in Walters' peepstone); Jason Treadwell, an "intimate friend and neighbor of Isaac Hale[,] convicted murderer of Oliver Harper, [and a] money-digging partner of Joseph Smith Jr." (Harper's widow, like Joseph Jr. and Joseph Sr., was contractually entitled to share in the proceeds from Josiah Stowell's Harmony, Pennsylvania, treasure-seeking project), and George Harper Jr., son of Oliver Harper.
    Other Smith Associates: Abraham Salisbury, "neighbor and relative of William Jenkins Salisbury," who was the "husband of Katherine Smith," Joseph Smith's sibling and Joseph and Hyrum's brother-in-law; William Smith, Joseph's brother, the "best friend and [yet another] brother-in-law of William Jenkins Salisbury"; Hyrum Smith, Patriarch and President of the Church and Joseph Smith's brother; Oliver Cowdery, a witness to the Book of Mormon; David Whitmer, a witness to the Book of Mormon; Sidney Rigdon, First Presidency First Counselor; Lyman E. Johnson, Apostle; Luke S. Johnson, Apostle; Joe Keeler, a Mormon bishop in New Portage, Ohio; Warren Parrish, Joseph's scribe and one of the officers in the Kirtland anti-Banking Society. Marvel C. Davis, "gunsmith and temple music director"; Solomon Wilbur Denton, "hired gun"; Frederick G. Williams, Second Counselor in the First Presidency and Justice of the Peace; John Boynton, Apostle; Burton H. Phelps; Lyman Wight, the man who ordained Joseph Smith to the Melchizedek Priesthood, a Mormon Danite leader in Missouri, Joseph's second in command at Zion's Camp, a future Apostle and a member of the Council of Fifty; Sarah Cleveland, the polyandrous wife of Judge John Cleveland and Joseph Smith, then also Emma's Counselor in the Ladies' Relief Society; Julius Granger, "mentioned in [the] *Elder's Journal* as [a] principal bogus dealer"; Amasa Bonney, "Mormon elder and brother to counterfeiter turned

JOSEPH SMITH, CASHIER, KIRTLAND
SAFETY SOCIETY ANTI-BANK

It is promised that this important institution, like Aaron's rod, will swallow up all of the other banks. It will "grow and flourish, and spread from the rivers to the ends of the earth, and survive when all others should be laid in ruins." Investors are encouraged to look at a bank established by a revelation from God, and to the veracity of the officers of that bank – Sidney Rigdon, President, and Joseph Smith, Treasurer. The bank failed within a month. It opened for business in January 1837 and was in trouble three weeks later. Thirteen lawsuits were brought against Joseph Smith between June 1837 and April 1839, and he was arrested seven times in four months. Warren Parrish, Joseph's Kirtland Clayton, upon leaving the fold, summarized:

> *Knowing their extreme poverty when they commenced this Mormon speculation, I have been not a little surprised to hear them assert that they were worth from three to four hundred thousand each, and in less than ninety days after become insolvent without any change in their business affairs.*[97]

> *I have been astonished to hear him [Joseph Smith] declare that we had 60,000 Dollars in specie in our vaults, and $600,000 at our command, when we had not to exceed $6,000 and could not command any more; also that we had about ten thousand Dollars of our bills in circulation, when he, as Cashier of the*

---

bounty-hunter, Edward Bonney"; Orrin Porter Rockwell, "Smith's boyhood pal" and "bodyguard"; Joseph Jackson, "Smith's real estate agent and *aide-de-camp*"; Brigham Young, the Senior Apostle and a future prophet; and Heber C. Kimball, an Apostle and a future First Presidency Counselor. (Ibid., 299-300).

One might add to that list (some of whom were indicted or jailed and some of whom were not), and as other alleged offenders, John Taylor, an Apostle and a future prophet; Peter Haws; Marinus Eaton; John Bernhisel; George Q. Cannon; George A. Smith and Theodore Turley.

[97]"To the Editor of the Painesville Republican," *Painesville Republican 2* (15 February 1838), signed by M. (should be W.) Parrish, certified by two of the Twelve Apostles, Luke Johnson and John Boynton, and two former presidents of the Seventies, Sylvester Smith and Leonard Rich, emphasis added.

institution, knew that there was at least $150,000.[98]

Warren Parrish, an officer in the bank with Rigdon and Smith, decried wild speculations calculated by Smith and Rigdon to "aggrandize themselves and founders" at the expense of "followers" reduced to "wretchedness and want." Having "knowledge of their private characters and sentiments," Parrish told the Painesville paper that, "I believe them to be confirmed Infidels, who have not the fear of God before their eyes . . . ."[99]

The Kirtland bank, which had no charter, was illegal from the day it opened. The Kirtland notes were printed with the promise that the bearer was entitled to gold or silver in the designated amount from the issuing bank, like other bank notes at that time. Legitimate banks in Ohio and elsewhere had agreements to honor the notes of other reputable banks. Deciding which banks were reputable and which of them were not was a subjective determination. Banks without gold and silver on hand to redeem their outstanding notes were considered "wildcat." The Kirtland Anti-Bank, "though capitalized at the outrageously high amount of $4,000,000 (most new banks were authorized for up to $100,000) according to its ledger book had sold stock at a face value of approximately $3,854,000, yet the paid up reserve totaled a meager $20,725."[100] The Kirtland Safety Society Anti-Banking Society was a fraudulent enterprise.

JOSEPH SMITH AND KIRTLAND REAL ESTATE

"John Johnson donated the land upon which the [Kirtland] temple was built to Smith . . . ."[101] Smith then proceeded to borrow money to buy more land near the temple, and so did some of the other leaders, "mostly on credit." For what purpose? To profit on the backs of the society's resettling emigrants. The more people Joseph and Hyrum could draw into their newly formed Zion, the better the land speculation might be expected to work. The leaders laid out a

---

[98]Ibid., emphasis added.
[99]Ibid.
[100]Melonakos, *Secret Combinations*, 284-85.
[101]Ibid., 277.

large city on paper and divided it into city lots projected to sell at exorbitant prices, from $100 to $200 each.[102] Besides the property Joseph already owned, more than one hundred forty acres adjoining the temple and four acres of business property on the Chillicothe Road, he then proceeded to make at least two other large acquisitions to be used for selling inheritances to the incoming Saints.[103] Smith's later purchases, by himself and with others, from Peter French, Alphaeus Russell and Samuel Canfield involved nearly four hundred fifty acres.

The most important purchases in 1836 were made by five people looking to profit by selling housing lots. Those entrepreneurs were: John Boynton, a Mormon apostle; Jacob Bump, a Master Mason and a Mormon; John Johnson, the father of two apostles, Luke and Lyman Johnson; Joseph Smith, Jr.; and Joseph's uncle, John Smith, a future Patriarch. For some of the large acquisitions, the Mormon prophet associated himself with Jacob Bump and Reynolds Cahoon.[104] It is said that he bought lots as often as every two weeks. Soaring prices promised soaring profits. "According to the *Painesville Telegraph* Joseph estimated [the value of] his own land in Kirtland at $300,000," a monumental amount at the time.[105] It was a time when the average family "earned $400 [a] year."

It is no wonder that the bank failed, Joseph's schemes collapsed and he was literally run out of town – fleeing Kirtland in the dead of night – in February 1838.

BLOOD ATONEMENT AND TEMPLES

Joseph Smith informed his followers that the Lord accepted this house (the Kirtland Temple), that his name should be in that house, and that he would manifest himself to his people and speak to them there. Jesus said that if the people did not pollute that holy house

---

[102]Ibid.

[103]Robert Kent Fielding, "Ph.D. Dissertation for Indiana University," quoted in Tanner and Tanner, *Mormonism: Shadow or Reality*, 528.

[104]Ibid.

[105]*Painesville Telegraph*, 27 January 1837, quoted in Brodie, *No man knows my history*, 195.

that the hearts of thousands and tens of thousands would greatly rejoice in consequence of the blessings associated with the endowment. "[T]he fame of this house shall spread to foreign lands; and this is the beginning of the blessings which shall be poured out upon the heads of my people."[106] The promises for the temple were not unlike the promises for the Kirtland Safety Society's failed bank.

Despite the fact that Joseph Smith informed his followers that he and Oliver Cowdery had seen the Lord, Moses, Elias and Elijah in the Kirtland Temple, the supposedly sacred venue rather abruptly became the scene of irresistible turmoil. "An open battle between Smith loyalists and dissenters took place in the temple, complete with pistols and bowie knives." With the passage of time (a very brief period of time), despite the efforts of a council led by Brigham Young to discipline the prophet's "ecclesiastical enemies," "nothing could still the opposition."[107] Smith and Rigdon left the divided Kirtland in disgrace – abandoning the temple, a printing press and a failed bank – in the middle of the night to escape creditors and dissidents. Cowdery (who was excommunicated in Missouri in 1838) left the Mormons, then later "renounced Mormonism" and joined the Methodist Church, where he served in 1844 as the secretary to a start-up congregation in Tiffin, Seneca County, Ohio.[108] After Joseph Smith's death on June 27, 1844, Emma and the Smith's children also attended the Methodist Church.

---

[106]Doctrine and Covenants 110:7-10.

[107]Turner, *Brigham Young: Pioneer Prophet*, 53.

[108]Statement, Judge Gabriel J. Keen to Arthur B. Deming, 14 April 1885, Vogel, ed., *Early Mormon Documents*, 2:504-6. Keen Affidavit, April 14, 1885: "I was well acquainted with Oliver Cowdery, who formerly resided in this city." When in a few years Cowdery "expressed a desire" to join a "'Methodist Protestant Church,' we waited on Mr. Cowdrey at his residence in Tiffin, and there learned his connection, from him, with that order [Mormonism], and his full and final renunciation thereof." When asked "to make a public recantation," he said that such recitals would "draw public attention, invite criticism and bring *him* into contempt." He would submit (recant), he said, "if the church require it." It did not. "We did not demand it . . . ." At a meeting he stood, addressed the audience, "admitted his error and implored forgiveness, and said that he was sorry and ashamed of his connection with Mormonism." At Tiffin he became the superintendent of the Sabbath school. There, according to Keen, he "led an exemplary life." Later on and in 1848, after the death of Joseph Smith and just

Joseph Smith was the first Latter-day Saint to articulate the doctrine of blood atonement.

> *In debate, George A. Smith said imprisonment was better than hanging. I replied, I was opposed to hanging, even if a man kill another, I will shoot him, or cut off his head, spill his blood on the ground, and let the smoke thereof ascend up to God; and if I ever have the privilege of making a law on that subject, I will have it so.*[109]

Joseph Smith and Brigham Young formulated supposedly unchangeable deity-driven temple ceremonies (including Brigham Young's Last Testament, the "Lecture at the Veil") that, until they were changed, contained highly incendiary rituals that prominently featured acrimonious attacks on evangelical Christianity, under the shield nudity, blood oaths, then gruesome penalties and covenants made without informed consent. The temple ceremony further required the misogynistic subservience of veiled women to men. The Lecture at the Veil promoted Adam as God. The hateful nature of the supposedly inviolable *original* ceremony and its effect on shell-shocked participants necessitated dramatic changes in the supposedly infallible drama near the end of the twentieth century. It was not a pretty thing.

---

shortly before his own death, Cowdery left the Methodists and rejoined the Mormons. He traveled to Council Bluffs and was rebaptized by Orson Hyde.

[109]"The Questions of 'Currency' and Blood Atonement, in the Nauvoo City Council" (March 1843), Roberts, ed., *History of The Church of Jesus Christ of Latter-day Saints*, 5:296, emphasis added.

Lieutenant-General Joseph Smith

FAILED PROMISES AND PROPHECIES
CONCERNING ZION

PROMISE: The Lord will tell you when the city of the New Jerusalem shall be prepared. When it is prepared you shall gather there, where you shall be his people and he shall be your God.

PROMISE: The Lord promises the faithful that they shall be preserved and rejoice together in the land of Missouri, and says he cannot lie. "Behold, I, the Lord, have brought you together that the promise might be fulfilled, that the faithful among you should be preserved and rejoice together in the land of Missouri. I, the Lord, promise the faithful and cannot lie."

PROMISE: The Lord holds Zion in his own hands. "And now, behold, this is the will of the Lord your God concerning his saints, that they should assemble themselves together unto the land of Zion, not in haste, lest there should be confusion, which bringeth pestilence. Behold, the land of Zion – I, the Lord, hold it in mine own hands."

PROMISE: Zion shall flourish, and the glory of the Lord shall be upon her. The Lord hath spoken it.

PROMISE: The Saints shall gather and stand upon Mount Zion, the city of the New Jerusalem. The Lord hath spoken it.

PROMISE: Zion shall be an ensign unto the people, who shall flock to her out of every nation under heaven. The Lord hath spoken it.

PROMISE: "And, behold, there is none other place appointed than that which I have appointed; neither shall there be any other place appointed than that which I have appointed, for the work of the gathering of my saints."

MORMONS IN MISSOURI ZION

"In 1833 angry Jackson County vigilantes attacked Mormon leaders, destroyed their printing press, and drove the Saints out of their homes." The refugees were not allowed to return to the only place of refuge reserved by Joseph's Lord for the gathering of his Saints in the advent of the end times. The old Missouri settlers resented the Mormons' insularity (they were "God's chosen people"). The Missourians suspected that the Saints were tampering with their slaves and stirring up the Indians . . . ," and they "distrusted the Saints communitarian economic system [the "idea of equality"]." The new society "bought land and started businesses with Church funds." "[T]he Missourians feared that the Mormons would dominate local politics . . . ." (Stephen C. LeSueur, 16-17)

The Mormons, who were busy establishing the Kingdom of God in Jackson County, claimed that they would "tread upon the ashes of the wicked after they are destroyed from off the face of the earth," that "it was folly for them [the Missourians] to improve their lands." God told the Mormons, who repeated his words, that he would "consecrate the riches of the Gentiles [non-Mormons] unto my people which are of the house of Israel." (LeSueur, 18). Joseph's God, a god of vengeance, anger and ego, referred to the old settlers as the "enemies" of the members of his bold new society.

THE REDEMPTION OF ZION

"[T]he time is near when the sun will be darkened, and the moon turn to blood, and the stars fall from heaven, and the earth reel to and fro . . . if we are not sanctified and gathered to the places God has appointed . . . we must fall." (Joseph Smith)

"A FOOL'S ERRAND"

Zion's Camp

William E. McLellin: *"After the mobbing here [at Independence in Jackson County] in 1833, Joseph delivered a revelation containing these words, 'Renounce war and proclaim peace' [Doctrine and Covenants 98:16]; but in about two months they held a council in Kirtland, comprising the highest authorities of the church, and determined on war; and sent Orson Hyde and John Gould all the way to Zion to tell the men to stand up and fight if oppressed by a mob. 'Fight in defense of pure religion.' We did fight; and that was the great reason why the church was driven from this county and never allowed to return again."*

"Joseph transgressed so as to be rejected in 1834." In that year, when the name of the church was changed, when the leaders *"took the spirit of war for the entire church in the winter of 1833-4"* (when they prepared the militia known as *"Zion's Camp"*), Satan rejoiced and God rejected the church. With a new *"false name"* appointed on May 3, 1834 (*"The Church of the Latter Day Saints"*), a change that eliminated the name of *"Christ"* in order to more accurately reflect the military aspirations of the pugnacious prophet and his increasingly violent society, Joseph Smith, who betrayed the Lord and many of the saints, fell from grace. McLellin described what he considered to be a sad, unholy affair. *"[T]he Lord to show his disapproval of their entire cause suffered the cholera to afflict . . . Joseph's 'braves,' and some . . . died in their warrior tramp – starting from Kirtland on the next day after their name was altered!"*

"[T]he day they [the Zion's Camp militia led by Joseph Smith] reached Clay Co[unty], about seventy were taken with Asiatic Cholera, and fourteen died. Joseph disbanded his men, and most of them returned home. Thus all their calculations of redeeming Zion by the sword were blasted; and evil, and only evil, attended that warrior tramp of some one thousand miles, on a fool's errand . . . ."

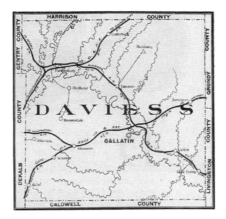

MAKING DAVIESS COUNTY A PLACE OF REFUGE,
CONSECRATED AND SACRED IN ITS OWN PECULIAR WAY

When the Mormons were driven from the city of Independence in Jackson County, Missouri, the only place the Lord allowed to become the New Jerusalem, they sought other sites of spiritual significance in yet other Missouri Counties (Caldwell, Carroll and Daviess). "In May 1838 the Mormons laid out a town in Daviess County, which the Prophet named Adam-ondi-Ahman . . . . Joseph Smith taught that the Garden of Eden was located in Jackson County, and that Adam and Eve fled to Adam-ondi-Ahman after their fall from grace. Adam-ondi-Ahman, said the Prophet, means 'the place where Adam dwelt.' Smith reportedly identified an altar built by Adam near the town and prophesied that Adam would return to bless his posterity at Christ's Second Coming." (Stephen C. LeSueur)

GOVERNOR LILBURN W. BOGGS

VILLAINS ALL

"With both Missourians and Mormons taking the law in their own hands [in 1838], mob and militia became indistinguishable, and Governor Lilburn W. Boggs himself declared: 'The quarrel is between the Mormons and the mob, and they can fight it out.' Both sides had become too desperate to reason."

Governor Lilburn W. Boggs

Missouri State Militia at Far West

JOHN CORRILL TESTIFIES

"The Mormon Church has been represented as being the little stone spoken of by Daniel, which should roll on and crush all opposition to it, and ultimately should be established as a temporal as well as a spiritual kingdom. These things were to be carried out through the instrumentality of the Danite band, as far as force was necessary; . . . . The teachings of that society led them to prohibit the talkings of any persons against the presidency; so much so, that it was dangerous for any man to set up opposition to any thing that might be set on foot, and I became afraid to speak my own mind."

"On Monday, Joseph Smith, jr., made a speech; and some resolutions were passed, purporting that those persons who would not engage in their undertaking [the 1838 Mormon Missouri War], their property should be consecrated (confiscated) to the use of those who did engage in their undertaking. On Sunday, Joseph Smith, jr., in his discourse, spoke of persons taking, at some times, what, at other times, it would be wrong to take; and gave as an example the case of David eating the shewbread, and also of the Saviour and his apostles plucking the ears of corn and eating, as they passed through the cornfield . . . . On the Monday . . . President Rigdon, in a speech, said that those who were unwilling to go into the war ought to [be] put upon their horses with guns and bayonets, and forced into the front of the war – having reference to those who heretofore had been backward in defending themselves and families. No persons were suffered to leave the county in this extreme time . . . ." (Testimony, John Corrill, Senate Document 189, 13).

"I think the original object of the Danite band was to operate on the dissenters; but afterwards it grew into a system to carry out the designs of the presidency; and, if necessary to use physical force to upbuild the kingdom of God; it was to be done by them. ... It was my understanding that Dr. Avard's teaching in the Danite society proceeded from the presidency." (Testimony, John Corrill, Richmond, Missouri, 1838; Ibid., 14). Ezra Booth: "The plan is . . . ingeniously contrived, having for its aim one principal point, viz: the establishment of a society in Missouri, over which the contrivers of this delusive system, are to possess unlimited and despotic sway."

THE DANITE COVENANT (ARM TO THE SQUARE)

"'In the name of Jesus Christ, the Son of God, I do solemnly obligate myself ever to conceal, and never to reveal, the secret purposes of this society called the Daughters of Zion. Should I ever do the same, I hold my life as the forfeiture.' The prophet Joseph Smith, jr., together with his two counsellors, (Hiram Smith and Sidney Rigdon), were considered as the supreme head of the church; and the Danite band feel themselves as much bound to obey them, as to obey the Supreme God. Instruction was given by Joseph Smith, jr., that if any of them should get into a difficulty, the rest should help him out; and that they should stand by each other, right or wrong. This instruction was given at a Danite meeting, in a public address." *(Sampson Avard, 1838, Senate Document 189, 2).*

Joseph Smith and Adam Black, Image source: https://mormonitemusings.com
/2016/04/28/eliza-snow-the-mormon-war-her-alleged-gang-rape/

SAMPSON AVARD ON MISSOURI JUDGE ADAM BLACK

"At the election last August [1838], a report came to Far West [the Mormon enclave] that some of the brethren in Daviess county were killed. I called for twenty volunteers to accompany me to see into this matter. I went; and about one hundred and twenty Mormons accompanied me to Adam on Diahmon [the place where Adam and Eve lived after being expelled from the Garden of Eden] – Mr. Joseph Smith, jr., in company. When I arrived there, I found the report exaggerated. None were killed. We visited Mr. Adam Black [Judge Adam Black] – about 150 or 200 men of us armed. Joseph Smith was commander; and if Black had not signed the paper he did, it was the common understanding and belief that he would have shared the fate of the dissenters. Sidney Rigdon and Lyman Wight were at Adam when we went to Black, and advised the movement." *(Ibid.).*

After meeting with Joseph Smith, and after being threatened by a large number of armed and hostile Mormon men, Black signed a document stating that he was "not attached to any mob, nor will attach himself to any such people, and so long as they [the Mormons] will not molest me, I will not molest them." *(Adam Black, J.P., August 8, 1838, LeSueur, 66).*

MISSOURI THEFT AND WASTE

William McLellin, Image source: Public domain via Wikimedia Commons.

William E. McLellin to John L. Traughber: *"During the wars, back and forth [in Missouri in 1838], J. Smith took about sixty men, well armed, and went out into Davis [Daviess] Co., as much as 60 miles, and scared away the inhabitants and gathered their household and farm goods and hauled them in wagons into Far West. But when ~~they~~ the army came near Far West, they hauled those goods about half a mile N.W., near the stone quarry, and threw them in piles in a little bottom. I myself, went to [page 10:] see them, and saw an old man who said he came about 60 miles for his goods. I think there were as many as ten wagon loads of goods scattered in that little bottom. I marvelled greatly to see them."*

THE SHORT, NASTY MISSOURI WAR

After the Mormons were roughly evicted from Jackson County, and even before the failed redemption adventure of the armed militia known as Zion's Camp, "Mormon exiles fled to neighboring Clay County, where they were treated with kindness and respect." In 1836, having worn out their welcome there, they agreed to leave the area at the request of those who had previously welcomed them. Following that benign expulsion, the Missourians created a new County, Caldwell County, where the Mormons created a new city, Far West, and lived for a time in relative isolation in a condition of "perfect peace." Mormon expansion, unwelcome expansion into surrounding counties, and other then recurring frictions, soon led to further conflicts between the Mormons and Missouri. In the summer of 1838, the Mormon people suffered death and defeat, in what was called the Mormon War, a short, brutal, nasty encounter. With that the Saints, who fought and plundered but lost, reluctantly left their promised land in the state of Missouri and their leaders were put in jail.

When the Mormons expanded their settlements to Daviess and Carroll Counties, and to a lesser extent to Clinton, Chariton, Ray and Livingston Counties, after they had agreed that they would not, the die was cast. Things would never be the same.

BRUCE R. McCONKIE: JOSEPH SMITH'S INSPIRED TRANSLATION OF THE KING JAMES VERSION OF THE ENGLISH BIBLE

Bruce R. McConkie: *"It can scarcely be stated with too great an emphasis. The Joseph Smith Translation, or Inspired Version, is a thousand times over the best Bible now existing on earth. It contains all that the King James Version does, plus pages of additions and corrections and an occasional deletion. It was made by the spirit of revelation, and the changes and additions are the equivalent of the revealed word in the Book of Mormon and the Doctrine and Covenants [the Inspired Revisions included in the Pearl of Great Price, the Book of Moses and parts of the gospel of Matthew are canonized]."* *("The Bible, a Sealed Book" [lds.org, 2004], 123-32).*

SHOCK AND AWE

In 2017, scholars at Brigham Young University published research suggesting Smith borrowed heavily from Methodist theologian Adam Clarke's famous Bible commentary: "Our research has revealed that the number of parallels between Smith's translation and Adam Clarke's biblical commentary are simply too numerous [hundreds of exemplars] and explicit to posit happenstance or coincidental overlap." (Wilson, Wayment, Brigham Young University Journal of Undergraduate Research, 16 March 2017).

Neither Smith nor Rigdon chose to connect this shameful confiscation with the prophet's so-called "translation." "What is noteworthy in detailing the use of this source is that Adam Clarke's textual emendations come through Smith's translation as inspired changes to the text." (Ibid.). Smith blessed his "inspired" ministry with Adam Clarke's insights.

"This new evidence effectively forces a reconsideration of Smith's translation projects, particularly his Bible project, and how he used academic sources while simultaneously melding his own inspiration into the resulting text." (Ibid.).

On "[T]he Other Translations [Bible Translations] of the World": *"Forget them; they are of so little value that it is almost a waste of time to delve into them. We take a generous view to even rate them as one on our scale [a scale of one to ten]. They are not binding on us, and in general they simply set forth the religious predilections of their translator."* (McConkie, A Sealed Book, 10).

On the Bible and the Book of Mormon: *"It is time we learned, not that the Book of Mormon is true because the Bible is true, but just the reverse. The Bible is true, insofar as it is, because the Book of Mormon is true."* (Ibid., 13).

On Celestial Marriage, Elias and Elijah: *"Celestial marriage has always existed. Indeed such is the heart and core of the Abrahamic covenant. Elias and Elijah came to restore this ancient order and to give the sealing power, which gives it eternal efficacy."* (Ibid., 14). *Before their visits (Elias and Elijah's visits) on April 3, 1836 (think here of Fanny Alger), such unions had no "eternal efficacy."*

On Ancient Scripture: *"I have often wished the history of ancient Israel could have passed through the editing and prophetic hands of Mormon. If so, it would read like the Book of Mormon, but I suppose that was the way it read in the first instance anyway."* (Ibid.).

On Teachings from the Source: *"Use the scriptures themselves . . . . Streams of living water flow from the Eternal Fountain, and they flow in scriptural channels prepared by the prophets. Here is a bit of wisdom most of you will understand: Don't drink below the horses, particularly the horses of sectarianism [that is to say below other Christians]."* (Ibid., 15).

On an Ethnocentric Church: *The gospel is and must be and can only be taught by the gift of the Holy Ghost. That gift is given to us as the Saints of the Most High and to none other. We stand alone and have given a power the world does not possess. Our views on religious and spiritual matters are infinitely better than theirs because we have the inspiration of heaven."* (Ibid., 16-17).

On Apostles and Prophets: *"Apostles and prophets are also teachers, and what greater commission can anyone have from the Lord than to stand in His place and stead, saying what he would say if he personally were present, and doing it because the words uttered flow forth by the power of the Holy Ghost."* (Ibid., 16).

Astrayals: Brigham Young

Epilogue

"Astrayals": Brigham Young

GOD ISSUES

Brigham Young, October 9, 1859: "The Being whom we call Father, was the Father of the spirit of the Lord Jesus Christ, and he was also his Father pertaining to the flesh. Infidels and Christians, make all you can of this statement."[1] Adam, the Father and God, was the father of Jesus Christ. An 1845 Proclamation of the Quorum of the Twelve Apostles – an epistle that quickly followed the death of Joseph Smith on June 27, 1844 – referred to the *"great Eloheim Jehovah."*[2] Brigham Young's Jesus, the Quorum of the Twelve's Jesus, Joseph Smith's Jesus, wasn't Jehovah. Adam was the father of Jesus in *the spirit* and in *the flesh.*

"Both American Protestants and early Mormons often conflated [combined] Elohim and Jehovah, two Anglicized renditions of Hebrew words for God." Brigham Young and the other members of the Quorum conflated Elohim ("Eloheim") and Jehovah, treating those names as interchangeable in their pretentious April 6, 1845, Proclamation of the Twelve "To all the Kings of the World; to the President of the United States of America; to the Governors of the several States; And to the Rulers and People of all Nations." The Quorum's 1845 Proclamation treating Eloheim/Jehovah as one God is further described at Appendix F. The *"great [interchangeable] Eloheim Jehovah"* by this high visibility reckoning was just then *one* indivisible person.[3] Modern Mormons (since 1915 or 1916) have

---

[1]Sermon, "Intelligence, Etc.," *Journal of Discourses*, 7:282-91, reproduced at *The Essential Brigham Young*, with a foreword by Eugene E. Campbell (Salt Lake City: Signature Books, 1992), 127.

[2]Proclamation of the Twelve, April 6, 1845, James R. Clark, comp., *Messages of the First Presidency of The Church of Jesus Christ of Latter-day Saints*, 6 vols. (Salt Lake City: Bookcraft, 1965-75), 1:, p. 252-66; c.f., Turner, *Brigham Young: Pioneer Prophet*, 128, emphasis added.

[3]"By contrast, the temple ceremony suggested a hierarchy of distinct divine beings, including Michael Adam." As evidence of some confusion, and as opposed

chosen to separate the interchangeable *"great Eloheim"* from the interchangeable *"great Jehovah,"* making one person then two persons now. One the Father, the other the Son. They have chosen to describe Jehovah as the preexistent Christ and the God of the Old Testament. Joseph Smith and Brigham Young both said Adam was God.

In Mormonism's later theology, Jesus became Jehovah, the God of Abraham, Isaac, Jacob *and Adam*. That tardy development meant that God wasn't really the "great Eloheim Jehovah" identified in the Quorum's 1845 Proclamation sent to the world at large. Brigham Young's son of Adam, Brigham's Jesus, became modern Mormonism's father of Adam, today's Jehovah. In the Dedication Prayer for the Kirtland Temple, Section 109 of the Doctrine and Covenants (a canonized "revelation"[4]), Joseph Smith identified Jehovah as the Father and Jesus as the Son. In Joseph and Brigham's church Adam was God, Michael and "Yahovah," and "Yahovah" (Jehovah) wasn't Jesus. Mormonism's slowly evolving metaphysical system reflected incontestable confusion on the part of the prophets, both early and late, about the name and nature of God. Those prophets proved over and over again that they didn't know Him.

By ignoring the Quorum's pretentious 1845 Proclamation issued when he was the Senior Apostle, Brigham Young separated "Eloheim" (Elohim) from Jehovah and Jesus. Elohim, Brigham's "High God," wasn't Jehovah, Brigham's "Father God." Furthermore, Elohim is a plural term in Hebrew usage. Adam was Brigham's Father God for this particular earth. Elohim outranked Adam but wasn't the Father God of this particular earth. *Adam/Michael/Yahovah,* one person called different names at different times, was Brigham's Father God, and Jesus was Father Adam's Son. Jesus Christ was Adam's spiritual son with Mother Eve. In the 1830 first edition of the Book of Mormon, Mary was the *mother of God* after the manner of the flesh. *The mother of a Father who became the Son.* In the 1837 second edition of the Book of Mormon, an amended Mary became the *mother of the Son of God*

---

to the proclamation of the twelve apostles, the ceremony separated Elohim, Jehovah and Michael [Adam]. (Ibid.).

[4]Preamble, Section 109, Doctrine and Covenants (1957 edition).

after the manner of the flesh. *The mother of a Son separate from the Father.* In the first 1830 edition of the Book of Mormon, Mary gave birth to an undivided deity, an essentially trinitarian God defined "as an absolute personage of spirit who, clothed in flesh, revealed himself in Jesus Christ." The first edition of the Book of Mormon speaks of only one God who could manifest himself either as the Father or the Son.

There were many gods for Brigham's other earths, multipliers of many, but Adam, he said, and not a separate Elohim, was the only God with whom the inhabitants of this particular earth had anything to do. *Adam/Michael/Yahovah* wasn't Brigham Young's subordinate Messiah. Brigham's Jesus was the son of Father Adam in *the spirit* and in *the flesh.* Brigham's Adam was the Father in *the spirit* and in *the flesh* of every other man and woman on this particular earth. His preexistent Christ wasn't Adam, or Jehovah, the God of the Old Testament or the Father of this earth. Adam, not Elohim, was Brigham's Father God. In this twenty-first century, the true disciples of Joseph Smith and Brigham Young, Mormonism's Fundamentalists, continue to believe that Adam is God and that polygamy is the most holy and important principle ever revealed to man on earth, as essential to the exaltation of humankind as an efficacious baptism.

Brigham Young taught his followers that Adam was *the literal Father* of Jesus Christ, a finite divinity created by *the spiritual union* of Adam and Eve, and *the temporal union* of Adam and Mary. Because created in the spirit in the preexistence with Eve, and in the flesh on earth with Mary, one of his spiritual sisters, Brigham's untraditional Jesus had multiple beginnings and wasn't eternal. Brigham Young, like Joseph Smith, chose to "refute the idea that God was God from all eternity." He *was* Adam; he had been like us but then *became* the resurrected Father.

Brigham Young:

> *When the Virgin Mary conceived the child Jesus, the Father had begotten him in his own likeness. He was not begotten by [or in the likeness of] the Holy Ghost. And who is the Father? He is the first of the human*

> *family . . . . Jesus, our elder brother, was begotten in*
> *the flesh by the same character that was in the garden*
> *of Eden, and who is our Father in Heaven.*[5]

Not the only Father. Not the only God. Not the highest God. Not the God of every earth. Adam was the Father of this particular family for this particular earth, *"the only God with whom we [the members of the Church and the citizens of this world] have to do."*[6] This Adam was a God of beginnings, *"mother[s], father and descent."* Brigham Young taught his followers on July 24, 1853, that, *"The Father came down in his tabernacle and begot Jesus."*[7] "The birth of the Savior," he then later said, "was as natural as are the births of our children . . . ." By July 24, 1853, Young had rejected traditional Christianity's "Virgin Birth" and thought to assert "that God has a body capable of sexual intercourse."[8]

> *Now, let all who may hear these doctrines, pause*
> *before they make light of them, or treat them with*
> *indifference, for they will prove their salvation or*
> *damnation . . . . Now remember from this time forth,*
> *and forever, that Jesus Christ was not begotten by the*
> *Holy Ghost.*[9]

"Adam is my Father,"[10] Brigham said. *"[W]hen you see your Father in the heavens, you will see Adam; when you see your mother that bears your spirit, you will see mother Eve."*[11]

Mary's relationship with Adam was sexual. In the 1830 first edition of the Book of Mormon, Mary, a virgin, became "the mother of

---

[5]Brigham Young, in a sermon entitled in pertinent part, "Adam, Our Father and God," 22nd Annual Conference (9 April 1852), *Journal of Discourses*, 1:50-51, emphasis retained and added.

[6]Ibid., emphasis retained.

[7]Quinn, *The Mormon Hierarchy: Extensions of Power*, 751.

[8]Ibid., 759.

[9]Brigham Young, "Adam, Our Father and God," 22nd Annual Conference (9 April 1852), *Journal of Discourses*, 1:51, emphasis added.

[10]28 August 1852, *Journal of Discourses*, 6:275.

[11]Sermon, Brigham Young, Brigham Young Papers (LDS Church History Library), 8 October 1854, 24th Semiannual General Conference, emphasis added. These recitals are from a typescript version, an unofficial transcription.

God, after the manner of the flesh."[12] "[T]he Book of Mormon tended to define God as an absolute personage of spirit who, clothed in flesh, revealed himself in Jesus Christ."[13] *The Father was the Son.* "The Book of Mormon speaks of only one God who could manifest himself either as the Father or the Son."[14] How did Brigham Young deal with that, and where did he come to rest? Brigham's Father God didn't reveal himself in Jesus Christ. He was the father of Mary in the spirit with Eve, one of his wives. He was the father of Jesus in the spirit with Eve, one of his wives. He was the father of Jesus in the flesh with Mary, one of his daughters. Adam was the father of Jesus, *the spiritual son* of Adam and Eve and *the temporal son* of Adam and Mary. Adam was the literal father of a twice-created less than eternal Jesus and the God of this particular earth. The Son was subordinate to the Father who created him.

In January 1860 the Quorum of the Twelve Apostles and President Brigham Young investigated Apostle Orson Pratt "for rejecting Brigham Young's Adam-God teachings." This particular inquiry revisited issues raised in an earlier trial in March 1858. Faced with evidence of the Apostle's continuing offense, the Quorum "voted to drop Pratt"[15] precisely because he rejected Adam as God. Young spoke of that decision in public, but later. On May 4, 1867, "Brigham Young 'preaches' that Apostle Orson Pratt 'would have been cut off from the Church long ago had it not been for me.' This refers to their long dispute over [the] Adam-God theory [*better described as the Adam-God doctrine*]."[16] That is to say that Pratt would have been excommunicated in 1860 by a Quorum that said Adam was God and that the Adam/God doctrine was Joseph's doctrine, if Brigham Young hadn't intervened. As it was, the Apostles, in league with their prophet and because of the "*Adam-God doctrine*," did not restore Pratt to full fellowship for more than two months.

---

[12]Book of Mormon, 1 Nephi 11:18, 25.

[13]Thomas Alexander, "The Reconstruction of Mormon Doctrine," *Sunstone*, vol. 5 no. 4 (July-August 1980): 25.

[14]Boyd Kirkland, "Jehovah as the Father: The Development of the Mormon Jehovah Doctrine," *Sunstone* (9.2): 37.

[15]Quinn, *The Mormon Hierarchy: Extensions of Power*, 759.

[16]Ibid., 764.

As against the Quorum and Brigham, Pratt had claimed that Adam wasn't God. He had contended that Adam didn't walk and talk with himself in the Garden of Eden. While that may seem to make sense, it didn't carry the day. On July 25, 1860, the *Deseret News* published Pratt's confession of error containing humiliating revisions the Quorum required Pratt to include.[17] As reflected in the 1860 Minutes of the Quorum of the Twelve Apostles, Pratt had previously rejected not only Brigham's doctrine, but that of the prophet Joseph Smith, the man supposed by that Quorum and its leaders to have been first to teach that Adam was God. The Church denied for many years, and until such assertions became impossible, that Brigham Young ever taught that Adam was God. The Church denies to this day that Joseph Smith ever taught that Adam was God. In 1860 the Minutes of the Quorum of the Twelve, the body that investigated the intransigent Pratt, reported that, "*It was Joseph's doctrine that Adam was God . . . .*"[18] It was "*Joseph's doctrine.*" It wasn't a *hunch*; it wasn't a "*theory*"; it was a "*doctrine.*" *Joseph's doctrine.* That confirmed by what became unanimous consent that it was what Brigham said that it was. A then less than fully fellowshipped Orson Pratt came close to excommunication for rejecting Joseph and Brigham's doctrine.

Faced with some recalcitrants outside of the Quorum, Brigham Young doubled down. "Some years ago, I advanced *a doctrine* with regard to Adam being our father and God . . . . *It is one of the most glorious revealments of the economy of heaven . . . .*"[19]

> *How much unbelief exists in the minds of Latter-day Saints in regard to one particular doctrine which I revealed to them, and which God revealed to me –*

---

[17]Ibid., 759.

[18]Minutes, 4 April 1860, Quorum of the Twelve Apostles (LDS Church History Library), emphasis added.

[19]"A Few Words of Doctrine," unpublished manuscript in the Brigham Young Collection (LDS Church History Library), as cited in Discourse, October 8, 1861, Brigham Young Collection (LDS Archives), as cited in David John Buerger, "The Adam-God Doctrine," *Dialogue: A Journal of Mormon Thought*, vol. 15 no. 1 (Spring 1982): 29, quoted in Sharon I. Banister, *For Any Latter-day Saint: One Investigator's Unanswered Questions* (Fort Worth, TX: Star Bible Publications, 1988), 106, emphasis added.

namely that Adam is our father and God . . . .[20]

At a meeting of the School of the Prophets, Brigham Young said that,

> *Adam was Michael the Archangel, & he was the Father of Jesus Christ & was our God & that Joseph taught this principle.*[21]

What faithful member of Brigham's branch of the Church of Jesus Christ of Latter-day Saints has leave to disregard these solemn declarations, inspired utterances from an unimpeachable source? From the prophet who said, "I will never mislead you"? And in the end from every member of the Quorum of the Twelve Apostles? Brigham's Jesus, Joseph's Jesus, was a finite creature, the conglomerate son of two different mothers and a god of beginnings, subordinate to God the Father and less than eternal, an earthbound God in a grove.

On February 7, 1877, a few months before he died, Brigham Young delivered "his last Adam-God sermon" as the final lecture of the endowment ceremony at the first Utah Territory Temple. The Lecture at the Veil then remained in its appointed place as an element of the endowment ceremony for many years.[22] "In late 1876 Young ordered the closure of the Endowment House at Temple Square in Salt Lake City [a facility that had long functioned like a temple], and on New Year's Day 1877 [the year of his death] church leaders dedicated the St. George Temple." Near the end of his life, Young "spent . . . two months attempting to perfect the endowment ceremony," which included the "lecture at the veil" where the "officiator explained" the plan of salvation to temple ceremony participants.

"In Young's St. George temple formulation, Adam came to earth as a resurrected, exalted, and immortal God, accompanied by his wife

---

[20]*Deseret News*, 18 June 1873, reproduced in Banister, *For Any Latter-day Saint*, 86, cf 113, emphasis added.

[21]Woodruff, *Wilford Woodruff's Journal* (ed. Kenney), 16 December 1867, emphasis added.

[22]Quinn, *The Mormon Hierarchy: Extensions of Power*, 772.

Eve." The previously resurrected couple revisited mortality by partaking of the "forbidden fruit." "Adam and Eve's transgression enabled the embodiment of spirit children they had already created 'in the celestial world.'" After Adam "eventually returned to the spirit world . . . he returned 'in the spirit [more correctly said "*in his tabernacle*"] to Mary and she conceived.'" *The Lecture at the Veil provided sophisticated amplification of Young's "earlier identification of Adam as humanity's god" to the patrons of Utah's first and then only temple.*[23]

Joseph Smith and Brigham Young were not alone in preaching Joseph's doctrine that Adam was God. Prominent early leaders who believed or taught Adam was God included Joseph Smith, Brigham Young, Wilford Woodruff, Lorenzo Snow, Heber C. Kimball, Daniel H. Wells, George Q. Cannon, Joseph F. Smith, Brigham Young Jr., Abraham H. Cannon, Franklin D. Richards, Orson Hyde, Eliza R. Snow, Abraham O. Smoot, George Albert Smith, every 1860 Apostle but Orson Pratt (who later recanted), and very many more ordinary others. Adam God was always a great deal more than Brigham's particular doctrine. Wilford Woodruff offered this remarkable tribute to his leader on October 8, 1854: "I Believe that He preached the greatest sermon that was ever Deliverd to the Latter Day Saints since they have been a People."[24] The speaker: *Brigham Young*. The subject: *Adam is God*.

Brigham Young told his followers that Adam and Eve and all plant and animal life had been transported to this earth from some other planet. "[T]here is lords many, and gods many . . ." and there are worlds. "Every world has had an Adam, and an Eve," he said. "[T]he first man is always called Adam, and the first woman Eve . . ."[25] he said. Eliza R. Snow, one of Joseph's wives and one of Brigham's wives, repeated those sentiments. Joseph Smith and the

---

[23]Turner, *Brigham Young: Pioneer Prophet*, 402-3, emphasis added.

[24]*Wilford Woodruff's Journal* (ed. Kenney), October 8, 1854, Appendix 5, 752.

[25]"I Propose to Speak Upon a Subject that does not Immediately Concern Yours or My Welfare," a Sermon Delivered on October 8, 1854, taken from *The Teachings of President Brigham Young*, vol. 3 (Salt Lake City: Collier's Publishing Co., 1987), as quoted in *The Essential Brigham Young* (foreword by Campbell), 92-93.

Doctrine and Covenants taught that Adam was Michael, the prince, the archangel ("thou art a prince over them [a multitude of nations] forever").[26] Brigham's great insight (as he improved on Moses) was that Adam was made of the dust of "the earth where on he was born in the flesh," but not of the dust of this earth. *"When Yahovah Michael had organized the world,"* according to Brigham, "and brought from another kingdom [meaning from some other planet] the beasts[,] fish, fowl, and insects, and every tree, and plant . . . when He had filled the Earth with animal and vegetable life, *Michael or Adam [*"Yahovah Michael"*]* goes down to the new made world, and there he stays."[27]

The Mormon prophets and the voice of the Lord in the Doctrine and Covenants have taught the members of the Church that Adam lived in Jackson County, Missouri, no more than seven thousand years ago,[28] that life on earth did not evolve from the lower forms of the animal creation,[29] and that death didn't precede Adam and Eve on earth. The Church still teaches that Adam and Eve, Noah, the Ark, a Global Flood, the Tower of Babel, the Jaredite dispersion, and the hegira of the Book of Mormon's Hebrews involved actual people and literal events, but not that Adam is God. In the nineteenth century, Adam was God. In the modern Mormon Church, that "glorious revealment" is forgotten and false. Anyone who dares to preach that Adam is God in the twenty-first century Church puts his or her membership at risk.

MIRACLES

Brigham Young and glossolalia: "[I] [Brigham Young] preacht as

---

[26]Doctrine and Covenants 107:54.

[27]"I Propose to Speak Upon a Subject that does not Immediately Concern Yours or My Welfare," as quoted in *The Essential Brigham Young* (foreword by Campbell), 94-95, emphasis added.

[28]"Q. What are we to understand by the book which John saw, which was sealed on the back with seven seals? A. We are to understand that it contains the revealed will, mysteries, and works of God; the hidden things of his economy concerning this earth *during the seven thousand years of its continuance, or its temporal existence.*" (Doctrine and Covenants 77:6, cf. 77:10-13, emphasis added).

[29]First Presidency Statement, November 1909, reaffirmed (*Ensign*, February 2002).

opertunity prezented." The new Mormonite exercised his first great spiritual gift, speaking in tongues, enthusiastically. "Young caught the contagious fire . . . ." While praying with Elder Alpheus Gifford at Heber C. Kimball's home, Gifford and then Young "commenced speaking in tongues." That unusual gift became Brigham Young's earliest and preferred method of spiritual expression. It provided him, a man of only limited education, with a place impervious to disputation at the spiritual table. "[T]he spirit came on me like an electric shock to speak in an unknown tongue . . . ." Not many mainstream Christians spoke in unknown tongues. "Brigham Young's practice of this New Testament spiritual gift marked him as having moved to a place very much on the fringes of American religion."[30] The Pentecostal gift of tongues, although said to have been prominent in the early Church, is just as unwelcome as Adam/God in the modern Church.

In April 1830, under the administration of Joseph Smith and at the home of Joseph Knight at Colesville, Broome County, New York, "the first miracle was wrought in this dispensation." The event involved a volatile issue of spirit possession, specifically "casting out devils" from a then unbaptized victim by the name of Newel Knight. By June 1830, when the Church held its first conference at Fayette, "the Holy Spirit was poured out in a miraculous manner, many of the Saints prophesied and Newel Knight and others had heavenly visions."[31] Brigham Young's early ministry, shared with Heber C. Kimball, involved travel to "nearby towns to preach, baptize, speak in tongues, and help converts receive the Holy Ghost."[32] Young's infatuation with speaking in tongues (something he carried to Kirtland), although early, pronounced and emphatic, did not long

---

[30]Turner, *Brigham Young: Pioneer Prophet*, 30. Dale Morgan, speaking of the appetites of the early Saints, reported as follows: "Their hunger for miracle, their thirst for the marvelous, their lust for assurance that they were God's chosen people, to be preserved on the great and terrible day, made them hardly less than Joseph, the authors of his history. His questionable responsibility is the faithful image of their own." (Dale Morgan, *Dale Morgan on Early Mormonism: Correspondence & A New History*, ed. John Phillip Walker, with a Biographical Introduction by John Phillip Walker and a Preface by William Mulder [Salt Lake City, UT: Signature Books, 1986], 260).

[31]Andrew Jenson, comp., *Church Chronology: A Record of Important Events Pertaining to the History of the Church of Jesus Christ of Latter-day Saints*, 2d ed., rev. and enlarged (Salt Lake City: Deseret News, 1914) 4.

[32]Turner, *Brigham Young: Pioneer Prophet*, 31.

endure. It was an entry level process, a gift that a more accomplished Young later mostly abandoned for himself and others.

MARRIAGE AND POLYGAMY

Brigham Young taught his followers that Adam, God the Father, was a polygamist, that Jesus, God the Son, was a polygamist, and that polygamy was the heavenly order of marriage on the earth and in the life to come. "The only men who become Gods, even the sons of God," according to Brigham, "are those who enter into polygamy."[33] God spoke to a certain selected few, through the prophet Joseph, in these terms: "For behold, I reveal unto you a new and an everlasting covenant [polygamy]; and if ye abide not that covenant, then are ye damned; for no one can reject this covenant and be permitted to enter into my glory."[34] What Young taught in public (after 1852), Joseph Smith taught in private from 1831 until his death in 1844. The first seven prophets of the Mormon Church (those who served consecutively from 1830-1945) actually practiced polygamy with about one hundred forty women. With those wives, those same seven polygamous prophets fathered about two hundred thirty-three children.

Brigham Young married about fifty-six women, including ten teenagers, and had about fifty-seven children. His wives included women who were married to about thirty-nine other men before or after they married him, including women who were legally married to other men and undivorced when they married him.[35] Brigham Young was divorced or separated at least fifteen times from about fourteen or fifteen different women.[36] His particularly favored son,

---

[33]Brigham Young, *Journal of Discourses*, 11:269.

[34]Doctrine and Covenants 132:4.

[35]George D. Smith, *Nauvoo Polygamy*, 635-37.

[36]Brigham Young – *Divorced:* Elizabeth Fairchild; Mary A. Clark (Powers); Mary Ann Turley; Mary de la Montague (Woodward); Eliza Babcock; Mary J. Bigelow; Ann Eliza Webb (Dee). One of these women (Mary de la Montague (Woodward)) returned to Young in 1851. *Separated:* Diana Chase; Maria Lawrence (Smith); Emily Haws (Chesley) (Whitmarsh); Julia Foster (Hampton); Abigail Harback (Hall); K.J. Carter (Twiss); Mary E. Rollins (Lightner) (Smith); and Lucy Augusta Adams (Cobb). Two of these women (Diana Chase and Maria

John Willard Young, was perfectly situated for leadership as the First Counselor in the First Presidency when Brigham Young died. He seemed to have been Brigham's preferred successor (secretly ordained by his father to the office of apostle at the age of eleven). John Willard Young was divorced or separated at least eight times from the five different women (every one of his wives) who delivered his eighteen children.[37] Brigham Young and his First Counselor in his last First Presidency, John Willard Young, father and son misogynists, were divorced or separated between the two of them nearly twenty-five times.

"Brigham Young was a missionary when he met Augusta Cobb in Boston in 1843. A married woman with seven children, she agreed to leave her husband and two oldest children and move to Nauvoo to live with Young. Her traveling companion, eighteen-year old Harriett Cook, was 'sealed' to Brigham in the same ceremony in what was in essence a time-saving double marriage."[38] "As Joseph Smith had done on many occasions, Young also married women who already had husbands." By virtue of their sealings, those women and their biological children with their legal husbands belonged to Brigham Young (and not to their legal husbands) in the life to come. "Out of his approximately fifty three plural wives [more probably fifty-six], around fifteen women were legally

---

Lawrence (Smith)) remarried Young. One of the reported women (Lucy Augusta Adams (Cobb)) requested the cancellation of her sealing (the equivalent of an eternal divorce). (Quinn, *Origins of Power*, 607-8).

[37]John Willard Young – *Separated before divorce:* Lucy M. Canfield (four children). *Separated before reconciliation and divorce:* Elizabeth Canfield (four children). *Divorced:* Lucy Luella Cobb (four children); *Separated and divorced:* Bertha Christine Damcke (two children). *Separated:* Clara L. Jones (four children). John Willard Young's engagement to a New York City debutante was cancelled by her mother in 1903 due to a terrible scandal involving his son, William Hooper Young (the murder of Anna Pulitzer). (Quinn, *The Mormon Hierarchy: Extensions of Power*, 720).

[38]George D. Smith, *Nauvoo Polygamy*, dust jacket. In 1843, Bishop Edwin Woolley, "a missionary in Connecticut, met Louisa Rising and convinced her to marry him." She, like other plural wives, married Woolley "without first divorcing her legal husband." (Ibid.). Men like William Clayton, Heber C. Kimball and Parley Pratt "courted potential plural wives on their missions." George D. Smith concludes that "it has to be acknowledged that they were as enthusiastic about their marital arrangements as they were about their gospel message." (Ibid.). At the same time, their respect for the civil covenants of others left something to be desired.

married to other men at the time of their sealings to Young.[39] Some of those prior marriages had failed, others were in the process of failing, but others persisted for many decades."[40] Brigham Young, the leader of the Utah faction of the Church of Jesus Christ of Latter-day Saints from about 1845 to 1877, was married (and sealed) during his lifetime to approximately fifteen women who were already legally married to other men and undivorced. Brigham Young's polyandry was sexual, as he proved with Zina Huntington (Jacobs) (Smith) (Young), the mother of Young's daughter Zina, and with the undivorced Lucy Decker (Seeley).[41] In 1886, the United States Supreme Court sustained the decision of a lower Utah court which defined the crime of "'cohabitation' as not requiring proof of sexual intercourse but rather of marital relationship."

Brigham Young addresses his followers on the subject of adultery: "[I]t is one of the laws of that kingdom [the celestial kingdom] where our Father dwells, that if a man was found guilty of adultery, he must have his blood shed, and that is near at hand."[42] "[T]he time will come . . . when those who profess our faith, if they are guilty of what some of this people are guilty of, will find the axe laid at the root of the tree, and they will be hewn down. What has been must be again . . . ."[43] Young was not hesitant to proudly proclaim his own stunning indiscretions.

> *Moses made the Bible to say his wife was taken out of his side, was made of one of his ribs . . . . The Lord knows if I had lost a rib for each wife I have, I should*

---

[39]Brigham Young's *fifteen* polyandrous wives: Augusta Adams (Cobb); Jemima Angell (Stringham); Amanda Barnes (Smith); Clarissa Blake (Homiston); Mary Ann Clark (Powers); Amy Cooper (Aldrich); Lucy Decker (Seeley); Lydia Farnsworth (Mayhew); Emily Haws (Whitmarsh); Zina Huntington (Jacobs); Mary de la Montague (Woodward); Phebe Morton (Angell); Margaret Pierce (Whitesides); Mary Elizabeth Rollins (Lightner); Hannah Tapfield (King).

[40]Turner, *Brigham Young: Pioneer Prophet*, 136, cf. 441-42 n 56.

[41]Lucy Decker (Seeley) had two children (Isaac Joseph Seeley and Harriet Christina Seeley) with her legal husband, William Seeley, from whom she was said to have been separated but not divorced when she married Brigham Young. She appears to have had seven children with Brigham Young while still legally married to William Seeley.

[42]Blood Atonement, 8 February 1857, *Journal of Discourses*, 4:215-21.

[43]Ibid.

*have had none left long ago. Some try to say how
many wives the Governor of Utah has, but if they can
tell, they can tell more than I can, for I do not know
how many I have; I have not counted them up for
many years. I did not know how many I had before I
left the United States I had so many. I heard that I
had ninety. Why bless your souls, ninety is not a
beginning. You might ask me if I have ever seen them
all; I answer no; I see a few of them I pick up myself
here. I have lots, and scores I never see nor shall not
until the morning of the resurrection.*[44]

Brigham Young considered "sexual access" a "patriarchal privilege." John G. Turner, Brigham Young's twenty-first century biographer, recounted this:

*"It is perfectly right," Young taught at Winter
Quarters, "that you enjoy a woman all you can to
overflowing & tell her to keep all about her clean &
neat." When a December 1847 council condemned
Young's adopted son John D. Lee for his cruel
treatment of his wives, including Lee's purported
boast that he had "frigged [Young's sister-in-law]
Louisa Free 20 times in one night," Young joined in
upbraiding Lee but seemed to make light of some
allegations. "[T]hats the matter with John," Young
laughed, "he has loved his women too much & frigged
them too much."*[45]

When Brigham Young promoted the hated reformation in the Utah Territory, he also stood behind the oppressive Mormon catechism, a list of deeply personal questions addressed by surrogates (visiting instructors) to all of the Latter-day Saints. The Reformation, a ritual-led recleansing, started in 1855 and flowered in the fall of 1856 with violent descriptions of the shortcomings of the Saints. At

---

[44]"I Propose to Speak Upon a Subject that does not Immediately Concern Yours or My Welfare," 343-68, as quoted in *The Essential Brigham Young* (foreword by Campbell), 94-95, emphasis added.

[45]Turner, *Brigham Young: Pioneer Prophet*, 158-59, emphasis added. "Frigged" was an early Mormon parody of the "f" word.

some point it progressed to the frenzied rebaptism of sinners, described to mean almost everyone. The Saints embraced the cleansing with manic intensity. The leaders preached the doctrine of blood atonement – human sacrifice for unatonable transgressions – from the pulpit in the Tabernacle. Heber C. Kimball "declared to the people that Brigham Young was his God, and their God, and the only God they would ever see if they did not obey him."[46] This frenetic period involving public confessions and extraordinary public meetings of the Priesthood resulted in a reign of terror, shocking outrages upon various citizens and a crusade against intellectual societies.[47] Last, but not least, people were asked deeply personal questions that put their private thoughts and acts in the public forum for humiliating review.[48] In the final analysis, this unsettling rebirth and all that it entailed was an important factor among other factors that contributed to cause the horrendous Mountain Meadows Massacre involving the deaths of about one hundred and twenty men, women and children traveling to California in a wagon train in the fall of 1857.[49]

Brigham Young taught his followers that a woman could leave a less distinguished but faithful man to marry a more distinguished faithful man who held a higher office in the priesthood if the more distinguished man was disposed to take her. Such a woman,

---

[46]T.B.H. Stenhouse, *The Rocky Mountain Saints: A Full and Complete History of the Mormons, from the First Vision of Joseph Smith to the Last Courtship of Brigham Young* (New York: D. Appleton and Company, 1873) 294. "Joseph Smith was God to the inhabitants of the earth when he was amongst us, and Brigham is God now."

[47]Ibid., 292. "26 Nov. [1856], *Deseret News* publishes new Hymn, 'The Reformation,' with fourth verse 'We ought our bishops to sustain, / Their counsels to abide / And knock down every dwelling / Where wicked folks reside." (Quinn, *The Mormon Hierarchy: Extensions of Power*, 753).

[48]Among those questions: "Have you ever committed murder, shed innocent blood, or given your consent thereto? Have you ever committed adultery? Have you ever spoken evil of the church authorities or anointed of the Lord? Have you ever betrayed your brethren? Have you ever stolen or taken anything that was not your own? Have you ever taken the name of God in vain? Have you ever been drunk? Do you pay all your tithing? Do you teach your children the gospel? Do you pray in your family night and morning? Do you attend your ward meetings? Do you pray in secret? Do you wash your bodies once a week?" (Quinn, *The Mormon Hierarchy: Extensions of Power*, 753).

[49]Will Bagley, *Blood of the Prophets: Brigham Young and the Massacre at Mountain Meadows* (Norman, OK: University of Oklahoma Press, 2002).

according to Young, didn't need to be divorced. Young took the
legal wife and biological children of Henry Jacobs, and the time and
eternity spiritual wife of a deceased Joseph Smith, Zina Huntington
(Jacobs) (Smith), the mother of Jacobs' children, on such terms. He
was, he said, Joseph's proxy. Jacobs, who walked in another man's
shoes, would need to find another wife. Only three women were
mentioned by name in the Book of Mormon, and they were
distinguished by their insignificance.

Joseph Smith married Zina Huntington (Jacobs) following extended
persistent courting before and after she married Jacobs and before
she married Brigham Young. Zina married Joseph Smith,
becoming the wife of two husbands, when she was six or seven
months pregnant with Henry Jacobs' child. In 1841 when she was
twenty and Smith was thirty-five, Zina received (while courting
Jacobs) a secret proposal from the Mormon prophet, who explained
that God was restoring the ancient order of plural marriage. She
declined the proposal and married Jacobs. Smith then later told
Zina, through her brother Dimick, that an angel with a drawn
sword told him that if he did not establish the plural marriage
principle (in her case polyandry) that he would lose his position and
his life.[50] Joseph's God is thus supposed to have insisted upon
Joseph's polyandry. When Zina also married Joseph Smith, she
was pregnant with Jacob's child. After she was married to Smith,
she didn't live with him. She had a second child with Jacobs after
the death of Joseph Smith and before she married and had yet
another child with Brigham Young. Young, while claiming her for
time and as Joseph's proxy, sent the heartbroken Jacobs (who was
ill at the time) away on a mission. "In all his previous missions he
had stayed in America, usually in Illinois, but now [in a call
imposed while Henry and Zina were trailing west] he was sent
overseas to England."[51]

Zina belonged to Henry Jacobs for time and to Joseph Smith for
time and eternity, but until Smith died she lived with her child and
Henry Jacobs. When Joseph Smith died in 1844, and while the
Saints, including the pregnant Zina and Henry, were traveling west,
Brigham claimed Henry's wife for time in his own right and as

---

[50]Compton, *In Sacred Loneliness: The Plural Wives of Joseph Smith*, 77-82.
[51]Ibid.

Joseph's proxy.   Zina later became the ranking woman in the
Mormon Church, where she served as the President of the Relief
Society from 1888 to 1901.   In her case, Young simply claimed,
because he could, what might be called a life estate. In the Mormon
afterlife, Zina and her children, including Brigham's child and
Henry's children, will belong to Joseph Smith, the man to whom
Zina was sealed but with whom she had no children. When Joseph
Smith sealed his already married polyandrous wives to himself, he
acquired not only the women, but also their progeny. Those wives
and their children belonged to him, and not to their legal husbands
and biological fathers, in a Mormon afterlife. Orson Hyde's ten
children with Marinda Nancy Johnson (Hyde) (Smith) will belong
to Joseph Smith in the life to come.

ACCUSATIONS, ADULTERY, RECLEANSING
AND ADOPTION

Brigham Young taught the Latter-day Saints that death or
castration was the appropriate punishment for fornication and
adultery and allegedly ordered the assassinations of apostates (and
some few equally unlikable others).

Brigham Young was indicted by a federal grand jury in 1871 for
"lascivious cohabitation," and for the "murder" of one Richard
Yates.   William ("Wild Bill") Hickman, one of Brigham's Utah
Territory enforcers, implicated his former leader "in the 1857 death
of non-Mormon trader Richard Yates." "Suspected of a long train
of church-ordered as well as freelance murders, Hickman met with
Deputy U.S. Marshall Sam Gilson and turned state's evidence."[52]
He ultimately admitted to committing a great many murders.

"Wild Bill" Hickman had ten wives and thirty-nine children. "Most
of his wives divorced him in 1867." Only one of his wives (his first
wife) remained with him. Hickman was baptized by John D. Lee,
the executor of the Mountain Meadows Massacre and an adopted
son of Brigham Young. He had been ordained a Seventy by Joseph
Smith himself. He was a bodyguard for Joseph Smith and a loyal

---

[52]Turner, *Brigham Young: Pioneer Prophet*, 364-66.

friend to Smith's volatile, promiscuous younger brother William Smith. Hickman, who had generous access to Brigham Young in the Utah Territory, "testified that 'Brigham Young had *ordered* him to kill Yates . . . .'" "Brigham Young and others were indicted on testimony provided by Hickman." Later Latter-day Saint leaders, long after the death of Hickman, restored the particularly violent man to a position of grace posthumously. Because of those extraordinary proceedings, "Wild Bill" Hickman is now a celestial Saint. His calling and election was made sure many years after the fact. *"1934, May 5: As authorized by President Heber J. Grant, all former priesthood and temple blessings were restored."*[53]

In 1870 a new Territorial Governor, J. Wilson Shaffer (an appointee of President Ulysses S. Grant) wrote to Secretary of State Hamilton Fish. "I am fully satisfied," he said, "that this people are worse than their enemies ever charged." Shaffer then alleged that Young, the man in charge, had sanctioned murders and assassinations. Then, finally, he discussed a terribly difficult fact. "As the law now stands the Mormons have entire control, and a verdict in favor of the Government or a Gentile cannot be had."[54] The new Territorial Chief Justice James McKean, ignoring judicial niceties in search of a solution, determined that the federally appointed U.S. Marshal would impanel juries in his court. That decision, which was contrary to territorial law, allowed the judge to stack the juries with non-Mormons.[55] Meanwhile Alderman Jeter Clinton, a Mormon bully, "ordered the destruction of $20,000 worth of liquor owned by non-Mormons who had refused to pay the city's steep licquor license fee." In a trial that followed in Judge McKean's court, "an entirely non-Mormon jury . . . convicted Clinton of malicious destruction of property." The United States Supreme Court "overturned the conviction, ruling that McKean had violated territorial law through his jury-selection process." The *Engelbrecht v. Clinton* decision "quashed all of the pending indictments," including the lascivious cohabitation and Yates murder charges against Brigham Young.[56]

---

[53]Richard S. Van Wagoner and Steven C. Walker, *A Book of Mormons* (Salt Lake City: Signature Books, 1982), 118-24, emphasis retained.

[54]Shaffer, quoted in Turner, *Brigham Young: Pioneer Prophet*, 363.

[55]Ibid., 363-64.

[56]Ibid., 367-68.

Before the Supreme Court's decision, Young faced an indictment for the murder of Yates (based on the testimony of the formerly trusted Hickman) and the prospect of a trial in the court of a hostile judge (Territorial Chief Justice James McKean). Faced with those uncomfortable facts, Young "slipped out of the city late at night."[57] Until his indictment and all other pending indictments were later quashed, Young acted like a person guilty as charged. "He briefly considered fleeing further south," thinking to "continue a line of settlements into Mexico . . . ." He asked his non-Mormon protector Thomas Kane to "investigate the possibility of securing a tract of land in British Columbia and a corresponding guarantee of religious freedom from the British government . . . ." Kane rejected those suggestions as "impossible." Mormon leaders then looked for ways to get Judge McKean removed or to "obstruct the trials."[58] The quashed indictments made those increasingly desperate maneuvers less inevitable. Brigham Young's death in 1877 put an end to the prosecutions.

Brigham Young taught and practiced "the law of adoption," a doctrine that allowed more powerful men to ritually adopt less powerful men into their families, a practice by means of which the greater men became the spiritual equivalent of biological parents. In this the lesser men, together with their lesser wives and lesser children, became the earthly and eternal recipients of the greater man's more eternally marketable virtue. This, like the fabled second anointing, was yet another Mormon indulgence, one more nineteenth-century sin.

John D. Lee, who was executed for his crimes at Mountain Meadows in 1877, was restored to all of his priesthood and temple blessings in 1961. Lee's restoration included all of the blessings associated with the vaunted second anointing, in his peculiar case that meant salvation/exaltation *despite* the shedding of *innocent blood*.[59] John D. Lee, who was Brigham Young's adopted son,

---

[57]Ibid., 366.

[58]Ibid.

[59]John D. Lee: "I was among the first to receive my washings and anointings, and even received my second anointing, which made me an equal in the order of the Priesthood . . . . There were about forty men who attained to that order in the Priesthood, including the twelve Apostles and the first presidency, and to them was

sometimes signed his name like the dutiful son of his spiritual father. He was, because of that spiritual protocol, John D. Lee "Young." Lee's "calling and election" was made sure in 1961 by reason of those rehabilitating posthumous proceedings. John D. Lee will be a King in the Kingdom of Heaven, a priest, a celestial saint and a god in the afterlife. Lee's brave biographer (faithful Latter-day Saint Juanita Brooks), after doing much heavy lifting and later in her life, privately came to feel that Brigham Young was directly responsible for the Mountain Meadows Massacre. She concluded that John D. Lee, although executed for his crimes, "would make it to heaven before Brigham Young."[60]

POWER

On February 12, 1849, shortly after the entry of the Mormon pioneers into the Salt Lake Valley, Brigham Young, who had been ordained to the office by the Council of Fifty, referred to himself as "King & Prest," acknowledging his appointment "to [the] theocratic office of King."[61] Young, who led the Latter-day Saints from 1844-1877, thus became the King of the Kingdom of Israel on Earth. He was, because of that appointment, the Mormon Pope.

When Brigham Young took his followers west, and when Mormons controlled the Utah Territory, Young "gave instruction to local Mormon leaders to be sure that elections produced the desired results." Utah voters, in common with voters in some other states, cast numbered ballots and election officials recorded their names. "The procedure added an element of coercion to Utah elections . . . ." More than any other American state or province, the Utah Territory represented a "union of political and ecclesiastical authority. Utah's elections were the nation's least suspenseful . . .

---

intrusted the keeping of the records. I was the head clerk; Franklin D. Richards was my assistant clerk. My office was in room number one, at President Young's apartments." (John D. Lee, *Mormonism Unveiled; Or, The Life and Confessions of the Late Mormon Bishop, John D. Lee* [St. Louis, MO: Bryan, Brand & Company; New York: W.H. Stelle & Co., 1877; photomechanical reprint of the original 1877 edition, Salt Lake City: Modern Microfilm Co.], 169, emphasis added).

[60]Karl Brooks, author (Will Bagley) interview note, 12 January 1996 (St. George, UT). Bagley, *Blood of the Prophets*, 363.

[61]Quinn, *The Mormon Hierarchy: Extensions of Power*, 747.

."[62]   Church-supported candidates in Utah continued to win elections "after the 1878 adoption of a secret ballot." Brigham Young died in 1877, a year before the adoption of a secret ballot.[63]

On 22 November 1855, Brigham Young secretly ordained two of his sons, John Willard Young (age eleven) and Brigham Young Jr. (age eighteen) to office as apostles in connection with receiving the endowment. "The Twelve doesn't learn of these ordinations for almost nine years. In later years he secretly ordains two other sons [Joseph A. Young and Heber Young] as apostles."[64] Joseph Smith had himself envisioned that his sons would one day lead a Patriarchal Church. Young ignored the prophet's children's patriarchal claims.

On 6 October 1870, "Brigham Young tells general conference that his published talks are scripture."[65] Why would any presently active member of the Brighamite faction of Joseph Smith's fractured following choose not to believe his or her "American Moses"? The Chancellor of the Lord's universities? The King of the Kingdom of Israel on Earth? When Brigham Young iterated his Adam/God doctrine in one of the published sermons in which it is most aptly described, it was specifically denoted as scripture. According to the prophet, "*I feel inclined here to make a little scripture.*"[66] He clearly meant to say that he was a prophet acting while duly inspired by the gift and power of God. That Adam was our Father and God, according to the Mormon leader, was "one of the most glorious revealments of the economy of heaven . . . ." It was something, he said more than once, that God had said to him.

On September 1, 1858, Young writes to Thomas L. Kane "that the

[62]Turner, *Brigham Young: Pioneer Prophet*, 243.

[63]The Church isn't a democracy, and the members don't elect its leaders. The theocratic process is properly called "the sustaining of the authorities." In the beginning, the ratification of the leadership was subject to a standing vote. At present members raise their arms to the square in favor of every request.

[64]Quinn, *The Mormon Hierarchy: Extensions of Power*, 752-53.

[65]Ibid., 767.

[66]"I Propose to Speak Upon a Subject that does not Immediately Concern Yours or My Welfare," a Sermon Delivered on October 8, 1854, taken from *The Teachings of President Brigham Young*, 343-68, as reproduced in *The Essential Brigham Young* (foreword by Campbell), 90, emphasis added.

time is not far distant when Utah shall be able to assume her rights and place among the family of nations."[67] On "9 Aug. [1874], Brigham Young dictates [a] revelation on [the] communitarian United Order. It is officially published in [the] *Deseret News* and *Journal of Discourses* but never canonized."[68] Brigham Young sought to organize and administer a separate theocratic kingdom in the west that would not be subject to the federal government's laws, traditions and restraints. He ignored western civilization's common law, established religious tribunals (probate courts) and repeatedly challenged the authority of the federal judiciary. His minions terrorized federal officials sent to conduct the affairs of the Territorial Government. Young sought by his actions to create an independent theocratic nation or an essentially sovereign theocratic state.

SLAVERY

The Utah Legislature, which functioned under the absolute control of Brigham Young, codified slavery in 1852 because the Mormon leader told his people that "we must believe in slavery."[69] Utah was the only territory assimilated as part of the Mexican cession seen to codify the practice of slavery.[70] Utah became "the only western territory where African-American slavery and slave-sales were protected by territorial statute."[71] Brigham Young took a slave as

---

[67]Quinn, *The Mormon Hierarchy: Extensions of Power*, 757.

[68]Ibid., 770.

[69]Ibid., 749.

[70]"Brigham Young had power to pass any measure he saw fit. He was pupet king and sole law giver of the Mormon world. By his council any man might or might not be sent to the legislature – and no member dare to oppose any measure that the prophet saw fit to have brought forward." (George Armstrong Hicks, quoted in Polly Aird, Jeff Nichols and Will Bagley, eds., *Kingdom in the West: The Mormons and the American Frontier, Volume 13 – Playing with Shadows: Voices of Dissent in the Mormon West* [Norman, OK: The Arthur H. Clark Company, 2011], 130).

[71]Quinn, *Origins of Power*, 659. "By 1850, approximately eighty enslaved and thirty free black men and women lived in Utah, the slave population augmented by a group of Mississippi Mormons that brought their human property to the valley in 1848." An 1851 census unsurprisingly understated their numbers and "falsely suggested all would soon go to California." (Turner, *Brigham Young: Pioneer Prophet*, 223). 1850s "Mormons are prohibited from owning Indian slaves, but can

tithing and selected William Hooper, another slaveholder, to be the U.S. Congressional Delegate for the Territory of Utah's at-large district in 1859. Hooper, who had been the Secretary of the Utah Territory in 1857 and 1858, became a Member of the Council of Fifty in 1867. Apostle John Willard Young, that favored son of an autocratic father, named one of his sons William Hooper Young.

Jane Elizabeth Manning James was the mother of the first black child born in the Utah Territory. After she joined the Church, she became a servant in the homes of Joseph Smith and Brigham Young. Manning petitioned the First Presidency to be endowed and sealed (with her children) to Walker Lewis, an African-American Elder. "Her petitions were consistently ignored or refused." In 1894 she was adopted into the family of Joseph Smith in a special ceremony. In a temple she was not permitted to enter, Jane Manning James was "attached as a Servitor for eternity to the prophet Joseph Smith . . . ." "Not satisfied to be an eternal servant in the Smith family, she continued to petition to receive her own temple endowment." In 1979, nearly seventy-two years after her death and long after that earlier procedure (Servitorship), James was posthumously endowed by proxy.[72]

"As was the case in most western states and territories, Utah blacks could not vote, hold territorial offices, serve on juries, or serve in the state militia."[73] Brigham Young, who "believed that God had cursed black people with inferiority and servitude, viewed American Indians as savages inclined toward idleness, and –

___

own African-American slaves." (Quinn, *The Mormon Hierarchy: Extensions of Power*, 750). As of March 7, 1852, "Utah law allows whites to 'purchase' Native Americans [Lamanites] from Indian or Mexican slave-owners in order to prevent these captives from being killed. Purchaser must 'immediately go' before county selectmen or probate judge who will 'bind out the same by indenture for the term of not exceeding twenty years.'" (Ibid.). It was out of the pot and into the fire.

[72]"Jane Manning James" (accessed 11 December, 2018), available from https://en.wikipedia.org/wiki/Jane_Manning_James; Internet, p. 3 of 7.

[73]Turner, *Brigham Young: Pioneer Prophet*, 223. "Young announces this policy in connection with the Utah legislature's legalization of African-American slavery. The law provides for only one interference with property rights of slave-owners: 'if any master or mistress shall have sexual or carnal intercourse with his or her servant or servants of the African race, he or she shall forfeit all claim to said servant or servants to the commonwealth . . . .'" (Quinn, *The Mormon Hierarchy: Extensions of Power*, 749-50).

especially until his later years – made misogynistic comments about women."[74] On August 2, 1857, "Brigham Young preaches, 'There are probably but few men in the world who care about the private society of women less than I do.'"[75]

> *When the servants of God in any age have consented to follow a woman for a leader, either in public or a family capacity, they have sunk beneath the standard their organization has fitted them for: when a people of God submit to that, their Priesthood is taken from them, and they become as any other people. ... Let our wives be the weaker vessels, and the men be men, and show the women by their superior ability that God gives husbands wisdom and ability to lead their wives into his presence.*[76]

Brigham Young decried miscegenation and instructed the members of his Church never to marry a black: "Shall I tell you the law of God in regard to the African race? If the white man who belongs to the chosen seed mixes his blood with the seed of Cain, the penalty, under the law of God, is death on the spot.[77] This will always be so."[78] "[N]egroes are the children of old Cain . . . . [A]ny man

---

[74]Turner, *Brigham Young: Pioneer Prophet*, 5. "11 Dec. [1866], Brigham Young Jr. writes in his diary that 'a nigger' is found dead in Salt Lake City with this note penned to [his] corpse: 'Let this be a warning to all niggers that they meddle not with white women.'" (Quinn, *The Mormon Hierarchy: Extensions of Power*, 764). Brigham Young presided "over a secret parliament composed of the same Mormon representatives who served in the legislature. When the shadow government approved a measure, it was immediately approved by the legislature; whatever the Council of Fifty disapproved, the legislature rejected." (George D. Smith, *Nauvoo Polygamy*, 298).

[75]Quinn, *The Mormon Hierarchy: Extensions of Power*, 755.

[76]"The Love of Truth and Righteousness Implanted in the Natural Man – Kindness and Firmness in Governments," Remarks made by President Brigham Young, Tabernacle (Salt Lake City: 15 June 1862), reported by G.D. Watt, *Journal of Discourses*, 9:308, emphasis added.

[77]The law of Utah in regard to the African race: "[I]f any white person shall be guilty of sexual intercourse with any of the African race, they shall be subject, on conviction thereof, to a fine of not exceeding one thousand dollars, nor less than five hundred, . . . and imprisonment not exceeding three years." (Statute, quoted in Quinn, *The Mormon Hierarchy: Extensions of Power*, 749-50).

[78]"The Laws of God Relative to the African Race," *Journal of Discourses*, 10:110.

having one drop of the seed of Cain in him cannot hold the priesthood."[79] Joseph Smith's controversial "Book of Abraham" gave scriptural warrant to the priesthood ban.[80]

VIOLENCE

Brigham Young informed the Latter-day Saints that blood atonement was the law of God. "The wickedness and ignorance of the nations forbid this principle's being in full force, but the time will come when the law of God will be in full force." "I have seen scores and hundreds of people for whom there would have been a chance (in the last resurrection there will be) if their lives had been taken and their blood spilled on the ground as a smoking incense to the Almighty, but who are now angels to the devil, until our elder brother Jesus Christ raises them up – conquers death, hell, and the grave."[81]

Brigham Young incorporated the oath of vengeance into the temple ceremony, where it remained as a particularly violent element of that particularly violent Mormon ritual until February 15, 1927, fifty years after his death. The oath read as follows: "You and each of you do covenant and promise that you will pray and never cease to pray to Almighty God to avenge the blood of the prophets upon this nation, and that you will teach the same to your children and to your children's children unto the third and fourth generation."[82] This generational hatred was passed to vulnerable children by

---

[79]Quinn, *The Mormon Hierarchy: Extensions of Power*, 749.

[80]". . . Noah . . . blessed him [Pharaoh] with the blessings of the earth, and with the blessings of wisdom, but cursed him as pertaining to the Priesthood." (The Pearl of Great Price, Abraham 1:26). ". . . Pharaoh being of that lineage by which he could not have the right of Priesthood, notwithstanding the Pharaohs would fain claim it from Noah, through Ham . . . ." (*Journal of Discourses*, 1:27).

[81]"To Know God is Eternal Life – God the Father of Our Spirits and Bodies – Things Created Spiritually First – Atonement by Shedding of Blood," Sermon Delivered 8 February 1857, *Journal of Discourses*, 4:215-21, reproduced at *The Essential Brigham Young* (foreword by Campbell), 110.

[82]"*Proceedings Before the Committee on Privileges and Elections of the United States Senate in the Matter of the Protests Against the Right of Hon. Reed Smoot, a Senator from the State of Utah, to Hold His Seat*," 59th Congress, 1st Session, Senate Document No. 486, 4 vols. (1 vol. index), (Washington; Government Printing Office, 1904) (see https://archive.org/details/proceedingsbefor01unitrich/page/n5).

means of indoctrination at difficult times. The indoctrination was reminiscent of Arabia's Wahhabism.[83]

In Brigham Young's Utah (and extending on to 1896 and statehood), there are as many lynchings (eleven) "as there are judicial executions (eleven)." The lynchings are primarily the work of Mormon "mobs."[84] These brutal events, which ignored the moral strictures of the law, were said to have operated "upon a more speedy, economical and salutary principle . . . ."[85] There were, in addition to the lynchings, an untold number of murders in the territory. Most of the many murders (apostates and Gentiles were favored victims[86]) went unpunished according to the principles of "mountain common law," a phrase popularized by Joseph Smith's influential cousin, Apostle George A. Smith. *Deseret News*, May 23, 1860: "Murder after murder has been committed with impunity within the precincts of Great Salt Lake City, till such occurrences do not seemingly attract much attention, particularly when the murdered have had the reputation of being thieves and murderers or associating with such characters from day to day . . . ."[87] One of the persons lynched by a Mormon mob (for the murder of an unarmed man in Logan, Utah) was Charles A. Benson, the

---

[83]The Father of Utah Journalism (Stenhouse) saw Islamic parallels in 1873: "Not inaptly or without logical force has Joseph Smith been designated the Mohammed of America. Between the prophet of Arabia and the prophet of Nauvoo (each claiming divine prophetic powers) there is a strong family resemblance and a more than singular coincidence of expression." (Stenhouse, *The Rocky Mountain Saints*, 203).

[84]Quinn, *The Mormon Hierarchy: Extensions of Power*, 759.

[85]Ibid. July 11, 1860. The *Deseret News* "favorably reports [the] lynching of horse-thief A.B. Baker by [a] posse deputized to arrest him." Calling this "summary justice," the Church publication admits the procedure was "not exactly according to law." The territorial authorities, under Mormon control, were themselves agents of abuse. "1 Feb. [1860], *Deseret News* reports that Orrin Porter Rockwell [Joseph's bodyguard and Brigham's "B'Hoy"] shoots Martin Oats to death after Oats accuses him [Rockwell] of stealing cattle. Rockwell reports [the] incident to Lehi authorities who dismiss him without further action." (Ibid., 759).

[86]"3 May [1854], [a] month after Brigham Young publicly condemns and excommunicates lawyer Jesse T. Hartley, he starts for [the] eastern states apparently without Young's safe-conduct pass. William Hickman murders him during [the] trip with Apostle Orson Hyde and Hosea Stout in [a] canyon. Stout's diary verifies Hickman's later account of this." (Ibid., 751).

[87]*Deseret News*, Editorial, quoted in Quinn, *The Mormon Hierarchy: Extensions of Power*, 759.

eldest son of a deceased apostle, the early Ezra T. Benson.[88]

Brigham Young's militia, under the local command of Brigham Young's Iron County militia commander William Dame[89] and stake president Isaac Haight, massacred approximately one hundred twenty emigrants from Arkansas, more than two-thirds of them women and children, at the scene of the Mountain Meadows Massacre in southern Utah on September 11, 1857. The perpetrators of that bloody deed were a body of radical men totally loyal to Brigham Young and directed on the ground by his adopted son, John D. Lee, Young's former bodyguard, emissary, clerk, brother-in-law, son-in-law and trusted friend (a member of the Council of Fifty who had earlier received the vaunted second anointing). The assailants stole the massacred emigrants' substantial belongings, including clothing from the bodies of the dead. They provided some small part of the loot ("which included 1,000 head of cattle") to the Indians who assisted them, then failed to bury their victims' bodies (because Indians didn't bury their victims' bodies). Indian agent Brigham Young and Indian specialist Jacob Hamblin charged the government for the upkeep and location of seventeen orphans under the age of five – children allowed to survive because it was thought that they were unable to report the details of the atrocity because they were of tender age. The children were initially placed in the homes of their parents' assailants, one small boy by the name of Fancher in the home of John D. Lee.

Approximately four months after these horrendous events (in

---

[88]F. Ross Peterson, "A History of Cache County," *Utah Centennial County History Series*, 95-99. When Benson, "a young man with a mean reputation" was caught, he "was taken to the jail in the rear of the original county building." Members of the posse that apprehended him, and citizens of Logan who failed to disperse, rushed the building, broke into the cell, dragged the prisoner out and strangled him with a rope draped over "the Cache County courthouse signposts." (Ibid.). No one paid any price for this extrajudicial lynching event.

[89]"20 Feb. [1854, before the Mountain Meadows Massacre], William H. Dame receives [this] patriarchal blessing: 'Thou shalt be called to act at the head of a portion of thy brethren and of the Lamanites [Native Americans] in the redemption of Zion and the avenging of the blood of the Prophets.'" According to historian D. Michael Quinn, "He orders the Mountain Meadows Massacre." (Quinn, *The Mormon Hierarchy: Extensions of Power*, 751). This author considers that conclusion highly unlikely.

January 1858), Brigham Young (whose consent to plurally marry was required) rewarded Lee and Isaac Haight (the executors of the massacre) by marrying them, with some few days between, Lee to Emma Batchelder (who was already married to another Mormon man whose domestic entitlement Young abruptly arranged to dismiss), and Haight to Elizabeth Summers. The two conspirators were married to their exciting new plural wives in the generous prophet's private sealing room.[90] When knowledgeable others, including one of the bridegrooms, sought to inform Young of the details surrounding the atrocity after the murders, Young said he told his reporters to say no more about it.[91] There were no church trials and there was no private or public condemnation of this monstrous early American crime. The Mormons placed the blame for the massacre at the time and for a long time after on the Indians. Because of that, they didn't bury the bodies.

After the fact, according to historian Michael Quinn,

> *[Brigham Young] tells participants that he approves of the [Mountain Meadows] massacre and lets them know he expects them to exonerate each other in [a] court of law. He publicly intimidates anyone who is inclined to give evidence against Mormon participants. He refuses to give federal authorities*

---

[90]"In 1858, Brigham Young gave me [John D. Lee] my seventeenth wife, Emma Batchelder. I was sealed to her while a member of the Territorial Legislature [and a few months after the massacre]. Brigham Young said that Isaac Haight, who was also in the Legislature, and I, needed some young women to renew our vitality, so he gave us both a dashing young bride. In 1859 I was sealed to my eighteenth wife, Terresa Morse. I was sealed to her by order of Brigham Young . . . . After 1861 I never asked Brigham Young for another wife. By my eighteen real wives I have been the father of sixty-four children." (Lee, *Confessions*, 289).

[91]"[Question:] Did John D. Lee report to you at any time after this massacre what had been done at that massacre, and if so, what did you reply to him in reference thereto? Answer – Within some two or three months after the massacre he called at my office and had much to say with regard to the Indians, their being stirred up to anger and threatening the settlements of the whites, and then commenced giving an account of the massacre. I told him to stop, as from what I had already heard by rumor, I did not wish my feelings harrowed up with a recital of detail." ("Deposition of Brigham Young Regarding the Mountain Meadows Massacre" [July 30, 1875], reproduced at Lee, *Confessions*, 303-6).

> *information that would implicate nearly all [of the]*
> *adults of [a] small Mormon community in [the]*
> *massacre and division of victims' property. Then*
> *when total denial becomes impossible, Young*
> *scapegoats three men through excommunication and*
> *arranges for participants to testify against (and*
> *jurymen to convict) only John D. Lee, Brigham*
> *Young's adopted son and Council of Fifty member.*[92]

Lee, it should be remembered, is the same man who got the "dashing young bride" to "renew" his "vitality" in the prophet's private sealing room shortly after the massacre.

On September 8, 1886, Isaac Haight, one of the three men excommunicated for his role in the Mountain Meadows Massacre, died in Arizona. Haight (like Lee but earlier) was "fully reinstated in the church sixteen years after his excommunication for [allegedly] ordering [the] Mountain Meadows Massacre."[93] Many people, including this author, think that Brigham Young ordered the Mountain Meadows Massacre.

> *30 May [1861], Brigham Young preaches to [a]*
> *southern Utah congregation filled with participants in*
> *[the] Mountain Meadows Massacre: "Pres. Young*
> *said that the company that was used up at the*
> *Mountain Meadows were the Fathers, Mothers, Bros.,*
> *Sisters & connections of those that Murdered the*
> *Prophets; they Merit[ed] their fate, & the only thing*
> *that ever troubled him was the lives of the Women &*
> *children [about two-thirds of the about one hundred*
> *and twenty victims], but that under the circumstances*
> *[that] could not be avoided. Although there had been*
> *[some] that want[e]d to betray the Brethren into the*
> *hands of their Enemies, for that thing [such] will be*
> *Damned & go down to Hell. I would be Glad to see*
> *one of those traitors . . . ."*[94]

---

[92]Quinn, *The Mormon Hierarchy: Extensions of Power*, 755-56, emphasis added.

[93]Ibid., 786.

[94]Ibid., 760, emphasis added.

In 1849, shortly after the Mormons arrived, Brigham Young initiated plans for the colonization of the Utah Valley – "the single most important Northern Ute stronghold." Soon after thirty men and their families forced their way upon Indian land making solemn promises they didn't intend to keep.   The settlers immediately commenced building a fort. When an Indian stole a shirt from one of the settlers, he was confronted by three Mormons led by one Richard Ivie. The Mormon men killed the thief, "ripped out the dead man's entrails filled his abdominal cavity with rocks, and sank the body in the Provo River," where it was soon discovered by Ute fishermen. Utes then killed and stole Mormon cattle. Settlers demanded the right of reprise. Brigham Young sent one hundred fifty militiamen to confront the contentious Utes. In bad weather, in particularly brutal encounters three years after the Mormons arrived in the Salt Lake Valley, Young's militia killed sixty or seventy Indians on historic Indian gathering grounds near the Provo River, after which Mormon men in company with a military physician decapitated forty or fifty of the victims.[95] It was intended that their heads, after being put on public display, should be used for "scientific experimentation."[96] The putrification of the

---

[95]John Alton Peterson, *Utah's Black Hawk War* (Salt Lake City: University of Utah Press, 1998), 50-58. "Reportedly 40 or so heads were boxed up and taken to the fort, where for several weeks they were openly viewed as curiosities by the settlers."

[96]Another Indian massacre only recently discovered has been described as follows: In August 2006 an excavation disclosed the remains of seven native American men about thirteen to thirty-five years old, who were allegedly executed by early Mormon settlers sent to Manti, Utah by Brigham Young. The victims were found in a shallow grave at a construction site in Nephi, Utah. Several of the victims were shot point-blank in the head. "The hands of one Indian were tied behind his back. Several showed evidence of blunt-force trauma." The victims are thought to have been "peace-loving" members of the Goshute tribe "who became casualties of the Walker war."   After white fatalities at a massacre at Uintah Springs, the settlers "counseled by Father [Isaac] Morley" (a regional leader) perpetuated "quite as barbarous an act the following morning . . . ." An eyewitness (Martha Spence Haywood), "a polygamous wife" of the absent Territorial Marshal and leader of the Nephi colony, reported as follows: "This barbarous circumstance" (an Indian massacre at Uintah Springs) caused regional leaders to respond in kind. "Nine Indians coming into our Camp looking for protection and bread with us, because we promised it to them and without knowing they did the first evil act in that affair [Uintah Springs] or any other, were shot down without one minute's notice." (Myrna Trauntvein, "Burial Site?" *The Times News* [Nephi, UT: 6 June 2007]). Morleys were classmates of this author in Price, Utah.

decapitated members made experimentation impossible. Native Americans held captive after the "Mormon attack" viewed "the grisly images" of their dead men, women and children. The attractive Indian wife of Old Elk, one of the headless Chiefs (William Hickman beheaded the dead Chief), either fell or leaped to her death from what has since come to be called Squaw Peak.

"23 Apr. [1866], 'Circleville Massacre,' in which local Mormon militia shoots hand-tied Piede Indian men, then slits throats of their women and children one-by one."[97] "The attack claimed the lives of as many as 30 men, women and children of the Paiute Tribe's Koosharem band . . . ." "After shooting captives who had attempted to escape, settlers struck the remaining prisoners on the back[s] of their heads before slitting their throats."[98] The Tribe's spokesperson, Dorena Martineau, speaking on the one hundred and fifty year anniversary of the massacre, noted that, "It's not taught in schools, it's not in the books . . . ." Jedediah Rogers, a senior historian with the Utah Division of State History, further reported that the story is "about a peaceful band of indigenous Utah Indians, the Paiute Tribe, being slaughtered by local Mormon settlers." After noting that following the horrific event the community "essentially dissolved," LDS Church historian Richard Turley reported that "[p]eople left for other parts, and I think it was one of those events that people were ashamed of – didn't want to talk about." Ms. Martineau said, "Utah's history includes many massacres, but few match the cultural devastation of the event in Circleville."[99] Speaking of this dark period in LDS history at the time, "[Nauvoo Legion] . . . commanding general Daniel H. Wells [who later became Young's Counselor in the First Presidency] writes that these 'brethren' did what was necessary."[100]

"BLEEDING THE BEAST"

Brigham Young (an alleged indicted counterfeiter) and a high

---

[97]Quinn, *The Mormon Hierarchy: Extensions of Power*, 763.
[98]Benjamin Wood, "'Forgotten' massacre of Utah Paiute group recalled with new monument," *Salt Lake Tribune* (22 April 2016).
[99]Ibid.
[100]Quinn, *The Mormon Hierarchy: Extensions of Power*, 763.

council at Kanesville, Iowa, take no action against four highly
prominent Mormons, allegedly counterfeiters: John M. Bernhisel,
"who transports counterfeiting equipment to Iowa"; Theodore
Turley, a "mechanic who works with the dies and press"; George A.
Smith, the prophet's first cousin, an Apostle and a future member
of the First Presidency; and Apostle Ezra T. Benson.[101] Turley, one
of Brigham Young's many fathers-in-law, was known to have also
been close to Joseph Smith. Benson and Smith "allude to their
[counterfeiting] involvement in [a] letter to the First Presidency on
27 Mar [1849]." Two of these early leaders, John M. Bernhisel and
Theodore Turley, were prominent members of the Council of Fifty
and leaders in the community, and the other two were Mormon
apostles. Two other inconsequential (less prominent) Mormons
were excommunicated for counterfeiting coins by the Kanesville,
Ohio, High Council. In further search of easy money, and on
October 7, 1849, Brigham Young delegated to the Presiding
Patriarch John Smith,[102] Joseph Smith's uncle, the selection of
"fifty gold-digging Mormon missionaries" to go to California as
"forty-niners." They were to serve a "Gold Mission for the
Church."

"Under Brigham Young, reports of counterfeiting followed the LDS
Church as relentlessly as the allegations that its members practiced
polygamy." In 1846 Young and other Mormon leaders "fled
Nauvoo after the federal circuit court of appeals in Illinois indicted
them for counterfeiting U.S. coin: *Niles National Register* reported
that the indictment alleged that Joseph Smith 'used to work with
his own hands at manufacturing those counterfeits.'"[103]

In the Utah Territory in Salt Lake City, twenty-five year old David
McKenzie engraved copper plates for the currency used by the
Deseret Currency Association (an alleged fraudulent enterprise)
while working in the tithing office. "McKenzie's plates made such

---

[101]Ibid., 746-47. John M. Bernhisel both preceded and succeeded slaveholder
William H. Hooper as the delegate to the United States House of Representatives
from the Utah Territory's at-large congressional district. ("John Milton
Bernhisel," [accessed 31 May 2018], available from https://en.wikipedia.org/wiki/
John_Milton_Bernhisel; Internet, 3 pages). A polygamist, six of his seven wives
later left him for various reasons.

[102]Ibid., 748.

[103]*Niles National Register*, 3, January 1846.

attractive currency" that he and others concocted "a scheme to pass hundreds of thousand[s] of dollars' worth of bogus U.S. Treasury drafts throughout the United States." When a McKenzie colleague "sold a counterfeit quartermaster's check for $368" to someone at Camp Floyd, he and McKenzie were both arrested. McKenzie's engraving, and the printing, was done in a church building in Brigham Young's compound within a few steps of the prophet's residence. The Marshal discovered the plates, and the paper intended for the Deseret Currency, on Young's premises. The engraving in the tithing office took more than a month to complete. McKenzie "pleaded not guilty but mounted no defense." He said that he "had consulted Brigham Young who frowned upon the enterprise and disapproved." McKenzie was sentenced "to two years' hard labor in the territorial penitentiary," after which he promptly returned to Mormon acceptance, favor and acclaim.[104]

TEMPLES

"28 July [1847]. [Brigham] Young selects the site of the Salt Lake Temple by using Oliver Cowdery's divining rod."[105] August 22, 1862: After saying he wanted the Salt Lake Temple nearly done "before we go to Jackson County [Missouri] [–] the way things are going the way will soon be clear [–]," Brigham Young makes two predictions: (1) "I think It [the Saints' return to Independence, Missouri] will not be more than seven years . . . ," and (2) that "no Temple will be finished until the one pointed out in Jackson County, Missouri, by Joseph Smith."[106] These predictions (prophecies) never came to pass. "On 8 July 1861 he said this temple complex will cover ten acres of land." On July 7, 1863, Brigham Young describes a future complex of twenty-four temples in Independence, Missouri. These projects would never be built.

---

[104]David L. Bigler and Will Bagley, *The Mormon Rebellion: America's First Civil War, 1857-1858* (Norman: University of Oklahoma Press, 2011), 346-48.

[105]Quinn, *Origins of Power*, 659. Cowdery, a Book of Mormon witness and scribe, was a counterfeiter. Sidney Rigdon, Hyrum Smith and eighty-four other prominent Mormon men, those who knew him best, described his counterfeiting in the Danite Manifesto.

[106]Quinn, *The Mormon Hierarchy: Extensions of Power*, 762.

HERITAGE

Brigham Young taught the Latter-day Saints that Joseph Smith was descended from Ephraim, the ancient Egyptian patriarch Joseph's younger son, and that Mormonism's prophet/founder was a "pure Ephraimite." Brigham Young taught his followers (the Brighamite faction) that he too was an Ephraimite of "the House of Israel, of the royal seed, of the royal blood."[107] Brigham Young revealed that Joseph Smith was the source of a doctrine known to provide "that the Gentile blood was actually cleansed" from a believing Mormon's veins, "and the blood of Jacob made to circulate in them." That physical exchange was described as being so abrupt and decisive as to cause those affected "to think they were going into fits."[108] "It is Ephraim that I have been searching for all the days of my preaching," Brigham said, "and that is the blood which ran in my veins when I embraced the gospel."[109] That premise, concerning Latter-day Saints who were not initially Ephraimites (the exchange of blood by some literal mystical process), might be easy to test. DNA testing can detect if the blood of these so-called mystical "Israelites" has a Semetic component.

When Joseph Smith, Brigham Young and John Taylor (the first

---

[107]Young, in *Journal of Discourses*, 2:268-69, cited in Richard Abanes, *One Nation Under Gods: A History of the Mormon Church* (New York, NY: Thunder's Mouth Press, 2003), 108-9.

[108]Brigham Young, *Journal of Discourses*, 2:269, cited in Abanes, *One Nation Under Gods*, 109-110. The metamorphosis of the Latter-day Saints from the status of Gentiles to the actual in-fact status of affinity Jews is not the product of science. It is the gift of a gracious God. Joseph Smith said the Lord told him that: "[T]he rebellious are not of the blood of Ephraim . . . ." (Doctrine and Covenants 64:36, quoted in Abanes, *One Nation Under Gods*, 109. *See, e.g.*, Doctrine and Covenants 86:8-10). Those who are obedient become the issue of Ephraim, or perhaps Manasseh; those who are rebellious do not. The body and blood of a Gentile literally becomes the body and blood of an Israelite, when one who is not "rebellious" accepts the gospel, is baptized for the remission of sins and confirmed to receive the Holy Ghost. Some people are Israelites by blood and biology; others become Israelites by means of some kind of mystical convention. Mormons can not in good conscience dismiss transubstantiation (as they most defiantly do). The notion that followers were Israelites also graced the Woodscrape, a Mormon-like society that preceded the Mormons in a number of important particulars. Oliver Cowdery's father was a member of the Woodscrape.

[109]Brigham Young, in *Journal of Discourses*, 2:268-69, cited in Abanes, *One Nation Under Gods*, 108-9 n 28, 523.

three Mormon prophets) had themselves ordained Kings, Priests, and Rulers over Israel on Earth, each in their time, they mostly did what they did as affinity Jews. The Book of Mormon's Native Americans, the descendants of Lehi, Nephi, Laman and Lemuel, were "Israelites," Hebrews (then depreciated Lamanites) by blood and by birth. The Caucasian founders of the Mormon Church, in the main (Joseph and Brigham, Ephraimites, excepted), were not Hebrews by blood or by birth. With Smith's prodding, "The Saints gradually came to embrace the notion that they were true Israelites descended from the biblical Joseph, son of the Hebrew Patriarch, Jacob."[110] Joseph Smith taught his followers this:

> *[A]s the Holy Ghost falls upon one of the literal seed of Abraham [say Jewish converts or Lamanites], it is calm and serene . . . while the effect of the Holy Ghost upon a Gentile [other Mormon converts], is to purge out the old blood, and make him actually of the seed of Abraham. That man that has none of the blood of Abraham (naturally) must have a new creation by the Holy Ghost. In such a case, there may be more of a powerful effect upon the body, and visible to the eye, than upon an Israelite . . . .*[111]

BIG BROTHER BRIGHAM

In the Utah Territory, people "churched together, kept watch on one another, and left the communal core only to labor on their peripheral farming plots. There were military and police forces, secret assassins with total allegiance to the monarch, and terrorist tactics." There were no public schools. "[C]lasses were held in Mormon church buildings and taught by Mormons using Mormon scripture for curriculum." Free discussion and criticism was

---

[110]Abanes, *One Nation Under Gods*, 108. Young said that Joseph Smith, Mormonism's prophet-founder, was a "pure Ephraimite." And that he, Brigham Young, like other Mormons, was of "the House of Israel, of the royal seed, of the royal blood." (Young, *Journal of Discourses*, 2:268-69).

[111]"The Prophet's Instructions on Various Doctrines," Joseph Smith, Roberts, ed., *History of The Church of Jesus Christ of Latter-day Saints*, 3:379-80, emphasis added.

restricted. "There was a single political party, surveillance of the voting process by numbered ballots, an all-embracing ideology, and means of mass communication. ... Control and limitations were placed on entry and exit across [the] geographical boundaries of [the] Utah Territory."[112]

Like authoritarian leaders in every age, Young changed history to his liking. He falsely depicted the history of the Mormon Battalion. He characterized its salutary (benevolent) contribution to the welfare of the penniless pioneers "into an unreasonable demand forced upon the Mormon people to their detriment." "The tragic fiasco [colossal failure] of the starving, late-arriving Martin and Willie 1856 handcart companies, which resulted in the suffering and death of hundreds, was lost in its transformation into a faith-promoting tale of courage and endurance." "The Mormon leaders' several prophecies of good weather, promises of safe passage, and the organizational errors of the failure are all but forgotten."[113] Prior to those ill-advised and disastrous misadventures in 1856, some 250,000 people had made that trip in relative safety.

"In 1861 Young instructed George Q. Cannon, then in charge of the LDS Saints in Liverpool, England, to destroy, or sell as wastepaper, all volumes of Joseph Smith's history written by Mother Lucy Smith. In 1865 Young commanded that all copies of her accounts then held by the Saints in Utah be given to him or burned. The events of the Mountain Meadows murders continue to be revised."[114] Author John Gary Maxwell chose to describe "the undeniable climate of fear created by violent preaching, intrusive interrogation, condoning of murder, harassment of dissidents, and secret paramilitary networks within an enforced 'culture of impunity and silence.'" In a theocratic society holding little respect for its democratic benefactor, Brigham Young was God.[115]

---

[112]John Gary Maxwell, *Robert Newton Baskin and the Making of Modern Utah (Western Frontiersmen Series)* (Norman, OK: The Arthur H. Clark Company, 2013), 81.
[113]Ibid.
[114]Ibid.
[115]Ibid., 82.

WALLACE STEGNER

Stegner, often called "The Dean of Western Writers," wrote two histories of the Mormon settlement in Utah. He concluded that the Mormon movement left much to be desired. "More and more I come to a condition of astonishment at the parallelism in methods between Utah in the early days, and any totalitarian state today. The whole thing is there – private army, secret police, encirclement myth, territorial dynamism, self sufficiency, chosen people, absolute dictatorship operating through party rule, group psychology, esoteric symbols and distinguishing uniforms (garments), New Order and all." (Baskin, Maxwell, 80)

Image source: Public domain via Wikimedia Commons.

"GIVE ME YOUR ROCKY MOUNTAINS"

Council of Fifty Minutes: Brigham Young said, "[I]n regard to going beyond the rocky mountains, he dont feel like it, it is so far to go there, and have to come back to kill off these cursed scoundrels [mobbers, apostates] . . . . If ever we get the City of Zion once organized the idea of men going and telling tales to our enemies will be put an end to. Let us get by ourselves and in a little while the Indians will join in with us, and as soon as we get cousin Lemuel [Native Americans] converted I dont fear."

"THIS RULE OF UNANIMITY"

Chairman Brigham Young: *"Brigham Young expounded upon this rule of unanimity ["decisions needed to be reached by the unanimous vote of each member present"]: 'In the event of a negative vote being given on any subject, the member voting in the negative is called upon to give his reasons for thus voting . . . . If a member should persist in his opposition after it is proved to him that he is in the wrong, his opposition would sever him from the Council.' The requirement that every decision be made by unanimous vote followed the pattern of the quorums of the Twelve Apostles and the Seventy."*

Council of Fifty Minutes

STEPHEN A. DOUGLAS

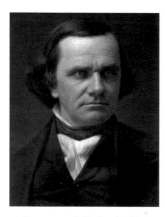

Image source: Public Domain, via Wikimedia Commons.

"As circuit judge in Illinois, that honourable gentleman had befriended the founder of Mormonism, when he was the victim of an erring interpretation of the law, or the subject of unwarrantable interference. The Mormons looked upon the judge very kindly, and in after-years, when he became senator, every delegation from Utah to Congress was certain to consult and listen to his suggestions and counsels." *"In the spring of 1856 [after the death of Joseph Smith and during the reign of Brigham Young] Senator Douglas delivered a great speech at Springfield, Illinois. It was the announcement of his platform before the assembling of the conventions that were to nominate the successor of President Pierce. In that speech the senator characterized [Utah Territory] Mormonism as 'the loathsome ulcer of the body politic' and recommended the free use of the scalpel as the only remedy in the hands of the nation."* *(T.B.H. Stenhouse)*

The Prophet, Priest and King of the Kingdom of God and his Laws Responds:
"Brigham alone could determine what course, if any, should be adopted in respect to the Springfield speech. Before long, the Deseret News, Brigham's official organ, presented to the world a reply to Senator Douglas. The priesthoods phials of wrath were poured out without stint or mercy upon the head of their quondam friend and defender. All the good that he had ever done was in a moment forgotten, and all their obligations were in an instant cancelled for ever." *(Ibid.)*

BILL HICKMAN

Image Source: Public domain, via Wikimedia Commons.

"Wild Bill" Hickman was the husband of ten wives, most of whom later left him, and the father of thirty-nine children. (George D. Smith). Baptized by John D. Lee, ordained to the office of seventy by Joseph Smith, he served as one of the prophet's life guards. Hickman decapitated Chief Big Elk after a conflict with the Indians in 1849. He said he killed a half-breed for Brigham Young at Council Bluffs, Iowa. "I found him, used him up, scalped him, and took his scalp to Brigham Young, saying: Here is the scalp of the man who was going to have a war-dance over your scalp; you may now have one over his, if you wish. He took it and thanked me very much. He said in all probability I had saved his life, and that some day he would make me a great man in the kingdom." Hickman killed one horse thief for Orson Hyde, then another for himself, then also one "Spanish Frank" who had seduced one of his wives. He was appointed sheriff, prosecuting attorney, and assessor for Green River County (later Wyoming) by Brigham Young, and he was elected to serve as a member of the Utah Territorial Legislature, like John D. Lee and Isaac Haight. Hickman turned on Brigham Young and accused the prophet of instigating murders, including the 1857 murder of Richard Yates (Hickman said Young ordered him to kill Yates), and the murder of Jesse Hartley (Hickman killed Jesse Hartley and more than half a dozen others). Brigham Young was indicted in 1871 on the basis of testimony provided to federal territorial authorities by Hickman, who had generous access to the Mormon leader as one of Brigham's "B'Hoys." Hickman was the grandfather of the western artist Minerva Teichert.

"1934 May 5: As authorized by President Heber J. Grant all [of the previously excommunicated Hickman's] former priesthood and temple blessings were restored." (Van Wagoner and Walker, A Book of Mormons).

THE COURSE OF THE GENTILES

Council of Fifty Minutes, 11 March 1845, Chairman Brigham Young: *"His feelings are that our time is short among the gentiles, and the judgment of God will soon come on them like whirlwind. He dont care about preaching to the gentiles any longer . . . he feels as Lyman Wight said let the damned scoundrels be killed, let them be swept off from the earth, and then we can go and be baptized for them, easier than we can convert them. The gentiles have rejected the gospel; they have killed the prophets . . . ."*

JOHN D. LEE, YOUNG'S ADOPTED SON

On April 20, 1961, the First Presidency and the Quorum of the Twelve Apostles (posthumously) authorized the restoration of the membership, priesthood and temple blessings of John D. Lee, a Mountain Meadows murderer. "Temple worker Merrit L. Norton . . . was baptized for his dead grandfather, and on May 9 Apostle Ezra Taft Benson officiated in the endowment and sealing ceremonies at the Salt Lake Temple." (Bagley).

Benson managed these unexpected events less than four months after he completed his service as the United States Secretary of Agriculture, and before he became the Thirteenth President of the Church of Jesus Christ of Latter-day Saints. These peculiar ceremonies included the restoration of the privileges and blessings associated with Lee's second anointing. Four of Lee's descendants have been United States senators from four different states. One of them has been a member of the House of Representatives and the Secretary of the Interior; another was the Solicitor General of the United States and the President of Brigham Young University. Another member of Congress, and another Lee descendant, became a candidate for the office of the Presidency of the United States and delivered the keynote address at the 1980 Democratic Convention. Lee's prominent descendants include a judge on the 9th Cirtcuit Court of Appeals, and a Justice on the Utah Supreme Court. Some of Lee's high achieving progeny left the Church. Lee became a despised pariah because of his allegiance to the Church and its authoritarian leader, his adoptive father, Brigham Young.

GEORGE ARMSTRONG HICKS

"On the seventh day of April 1874 [seventeen years after the Mountain Meadows Massacre, and before the apprehension and execution of John D. Lee], I saw John D. Lee by the side of Brigham Young's carriage, and reported the same to The Tribune [a Gentile newspaper in Salt Lake City]. I was suspected of so doing. Bishop Henry Lunt of Cedar City, questioned me on the subject. I did not deny the fact, and was immediately cut off [from the Church] without even a hearing of any kind."

"[I]f I had only been a pious murderer I might have rode 'cheek by jowl' with the Prophet as Lee has done, and been in good standing in the Church."

"When men of brutal dispositions get into power in the church, they worship a brutal god and they teach a brutal faith . . . ."

BRIGHAM CONFISCATES ZINA

"[W]ithin the hearing of many Saints . . . [Brigham Young] ordered those walking in other men's shoes to step out of them. 'Brother Jacobs,' Young declared, 'the woman you claim for a wife does not belong to you. She is the spiritual wife of brother Joseph, sealed up to him. I am his proxy, and she is, in this behalf, with her children [Henry's two sons] my property. You can go where you please and get another . . . .'" (T.B.H. Stenhouse). *Brigham fathered a daughter with Zina, a polyandrous wife, and one of his more than fifty other wives. His polyandry with Zina was sexual.*

ZINA DIANTHA HUNTINGTON (JACOBS, HENRY) (SMITH, JOSEPH) (YOUNG, BRIGHAM)

She taught her polygamous peers that a "successful polygamous wife 'must regard her husband with indifference, and with no other feeling than that of reverence, for love we regard as a false sentiment; a feeling which should have no existence in polygamy.'" (A Book of Mormons). She became the third President of the Relief Society of the Church of Jesus Christ of Latter-day Saints.

Image source: James H. Crockwell [Public domain], via Wikimedia Commons.

Image source: https://history.lds.org/missionary/individual/henry-b-bailey-jacobs-1817?lang=eng.

HENRY JACOBS

He was the legal husband of Zina Diantha Huntington (Jacobs) (Smith) (Young) and the father of two of her three children. Her children with Henry Jacobs and her child with Brigham Young will belong to Joseph Smith in the life to come. Henry spoke of his loss: "I do not Blame Eny person . . . . [M]ay the Lord our Father bless Brother Brigham . . . . [A]ll is right according to the law of the Celestial Kingdom of our God Joseph." "But I feel alone & no one to speak to to call my own I feell like a Lamb without a Mother." (Todd Compton)

LEADERSHIP

George Armstrong Hicks: *"No man in the last century has had as good an opertunity to build up a good and virtuous community as Brigham Young has had. For many years he was the sole dictator of all classes of society. At the beginning and during the first stages of the Reformation [a call to the people for repentance], the people of Utah believed as he did, thought as he thought, and wept or smiled when he smiled. When he said Adam was the god of this world, the people believed it or pretended to . . . . In all mat[t]ers he was the sun of our system . . . . Ignorance and superstition generaly go hand in hand and we were at that time afflicted with both."* (Kingdom in the West, vol. 13)

Brigham Young: *"[i]nasmuch as I believe in the Bible, inasmuch as I believe in the ordinances of God, in the Priesthood and order, and decrees of God, I must believe in slavery." "I am a firm believer in slavery."* (John G. Turner)

Brigham Young: *"Any man having one drop of the seed of Cane in him Cannot hold the priesthood & if no other Prophet ever spake it Before I will say it now in the name of Jesus Christ."* (Ibid.)

Jenie Airey / Cultura / Visualphotos

Bruce R. McConkie: *"All races of men stem from certain common ancestors . . . . Racial degeneration, resulting in differences in appearance and spiritual aptitude have arisen since the fall. We know the circumstances under which the posterity of Cain (and later of Ham) were cursed with what we call negroid racial characteristics (Moses 5:16-41; 7:8, 12, 22; Abra. 1:20-27) [Mormon Scripture]. The Book of Mormon explains why the Lamanites received dark skins and a degenerate status . . . [A]ll these changes from the physical and spiritual perfections of our common parents have been brought about by departure from the gospel truths."* (Mormon Doctrine)

THE HANDCART FIASCO

Mormon Pioneer handcart. Image source: Torleif S. Knaphus,
Public domain, via Wikimedia Commons.

Brigham Young: *"If any man or woman complains of me or of my Counselors, in regard to the lateness of some of this season's immigration, let the curse of God be on them, and blast their substance with mildew and destruction, until their names are forgotten from the earth." (Kingdom of the West, vol. 13). More than one hundred fifty handcart pioneers died en route.*

THE PROPHET IS PAID

George Armstrong Hicks: *"I heard Prest. Brigham young boast at this time that he was worth $80,000 [general conference, October 1852]. He told us what fine abilities he had for making money. I was somewhat surprised to hear him, for I had known him to be a poor man in Nauvoo and I knew it was said of him that he had to be helped from Winter Quarters . . . how could a man in that short space of 5 years accumulate the vast sum of $80,000 without the benefit of trade, at the same time situated 1000 miles from any commercial center? It is no mystery at the present time. The $80,000 was tithing that he had filched from his honest but ignorant followers . . . ." Brigham Young's boasting does not appear in the edited records of the fall conference." (Ibid.)*

George Q. Cannon, 1875: *"It is felt that the funds of the Church have been used with a freedom not warranted by the authority which he [Brigham Young] held." (Ibid.)*

James Allen and Glen Leonard (LDS historians): *"It was finally determined that [Brigham Young's] estate [upon his death in 1877] was worth approximately $1,626,000, but obligations of more than a million dollars to the Church plus other debts and executor's fees reduced the family's claim to $224,000. When seven of his dissatisfied heirs challenged this settlement, however, that matter was settled out of court and the Church agreed to give the heirs an additional $75,000." The estate today would be worth $39,665,573. (The Story of the Latter-day Saints)*

JOHN WILLARD YOUNG

*On November 22, 1855, Brigham Young secretly ordained two of his sons, John Willard
Young (age eleven) and Brigham Young Jr. (age eighteen) to the office of Apostle. "The
Twelve doesn't learn of these ordinations for almost nine years. In later years he secretly
ordains two other sons [Joseph A. Young and Heber Young] as apostles." (D. Michael
Quinn). John Willard Young (the First Counselor in Brigham Young's last First
Presidency) was divorced or separated at least eight times from the five different women
(every one of his wives) who delivered his eighteen children. He was ordained to the
office of First Counselor in the First Presidency in October 1876 (one year before
Brigham Young died in 1877). John Willard Young, the apparent successor to the office
held by his powerful father, was positioned to become the President of the Church. The
Salt Lake Tribune incorrectly predicted his ascent to the office vacated by his father's
death. This privileged son died a pauper. In New York, late in his life, he became "an
elevator operator in an exclusive hotel where he once lived." His son, William Hooper
Young, pleaded guilty to second degree murder for a crime (the death of Anna Pulitzer)
that appeared to have been committed in his father's apartment.*

Heber J. Grant: *"I wish I had confidence in him but I have not and never hear his name
mentioned in connection with our efforts for Statehood but what It decreases my faith in
the success of our efforts. If the Lord is going to use a man with a dishonest financial
record, to give the people liberty, it looks to me as though He was placing a premium on
dishonest methods." (Todd Compton, "John Willard Young, Brigham Young, and the
Development of Presidential Succession in the LDS Church")*

Astrayals: Other Prophets

Astrayals: Other Prophets

POLYGAMY, POLYANDRY, INCEST, "MANY WIVES AND CONCUBINES"

The Church published the Manifesto (suspending the practice of polygamy) in 1890, and it was accepted by the membership on October 6. Wilford Woodruff officially reported on September 24 and 25, 1890, that charges made in certain "Press dispatches" had all been false. Those charges were (1) that "plural marriages are still being solemnized," (2) that "forty or more such marriages have been contracted in Utah since last June or during the past year," and (3) that the leaders of the Church have publicly "taught, encouraged and urged the continuance of the practice of polygamy." Woodruff denied those claims with emphasis.

> *I, therefore, as President of the Church of Jesus Christ of Latter-day Saints, do hereby, in the most solemn manner, declare that these charges are false. We are not teaching polygamy or plural marriage, nor permitting any person to enter into its practice, and I deny that either forty or any other number of plural marriages have during that period been solemnized in our Temples, or in any other place in the Territory.*[1]

Later, in refutation to Woodruff's claims and in 1909 and 1910, the *Salt Lake Tribune* published the names and marriage information for more than two hundred Mormon men who had entered into (or continued) the "practice" of plurality by taking polygamous wives after Woodruff's Manifesto.[2]

In July and September of 1870, three prominent Mormon leaders – Joseph F. Smith and Wilford Woodruff, both future prophets, and

---

[1]Doctrine and Covenants, Official Declaration (dated 24 September 1890), emphasis added.

[2]*Salt Lake Tribune* (8 October 1910), 6.

First Presidency Counselor Daniel H. Wells, each on different dates, sealed Scotland's (deceased) Queen Maud, and "eight political heroines or female rulers including Charlotte Corday (who murdered the radical Jacobin Marat during [the] French Revolution), to be eternal wives to the martyred prophet Joseph Smith.   Other wives included Empress Josephine (wife of Napoleon), Saint Helena (the mother of Constantine) and a monastic Carmelite reformer Saint Theresa of Spain. "These are [the] first women of international prominence sealed as wives to Joseph Smith, but during fifty years after his death hundreds of deceased women are similarly joined to him, even though many had husbands during their lifetimes."[3]   Who can honestly say that polygyny (multiple wives) and polyandry (multiple husbands) are not elements of the Mormon afterlife? Apostle Bruce R. McConkie, the modern author of the Introduction to the Book of Mormon, posited a state of eternal polygamy in his theological epistle, *Mormon Doctrine*. "*Obviously*," according to McConkie, "*the holy practice [the law of heaven] will commence again after the Second Coming of the Son of Man and the ushering in of the millennium. (Isa. 7).*[4]

Some Mormon leaders publicly denied the practice of polygamy even before the notorious Manifesto. *In 1880* George Q. Cannon, soon to become the *de facto* leader of the Church of Jesus Christ of Latter-day Saints and a towering figure in the nineteenth-century Church, informed the *Omaha Herald* that, "Polygamous marriages have ceased entirely so far as I know."   "In fact, in [the] Endowment House alone, 107 men married polygamously in 1879 and 136 in 1880 . . . ."   Most of those marriage ceremonies (marriages in the newly constructed St. George Temple were not included) were "performed by general authorities."[5]

John Taylor, the third Mormon prophet, announced on October 13, 1882, by way of a "revelation," that plural marriage (the *everlasting* covenant) was a requirement for all of the presiding officers of the Church.   Taylor's revelation was accepted by the First Presidency and the Quorum of the Twelve on October 14, 1882.   Taylor's

---

[3]Quinn, *The Mormon Hierarchy: Extensions of Power*, 766.
[4]McConkie, "Plural Marriage," *Mormon Doctrine*, 578, emphasis added.
[5]Quinn, *The Mormon Hierarchy: Extensions of Power*, 777.

divine edict was published as a pamphlet in Salt Lake City and in the Swedish, German and Danish editions of the Doctrine and Covenants. In some cases (German 1893, 1903, 1920; Danish 1900), the revelation continued to be published until long after the Manifesto. Taylor's revelation was not canonized by a vote of the conference, nor was it added to the English language editions of the Doctrine and Covenants.[6] But at a conference priesthood meeting on April 5, 1884, four years after George Q. Cannon misrepresented the facts to the *Omaha Herald* in 1880, John Taylor said that "all presiding officers must marry polygamously or resign their positions."[7] Taylor called out three monogamous stake presidents, and one of them, William W. Cluff, resigned.

Michael Quinn writes that on

> *15 July [1886], Apostle [and future prophet] Lorenzo Snow says that in future "brothers and sisters would marry each other in this church. All our horror at such a union was," he said, "due entirely to prejudice, and the offspring of such unions would be as healthy and pure as any other. These were the decided views of Pres. [Brigham] Young, when alive, for Bro. S[now] talked to him freely on this matter."*[8]

On October 8, 1854, Young reported that Adam was God before he addressed the subject of incest:

> *. . . I reckon that the children of Adam and Eve married each other . . . . I believe in sisters marrying brothers, and brothers having their sisters for wives. . . . Our spirits are all brothers and sisters, and so are our bodies; and the opposite idea to this has resulted from the ignorant, and foolish traditions of the nations of the earth.*[9]

---

[6]Ibid., 780-81.

[7]Ibid., 782-83.

[8]Ibid., 786, emphasis added.

[9]"I Propose to Speak Upon a Subject that does not Immediately Concern Yours or My Welfare," a Sermon Delivered on October 8, 1854, taken from *The Teachings of President Brigham Young*, vol. 3 (Salt Lake City: Collier's Publishing

On January 5, 1852, George D. Watt, Mormonism's first English convert, and by then Brigham Young's stenographer and private clerk, married his half-sister, Jane Brown, with Brigham Young's consent.[10] The canonized revelation on polygamy, Section 132 of the Doctrine and Covenants, remains in its protected place, impervious to the criticisms of the laity. That canonized revelation, although temporarily suspended, specifically allows both "wives and concubines." All of Mormonism's plurally married leaders (including twelve prophets), sealed to multiple women, various apostles and many laymen, expect to claim their plural wives in the life to come.

MONEY AND BRIBES

On December 31, 1884, the First Presidency authorized $25,000 for the payment of a bribe to the incoming administration of President Grover Cleveland. The men specifically authorized to execute this prohibited temporal outreach were Brigham Young Jr., a future President of the Quorum of the Twelve Apostles, and Charles W. Penrose, a future First Counselor in the First Presidency, a member of the Council of Fifty and one of the authors of a still undrafted 1890 Manifesto. (The "Quorum of the Twelve agrees to these arrangements on 4 Jan. 1885 [there will be other under-the-table negotiations], but [this particular] effort proves to be [an] attempt by imposters to defraud [the] church."[11])

On January 7, 1886, the United States Supreme Court sustains a definition of "'cohabitation' as not requiring proof of sexual intercourse but rather of marital relationship." Two Justices, Miller and Field, "dissent on grounds that Congress intended [the] law to prohibit 'unlawful habitual sexual intercourse' with more than one woman. Justice Field [an Associate Justice of the United

---

Co., 1987), as quoted in *The Essential Brigham Young* (foreword by Campbell),98-99, emphasis added.

[10]"Jane Brown Watt Saladen" (accessed 1 March 2019), available from http://browngenealogy.org/1952debbieholtzendorff/1777josephbrown/1828jane.ht ml; Internet, p. 1 of 1. Jane was George's second wife and they had three children: Joseph, Robert and Margaret. (Ibid.).

[11]Quinn, *The Mormon Hierarchy: Extensions of Power*, 783.

States Supreme Court] is [alleged to have been] on [the] secret payroll of [the] First Presidency."[12]

On 25 January 1886, the federal court begins hearings on the efforts of two men to bribe U.S. Deputy Marshal E.A. Franks "to give advance warning of efforts to arrest Mormon polygamists." By 1888 Deputy Franks is alleged (supposed) to have been on the First Presidency's payroll as a "bribed informer."[13]

On January 19, 1887, President "John Taylor has $40,000 removed from the First Presidency's safe to bribe influential members of Congress to oppose [the] Edmunds-Tucker bills and support Utah statehood."[14] At the time of this withdrawal, the polygamous Taylor is in hiding as a fugitive from justice, and there is a reward posted for information leading to his capture.

On October 23, 1888, President Wilford Woodruff and the apostles "approve sending $20,000 to bribe democratic members of Congress to help [the] Utah Mormon cause."[15] Speaking in favor of such efforts on October 18, 1890, Abraham H. Cannon, a rising star in the leadership, said this: "Thus with a little money a channel of communication is kept open between the government offices and the suffering and persecuted Church members."[16]

On August 12, 1887, the Quorum of the Twelve (members of which are sustained at General Conference on April 8, 1887, as prophets, seers & revelators) are alleged to have permitted the former Presidency (surviving Counselors George Q. Cannon and Joseph F. Smith) to complete already pending arrangements for pro-Mormon coverage from some of the leading papers in New York and other cities, by paying their newspaper editors $75,000 cash in advance, with an added $70,000 after Utah gains statehood.[17]

---

[12]Ibid., 785.
[13]Ibid.
[14]Ibid., 787.
[15]Ibid., 788.
[16]Ibid., 792.
[17]Ibid., 787.

BRIGHAM YOUNG'S ESTATE

When Brigham Young died, the *Salt Lake Tribune* described his will as, "One of the Most Remarkable Documents in the World." "The twelve-page instrument had apportioned the estate among nineteen classes of wives and children, 'reminding one,' the *Trib* said, 'of the premium lists of an agricultural fair.'" The *Tribune* reported *"Millions of the Peoples Tithing Divided Among His Families."* What the *Tribune* didn't know, and what the people didn't know, was that Brigham Young had a number of additional wives who were "not mentioned . . . in the will." No official provision appeared to have been made for their support.[18]

What Brigham Young claimed for himself and bequeathed to his heirs "as his personal assets" was referred to in his will by legal description. Those confusing descriptions directed to various questionable bequests, on first glance and for many, made the subjects of Brigham's bounty greatly less visible. After checking the legal descriptions against a lot map of the city, it became clear that what Brigham claimed and hoped to safely quietly pass included the Social Hall, "the LDS Museum, the President's Office . . . 'the Council House . . . ; the Constitution building . . . ; and . . . the Salt Lake Theater.'" Brigham also purported to pass a one-third interest in ZCMI valued at $118,000, and stock in the city's street railway and gas companies, valued at $113,500, if some ownership issues could be successfully addressed.[19]

All that Brigham claimed and hoped to pass didn't get to his disappointed heirs (through no fault of his own). Brigham's successor John Taylor intimidated heirs who thought to assert their legal claims in civil court and by other means. Taylor managed to significantly reduce the size of the dead prophet's massive estate. That was bad for Brigham, but good for the Church. The value of the estate he had hoped to pass, property he said he owned, if calculated in U.S. dollars in the year 2015, was about $36,954,545 (in 1877, at the time of his death and before any of Taylor's

---

[18]Samuel W. Taylor, *The Kingdom or Nothing: The Life of John Taylor, Militant Mormon* (New York: MacMillan Publishing Co., Inc., 1976), 264.
[19]Ibid., 264-65.

unwelcome reductions, the figure was $1,626,000).[20]

TEACHINGS

On April 18, 1880, Apostle (and future prophet) Joseph F. Smith writes that he believes that the measurements of the Great Pyramid "predict future events."[21] "21 Nov. [1875], local bishop reports that first counselor [First Presidency Counselor] 'George A. Smith preached in Salina Sevier County last year and said that *The Savior Jesus Christ* will be here on Earth in 1891 . . . .'"[22] 27 December 1879: Apostle Wilford Woodruff tells stake conference at Snowflake, Arizona, that, "There will be no United States in the year 1890."[23] On July 3, 1885, "Apostle Heber J. Grant records that [the] First Presidency authorizes half-masting of American flags on Salt Lake city hall, court house, and at church-owned ZCMI on July 4."[24] In 1885 nine apostles and two members of the Council of Fifty "anoint and ordain John Taylor as King, Priest, and Ruler over Israel on Earth."[25] Taylor, like Joseph Smith and Brigham Young (both of whom were also so ordained), was then the undisputed theocratic magistrate.

John Taylor described Jehovah as the Father of Jesus. Jesus wasn't Jehovah to John Taylor. *Joseph Smith and Brigham Young described Jehovah as the Father of Jesus.* Jesus wasn't Jehovah to Joseph Smith or Brigham Young. But Taylor separated God the Father ("Jehovah") from Elohim and Adam. The modern Church, unlike those early leaders, teaches that the preexistent Jesus was Jehovah, the God of Abraham, Isaac, Jacob *and Adam. In Joseph*

---

[20]D. Michael Quinn, *The Mormon Hierarchy: Wealth and Corporate Power* (Salt Lake City: Signature Books, 2017), 174. "It was finally determined that his estate was worth approximately $1,626,000, but obligations of more than a million dollars to the Church plus other debts and executor's fees reduced the family's claim to $224,000. When seven of his dissatisfied heirs challenged this settlement, however, that matter was settled out of court and the Church agreed to give the heirs an additional $75,000." (James Allen and Glen Leonard, *The Story of the Latter-day Saints*, 2nd ed. [Deseret Book, 1992], 385).

[21]Quinn, *The Mormon Hierarchy: Extensions of Power*, 778.

[22]Ibid., 771.

[23]Ibid., 777.

[24]Ibid., 784.

[25]Ibid., 783.

and Brigham's church, Adam was God, and Jehovah, and the Ancient of Days, but not Jesus. Hear Taylor ignore Adam and Elohim and separate Jehovah as Father from Jesus as Son in the lyrics to a hymn he composed before he succeeded Brigham Young as King, Priest and Ruler over Israel on Earth.

> *As in the heavens they all agree,*
> *The records given there by three,*
> *Jehovah, God the Father's one*
> *Another His Eternal Son,*
> *The Spirit does with them agree,*
> *The witnesses in heaven are three.*[26]

John Taylor prayed to Jehovah, God the Father and the Father of Adam and Jesus. Brigham Young prayed to Adam, the Father of Jesus and the God of this particular earth (the only God with whom we have to do). Heber C. Kimball and Daniel H. Wells prayed to Adam, the Father of Jesus.[27] Wilford Woodruff, George Q. Cannon and Eliza R. Snow prayed to Adam, the Father of Jesus. Joseph Smith sometimes prayed to "Jehovah-God-Thou Eloheim," two interchangeable names for one indivisible person and the Father of Jesus. And in the canonized provisions of Section 109 of the Doctrine and Covenants (the Kirtland Temple Dedication Prayer), Joseph Smith prayed to "Jehovah" "in the name of Jesus Christ, the

---

[26]Lyrics reproduced at Boyd Kirkland, "Jehovah As Father: The Development of the Mormon Jehovah Doctrine," *Sunstone* (1984), 9.2, 5, emphasis added.

[27]April 30, 1862, Heber C. Kimball, First Counselor in the First Presidency: "[T]he Lord told me that Adam was my father and that he was the God and father of all the inhabitants of this Earth." (*On the Potter's Wheel : The Diaries of Heber C. Kimball*, Stanley B. Kimball, ed. [Salt Lake City: Signature Books, 1987], Appendix A, Memorandum Book). 1873, Daniel Wells, Second Counselor in the First Presidency: (Regarding the doctrine of Adam being our Father and our God): President Wells "bore a powerful testimony to the truth of the doctrine, remarking that if ever (anyone) had received a testimony of any doctrine in this Church he had of the truth of this." (Daniel H. Wells, Salt Lake School of the Prophets – Minutes: 9 June 1873, in Fred C. Collier, *President Brigham Young's Doctrine on Deity*, vol., 1 [Salt Lake City: Collier's Publishing Co., 1999], 370). Brigham Young, the President of the Church, "was positive of the truth of the doctrine" (that Adam was God). (Ibid.). The doctrine was approved or endorsed by Henry Grow, D.B. Huntington, Joseph F. Smith, John Lyon and George B. Wallace. (Ibid., 370-71).

Son of thy bosom."[28]   Jehovah wasn't Jesus to Joseph.   David O. McKay, Howard W. Hunter, Thomas S. Monson, Gordon B. Hinckley and others prayed to Elohim, the Father of Jehovah. Their amended Jehovah came to rest as Jesus, the God of Abraham, Isaac and Jacob and the father of Adam.   Since about 1916 Mormonism's modern prophets have prayed to Elohim, the Father of Jehovah, who became Jesus by arbitrary fiat many years after the deaths of Joseph Smith and Brigham Young.[29]

John the Beloved said: "And this is life eternal, that they might know thee the only true God, and Jesus Christ, whom thou has sent."[30]   Apostle McConkie added this: "True religion is found only where men worship the true and living God. False religion always results from the worship of false gods. Eternal life itself, which is the greatest of all the gifts of God, is available to those and those only who know God and Jesus Christ whom he hath sent."[31]   In the twentieth century, the Church changed its slowly evolving theology to declare that Jehovah, the God of Abraham, Isaac and Jacob, was the preexistent Jesus and that Elohim, a higher god, was God the Father and the Father of Jesus.

First Presidency Counselor George Q. Cannon disclosed in 1898, in an important but seldom mentioned report, "that he had seen God and Jesus Christ and heard their voices."   Cannon's vision was supposed to have occurred before the Church decided that the Holy

---

[28]Joseph Smith described a "holy Father" identified repeatedly as "O Jehovah" in the Dedication Prayer at the Kirtland Temple on March 27, 1836. "According to the Prophet's written statement, this prayer was given to him by revelation." The canonized dedication prayer became Section 109 of the Doctrine and Covenants. Jehovah, the "holy Father" of Jesus (the Son of his "bosom"), *isn't Jesus* in Section 109 of the Doctrine and Covenants. *In Joseph and Brigham's Church, Adam was God (and Jehovah), and Jehovah wasn't Jesus.*

[29]1916 First Presidency Statement (The First Presidency and the Council of the Twelve Apostles of the Church of Jesus Christ of Latter-day Saints) on the Father and the Son. "'Elohim' is the literal Parent of our Lord and Savior Jesus Christ and of the spirits of the human race." This 1916 Statement identified "Elohim" as God the Father and "Jehovah" as the Son, Jesus Christ.

[30]John 17:3.

[31]McConkie, Conference Report (October 1980), quoted in "Bruce R. McConkie's Letter of Rebuke to [BYU] Professor Eugene England" (19 February 1981, accessed 8 September 2009), available from http://www.myplanet.net/mike/ LDS/McConkie_England_letter.html; Internet, 4.

Ghost was a personage. What the Holy Ghost was seen to become was what a now amended anthropomorphic Father had earlier been (*"a personage of spirit"*). The *Lectures on Faith* reported in 1834-35 that there were *only two personages* in the godhead, the Father and the Son. Not three, and not the Holy Ghost. Those provisions remained as part of the Doctrine and Covenants until 1921. In those *Lectures*, the doctrine part of the Doctrine and Covenants, the Holy Spirit was a member of the godhead but not a personage. The Holy Spirit was first described as the common mind of a spirit Father and an anthropomorphic Son. In 1899, Cannon (an Adam/God Apostle) reported "that he had heard [the] audible voice of [the] Holy Ghost as [a] separate personage."[32] The Church then started a process that came forth to declare that the Holy Ghost, which was not a personage in 1834-35 when the *Lectures on Faith* were published, was a personage now. In the canonized *Lectures on Faith*, the original Holy Ghost was the noncorporeal presence of a shared mind. After the death of Joseph Smith, and with an assist from George Q. Cannon, once described as "a savvy political operative" who was "stout of flesh, low of stature, rubicund of countenance, and ready of tongue,"[33] the amended Holy Ghost slowly evolved to become what the amended anthropomorphic Father had earlier been, *a personage of spirit.*

At General Conference on or after April 9, 1852, Heber C. Kimball, the First Counselor in the First Presidency, said "the Lord told me that Adam was my father and that he was the God and father of all the inhabitants of this earth."[34] One of Kimball's descendants, a twentieth-century prophet, denounced Joseph, Brigham, Heber, Wilford, Daniel and Eliza's Adam/God doctrine. Heber's nineteenth-century revelation ("The Lord told me that Adam was my father. . .") became Spencer W. Kimball's twentieth-century heresy. Spencer W. Kimball denied Adam was God and described the doctrine as false.

On April 4, 1897 (twenty years after the death of Brigham Young

---

[32]Quinn, *The Mormon Hierarchy: Extensions of Power*, 647.

[33]*New York Tribune* (22 November 1871), quoted in Turner, *Brigham Young: Pioneer Prophet*, 368.

[34]Heber C. Kimball, 30 April 1862, quoted in Solomon F. Kimball, "Sacred History," *Solomon F. Kimball Journal* (Church Historian's Office).

and close to the end of the nineteenth century), the prophet Wilford Woodruff reiterated his belief in the doctrine that Adam was God: "Adam is our Father and God and no use to discuss it with Josephites [Trinitarians] or anyone else."[35]   Joseph, Brigham, Heber, Wilford and George Q. Cannon *used to believe* that Adam was God.   The Fundamentalists, today's faithful followers of Joseph, Brigham, Heber, Wilford and George, *still believe* that Adam is God.   For those disciples who drink from ancient springs, Adam is God and polygamy is the most distinctive signature of the twenty-first century church.

First Presidency, 1909, Reaffirmed 2002:

> *It is held by some that Adam was not the first man upon this earth and that the original human being was a development from lower orders of the animal creation.   These, however, are the theories of man. The word of the Lord [which is not a theory] declared that Adam was "the first man of all men (Moses 1:34) [Mormon scripture produced by Joseph Smith], and we are therefore bound to regard him as the personal parent of our race."*[36]

The Church continues to embrace a literal Adam, a literal Eve, a literal Flood, a literal Noah, a literal Ark, Jaredites, a Tower of Babel, Nephites, Lamanites and an American Jesus.

Jesus didn't become Jehovah in Mormon theology, meaning a lesser God beholden to a greater God by the name of Elohim, a Jehovah son to an Elohim father, until many years after the death of Joseph Smith.   In some two hundred fifty-six references to Elohim and Jehovah, and to the God of the Old Testament in the Journal of

---

[35]Wilford Woodruff, Brigham Young Jr.'s Journal (4 April 1897, accessed November 2015), available from mormonhandbook.com/home/adam-god-doctrine.html; Internet, 5. At the time of this statement, Woodruff, who died in 1898, had been the prophet for eight years.   Brigham Young described the Adam/God doctrine at General Conference in 1852, fully forty-five years before Woodruff reaffirmed his belief in that controversial doctrine in 1897.   Woodruff was one of Brigham Young's first and most ardent Adam/God converts.

[36]First Presidency Statement, *Improvement Era*, November 1909, reaffirmed, *Ensign*, February 2002, emphasis added.

Discourses (representing the sermons of the members of the First Presidencies and Quorums of the Twelve), the title Jehovah is specifically applied to Jesus only once.[37] That obscure reference did not occur until 1885 (which was also after the death of Brigham Young) when the strange new doctrine (that Jesus was Jehovah) (which was not clarified until about 1916) was only just beginning to develop.

The Book of Mormon

The prophets have taught that the Book of Mormon is the most correct of any book on earth. They said it was *translated* from ancient inscriptions on golden plates by the prophet Joseph Smith with the aid of the Urim and Thummim by the gift and power of God. Those Urim and Thummim interpreters, according to Smith, were found in the concrete box that contained the golden plates. Who knew that Joseph Smith translated the Book of Mormon without the Urim and Thummim while the plates were covered with cloth or out of the room and in the woods?

In this twenty-first century, in what has been a painful and dishonest reversal, Smith is now said to have translated the book by looking at a chocolate-colored stone found deep in the ground while digging a well – the same stone he previously used to tell fortunes and search for buried treasure. Twenty-first century Mormons have changed course to say that Smith translated the Book of Mormon without the Urim and Thummim by looking at a peepstone in a stovepipe hat. History changed to say that it was done through the stone without really looking at the plates the Lehites killed Laban to secure. Thousands of graphic depictions strategically placed in houses of worship (and in instructional materials) have deceptively reflected the disingenuous historical view. Until recently, and even still today, Joseph Smith is depicted as having translated the Book of Mormon without the stone, but with the aid of those magic interpreters from visible plates.

The Book of Mormon is "a volume of holy scripture comparable to

---

[37]Kirkland, "Jehovah As Father," *Sunstone* (1984), 9.2, 5.

the Bible" and "a record of God's dealings with the ancient inhabitants of the Americas." All of the early prophets said it contained "the fulness of the everlasting Gospel" as delivered by an *historically invisible Savior* to the ancient inhabitants of the American continent. It is believed that no modern Mormon scholar or leader would now, because of the twists and turns of the everchanging theology, be willing to say what the angel was supposed to have said, that the Book of Mormon contained the "fulness of the everlasting Gospel."

All of the early LDS prophets, starting with Joseph Smith and then Moroni, the Book of Mormon and a great Proclamation to the world at large (Appendix F), taught the laity that the Book of Mormon was a history of the inhabitants of the Western Hemisphere and that the Native Americans were Lamanites, North and South American Hebrews. In the Doctrine and Covenants, Joseph's God described the ancient inhabitants (Native Americans) as Lamanites at least eleven times. From the earliest days, the leaders of the Church have described Native Americans as Lamanites. From 1981 to 2007, the Introduction to the Book of Mormon identified the Lamanites as *"the principal ancestors of the American Indians."* Since 2007 "Mormon Scholars who favor a limited geography model have been disclaiming any significant genetic connection between Lamanites and any modern people."[38]

The Church has only recently been forced to admit in an undated unsigned essay published in 2014 that DNA science does not support the proposition that the Native Americans came from the Middle East. Perfectly overwhelming evidence has caused the Church to change that historical tune. The Church has been forced to say that, "The evidence assembled to date suggests that the majority of Native Americans carry largely Asian DNA."[39] Uncorrelated DNA science obliterates that principal tenet of the Book of Mormon, Hebrew (Semetic) origins. "[I]f the Book of Mormon was not brought forth, as Joseph Smith insisted, by the hand of God, in very fact an account of God's involvement with ancient Americans

---

[38]"Lamanites" (accessed August 2014), available from wikipedia.com.
[39]"Book of Mormon and DNA Studies," one of a number of unsigned and undated Essays published by The Church of Jesus Christ of Latter-day Saints in 2014.

descended from the people of ancient Judah, then the Church and its priesthood and Mormonism as a religion are abject frauds."[40]

Simon Southerton, a former Mormon bishop and an expert on the Book of Mormon and DNA, has discussed the extent of the majority the Church has only recently been forced to concede. "The DNA studies support the conclusion that greater than 99.994% of the DNA of the Maya [the population central to modern Mormonism's Book of Mormon limited geography model] is derived from Asian migrations over 15,000 years ago" ("Semitic DNA has escaped detection").[41] The Book of Mormon unequivocally claims that the Native Americans came from the Middle East. The book stands or falls upon that vitally important assumption. The Doctrine and Covenants clearly claims, in the voice of the Mormon God, that the Native Americans are Lamanites.

Until very recently the Mormon prophets taught their followers that the Native Americans, descendants of "the former inhabitants of this continent," were Hebrews from the loins of Lehi, a remnant of Jacob and Lamanites. The premise was that the Native Americans were the descendants of the Hebrew colonizers of the hemisphere. The historical foundations of the Book of Mormon are crumbling in the face of the advance of DNA science.[42] Modern molecular genealogy can separate the Hebrews from the

---

[40]Sterling M. McMurrin, Foreword, in B.H. Roberts, *Studies of the Book of Mormon* (Salt Lake City: Signature Books, 1985), xv.

[41]Simon Southerton, "Simon's DNA Musings: DNA vs. the Mesoamerican Limited Geography" (accessed 28 February 2014); available from http://simon southerton.blogspot.com/2014/02/lose-limited-geography.html#comment-form, 6.

[42]"Scientists have failed to uncover genetic links to the Middle East among Native Americans in general and Mesoamericans specifically." (Ibid., 1). LDS apologist scholars, speaking for apostles and prophets who fail to speak for themselves, have centered their limited geography theories upon "the complex civilizations of the Maya." The Mayan populations "were large," the Mayans "lived at the right time," and the Mayans were the only New World culture with a system of writing. But even the Mayan writing, which can now be interpreted, shows no relationship to anything in the Book of Mormon. "The 20th century saw an explosion in scientific understanding of the prehistoric colonization of the Americas." "The latest whole genome marker studies have revealed in high resolution the complete absence of Semitic DNA in the Maya. At least 99.99% of the pre-Columbian DNA of the Maya is of Siberian origin." (Ibid.).

Lamanites.[43]   It can also discern a forty thousand year-old Neanderthal inheritance to which it can ascribe a percentage. "As only Mormons consider the Book of Mormon to have any ancient historical basis, Lamanites are not considered to be a valid category of people by mainstream scholars"[44] anywhere in the world. "Scholars outside Mormonism do not . . . accept the Book of Mormon as a valid source of ancient American history."[45]

All Mormon prophets have taught that the biblical Tower of Babel and the dispersion were literal rather than metaphorical events. Without a literal Tower of Babel, the confusion of language and a dispersion, there would be no Jared, no great epiphany, no brother of Jared, no Jaredites, no Book of Ether and no Book of Mormon.

All of the early Mormon prophets taught without equivocation that the ancient inhabitants of the Americas, specifically those who came with the migration of the Lehites in about 600 BC, were Hebrews, that they separated into two nations (Nephites and Lamanites) and inhabited a previously empty hemisphere. Until recently, all Mormon prophets have taught that the survivors of those two nations ("After thousands of years all were destroyed except the Lamanites . . .") were "the principal ancestors of the American Indians."[46] DNA research has caused the prophets to quietly

---

[43]With the whole genome population studies available to scientists in 2014, "It is now possible to scan entire genomes for hundreds of thousands of DNA markers and to detect traces of historical mixing between ancient populations with incredible clarity." (Ibid., 2). Using methods described in the February 2014 issue of *Science*, researchers (Hellenthal et al.) "examined over 400,000 DNA markers on 22 pairs of chromosomes," which is "almost the entire human genome." Earlier mtDNA studies, which traced "maternal lineages," by way of contrast, used only a few dozen markers. The Hellenthal study "outlines sophisticated methods for identifying evidence of historical inbreeding between populations." (Ibid., 4). "Ancestry.com (Provo, Utah) will now test your autosomal DNA at 700,000 markers [almost twice the number of markers used in the Hellenthal study] . . . then compare your DNA to samples from around the world to reveal your genetic background and ethnic history. Using the methods published in the Hellenthal study they could tell you exactly where your ancestors lived during the past 4000 years." (Ibid.).

[44]"Lamanites" (accessed August 2014), available from wikipedia.com.

[45]Ibid.

[46]*The following reflects the unanimous teachings of the recent past before DNA research. Boyd K. Packer, 1964:* "Today thousands of Lamanites are coming into the Church [*"In fulfillment of Nephi's prophetic words, the Lamanites in our day*

abandon that doctrine without so much as ever saying so. Apologists, not prophets and apostles, have put their shoulders to this collapsing wheel. There is now not one specifically discernible Lamanite to be found anywhere on Mormon earth. And yet the Book of Mormon reports (on its title page) that it is *"Written to the Lamanites, who are a remnant of the House of Israel . . . ."*[47]

Spencer W. Kimball, various other prophets, and thousands of leaders, members and missionaries have taught that Native Americans (constituting all of "the indigenous peoples of the Americas"), and (more recently) the Polynesians, collectively embracing many millions of people, were direct descendants of Laman, a principal ancestor of the Native Americans. The Lord has repeatedly reported in canonized Mormon scriptures that the Native Americans are the descendants of the Lamanites.

Discernment

Gordon B. Hinckley and other leaders have purchased and/or otherwise acquired or tried to acquire various fraudulent documents believed to have been authentic at a striking cash and in-kind cost from Mark Hoffman, a now convicted murderer and an accomplished forger. They did this in order to keep such documents from being brought to light. A case in point: A forged

---

are, indeed being restored to their rightful place in the House of Israel"]. More than one hundred Lamanite branches have been organized among the stakes and within the missions. In many of these branches the leadership is provided by the Lamanite members. They are the branch presidents, the teachers, the auxiliary leaders, the music directors . . . . In the small Paiute Indian settlement near Cedar City, Utah, a beautiful new chapel points its spire to the sky . . . . The work in behalf of our Lamanite brothers and sisters must go forward." (Boyd K. Packer, Assistant to the Council of the Twelve [speaking before DNA], "For the Blessing of the Lamanites," *Relief Society Magazine*, vol. 51 no. 8 [August 1964]: 565, 567). There were Lamanites everywhere then; today there are none.

[47]Book of Mormon, Title page, emphasis added. The title page of the Book of Mormon is "an account written by the hand of Mormon upon plates taken from the plates of Nephi." Those words, not the words of any nineteenth-century Saint, are part of the "original translation from the plates into English by Joseph Smith, Jun." The words on the Book of Mormon's title page (*"written to the Lamanites who are a remnant of the house of Israel . . ."*) are not negotiable. If there are no Lamanites, the Book of Mormon fails to serve its carefully stated purpose.

letter supposed to have been sent to Josiah Stowell by Joseph Smith. If that letter had proved to be authentic, it would have been Joseph Smith's earliest known holograph. Hinckley personally purchased the letter privately from Hoffman for the sum of $15,000, claimed to have owned it outright and consigned it to the Church's vault. Even with the aid of professional Mormon historians, the Church's highest leaders proved themselves utterly incapable of detecting Hoffman's continuing deceptions. They were willing to purchase and conceal what they thought to be harmful historical documents. Their reliance upon the fraudulent representations of the now discredited forger present a formidable challenge to the vaunted notion that the highest leaders of the LDS Church exercise special powers of "discernment."

DISCRIMINATION, MISOGYNY AND PRIESTHOOD

Joseph Smith was the first Latter-day Saint to bar the Negro race from holding the priesthood, although he once allowed the ordination of a black man by the name of Elijah Abel. Smith taught racially charged exclusionary doctrine and claimed it was revealed to him by God. He also produced racially charged scripture. On one occasion the Mormon prophet proclaimed: "Had I anything to do with the negro I would confine them by strict law to their own species, and put them on a national equalization."[48] A black woman was sealed to Smith in a temple she was not allowed to enter as a servitor for eternity.

On February 5, 1852, Brigham Young declared that "negroes are the children of old Cain." Young's declaration occurred "in connection with [the] Utah legislature's legalization of African-American slavery,"[49] an initiative for which the Mormon prophet had been the indispensable sponsor. The codification of slavery, an inflammatory development, was overlooked in the clamor surrounding the disclosure that same year that the Church was practicing polygamy. On August 9, 1857, Apostle (and future prophet) John Taylor reported that, "This [Horace] Greeley is one

---

[48]Joseph Smith Jr., 2 January 1843, Roberts, ed., *History of The Church of Jesus Christ of Latter-day Saints*, 5:217-18.
[49]Quinn, *The Mormon Hierarchy: Extensions of Power*, 749-50.

of their popular characters in the East, and one that supports the stealing of niggers and the underground railroad."[50] On October 6, 1863, Young prophesies at general conference: "Will the present struggle [the U.S. Civil War] free the slave? No . . . and men will be called to judgment for the way they have treated the negro."[51] Young believed in slavery, and firmly said so, but also said that slaves should be treated better. The Latter-day Saints sat out of the Civil War. They believed the war would destroy the Union and that that was in the best interest of the Kingdom of God.

Joseph Smith, Brigham Young and the prophets who succeeded them – until the administration of Spencer W. Kimball in 1978 – taught that Mormonism's racial doctrine was revealed to the prophets of God. Blacks were excluded from the priesthood and from the temple and from exaltation by divine edict because they were less valiant in the preexistence. These doctrines were revealed to Smith, and they were memorialized in canonized Mormon scripture produced by Smith and the God he said he served.

In what are thought to have been more than forty printings of his book *Mormon Doctrine* (1958-2010, three editions), Apostle Bruce R. McConkie defined Mormonism's controversial racial tenets. Acknowledging humanity's similarities, McConkie contended that "All races of men stem from certain common ancestors [specifically Adam and Eve and Noah]." By Noah's sons Shem, Ham and Japheth "was the whole earth overspread."[52] "Racial degeneration resulting in differences in appearance and spiritual aptitude, has arisen since the fall." By reference to uniquely peculiar Mormon resources produced by Joseph Smith, with the aid and assistance of the Mormon God – specifically the Book of Mormon, the Book of Moses and the Book of Abraham – McConkie explains that Latter-day Saints know things about the races that the sectarians (Protestants) do not. "We know the circumstances under which the posterity of Cain (and later of Ham) [Noah's son who survived the Flood] were cursed with what we call negroid racial

---

[50]Ibid., 755.
[51]Ibid., 762.
[52]Genesis 9:19, quoted in Bruce R. McConkle, "Races of Men," *Mormon Doctrine*, 2d ed. (Salt Lake City, UT: Bookcraft, 1966), 616.

characteristics."[53]   We know these things because of those extraordinary Mormon scriptures brought to light by the Prophet Joseph Smith.[54]

Furthermore, according to McConkie and other faithful apologists who proceeded in lockstep to assist the leaders of the Church in the articulation and defense of those racially discriminatory doctrines until 1978: "The Book of Mormon explains why the Lamanites received dark skins and a degenerate status."[55]   In the absence of perfect knowledge ("detailed information" for the record is not entirely clear), there is one overarching general principle to guide the faithful pending some further clarification. "[W]e know only the general principle that all these changes from the physical and spiritual perfections of our common parents have been brought about by departure from the gospel truths . . . ."[56]   The Lord caused a cursing to come upon them because of their iniquity.

> *[W]herefore, as they were white, and exceedingly fair and delightsome, that they might not be enticing unto my [Nephi's] people, the Lord God did cause a skin of blackness to come upon them.   And thus saith the Lord God: I will cause that they shall be loathsome unto thy people, save they shall repent of their iniquities.*[57]

Those who "mixeth with their seed" shall be cursed to be like them. "[T]he Lord spake it, and it was done." Because of the curse "they did become an idle people, full of mischief and subtlety . . . ." "The race and nation in which men are born in this world is a direct result of their pre-existent life. All the spirit hosts of heaven deemed worthy to receive mortal bodies were foreordained to pass through this earthly probation in the particular race and nation suited to their needs, circumstances and talents . . . . [G]roups were

---

[53]Ibid.

[54]The Pearl of Great Price, Moses 5:16-41; 7:8, 12, 22; Abraham 1:20-27.

[55]Book of Mormon, 2 Nephi 5:21-23.

[56]McConkie cites for his authority here ("Races of Men," *Mormon Doctrine*, 616) the *Doctrines of Salvation*, 1:148-51; 3:313-26 (authored by his father-in-law, Joseph Fielding Smith, yet another leader (and a future prophet) of the Church of Jesus Christ of Latter-day Saints).

[57]Book of Mormon, 2 Nephi 5:21-23, emphasis added.

thus foreknown and their total memberships designated in the premortal life."[58]

In the war in heaven in the preexistence, one-third of the spirit hosts rebelled against God and were cast out without bodies, becoming the devil and his angels. The other two-thirds stood for Christ. "Of the two-thirds who followed Christ . . . some were more valiant than others." Those more valiant souls were blessed to receive a better placement. "Those who were less valiant in [the] pre-existence and who thereby had certain spiritual restrictions imposed upon them during mortality are known to us as the *negroes*. Such spirits are sent to earth through the lineage of Cain, the mark put upon him for his rebellion against God and his murder of Abel being a black skin." All as described in Mormonism's unique and particular scripture (Moses 5:16-41; 7:8, 12, 22). "Noah's son Ham married Egyptus, a descendant of Cain, thus preserving the negro lineage through the flood." All as described in other unique and particular Mormon scripture (Abraham 1:20-27).[59] By Mormon reckoning, God, through his prophet Joseph Smith, is the author of this:

> *Before 1978 Negroes were denied the priesthood in this life.*

> *Before 1978 Negroes were deprived the blessings of the temple.*

> *Before 1978 the gospel message of salvation was not carried to them.*

> *Before 1978 the insufficiently devoted Negroes got what they got as a result of their long and unsuccessful pre-mortal probation in the presence of the Lord.*

Black Latter-day Saints were not married for time and eternity, and black families were not forever. McConkie and other leaders of the Church asked members and critics of the Church to remember that, "[T]his inequality is not of man's origin. It is the Lord's doing . . . based on his eternal laws . . . and grows out of the lack of

---

[58]McConkie, "Races of Men," *Mormon Doctrine*, 616.
[59]McConkie, "Negroes," *Mormon Doctrine*, 526-28.

spiritual valiance of those concerned in their first estate."[60] "Excluded from the church's most sacred rituals, black Mormons would thus not share celestial glory with their white counterparts . . . . [T]he exclusion of black Mormons from church offices and most rituals meant the eternal perpetuation of earthly iniquities."[61] Joseph Smith informed the Saints that this "inequality" was "the Lord's doing."

Brigham Young (1852): "*Any man having one drop of the seed of Cane [sic] in him Cannot hold the priesthood & if no other Prophet ever spake it Before I will say it now in the name of Jesus Christ.*"[62] According to Brigham Young, blacks were "cursed," "uncouth," "uncomely," "disagreeable," "wild," "deprived of intelligence, and preordained to be servants."[63] Young:

> *[I]nasmuch as I believe in the Bible, inasmuch as I believe in the ordinances of God, in the Priesthood and order, and decrees of God, I must believe in slavery.*[64]

Brigham Young disliked the Union and several American presidents (Zachary Taylor was going to be his bootblack in the life to come). Young favored the cause of the South in the Civil War and denied the priesthood to emancipated Negroes. He informed the Latter-day Saints that what he taught about God and race he first learned from Joseph Smith. Eleven consecutive Mormon prophets, including Joseph Smith, untouched by the injustices that surrounded them and blind to a better way, perpetuated Joseph and Brigham's discriminatory racial doctrines for more than one hundred and thirty years, from the early days of the Church until 1978.[65]

---

[60]Ibid.

[61]Turner, *Brigham Young: Pioneer Prophet*, 223.

[62]Ibid., 226, emphasis added.

[63]Publisher's Preface, *The Essential Brigham Young* (foreword by Campbell), xiii. "I should feel myself more degraded in the eyes of the Lord to be acting [in a state militia] under a commission from Gov[ernor] Ford, than I should to be changed into an affrican." (Turner, *Brigham Young: Pioneer Prophet*, 124).

[64]Ibid., 225, emphasis added.

[65]The eleven prophets: Joseph Smith, Brigham Young, John Taylor, Wilford Woodruff, Lorenzo Snow, Joseph F. Smith, Heber J. Grant, George Albert Smith,

The First Presidency directly addressed the issue of race in 1949 ("First Presidency Statement," August 17, 1949, President George Albert Smith):

> *The attitude of the Church with reference to Negroes remains as it has always stood. It is not a matter of the declaration of a policy but of direct commandment from the Lord, on which is founded the doctrine of the Church from the days of its organization, to the effect that Negroes may become members of the Church but that they are not entitled to the priesthood at the present time . . . .*[66]

> The First Presidency

The First Presidency and the Quorum of the Twelve Apostles revisited the issue of race in 1969:

> *[M]atters of faith, conscience, and theology are not within the purview of the civil law. . . . "Congress shall make no law respecting an establishment of religion, or prohibiting the free exercise thereof."*

> *The position of the Church of Jesus Christ of Latter-day Saints affecting those of the Negro race who choose to join the Church falls wholly within the category of religion. It has no bearing upon matters of civil rights. In no case or degree does it deny to the Negro his full privileges as a citizen of the nation.*[67]

David O. McKay, Joseph Fielding Smith and Harold B. Lee.

[66]Statement of the First Presidency of The Church of Jesus Christ of Latter-day Saints, 17 August 1949 (LDS Archives, Salt Lake City), emphasis added.

[67]Hugh B. Brown and N. Eldon Tanner (President David O. McKay being ill at the time), Letter dated December 15, 1969, "First Presidency Statement," *Priesthood Bulletin* (February 1970). Until federal law undid slavery in the U.S. territories in 1862, "some African-American slaves are paid as tithing," meaning "bought, sold, and otherwise treated as chattel[s] in Utah." On September 7, 1859, the "Salt Lake City Clerk records [the] sale of [a] twenty-six year old 'Negro boy' for $800 to William H. Hooper." One month before this transaction, Hooper was elected as "Utah's delegate to Congress." (Quinn, *The Mormon Hierarchy: Extensions of Power*, 758).

This position "has no relevancy whatsoever to those who do not wish to join the Church." Those who do not believe in the "divine origin and nature of the Church," or that the Church has "the priesthood of God[,] . . . should have no concern with any aspect of our theology on priesthood so long as that theology does not deny any man his Constitutional privileges." The Church accepts "the principle of continuous revelation."

> *From the beginning of this dispensation, Joseph Smith and all succeeding presidents of the Church have taught that Negroes, while spirit children of a common Father, and the progeny of our earthly parents Adam and Eve, were not yet to receive the priesthood, for reasons which we believe are known to God, but which He has not made fully known to man.*[68] *Our living prophet David O. McKay has said, "The seeming discrimination by the Church toward the Negro is not something which originated with man, but goes back into the beginning with God . . . . Revelation assures us that this plan antedates man's mortal existence, extending back to man's preexistent state."*

> Faithfully your brethren,
> The First Presidency[69]

Mormon Founder Joseph Smith:

> *[W]e unhesitatingly say . . . the project of emancipation is destructive to our government, and the notion of amalgamation is devilish! – And insensible to feeling must be the heart, and low indeed must be the mind, that would consent for a moment, to*

---

[68]Horace Greeley to Brigham Young: "H.G. What is the position of your church with respect to slavery?" "B.Y. We consider it of divine institution, and not to be abolished until the curse pronounced on Ham shall be removed from his descendants." (*New York Daily Tribune* (20 August 1859), quoted in Quinn, *The Mormon Hierarchy: Extensions of Power*, 758).

[69]Brown and Tanner, Letter dated 15 December 1969, "First Presidency Statement," *Priesthood Bulletin* (February 1970), emphasis added

> *see his fair daughter, his sister, or perhaps, his bosom companion, in the embrace of a NEGRO!* [70]

Mormon Prophet Joseph Fielding Smith:

> *It is true that the Negro race is barred from holding the Priesthood, and this has always been the case. The Prophet Joseph Smith taught this doctrine, and it was made known to him . . . .* [71]

Ezra Taft Benson and other influential Mormon leaders strongly opposed integration and the American Civil Rights Movement. In 1978 Spencer W. Kimball claimed to have had an unpublished revelation reversing the discriminatory doctrine. In a recent undated and unsigned twenty-first century essay, "Race and the Priesthood," the Church implied that a sitting prophet can lead the church astray when, in a futile effort to protect the reputation of Joseph Smith, as always and at all costs, it assigned blame for the priesthood ban (only part of a larger discrimination package) on Brigham Young's nineteenth-century racism. In point of fact, Mormonism's failure to give black people the priesthood, and to treat them fairly, was a mistake which was "officially, authoritatively endorsed by First Presidencies and Quorums of the Twelve for 130 years." [72]

In a moment of candor in a letter he hoped would be destroyed, Joseph Smith told Miss Nancy Rigdon it was not for her to reason why.

> *Whatever God requires is right, no matter what it is,*

---

[70] Joseph Smith, *Messenger and Advocate*, vol. 2 no. 7 (April 1836), 300, emphasis added and retained. "Smith declares that slavery was ordained by God and consistent with the gospel of Christ." (Lynn K. Wilder, former BYU professor, author of "Unveiling Grace" [a video documentary, 2011]). Mormonism's racist posture "originated in the scripture and teachings that Joseph Smith brought forth," we may suppose, by the gift and power of God.

[71] Joseph Fielding Smith, *The Improvement Era*, 27 no. 6 (April 1924), 565, emphasis added.

[72] Tal Bachman, "Re the new 1st Presidency statement, here are MY questions (add yours here)" (28 June 2014; accessed August 2014); available from http://exmormon.org/phorum/read.php?2,1308419; Internet, 1.

although we may not see the reason thereof til long after the events transpire.[73]

Latter-day Saints subordinated their judgments to those of their leaders by essentially accepting everything these materials have just described. And when those unchangeable principles were changed by what was supposed to have been an unchangeable God and infallible prophets, they accepted the changes as well. T.B.H. Stenhouse, a prominent figure in the nineteenth-century Church, a man close to Mormon leaders and events, left the faith and said:

Those who have not lived under the influence of an "inspired prophet" can form no idea of the facility with which a religious people can be taught any doctrine, and be led on to lay aside their education, or their sense of morality, and thus be cast in the mould of a teacher's mind.[74]

---

[73]Jessee ed., *The Personal Writings of Joseph Smith*, 507-09, emphasis added.
[74]Stenhouse, *The Rocky Mountain Saints*, 184, emphasis added.

Appendices

MORMON EUGENICS: 1857

George Q. Cannon (1827-1901) was a Counselor to four Mormon prophets and had a commanding presence under and after Brigham Young in Utah. He was a most important and powerful nineteenth-century Saint. Cannon had six wives and forty-three children. "The physical nature of man is animal," according to Cannon. "The laws of generation, development, sustenance and health which apply to the lower orders of animals apply also to him." Noting that mankind paid more attention to the "natural laws" that governed "the propagation of animals" than to the natural laws that governed the propagation of humankind, Cannon offered a solution in the name of the Church in a Mormon publication. "Doubtless it is and ought to be the duty of legislators and conservators of our race, to introduce such regulations and laws, and enforce them as are best calculated to develop our physical nature." With that, he also said that, "A well formed, healthy, vigorous race should be the end sought," after which he previewed the model for society that he, his publication, the Church and its polygamous principals (notably Joseph Smith) envisioned. "Cannon argued that polygamy should be implemented through a careful management of all sexual relationships by the state."[1]

"The ancient Spartans acted upon this policy [regulations and laws calculated to develop mankind's physical nature], and the happy result was the production of a nation of the noblest men and women the world ever saw." Cannon envisioned a world and a universe inhabited by noble men and women. "No diseased and effeminate person was permitted to marry and curse the world with a tainted offspring." It took a village. "The children of the entire republic belonged to the Government, which appointed competent persons to superintend their physical and mental training, and when the fit time arrived they married them as they saw fit, keeping constantly

---

[1]George Q. Cannon, "Improvement of Our Species," *Western Standard*, George Q. Cannon, ed., 7 August 1857 (2/4-6), 2:22, reproduced at B. Carmon Hardy, ed., *Doing the Works of Abraham: Mormon Polygamy – Its Origin, Practice, and Demise (Kingdom in the West: The Mormons and the American Frontier)*, Will Bagley, ed., vol. 9 (Norman, OK: The Arthur H. Clark Company, 2007), 106-9.

in view the improvement of the race." Racial purity, a concept of some importance in the twentieth century, was central to the emerging society's new cosmology. "It was early and constantly impressed upon the minds of the youth, that it was a duty which they owed to the nation to preserve the fountain of life pure within themselves and so to transmit it to their offspring." In this historical model the Latter-day Saints saw hope for their own regulated non-monogamous future. "Those were the days of wise thoughts and noble deeds; and Pagan though they were, they [the ancient Spartans, a warrior class] were incomparably more virtuous than is modern Christendom."[2]

Describing the spiritual and the physical as indissoluble, Cannon suggests that the full exercise of the spiritual depends materially upon the perfect development of the physical. A mal-formed man will have a mal-formed mind. It is, he said, "utter folly" to attempt to improve "the moral condition of the world while its physical remains unimproved."[3] Now, on behalf of the Church in its west coast publication, editor George Q. Cannon describes a Mormon vision of the true order of things: *This state of things [the moral and physical decline of the world] must continue, until moralists and legislators find out that a true and effectual reform must begin in the marriage bed.*"

> *License to marry should not come from the priest but from the physician. It will be when the law forbids the unhealthy to beget children – when it compels every healthy man to marry – when a refusal to this will debar him from holding office – from voting – from sueing at courts at law – from making contracts – from following any learned profession – when it suffers no healthy girl to remain single after she becomes of proper age – when no whore shall be permitted to live – when illicit intercourse shall be punished with death, that we shall witness any improvement in the morals of the age.*[4]

---

[2]Ibid.
[3]Ibid., 107.
[4]Ibid., 107-8, emphasis added.

"This" Cannon said, "is precisely what the Saints in the valleys of the mountains are endeavoring to accomplish. Joseph Smith had penetration enough to know, that so long as the bodies of men are weak, degenerate, and tainted with impurities inherited from their fathers for a thousand generations, it is impossible to accomplish with them any great moral improvement, or indoctrinate them with many divine truths."   Cannon opined that these enlightened principles "would come in contact with the ridiculous sentimentality of the age which, "heaven knows if that could be overturned and rooted out, it would be a substantial blessing."

Cannon laid his analysis squarely on the shoulders of Joseph Smith. "He [Smith] taught that none but healthy men should marry – that a man should know his wife for the purpose of procreation and for that only – that he should keep himself apart from her during the carrying and nursing periods . . . ." Cannon credited Joseph Smith for teaching "that it is lawful and right, God commanding, for a man to have more than one wife – that adultery should be punishable with death – [and] that whoredom should not be tolerated under any consideration . . . ." What Cannon described was, he reported, the actual "practice" of the Utah Saints. "This theory is reduced to practice in Utah Territory; and it is remarked by immigrants passing through Salt Lake City, that the proportion of children is unusually great, and they are uncommonly robust and healthy." Why shouldn't the world see what the Latter-day Saints saw? "Who cannot see that the mental vigor of those children will be in proportion to their physical perfection and that a generation is rising in the American interior, who will make their mark upon the history of their times?"

"There is not a whore in Utah, neither is there a single female but what can find a husband and home if she so desires: whereas in Christian cities harlots are numbered by the thousand."[5] Cannon told his audience what needed to be done to get there. "Human nature must be taken as it is. Legalize polygamy, abolish whoredom by the strong arm of the law, and punish adultery with death . . . ."[6] He then described the mournful consequences of failure – measure failure as monogamy. "[A]s long as monogamy is

---

[5]Ibid., 108, emphasis added.
[6]Ibid., 108-9.

the law, bastardy, whoredom, and degeneracy will exist; and also their concomitants, irreligion, intemperance, licentiousness and vice of every kind and degree."

HYRUM SMITH BLESSES JOAB –
GENERAL IN ISRAEL, JOHN C. BENNETT

On September 21, 1840, Patriarch Hyrum Smith, on fire at the time, lavished elaborate blessings on John C. Bennett's head and predicted the prized new recruit's glorious future, in the sacred name of Jesus Christ. Bennett was, he said, a son of Abraham. Hyrum blessed an errant husband, who had abandoned his undivorced wife and children, with all the graces and gifts of the holy priesthood, to include "wisdom in all the mysteries of God." Bennett told the Saints, including Hyrum, he was a single man.

"Thou shalt have," the Patriarch reported, "knowledge given thee and shalt understand the *keys* by which all mysteries shall be unlocked." "Thou shalt have," he said, "great power among the children of men," and "influence among the great and the noble," and thou shalt "bring them to the knowledge of the truth." Thou shalt "prevail over thy enemies."   "Many souls shall believe, because of the *proclamation* which thou shalt make." "The Holy Spirit shall rest upon thee . . . ." "[T]hy voice shall make the foundation on which thou standest to shake, – so great shall be the power of God."[1] Hyrum's unbounded undiscerning exuberance puts one in remembrance of God's failed revelatory blessing to another great rascal, Bennett's friend, Apostle William Smith. ". . . I will yet make him a polished shaft in my quiver, in bringing down the wickedness and abominations of men and there shall be none greater than he in his day and generation . . . ."[2] Joseph's God said that to Joseph's brother William Smith.

Does Hyrum know to whom he speaks? Has the Savior given voice to these noble and unconditional recitals? God's "favor shall rest

---

[1]"Patriarchal blessing of John C. Bennett given by Hyrum Smith on September 21, 1840," in H. Michael Marquardt, comp., *Early Patriarchal Blessings of The Church of Jesus Christ of Latter-day Saints* (Salt Lake City: Smith-Pettit Foundation, 2007), 197-98, emphasis added.

[2]Revelation, 3 November 1835 (Kirtland, Ohio), "Joseph Smith, 'Sketch Book for the use of Joseph Smith, jr.,' Journal, Sept. 1835-April 1836," Joseph Smith Collection (Church History Library), in *The Joseph Smith Papers*, 18.

upon thee in dreams and visions . . . ." "Beloved Brother, if thou art faithful, thou shalt have power to heal the sick; cause the lame to leap like an hart; the deaf to hear; and the dumb to speak . . . ." And, said the loquacious Hyrum, "their voice[s] shall salute thine ears . . . ."

"Thou shalt be like unto Paul." The visions of heaven shall open to Bennett even as they did to him. "Thy name shall be known in many nations . . . thy voice shall be heard among many people. Yea, unto many of the remnants of Israel shalt thou be known . . . . [T]hou shalt proclaim the gospel unto many tribes of the house of Israel."[3] Is this a one-of-a-kind blessing reserved for a runaway husband, an absent father, a discredited academic, an abortionist and a promiscuous adulterer? Is this the same man Joseph will come to describe to a large congregation in a violent speech in June of 1842 as "an adder in the path and a viper in the bosom"?[4] Is God behind these fortune telling platitudes?

"God is with thee," the Patriarch said. "God shall reward thee for thy kindness," he said. God wants you to "travel and labor for Zion," he said. That "is the mind and will of God," he said. God "shall shield thee forever. Angels shall guide thee . . . ." "Thou shalt have power over many . . . ." "[T]hey shall tremble when they hear thy words." "Thou shalt be blessed with the blessings of Abraham, Isaac and Jacob . . . ." What "thou shalt pronounce shall be sealed in heaven." And if "thou continue faithful and steadfast . . . thou shalt have power over the winds and the waves, and they shall obey thy voice when thou shalt speak in the name of Jesus Christ." "Thou shalt be crowned with immortality in the Celestial Kingdom, when Christ shall descend. Even so, Amen."[5]

This was a remarkable blessing given by Hyrum Smith to John C. Bennett, a man for all seasons.

---

[3]"Patriarchal blessing of John C. Bennett given by Hyrum Smith on September 21, 1840," in Marquardt, *Early Patriarchal Blessings of The Church of Jesus Christ of Latter-day Saints*, 197-98.

[4]*Times and Seasons*, vol. 3 no. 19, whole no. 53 (1 August 1842), 868.

[5]Blessing excerpts from Wyl, *Mormon Portraits*, 129.

TIMELINE: JOHN C. BENNETT

August, September 1840: "Dr. John C. Bennett . . . located himself in the city of Nauvoo, about the month of August, 1840 [probably September], and soon after joined the church."[1]   Bennett was baptized by Joseph Smith.

August, September 1840: Joseph Smith knows (no later than August or September 1840) that John C. Bennett is representing himself to the Church in Nauvoo as a single man without ever mentioning a wife or children. For thirty-nine weeks Bennett lives with Joseph and Emma. After he leaves those temporary quarters, he continues to take his meals there.

1840: Joseph received a letter (which is not described until 1842) from "a person of respectable character residing in the vicinity where Bennett had lived. This letter cautioned us against him, setting forth that he was a very mean man, and had a wife and two or three children in McConnelsvill[e], Morgan county, Ohio . . . ." Knowing "that it is no uncommon thing for good men to be evil spoken against," the letter was "kept quiet, but held in reserve."[2]

December (or pre-December) 1840:

> *He had not been long in Nauvoo before he began to keep company with a young lady, one of our citizens: and she, being ignorant of his having a wife living, gave way to his addresses, and became confident from his behavior towards her, that he intended to marry her; and this he gave her to understand he would do. I [Smith], seeing the folly of such an acquaintance, persuaded him to desist, and on account of his*

---

[1]Joseph Smith, "An Address to the Church of Jesus Christ of Latter-day Saints and to all the Honorable Part of the Community," *History of the Church*, 5:35.

[2]Ibid., *History of the Church*, 5:36.

*continuing his course, finally threatened to expose
him if he did not desist. This, to outward appearance,
had the desired effect, and the acquaintance between
them was broken off.*[3]

Joseph said (but not until 1842) that Bennett continued his wicked
course, but in secret, teaching innocent women "who knew nothing
of him but as an honorable man" that "promiscuous intercourse
between the sexes was a doctrine believed in by the Latter-day
Saints, and that there was no harm in it . . . ." "[T]his failing,"
Bennett told these women that Joseph Smith "and others of the
authorities of the Church, not only sanctioned but practiced the
same wicked acts . . ."[4] while keeping them secret. "After the two
men broke completely, Joseph said in a guarded public statement
that he had caught Bennett preaching promiscuous intercourse as
early as December 1840 and had let him off with a severe rebuke."[5]

That this "wicked" course started in 1840 (and even earlier than
December) was confirmed in a letter Joseph Smith sent to Illinois
Governor Thomas Carlin on *June 24, 1842.* "More than twenty
months ago," Smith said (*meaning even earlier than October 1840*),
"Bennett went to a lady in the city and began to teach her that
promiscuous intercourse between the sexes was lawful and no harm
in it, and requested the privilege of gratifying his passions . . . ."
Though the woman first refused, and "in the strongest terms,"
when told "that men in higher standing in the Church than himself .
. . both taught and acted in the same manner," she, and then also
others, acquiesced. Women were seduced by these wicked means,
then "subjected" to "public infamy and disgrace."[6]   These

---

[3]Ibid., emphasis added.

[4]Ibid.

[5]Fawn M. Brodie, *No Man Knows My History: The Life of Joseph Smith the
Mormon Prophet*, 2d ed., rev. and enl. (New York, NY: Alfred A. Knopf, 1972), 309.
December 16, 1840, is the date when Bennett got the charter for the city of Nauvoo
passed into law by the Illinois legislature. On and after that date, John C. Bennett
was the toast of the town.

[6]Letter, Joseph Smith to Thomas Carlin, Governor of the State of Illinois, 24
June 1842, *History of the Church*, 5:42. Smith further represented that, "About the
early part of July, 1841, I received a letter from Pittsburg, Pennsylvania [the letter
from Hyrum Smith and William Law]; in it was contained information setting
forth that said Bennett had a wife and two or three children then living." (Ibid.,
5:42-43). In his letter to the Governor he does not mention a much earlier letter (in

promiscuous intercourse events – multiple events – preceded the Lord's revelation to Joseph praising Bennett on January 19, 1841, and Bennett's ostentatious 1841 appointment to the office of Assistant President of the Church of Jesus Christ of Latter-day Saints, an appointment made at a session of the Church's General Conference on April 8, 1841.

January 19, 1841: Shortly after that 1840 letter and those 1840 events, Joseph's God directs a revelation to John C. Bennett, Doctrine and Covenants, 124:16-17:

> *[L]et my servant John C. Bennett help you in your labor in sending my word to the kings and people of the earth, and stand by you, even you my servant Joseph Smith, in the hour of affliction; and his reward shall not fail if he receive counsel. And for his love he shall be great, for he shall be mine if he do this, saith the Lord. I have seen the work which he hath done, which I accept if he continue, and will crown him with blessings and great glory.*[7]

March 2, 1841: Bishop George Miller is sent to Ohio, at the request of Joseph Smith, to discover the truth about John C. Bennett, his wife and his children. Miller describes his findings in a letter to Smith dated March 2, 1841. Bennett, he says, is a "superficial character, always uneasy," who moves from place to place. He has lived in not less than "twenty towns" at "different times." He believes "he is the smartest man in the nation . . . ." "[H]e is always ready to fall in with whatever is popular; . . . ." "[B]y the use of his recommendations he has been able to put himself into places and situations entirely beyond his abilities . . . ." For many years, Bishop Miller continues, "his poor but confiding wife, followed him from place to place, with no suspicion of his unfaithfulness to her; at length however, he became so bold in his departures, that it was evident to all . . . that he was a sore offender . . . ." Mrs. Bennett, who now lives with her father, has "left him under satisfactory

---

1840) "received at Nauvoo from a person of respectable character residing in the vicinity where Bennett had lived," or the detailed letter containing various other allegations that he received from Bishop George Miller on March 2, 1841.

[7]Doctrine and Covenants 124:16-17, emphasis added.

evidence of his adulterous connections." Bennett has two children who live with their mother and her father, and the couple "has buried one or two." It has been Dr. Bennett's wish that his wife "should get a bill of divorcement, but as yet she has not." "*[I]n fine,*" Bishop Miller reports, "*he is an imposter, and unworthy of the confidence of all good men . . . .*"[8]

April 8, 1841: John C. Bennett is appointed Assistant President of the Church of Jesus Christ of Latter-day Saints until "President [Sidney] Rigdon's health should be restored." Bennett is presented, with the First Presidency, to the "presidents of all the Quorums," to the High Council, High Priests, Seventies, Elders, and Lesser Priesthood "for their acceptance or rejection."[9]

July 1841: Joseph receives a letter dated June 15, 1841 (that is not received until July), from Hyrum Smith and William Law corroborating the facts revealed to Smith by Bishop George Miller on March 2, 1841. The letter "contained the particulars of a conversation betwixt them and a respectable gentleman from the neighborhood where Bennett's wife and children resided." It further confirmed that Bennett's wife had left him because he had treated her badly. "This letter was read to Bennett, which he did not attempt to deny; but candidly acknowledged the fact."[10] In the July 1841 letter, Joseph is supposed to have discovered that John C. Bennett has seduced innocent women in the name of the prophet[11] with a degree of "success" that is "humiliating to confess."[12]

When Smith discovered in mid-July 1841 that Bennett – who had been preaching "promiscuous intercourse" as early as or earlier than December 1840 (Carlin letter, 24 June 1842) – was seducing "innocent women, this time in the name of the prophet and with the promise of marriage,"[13] he claimed to have confronted Bennett.

---

[8]*Times and Seasons* 3 (1 July 1842), 842, emphasis added. *RLDS History of the Church*, 2:591-92.

[9]*History of the Church*, 4:339-41, emphasis added.

[10]*History of the Church*, 5:36-37.

[11]Ibid.

[12]T.B.H. Stenhouse, *The Rocky Mountain Saints: A Full and Complete History of the Mormons, from the First Vision of Joseph Smith to the Last Courtship of Brigham Young* (New York, NY: D. Appleton and Company, 1873), 184.

[13]Brodie, *No Man Knows My History*, 309.

"Joseph said that when he confronted Bennett with the evidence and also with letters showing him to be a wife-deserter, Bennett in despair took poison – not enough to kill himself (though he was physician enough to be able to measure the correct dose), but enough to convince everyone that his repentance was sincere."[14] "Dr. Bennett made an [unsuccessful] attempt at suicide, by taking poison . . . . The public impression was, that he was so much ashamed of his base and wicked conduct, that he had recourse to the above deed to escape the censures of an indignant community."[15] Until 1842, whatever the *Times and Seasons* said, this event, if it did in fact occur, was unknown to the laity.

1840-1842: Postings, Praise and Appointments

Bennett's extraordinary rise in the society of the Saints after his baptism in August or September of 1840 followed notice to Smith that Bennett was a married man who had abandoned his wife and children. While Joseph knew (because of the 1840 letter that he "held in reserve"), others did not. Bennett said he was a single man, but Joseph knew that he was not. It hadn't mattered. Bennett lied; Joseph knew that he did and didn't care. Every important posting followed the notice of those facts to Joseph Smith. On January 19, 1841, the Lord pronounced a revelatory blessing on John C. Bennett. Didn't the Lord know that Bennett was "an adventurous malcontent"? Didn't the Lord know he was "preaching promiscuous intercourse" in 1840? Didn't the Lord know that his marriage failed because of his repeated infidelities? That he was probably "the greatest scamp in the western country"?[16]   That he was "everywhere accounted the same debauched, unprincipled and profligate character"?[17] That he was "Joseph's Judas"?[18]

---

[14]*History of the Church*, 5:37, 42 (*sic*, 43), quoted in Brodie, *No Man Knows My History*, 309.

[15]*Times and Seasons* 3 (July 1, 1842), 840.

[16]Governor Thomas Ford, *A History of Illinois* (Chicago: 1854), 263.

[17]Ibid.

[18]Richard Lyman Bushman, with the assistance of Jed Woodworth, *Joseph Smith: Rough Stone Rolling* (New York: Alfred A. Knopf, 2005), 459.

After the Lord praised his work on January 19, 1841, Bennett is *"unanimously"* elected with thousands of votes to the office of mayor in the City of Joseph.[19] On April 8, 1841, "General John C. Bennett" is appointed to be the Assistant President of the Church of Jesus Christ of Latter-day Saints. After February of 1841, Mayor John C. Bennett is appointed Chancellor of the University of Nauvoo, Major General of the Nauvoo Legion, Master in Chancery for Hancock County, Chief Justice of the Nauvoo Municipal Court, Grand Secretary of the Nauvoo Masonic Lodge, and to office as a Director of the Nauvoo Agricultural and Manufacturing Association. Prior to the conferral of those honors and postings, Bennett "was instrumental in moving the Nauvoo City charter through the Illinois legislature."[20]

April 1841: On April 7, 1841, after President Don Carlos Smith arose "and gave an exhortation to the assembly," Bennett addressed the Mormon Conference:

> *General John C. Bennett then spoke at some length on the present situation, prospects, and condition of the Church, and remarked that the hand of God must indeed be visible, in accomplishing the great blessings and prosperity of the Church, and called upon the Saints to be faithful and obedient in all things, and likewise forcibly and eloquently urged the necessity of being united in all their movements; and before he sat down, he wished to know how many of the Saints who were present felt disposed to continue to act in concert and follow the instructions of the First Presidency;*

---

[19]John C. Bennett, *The History of the Saints: Or, an Expose of Joe Smith and Mormonism* (Boston: Leland & Whiting, 1842; photomechanical reprint of 1842 original, Salt Lake City: Modern Microfilm Company), 19. Bennett was elected to be the first Mayor of Nauvoo on February 8, 1841. "The mayor held a position of supreme power, for he formulated laws as a member of the city council, interpreted laws as a member of the court, and enforced them through the militia, known as the Nauvoo Legion." [Linda King Newell and Valeen Tippetts Avery, *Mormon Enigma: Emma Hale Smith, Prophet's Wife, "Elect Lady," Polygamy's Foe – 1804-1879* (Garden City, N.Y.: Doubleday & Company, Inc., 1984), 92].

[20]John L. Brooke, *The Refiner's Fire: The Making of Mormon Cosmology, 1644-1844* (Cambridge, United Kingdom: Cambridge University Press, 1994; reprinted 2001), 251.

and called upon all those who did so, to arise on their feet – when immediately the Saints, almost without exception, arose.[21]

At that Conference and on April 8, "President Rigdon arose and stated that, in consequence of weakness from his labors of yesterday, he would call upon General John C. Bennett to officiate in his place."[22] In order to become the effective successor to Rigdon, Bennett is appointed to the office of Assistant President. On April 8, in the Thursday morning session of the Conference, "John C. Bennett was presented, with the First Presidency . . . ."[23] *So in April 1841, the Lord, who had praised Bennett in a revelation in January, now calls* Bennett to serve in the powerful place of the ailing Rigdon, after which Bennett then becomes, for all intents and purposes and for so long as Rigdon is indisposed and until the days of his disgrace, Joseph's "bosom" friend and the second most powerful man in the Mormon Church.

In the face of what became a profusion of incriminating disclosures, the resilient Bennett, because of his powerful patron, does not lose any of his civil or religious investitures. Even after Joseph discovers that Bennett had been preaching "promiscuous intercourse" with a "success" that is "humiliating to confess," and even after he is supposed to have ingested poison "to escape the censures of an indignant community," General Bennett retains all of his postings.

"And for his love he shall be great, for he shall be mine if he do this, saith the Lord. I have seen the work which he hath done, which I accept if he continue, and will crown him with blessings and great glory."[24] Does the Lord really believe Bennett will be great because of "his love"? Does the Lord really accept Bennett's "work" and want to see it continued? When this revelation is pronounced, the undivorced Bennett, a wandering pariah who has abandoned his wife and children, is actively "preaching promiscuous intercourse." His wife had "left him under satisfactory evidence of his adulterous

---

[21]*History of the Church*, 4:340, emphasis added.
[22]Ibid., 4:339.
[23]Ibid., 4:340-41.
[24]Doctrine and Covenants 124:15-17.

connections." He is a married man representing himself as a single man. He has lived in twenty different localities. He is in possession of medicines and instruments to be used for the purpose of abortion, a procedure he claimed to be able to perform with perfect safety to the mother at any stage of pregnancy. He has "peddled degrees in medicine, law and theology" to anyone willing to pay at Christian College in New Albany, Indiana. He has been fired from the faculty at Chagrin College and expelled from his Missouri Masonic Lodge for "misconduct." He is a "mean" man with a glib tongue and low morals found to be teaching various gullible women that when there is no accusation there is no crime. *Does Joseph's Lord know nothing of any of this?*

Does Joseph act on Bishop George Miller's March 2, 1841, indictment? Not until more than a year has passed. Bennett exercises enormous power in the Mormon community after the "promiscuous intercourse" in 1840 and after the first letter in 1841. Bishop Miller's sobering report "did not prevent the prophet from appointing Bennett assistant president to the church in early April 1841."[25] And Hyrum Smith and William Law's later report did not cause the prophet to remove Bennett from that important appointment in July 1841. From August or September 1840, when Bennett is baptized, to May and June of 1842, when Bennett is displaced, the high visibility leader holds his posts, does what Sidney Rigdon had done, and is Smith's most trusted confidant and principal adviser. Smith and Bennett, Captain Oliver Olney says, "moved together hart and hand in all their windings." "If Bennett had not moved quite so fast," Olney said, "all would have be[e]n well now . . . ."[26]

William Law, the Second Counselor in the First Presidency, didn't know in 1842 that Joseph was teaching polygamy but later said he thought that Bennett did. "I believe now," years later he said, that Bennett did know, "for he at that time was more in the secret

---

[25]Richard S. Van Wagoner, *Mormon Polygamy: A History* (Salt Lake City: Signature Books, 1986), 18.

[26]Oliver Olney, Journal, 18 June 1842 (City of Nauvoo), in The Oliver Olney Papers (originals at Yale; Microfilm in LDS Church Archives, MS 8829, Item 8).

confidence of Joseph than perhaps any other man in the city."[27] On January 25, 1842, and after nearly all of this, almost every distasteful bit, President Joseph Smith and Assistant President John C. Bennett engage in a friendly public debate in Nauvoo on the subject of "Lamanites and Negroes,"[28] after which Joseph reports that Dr. Bennett as an orator is superior to the Apostle Paul. Until May 11, 1842, Bennett continues to hold all of his various postings, serving until then as "The Assistant President of the Church of Jesus Christ of Latter-day Saints."

---

[27]Letter, William Law to T.B.H. Stenhouse, November 24, 1871, quoted in Stenhouse, *The Rocky Mountain Saints*, 198.

[28]*History of the Church*, 4:501.

JOSEPH'S RESPONSE TO DR. JOHN C. BENNETT

William Marks

On August 12, 1843, a well-connected William Marks was the Stake President of the Nauvoo Stake of Zion. After Joseph Smith's death on June 27, 1844, Emma Smith favored Marks to be the successor to her dead husband.[1] As a most recent President of the Nauvoo High Council, the governing body under the prophet at the headquarters of the Church in Nauvoo, such a claim was plausible.

On August 12, 1843, the day Hyrum Smith read the revelation on polygamy to the High Council threatening damnation to those who didn't accept that controversial doctrine, three of the members, William Marks, Austin Cowles and Leonard Sobey, expressed their opposition. Marks' objections to polygamy and his support for Sidney Rigdon to replace the murdered prophet ultimately doomed any chance he may himself have had to succeed to Joseph and Hyrum's job. Other leaders who supported polygamy "feared that Marks would end plural marriage and other ordinances that they saw as crucial to the afterlife."[2] Brigham Young wanted Marks excommunicated, but the Nauvoo High Council rejected that request, and the inhumane procedure never occurred.

On August 31, 1842, when the "Affidavits and Certificates Disproving the Statements and Affidavits Contained in John C. Bennett's Letters" were assembled in a now notorious broadside for the misuse of hundreds of Elders, William Marks didn't seem to know that Joseph Smith was married to more than fifteen women. He may not have known about the doctrine of polygamy until on and after August 12, 1843. Thus, in a certificate dated July 26, 1842, William Marks said in materials to be included in Smith's disingenuous broadside (a challenge to Bennett's recitals) that he knew "many of his [Bennett's] statements to be false." Marks went

---

[1]"William Marks," (accessed 26 March 2018), available from https://en.wikipedia.org/wiki/William_Marks_(Latter_Day_Saints); Internet, p. 3 of 5.
[2]Ibid.

further to say that he believed "them to be the offspring of a base and corrupt heart . . . without the least shadow of truth . . . ." Noting that Bennett had used his name without his permission, he said he believed his prophet's former friend (and Nauvoo's former unanimously-elected Mayor) "to be a vile and wicked adulterous man, who pays no regard to the principles of truth or righteousness, and is unworthy the confidence of a just community."[3]

William Marks:

> *I would further state that I know of no Order in the church which admits of a plurality of wives, and do not believe that Joseph Smith ever taught such a doctrine, and further, that my faith in the doctrines of the Church of Jesus Christ of Latter-day Saints, and in Joseph Smith, is unshaken.*

William Marks,[4] July 26, 1842

On June 29, 1842, some few days after John C. Bennett left Nauvoo, Joseph Smith married Eliza Roxcy Snow, his fourteenth wife. On July 27, 1842, one day after William Marks prepared the entry found in Joseph Smith's broadside, a thirty-six year-old Joseph Smith married seventeen-year-old Sarah Ann Whitney, who then became the prophet's sixteenth wife. Of those first fifteen plural wives (not including Emma or Fanny Alger), ten were married wives of other men, and two were widows.

On August 26, 1842, Joseph told his followers through some favored few surrogates that "it was wisdom in God that the Elders should go forth and deluge the States with a flood of truth . . . ."[5] Whatever

---

[3]"Affidavits and Certificates, Disproving the Statements and Affidavits Contained in John C. Bennett's Letters. Nauvoo Aug. 31, 1842," re-composed copy of a broadsheet issued in 1842 by the *Times and Seasons* of Nauvoo, prepared from a transcript by H. Michael Marquardt (Salt Lake City: Signature Books, 2006) (accessed 1 April 2018); available from https://archive.org/details/AffidavitsAnd Certificates; Internet, 2 pages.

[4]"Affidavits and Certificates, Disproving the Statements and Affidavits Contained in John C. Bennett's Letters. Nauvoo Aug. 31, 1842," p. 2 of 2, emphasis added.

[5]Jessee, ed., *The Papers of Joseph Smith: Journal*, 1842-44, 443.

William Marks knew or may have suspected at the time, one thing is certain: There was one man who knew the truth, every damning thing, and that was Joseph Smith.

Sidney Rigdon

On or about July 25, 1842, and just days before Joseph Smith secretly married Miss Whitney, his seventeen-year-old sixteenth wife, Sidney Rigdon presented the following Certificate, containing recitals to be published in the prophet's notorious broadsheet. Rigdon knew his words were going to be used by nearly four hundred elders to dispute the claims of General John C. Bennett. Bennett had previously had Rigdon's full support in 1841 when he temporarily assumed a then ailing Rigdon's duties (and was appointed to be the Assistant President of the LDS Church).

> *As there seems to be some foolish notions that I have been engaged with J.C. Bennett, in the difficulties between him and some of the citizens of this place, I merely say in reply to such idle and vain reports that they are without foundation in truth.*
>
> Sidney Rigdon[6]

Rigdon was, he said, out of the loop.

On August 27, 1842, Sidney Rigdon wrote a letter to the perpetually angry editor of *The Wasp*. From April to December 1842, William Smith, a member of the founding Quorum of the Twelve Apostles and Joseph Smith's brother, was the editor of *The Wasp* (a secular pro-Mormon newspaper published in Nauvoo, Illinois). In his letter Rigdon claimed that General Bennett's publication of certain information "which has appeared in the *Sangamo Journal*" (a newspaper published in Springfield, Illinois) concerning Rigdon's daughter, Miss Nancy Rigdon, and most specifically the publication of a letter "purporting to have been written by Mr. Joseph Smith to

---

[6]"Affidavits and Certificates, Disproving the Statements and Affidavits Contained in John C. Bennett's Letters. Nauvoo Aug. 31, 1842," p. 2 of 2, emphasis added.

her," had been "unauthorized."

Speaking for his daughter, Rigdon claimed that Nancy never told Bennett "or any other person, that said letter was written by said Mr. Smith, nor in his hand writing, but by another person, and in another person's hand writing." Rigdon knew exactly who the letter was from and why it was penned by someone other than Smith. Miss Rigdon, he said, had "never at any time authorized Gen. Bennett to use her name in the public papers, as he has done . . . ." Rigdon said that Bennett (with whom he was formerly known to have been on friendly terms) had been guilty of wounding Nancy's feelings, in what was a flagrant violation of the rules of gallantry. Miss Rigdon wanted the public to know "that the obtruding of her name in the manner in which it has been done . . . cannot avoid to insult her feelings." Then further, on behalf of his colleague of about twelve years, Sidney wanted this to be known: "*I would further state that Mr. Smith denied to me the authorship of that letter.*"[7] Sidney could not have possibly thought that to be the case. As he proved yet again, in this most curious circumstance, he, like Smith, Cowdery and a cadre of others, could be trusted not to tell the truth.

In a letter written on July 27, 1842 (the same day that Joseph Smith married Sarah Ann Whitney), Nauvoo Legion General George W. Robinson, Sidney Rigdon's son-in-law and Nancy Rigdon's brother-in-law, told General James Arlington Bennet how Nancy Rigdon came home from her meeting with Smith (and with Mrs. Orson Hyde), which occurred in the "under rooms of the printing office." According to Robinson, Miss Rigdon "told her father of the transaction; upon which Smith was sent for. He came." When he came, Nancy Rigdon recounted how she went to Mrs. Hyde's house (the Printing Office) to see the prophet at his request and just exactly what had happened there. Robinson, who was present at the meeting between Smith and the Rigdons after the meeting between Smith and Miss Rigdon at the Printing Office, heard those issues discussed. "I have reason," General Robinson said, "to believe General Bennett's story in his disclosures of Smith's rascality; although I am not a witness to all of the facts, yet I am to

---

[7]Ibid., emphasis added.

some."[8] The man who penned the 1838 account of the First Vision of the Father and the Son had lost his faith in his prophet.

Sidney Rigdon, who summoned the prophet to come to his house to explain the prophet's "base attempt" upon Miss Nancy's "virtue," was not only "engaged with J.C. Bennett, in the difficulties between him and some of the citizens of this place," "foolish notions" or not, but was rather a central figure in the controversy at the heart of the breach.   According to John Rigdon, Sidney's son, the fact that Joseph Smith had made a proposition to his sister, Nancy Rigdon, inviting her to become his wife, had caused quite the disturbance.[9] General George W. Robinson, who knew all about the prophet's letter, saw the forest for the trees.   "I liked to have forgotten to state," he said, "that the affair with Miss Rigdon was the cause of Smith's coming out so on Bennett, he having suspicion that Bennett had cautioned her on the matter . . . ."[10]

Rigdon was not divorced from these events, but rather consumed by them. By July or August of 1842, and before four hundred Elders left to "support the character of the Prophet,"[11] "wisely, humbly setting forth the truth as it is in God . . . ,"[12] Rigdon had to know, however he chose to plead and because of the events concerning his daughter, that there was a secret marriage system in the City of Joseph. That is what the prophet's proposal to Miss Rigdon, as the letter she presented to her family in the prophet's presence, and in Sidney Rigdon's presence, was seen to suppose. His daughter's dilemma and the letter dictated by the prophet and delivered by Willard Richards made the prophet's private case.

---

[8]George W. Robinson, quoted in John C. Bennett, *The History of the Saints: Or, an Expose of Joe Smith and Mormonism* (Boston: Leland & Whiting, 1842; photomechanical reprint of 1842 original, Salt Lake City: Modern Microfilm Company), 246.

[9]John Rigdon Affidavit, in *Blood Atonement and the Origin of Plural Marriage – A Discussion*, correspondence between Elder Joseph F. Smith, Jr., of the Church of Jesus Christ of Latter-day Saints, and Mr. Richard C. Evans, Second Counselor in the Presidency of the "Reorganized" Church (Salt Lake City: The Deseret News Press, 1905), 81-84.

[10]Robinson, letter reproduced in *The History of the Saints*, 246, emphasis added.

[11]"History, 1838–1856, volume D-1" (29 August 1842), *The Joseph Smith Papers*, 1389.

[12]Ibid., (27 August 1842), 1387.

After the death of the prophet in June of 1844, and as early as October 1844, Rigdon, then out of the Church and opening up, spoke in scathing terms of hellish wickedness, citing prevaricating polygamists and secret polygamy. *"How often,"* he said, *"have these men and their accomplices stood up before the congregation, and called God and all the holy Angels to witness, that there was no such doctrine taught in the church, and it has now come to light . . . ."*[13] Rigdon said they "dared heaven and insulted the world." "[T]here were multitudes of their followers in the congregation at the time who knew it . . . ," one of whom, to be generous, should have been Sidney Rigdon because of his position in the leadership, then also because of his daughter and her event.[14] Nauvoo polygamy, however Rigdon negotiated his own monogamous path, should not have escaped his scholarly glance.

In an Affidavit which became part of the elders' broadside (Joseph's response to Bennett's claims), Sidney described "the letter" Richards delivered to "Miss Nancy" the day after her meeting with Smith as only "purporting to have been written by Mr. Joseph Smith." It was a lame attempt to deny something perfectly obvious to anyone who had knowledge of the facts. Rigdon knew, perhaps better than anyone, that Smith seldom wrote anything himself. Sidney Rigdon, Nancy Rigdon, John Rigdon,

---

[13]Sidney Rigdon, *Messenger and Advocate*, no. 1 (Pittsburgh: 15 October 1844): 14, emphasis added. "I could bring facts which can be established in any court of justice, in relation to these vile abominations practiced under the garb of religion that would make humanity blush." (Ibid.).

[14]Ibid. In the early 1830s, Sidney Rigdon, Oliver Cowdery and Frederick G. Williams joined together at the prophet's request to meet with and pacify an angry Emma over matters concerning a "transaction" between Joseph and Emma's household helper, Miss Fanny Alger, a transaction that occurred on a hay mow in the parties' barn. Miss Alger, who lived with the Smiths, may have been involved with Joseph Smith as early as 1831, at which time she was only fourteen years old. Sidney Rigdon knew the details of that transaction and was a party to the reconciliation that followed. If he didn't know that Smith married Miss Alger (there is no contemporaneous record of that), then he had to think that the relationship was adulterous. If he did know of a marriage, then he knew many years before the Bennett fiasco that there was a "secret marriage system." Furthermore, he had to have known that "the doctrines and principles relating to plural marriage were revealed to Joseph Smith [and to the missionaries to the Lamanites] as early as 1831." And to the members of the Quorum of the Twelve Apostles in 1841. (*Teachings of Presidents of the Church – Joseph Smith* [Salt Lake City: The Church of Jesus Christ of Latter-day Saints, 2007], xii).

Athalia Rigdon (Robinson), Athalia's husband (General George Robinson) and Nancy's mother knew that Joseph Smith composed the incredible letter. He admitted that to them on the occasion of their meeting. Smith's unusual letter was a written defense of the never publicly discussed doctrine of polygamy, something Smith cautioned Miss Rigdon to read and destroy. When Rigdon claimed that Nancy never told Bennett "or any other person, that said letter was written by said Mr. Smith, nor in his hand writing, but by another person, and in another person's hand writing," everyone knew Joseph, who dictated his thoughts, used a scribe. He told the Church that he did. The letter carried to "Miss Nancy" by the prophet's messenger, Willard Richards, while penned by Richards, was not composed by Richards. The revelations in the Doctrine and Covenants were not penned by Smith, nor either the contents of the Book of Mormon, but rather by more educated better prepared others.

When Rigdon essentially encouraged four hundred elders who left Nauvoo to tell the world that the society was monogamous (that there was no secret wife system, and that there were no plural wives), and when Sidney then proceeded to say that he would "further state that Mr. Smith denied to me the authorship of that letter," Rigdon knew better, and so did Joseph Smith. All of those four hundred elders shared those falsified insights with everyone wherever they went.

Chauncey L. Higbee and William Smith

On May 17, 1842, Joseph Smith had twelve wives, about nine of whom had living husbands in addition to Joseph. A tenth was his dead brother's widow.[15] On that day, Chauncey L. Higbee prepared an affidavit that was also attached to Joseph's broadside (the document furnished to the nearly four hundred elders sent forth to "deluge the States with a flood of truth"). Higbee, a Missouri Danite, a Nauvoo alderman, and Major General John C. Bennett's *aide-de-camp*, being duly sworn and then deposed (procedures without meaning for oath-bound Danites), proceeded to

---

[15]George D. Smith, *Nauvoo Polygamy . . . But We Called It Celestial Marriage* (Salt Lake City: Signature Books, 2008), 621-22.

say that Joseph Smith "never did teach" him "in private or public that an illicit intercourse with females was, under any circumstances, justifiable and that he never knew him so to teach others." According to Higbee, he was never taught "any thing in the least contrary to the strictest principles of the gospel . . . ."[16]

The broadsheet left the impression that Chauncey L. Higbee and Joseph Smith, student and teacher, were squeaky clean. On May 21, 1842, however, barely four days after the date of the Affidavit attached to Joseph Smith's broadside, that intentionally misleading document published by the *Times and Seasons*, Bishop George Miller preferred meritorious charges against Higbee "for unchaste and un-virtuous conduct with the widow [Sarah Miller] and others." The charges were lodged with the Nauvoo High Council, and they resulted in church discipline. Three witnesses testified that Higbee had seduced several women by teaching them it was right to have free intercourse with women if the parties kept the proceedings secret. Higbee's accusers reported, contrary to everything he said in the broadside's affidavit, that he told them that the prophet Joseph Smith "autherised him to practise these things." Hyrum Smith moved that Higbee "be expelled from the Church" and that the proceedings "be made public through the medium of the *Times and Seasons*."[17] For the best of all good reasons, that didn't occur. Joseph Smith, who didn't need the exposure, was the editor of the *Times and Seasons* at the time.

Higbee's representations to the women concerning the prophet and consensual sex preceded the affidavit Higbee attached to the broadside in an effort to clear himself and the prophet. The widow Miller reported in the High Council proceedings that, "*When he [Chauncey L. Higbee] came again* [in support of sex without commitment], *William Smith come with him & told me that the doctrine which Chancy Higbee had taught me was true.*" *William said that what Chauncey had said was what the prophet had said. Chauncey told Sarah Miller that if the sex had a consequence, "Dr.*

---

[16]"Affidavits and Certificates, Disproving the Statements and Affidavits Contained in John C. Bennett's Letters. Nauvoo Aug. 31, 1842," p. 2 of 2.
　　[17]*The Nauvoo City and High Council Minutes*, John S. Dinger ed. (Salt Lake City: Signature Books, 2011), 413-15.

Bennett . . . would come and take it away . . . ."[18]

Danites Speak; Elders Follow

Thirteen members of the City Council in Nauvoo signed an Affidavit on July 20, 1842, in which they said, among other things: "We do further testify that there is no such thing as a Danite Society in this city nor any combination, other than the Masonic Lodge, of which we have any knowledge." Among these testators were five men – Vinson Knight, John P. Green, George A. Smith, George W. Harris, and Charles C. Rich – who were Danites then and always, men who had taken the oath. Men pledged to lie, when need be, with reckless impunity. Although Brigham Young, one of those signators, was not a member of the Danite band, two of his brothers Lorenzo and Phineas were, and his brother-in-law, John P. Green.[19]

"Justus Morse told how, as a Danite in Missouri in 1838, he and others were directed to assist each other when in difficulty by lying, 'and to do it with such positiveness and assurance that no one would question our testimony.'"[20]

The hands of no less than twelve Danites, including their leaders, Smith and Rigdon, spilled out upon the pages of Joseph Smith's anti-Bennett "Affidavits and Certificates" intended for the use of the Church's elders. The names of those subscribers were Elias Higbee, Vinson Knight, John P. Green, George A. Smith, Charles C. Rich, G.W. Harris, Francis M. Higbee, Joseph Smith, Sidney Rigdon, Stephen Goddard, Ebenezer Robinson and Chauncey L. Higbee.

---

[18]Ibid., 415-16, emphasis added.

[19]"Danites in 1838, A Partial List," Appendix 3 in D. Michael Quinn, *The Mormon Hierarchy: Origins of Power* (Salt Lake City: Signature Books in association with Smith Research Associates, 1994), 479-85. These men had been Vinson Knight (a bishop at Adam-ondi-Ahman), John P. Green (High Council at Far West), George A. Smith (High Council at Adam-ondi-Ahman, son of the Stake President and Joseph Smith's first cousin), G.W. Harris (High Council at Far West), and Charles C. Rich (President of the High Priest Quorum at Far West).

[20]B. Carmon Hardy, *Solemn Covenant: The Mormon Polygamous Passage* (Urbana, Chicago: University of Illinois Press, 1992), 366.

RECORD KEEPING QUESTIONS

What does the Church count in its published membership totals?

What criteria does the Church apply to determine whether a member is active or not?

Does the record keeping system used by the LDS Church include the records of everyone who has ever been blessed as a baby in a Mormon meeting?

Are those babies, once they are blessed and before they are baptized and confirmed, counted as members in the statistical report of the membership?

Are children of members of record who are never blessed, baptized or confirmed included as members in the statistical report of the membership? If so, when and by what means are they ever excluded?

Are all those infants, children who are blessed but not baptized and confirmed, and children of members of record who are never blessed, baptized and confirmed, treated as members on the records of the Church?

Will the memberships of such persons continue to be recognized and published in statistical form on the records of the Church until they achieve the theoretical age of one hundred and ten years?

Are the records of the members who resign their membership actually removed from the record keeping system when those members resign, or do they continue there to be counted as members in the statistical report of the membership?

Is it true that once a person is included in the Church's record keeping system that such a person never gets out, whether or not they are blessed, baptized, or confirmed, and no matter that they resign?

Does the Church deduct the number of members who resign from the statistical reports of the membership presented to the members of the Church at the end of each reporting period?

Will the memberships of those persons continue to be recognized and published in statistical form on the records of the Church until they achieve the theoretical age of one hundred and ten years?

Does the Church deduct the number of members who die from the statistical reports of the membership presented to the members of the Church at the end of each reporting period?

How are such reductions, those concerned with resignation or death, accounted for at the end of the reporting period? What procedure has the Church historically followed in that respect?

Does the Church in some way mark or annotate the records of evacuees, dissidents or apostates, noting those records for sin and/or transgression?

Is it the position of the Church that the records it keeps are sealed on earth and in heaven "to be presented to God as an offering of the Sons of Levi"?

Is it the position of the Church that if a member's record is in some way marked or annotated for sin and/or transgression that such a person will be damned in his or her progression and thus removed from the sealing chain back to a literal Adam and Eve?

Is it the position of the Church that God is bound by the annotations appended to a member's record by that member's leaders, and that each member's salvation depends upon those markings, and upon the approval of their leaders, when those records are presented to God?

Appendix   F

PROCLAMATION OF THE TWELVE APOSTLES
A MESSAGE TO THE WORLD
APRIL 6, 1845

PROCLAMATION of the Twelve Apostles of the Church of Jesus Christ of Latter-day Saints. To all the Kings of the World; To the President of the United States of America; To the Governors of the several States; And to the Rulers and People of all Nations; GREETING: KNOW YE THAT the kingdom of God has come: as has been predicted by ancient prophets, and prayed for in all ages; even that kingdom which shall fill the whole earth, and shall stand for ever.

> *The great Eloheim Jehovah has been pleased once more to speak from the heavens; and also to commune with man upon the earth, by means of open visions, and by the ministration of HOLY MESSENGERS.*

Jesus Is Not Jehovah

On April 6, 1845, the Quorum of the Twelve Apostles proclaims that Eloheim Jehovah is one person, not the Father *and* the Son. On this particular day in this high profile message, closely following the death of Joseph Smith, on June 27, 1844, "Eloheim Jehovah" is a term seen to identify one indivisible person. The names here, as they sometimes were in Hebrew scripture, and as they were in Mormon scripture for many years, were interchangeable. In 1916 a Doctrinal Exposition by the First Presidency declared that Elohim, one person, was the Father and that Jehovah, another person, was the Son.[1] Jesus didn't become Jehovah in Mormon theology, meaning a lesser God beholden to a greater God by the name of Elohim, and one of two gods, a Jehovah/Son to an Elohim/Father, until long after the deaths of Joseph Smith and Brigham Young. In some two hundred fifty-six references to Elohim and Jehovah, and

---

[1]"A Doctrinal Exposition by the First Presidency and the Quorum of the Twelve Apostles," dated June 30, 1916, *Improvement Era* (August 1916): 934-42.

to the God of the Old Testament in the Journal of Discourses (representing the sermons of the members of the First Presidencies and Quorums of the Twelve), the title Jehovah is applied to Jesus only once. (Kirkland, "Jehovah as Father"). That obscure reference did not occur until 1885, when the strange new doctrine (that a preincarnated Jesus was Jehovah) was beginning to develop.

There Is One Path to Salvation

The great and eternal High Priesthood after "the Order of his Son" (after the Order of Jesus, the son of "Eloheim Jehovah") "has been restored; or, returned to the earth" by the ministration of HOLY MESSENGERS. It is the power "to bind on earth that which shall be bound in heaven . . . ." It is the power to organize, direct and administer the affairs of the kingdom of God. "We testify that the foregoing doctrine [the doctrine of the Church] is the doctrine or gospel of Jesus Christ, in its fulness; and that it is the only true, everlasting, and unchangeable gospel; and the only plan revealed on earth whereby man can be saved."

The Indians of North and South America Are a Remnant of the Tribes of Israel

"We also bear testimony that the 'Indians' (so called) of North and South America are a remnant of the tribes of Israel; as is now made manifest by the discovery and revelation of their ancient oracles and records. And that they are about to be fathered, civilized, and made one nation in this glorious land." "[T]hey will also come to the knowledge of their forefathers, and of the fulness of the gospel; and they will embrace it, and become a righteous branch of the house of Israel." "A great, a glorious, and a mighty work is yet to be achieved, in spreading the truth and kingdom among the Gentiles – in restoring, organizing, instructing and establishing the Jews – in gathering, instructing, relieving, civilizing, educating and administering salvation to the remnant of Israel on this continent . . . ."

Zion Is to Be Built on Indian Land

"He will assemble the Natives the remnants of Joseph in America; and make of them a great, and strong, and powerful nation; and he will civilize and enlighten them and will establish a holy city, and temple, and seat of government among them, which shall be called Zion."

The Book of Mormon Is a History of the Origins of the "aboriginal tribes of America"

"The despised and degraded son of the forest, who has wandered in dejection and sorrow, and suffered reproach, shall then drop his disguise, and stand forth in manly dignity, and exclaim to the Gentiles.. . . I am a descendant of that Joseph who was sold into Egypt . . . and am heir to the inheritance, titles, honors, priesthood, sceptre, crown, throne, and eternal life and dignity of my fathers who live for evermore." "He shall then be ordained, washed, anointed with holy oil and arrayed in fine linen, even in the glorious and beautiful garments and royal rob [robe] of the high priesthood, which is after the order of the Son of God; and shall enter into the congregation of the Lord, even into the Holy of Holies, there to be crowned with authority and power which shall never end."

"He has revealed the origin and the Records of the aboriginal tribes of America, and their future destiny. – And we know it."

"He has revealed the fulness of the gospel, with its gifts, blessings, and ordinances. – And we know it."

The Words of This Proclamation Shall Be Fulfilled

"[B]e ye sure of this, that whether we live or die the words of the testimony of this proclamation which we now send unto you, shall all be fulfilled."

"Heaven and earth shall pass away, but not one jot or tittle of his revealed word shall fail to be fulfilled."

Promises

This kingdom will fill the earth and stand forever. You shall receive the gift of the Holy Spirit. You shall heal the sick and expel Demons. You shall see visions and converse with Angels and spirits from the unseen world. You shall escape the day of desolation and stand before the Son of Man, for his coming is near at hand. He will descend from heaven. He will stand upon the Mount of Olives which shall "cleave in sunder." He has brought about "the restoration of all things, and he has revealed the fulness of the gospel. The Jews will gather in Jerusalem. The Ten Tribes of Israel shall be revealed in the North Country. "Thrones will be cast down and Kingdoms will cease to be."

(Messages of the First Presidency, James R. Clark, comp. [Bookcraft, 1965-75], 1:252-66).

Bibliography

SOURCES CITED

"1835 Doctrine and Covenants denies polygamy – D&C 101 (original)" (accessed 15 December 2015), available from https://www.fairmormon.org/answers /Mormonism_and_polygamy/1835_Doctrine_and_Covenants_denies_ polygamy; Internet, 5 pages.

Abanes, Richard, *One Nation Under Gods: A History of the Mormon Church* (New York, NY: Thunder's Mouth Press, 2003).

"Adam-God Doctrine," Manuscript Addresses of Brigham Young, G.D. Watt transcriber, 8 October 1861, "with minor misspelling corrected," (accessed 16 July 2014), available from wikipedia.com.

Aird, Polly, Jeff Nichols and Will Bagley, eds., *Kingdom in the West: The Mormons and the American Frontier, Volume 13 – Playing with Shadows: Voices of Dissent in the Mormon West* (Norman, OK: The Arthur H. Clark Company, 2011).

Alexander, Thomas G., "The Reconstruction of Mormon Doctrine: From Joseph Smith to Progressive Theology," *Sunstone*, vol. 5 no. 4 (July-August 1980).

Allen, James B., "Eight Contemporary Accounts of Joseph Smith's First Vision," *Improvement Era* (April 1970).

—— "The Significance of Joseph Smith's 'First Vision' in Mormon Thought," *Dialogue: A Journal of Mormon Thought*, vol. 1 no. 3, (Autumn 1966).

Allen, James, and Glen Leonard, *The Story of the Latter-day Saints*, 2nd ed. (Deseret Book, 1992).

Arrington, Leonard J., *Brigham Young: American Moses* (New York: Knopf, 1985).

Bachman, Tal, "Re the new 1st Presidency statement, here are MY questions (add yours here)" (28 June 2014; accessed August 2014); available from http://exmormon.org/phorum/read.php?2,1308419; Internet, 14 pages.

Bagley, Will, *Blood of the Prophets: Brigham Young and the Massacre at Mountain Meadows* (Norman, OK: University of Oklahoma Press, 2002).

Banister, Sharon I., *For Any Latter-day Saint: One Investigator's Unanswered Questions* (Fort Worth, TX: Star Bible Publications, 1988).

Beadle, John Hansen, *Life in Utah; or the Mysteries and Crimes of Mormonism* (National Publishing Company, 1870).

Bennett, John C., *The History of the Saints: Or, an Expose of Joe Smith and Mormonism* (Boston: Leland & Whiting, 1842; photomechanical reprint of 1842 original, Salt Lake City: Modern Microfilm Company).

Bergera, Gary James, *Conflict in the Quorum* (Salt Lake City: Signature Books, 2002).

—— "The Earliest Eternal Sealings for Civilly Married Couples Living and Dead," *Dialogue: A Journal of Mormon Thought* 35 (Fall 2002).

—— "'Illicit intercourse,' Plural Marriage and the Nauvoo Stake High Council, 1840-44," *The John Whitmer Historical Association Journal* 23 (2003).

—— "The Orson Pratt-Brigham Young Controversies: Conflict Within the Quorums, 1853 to 1864," *Dialogue: A Journal of Mormon Thought*, 13(2) (1980): 41.

—— "'Weak-Kneed Republicans and Socialist Democrats': Ezra Taft Benson as a U.S. Secretary of Agriculture, 1953-61, Part 2," *Dialogue: A Journal of Mormon Thought*, vol. 41 no. 4 (Winter 2008), 55-95.

Bigler, David L., and Will Bagley, *The Mormon Rebellion: America's First Civil War, 1857-58* (University of Oklahoma Press: Norman, 2011).

Blood Atonement and the Origin of Plural Marriage – A Discussion, correspondence between Elder Joseph F. Smith, Jr., of the Church of Jesus Christ of Latter-day Saints, and Mr. Richard C. Evans, Second Counselor in the Presidency of the "Reorganized" Church (Salt Lake City: The Deseret News Press, 1905).

"Book of Mormon and DNA Studies," one of a number of unsigned and undated essays (The Church of Jesus Christ of Latter-day Saints, 2014).

Brigham Young Jr.'s Journal (4 April 1897, accessed November 2015), available from mormonhandbook.com/home/adam-god-doctrine.html; Internet, 5.

Bringhurst, Newell G., and Craig L. Foster, *The Persistence of Polygamy: From Joseph Smith's Martyrdom to the First Manifesto, 1844-1890* (USA: John Whitmer Books, 2013).

Brodie, Fawn McKay, *No Man Knows My History: The Life of Joseph Smith the Mormon Prophet*, 2d ed., rev. and enl. (New York, NY: Alfred A. Knopf, 1972).

Brooke, John L., *The Refiner's Fire: The Making of Mormon Cosmology, 1644-1844* (Cambridge, United Kingdom: Cambridge University Press, 1994; reprinted 2001).

Brooks, Juanita, to Roger B. Mathison, 21 November 1968, Brooks Papers (University of Utah Marriott Library, 1974).

Brooks, Karl, Will Bagley interview note, 12 January 1996 (St. George, UT).

Brown Hugh B., and N. Eldon Tanner, "First Presidency Statement," 15 December 1969 (accessed 18 February 2019); available from https://www.fair mormon.org/answers/Mormonism_and_racial_issues/Blacks_and_the_pries thood/Statements; Internet, 5 pages.

Brown, Hugh B., and N. Eldon Tanner, Letter dated December 15, 1969, "First Presidency Statement," *Priesthood Bulletin* (February 1970).

"Bruce R. McConkie's Letter of Rebuke to [BYU] Professor Eugene England" (19 February 1981, accessed 8 September 2009), available from http://www.myplanet.net/mike/LDS/McConkie_England_letter.html; Internet.

"Buckeye's Lamentation for Want of More Wives," *Warsaw Message* (7 Feb. 1844); *Warshaw Signal* (name change) (25 April 1844).

Buerger, David John, "The Adam-God Doctrine," *Dialogue: A Journal of Mormon Thought*, vol. 15 no. 1 (Spring 1982).

—— *The Mysteries of Godliness: A History of Mormon Temple Worship* (San Francisco, CA: Smith Research Associates, 1994, 2002).

Bushman, Richard Lyman, with the assistance of Jed Woodworth, *Joseph Smith: Rough Stone Rolling* (New York: Alfred A. Knopf, 2005).

—— *"The Visionary World of Joseph Smith," Brigham Young University Studies* 37, no.1 (1997-1998).

Callister, Tad R., *The Inevitable Apostasy and the Promised Restoration* (Salt Lake City: Deseret Book Company, 2006).

Campbell, Eugene E., *Establishing Zion: The Mormon Church in the American West, 1847-1869* (Salt Lake City: Signature Books, 1988).

Campbell Eugene E., and Bruce L. Campbell, "Divorce among Mormon Polygamists: Extent and Explanations" (paper read at the Annual Meeting of the Utah State Historical Society, September 17, 1977, Salt Lake City), *Utah Historical Quarterly*, vol. 46 no. 1 (winter 1978).

Candid Insights of a Mormon Apostle: The Dairies of Abraham H. Cannon, 1889-1895, ed. Edward Leo Lyman (Salt Lake City: Signature Books in association with the Smith-Pettit Foundation, 2010).

Canham, Matt, "Mormon Portion of Utah Population Steadily Shrinking," *Salt Lake Tribune* (2005).

—— "Salt Lake County is now minority Mormon, and the impacts are far reaching," *Salt Lake Tribune* (9 December 2018).

Cannon, Donald Q., and Lyndon W. Cook, eds., *Far West Record: Minutes of the Church of Jesus Christ of Latter-day Saints, 1830-1844* (Salt Lake City: Deseret Book Co., 1983).

Cannon, George Q., "The Improvement of Our Species," *The Western Standard,* a Mormon newspaper (7 August 1857 [2/4-6]), 2.

Charles L. Walker Diary (Harold B. Lee Library, Brigham Young University, 1855-1902).

Cheesman, Paul R., "An Analysis of the Accounts Relating Joseph Smith's Early Visions" (Master of Religious Education Thesis, Brigham Young University, 1965).

Clark, Gregory A., "Commentary: Students must be taught what science is. And is not." *The Salt Lake Tribune* (Salt Lake City: 20 January 2019).

Clayton, L. Whitney, "Getting and Staying Connected," BYU Commencement Speech (21 April 2016, accessed 16 March 2018), available from https://speeches.byu.edu/talks/l-whitney-clayton/getting-staying-connected/; Internet, 3 pages.

Clayton, William, *An Intimate Chronicle: The Journals of William Clayton*, ed. George D. Smith (Salt Lake City: Signature Books in association with Smith Research Associates, 1995).

—— "William Clayton's Testimony," *The Historical Record: A Monthly Periodical* (May 1887).

Collier, Fred C., comp., *The Nauvoo High Council Minute Books of the Church of Jesus Christ of Latter-day Saints,* 1 ed. (Hanna, UT: Collier's Publishing Co., 20 May 1842, additional copyright December 2005).

—— *President Brigham Young's Doctrine of Deity, Volume 1* (Hanna, UT: Collier's Publishing Co., 1999)

Compton, Todd, *In Sacred Loneliness: The Plural Wives of Joseph Smith* (Salt Lake City: Signature Books, 2001).

"Counting Mormons," *Salt Lake Tribune* (11 January 2014).

Cowdery, Oliver (and Joseph Smith), "Letter to W.W. Phelps, Esq." (Oliver Cowdery and Joseph Smith's 1834-35 History), *Messenger and Advocate*, vol. 1 no. 1 (October 1834): 13-16.

—— "Letter III To W.W. Phelps, Esq." (Oliver Cowdery and Joseph Smith's 1834-35 History), *Messenger and Advocate*, vol. 1 no. 3 (December 1834): 41-46.

—— "Letter IV To W.W. Phelps, Esq." (Oliver Cowdery and Joseph Smith's 1834-35 History), *Messenger and Advocate*, vol. 1 no. 5 (February 1835): 77-80.

Dehlin, John, "Episode #985: Truth Seeking with Hans and Birgitta Mattsson, Pt. 2," Mormon Stories, hosted by Dr. John Dehlin (published 27 September 2018).

—— "Kirk and Lindsay Van Allen – Facing Church Discipline for Rejecting Polygamy D&C 132)," Episode 530 (8 April 2015, accessed 6 February 2018), available from http://www.mormonstories.org/kirk-and-lindsay-van-allen-facing-church-discipline-for-rejecting-polygamy-dc-132/; Internet, 22 pages.

—— "Tom Phillips, The Second Anointing, and LDS Apostle Jeffrey R. Holland," Mormon Stories (27 April 2015).

Deseret News (Salt Lake City, UT).

Dialogue: A Journal of Mormon Thought (Salt Lake City, UT).

The Discourses of Wilford Woodruff, G. Homer Durham, comp. (Salt Lake City: Deseret Book Company, 1946; reprinted by Bookcraft, 1990).

"A Doctrinal Exposition by the First Presidency and the Quorum of the Twelve Apostles," dated June 30, 1916, *Improvement Era* (August 1916): 934-42.

"Doctrine and Covenants" (accessed 1 December 2015), available from https://en.wikipedia.org/wiki/ Doctrine_and_Covenants; Internet, 36 pages.

"Document Showing The Testimony Given Before the Judge of the Fifth Judicial District of the State of Missouri, on the Trial of Joseph Smith, Jr., and others, for High Treason and Other Crimes Against that State," Senate Document No. 189 (Washington D.C.: Blair & Rives; photomechanical reprint of 15 February 1841, Salt Lake City: Utah Lighthouse Ministry).

Ehat, Andrew F., and Lyndon W. Cook, *The Words of Joseph Smith: The Contemporary Accounts of the Nauvoo Discourses of the Prophet Joseph Smith* (Provo, UT: Religious Studies Center, Brigham Young University, 1980).

Ellis, Jonathan, "Transcript of Claudia and Richard Bushman's Remarks at Faith Again" (12 June 2016, accessed 6 February 2018), available from https://medium.com/@jellistx/transcript-of-claudia-and-richard-bushmans-remarks-at-faith-again-e9d03bdea0e3; Internet, 42 pages.

Emerson, Ralph Waldo, *Selected Writings of Ralph Waldo Emerson*, William H. Gilman ed. (New York, Toronto: The New American Library, 1965).

The Essential Brigham Young, with a foreword by Eugene E. Campbell (Salt Lake City: Signature Books, 1992).

Evans, Arza, *The Keystone of Mormonism* (St. George, UT: Keystone Books Inc., 2003).

"Fanny Alger" (n.d., accessed 19 February 2019), available from https://www.lds.org/study/history/topics/fanny-alger?lang=eng; Internet, 2 pages.

Faulring, Scott H., *An American Prophet's Record: The Diaries and Journals of Joseph Smith* (Salt Lake City, UT: Signature Books and Smith Research Associates, 1987).

"Fawn M. Brodie" (accessed 13 July 2014), available from wikipedia.com; Internet.

First Presidency Statement, The Church of Jesus Christ of Latter-day Saints, November 1909, reaffirmed (*Ensign*, February 2002).

Ford, Thomas A., *History of Illinois, From Its Commencement as a State in 1814 to 1847*, Applewood's Series Historiography (Applewood Books, 2010).

"George Darling Watt" (accessed 18 December 2018), available from http://browngenealogy.org/1952debbieholtzendorff/1790jamesdwatt/1812george.html; Internet, 1 page.

Givens, Terryl L., *By the Hand of Mormon: The American Scripture that Launched a New World Religion* (*n.p.*: Oxford University Press, Inc., 2002; reprint, New York, NY: Oxford University Press paperback, 2003).

"Gordon Hinckley: Distinguished Leader of the Mormons," *Larry King Live* [aired September 8, 1998], available from mormonhomeevening. blogspot.com).

Groat, Joel B., "Joseph Smith Statements Denying Polygamy: WWCB Series (Why We Can't Believe) (Institute for Religious Research, accessed December 2015), available from mit.irr.org/joseph-smith-statements-denying-polygamy); Internet, 5 pages.

Gunnison, Lieut. John W., *The Mormons, or Latter-day Saints, in the Valley of The Great Salt Lake: A history of their rise and progress, peculiar doctrines, present condition, and prospects, derived from personal observation, during a residence among them* (Freeport, NY: Books for Libraries Press, 1852, 1972).

Hales, Brian C., "Encouraging Joseph Smith to Practice Plural Marriage: The Accounts of the Angel with a Drawn Sword," *Mormon Historical Studies*, vol. 11 no. 2 (Fall 2010).

—— *Joseph Smith's Polygamy, Volume 1: History* (Salt Lake City, UT: Greg Kofford Books, 2013).

—— "The Joseph Smith-Sylvia Sessions Plural Sealing: Polyandry or Polygyny?" in *Mormon Historical Studies*, 9/1 (Spring 2008), 41-57.

—— "A response to D. Michael Quinn's, 'Evidence for the Sexual Side of Joseph Smith's Polygamy,' Comments on a Session #2A Reconsidering Joseph Smith's Marital Practices Mormon History Association's Annual Conference, Calgary, Alberta, Canada, June 29, 2012, (unabbreviated version, revised during July)" (25 August 2012).

Hales, Brian C., and Laura H. Hales, *Joseph Smith's Polygamy: Toward a Better Understanding* (Draper, UT: Greg Kofford Books, 2015).

Hansen, Klaus J., "The Metamorphosis of the Kingdom of God: Toward a Reinterpretation of Mormon History," *Dialogue: A Journal of Mormon Thought*, vol. 1 no. 3 (Autumn 1966).

Hardy, B. Carmon, ed., *Doing the Works of Abraham: Mormon Polygamy – Its Origin, Practice, and Demise*, vol. 9 of *Kingdom in the West: The Mormons and the American Frontier* (Norman, OK: The Arthur H. Clark Company, 2007).

—— *Solemn Covenant: The Mormon Polygamous Passage* (Urbana, Chicago: University of Illinois Press, 1992).

Hill, Donna, *Joseph Smith: The First Mormon* (USA: Doubleday & Company, Inc., 1977; reprint, Salt Lake City: Signature Books, 1977, 1982, 1999).

Hill, Marvin S., Hill, "The First Vision Controversy: A Critique and Reconciliation," *Dialogue: A Journal of Mormon Thought*, vol. 15 no. 2 [Summer 1982]: 31-47.

—— "Joseph Smith and the 1826 Trial: New Evidence and New Difficulties," *BYU Studies*, 12 (Winter 1972).

Hinckley, Gordon B., Gordon B. Hinckley, "The Marvelous Foundation of our Faith," *Ensign* (October 2002).

—— "Messages of Inspiration from President Hinckley," *Church News* (1 February 1997).

"Hogamous, Higamous, Man is Polygamous, Higamous, Hogamous, Woman is Monogamous" (8 March 2012, accessed 28 December 2018), available from https://quoteinvestigator.com/ 2012/03/28/hogamous/; Internet, 9 pages.

The Holy Bible, Containing the Old and New Testaments (translated out of the original tongues: and with the former translations diligently compared and revised, by His Majesty's special command; specially bound for The Church of Jesus Christ of Latter Day Saints, Deseret Book Company, 1956).

Howe, Eber D., *Mormonism Unvailed: Or, A Faithful Account of That Singular Imposition and Delusion* (Painesville, OH: E.D. Howe, 1834; reprint, New York: AMS Press Inc., 1977).

The Improvement Era (The Church of Jesus Christ of Latter-day Saints, 1897-1970).

Jackson, Joseph H., *A Narrative of the Adventures and Experience of Joseph H. Jackson in Nauvoo* (Morrison, IL: K. Yost, 1844, reprint 1960).

"Jane Brown Watt Saladen" (accessed 1 March 2019), available from http://brown genealogy.org/1952debbieholtzendorff/1777josephbrown/1828jane.html; Internet, 1 page.

"Jane Manning James" (accessed 11 December, 2018), available from https://en.wikipedia.org/wiki/Jane_Manning_James; Internet, 7 pages.

Jenson, Andrew, comp., *Church Chronology: A Record of Important Events Pertaining to the History of the Church of Jesus Christ of Latter-day Saints*, 2d ed., rev. and enlarged (Salt Lake City: Deseret News, 1914).

—— "Plural Marriage," *Historical Record* (May 1887), 6:225.

Jessee, Dean C., "The Early Accounts of Joseph Smith's First Vision," *BYU Studies* 9, no. 3 (Spring 1969).

"John Milton Bernhisel," [accessed 31 May 2018], available from https://en. wikipedia.org/wiki/ John_Milton_Bernhisel; Internet, 3 pages.

"Joseph Smith Translation of the Bible" (accessed March 2018), available from Wikipedia.com; Internet, 7 pages.

The Joseph Smith Papers: Revelations and Translations Volume 2: Published Revelations, eds. Robin Scott Jensen, Richard E. Turley Jr., and Riley M. Lorimer (Salt Lake City: Church Historian's Press, 2011).

Journal of Discourses, 26 vols. (Liverpool, England: F.D. Richards, 1855-1886).

Kimball, Heber C., 22nd Annual General Conference, April 10, 1852.

—— *On the Potter's Wheel: The Diaries of Heber C. Kimball*, Stanley B. Kimball, ed. (Salt Lake City: Signature Books, 1987).

Kimball, Solomon F., "Sacred History," *Solomon F. Kimball Journal* (Church Historian's Office).

"Kinderhook Plates" (accessed 14 February 2019), available from Wikipedia.com.

Kirkland, Boyd, "Jehovah As Father: The Development of the Mormon Jehovah Doctrine," *Sunstone* (1984).

"Lamanites" (accessed August 2014), available from wikipedia.com.

The Latter Day Saint's Messenger and Advocate (Pittsburgh, PA: 15 October 1844).

The Latter-day Saints Millennial Star (Liverpool: Great Britain, 1840-1970).

Lattin, Don, "Sunday Interview – Musings of the Main Mormon/Gordon B. Hinckley, 'president, prophet, seer and revelator' of the Church of Jesus Christ of Latter-day Saints, sits at the top of one of the world's fastest-growing religions," *The San Francisco Chronicle* (13 April 1997), 3/Z1.

Law, William, Letter to Dr. Wyl, Letter I, "Three Letters from William Law on Mormonism: An Honest Man's View and Remorse," *The Daily Tribune,* 3 July 1887 (Salt Lake City, accessed 12 June 2018), available from http://www.william-law.org/publications/the-mormons-in-nauvoo-three-letters-from-william-law-on-mormonism-an-honest-mans-view-and-remorse-the-daily-tribune-salt-lake-city-july-3-1887; Internet, 8 pages.

LDS Church News (Salt Lake City, UT).

Lee, John D., *Confessions of John D. Lee* (New York: Bryan, Brand & Company: W.H. Stelle & Co., 1877; photomechanical reprint of 1877 original, Salt Lake City, UT: Modern Microfilm).

—— *Mormonism Unveiled; Or, The Life and Confessions of the Late Mormon Bishop, John D. Lee* (St. Louis, MO: Bryan, Brand & Company; New York, NY: W.H. Stelle & Co., 1877; photomechanical reprint of the original 1877 edition, Salt Lake City: Modern Microfilm Co.).

Marquardt, H. Michael, *Early Patriarchal Blessings of The Church of Jesus Christ of Latter-day Saints* (Salt Lake City: Smith-Pettit Foundation, 2007).

—— *The Rise of Mormonism: 1816-1844* (Longwood, FL: Xulon Press, 2005).

—— *The Strange Marriages of Sarah Ann Whitney to Joseph Smith, the Mormon Prophet, Joseph C. Kingsbury and Heber C. Kimball* (first published 1973; revised 1982; web version © 2001).

Marquardt, H. Michael, and Wesley P. Walters, *Inventing Mormonism: Tradition and the Historical Record* (n.p.: Smith Research Associates, 1998).

"Martin Luther King Jr." (accessed 1 January 2016), available from http://www.brainyquote.com/ quotes/quotes/m/martinluth103526.html; Internet, 1.

Matthews, Robert J. (Assistant Professor of Ancient Scripture), "Joseph Smith's Inspired Translation of the Bible," Brigham Young University (accessed March 2018), available from htpps://www.lds.org/ensign/1972/12/Joseph-Smiths-Inspired-Translation-of-the-Bible?/lang=eng; Internet, 9 pages.

Maxwell, John Gary, *Robert Newton Baskin and the Making of Modern Utah* (Norman, OK: The Arthur H. Clark Co., 2013).

McConkie, Bruce R., "The Bible, a Sealed Book," *Teaching Seminary: Preservice Readings* (2004), 123-32 (accessed March 2018), available from https://www.lds.org/manual/teaching-seminary-preservice-readings-religion -370-471-and-475/the-bible-a-sealed-book?lang=eng; Internet, 17 pages.

—— *Mormon Doctrine*, 2d ed. (Salt Lake City: Bookcraft, 1966).

Melonakos, Kathleen Kimball, *Secret Combinations: Evidence of Early Mormon Counterfeiting 1800-1847* (Lyrical Productions, 2016).

Messenger and Advocate (Kirtland, Ohio 1834-1836; Salt Lake City: Utah Lighthouse Ministry, photo reprint of Early LDS Magazine).

Mill, John Stuart, *On Liberty* (London, England: J.W. Parker, 1859).

"Millennial Star" (accessed 8 September 2014), available from https://en. wikipedia.org/wiki/Millennial_Star; Internet, 4 pages.

Milman, Henry H., D.D., *The History of Christianity: From the Birth of Christ to the Abolition of Paganism in the Roman Empire*, vol. 2 (London: William Clowes and Sons, 1867).

Minutes, 4 April 1860, Quorum of the Twelve Apostles (LDS Church History Library).

Mithryn (anonymous contributor), "Exploring Mormonism" (accessed 13 November 1842, posted 2 September 2013), available from exploring mormonism.com/polygamy-timeline; Internet, 41 pages.

—— "Greg Trimble, the word is 'Adultery,'" Exploring Mormonism (accessed 25 November 2014), available from https://exploringmormonism.com/greg-trimble-the-word-is-adultery/; Internet.

—— "Joseph Smith, Orson and Sarah Pratt -- A timeline" (posted 31 January 2013, 2012, accessed 11 October 2018), available from https://www.reddit. com/r/ mormon/ comments/ xe69p/ orson _ pratt _ sarah _ pratt _ and _ joseph _smith_a/; Internet, 4 pages.

Morgan, Dale, *Dale Morgan on Early Mormonism: Correspondence & A New History*, ed. John Phillip Walker, with a Biographical Introduction by John Phillip Walker and a Preface by William Mulder (Salt Lake City: Signature Books, 1986).

Mulder, William, and A. Russell Mortensen, eds., *Among the Mormons: Historic Accounts by Contemporary Observers* (New York, NY: Alfred A. Knopf, 1958).

The Nauvoo City and High Council Minutes, John S. Dinger, ed. (Salt Lake City: Signature Books, 2011).

Nauvoo Neighbor, John Taylor, ed. (Nauvoo, IL: 1843-1845).

Newell, Linda King, and Valeen Tippets Avery, *Mormon Enigma: Emma Hale Smith, Prophet's Wife, "Elect Lady," Polygamy's Foe – 1804-1879* (Garden City, N.Y.: Doubleday & Company, Inc., 1984).

Niles National Register, (Baltimore, MD: Hezekiah Niles, 1811-1849).

Oaks, Dallin H., Interview, *LDS Newsroom*, PBS documentary (20 July 2007).

The Oliver Olney Papers (originals at Yale; microfilm in LDS Church Archives, MS 8829, Item 8).

"Orson Hyde," (accessed 25 May 2018), available from https://en.wikipedia.org/ wiki/Orson_Hyde; Internet, 6 pages.

Packer, Boyd K., "For the Blessing of the Lamanites," *Relief Society Magazine*, vol. 51 no. 8 (August 1964): 565.

—— Talk to the All Church Coordinating Council (18 May 1993).

Palmer, Grant H., *An Insider's View of Mormon Origins* (Salt Lake City: Signature Books, 2002).

—— "Sexual allegations against Joseph Smith, 1829-35," typescript, n.d. (after 1999), UU_Accn0900, H. Michael Marquardt Collection, Marriott Library (photocopy in possession of Joel M. Allred).

—— "Sexual Allegations against Joseph Smith and the Beginnings of Polygamy in Nauvoo" typescript, n.a. [after 1999], UU_Accn 0900, H. Michael Marquardt Collection, Marriott Library, photocopy in possession of Joel M. Allred).

Park, Lindsay Hansen, "Who Are the Real Mormons?" (22 August 2016, accessed 18 September 2018), available from http://www.patheos.com/blogs/yearof polygamy/2016/08/many-mormonisms/; Internet, 8 pages.

Parrish, Warren, "To the Editor of the Painesville Republican," *Painesville Republican 2* (15 February 1838):3.

Pearson, Carol Lynn, *The Ghost of Eternal Polygamy: Haunting the Hearts and Heaven of Mormon Women and Men* (United States: Pivot Point Books, 2016).

Petersen, LaMar, *The Creation of the Book of Mormon: A Historical Inquiry* (Salt Lake City: Freethinker Press, 2000).

Peterson, F. Ross "A History of Cache County," *Utah Centennial County History Series*.

Peterson, John Alton, *Utah's Black Hawk War* (Salt Lake City: University of Utah Press, 1998).

Peterson, H. Donl, "Moroni, the Last of the Nephite Prophets" in *Fourth Nephi, From Zion to Destruction*, ed. Monte S. Nyman and Charles D. Tate Jr. (Provo, UT: Religious Studies Center, Brigham Young University, 1995).

Phelps, W.W., Letter to Brigham Young, 12 August 1861 (LDS Archives).

"Plural Marriage in Kirtland and Nauvoo" (2014, accessed 15 March 2016), available from https://www.lds.org/topics/plural-marriage-in-kirtland-and-nauvoo?lang=eng; Internet, 8 pages.

Proceedings Before the Committee on Privileges and Elections of the United States Senate in the Matter of the Protests Against the Right of Hon. Reed Smoot, a Senator from the State of Utah, to Hold His Seat," 59th Congress, 1st Session, Senate Document No. 486, 4 vols. (1 vol. index), (Washington; Government Printing Office, 1904) (see https://archive.org/details/proceedingsbefor01 unitrich/page/n5).

Proclamation of the Twelve, April 6, 1845, James R. Clark, comp., *Messages of the First Presidency of The Church of Jesus Christ of Latter-day Saints*, 6 vols. (Salt Lake City: Bookcraft, 1965-75).

Quinn, D. Michael, *Early Mormonism and the Magic World View* (Salt Lake City: Signature Books, 1987).

—— "Evidence for the Sexual Side of Joseph Smith's Polygamy," presented to the Mormon History Association's Annual Conference (Calgary, Alberta, Canada: 29 June 2012; expanded, finalized 31 December 2012; circulated mid-2013).

—— "LDS Church Authority and New Plural Marriages, 1890-1904," *Dialogue: A Journal of Mormon Thought*, vol. 18 no. 1, (Spring 1985): 9-105.

—— "Latter-day Prayer Circles," *BYU Studies*, 19 (Fall 1978).

—— *The Mormon Hierarchy: Extensions of Power* (Salt Lake City: Signature Books in association with Smith Research Associates, 1997).

—— *The Mormon Hierarchy: Origins of Power* (Salt Lake City: Signature Books in association with Smith Research Associates, 1994).

—— *The Mormon Hierarchy: Wealth and Corporate Power* (Salt Lake City: Signature Books, 2017).

—— "Organization Development and Social Origins of the Mormon Hierarchy, 1832-1932: A Prosopographical Study" (M.A. thesis, University of Utah, 1973).

Randyj, "Recovery from Mormonism" (accessed 2 December 2014); Internet, available from http://www.exmormon.org; Internet, 3 pages.

Read, Waldemer P., "What Freedom is Found in the Local Culture," *Great Issues Concerning Freedom* (Salt Lake City, UT: University of Utah Press, 1962).

Riess, Jana, "Mormon growth continues to slow, especially in the US" [13 April 2018, accessed 30 July 2019], available from https://religionnews.com/2018/04/13/mormon-growth-continues-to-slow-especially-in-the-u-s/; Internet, p. 2 of 4

Roberts, Brigham H., *A Comprehensive History of the Church of Jesus Christ of Latter-day Saints*, 6 vols. (Provo, UT: Brigham Young University Press, 1965).

—— *Studies of the Book of Mormon* (Salt Lake City: Signature Books, 1985).

Robinson, Ebenezer, "Items of Personal History of the Editor," *The Return*, vol. 3 no. 2 (Davis City, IA: February 1891).

Roper, Matthew, Paul J. Fields and Atul Nepal, "Joseph Smith, the *Times and Seasons*, and Central American Ruins," *Journal of the Book of Mormon and Other Restoration Scripture*, vol. 22 no. 2 (2013): 84-97.

Russell, Bertrand, *The Basic Writings of Bertrand Russell*, Robert E. Egner and Lester E. Denonn, ed. (London: George Allen & Unwin Ltd., 1961).

—— *Why Men Fight* (New York: The Century Co., 1917; reprint 1920).

The Saints Herald (Plano, IL: Reorganized Church of Jesus Christ of Latter-day Saints, 1 October 1879).

Salt Lake Temple Sealing Records, Genealogical Society (GS) film (LDS Family History Library).

Salt Lake Tribune (Salt Lake City, UT).

Sangamo Journal (Springfield, IL: 1831-1847).

"Series of Articles Challenges LDS Claim to Be 'Fastest Growing Religion,'" *Sunstone*, issue 138 (September 2005).

Smith, Andrew F., *The Saintly Scoundrel: The Life and Times of Dr. John Cook Bennett* (Urbana and Chicago: University of Illinois, 1997).

Smith, George D., *Nauvoo Polygamy: " . . . but we called it celestial marriage"* (Salt Lake City: Signature Books, 2008).

—— "William Clayton: Joseph Smith's 'Private Clerk' and Eyewitness to Mormon Polygamy in Nauvoo," *Sunstone* (December 1991): 32-35.

Smith Jr., Joseph, comp., *A Book of Commandments, For the Government of the Church of Christ, Organized According to the Law, on the 6th of April, 1830* (Zion, MO: W.W. Phelps, 1833).

—— trans., *The Book of Mormon: An Account Written by the Hand of Mormon, Upon Plates Taken from the Plates of Nephi* (Salt Lake City: The Church of Jesus Christ of Latter-day Saints, 1957).

—— trans., *The Book of Mormon: Another Testament of Jesus Christ*, first English edition (Palmyra, NY: n.p., 1830; reprint, New York, NY: Doubleday, 2004).

—— *Diary of Joseph Smith, Jr.* (1832-1834) in LDS Church Archives.

—— comp., *Doctrine and Covenants of the Church of Jesus Christ of Latter-day Saints: Containing Revelations Given to Joseph Smith, the Prophet, with Some Additions by His Successors in the Presidency of the Church* (Herald Publishing House, 1835).

—— comp., *Doctrine and Covenants of the Church of Jesus Christ of Latter-day Saints: Containing Revelations Given to Joseph Smith, the Prophet, with Some Additions by His Successors in the Presidency of the Church* (Salt Lake City: The Church of Jesus Christ of Latter-day Saints, 1957; reprint 1981; reprint 2013).

—— *History of The Church of Jesus Christ of Latter-day Saints*, B.H. Roberts, ed., 7 vols., 2d ed., rev., (Salt Lake City: The Deseret Book Company, 1978).

—— *[Inspired] Translation of the Bible*.

—— *Lectures on Faith: Prepared by the Prophet Joseph Smith, Delivered to the School of the Prophets in Kirtland, Ohio, 1834-35* (Salt Lake City: Deseret Book Company, 1985).

—— Letter to Newel K. Whitney, 27 July 1842 (accessed 5 June 2018), available from https://www.reddit.com/r/exmormon/comments/1ah2lw/here_is joseph_smiths_letter_to_ newel_k_whitney/; Internet, 4 pages.

—— *The Papers of Joseph Smith: Volume 1, Autobiographical and Historical Writings*, ed. Dean C. Jessee (Salt Lake City: Deseret Book Company, 1989).

—— *The Papers of Joseph Smith: Journal, 1832-1842*, ed. Dean C. Jessee (Salt Lake City: Deseret Book Company, 1989-1992).

—— *The Pearl of Great Price: Being a Choice Selection from the Revelations, Translations, and Narrations of Joseph Smith, First Prophet, Seer and Revelator to the Church of Jesus Christ of Latter Day Saints* (Liverpool, UK: F.D. Richards, 1851).

—— *The Personal Writings of Joseph Smith*, ed. Dean C. Jessee (Salt Lake City: Deseret Book, 1984).

Smith, Joseph Fielding, *Doctrines of Salvation*, ed. Bruce R. McConkie, 3 vols. (Salt Lake City: Bookcraft, 1956).

Smith, Joseph F., John R. Winder, Anthon H. Lund, "The Origin of Man: 1909 First Presidency Message," *Improvement Era* (November 1909), 75-81, reaffirmed in *Ensign* (February 2002).

Smith, Lucy Mack, *Biographical Sketches of Joseph Smith the Prophet, and His Progenitors for Many Generations* (Liverpool, UK: S.W. Richards, 1853).

—— *History of Joseph Smith by His Mother, Lucy Mack Smith: The Unabridged Original Version – An Up-To-Date Reprint of the Original 1853 Edition in Its Entirety, With Additional Information from the Rough-Draft Manuscript and Corrections Resulting from Subsequent Research*, comp. R. Vernon Ingleton, with a foreword by Richard Lloyd Dewey (Arlington, VA; Provo, UT: Stratford Books, 2005).

Snow, Eliza R., "The Ultimatum of a Human Life" in *Poems: Religious, Historical, and Political*" (Salt Lake City: printed at the Latter-day Saints' Printing and Publishing Establishment, 1877).

—— "We Believe In Our God" in *Sacred Hymns and Spiritual Songs for the Church of Jesus Christ of Latter-day Saints*, 11th ed. (Liverpool, England: Franklin D. Richards, 1856

Southerton, Simon G., *Losing a Lost Tribe – Native Americans, DNA, and the Mormon Church* (Salt Lake City: Signature Books, 2004).

—— "Simon's DNA Musings: DNA vs. the Mesoamerican Limited Geography" (accessed 28 February 2014); available from http://simonsoutherton. blogspot.com/2014/02/lose-limited-geography.html#comment-form, 6.

Stack, Peggy Fletcher, "Brazil Mystery: Case of the missing Mormons (913,045 of them, to be exact)," *Salt Lake Tribune* (Salt Lake City, 16 July 2012).

—— "Wayward LDS Invited Home," *Salt Lake Tribune* (7 April 2008).

Statement of the First Presidency of The Church of Jesus Christ of Latter-day Saints, 17 August 1949 (LDS Archives, Salt Lake City).

Stenhouse, T.B.H., *The Rocky Mountain Saints: A Full and Complete History of the Mormons, from the First Vision of Joseph Smith to the Last Courtship of Brigham Young* (New York, NY: D. Appleton and Company, 1873).

Stewart, David, "LDS Church Growth, Member Activity, and Convert Retention: Review and Analysis: Chapter IV-06: Member Activity and Convert Retention" (accessed May 2019), available from http://cumorah.com/index. php?target=church_growth_articles; Internet, 1 page.

Stewart, David, and Matt Martinich, *Reaching the Nations: International Church Growth Almanac 2014 Edition* (David Stewart, 2013).

Talmage, James E., *The Great Apostasy* (Salt Lake City: Deseret Book Company, 1953).

Tanner, Jerald, and Sandra Tanner, *The Changing World of Mormonism: A Behind-the-Scenes Look at Changes in Mormon Doctrine and Practice* (Chicago, IL: Moody Press, 1979).

—— *Mormonism – Shadow or Reality?* (Salt Lake City: Utah Lighthouse Ministry, 1987).

Taylor, Samuel W., *The Kingdom or Nothing: The Life of John Taylor, Militant Mormon* (New York: MacMillan Publishing Co., Inc., 1976).

—— *Nightfall at Nauvoo* (New York, NY: Avon Books, 1971).

Teachings of Presidents of the Church – Joseph Smith (Salt Lake City: The Church of Jesus Christ of Latter-day Saints, 2007).

thingsithink (Anonymous informant), "Re: The Morg's lawyers dodging the issues," *Recovery from Mormonism* (posted and accessed 15 March 2014), available from exmormon.org/phorum/read.php?2,1204555, 1204663,quote=1; Internet.

"Three Nights' Public Discussion between Revds. C.W. Cleeve, James Robertson, and Philip Cater and Elder John Taylor, of the Church of Jesus Christ of Latter-day Saints, at Boulogne-Sur-Mer, France" (Liverpool, UK: John Taylor, 1850).

Times and Seasons (Nauvoo, IL: 1839-1846).

Tomasi, Rollo, "FWIW: My Thoughts on 'Plural Marriage in Kirtland and Nauvoo' Essay" (revised 13 November 2014).

Toscano, Paul James, *The Sacrament of Doubt* (Salt Lake City: Signature Books, 2007).

Trauntvein, Myrna, "Burial Site?" *The Times News* (Nephi, UT: 6 June 2007).

Tucker, Pomeroy, *Origin, Rise and Progress of Mormonism: Biography of the Founders and History of Its Church* (New York: Appleton and Company, 1867).

Tullidge, Edward W., *The Women of Mormondom* (New York: 1877).

Turner, John G., *Brigham Young: Pioneer Prophet* (Belknap Press of Harvard University Press, 2012).

Van Biema, David, "Kingdom Come," *Time Magazine*, vol. 150 no. 5 (4 August 1997).

Van Wagoner, Richard S., *Mormon Polygamy: A History* (Salt Lake City: Signature Books, 1986).

—— "Orrin Porter Rockwell: Lehi Yesteryears" (accessed 2 July 2018), available from https://www.lehi-ut.gov/wp-content/uploads/2014/03/PorterRockwell byRichardVanWagonerweb.pdf; Internet, 5 pages.

—— *Sidney Rigdon: A Portrait of Religious Excess* (Salt Lake City: Signature Books, 1994; paperback 2006).

VanWagoner, Richard S., and Steven C. Walker, *A Book of Mormons* (Salt Lake City: Signature Books, 1982).

Vogel, Dan, ed., *Early Mormon Documents*, 5 vols. (Salt Lake City: Signature Books, 1996-2003).

—— *Joseph Smith: The Making of a Prophet* (Salt Lake City: Signature Books, 2004).

"The Voice of Innocence from Nauvoo, A Denunciation of Polygamy" adopted by the Relief Society, published in the *Nauvoo Neighbor* (20 March 1844), "Book of Abraham Project," available at Archive.org; Internet, 4 pages.

Walker, Lucy, 17 December 1902 (Salt Lake County, State of Utah: LDS Archives, MS 3423, CHL).

Walker, Ronald W., *Wayward Saints: The Godbeites and Brigham Young*, foreword by Jan Shipps (Urbana and Chicago: University of Illinois Press, 1998).

Walters, Wesley P., "Joseph Smith's Bainbridge, N.Y., Court Trials," reprinted by permission from the *Westminster Theological Journal* 36, no. 2 (Winter 1974) (Salt Lake City: Utah Lighthouse Ministry, 1974 and 1977).

The Wasp, William Smith, ed. (Nauvoo, IL: April 1842-April 1843).

Where Does it Say That? Photo Reprints of Hard-To-Get Mormon Documents, Bob Witte, comp. (Michigan: Institute for Religious Research).

Whitmer, David, *An Address to All Believers in Christ: by A Witness to the Divine Authenticity of The Book of Mormon* (Richmond, MO: n.p., 1887; photographic reprint, Concord, CA: Pacific Publishing Company, 1993).

Wilder, Lynn K., "Unveiling Grace" (a video documentary, 2011).

The William E. McLellin Papers: 1854-1880, eds. Stan Larson and Samuel J. Passey, foreword by George D. Smith (Salt Lake City: Signature Books, 2008).

"William Hooper Young" (accessed 15 July 2014), available from wikipedia.com.

"William Law [Latter Day Saints]," (accessed 25 June 2018); Internet, available from https://en.wikipedia.org/wiki/WilliamLaw_%28Latter_Day_Saints %29#cite _note-wife 19-4, 4 pages.

Williams, John K., "Concise Dictionary of Mormonism: Joseph Smith-History" (26 April 2012, accessed 13 September 2018), available from https://runtu.word press.com/?s=joseph+smith+thwarted+mob; Internet, 3 pages.

Willis, Stacey A., *Las Vegas Sun* (4 May 2001).

Wilson, Haley, and Thomas Wayment, "A Recently Recovered Source: Rethinking Joseph Smith's Bible Translation" (Brigham Young University Journal of Undergraduate Research, Department of Ancient Scripture, 16 March 2017).

Wood, Benjamin, "'Forgotten' massacre of Utah Paiute group recalled with new monument," *Salt Lake Tribune* (22 April 2016).

Woodruff, Wilford, *Wilford Woodruff's Journal, 1833-1898: Typescript,* ed. Scott G. Kenney (Signature Books, 1983).

Wyl, Dr. W. (pen name, real name of Wilhelm Ritter von Wymetal), "Interview with Wm. Law, March 30, 1887," *Salt Lake Tribune* (1 July 1887).

—— *Mormon Portraits or, The Truth About the Mormon Leaders From 1830 to 1866: Volume First: Joseph Smith, The Prophet, His Family and Friends, A Study Based on Facts and Documents* (Salt Lake City, UT: Tribune Printing and Publishing Company, 1886).

Young, Ann Eliza, *Wife No. 19* (Dustin, Gilman and Co., 1875; reprinted CreateSpace Independent Publishing Platform, 2014).

Young, Brigham, "Adam, Our Father and God," sermon delivered at the 22nd Annual Conference (9 April 1852), *Journal of Discourses,* 1:50-51.

—— Address, Semiannual Conference (7 October 1866), *Brigham Young Papers* (LDS Archives).

—— "Deposition of Brigham Young Regarding the Mountain Meadows Massacre" (July 30, 1875).

—— *Deseret News* (6 August 1862).

—— "A Few Words of Doctrine," unpublished manuscript in the Brigham Young Collection (LDS Church History Library)

—— General Conference, 8 October 1854, LDS Church Archives, *Brigham Young Papers* (Ms d 1234, ff marked: Addresses-1854, July – October).

—— "I Propose to Speak Upon a Subject that does not Immediately Concern Yours or My Welfare," a Sermon Delivered on October 8, 1854, taken from *The Teachings of President Brigham Young,* vol. 3 (Salt Lake City: Collier's Publishing Co., 1987).

——— "Intelligence, Etc." A Sermon delivered by Brigham Young on 9 October 1859, from *Journal of Discourses* (Liverpool, England: F.D. Richards, 1855-1886), 7:282-291.

——— "The Love of Truth and Righteousness Implanted in the Natural Man – Kindness and Firmness in Governments," Remarks made by President Brigham Young, Tabernacle (Salt Lake City: 15 June 1862), reported by G.D. Watt, *Journal of Discourses, 9:*308

——— Sermons, *Journal of Discourses*, 26 vols. (Liverpool, England: F.D. Richards, 1855-1886).

——— *Times and Seasons* (1 July 1845).

Index

INDEX